'A valuable resource! It reflects the global diversity and cultural sensitivity of social work. In this handbook, contributing authors from Africa, Asia, and Latin America share their experiences in organising study placements and practice learning of students. The authors also discuss local models for field education under social realities of countries facing poverty, inequality, and human rights violations, sometimes with insufficiently institutionalised social work as a profession. The text provides practical examples to guide universities and social services. I consider that social work educators will find this reflexive book useful'.

Tetyana Semigina, *Professor, Academy of Labour, Social Relations, and Tourism, Kyiv, Ukraine, and former Secretary of the International Association of Schools of Social Work*

'As a profession that requires direct contact with clients who may be vulnerable, disadvantaged, and low resourced, being acculturated into the practice environment through field work is absolutely important. This global handbook on how field work is being organised in different socio-economic-political contexts is a unique contribution to social work education. This book is an invaluable contribution in field work in the global south and I would strongly recommend it to all social work education programmes as populations are moving around and the training under different cultural context should be world knowledge'.

Cecilia Lai Wan Chan, *Professor Emeritus, Department of Social Work and Social Administration, The University of Hong Kong*

The Routledge Handbook of Social Work Field Education in the Global South

This handbook provides an authoritative account of social work field education in the global south. It presents an overview of various aspects of theory and practice modules in the social work curriculum and advances in research in social work field education in the developing world through in-depth analyses and global case studies.

Key features:

- Discusses critical issues and new directions in the theory and practice of social work field education, challenges in field work education, decolonising field work training, developing competent social work graduates, aligning fieldwork with cultural practices in indigenous communities, the idea of clinical social work, and a comparative analysis of social work field supervision.
- Integrates theory and practice of social work field education for students and teachers from diverse geographical and cultural contexts across the global south, including countries from South Asia and Asia, Africa, and Latin America and the Caribbean, covering India, Bangladesh, Pakistan, Nepal, Sri Lanka, China, Georgia, Philippine, Turkey, Papua New Guinea, Eswatini, Republic of Trinidad & Tobago, Kenya, Nigeria, South Africa, Botswana, Chile, and Barbados.
- Brings together international comparative perspectives on field work education in social work from leading experts, social work educators, and social work professionals.

This handbook will be an essential resource for scholars and researchers of social work, development studies, social anthropology, sociology, education, South Asian studies, and Global South studies. It will also be useful to educators and practitioners of social work in global institutions of higher studies as well as civil society organisations.

Rajendra Baikady is URC Special Post-Doctoral Fellow and Senior Research Associate at the Department of Social Work and Community Development, University of Johannesburg, South Africa, and a fellow of the Royal Society of Arts, London, UK.

Sajid S.M. is a senior social work educator and Professor of Social Work at Jamia Millia Islamia, New Delhi, India.

Varoshini Nadesan is Lecturer and Postgraduate Supervisor at the Department of Social Work and Community Development, Faculty of Humanities at the University of Johannesburg, South Africa.

M. Rezaul Islam is Professor in Social Work at the Institute of Social Welfare and Research, University of Dhaka, Bangladesh.

The Routledge Handbook of Social Work Field Education in the Global South

Edited by Rajendra Baikady, Sajid S.M., Varoshini Nadesan, and M. Rezaul Islam

LONDON AND NEW YORK

Cover image credit line: @gettyimages

First published 2022
by Routledge
4 Park Square, Milton Park, Abingdon, Oxon OX14 4RN

and by Routledge
605 Third Avenue, New York, NY 10158

Routledge is an imprint of the Taylor & Francis Group, an informa business

© 2022 selection and editorial matter, Rajendra Baikady, Sajid S.M., Varoshini Nadesan and M. Rezaul Islam; individual chapters, the contributors

The right of Rajendra Baikady, Sajid S.M., Varoshini Nadesan and M. Rezaul Islam to be identified as the authors of the editorial material, and of the authors for their individual chapters, has been asserted in accordance with sections 77 and 78 of the Copyright, Designs and Patents Act 1988.

All rights reserved. No part of this book may be reprinted or reproduced or utilised in any form or by any electronic, mechanical, or other means, now known or hereafter invented, including photocopying and recording, or in any information storage or retrieval system, without permission in writing from the publishers.

Trademark notice: Product or corporate names may be trademarks or registered trademarks, and are used only for identification and explanation without intent to infringe.

British Library Cataloguing-in-Publication Data
A catalogue record for this book is available from the British Library

Library of Congress Cataloging-in-Publication Data
A catalog record has been requested for this book

ISBN: 978-1-032-13718-6 (hbk)
ISBN: 978-1-032-19261-1 (pbk)
ISBN: 978-1-003-27011-9 (ebk)

DOI: 10.4324/9781003270119

Typeset in Bembo
by Deanta Global Publishing Services, Chennai, India

To Professor Marion Bogo,
who wrote an encouraging Foreword to this handbook,
but left us before the book could see the light of the day.

Contents

List of Figures *xiii*
List of Tables *xiv*
List of Contributors *xv*
Foreword *xxiii*
Acknowledgements *xxv*

    Introduction: New Directions to Field Work Education in Social Work:
    A Global South Perspective 1
    Rajendra Baikady, Varoshini Nadesan, S.M. Sajid, and M. Rezaul Islam

PART I
Developing Practice and Rethinking Perceptions: Field Education in South Asia 11

1 Revisiting Praxis as a Model for Field Education in Social Work 13
   Febna Reheem, Sojin P. Varghese, and Richa Bhardwaj

2 Swastyayan, a Commitment: Fieldwork through Community Engagement 26
   Victor Narzary, Bibharani Swargiary, Riju Sharma, and Alice K. Butterfield

3 Impact of the Competency-Based Field Work Practicum on Students' Learning 39
   Pradipta Kadambari and Nalini Lama

4 Challenges Faced in Field Work: An Indian Perspective 54
   Deepshikha Carpenter

5 Concurrent Fieldwork in Macro Practice: Cases from the South Indian Context 65
   S. Kanagaraj

6 Field Work in Social Work Education: An Account of the
   Sri Lankan Experience   76
   Shamila Sivakumaran and S. Jeevasuthan

7 The Need for Decolonising Field Work Training in Social Work in India   92
   Bishnu Mohan Dash

8 A Critical Reading of Community Social Work Methods and
   Practices Employed within Urban Underserved Communities
   in Sri Lanka   102
   H. Unnathi S. Samaraweera

9 Social Work Education and Practice in Pakistan: Mapping the Terrain
   and Missing Links   116
   Sakina Riaz

10 Social Work Practice in India: In Search of a New Direction   138
   Poonam Gulalia and Chittaranjan Subudhi

PART II
New Insights into Social Work Field Education in Developing Asia   151

11 Practice Teaching in the Social Work Master's Degree Programme:
   Fostering the Third Mission of Universities: The Case of Georgia   153
   Shorena Sadzaglishvili

12 Field Work as a 'Crucible of Practice' in the Pursuit of Social Justice and
   Defence of Human Rights: The Philippine Context   170
   Gil 'Jake' I. Espenido

13 Social Work Field Education in Turkey   182
   Eda Beydili Gürbüz, İlkay Başak Adıgüzel, and Sinan Akçay

14 Social Work Field Education in India and China: A Comparison   197
   Rajendra Baikady and Varoshini Nadesan

PART III
Field Work Education in the Latin American and the Caribbean Context   207

15 Clinical Social Work in Chile   209
   *Carolina Muñoz-Guzmán, María Olaya Grau,
   Karla González Suitt, and Valentina Garrido López*

16 Cultural Practices in Indigenous Chilean Communities: New Findings for Social Work Practice 223
Lorena P. Gallardo-Peralta, Julio Tereucán Angulo, Abel Soto-Higuera, and Esteban Sánchez-Moreno

17 Social and Field Work Abilities of Teaching Professors 239
Claudia Reyes-Quilodran, Paula Miranda, and Liliana Guerra-Aburto

18 The Block Placement in Social Work Field Education: A Barbados Case Study 252
Thérèse Odle-James and Letnie F. Rock

19 Constructing a Culturally Relevant Social Work Curriculum in Papua New Guinea: Connecting the Local and Global in Field Education 265
Dunstan Lawihin

20 Social Work Practicum in Chile: The Role of Field Supervisors in a Neoliberal Context 287
Daniela Díaz-Bórquez, Magdalena Calderón-Orellana, and Rafael Araya-Bugueño

21 Let Me Count the Ways: Multiple Discourses in Understandings of Readiness for Practice in Social Work 299
Karene-Anne Nathaniel

22 Mental Shortcuts: Representativeness Heuristics in Evaluations and Social Work Practice Assessment 313
Karene-Anne Nathaniel

PART IV
Developing Competent Social Work Graduates: African Perspectives on Field Work Education **327**

23 Contextualising Social Work Fieldwork Practicum: Innovations, Challenges, and Perspectives from Nigeria 329
Uzoma O. Okoye and Samuel O. Ebimgbo

24 Social Work Field Education in Africa: The Case of Botswana 343
Lengwe-Katembula J. Mwansa

25 Social Work Field Instruction in an Open and Distance Learning (ODL) Context 357
Boitumelo Joyce Mohapi

26 Fieldwork Practice in Countries with Recently Introduced Social Work
    Training: Lessons from Lesotho   371
    Sophia Thabane, Pumela Nomfundo Mahao, and
    Tšepang Florence Manyeli

27 Social Work Field Education: A Comparative Study of South Africa
    and Eswatini   388
    Boitumelo Joyce Mohapi, Felicity Besong Tabi, and Zee Catherine Masuku

28 Professionalisation of Social Work in Eswatini: A Comparative Study
    Between South Africa and Eswatini   403
    Boitumelo Joyce Mohapi, Felicity Besong Tabi, and Zee Catherine Masuku

Index   *419*

Figures

3.1	KMC Competency-Based Field Work Practicum Pedagogy 2016	51
3.2	Conceptual Framework: Impact Pyramid of the Competency-Based Field Work Practicum in Student Learning	52
5.1	Stakeholders of community open setting fieldwork as part of departmental fieldwork	66
8.1	Example of risk analysis method	109
9.1	Geographical distribution of the respondents (n = 122)	122
9.2	Demographic distribution of the respondents (n = 122)	123
9.3	Professional challenges (n = 122)	125
9.4	Social work association and importance (n = 122)	127
9.5	Administrative issues (n = 122)	129
9.6	Field work practice (n = 122)	131
16.1	Percentage of population in poverty and social exclusion in indigenous population	226
19.1	How to integrate the local and the global aspects of field education	278

Tables

2.1	MSW fieldwork structure	28
2.2	Community Engagement Programme of ADBU	31
4.1	A sample of field work guidelines as observed from the course of study	56
6.1	Field work practicum subjects offered at the NISD at a glance	89
8.1	Example of SWOT analysis method conducted in an underserved fishing community	107
11.1	Assessment criteria for field education of MSW programmes	160
11.2	Distribution of filed hours per semester	164
11.3	32 hours of university classroom field seminar conducted by a Practice Coordinator	164
16.1	Participant's characteristics	228
16.2	Chi-square analysis with respect to indigenous cultural practice	230
16.3	Differences between ethnic groups for the domains of subjective wellbeing	230
16.4	Differences in SWB depending on the maintenance of cultural practices	231
17.1	Professor skills	247
17.2	Basic elements of successful supervision and professor skills	248
17.3	Munson's activities and skills identified by professors	248
19.1	The data collection methods and number participants for this study	271
20.1	Field Supervisor Knowledge and Skill Required	292
24.1	Timetable for fieldwork	353
25.1	SACSSP Norms and Standards for Bachelor of Social Work Field Instruction	364
26.1	Bachelor of Social Work Graduates from 2004/05 to 2018/19 academic years	374
26.2	Summary of above-recommended fieldwork format	384
Annexure I: NUL Fieldwork Practice Guidelines		386
Annexure II: NUL Fieldwork Practice Assessment Format		386

Contributors

Rajendra Baikady, PhD, FRSA holds a dual appointment as a URC special Post-Doctoral Fellow and as a Senior Research Associate at the Department of Social Work and Community Development, University of Johannesburg, South Africa. He is also a Principal Investigator (Summer Research Fellowship) at the International Socioeconomics Laboratory, Harvard University, USA. He completed his first post-doctoral fellowship at the Hebrew University of Jerusalem, Israel, and was awarded a Golda Meir Fellowship by the Lady Davis Trust at the Hebrew University of Jerusalem.

S. M. Sajid has been Senior Social Work Educator for 35 years and is Professor of Social Work at Jamia Millia Islamia, New Delhi, India. He has also served as registrar, pro-vice-chancellor and officiating vice-chancellor of Jamia Millia Islamia. In addition, he has held positions of Honorary Advisor at the Centres of Higher Learning and Research, Jamia Millia Islamia, and as Director at the Academic Staff College, Jamia Millia Islamia. He established the Nelson Mandela Centre of Peace and Conflict Resolution, JMI and was its Founding Director.

Varoshini Nadesan (BSW, MCYC, D Litt et Phil) holds postgraduate qualifications in both Social Work and Child and Youth Care. She has 20 years' graduate experience as a Social Work Practitioner at the Department of Social Development in KwaZulu/Natal, six years at the South African Council for Social Service Professions (SACSSP) in Pretoria as National Manager for Professional Conduct, and nine years as lecturer and senior lecturer at the University of Johannesburg, South Africa.

M Rezaul Islam, PhD, is Professor in Social Work at the Institute of Social Welfare and Research, University of Dhaka, Bangladesh, International Academic Adviser at the Department of Social Administration and Justice, University of Malaya, Senior Research Associate, Department of Social Work, University of Johannesburg, South Africa, and Academic Fellow at the Faculty of Arts and Social Sciences, University of Sains, Penang, Malaysia. He has been visiting professor at the University of Malaya, Malaysia.

Febna Reheem is Assistant Director of I-YwD, a programme that aims to facilitate innovative entrepreneurship in Youth with Disabilities in Kerala, India. She is a social worker and researcher working on learning designs that are effective, inclusive, and accessible. She is also a trainer on psychosocial health issues.

Sojin P. Varghese has earned a doctorate in Social Work from the University of Kerala, Trivandrum, India, and has completed a Master of Social Work with specialisation in Medical and

Psychiatry from Mahatma Gandhi University, Kottayam, India. His areas of engagement include public policy analysis, sociopolitical advocacy, research, and consultation. Being a member of the Georgia Society for Clinical Social Workers (GSCSW) Professional Education Committee, Atlanta, USA as well as the Kerala Association of Professional Social Workers (KAPS) India, he has wider experience in the field of social work to his credit.

Richa Bhardwaj is pursuing a PhD and is working on the project Towards Sustainable Sanitation in India and Brazil at TISS, Mumbai, India. She is a development professional and Researcher with interests in urban poverty, planning, and governance. Having completed her MA in Social Work and M. Phil in Habitat Studies from TISS, she has been part of various international collaborative research projects.

Victor Narzary is an Officer on Special Duty (Education) to the Chief of Bodoland Territorial Region, India. He has an MA in Social Work from Tata Institute of Social Sciences, Mumbai, and is pursuing a PhD in Social Work from Assam Don Bosco University (ADBU), Assam, India. He served first as a Programme Officer and later on as Teaching Associate at the Tata Institute of Social Sciences Guwahati. He held the position of Assistant Professor at the Department of Social Work, Assam Don Bosco University. He has successfully completed several national and international assignments on teaching, research, and consultancies in the field of social work.

Bibharani Swargiary is Assistant Professor at the Department of Social Work, Assam Don Bosco University, India. A native from Bodoland living in Guwahati, she has worked with North-Eastern Social Research Centre at Guwahati, and Foundation for Social Transformation: Enabling Northeast India, Assam. She completed her MA in Social Work from Tata Institute of Social Sciences, Mumbai. She specialises in the field of tribal/indigenous social work in India and has been researching tribal/Adivasi women who have been widowed as a result of violence perpetrated in tribal/Adivasi areas.

Riju Sharma is Associate Professor and Dean of School of Humanities and Social Science at Assam Don Bosco University, India. She completed her Master's in Political Science at Delhi University, Master's in Human Rights at Pondicherry University, and PhD from Gauhati University. Her areas of specialisation are Human Rights, Social Legislations and Social Justice and Conflict Management, and Peace Building. She has worked extensively in the Juvenile Justice sector and had been actively involved in training and building capacities of the Juvenile Justice Functionaries in the State. She has initiated several national and international collaborations and joint projects with institutions of higher education thereby creating an enabling environment for co-teaching, research, joint courses, consultancies, and community engagement.

Alice K. Butterfield is Professor at Jane Addams College of Social Work, University of Illinois Chicago, USA. Her scholarship focuses on homelessness, social policy, international social work education, and community development. She is the author of *Incorporating Engaged Research in Social Development: Exemplars and Guidelines for Social Work and Human Services* (2021); *Practicing as a Social Work Educator in International Collaboration* (2017); *Dynamics of Family Policy* (2010); *Social Development and Social Work: Learning from Africa* (2013); *Interdisciplinary Community Development* (2007); *and University-Community Partnerships* (2005).

Contributors

Pradipta Kadambari is a social work educator, founding member and Principal of Kadambari Memorial College, School of Social Work, Kathmandu, Nepal. She has been involved in training social work students, revising the social work curriculum for Paranuchal University, and collaborating with the international social work fraternity to establish and strengthen social work as an academic discipline and profession in Nepal.

Nalini Lama is the coordinator of the Centre of Research, Development, and Innovation at Kadambari Memorial College, School of Social Work, Kathmandu, Nepal. She is also a founder of the Lagu Foundation, a research-based organisation which focuses on promoting partnership to ensure and act upon lifelong learning opportunities for all.

Deepshikha Carpenter is Assistant Professor, Department of Social Work, Mahapurusha Srimanta Sankaradeva Viswavidyalaya, Guwahati, India. Her doctoral thesis is 'A critical study of various legal provisions related to domestic violence in Assam' from the Department of Women's Studies, Gauhati University. She specialises in social work, gender studies, and disability studies.

Kanagaraj S. is Field Coordinator at the Department of Social Work, Amrita Vishwa Vidyapeetham, Coimbatore campus, India. He has qualified for the UGC-NET and SET (State Eligibility Test) in Social Work. He has a rich field experience and networking with stakeholders, grass-root level interventions in the community, and guided many social work students through field projects.

Shamila Sivakumaran holds a Master of Social Work from the University of Madras, India. She has extensive experience in working with different communities in Sri Lanka since 2006. She works as a Technical Consultant (MHPSS) for The Good Practice Group. She has been a lecturer at the National Institute of Social Development. Her research interest focuses on social work education and practice, social problems, and community development.

S. Jeevasuthan is a senior academic at the Department of Sociology, University of Jaffna, Sri Lanka. He holds a PhD in Sociology from University Sains, Malaysia and a Master in Social Work from the University of Madras, India. His research interests include research on the Tamil diaspora and the engagement in Jaffna's development, transnationalism, sociology of aid, transitional justice, war recovery, and post-war relocations.

Bishnu Mohan Dash, M.S.W., M.Phil, PhD, ICSSR Post-Doctoral Fellow, is Associate Professor, Department of Rural Development, Indira Gandhi National Open University, Delhi, India. He is the recipient of Best Teacher Award from Government of Delhi, 2019–20 and University of Delhi Excellence award for teachers in colleges in Service, 2021. He is also General Secretary of Bharatiya Samaj Karya Parishad (a national association of social workers) promoting the Indianisation of social work education in India.

H. Unnathi S. Samaraweera is a senior lecturer attached to the Department of Sociology, University of Colombo, Sri Lanka. She obtained her MA (Sociology) degree from the South Asian University, New Delhi, India and BA (Sociology Honours) degree from the University of Colombo, Sri Lanka. Her research interests involve gender sexuality and LGBTQI community, disaster resilience, and social work.

Contributors

Sakina Riaz is Assistant Professor in the Department of Social Work, University of Karachi, Pakistan. She has had a distinguished career in higher education that includes teaching, administration, and research. In her professional career involving teaching as well as extensive research work, she has been associated with a number of key academic institutions and organisations. She has been the recipient of several awards and fellowships.

Poona Gulalia, PhD is Field Work Coordinator at the School of Social Work in Tata Institute of Social Sciences (TISS) Mumbai, India. She also teaches a core paper on 'Social Case Work – Working with Individuals' at the School of Social Work. She worked as Education Social Worker and Community Social Worker with UNHCR, New Delhi for over eight years. She also worked with CASP PLAN, Nehru Yuva Kendra Sangathan, and Springdales School. Her more recent achievements include coordinating the development of various modules on 'Field and Field Supervision' along with a colleague. This was an initiative of the MHRD, Government of India (INFLIBNET). She has extensive experience and has been working as a practising professional for over three decades.

Chittaranjan Subudhi, PhD is Assistant Professor in the Department of Social Work, the Central University of Tamil Nadu (by an Act of Parliament) Thiruvarur, India. He has a Bachelor degree in Commerce and a Master degree in Social Work from the Utkal University of Odisha, India. He completed his PhD at the Department of Humanities and Social Sciences, National Institute of Technology Rourkela, India. He has researched various areas like health and mental health, medical anthropology, family and child welfare, disability studies, and tribal health issues. He teaches Psychiatric Social Work, Working with Individuals and Communities, Qualitative Research, ICTs in Social Development, and Health System Management.

Shorena Sadzaglishvili, MSW, PhD, directs MSW and PhD programmes and the Research Center at Ilia State University, Georgia. She is also the founder of the first MSW Programme in Georgia. She is a Chairperson of the Georgian Association of Social Workers. Her recent research interests focused on homeless youth, deinstitutionalisation, IDPs, HIV/AIDS, and mental health.

Gil 'Jake' I. Espenido is a full-time faculty of the Department of Social Work, College of Social Work and Community Development (CSWCD) of the University of the Philippines Diliman campus, Philippines. He finished his BS Social Work in the CSWCD in 1981 and passed the board exam of social work on the same year. He also completed his master's degree in Public Affairs with a major in Agrarian and Rurban Development Studies at the College of Public Affairs and Development (CPaf) at the University of the Philippines, Los Banos. His articles on social work and human rights and progressive community organising are published locally and internationally.

Eda Beydili Gürbüz is Assistant Professor (PhD) at the Department of Social Work, Düzce University Faculty of Health Sciences, Turkey. She has been teaching social work theory, violence against women, gender, and social work interview courses at undergraduate level. Her major research interests are gender, social work education, social problems, and social policy.

İlkay Başak Adıgüzel is Research Assistant (PhD) at the Department of Social Work, Hacettepe University FEAS, Turkey. She has been teaching social work theory and human behaviour and social environment courses since 2019 at the same department. She is a psychodramatist. She is interested in feminist social work, violence against women, working with the perpetrator of violence and group psychotherapy.

Sinan Akçay is Associate Professor (PhD) at the Department of Social Work, Selcuk University Faculty of Health Sciences, Turkey. He has been teaching social work theory, gender and social work, qualitative research methods, psychiatric social work courses at undergraduate and postgraduate levels. He is interested in psychiatric social work, gender, and qualitative research methods.

Carolina Muñoz-Guzmán is Associate Professor at the School of Social Work at Pontificia Universidad Católica de Chile, Santiago and has a PhD in Social Policy from University of Birmingham, England. Her research focus is on social policy, family, and children.

María Olaya Grau is Assistant Professor at the School of Social Work at Pontificia Universidad Católica de Chile, and has a PhD in Political Science from Universidad Complutense de Madrid. Her research focuses on migrant population, children, and families.

Karla González Suitt is Assistant Professor at the School of Social Work at Pontificia Universidad Católica de Chile, Santiago and has a PhD in Social Work from the University of Texas at Austin. Her research focuses on implementation science and clinical social work.

Valentina Garrido López is Teaching Professor at the School of Social Work at Pontificia Universidad Católica de Chile, and has a MSW from the University of Michigan, USA. Her research focus is on palliative care and clinical social work.

Lorena P. Gallardo-Peralta, PhD, is Associate Professor of Social Work and Social Services at Complutense University of Madrid (Spain) and Associate Researcher at Tarapacá University (Chile). Her research lines include social gerontology, quality of life, social networks and successful aging. In recent years, she has focused on the aging process of indigenous communities, currently leading the project 'Ethnic Diversity and Aging: Towards a Multicultural Map of Successful Aging in Chile'.

Julio Tereucán Angulo, PhD, is Associate Professor and Director of the Department of Social Work, at Universidad de la Frontera (Chile). His lines of research are ethnic identity in indigenous contexts, focusing on identity construction processes and associated cultural determinants; Mapuche reciprocity and exchange, especially from the analysis of social anthropology and cultural economy, and intergenerational social mobility in educational contexts of both secondary and higher education.

Abel Soto-Higuera, is Associate Professor of the Department of Social Work at University of La Frontera, Chile. His research lines include gender violence from an intercultural perspective and, in recent years, the study of the aging process on indigenous older adults in Chile, specifically on ethnic identity, quality of life, and support networks. Currently, he is a co-investigator of the Project; Ethnic Diversity and Aging: towards a multicultural map of successful Aging in Chile

Esteban Sánchez-Moreno, PhD, is Senior Lecturer and researcher, and Director of the Research Institute for Development and Cooperation, Universidad Complutense, Madrid, Spain. Dr Sánchez-Moreno has focused on two lines of research. The first line is defined by the social determinants of health, and specifically the impact of socio-economic inequalities. The second line consists of analysing the ageing process and the factors that influence the reproduction of social inequalities in said process, with particular attention to wellbeing and health.

Claudia Reyes-Quilodran is Associate Professor in the School of Social Work at Pontificia Universidad Católica de Chile. She received her PhD from Washington State University in 2009. Her areas of specialization include political psychology, criminal justice and Latin American studies. Her most recent research projects include juvenile delinquency and gender, prison violence, professional judgement in interventions with vulnerable families, and comparatives studies in juvenile restorative justice. She has extensive experience working with victims affected by severe human rights violations during the Chilean military regime, and she has worked in the National Child Social Service and in state agencies to prevent crime and violence in Chile.

Paula Miranda is Professor in undergraduate programmes, certificate programmes for professionals and the Chilean government capacity-building organization, and CORFO for entrepreneurs and social innovators. Currently, she is conducting a study on the entrepreneurial talent of indigenous Mapuche entrepreneurs in Chile. She is also carrying out research on the monitoring and evaluation systems for criminal mediation for the Juvenile Social Rehabilitation Service. She has written and studied other social topics, including the way in which third and fourth sector organizations relate to social innovation, entrepreneurship and social services. She is a member of the OCULAB-Laboratory of Social Innovation in Visual Disability, UC Board of Directors/Researcher, and Deputy Director of the Continuing Education, Communications and Extension Department at UC School of Social Work.

Liliana Guerra-Aburto is Associate Professor and received her PhD in Latin American studies, University of Chile, and Master's in social work, Pontifical Catholic University of Chile. She has her postgraduate degree in family studies, Pontificia Universidad Católica de Chile, and her undergraduate degree in social work at Pontifical Catholic University of Chile. Her research projects include culture and family, family intervention, social policies and family.

Thérèse Odle-James is a Clinical Social Worker, Lecturer in Social Work, Director of Field Education and Undergraduate Programme Coordinator at The University of The West Indies, Cave Hill Campus, Barbados, West Indies. She is also an Executive Member of The Association of Caribbean Social Work Educators (ACSWE) and a Member of The International Association of Schools of Social Work (IASSW).

Letnie F. Rock, PhD, is a former senior lecturer in Social Work with The University of the West Indies Cave Hill Campus, Barbados where she was Head of the Department of Government, Sociology, Social Work and Psychology and Acting Head of the Institute for Gender and Development Studies: Nita Barrow Unit. She was President of the Association of Caribbean Social Work Educators.

Dunstan Lawihin is Lecturer and Field Education Coordinator in Social Work at the University of Papua New Guinea and has more than 15 years professional experience. His main research and teaching interests are culturally relevant social work education, field education, NGOs and community work, social policy, service delivery, social service workforce and socially inclusive community development interventions.

Daniela Díaz Bórquez is Adjunct Professor, School of Social Work, Pontificia Universidad Católica de Chile and current president of the Childhood and Adolescence Observatory of Chile. Master in Sociology and Social Work at Universidad Católica de Chile.

Magdalena Calderón-Orellana is Adjunct Assistant Professor, School of Social Work, Pontificia Universidad Católica de Chile; and has a Master in Public Management, Universidad Católica de Valparaiso; Social Worker, Universidad Católica de Chile.

Rafael Araya-Bugueño is Public Administrator and has a Master in Politics and Government He has 20 years of experience in public management. Currently, he works as Head of Audit Office at Secretary of cultures, arts, and heritage. He has led teams in planning, public policy monitoring, participation, transparency, and public innovation.

Uzoma O. Okoye, is Professor in the Department of Social Work, University of Nigeria, Nsukka (UNN) was a Fulbright Scholar and a Dick Splane Scholar. She has attended many conferences, workshops, and authored over a hundred journal articles and book chapters. She has graduated over fifty MSc and PhD students. Her current research interests include gerontology, public health, child protection, migration, and internal displacement.

Samuel O. Ebimgbo is Lecturer II and a PhD student in the Department of Social Work, University of Nigeria, Nsukka (UNN), Nigeria. He studied Social Work in Diploma and B.Sc. from the University of Nigeria, Nsukka (UNN). He obtained M.Sc. in Social Work from UNN. He has published some studies in gerontology in peer review journals.

Karene-Anne Nathaniel is a social work educator and workshop facilitator with several years as a lecturer and trainer in the Caribbean at all levels. Her areas of interest include pedagogy for helping professionals, professional socialization and identity development. She has served on the executive of the Caribbean and International associations for social work education over the last eight years.

Lengwe-Katembula J. Mwansa is Professor at the University of Botswana, Department of Social Work. He teaches various course offerings at Diploma, Bachelor of Social Work, Master of Social Work, and PhD levels. He started his teaching career at the University of Zambia in 1979 as a Staff Development Fellow and continued after successfully completing his Master's degree in Social Work at McGill University, Canada and PhD at Heller Graduate School, Brandeis University, USA.

Boitumelo Joyce Mohapi is a senior lecturer in the Department of Social Work at the University of South Africa (UNISA). She has experience in research, project management, learning materials development, career guidance, and training. She obtained a D.Phil. from the University of Pretoria, and a Certificate in Project Management from Management for Development Foundation (MDF) in the Netherlands. She has presented conference papers nationally and internationally. She has travelled to Australia, Senegal, the United States of America, Lesotho, the Netherlands, Namibia, England, Kenya, Botswana, Brazil, and Uganda.

Sophia Thabane is a social work lecturer at the National University of Lesotho (NUL), Roma. She holds a PhD (Social Work), MSW (UKZN), and BSW (UZ). Before joining NUL, she worked for the Department of Social Welfare and as a lecturer and researcher for the University of Kwa-Zulu Natal. Apart from practical and teaching experience in social work, she has published in the areas of psychosocial factors aggravating the spread of HIV in Lesotho as well as the protection/welfare of vulnerable populations such as older people and children.

Pumela Nomfundo Mahao is a Social Work Lecturer at NUL. She holds an MA (Social Work) and Bachelor of Arts (Sociology and Public Administration) both conferred by National University of Lesotho (NUL) and is a former Community Work Lecturer at the University of South Africa (UNISA) in the Department of Social Work. She worked in various public and private sector organisations in Lesotho and South Africa where she gathered a lot of experience in project management, community work, and socioeconomic development issues.

Tšepang Florence Manyeli is Senior Lecturer in Social Work at the National University of Lesotho and a former Head of Department. She previously worked as a social worker and head of humanitarian relief services. She has also undertaken consultancies and done empirical research in various fields related to people's general well-being including vulnerability and social welfare. In line with this she produced reports and published journal articles.

Felicity Besong Tabi, BSW, MSW, MCHPR, is an Eswatini citizen, a qualified social worker, a child protection specialist, and a play therapist. She is a registered social work practitioner with the South African Council for Social Service Professions (SACSSP) and a member of the International Association for Social Work with Groups (IASWG). She holds two social work-related master's degrees: an MSW (social work with a specialisation in play therapy) from the University of Pretoria (UP), South Africa and MCHPR (child care and protection [law and social work]) from the University of Kwa-Zulu Natal (UKZN), Durban, South Africa.

Zee Catherine Masuku BSW, MSW, is an Eswatini citizen, a qualified social worker with more than 25 years of experience in direct social work practice, policy, strategy development, legislation, and implementation of systems to guide child protection and social service delivery. Ms Masuku is the founder and director of the Regional Social Work Centre of Excellence, an NGO whose overall goal is social work system strengthening and has introduced a dignity package. The dignity package consists of dignity packs, health education, and motivational speeches to 130 girls in the juvenile facility under the Correctional Services in Eswatini.

Foreword

Across the globe, graduates of social work programmes generally credit their field work experience as the most significant component of their education. This is likely a result of students' motivation to enter social work committed to helping individuals, families, groups, and communities in a range of ways. Many students aim to work to ensure that all members of their society experience equity, fairness, and social justice. This includes having access to services that provide support and resources when faced with urgent needs and hardships. As well, social workers hope to contribute to efforts to achieve safety, peace, and environmental sustainability. This is especially true in regions where human events and natural disasters pose challenges to good health and well-being.

Over the past many decades, a rich and varied literature about field education has developed. This literature encompasses conceptual, empirical, and practice wisdom contributions. Educators have drawn upon a wide range of pedagogical concepts including adult learning and experiential learning, situational learning, attachment theory, and more recently contributions from neuro-science research. Culling from studies of students' and field instructors' perceptions of what facilitates learning in field education, best practices have been identified in reviews in social work and related human service professions. These include the presence of a supportive and positive context in the service setting and with the field instructor, opportunities to observe experienced practitioners, and to be observed as students learn to practise. With observation of students' practice, field instructors can provide focused and specific feedback. Students then use that feedback in subsequent situations and through repetitive practice develop increased competence. Reflective discussions with their supervisors bring theory and practice together so that students learn not only *about* social work concepts, but importantly how to actually *do* social work (Bogo et al., 2020).

These principles, however, are largely based on literature from Western countries, especially the United States, Canada, England, Ireland, Scotland, Australia, New Zealand, and countries influenced by Western perspectives such as Hong Kong and more recently China. Since knowledge-development and social work practices are highly contextual, they reflect the societies in which they arose. The transfer of knowledge between differing contexts is both challenging and not always appropriate. Nevertheless, field educators are interested in learning from each other so as to expand their repertoire of possible effective teaching and learning models. This is evident in the attendance at international conferences where presentations and informal discussions stimulate such exchanges.

Sorely lacking, however, has been a comprehensive text that offers understanding and insights about social work field education from the global south. As a result, this handbook, the first volume of its kind, fills an important gap. It presents a wide range of relevant and interesting contributions that provide information about social work field education in a multitude of countries from South Asia, developing Asian countries, South Latin American countries, and the African continent.

Concerns such as the structure and organisation of the curriculum are discussed in some chapters and this topic is of interest to all those engaged in field education, regardless of location. As has been the case in Western countries, academic courses and theoretical learning can take precedence over learning to practice. This is ironic as students have entered these programmes to prepare them for careers in practice. The importance of universities offering solid administration and resources for field education can be supported by the contributions in this text. This provides administrators of field programmes with the necessary information to use in advocating for what they need to produce quality education.

Topics in the chapters address many salient issues such as the challenges of finding quality field placements and the importance of collaborative relationships and local models created between community settings and the social work school. The need for local models that are context-specific, culturally meaningful, and indigenised is offered in examples from many regions. Where local approaches to social work are still developing educators are at the same time faced with creating field models and finding field instructors who can impart these new practices to students. Different regions in the global south present particular issues. For example, while some regions focus on community development others incorporate clinical social work practice. This diversity in practice highlights the rich and varied approaches to social work practice and related field education across the globe.

The creative and diverse collection of materials in this text has much to offer the social work education community. While presenting local issues it also includes field education concerns that are universal. Readers from schools in all locations will surely benefit from this comprehensive collection.

Marion Bogo, *O.C., LL.D., MSW, RSW*
Professor, Factor-Inwentash Faculty of Social Work
University of Toronto
Toronto, Canada

Reference

Bogo, M., Sewell, K. M., Mohamud, F., & Kourgiantakis, T. (2020). Social work field instruction: A scoping review. *Social Work Education*. doi: 10.1080/02615479.2020.1842868

Acknowledgements

We are grateful to each of the volumes' contributors, all of whom are eminently qualified to write about social work field education in their own countries, regions, and regimes. We acknowledge their enthusiasm, cooperation, and expertise in bringing out this remarkable handbook on social work field education in the global south.

We acknowledge the difficulties we all experienced during the time this book was conceived, developed, and put into production. This was the most difficult time for billions of lives all across the globe. COVID-19 hit the world and profoundly impacted the lives and livelihoods of people including the authors and their family, as well as the production process of the book that you are now reading. Overnight, countries across the globe announced complete lockdowns, and schools, colleges, and educational institutions across the globe started functioning remotely, with students and educators experiencing innumerable challenges in their learning and teaching activities. We acknowledge those who lost their lives, those who lost their loved ones, and those who are working relentlessly in rebuilding a 'new normal' society.

Rajendra Baikady gratefully acknowledges support from the Hebrew University of Jerusalem, Israel in the form of a post-doctoral fellowship in the year 2019–2020 during which the idea of this handbook project was conceived and initiated. He is also thankful to his supervisor Professor John Gal for his continued support and encouragement.

Finally, we are thankful to Antara Ray Chaudhary and Shashank Shekhar Sinha for providing an opportunity to put together this handbook and Rimina Mohapatra and her team at Routledge for their editorial support and cooperation in producing this handbook. Choosing Routledge as the best possible publisher for this handbook was justified at every stage of work with these colleagues.

Rajendra Baikady
Sajid S.M
Varoshini Nadesan
M. Rezaul Islam

Introduction: New Directions to Field Work Education in Social Work

A Global South Perspective

Rajendra Baikady, Varoshini Nadesan, S.M. Sajid, and M. Rezaul Islam

The recognition of field work as the signature pedagogy by the Council on Social Work Education (CSWE) in 2008 spurred debate and discussion on the immense value of this training component in social work education (CSWE, 2008). Field work is where students engage in practical training in their journey towards becoming social workers. Students are afforded the opportunity to test their practice abilities in the field work settings by transferring theoretical lessons learnt in the class into real-life situations. Thus, field work practice prepares students to provide direct intervention, support, and help in the lives of humankind. Of course, this would require close monitoring and guidance as these soon-to-be social workers are required to intervene in real-life situations in the micro, meso, and macro environments. Thus, social work students are expected to undertake field work practicum under the direct supervision of a faculty supervisor and agency supervisor (Nadesan, 2020).

Over the last five decades immense literature has been produced on different aspects of social work education and in particular field work education. This literature has been largely from writers based in developed countries, based on western ideologies. However, the western dominance in theory and practice knowledge is criticised extensively in social work across the globe. This western hegemony dominates nonwestern academia in the form of reading materials and texts, underplaying the value of indigenous knowledge systems in social work intervention. Additionally, a spate of recent literature has raised arguments of social work education and practice across the globe being influenced by western ideologies and theoretical knowledge (Sajid et al. 2020). These western theories and practice models, advanced under the context of western ideologies and developed countries and previously unwittingly and inadvertently used in global south social work academia, provided initial grounding for teaching and learning. However, debates are ongoing as to the unsuitability of such ideologies in developing countries and indigenous communities. Thus, academic imperialism in all aspects of social work practice, including international social work, is discussed extensively at many academic fora (Mabvurira, 2018; Shokane & Masoga, 2019; Sajid , et al. 2020; Harms Smith, 2020; Yadav & Yadav, 2020).

Societies in the global south have unique characteristics that are not found in a western context, in addition to this the problems experienced by people, communities, and societies in the global south are not comparable with western society. Societal realities and challenges faced by the countries in the global south are very different to those of developed countries; social work education in the developing world needs context-specific practice teaching models. Further studies have also proposed integrating culture and tradition into social work teaching and learning as a part of developing culturally relevant social work (Allegritti & Gray, 2003; Gray & Allegritti, 2002). Also, there is limited literature on the social work field practicum in the global south. We assume that social work academics in each country in the global south have their own unique and context-specific social work practice model. Bringing together these practice literatures from social work educators and field supervisors in this volume helps them to collaborate and learn from each other's experiences.

Societies in the global south are facing unprecedented challenges such as poverty, inequality, human rights violation, gender-based violence, and disasters. A few countries in the South Asian and Middle East region are also struggling to establish peace and stability in their society. The social, political, and economic context of countries in the global south are in a state of transformation and social work as a human service profession needs to prepare its professionals to respond to the issues emerging as part of privatisation, globalisation, and economic and labour market restructuring. Social work educators also need to consider preparing future practitioners to work for establishing peace, equality, and social justice in the world. As social work believes in establishing a just society with equality and wellbeing, educational programmes in social work need to prepare their learners as expert contributors to the much-needed reconstruction process.

The *Routledge Handbook of Social Work Field Education in the Global South* brings together the best possible authors from the global south to discuss the present condition of social work education and field education in their respective countries. Authors in this volume examine various aspects related to social work education and practice in around 20 countries in the global south. This gives us an account of practices and procedures in conducting social work field practice in different developing countries across different regions. This also provides an opportunity for the editors, authors, and readers to gain transnational, comparative, and context-specific social work educational experience. Contributors of the handbook are eminently experienced and practice-oriented academics who are field work supervisors and social work educators. Hence their years of experience in teaching, supervision, and research shaping the discussion in this volume.

The biggest challenge for social work education in the global south is to prepare students who can respond to the diverse social realities. The challenge in educating resilient practitioners who can manage to serve in adverse situations and remain in the social work profession is a much experienced but less discussed issue in social work, especially in relation to field work education. A number of studies across the globe recommend resilience training for social work students to prevent workplace burnout (Grant and Kinman, 2011; Kinman and Grant, 2011) and teaching the required skills which may help the graduates to survive in the social work profession (Davidson, 2005; Collins, 2007; Wilks and Spivey, 2010). While discussing workplace burnout, the reluctance among graduates to practise social work, and the low level of professional identity and recognition, one should also make efforts in improving the prevailing diverse educational models, and deal with the lack of regulatory framework, trained educators, and available resources in developing countries. These make it difficult to achieve the required minimum standards set by the global community. As a result of these ongoing dilemmas there is a high level of reluctance to undertake social work education and thereafter to practise social work as a profession.

Several authors in this volume pointed out micro level innovations in imparting social work field education in their country's context. Contributions from South Asian countries discuss the importance of social work field education and challenges experienced by supervisors, institutions, and trainees. The handbook includes contributions from field instruction practices in social work education at different levels in the field across the global south. The volume aims to identify and define social work field education in various national and international spheres; the book is expected to be a major reference for expert reading. It includes specially commissioned chapters combining cutting edge research and review articles contributed by social work educators and field work supervisors.

Some of the authors in this handbook bring in discussion on current concerns about risk and uncertainty in field education in diverse contexts. Despite well-established theoretical education in many developing countries, field work education in social work is somewhat neglected or not substantially taught or intensively practiced. As a result, quality of social service delivery, professional practice, professional recognition, public trust in the professionals, and respectable pay are at stake. Scholars have also discussed the absence of service structure to support fieldwork education and employment of social work graduates in many countries (Leung, 2007; Lin & Chen, 2005; Gray & Yadav, 2015; Panic, 2016). While literature at local and global levels continues to discuss and recognise the importance, need, and uniqueness of field work practice many training institutions marginalise the field work practice while placing more weight on classroom teaching (Dhemba, 2012; D'Souza, 2012; Mallick, 2007; Kasake, 1990).

The *Routledge Handbook of Social Work Field Education in the Global South* is a collaborative effort in bringing out multiple stakeholder perspectives on challenges, prospects, and innovations in field work education in the global south. While reading many of the contributions in this volume we understand the progress achieved by social work education in many developing countries in spite of practical challenges such as lack of professional recognition, lack of regulatory mechanisms, low pay, and uncertain employment opportunities. Furthermore, several other authors give us the sense that field work in social work is neither integrated nor upgraded as much as it has been discussed in the literature (see Chapters 19, 22, and 27). However, as a collective effort in contributing to ongoing global discussion on enhancing, validating, and professionalising social work education and practice, this handbook makes an important contribution by giving recognition to global south voices.

Need for a Handbook on Field Work Education in the Global South

This handbook collects and examines the contemporary debates, research, challenges, opportunities, and innovations related to social work field education in the developing countries. Field work in social work learning occupies a central role as it is expected to prepare ethically competent social workers for future practice. However, despite its unique contributions in educating and preparing future social work practitioners, many institutions place little emphasis on practical training while giving greater importance to classroom teaching in their teaching approach (Baikady et.al 2022). In order to examine the contemporary challenges in social work field education this handbook brings together international scholars working and researching in South Asia, developing Asian countries, South Latin American countries, and the African continent. Hence the handbook is a representation of the social work education in the developing countries in the global south. We believe this handbook sets new examples of collaboration and co-learning in field work education across the regions and regimes represented in this volume. Contributions in this handbook reiterate the importance and need for providing experiential learning to social work students. Transforming practice teaching, bringing a sustainable relation between the field placement agency, school and the community, and developing local models of social work field education are the important issues discussed in this volume. While there may be innumerable benefits from this handbook for social work academics, practitioners, researchers, and students, we elaborate on the following significant takeaways from our experience in compiling and editing this handbook.

Building Tacit Knowledge

Social work education in general and field work practice in particular need a greater transformation in many countries in the global south. In addition to the many challenges faced by social work academia there is a need for developing a strong knowledge base for the profession. The need for documenting the experiences of educators, practitioners, and students' perspectives is important to understand and develop localised, context-specific, and culturally relevant literature that could help in training next-generation practitioners. Further research, discussion, and literature related to tacit knowledge building in social work practicum is a neglected area. Research so far appears to focus predominantly on tacit knowledge at a theoretical or conceptual level (De Roos, 1990; Dybicz, 2004; Gowdy, 1994; Imre, 1985; Klein & Bloom, 1995; Scott, 1990; Sheppard, 1995); whereas empirical research examining the tacit knowledge or practice wisdom is limited. Contributions in this handbook provide evidence-based understanding of the development, status, challenges, and innovations in the practice domain of social work. Further developing tacit and experiential knowledge in social work will have a greater impact on the ways social work professionals respond to social problems and issues in the global society. Tacit knowledge provides a deeper understanding of complex practice issues.

Strengthening the Linkages between Theory and Practice

The *Routledge Handbook of Social Work Field Education in the Global South* brings together 28 well-researched contributions covering 20 countries across the developing world. The authors in this volume address the contemporary challenges faced by social work education in their respective countries. One of the foci in the handbook is to examine, research, and reconceptualise the concept of theory and practice relationship in social work. The relationship between theory and practice is a long-standing debate in social work both in local and global contexts. Many researchers have tried to provide a deeper understanding of theory and practice relationship in social work (e.g., Osmond & O'Connor, 2004; Sheppard, 1995; Teater, 2017). However, confusion and lack of understanding on theory and practice relation in social work still persist in many countries' social work, which leads to an explicit focus on theoretical teaching while sidelining the field work component of social work education.

Developing Skills and Competences of Students and Practitioners

Preparing competent social workers who can address the growing injustice and inequality in the globalised world is the challenge that social work education is facing in the contemporary world. The main purpose of social work education is to equip graduates with the knowledge, values, and skills that are required for the effective discharge of core social work functions in their practice. Social work as a service profession aims to alleviate the distress and enhance the wellbeing of humankind. In order to prepare ethically competent social work practitioners, schools of social work need to train their graduates in reflective ability, empathy, and emotional intelligence. Further studies have highlighted that skills of reflection (Ferguson, 2018) and empathic ability (Gerdes & Segal, 2011) are the important skills to be imparted to social workers alongside other training and knowledge.

Building evidence-based knowledge, person-centred values, and inculcating the skills of effective intervention and assessment are the core purpose of social work. Furthermore, this book brings in discussion on competency-based field work practice (Chapter 3). Inculcating the quality of empathy is one of the important aspects that need to be discussed in social work education and practice teaching. Preparing future practitioners to be empathetic is inculcating the ability to understand and recognise the emotions of others (Badea & Pana, 2010) and this quality is considered to be an important aspect of care professions (Grant, 2014; Ioannidou & Konstantikaki, 2008) such as social work.

Knowledge Production

The *Routledge Handbook of Social Work Field Education in the Global South* is an attempt to develop high quality reference materials related to social work education and field work practice in the developing countries. Literature in the social work domain has been discussing the issue of western domination and imperialism for several years. Social work academics in the global south criticise western domination and western theories in their social work teaching as they do not seem to be applicable to the local realities. The need and challenges for developing indigenous teaching materials has been in discussion both at national and international levels in several countries(Sajid et al. 2020). For several years scholars have been demanding the development of a context-specific social work curriculum, pedagogy, and practice component in social work education.

Several authors in this handbook discuss the importance of developing indigenised, context-specific, and culturally relevant social work education and training programmes in developing countries. Social realities in the developing world are different to that of the developed world, hence many of the theories and teaching modules developed in the western context tend to be irrelevant and ineffective in responding to the social problems experienced in developing countries. Contributions in this handbook discuss decolonising social work practice (Chapter 7), cultural practices in indigenous communities (Chapter 16), building culturally relevant social work curriculum (Chapter 19), and contextualising social work field education (Chapter 22) across different regions and regimes. Further contributions result in the form of this handbook which is a rich source of literature focusing on developing countries and originating in the countries' context. This handbook is of additional value to the indigenous knowledge in each of the countries that are covered in this handbook.

Structure and Content of the Handbook

The aim of this handbook is to provide a comprehensive review of fieldwork education internationally. It is structured into 28 chapters and four parts, with each part focusing on a specific theme within fieldwork literature and research. The structure is as follows:

Part 1: Developing Practice and Rethinking Perceptions: Field Education in South Asia
Part 2: New Insights into Social Work Field Education in Developing Asia
Part 3: Field Work Education in the Latin American and the Caribbean Context
Part 4: Developing Competent Social Work Graduates: African Perspectives on Field Work Education

The Routledge Handbook of Social Work Field Education in the Global South fills the north-south gap by generating high quality academic contributions dealing with field education at different levels of social work education in universities and colleges across countries in the global south. Thus, the book is the first in social work academia to bring field education from the global schools under a single volume (please also see *The Routledge Handbook of Field Work Education in Social Work*). We provide an overview of what is covered under each of the four parts of the handbook.

Developing Practice and Rethinking Perceptions: Field Education in South Asia

In South Asia professional social work education is offered in five countries including India, Sri Lanka, Nepal, Bangladesh, and Pakistan. In addition to this the Kingdom of Bhutan has recently started a certificate course in Social Work. Despite decades of social work education and practice, the status of social work is not high and public recognition of social work is low. Social work field practicum is practised as an integral part of teaching programmes; however, western domination in the practice and teaching modules continues to be dominant and literature on social work education in these countries makes demands for the indigenisation and decolonisation of social work education and practice. Schools of social work in the South Asian region practise various models in field work education and the most commonly used model is the traditional placement model. In the traditional placement model students are placed at agencies in the community for practical learning (Lager and Robbins, 2004; Royse et al., 2003; Savaya et al., 2003). Furthermore, Chapter 2 discusses the field work practicum in community engagement programmes. Field work education in the South Asian region faces a number of challenges which are common to most of the countries. Lack of professional recognition, low pay, and low-profile jobs are the common challenges in all South Asian countries (Chapter 3 Nepal, Chapter 6 Sri Lanka, and Chapter 7 India) whereas a large number of schools offering social work programmes, increasing enrollment, and a limited number of field work agencies with trained supervisors are found in India, Bangladesh, and Pakistan. Chapters in this section also discuss decolonisation (Chapter 7), community social work methods (Chapters 2 and 8), competency-based field work practicum and its importance (Chapter 3), and challenges faced by social work education in the South Asian region. In sum, this section is a comprehensive overview of field work education in the South Asian region.

New Insights into Social Work Field Education in Developing Asia

Societies in the Asian region continue to experience several developmental challenges including poverty, unemployment, inequality, and human rights violations. Further political, economic, and development discourse in the region is influenced by the western legacy and people's lives are systematically controlled by the forces of globalisation and neoliberal policies. In the 21st century Asian developing countries experience extreme levels of poverty and inequality. Social work education and practice in the region need to incorporate the societal details in their teaching and prepare their professionals to provide the best possible intervention and service. Further literature also notes that the origin of social work was an institutional response to the public issues and private troubles experienced in many societies across the globe (Parsons, 1939). *The Routledge Handbook of Social Work Field Education in the Global South* is an attempt to collect such innovative and impact-making interventions and practices by the social work academics in the developing countries. This section of the handbook is a collection of four articles written by academics and practitioners from Georgia, the Philippines, Turkey, and India. Though there are only a few contributions this section provides a deeper understanding of practice teaching and its challenges in Georgia (Chapter 11), the role of social work field education in achieving social justice and human rights (Chapter 12), and the challenges and the prospects of social work field education in Turkey (Chapter 13). Chapter 14 in this section provides a comparative understanding of the development of and challenges faced by social work field education in India and China.

Other countries in the Asian region also experience issues related to irrelevant theories and practice models in their social work curriculum, pedagogy, and research. There is an ongoing demand for indigenisation and contextual social work development in most of the developing Asian countries. Chinese social work educators have also recognised development and professionalisation of the practice components in social work education as a crucial step in achieving indigenisation in social work (Tong, 2003) which appears to be true in many other countries across the globe. Furthermore, in terms of field work placements, block placement is the most common type of field placement for students in the Asian region. Block placement expects students to complete theoretical learning prior to embarking on field practice – which in other words is perceived as an obstacle to students' professional development as there is a gap between theoretical and practical learning. After theoretical input in the classroom, students spend four to five days a week conducting field work at a designated agency (Liu et al. 2013). Contributions in this handbook also discuss the challenges faced by schools of social work in terms of finding field work agencies, field work supervisors, and qualified agency supervisors. Scholars have suggested paying greater attention to the management of field education and programme structure (Grady, Powers, Despard, & Naylor, 2011) as these factors have a greater influence on the overall development and professionalisation of social work education and practice.

Field Work Education in the Latin American and the Caribbean Context

Tensions in social work development and demand for culturally relevant social work curriculum and practice are the most discussed issues in social work in the South Latin American context (see Chapters 16 and 19). Furthermore, societies in South Latin America continue to face issues such as poverty, inequality, and unemployment. Social work development in Latin America was an effort to professionalise the philanthropic practices followed in helping people. In the development of social work, culture also played an important role as cultural practices in Latin American countries were not supportive of economic growth programmes and that explains how the situation of poverty and inequality existed in society. Furthermore, Carolina Munoz-Guzman et al. in their contribution provide an understanding of clinical social work in Chile, and Claudia Reyes-Quilodran et al. discuss the issues related to social work and field work abilities in the teaching professionals. In general, this section provides an interesting and evaluative understanding of the development and challenges faced by social work in the contemporary South Latin American context.

Developing Competent Social Work Graduates: African Perspectives on Field Work Education

Social work in Africa was introduced only in the 1960s and is hence a relatively young profession. Due to the basic principle of the profession – 'establishing a just society' – social work professionals in Africa intervene in issues related to poverty, HIV eradication, gender equality, and self-led community empowerment. Africa is a continent with more than 50 countries; all these countries are experiencing social issues to more or less the same extent. Issues such as poverty, unemployment, and migrant population with communicable disease appear to be prevalent in some countries. Social work education is generally provided within the university system and the approach is largely remedial or curative in nature. This handbook brings together social work field practice evidence from South Africa (See Chapters 21 and 26), Nigeria (see Chapter 22), Trinidad and Tobago (see Chapters 23 and 24), Botswana (see Chapter 25), Lesotho (see Chapter 27), Eswatini (see Chapters 28 and 29). Furthermore, the last two chapters also provide a comparative understanding of field work education in South Africa and Eswatini (see Chapters 28 and 29). The contributions in this section address a variety of issues including: South African perspectives on field work education; innovations, challenges, and perspectives in Nigerian social work field education; understanding the readiness for practice in social work; challenges in assessing students practice; challenges and development of social work field education in Botswana; challenges and opportunities for offering social work field education through open and distance learning; development of social work field education in countries with newly developed social work programmes; the role of social workers in knowledge transfer; and challenges in the professionalisation of social work in the African continent.

All the nine chapters in this section are well-researched and conceptualised to bring out the best results of social work education in the African continent. The section provides an understanding of social work education and practice in six African countries where social work is practised and taught in universities and higher educational institutions. A comparative understanding among all these contributions also proves that social work in general and social work education and field education in particular is well established in South Africa as the country has a regulatory mechanism for both education and practice. Furthermore, all 28 chapters spread across 20 countries contribute to the knowledge base of international social work focusing on the global south.

Our point of departure in this volume is *co-learning* and *cooperation*. We believe that social work academia in the global south can develop indigenised, context-specific, culturally relevant, and socially responsible education and practice through collaboration and cooperation between and within countries. These collaborations will further help the countries in developing social work education and practice centred around social justice, human rights, equality, and national development. In conclusion, we would like to express our gratitude to the contributors for working with us to achieve the goal of an international handbook on fieldwork focusing on the global south. We have learnt a lot from each of the contributors and have noted the variety and diversity of practices and experiences across cultures and continents. One of the strengths of this handbook is bringing experiential learning and experts' perspectives from 20 countries across the global south. We believe social work across the globe and particularly in the global south is developing uninterruptedly and has all the strengths to respond to the social problems and concerns in contemporary society. Having said that, we are also reminded that social work must continue to grow and develop its knowledge base, so it remains relevant and helpful to its users.

References

Badea, L., & Pana, N. A. (2010). The role of empathy in developing the leader's emotional intelligence. *Theoretical and Applied Economics*, 2(543), 69–78.

Baikady, R., Sajid, S.M., Nadesan, V., & Islam, M.R. (2022). The Routledge Handbook of Field Work Education in Social Work (1st ed.). Routledge India. https://doi.org/10.4324/9781032164946

Collins, S. (2007). Social workers, resilience, positive emotions and optimism. *Practice*, 1(4), 255–269.

Council on Social Work Education. (2008). *Educational Policy and Accreditation Standards*. Alexandria, VA: CSWE. Retrieved from https://www.cswe.org/getattachment/Accreditation/Standards-and-Policies

/2008-EPAS/2008EDUCATIONALPOLICYANDACCREDITATIONSTANDARDS(EPAS)-08-24-2012.pdf.aspx

Davidson, J. C. (2005). Professional relationship boundaries: A social work teaching module. *Social Work Education*, 24(5), 511–533.

DeRoos, Y. S. (1990). The development of practice wisdom through human problem-solving processes. *Social Service Review*, 64(2), 276–287.

Dhemba, J.(2012). ―Fieldwork in social work education and training: issues and challenges in the case of eastern and Southern Africa.‖ Social Work & Society, 10(1): 464–80.

D'Souza, A. and Sebastin. K. (2012). ―Field practicum: need for evolving best practices.‖Deeksha,10(2): 33–42

Dybicz, P. (2004). An inquiry into practice wisdom. *Families in Society: The Journal of Contemporary Social Services*, 85(2), 197–203.

Ferguson, H. (2018). How social workers reflect in action and when and why they don't: The possibilities and limits to reflective practice in social work. *Social Work Education*, 37(4), 415–427.

Gerdes, K. E., & Segal, E. (2011). Importance of empathy for social work practice: Integrating new science. *Social Work*, 56(2), 141–148.

Gowdy, E. A. (1994). From technical rationality to participating consciousness. *Social Work*, 39(1), 363–370.

Grady, M. D., Powers, J., Despard, M., & Naylor, S. (2011). Measuring the implicit curriculum: Initial development and results of an MSW survey. *Journal of Social Work Education*, 47(3), 463–487. Fall 2011.

Grant, L. (2014). Hearts and minds: Aspects of empathy and wellbeing in social work students. *Social Work Education*, 33(3), 338–352.

Grant, L., & Kinman, G. (2011). Enhancing wellbeing in social work students: Building resilience in the next generation. *Social Work Education*. DOI: 10.1080/02615479.2011.590931

Gray, M., & Allegritti, I. (2002). Cross-cultural practice and the indigenisation of African social work. *Social Work/ Maatskaplike Werk*, 38(4), 324–336.

Gray, M., & Allegritti, I. (2003). Towards culturally sensitive social work practice: Re-examining cross-cultural social work. *Social Work/Maatskaplike Werk*, 39(4), 312–325.

Gray, M., & Yadav, R. K. (2015). Social work without borders: A Janus-faced concept. *Social Dialogue*, 11, 26–27. Retrieved September 26, 2016, from http://data.axmag.com/data/201508/20150818/U114409_F349450/FLASH/index.html

Harms Smith, L. (2020). Franz Fanon's revolutionary contribution. In C. Morley, P. Ablett, C. Noble, & S. Cowden (Eds.), *The Routledge Handbook of Critical Pedagogies for Social Work: New Perspectives on Educating for Social Change* (pp. 399–411). London: Routledge/Taylor Francis.

Imre, R. W. (1985). Tacit knowledge in social work practice. *Smith College Studies in Social Work*, 55, 137–149.

Ioannidou, F., & Konstantikaki, V. (2008). Empathy and emotional intelligence: What is it really about? *International Journal of Caring Sciences*, 1(3), 118–123.

Kaseke, E. (1990) Foreword, in: Hall, N. Social Work Training in Africa: A Fieldwork Manual. Harare, Journal of Social Development in Africa

Kinman, G., & Grant, L. (2011). Exploring stress resilience in trainee social practitioners: The role of emotional and social competencies. *British Journal of Social Work*, 41(2), 261–275.

Klein, W. C., & Bloom, M. (1995). Practice wisdom. *Social Work*, 40(6), 799–807.

Lager, P., & Robbins, V. (2004). Field education: Exploring the future, expanding the vision. *Journal of Social Work Education*, 40(1), 3–11.

Leung, J. C. B. (2007). An international definition of social work for China. *International Journal of Social Welfare*, 16, 391–397. DOI: 10.1111/j.1468-2397.2007.00495.x

Lin, J., & Chen, X. (2005, September 6). The embarrassment prospects of seeking appropriate positions for social work graduates. *China Youth Daily*, p. 3.

Liu, M., Sun, F., & Anderson, S. G. (2013). Challenges in social work field education in China: Lessons from the western experience. *Social Work Education*, 32(2), 179–196.

Mallick, A. (2007). ―Fieldwork training in social work curriculum.‖ The Indian Journal of Social Work,68(4): 573–80.

Nadesan, V. S. (2020). Challenges of social work students from historically disadvantaged universities during placements in semi-rural areas in South Africa. *Southern African Journal of Social Work and Social Development*, 32(3), 17. https://upjournals.co.za/index.php/SWPR/index

Osmond, J., & O'Connor, I. (2004). Formalizing the unformalized: Practitioners' communication of knowledge in practice. *British Journal of Social Work*, 34(5), 677–692.

Panic, G. (2016, August 19–21). *Mobilization of Graduated Social Workers for Alternatives in Social Work*. Paper presented at the 14th Annual TiSSA PhD Network, Gent, Belgium.

Parsons, T. (1939). The professions and social structures. *Social Forces, 17*(May), 457–467.

Royse, D., Dhooper, S. S., & Rompf, E. L. (2003). *Field Instruction: A Guide for Social Work Students*. United States of America: Pearson Education.

Savaya, R., Peleg-Oren, N., Stange, D., & Geron, Y. (2003). Congruence of classroom and field instruction in social work: An empirical study. *Social Work Education, 22*(3), 297–308.

Scott, D. (1990). Practice wisdom: The neglected source of practice research. *Social Work, 35*(6), 564–568.

Sheppard, M. (1995). Social work, social science and practice wisdom. *British Journal of Social Work, 25*, 265–293.

Shokane, A. L., & Masoga, M. A. (2019) Social work as protest: Conversations with selected first black social work women in South Africa, *Critical and Radical Social Work, 7*(3), 435–445. DOI: 10.1332/204986019X15695497335752

Sajid, S. M Baikady, R., Sheng-Li, C., & Sakaguchi, H. (2020). Introduction: Social work: A profession without boundaries: Debates on global and contextual social work. In S. M. Sajid, R. Baikady, C. Sheng-Li, H. Sakaguchi (eds), *The Palgrave Handbook of Global Social Work Education*. Cham: Palgrave Macmillan. DOI: 10.1007/978-3-030-39966-5_1

Teater, B. (2017) Social work research and its relevance to practice: "The gap between research and practice continues to be wide". *Journal of Social Service Research, 43*(5), 547–565.

Tong, M. (2003). Integration between theories and practice: Reflections on curriculum design of social work courses. In *Proceedings of the Fourth Annual Conference of the China Association for Social Work Education (CASWE)*. Beijing: Social Science Academic Press.

Vincent, M. (2018). Making sense of African thought in social work practice in Zimbabwe: Towards professional decolonization. *International Social Work, 63*(4), 419–430.

Wilks, S. E., & Spivey, C. A. (2010). Resilience in undergraduate social work students: Social support and adjustment to academic stress. *Social Work Education, 29*(3), 276–288.

Yadav R., & Yadav A. K. (2020) Decolonising social work education in Nepal. In S. M. Sajid, R. Baikady, C. Sheng-Li, H. Sakaguchi (eds), *The Palgrave Handbook of Global Social Work Education*. Cham: Palgrave Macmillan. DOI: 10.1007/978-3-030-39966-5_20

Part I
Developing Practice and Rethinking Perceptions: Field Education in South Asia

1
Revisiting Praxis as a Model for Field Education in Social Work

Febna Reheem, Sojin P. Varghese, and Richa Bhardwaj

The role of professional social worker is to be immersed in the field and engaged with the people, while respecting their agency. Under the current COVID-19 scenario, how do social work practitioners engage with the field without endangering themselves and the communities they work with? This is both a question of ethics of fieldwork as well as professional commitment and responsibility. The answer to this question is also one that has implications on the way social work education, especially field education, is conceptualised and organised.

This book is coming out at a time when the world is in a phase of uncertainties. Social work being a profession engaged in interventions across different domains and cultural contexts is one that is mired in ambiguities as to what are the best intervention strategies. The current COVID-19 crisis in the world makes it even more challenging to espouse the best field strategies, given the virgin terrain that is created by the combination of a new viral strain spreading on a hitherto unprecedented global scale. For India, the unprecedented crisis of the health pandemic is multifold, coupled with the tribulations of the economy within an already volatile terrain of majoritarian politics with simmering feelings of polarisation. The scenario is one that makes the work of social work professionals extremely challenging. How do social workers, supervisors, educators, and students approach fieldwork and community engagement in such contexts? How does social work fieldwork education prepare future professionals for such situations? There are many questions for practice in the immediate and current situation. But the implications for the organisation of education, especially field education, cannot be neglected.

A quick analysis of the response of social workers in Mumbai, one of the hardest hit areas in the initial phases of the COVID-19 pandemic in India, is one that provides new insights for the conduct of social work in the country. Social work is a profession that is deeply connected to the ebb of life (Ferguson 2001) of people in the community it is rooted in. The current crisis India and the world is facing is concurrently shaping the identity of social work practice. And as social work practice is changing and/or evolving, the requirements for the educational process that fashions social workers are to be adapted to match the needs of the context. Fieldwork education is the signature pedagogy of the social work profession (CSWE 2008). The new emerging realities from the field require that we look with a new perspective at the values, dispositions, and skills imparted during field education.

DOI: 10.4324/9781003270119-3

The core principle of fieldwork education is to be present with and available alongside people whenever there is a crisis. The training in community organisation, mobilisation, development, approaches of group work, and case work all stress empathy, engagement, and empowerment. Among the various models of social work, critical and structural social work is the need of the day in the Indian context. For such emancipatory social work the concepts of social justice and human rights are cardinal. The emphasis for interventions is on collaboration rather than prescription. How we can have a fieldwork education model that ensures that social work students are primed to imbibe this intricate matrix of values, skills, and dispositions is a pertinent question.

Given the diversity in the field of social work practice, it is simplistic to offer a prescriptive model for field education that encompasses the needs of different contexts —unless the pedagogical model itself is one that has adaptability and context-specificity built into it. The praxis model of social work is revisited as a possible intervention model to familiarise students with the praxis potential of social work. Praxis is conceptualised as a complex of thought and action in which reflexivity and critical and collaborative enquiry are integrated (Healy, 2001; Prabhakaran, 2005; Fook 1999).

The chapter explores how the principles of praxis can be woven into the fieldwork framework ranging from planning the fieldwork engagement, interaction between the supervisor and the student, placement of the practicum in the curriculum etc. A model of praxis intervention conducted in the village hamlets of Attapady, a tribal settlement in Kerala, elucidates that collaborative enquiry and action can facilitate community-desired and driven change. Emphasising praxis in the fieldwork engagements has the potential to provide long-term dividends to the profession. It can usher in the much-needed impetus to critical social work in India. Providing aptitude and tools for critical enquiry to budding social workers, the praxis model can also remedy the lack of a rigorous knowledge base in the profession.

Emerging Face of Social Work in India and Recent Lessons

The role and purpose of social work in general has been hotly contested since its inception and the diverse answers which have been provided have been categorised roughly into three types (Dominelli 1998). These are:

- Therapeutic helping approaches
- Maintenance approaches
- Emancipatory approaches

Among these three approaches, the paradigms based on the emancipatory approach are indispensable for social work in India. Those endorsing an emancipatory approach to social work have an explicit commitment to social justice (Dominelli 1998). Social change at both the individual and societal levels lies at the heart of an emancipatory approach. This is in sharp contrast to the managerial strand of social work as it is increasingly practised in the West. Managerialism is not just reflected in tools but also in the fundamental philosophies that define and inform social work practice (Prabhakaran 2011). To effectively honour the intentions of social work practice, we must adhere to a practice that looks beyond a narrow problem management perspective – to one that looks at the sociopolitical ecology of the problems handled by social work. (Prabhakaran 2005). Emancipatory approaches guide practitioners beyond the traditional goals of 'managing', 'controlling' and 'coping with crisis' that are there in therapeutic and maintenance approaches.

There are different progressive movements and trends within the paradigm of emancipatory social work (Dominelli 1998). Anti-oppressive practice, radical social work, feminist social work, anti-racist social work are some such strands. In toto, they are approaches that have social justice at their centre and they are cognisant of the structural nature of problems and solutions, giving them all a critical orientation in practice. What Healy (2001) says about critical social work is a summation that captures the various strands and practices in it, in that they all encompass

> a recognition that large scale social processes, particularly those associated with class, race and gender, contribute fundamentally to the personal and social issues social workers encounter in their practice; the adoption of a self-reflexive and critical stance to the often contradictory effects of social work practice and social policies; a commitment to co-participatory rather than authoritarian practice relations; and working with and for oppressed populations to achieve social transformation
>
> *(Healy, 2001)*

Because of the way these practices understand the structural basis of people's problems they have much to contribute to social work in Indian contexts. In India there is more at stake than the provision of services for people in need. Social work in the country should emerge as a progressive practice, which takes the side of people who have been subjugated by structural inequalities (Ramaiah 1998; Anand 2009). Poverty is a principal manifestation of the structural inequalities that social workers encounter and it is pervasive in India. Moreover, there is a complex interplay of identities and vulnerabilities rooted in those identities. The marginalisation of Dalits, tribes, the LGBTQI community, women, minorities, refugees, and environmental crises are all critical social justice issues to be addressed in the Indian social work field. Understanding the interplay of such vulnerabilities and working towards the elimination of structural inequalities that perpetuate them is essential for social work to fulfil its potential as an empowering profession in the country's context. Any social work intervention, whether gradual or immediate, has to take cognisance of these realities. The most effective interventions are effective, this is so because of such cognisance. The interplay of these identities and poverty was evident in the dynamics of the recent COVID-19 response in Mumbai.

A Snapshot of Social Work in Mumbai, as a COVID-19 Response

In March 2020, India went into a sudden countrywide lockdown, prompted by the impending increase in COVID-19 infections, which at that time were mostly concentrated in the big urban centres of the country. While the lockdown was meant to give the government administration and departments time to gear up their health infrastructure and protocols to deal with the challenge of increasing patients in the future, its impact on the marginalised population groups of the cities was immense.

One of the most urbanised states of India, Maharashtra and its premier city Mumbai, where, as per official figures about 42 percent of its population resides in slums (Census 2011), is the worst impacted. The working-class population of the city residing in these slums or informal settlements largely consist of the people from lower caste hierarchy, minority religions, and migrants from other states of India engaged in various forms of casual employment. The absence or paucity of basic amenities and extremely high population densities are some of the features of the everyday lived reality of people living in these informal settlements. Most of their work being of an informal nature does not allow these people the luxury of working from home. Therefore, within these pre-existing vulnerabilities, the impact of a sudden lockdown was unprecedented.

The prescription for prevention of COVID-19 is physical distancing, frequent handwashing, and wearing a mask, which in theory does not seem like a big thing to follow. However, the majority of social work practitioners and local community leaders understood the challenge of actually implementing these in the informal settlements of Mumbai. The approaches and strategies understood through online posts of many of the NGOs in Mumbai and conversations with development practitioners bring out how over a period, interventions were planned and protocols of fieldwork defined. The development practitioners, through past interventions and current discussions with the marginalised sections of the city, were privy to the economics of work, household expenditure, and savings of large sections of these people. While the threat of disease was imminent, the immediate concern for most people was how long they would be able to feed themselves and their families. Therefore, one saw many grassroots level NGOs commence with the distribution of dry ration kits, highlighting the plight of these communities and the need for redefining one's interventions in the field.

An interesting takeaway for the authors was how, while the approach of distribution of food was done by many organisations, there were few who incorporated in practice the changed protocols of physical distancing during distribution. A changed scenario required a change in intervention style. Some organisations engaged with community leaders and volunteers to identify the most vulnerable within the community on parameters such as the elderly living alone, widowed women, daily wage unskilled workers etc. and targeted distribution specifically to them. These organisations also ensured the creating of protocols for physical distancing during distribution i.e. placing food kits on stools, stepping back, and then calling the recipients one by one. Additional care was taken to avoid overcrowding at predefined distributions points by coordinating with people at stipulated slots. For these organisations food distribution was not seen as an end in itself. Over this period they engaged with the communities via video and phone calls coordinated through leadership nurtured at the grassroots level. Thus, a collaborative discussion was ensured for identifying the challenges, exploring the solutions, and mitigating the crisis. The paucity of basic amenities like access to water and clean toilets was simultaneously tackled through advocacy efforts with the concerned government departments. Thus, practical solutions were explored and implemented through coordination between the community, development practitioners, and the government.

Interestingly some of these organisations and concerned individuals also used this crisis to highlight the longstanding embedded structural issues with the way policies related to poverty alleviation, food distribution, migration, urban planning, housing, and basic amenities. They brought out the mono-rational conceptualisation of these policies which impacted their success when implemented on the ground and the negative repercussions of the same came to the forefront when the COVID-19-induced sudden lockdown came into operation.

The successes in the different phases of the COVID-19 response is telling of three things: 1) That understanding structural realities renders micro-interventions successful 2) Adaptability in response to emerging contexts is a crucial element to effective interventions and 3) Collaborative thought and action create sturdy support systems for people in need. This spirit of context-specific, collaborative adaptation was a new equation for social action and there are lessons in it for the task of reimagining fieldwork education in India.

Fieldwork as a Signature Pedagogy in Social Work Education

Every practice profession has a pedagogical mark that prepares its students in the profession's fundamental ways of thinking, performing, and acting with integrity (Wayne et al. 2013). This 'signature pedagogy' (Shulman 2005) comprises the characteristic forms of teaching and learning used in a particular profession. Each profession has a distinct signature pedagogy – akin to the medical rounds that form the signature pedagogy in medical practice. In the case of social work, it is field practice (CSWE 2008). This is because, in social work, students must not only gain a grasp of conceptual knowledge and emerging empirical findings and values but also learn to integrate and apply these dimensions through skilful and intentional practices.

Through fieldwork,

1) Students develop practice skills
2) Translate theory from the classroom into the reality of practice
3) Test their ability to be professional social workers

Despite field practice being the signature pedagogy in social work, there is no definite or pervasive frame that organises it across the different social work educational institutions in the world (Wayne et al. 2013).Different pedagogical principles are used from institution to institution and setting to setting and none of them are routine or pervasive or generic. What is pervasive and routine about social fieldwork education so far is that it is required of all students for the same minimum number of hours and that it must be supervised by a field instructor with a social work degree. We need more organising principles than that to ensure the signature pedagogy in social work maintains its integrity and vitality. This is all the more the case in social work education in India.

It could be argued that the increasing diversity in the field of social work makes a generic pedagogy impractical. However, it is possible to isolate intellectual, emotional, and skill-based learnings that every social work student, despite their specialisation or context of practice, can benefit from. There is merit in considering which, if any, pedagogical principles are worthy of becoming a universal component of social work education. Social work has fashioned its fieldwork practice's prominent pedagogical principles from several other disciplines, especially psychology. For example, psychodynamic theory was relied upon heavily to inform direct practice (from the 1930s to the 1960s) and the trend that resulted was the evolution of the tradition where the one-to-one supervisory relationship was viewed as a critical component of social work education (Wijnberg and Schwartz 1977). This model is relied on heavily in our social work field practice in education.

At a juncture where there is a coalescence of multiple identities, multiple issues, and global practice, social work as a profession must be steered towards a critical, emancipatory approach. And we need a model of social work field education that retains the signature of the progressive nature of social work practice. The field of practice is increasingly a complex terrain where the social workers or development professionals are required to navigate convoluted situations which often do not come with pre-set prescriptions. At the same time the response to such situations needs to be given within a short span of time. From the successful Mumbai response, it can be seen that it was the structural understanding of class, caste, migrant realities, and collaboration that allowed for the designing of service provisions that were effective in reaching out to the most marginalised in the most pertinent ways. In fieldwork placements, social work students should be facilitated to develop and employ such perspectives. The concept of praxis is suggested as an organising principle for field education that can engender that.

What is Praxis?

The theory of praxis goes back to the times of Aristotle. Aristotle classified the field of theory and action into three parts: 1) The theoretical (*theoria*) 2) The productive (*poesis*) and 3) The practical (*praxis*).Each of the three forms has a different *telos* (purpose) (Smith, 2011).

The purpose of a *theoria* (theoretical discipline) is the pursuit of truth through contemplation and its *telos* is the attainment of knowledge for its own sake. The purpose of *poesis* (the productive sciences) is to make something. Its *telos* is the production of some artefact. *Praxis* encompasses the practical disciplines which deal with ethical and political life. Their *telos* is practical wisdom and knowledge (Carr and Kemmis, 1989).

In view of this categorisation, the entire realm of whole social work practice falls under *praxis* and not *poesis*. The distinction he makes between *poesis* which can be equated to a 'productive' action and *praxis* which can be equated to 'practical action' is crucial for social work. *Poeisis* always results from the idea, image, or pattern of what the artisan wants to make. In other words the person has a guiding plan or idea. The *praxis* is the practical and cannot have such a concrete prescription. Instead, we begin with a question or situation. We then start to think about this situation in the light of our understanding of what is good or what makes for human flourishing (*phronesis*). *Poiesis* is about acting upon, doing to an entity. It is about working with definite objects/plans. *Praxis*, however, is creative: it is dialogical, seeking, and dialectical (Smith, M.K, 2011).

Different social scientists and philosophers since then have elucidated praxis, emphasising different aspects of the concept. Capturing the most common denominator among them, it could be said that praxis has been understood as a reflective practice.

August Cieszkowski was one of the earliest philosophers to use the term *praxis* to mean 'action oriented towards changing society' in his 1838 work *Prolegomena zur Historiosophie* (*Prolegomena to a Historiosophy*) (Prabhakaran 2005). Fleshing out the possibility of praxis for social change further, Paulo Freire defines *praxis* in *Pedagogy of the Oppressed* as 'reflection and action directed at the structures to be transformed' (Freire 1970, p. 126). This has two components: 1) The oppressed acquiring critical awareness of their condition 2) Their action towards liberation. Straddling a realm that comes in between pure theory and pure action, praxis encompasses a state where the individual reflectively engages with action in an iterative manner (Smith, M.K 2011). It's a dialectical concept that conceives the relationship between theory and practice as one intrinsically blended together. A description of such a praxis can be seen in the concept as explained by Mahilo Markovic, who stated that praxis is 'creativity instead of sameness, autonomy instead of subordination, sociality instead of massification, rationality instead of blind reaction and intentionality rather than compliance' (1974:64). Such a practice that is persistently in peoples' lived-in reality, always fresh to the context and needs of the situation, ensures that the work is one that is relevant and in congruence with the principle of freedom.

Praxis Model in the Field

Praxis accordingly has two forms – one that copies models and wishes to reproduce models is an 'imitative and bureaucratized practice'. In contrast to this is transforming practice that is 'essentially creative, daring, critical and reflexive' (Gadotti 1996). It is the second interpretation that holds potential as an organising principle for social work field education in India and thereby needs further elaboration in this chapter.

> It is not simply action based on reflection. It is action which embodies certain qualities. These include a commitment to human well-being and the search for truth, and respect for others. It is the action of people who are free, who are able to act for themselves. Moreover, praxis is always risky. It requires that a person 'makes a wise and prudent practical judgment about how to act in this situation'
>
> *(Carr and Kemmis 1986 :190)*

A field model from a tribal settlement in Kerala will help convey the potential of praxis more tangibly. The model will elucidate how the qualities mentioned by Gadotti and Carr and Kemmis were engendered on the field. Praxis intervention as a fieldwork model, in its prototypic version, can be seen in the intervention carried out in the tribal hamlets of Attapady in Kerala (Prabhakaran 2005). The intervention was aimed at working with the adults there to collectively enquire upon and take action on issues that were deemed relevant for themselves by the community. The endeavour was an amalgamation of 'research', 'reflection', and 'action' in that it combined elements that equipped the communities with perspectives and skills to undertake scrutiny of their own condition and initiate action on the same. The work had field research, workshops, classroom and fieldwork sessions integrated. The intervention had spontaneous and well-planned elements incorporated.

The fieldwork had components of week-long discussions with sociologists, ecologists, historians, anthropologists, activists, and philosophers. An example of one such interaction was the attempt to unravel the concept of 'Adivasi' collectively. Discussion sessions were arranged intermittently between month-long field explorations continuing for about nine months. Every session of the week-long discussion was preceded and followed by a workshop and an evaluation respectively. All the 35 participants native of the hamlets were oriented towards conducting research on the life condition of their fellow aboriginals with active participation of their respective hamlet dwellers. The systematic collective exploration of their life conditions prompted the hamlet dwellers to realise and tackle certain issues they felt possible. One such issue that they found had much salience from their research was the poor nutritional status of the community. The intervention undertaken with the community could initiate a process of gaining historical competence and for the first time in their life the aboriginal participants wrote their history collectively (Prabhakaran 2005).

This praxis intervention practice has much to offer for social work education. Ethical, critical, contextualised action is a hallmark of effective social work endeavour. The potential enrichment that praxis has to offer can be broken down into three components: 1) Experience that facilitates the intellectual and emotional dispositions to look at the self, client, and field critically 2) Experience that conditions the student to engage in collaborative action with the clientele/community 3) Because of the above two, experience that instils progressive, emancipatory values. When a social worker enters into a praxis intervention, s/he along with the clientele enters into a collective dialogical probing into problem ecology. The theory-practice interaction is engendered in fieldwork practice in many institutions. The placement of concurrent fieldworks is consciously designed so. But what can be reinforced to usher in the true practice of praxis is the reflexive, collaborative components.

The potential of the fieldwork period to be one of praxis can be enhanced when the student and supervisor create a field of thought and action that is critical. Critical thought as a vector can be placed in different constitutive components. Reflexivity (Healy 2001) and the critical perspective (Gadotti 1996) are aspects of informed thought in praxis. Collaborativeness (Fook) and flexibility (Prabhakaran 2005) are both components of the action part of praxis. To understand what each of them implies for a fieldwork student, we have to unpack them separately.

1) Being Reflexive

A cardinal, critical component of praxis is **reflection**. Healy (2001) points out that praxis fosters self-reflection. This concept has tremendous use for a social work student who has to unravel the biases and conditionings s/he holds to effectively engage in practice in a progressive way. Adhering to praxis necessitates that the student work on his/her own biases as well as that of the clientele. A frank, scientific audit of self as a human and as a social work agent will help the students to unravel class, caste, gender biases embedded in them their position in the intellectual field and in their respective social space and also their intellectual bias. The model provides opportunity for the social worker to undertake a reflexive inward journey to get rid of biases that affect his/her practice. A social work education based on praxis principles could shape the students and teachers to be self-reflexive and sensible. Similarly, when a community/client is empowered to undergo the same reflective processing, it can initiate the process of empowerment. Reflective praxis thereby builds on reflective awareness and action at both individual and collective levels.

This prescription in the praxis model to put the self of the social worker in the enquiring gaze is one that is conducive for a practice that is anti-oppressive. Rossiter (2005) observes how social workers are often involved in a 'messy' job of a civilising mission, one that produces the 'other' in need of help. For example, the very identity of a social worker that is sustained is that of a helping, good person. The 'client' is the needy, vulnerable one. Such identity creations and relations obscure the problem of power and privilege in the relations between the helper and the helped. So the critical gaze itself questions the innocence with which social work is taught and practised, and is highly called for. Such a questioning should come early in social work education. Praxis, with its explicit prescription for reflexivity and self-objectivation requires that. For instance, a social work student working with the issue of a Dalit woman in a village should be aware of the intellectual and dispositional biases s/he holds as a result of her/his class, caste, gender, locational positionings.

2) Having a Critical Perspective

Brechin et al.'s (2000) accounts are of critical action in social work settings as 'open-minded, reflective appraisal that takes account of different perspectives, experiences and assumptions'. The act of considering different perspectives, experiences, and assumptions requires that the social worker is competently versed in a thorough understanding of the sociopolitical contexts and theoretical perspectives that expound on them. Critical theories inform and enhance critical practice. However, as a discipline, social work has been perceived as one with an anti-theoretical orientation (Barbour, 1984). This comes from the conceptualisation of the field as a pragmatic profession that offers concrete, common sense solutions to problems occurring in the world (Mullaly, R. & Mullaly, B. 2007). There needs to be better integration in social work curriculum between theory and practice. Mullaly (2007)points out how there is a stark dichotomy between theory and practice in the minds of social workers and how they distance themselves from theory, perceiving it as esoteric, abstract, and 'something people discuss in universities'. The social work curriculum enforces that dichotomy, according to him. However, such dissociation from theory – as in when a social work practitioner strays away from what s/he perceives as 'theory' and engages in action – is dangerous. For then s/he is actually relying on 'personal constructed theory' that is a 'taken for granted reality' of her/himself. Such naïve positioning can lead to a perpetuation of structural inequalities. This is because underlying ideologies we unconsciously operate with starkly influence the biases we have, agendas we set, and the language we use (Adams, Dominelli and Payne, 2002). Many of such biases and agendas may be perpetrators of already existing structural inequalities. The transgressions could be in macro-policies or in micro-actions. For instance, a social worker working with 'homeless' communities assisting the registration for IDs that inadvertently label an individual as a 'homeless citizen' is acting as an agent of coercive State mechanisms. S/he is unaware of the larger structures of disciplining and labelling that jeopardises the condition of the clientele with the label of homelessness. A group of social work students welcoming a community for a group event with a performance and attires of the dominant caste is communicating in a language that disempowers the oppressed castes in the area. Such naïve positioning can lead to a perpetuation of structural inequalities. A reading of Foucault and his writing on governmentality or an understanding of Sanskritisation might be easily relegated to abstract, cold theory by many a social worker. But the sensitising capacity of such critical theoretical understandings in contexts such as the above-mentioned is immeasurably valuable. Such knowledge not only sanitises but also galvanises the agency of a social worker.

The praxis approach appreciates such critical theoretical engagement-mediating action. The scheme for such an engagement would give a student the nudge to constantly go back and forth between theory and field reality, thereby making firm connections between the two. Reflexivity and a theoretical understanding of the field are interrelated in that a key way the insights of critical theory are translated into practice occurs through the mechanism of critical reflection (Prabhakaran 2011).

In general, there needs to be better integration in social work curriculum between theory and practice. The praxis model offers a vital connecting paradigm that links both without falling into the danger of abstract theorisation. This is because a practice of praxis ties the thoughtful enquiry intimately to the practice at hand.

3) Being Collaborative

The result of the intervention at Attapady, where the community themselves became the interpreters and designers of their reality, is an example of empowering, collaborative practice. The framework of praxis allows for contextualised collaborative enquiry. As a world we are entering into uncertain times. Social workers across communities are engaged in practice that is mired in ambiguities as to what the best intervention strategies are. This has been the reality of the COVID-19 situation. In the action taken by NGOs in Mumbai, immense interdisciplinary collaboration and pooling of community resources and perspectives were the reasons for effective interventions. The paradigm of praxis is essentially useful here for all the ways it allows for and elicits contextualised (in time and space) practice. To understand the application of praxis in this context, we have to go back to the cardinal conception of *praxis* by Aristotle. As has been discussed earlier in the chapter, in Aristotelian *praxis*, there can be no prior knowledge of the right means by which we realise the end in a particular situation. Gadamer (1979) captures the spirit of such engagement as he observes,

> As we think about what we want to achieve, we alter the way we might achieve that. As we think about the way we might go about something, we change what we might aim at. There is a continual interplay between ends and means. In just the same way there is a continual interplay between thought and action. This process involves interpretation, understanding and application in 'one unified process.
>
> *(Gadamer 1979:275)*

Developing an attitude informed by this praxis orientation is a crucial learning for social work students. In situations where there are no prior prescriptions or theoretical or practical models of enquiry and action, such a paradigm for dialectical action becomes relevant.

Moreover, collaboration between social work students during fieldwork placements needs to be facilitated. Peer learning is a central, highly valued component of adult education theory and practice (Knowles, 1980). The active interaction with students and peers through the greater use of educational group structures would ensure accountability develops in students (Schulman 2005).Expanding the use of group learning structures in social work field education would bring the additional benefit of providing students with both the skills and mindset to engage in peer evaluation and accountability.

4) Facilitating Reflexivity, Critical Understanding, Collaboration with the Clientele

Praxis as a within-person endeavour has been discussed above. Equally cardinal is the exercise of facilitating the 'other' – the client or the community to engage in reflexivity, critical understanding, and collaboration. Critical action in praxis is necessary, as are endeavours to make the marginalised and subaltern probe their social reality and trajectory. Through praxis, the social work student understands, articulates, intervenes in the life world of the clientele with the clientele themselves. Such a probing should be the impulse for action. The profession needs social workers who can be critical and who empower those with whom they work by helping them to understand their situation. Praxis aids the social workers in empowering their 'clients' and communities to make connections between their personal plight and that of others, examine power relations and their impact on the specifics of their daily routines and acquire the knowledge and skills for taking control of their lives.

In the example of the praxis intervention in Attapady, one of the primary exercises was to create a critical consciousness in the participating group of individuals from the hamlet about the Adivasi identity and the dichotomy in language use of 'Adivasi' (tribal) and 'Vandavasi' (non-tribal). The ingrained as well as arbitrary nature of the identities were expressed and processed in dialogues surrounding the concepts exemplifying how such meta-thinking –usually a domain of academics – were fluidly handled by the tribal members in the intervention group. The presence of a local historian in the discussion sessions facilitated a discursive engagement with their local history, priming the group with tools to critically reflect on the community's past and current trajectories. Such perspective sharing is equivalent to power sharing, given the Foucauldian knowledge/power complex's action (Ramachandran, 2008).

India is a highly diverse nation. There are over 4000 distinct communities in the country, each with its own unique sociocultural and political dynamics. On successful completion of a course in social work, the graduate worker needs to be able to contextualise her/his action to the local reality, even being active in engaging with macro-narratives and structures. A forging of bonds with local communities as critical partners in search of knowledge and action models can help the professional in remaining relevant and effective. In the Indian context facts, frameworks, and skills to engage with social problems are still in wanting. Even as empirical enquiries into local realities are called for what is more imperative is that such research is done 'with' the marginalised instead of 'on' them. In a context where fabrication of meaning is more important than the meanings themselves (Bannet 1989:66), the community that a social worker with praxis orientation engages with gets an opportunity to fabricate meaning for themselves.

In the domain of action also, collaboration is valuable. Practice that is persistently centred in peoples' lived-in reality ensures that the work is one that responds to the issues and questions which are identified by the oppressed groups themselves. Increasingly, marginalised communities are rising up to assert their rights. New social movements for land rights and human rights are evolving. Marginalised people have created these organisational entities for themselves to challenge the inadequate services being meted out to them under the prevailing system. The role a social worker has there is to be a conscientious partner.

Dividends of Praxis

We need structural and critical approaches to social work to unearth the true empowering power of the profession. The roots of many social problems are systemic and these systemic influences spill over to different fields of social work practice. Ideology is extensively pervasive in the field of social and personal action. The language we use, the agendas we set, the judgments we make are all results of larger systemic structures. We need the eye and ear to discern the biases we have from these systemic influences. Reflexive praxis introduced through social work field education will prime students with the critical skills to identify and resolve that. This is essential considering the 'governmentality' and 'managerial' nature of various social work positions today (Prabhakaran 2011). An aptitude for praxis inculcated early in social work education will create cohorts of social workers who are disposed to critical and structural work – an orientation that is indispensable for the effective practice of the profession in the Indian context.

Another important need to be considered is the need for the field to have a more rigorous knowledge base. The discipline has difficulty articulating and demarcating an exclusive cognisance (Taylor and White, 2006). In social work, knowledge needs to incorporate both the practical and theoretical. Knowing about and knowing how to act are important in this knowledge base. Trevithick (2009) includes theoretical knowledge, factual knowledge, and practice knowledge as three subcomponents of the social work knowledge base. Social work in general is lacking in all these three dimensions. This is all the more applicable for social work in the diverse terrain that is India. The discipline has borrowed heavily from other social science disciplines. This dearth is a highly problematic one. For although social work is about action, that action it professes must be supported by theory. Moreover, for critical change to happen, the action must be informed by critical thought. There should be more theories and practice models based on a study of the field realities that inform the discipline. In a country with over 4600 unique communities, structural action needs to be informed by the sociopolitical contexts of these communities. The profession can grow in this regard only if a cadre of practitioners who have a research aptitude and the critical thinking endeavours to contribute to a system of knowledge and analysis, concurrent to their practice of social work. To facilitate the evolution of social workers who work in such a manner, we need a pedagogical model in social work education that emphasises the connection of theory to action. The familiarity in linking action to theory iteratively will facilitate social workers to act as social scientists.

Considering the need for critical social work and the need for knowledge building in the Indian context, it can be said that any new innovation in fieldwork practice should be a response to these needs. An introduction of pedagogy and the principles of praxis explicitly in the curriculum will further that.

Conclusions

Social work is a profession intimately connected to the ebbing life-politics of the clients and communities it engages with and one that has the power to legitimately intervene in the private lifespans of individuals. With such great proximity and access comes the greater need for continuous overhauls, accountability, and rigour in practice. Practitioners who can effectively transduce field realities to effective modes of action can facilitate such a transformation in the profession. The rigour can be engendered through an open-minded critical engagement with self as a social worker and the community. The fieldwork education has to be structured in such a way as to facilitate this. Fieldwork supervisors should lay critical emphasis on facilitating critical reflection by the students on their identities and positions. The mentorship process should be a central field for engendering praxis during fieldwork practice of students. Irrespective of specialisations, regardless of methods of social work employed, such a reflective practice will equip the students to shake off conditionings that are derivatives of their identities, ideological stances, and positioning as a social worker itself. Collaboration between students to embark on collective inquiry and action for related problem fields should be facilitated during fieldwork practice. In situations where there are no prior prescriptions or theoretical or practical models of inquiry and action to fall back on, such a paradigm for collaborative, inquiring action will prove useful. Abstracting theoretical implications from practice is significant in praxis. Having an approach that validates significance of everyday experience as a legitimate source of information in designing services equips the students to contribute to the profession in significant ways. Such an engagement is an endorsement of experiential knowledge as an important source of data. And the praxis of iteratively, critically learning from experiences will help the students to create a body of much-needed knowledge that furthers practice and research in the field.

References

Adams, R., Dominelli, L., &Payne, M. (2002). *Social Work: Themes, Issues and Critical Debates*. Basingstoke, UK: Palgrave.
Anand, M. (2009). Gender in social work education and practice in India. *Social Work Education, 28*(1), 96–105.
Bannet, E. (1989). *Structuralism and the Logic of Dissent*. London: Macmillan Press.
Barbour, R. (1984). Social work education: Tackling the theory-practice divide. *British Journal of Social Work*, 14 (6) 557–578.
Brechin, A., Brown, H., &Eby, M. (2000). *Critical Practice in Health and Social Work Care*. London: Sage.
Carr, W., &Kemmis, S. (1989). Becoming critical: Education, knowledge and action. *Journal of Educational Thought*, 43(3), 209–216.
Census. (2011), *Primary Census Abstracts, Registrar General of India*. Ministry of Home Affairs, Government of India, Available at: http://www.censusindia.gov
CSWE. (2008). *Educational Policy and Accreditation Standards*. Alexandria: Council on Social Work Education.
Dominelli, L. (1998). Anti-oppressive practice in context. In Dominelli, L.&AdamsR. (Eds.), *Social Work*. London: Palgrave.
Ferguson, H. (2001). Social work, individualization and life politics. *British Journal of Social Work, 31*, 41–55.
Fook, J. (1999). '*Critical Reflectivity in Education and Practice*'. *Transforming Social Work Practice: Postmodern Critical Perspectives*. (J. F.Job Pease, Ed.) London: Routledge.
Gadamer, H. (1979). *Truth and Method*. London: Shed & Ward.
Gadotti, M. (1996). *Pedagogy of Praxis*. New York: State University of New York Press.
Healy, K. (2001). Reinventing critical social work: Challenges from practice, context and postmodernism. *Critical Social Work, 2*(1), 1–13.
Knowles, M. (1980). *The Modern Practice of Adult Education: From Pedagogy to Andragogy*. Englewood Cliffs, NJ: Cambridge Adult Education.
Markovic, M. (1974). *From Affluence to Praxis*. Boston, MA: Beacon Press.
Mullaly, R., &Mullaly, B. (2007). *The New Structural Social Work*. Oxford: Oxford University Press.
Prabhakaran, M. (2005). *Towards a Praxis Model of Social Work: A Reflexive Account of 'Praxis Intervention' with the Adivasis of Attappady*. Kottayam: Mahatma Gandhi University.
Prabhakaran, M. (2011). Praxis Intervention: Towards a New Critical Social Work (February 20, 2011).. Available at SSRN: https://ssrn.com/abstract=1765143 or http://dx.doi.org/10.2139/ssrn.1765143
Ramachandran, R. (2008). Genetic Landscape. *Frontline Magazine, 90*.
Ramaiah, A. (1998). The plight of untouchables: A challenge to social work profession. *Indian Journal of Social Work, 59*(1), 124–146.
Rossiter, A. (2005). Discourse analysis in critical social work: From apology to question. *Critical Social Work*, 6(1).
Schulman, L. (2005). Signature pedagogies in the professions. *Daedalus, 134*(3), 52–59.
Smith, M. (2011). *What is Praxis?* Retrieved August 10, 2020, from The Encyclopedia of Pedagogy and Informal Education.

Taylor, C., & White, S. (2006). Knowledge and reasoning in social work: Educating for humane judgement. *British Journal of Social Work*, 937–954.

Trevithick, P. (2009). Revisiting the knowledge base of social work: A framework for practice. *British Journal of Social Work, 38*(6).

Wayne, J., Bogo, M., &Raskin, M. (2013, March). Field education as the signature pedagogy of social work education. *Journal of Social Work Education*, 327–339.

Wijnberg, M., &Schwartz, M. (1977). Models of student supervision: The apprentice, growth, and role systems models. *Journal of Education for Social Work*, 107–113.

2

Swastyayan, a Commitment

Fieldwork through Community Engagement

Victor Narzary, Bibharani Swargiary, Riju Sharma, and Alice K. Butterfield

---

Fieldwork is an essential component of social work education. It places the students in real-life situations providing them with opportunities for growing as professional social work practitioners. In the process, students are able to understand the complexities of society, learn the modalities of intervention for social change and development, network and liaison with practitioners in the field, and thereby, attain adequate preparation and skills for engaging in social work practice. While fieldwork education places primacy on students' learning, growth, and development, it also provides social work educators with the space and the scope for networking and collaborative engagement with communities.

Social work education in classrooms is inadequate as generally, it imparts only conceptual and theoretical knowledge. It is important for social work learners to be able to 'feel' and 'do' (Parasuraman et al. (2021). Fieldwork provides the avenues for continued feeling, doing, reflection, and critical thinking. The fieldwork component of social work education is essential in that it exposes the students to institutions and systems that liberate or oppress people. In this regard, social work education also aims at enabling students to 'enhance problem-solving, coping, and developmental capacities of people', promote humane systems, and link individuals to 'resources, services and opportunities' (Minahan, 1978, p. 183). Within the Indian context, bodhi (2014, p. 9) posits that the context holds primacy, and as such students need to learn, as part of their fieldwork, 'theoretical frames (emerging from a context) coupled with … concomitant practice skills (both macro and micro) in relation to the identified context'. This approach draws attention to the dangers that preplanned projects and programmes could harm rather than liberate groups and communities. Fieldwork education has to be organised as per the needs of a given context.

In the light of the dilemma and questions social work encountered at the turn of the 21st century, Powell (2001) suggests that social work practitioners need to be equipped with theory, skills, and values that draw a balance between consumerist social work practice on the one hand, and the uncertainties of radical social work practice on the other hand. This, he proposes, can be done by directing social work education and practice towards civic social work practice. For engaging in civic social work practice, students need to imbibe 'civic values based upon principles that are democratic, inclusive and communitarian' (p. 161). In line with this view, community engagement projects of the Assam Don Bosco University (ADBU) have the participation of people in the community at the core – from conception, throughout implementation, and including critical reflection. The Don Bosco way of education with its variety of community engagement projects and civic social work practice are in confluence. This chapter presents the case of social work students' fieldwork education in the community engagement projects of ADBU. The background, history, and learning from the field showcase a unique civic engagement model of social work education at the university.

This chapter is largely based on the authors' experiences and critical reflections on the development of social work education that is intimately linked to the community engagement projects of ADBU. Victor Narzary and Bibharani Swargiary are part of the coordination teams for different community engagement projects. Riju Sharma heads the School of Humanities and Social Sciences and has played a pivotal role in several community engagement projects. Alice K. Butterfield has been closely associated with the Department of Social Work and its community engagement projects ever since her visit to ADBU as a Fulbright Specialist in 2017. The chapter has been developed from the reports of several community engagement projects. A few scholarly journal articles and books are referenced to locate the community engagement projects of ADBU as fieldwork sites within the domain of social work education. Fieldwork reports and community engagement reports were analysed to project the learning and principles that have emerged.

Fieldwork Education at Assam Don Bosco University

Assam Don Bosco University (ADBU) is part of the worldwide family of Salesians of Don Bosco that caters to the educational and developmental needs of 15 million young people across 132 countries. It is serenely located in the midst of a multicultural milieu in North Eastern India. Beginning in 2011, ADBU addresses the higher educational needs of the youth from the region by offering programmes in engineering and technology, management studies, basic sciences, life sciences, and social sciences. The university envisages moulding 'intellectually competent, morally upright, socially committed and spiritually inspired persons, at the service of India and the world of today and tomorrow by imparting holistic and personalized education' (Assam Don Bosco University [ADBU], 2013). Apart from aspiring for academic excellence among the students and faculty, ADBU has been actively developing participatory community and civic engagement programmes.

The ADBU engagement projects are located on the outskirts of Guwahati city of Assam in three places: Dimoria Development Block, Rani Development Block, and Karghuli. Since 2013, the Social Work Department has implemented projects to address conditions that impede the development of indigenous communities in terms of employment, particularly the rapid loss of community land and livelihoods due to urban sprawl, degradation of environment, and deteriorating living conditions. Planned in alignment with the vision of the university, the fieldwork education of the graduate social work students has been purposefully intertwined with these projects.

The Structure of Fieldwork

The graduate programme in social work (titled 'Master's of Social Work') is a two-year long programme. The curriculum has been designed in a way that the graduating students may specialise in one of the four areas of concentration – Community Development, Medical and Psychiatric Social Work, Family and Child Welfare, or Management of Development Organisations. Fieldwork is structured to address the incremental learning needs of the graduate students. There are eight components with a total of 18 credits (one credit being counted as 15 hours) that make up the fieldwork education rubric. Fieldwork education is comprised of orientation visits, concurrent and continuous placements, rural practicum, study tour, and an internship in the form of a block placement (See Table 2.1).

Observation visits to human service agencies orient students to fieldwork education, issues concerning human society, and societal response to those issues. Organization observation visits to agencies are done through visiting different organisational visits, lectures by agency personnel, guided observations, discussions, analysis of agency reports, discussions with agency personnel and constituencies. Rural practicum provides the students with a platform for engaging in participatory action research. They are taken through the process of zeroing in on a place for organising the practicum, collaborating with the local community, and carrying out participatory

Table 2.1 MSW fieldwork structure

Semester	Module	Credit hours*	Placement/setting	Fieldwork focus
1	Observation visits	-	-	Orientation and induction to fieldwork
	Concurrent fieldwork	4	Communities, NGOs, and government agencies	Individuals, groups, and communities: issues, contexts, constraints, challenges, and latent opportunities
	Rural practicum	2	Rural communities	Rural exposure and participatory action and reflection
2	Concurrent fieldwork	4	Communities, NGOs, and government agencies	Service for individuals, groups, and communities: apply casework, groupwork, community organising, and research
3	Continuous placement	4	Communities, peoples' movements, NGOs, and government agencies	Area of Concentration chosen by the student
	Study tour	-	Educational tour	Different approaches to social development and innovative programmes for intervention at regional, national, or international levels
4	Continuous placement	4	Communities, peoples' movements, NGOs, and government agencies	Policy analysis and advocacy, taking lead in mobilisation of local human and physical resources; proficiency in the application of relevant methods, skills, and techniques for handling real situations in the field
	Internship (block placement)	-	Communities, peoples' movements, NGOs, and government agencies	Experience hands-on job situation

Source: Authors
Note: One credit hour is equivalent to 15 working hours

action research on issues faced by the community. The educational tour in the third semester is a student-led activity where they travel in groups based on their areas of interest to study the best practices of social work intervention in India and neighbouring countries. The internship at the end of the two-year programme is a hands-on practice situation.

The concurrent fieldwork in the first and the second semesters is by and large carried out in the community engagement projects of the ADBU. The students are expected to get a close feel of the community and community settings, understand the dynamics, diversity and issues there, and become aware of the mores and values of people while working with them. They are also entrusted with positions of responsibility and engage in coordinating and implementing identified participatory community projects. This provides them with the avenues for application of skills of leadership, group work, community organisation, and participatory tools in the community setting. Most importantly, by getting involved in community efforts, students develop critical awareness about society and social change processes. Fieldwork practice in the third and fourth semesters focuses on the Area of Concentration chosen by the students. During this period, students generally choose a field setting or a community engagement project where they are exposed to specialised methods in their selected Area of Concentration.

Community Engagement Projects of ADBU

Social work originated in response to various social problems faced in different epochs of time. Over the years, its approach evolved and shifted from charity, to welfare, to development (bodhi, 2014), and more recently, to civic engagement (Powell, 2001). The charity approach focused on providing service to the 'deserving poor'. The welfare approach mandated that the state provide for the vulnerable in the society. The development approach aims at improving the quality of life by way of enhancing social and economic participation and the well-being of the people (Midgley & Conley, 2010). At the core of the civic social work practice is the drive for social inclusion that views the 'client' or the 'service-users' as citizens by ensuring equality and participation (Powell, 2001). Civic social work strategises to remove the propensity of social work to perpetuate relationships of dependency and inequality between the service provider and the service-users. In the words of Powell (2001) 'the reconstruction of the client as citizen provides the basis for a civic approach to social work' (p. 161). The dilemma of social work in addressing clientisation and the dependency of service-users is reconfigured in terms of civic values along the lines of democracy, inclusion, and community.

As part of its Community Engagement Programme, the Department of Social Work at ADBU uses a multipronged strategy to address issues of poverty, health, education, drinking water, cleanliness, and gender disparity. The aim is to engage students in achieving local community and national development, as well as working toward the United Nation's Sustainable Development Goals 2030.

The first community engagement project of the ADBU was started by the Department of Social Work in the year 2013. Four graduate students, namely, Esalanmidaka, Veronica Nriamei, Habadei Kharsatti, and Stephani Nongkynrih, were placed in the community setting of the Azara Gaon Panchayat for fieldwork. The initial discussion among the four students and three faculty, Victor Narzary, Riju Sharma, and Jacob Islary, led to a series of meetings among the village committees led by Sarat Das, Village Headman, and Prabin Medhi, President, Azara Gaon Panchayat, the ADBU Management Team led by Fr. (Dr.) Stephen Mavely and the faculty of the Department of Social Work. The outcome was the community engagement programme, named *Swastyayan … a commitment* meaning a fight to eradicate the ills of our society, on 30 April 2013. The launch day was a special event attended by the children, women, and men from the villages. The opening ceremony provided space for the presentation of what *Swastyayan ... a commitment* was all about and how it would be operationalised. Its coordination was carried out by Victor Narzary and the fieldwork students placed under his supervision, with support from Jacob Islary and Riju Sharma. There was a Core Committee comprising the Vice-Chancellor, School Directors, and Community Leaders to provide direction to the project (Assam Don Bosco University [ADBU], 2013).

Initially, the programme began by extending educational support to the schoolchildren of the neighbouring villages. In the later years, two other components, namely, the Community Counselling Centre (CCC) and the Life Skill Education and Awareness Programme (LEAP) were included. The addition of these two components in *Swastyayan* was significant in the sense that the CCC drew expertise and support from the Department of Psychological Counselling, while the LEAP was a direct result of the participation of the graduate students of Human Rights (with specialisation in Child Rights). The CCC was introduced in response to the psychological problems faced by children as a result of negative experiences in their schools and homes. It provided the children and their families with counselling support. LEAP sought to impart life skills education to the children in their neighbourhoods, while conducting awareness programmes on child rights. These inputs transformed *Swastyayan* into multidisciplinary community engagement. The faculty and the students involved had to work intensely together to coordinate and provide meaningful services.

The aim of *Swastyayan* has been to make the university resources available to the needs and requests of vulnerable communities around the university and beyond. Victor Narzary, who has been coordinating the programme, reiterated this specifically during the Opening Ceremony by saying,

> *Swastyayan* sets its first foot forward today with an affirmed belief that all of us, especially the constituent members of the university, namely, faculty, staff and students, and also the community leaders and government agencies should contribute meaningfully to development and transformation in the society.

Swastyayan has been extending the education support programme by providing free tutoring in the ADBU classrooms. The university has opened its doors: classrooms, counselling rooms, administrative and financial support needed to implement the programme. Hundreds of university students and faculty have volunteered to tutor, provide counselling and life skills education to school children in the following years. *Swastyayan* expanded its work to the Sonapur vicinity under the Dimoria Development Block which is around the ADBU campus at Tapesia Gardens. There, the programme has been contextualised in order to be able to address schoolchildren's educational needs in their home environment. Faculty and students conduct tutorial sessions for groups of five to ten children in homes identified by the children and community leaders.

The efforts have received wide publicity and have been much appreciated. It has been recognised as a best practice against Sustainable Development Goal 10 'Reduced Inequalities' by the International Association of Universities (International Association of Universities, 2017). Most importantly, it has been able to provide meaningful fieldwork placement for graduate students of social work. Over the years, *Swastyayan* also paved the way for collaborative work with national and international development agencies thereby strengthening civic social work engagement in the community, while also providing avenues for students to engage in multicultural and transnational teamwork.

Similar to *Swastyayan ... a commitment*, there are now several other community engagement projects at the ADBU. It is beyond the scope of this chapter to present the case of each of these projects. However, in Table 2.2, some of the key community engagement projects are

Table 2.2 Community Engagement Programme of ADBU

Sl. No.	Community Engagement Programme	Key Activities
1.	Swastyayan … a commitment http://www.dbuniversity.ac.in/swastyayan.php	• Catered to the educational needs of schoolchildren in the neighbourhood: 150 children per year since 2013 • So far, 543 faculty and students have volunteered at an average of 108 per year • A certificate course on Computer Literacy has been availed of by 15 children • Groups of children have been taken for educational tours to Guwahati planetarium, Don Bosco Institute, and Cotton College • Personality development and life-skill sessions on career goals, life-skill development, gender justice, quitting tobacco, singing, dancing, and painting, etc. have been conducted annually • Has been recognised as best practice for sustainable development by the IAU • Expanded to include home-based tutorship by faculty and student volunteers for extremely poor high school students of Hatimura village in Dimoria Development Block
2.	Prajiwal https://www.dbuniversity.ac.in/prajjwal.php	• Average of 100 children's educational needs addressed every year since 2010 • Drawing & art competitions, memory tests, different outdoor games, etc. held among the students annually • Platform for developing singing (both individual and group), dancing (both individual and group), role-play, speeches, poetry recitation, etc. provided annually • Observation of important national and international days observed every year: Rangali Bihu, Friendship Day, Independence Day, Teachers' Day, Children's Day, Gandhi Jayanti Day, Prajjwal Family Get-Together, etc.
3.	Adult Literacy Project	• Basic English (reading and writing) class for 25–30 women provided every Thursday and Friday in 2017 • Workshops on Child Development and Parenting, Nutrition and Balanced Diet, Physical Health (communicable and non-communicable diseases) and Mental Health held for the women • Seven members of faculty of the ADBU involved in the project • Four student volunteers facilitated the sessions • Seven women finally graduated with the Certificate in Basic English (Reading and Writing) issued by the ADBU

(Continued)

Table 2.2 Continued

Sl. No.	Community Engagement Programme	Key Activities
4.	Computer Literacy Project for Women's Empowerment: Vanit Agrata http://www.dbuniversity.ac.in/ced.php	• Several groups of women have benefitted from the training since 2015 • The faculty of the Computer Science Engineering Department are wholly involved in the project • Women trained on basics: what is a computer, parts of a computer, application software, word document, calculations using spreadsheet, internet, emailing, etc.
5.	'Swabhalamban': Livelihood Training Programme for Youth http://www.dbuniversity.ac.in/swabalamban.php	• Free training for unemployed youths on Electronics and Information Technology Hardware, installation and maintenance of power backup systems and computer application training since 2015 • 50 youths trained so far • 50 staff and faculty from the School of Technology involved in the effort • Nine student volunteers involved in the mobilisation of participants
6.	ADBU-UCDVO Support programme for Anganwadi Centres http://www.dbuniversity.ac.in/isesi.php	• Anganwadis (early childhood care centres under the Integrated Child Development Services Scheme of Government of India) have been renovated with GI roofing, wall painting, floor repairs, teaching-learning materials, toys, etc. since 2015 • Awareness programme through Street plays on alcoholism, domestic violence, school non-attendance, health, and unemployment • Installation of drinking water facilities in Ural Basti for about 75 families • Cleaning of the drinking water tank at Hatimurah • Organised games and sports programme in the villages • Organised a series of Workshops on Understanding Child Growth and Development for 50 Anganwadi Workers and Helpers of Dimoria Development Block • A total of 125 faculty and students from University College Dublin Volunteers Overseas and Assam Don Bosco University have participated in the project • Enhancement in the understanding of volunteering from multicultural and intercultural perspectives both among the participants and the community members

7.	Disaster Response Programme https://www.dbuniversity.ac.in/crisisresponse.php	• Disaster Relief and Intervention Programmes carried out since 2013 to reach out to communities affected by conflicts and recurrent floods in Assam and Kerala • Trained 30 NGO leaders in Community-Led Disaster Risk Reduction Programme in collaboration with Indo Global Social Service society • 300 GI roofing sheets, 54 school bags and stationery kits, 17 new sets of textbooks for students, essential food items, 40 sets of utensils for families, reconstruction of 12 houses, rebuilding of a village road 150 m long, psycho-social services for women, children, and youths in Hahim (Kamrup Rural) in 2014 • 700 families have been helped with food packets in 2016 and 2017 • 500 children have been provided with stationery kits in 2017 • 50 families have been provided with relief support in Kerala in 2018 • Involvement of the whole university community: staff, students, faculty, and management.
8.	Bixudha Jal Asoni: Clean Water and Sanitation Support Programme	• Low-cost and green technology transfer to 12 villages in Dimoria Development Block (Sonapur) • Clean drinking water facility distributed free-of-cost to the 12 villages in community water sources • Training of unemployed educated youths on installation and maintenance of domestic units • Entrepreneurship training for youths
9.	Centre for Development Studies and Initiatives (CDSI): Community Animation Programmes http://www.dbuniversity.ac.in/cdi.php	• Participatory sustainable development process started in 12 villages of Dimoria Development Block • Implementation of the social development programmes of the Government of India, such as, Swacch Bharat Abiyan, Unnad Bharat Abhiyan, and Fit India Movement • Facilitation of faculty and students to channel their creative and innovative pursuits into meaningful social change projects • Conducted a Summer School Programme 2017 for Grade IX and X students of the neighbouring villages (Marangabari, Upper Tapesia, Jargoan, Patharkuchi, Kamarkuchi, and Hatimura), 24–28 July 2017 • 65 school students and 8 faculty members along with 10 student volunteers from ADBU participated in the Summer School Programme • Facilitated the alumni of Assam Don Bosco University to conduct a 5 Day Kiddies Day Camp at A. W. Thomas Girls Home for the children of 6–13 years old 29 January–2 February 2018 Health Outreach Programme. 38 girls benefitted from the programme • In the sports and well-being programme, 23 children participated in a Community Volleyball Coaching Camp (10–22 December 2017) • Health and Mental Health Outreach programme • Blood Donation Camps

Source: Authors, based on various sources

presented. The different schools at the university, namely, the School of Technology, School of Humanities and Social Sciences, School of Management, School of Life Sciences, and School of Basic Sciences have unique community engagement projects that harness the core disciplinary knowledge and skills associated with them. All of these projects have a similar structure: a Core Committee comprising representatives from the ADBU Management Team, the project coordinator(s), student coordinator(s), Community Leaders and representatives from Non-Government, as well as Government Agencies. Some of these projects also have sub-committees that look into the everyday functioning of the project activities (See Table 2.2). In sum, the community engagement projects of ADBU have played a fundamental role in forging a critical mass comprising academics, students, communities, non-government and government agencies needed for meaningful and sustainable social transformation and development. They have been strategically positioned to address key development concerns of children, women, youth, vulnerable families, and communities in India. While they are hinged around the university's vision of moulding socially committed individuals at the service of India and the world, they are aligned, as much, with the shared vision and ownership of the communities facilitated through a participatory process. The efforts have generated a network of inter-community, intra-community, university-community, university-business, intra and inter-institutional, and university-government agency partnerships at local, national, and international levels.

Discussion

The nature of students' fieldwork carried out in the community engagement projects of Assam Don Bosco University draws its strength from the value for social inclusion. In the words of Powell (2001), 'social work defines its role [here] in terms of civic engagement with the most vulnerable citizens as a basic democratic imperative grounded in socially inclusive practice' (p. 157). The fieldwork orientation, community immersion, practice, supervision, and evaluation are grounded in the imperative for social inclusion in the local contexts that call for social work interventions. They hold onto a value-based call for a 'critically reflexive anti-oppressive' stance (Brown, 2012, p. 34). This stance allows for faculty and students of social work to engage in a participatory process that centres on the voices of the community while drawing from the resources that the community itself and the university can provide to address issues of children, women, and men and the community in general. The learning that has emerged is presented briefly in the following paragraphs.

Peoples' Participation is the Key

The social work practice in a community setting can no longer be one-sided. It is essential to engage in a participatory process to identify and address community problems (Kumar, 2002). Drawing from the fieldwork education carried out in the community engagement projects of ADBU, giving participatory processes a foundational position in social work education and practice reaps desirable outcomes. It begins with the departmental orientation to fieldwork for students who join the social work programme from a variety of disciplines during their undergraduate studies. All along, the students and faculty are in the driver's seat in ensuring that there are no short cuts to or deviations from the participatory processes during the fieldwork engagement. The involvement of the fieldwork agency leaders in evaluating students further strengthens the participation of people in fieldwork education.

Dialoguing as a Way

It is not possible to engage in a participatory practice without dialoguing. Dialogue ensures equality between the social work practitioner and community members. Dialogue makes it possible for the oppressed and the most vulnerable to trust the practitioner (Freire, 1972). Thus, dialogue makes it essential for the practitioner to empathise and value diversity. At the ADBU, dialogical relationships established with the communities have contributed greatly towards making the projects community-owned and sustainable. It is imperative for the fieldwork education to train the students in dialogical processes.

Context-Specific Social Work Practice

Social work offers a great variety of models to choose from in dealing with problems in society (Doel, 2012). Practitioners often find it easier said than done to correctly employ a set of sophisticated theories, models, or skills that they are equipped with. In this light, bodhi (2014) posits the contextualisation of social work practice as quintessential in order to engage in anti-oppressive and critical social work practice. Fieldwork practice in community engagement projects entails a high degree of contextualisation, in the sense that students are provided with the opportunity to engage in a participatory and dialogical practice to address the fundamental issues that are identified by community members. The case example of *Swastyayan ... a commitment* highlights that fact that fieldwork students address a fundamental need identified in and by a community. Social work's value orientation, ethics, perspective, and skills revolve around the need identified in and by the community.

Competence in Practice

All community engagement projects of the university have been designed to facilitate multidimensional outcomes. These include positive changes in the community, meeting the learning requirements of students and faculty, building skills and developing attitudes that align with the profession of social work. First, the learning needs of the students and faculty are largely met because of participation in the projects. The projects support the experiential learning requirements of the students by providing them space to be involved in planning, implementing, monitoring, and evaluating innovative projects for sustainable development. All the projects are anchored by a committee comprising a faculty-in-charge and a group of student members that facilitate the involvement of the larger university community. Structuring them in this way allows for expression of leadership, innovation, teamwork, and creativity. This, therefore, contributes to the attitudinal development of cooperation, and the value base of social work and its ethical principles, as well as teamwork, communitarian practice, democracy, and diversity. The successful planning and implementation of the projects in a participatory manner allows for ideal student-teacher bonding and facilitates the development of harmonious aspirations and commitment to social change. It helps in identifying strengths, weaknesses, opportunities, and threats for engagement by students as well as faculty. Competence in practice also working towards excellence, keeping in mind the limitations and strengths of one another. Ideally, an environment of trust and mutuality is created. This is streamlined into meaningful and engaging relationships for academic excellence in the respective fields of study, and fruitful community engagement projects that lead to social change.

Partnerships

The ADBU community engagement projects have been successful thanks to a number of agencies for partnering in its social change and development efforts. These partnerships provide excellent avenues for fieldwork students. They are able to work closely with personnel from national and international agencies, network with them, and at the same time learn from their practice models. The involvement of students and faculty in initiating a community mental health programme in Guwahati is a case in point (Narzary, Sharma, Swargiary, & Butterfield, 2019).

Contribution to National Development

The students are moved towards nation-building and development by striving for strong and resilient communities where social justice and dignity of all prevails. This is mandated by the vision statement of the university that seeks 'to mould intellectually competent, morally upright, socially committed and spiritually inspired persons at the service of India' (ADBU, n.d.). With this objective, social work students and faculty engage in its wide-ranging community engagement projects. These projects focus on addressing multifarious social problems in the vicinity. While fulfilling the objective of developing a cadre of dependable human resources at the service of India and the world, they are strategically positioned to serve the needs, rights, and entitlements of vulnerable children, youth, women, and communities. The educational needs of children are addressed through *Swastyayan ... a commitment*, ADBU-UCDVO Support Programme for Anganwadi Centres, and Prajjwal projects. Swabalamban seeks to train unemployed youth in livelihood-oriented skills through low-cost technology. The Vanitagrata and Adult Literacy Programme for Women envisage the achievement of women's empowerment through education. Thus, all projects are aimed at addressing the needs of the vulnerable and the marginalised, and thereby, seek to build strong and resilient communities in India. In this way, fieldwork students are able to participate and meaningfully engage in civic social work practice.

Sustainability of the Projects

The sustainability of social commitment programmes in ADBU is largely dependent on the voluntary spirit, goodwill, and commitment of its faculty, staff, and students. The enthusiasm and zeal of the faculty and students towards engaging in free service for nation-building and social development have been hugely rewarding. Like-minded organisations have also extended timely partnerships and support in all different projects. All of the projects are participatory in nature and involve the target communities beginning with the visioning and planning stage. Community ownership is a major target to be achieved by each project. So far, the projects have been largely sustained by community participation, involvement, and ownership. In addition, the Centre for Development Studies and Initiatives (CDSI) is an apex centre at the university that has been put together to address the multiple objectives of catering to the implementation of the social development programmes of the Government of India and the World Sustainable Development Goals 2030. It has resulted in the creation of a space to nurture a 'socially committed' environment in the university, and as a place to seek out partnerships and resources.

Evaluation of Fieldwork in Community Engagement Project

The fieldwork evaluation at the ADBU is both formative and summative. Individual and group conferences of fieldwork students are carried out weekly in order to facilitate deeper engagement with the communities and also to mentor students towards civic social work values and principles in a non-threatening environment. The process records of fieldwork days and their time diaries are used for low stake formative assessment of the students. The community/agency fieldwork supervisors also carry out a summative evaluation of the performance of students at the end of the fieldwork placement. Finally, there is a viva-voce examination conducted by bringing in prominent social work educators and practitioners to examine the fieldwork practice of the students. It has been found that this style of evaluation of the fieldwork education facilitates the ongoing and incremental learning needs of the students throughout the fieldwork placement in community engagement projects. Besides serving the evaluation of fieldwork students, the formative assessment enables identification and close monitoring of the activities carried out in the communities.

Conclusion

Thus, the community engagement projects of ADBU are distinctive and equally benefit all stakeholders. Students and faculty enhance their learning and knowledge, the institution is kept aligned towards its vision, and communities benefit as their social problems are addressed participatorily. Another distinctive mark is the no-profit-no-loss and low-cost nature of all the activities. These projects have been largely sustained by community participation, involvement, and ownership, and active engagement of social work students and faculty. They also provide excellent avenues for carrying out fieldwork education. The approach in such settings has been to closely work with communities for social inclusion: vulnerable children's educational needs, training of youths for employment, adult literacy classes for gender justice, extending support to early child care and development centres, participatory clean drinking water projects, and digital literacy. Such an approach is closely aligned to the civic social work practice that Powell (2001) proposes for addressing social problems without falling prey to consumerist social work practice on one side of the spectrum and the radicalisation of social work practice on the other. Students, faculty, and the communities are mutually aligned for enhancing the strengths and resilience of both individuals and communities. Social work education can be made more meaningful, in this way, by addressing the issues and problems that are embedded in contexts and communities.

References

Assam Don Bosco University [ADBU]. (2013a). *Our vision*. Retrieved 12 June 2020, from http://www.dbuniversity.ac.in: http://www.dbuniversity.ac.in/vision.php

Assam Don Bosco University [ADBU]. (2013b). *Swastyayan*. Retrieved 23 July 2020, from http://www.dbuniversity.ac.in/: http://www.dbuniversity.ac.in/swastyayan.php

Bodhi, S. (2014). Defamiliarizing and deassembling social work methods: Four ways of seeing, reflecting and engaging from a DTSW perspective (part one). *Indian Journal of Dalit and Tribal Social Work, 2*(3), 1–10.

Brown, C. G. (2012). Anti-oppression through a postmodern lens: Dismantling the master's conceptual tools in discursive social work practice. *Critical Social Work, 13*(1), 34–65.

Doel, M. (2012). *Social work: The basics*. New York: Routledge.

Freire, P. (1972). *Pedagogy of the oppressed*. Harmondsworth: Penguin.

International Association of Universities. (2017). Higher education paving the way to Sustainable Development Goals 2030. Retrieved 10 June 2018, from International Association of Universities: http://iau-hesd.net/sites/default/files/documents/higher-education-paving-the-way-to-sd-iau-2017.pdf

Kumar, S. (2002). *Methods for community participation: A complete guide for practitioners*. New Delhi: Sage.

Midgley, J., & Conley, A. (2010). *Social work and social development: Theories and skills for developmental social work*. London: Oxford University Press.

Minahan, A. (1978). Summary of the report of the undergraduate curriculum project. *Social Work, 23*(3), 183–184.

Narzary, V., Sharma, R., Swargiary, B., & Butterfield, A. (2019). Ashadeep: A holistic intervention with homeless mentally ill persons in northeast India: Considering disability policy and creating a path for social work education. In R.M Channaveer, R. Baikady, S. Cheng, & S. Haruhiko (Eds.), *Social welfare policies and programmes in South Asia* (pp. 25–43). New Delhi: Routledge. https://doi.org/10.4324/9780429323041

Parasuraman, S., Jha, M., Gulalia, P., Nair, R., & Jaswal, S. (n.d.). *Reflection and critical thinking in fieldwork*. Retrieved 16 July 2020, from http://epgp.inflibnet.ac.in/: http://epgp.inflibnet.ac.in/epgpdata/uploads/epgp_content/S000032SW/P001701/M020357/ET/1496901814Q1M7-ReflectionandCriticalThinking-text.pdf

Powell, F. (2001). *The politics of social work*. New Delhi: Sage.

3

Impact of the Competency-Based Field Work Practicum on Students' Learning

Pradipta Kadambari and Nalini Lama

'Social work is a practice-based profession and an academic discipline that promotes social change and development, social cohesion, and the empowerment and liberation of people' (IFSW, 2020). To develop the graduates of social work ready to practice social justice, social work education follows a systematic approach of learning. It is built with two systems. First, a knowledge-building method, where theoretical knowledge including social work values, principles, ethics, and skill sets are taught in the classroom. The other technique is the practice system of the field work practicum, which allows students to engage in a professional social work environment and participate in the experiential learning process to develop as competent graduates through guided supervision. These two systems are interdependent with each other to maximise students' development as proficient social workers. Field work training of social work is considered a unique feature which distinguishes social work from other social sciences (Social Work Education: Fieldwork Practicum, n.d). Providing best learning pedagogy to the students during the field work practicum is instrumental for social work academic institutions as students are testing and experiencing their classroom learning to real-life situations and identifying problem, handling situations, and overcoming both the challenges of their clients and also those they encounter themselves during professional development. To facilitate these skills, a movement of outcome-based education began. This movement of assessing learning outcomes in higher education became a prerequisite to social work education in regional accrediting bodies of social work also as Council on Social Work Education, CSWE (McGuire & Majewski, 2011).

Kadambari Memorial College of Science and Management (KMC), as a pioneering social work institution in Nepal, has been running the Bachelor of Social Work (BSW) at Purbanchal University (PU) since 2005. From 2005 to 2015, KMC applied the AB learning method in the field work practicum where activities of the agency and social work trainee were at the core. The learning was based on activities which guided the knowledge and skill attainments of students. Competencies that the students developed were depended on what students were involved in. In 2015, PU upgraded the BSW to a four-year programme, revising the curricular structure from a general to a CB system. The ten core competencies identified by CSWE in 2008 were taken as the framework of the revised curriculum, (CSWE, 2012). This shift in curriculum led the KMC field work department to develop a competency-specific training pedagogy. Responding to the change, KMC scaled up its practicum to CB learning with the same ten core competencies as its competency framework. This shifted the learning approach from activity to CB, positioning students' competencies at the centre with well-defined competencies. A Field Work Practicum Learning Plan came into practice in 2016. The objective of the Learning Plan is to enable students to reflect, test, and analyse their classroom learning and theoretical understanding of real-life problems, situations, and challenges, hence identifying the best practices of their profession and demonstrating the competencies guided by the learning plan. This also equips supervisors to organise and conduct student supervision and offer support in understanding, integrating, and applying the competencies during the practicum.

This chapter presents the impact of the CB field work in terms of student ability to demonstrate the competencies during practicum. It collects students' reflection from interviews and assesses their ability to demonstrate their proficiency. It applies a triangulation method of data collection and analysis to validate the impact. Data gathered from field supervisors are used to evaluate development of the competencies and demonstration in agency, supervision, and examination and to see differences in the AB field practicum. Students' placement final scores are evaluated to see if the outcome measured by supervisors and illustrated by students are similar. In-depth interviews with 13 students representing 50% of the total population of the outgoing batch and three field work supervisors were conducted. The authors' own experiences are used to narrate the development of the field work practicum as social work educators of KMC.

This chapter is presented in six sections. The first section depicts the context in three subsections: the historical context of KMC social work and the field work practicum; the developmental context of KMC and CB pedagogy; and the evaluation context of the field practicum. The second section discusses the value of CB education as an educational approach in higher education and the latest developments in social work and presents the KMC model of the CB field work practicum. The third section presents the conceptual framework of this study as an impact pyramid of the CB field practicum of the KMC as it facilitates the data gathering and analysis of this study. The method of the study is described in the fourth section. The fifth section presents the discussion on the analysis and findings of the information followed by a conclusion in the sixth section.

Context

The context of this study is presented in three stages in a historical context: the KMC social work programme and its social work field practicum, in a developmental context; the KMC to CB pedagogy and evaluation context; and an assessment of the CB practicum.

Historical Context

The history of the social work academic programme began in 1996 in Nepal with the Bachelor of Arts in Social Work in Kathmandu University. In 2005, PU became the second university to begin a social work programme with the BSW and the Master of Social Work (MSW). In the same year, KMC was established as a private higher educational institute and became the second college of social work in Nepal.

Historically, 2006 was a significant year for Nepal, as a decade-long armed conflict involving the internal Maoist people's movement came to an end. Poverty and the exclusion of marginalised castes and ethnic groups in rural areas were the key drivers of the insurgency (Nikku, 2012). In the post-war situation, the government was in need of institutions, resources, and efficient human service practitioners to solve the spectrum of problems of marginalised and vulnerable people and communities affected by the armed conflict. The PU social work programme was developed on the back of this historical movement, realising the need for professional social workers as potential human resources to work with individuals, groups, communities, and the government at micro, mezzo, and macro levels. The three-year BSW curriculum was developed with a 15 credit practice course of a supervised field practicum. For the first two years, 800 hours of a supervised field practicum per year were carried out (Nikku, 2012). From 2009, the hours were reduced to 560 per year to match the practicality of the semester examination schedule. The total hours of field practicum totalled 1680 hours in a three-year period. The field work process followed the AB model. In this pedagogy, field agency and its activities, along with student observation and undertakings, were at the centre of the experiential learning.

In 2015, PU upgraded the three-year BSW to four years. The author, as a member of the subject committee, worked with other members in revising the curriculum. As social work is a practice-oriented education, the importance of demonstrability of the students' skills set was taken into consideration whilst revising the curriculum to that of a CB framework. The ten core social work competence of CSWE 2008 was adopted in order to build the curriculum as: Identify as a professional social workers and conduct accordingly (1); Apply social work ethical principles to guide professional practice (2); Apply critical thinking to inform and communicate professional judgments (3); Engage diversity and difference in practice (4); Advance human rights and social and economic justice (5); Engage in research-informed practice and practice-informed research (6); Apply knowledge of human behaviour and the social environment (7); Engage in policy practice to advance the social and economic well-being and to deliver effective social work services (8); Respond to contexts that shape practice (9); Engage, assess, intervene, and evaluate (10). Following the change, KMC also decided to change its field work practicum pedagogy from an AB to a CB learning framework which would be 20 credit practice courses with 1680 intensive hours of a supervised agency placement.

Developmental Context

From 2016, KMC started hosting an international social work field practicum in Nepal. Students from the USA, Canada, and Australia came to the programme at KMC. This exposure enabled the KMC field work department to practise the CB learning plan of the respective universities. As internal supervisors of the international social work students, the field work supervisors enhanced their capacity in supporting and assessing students to demonstrate their social work competency. This development inspired KMC to follow the developing educational trend of international universities. In the same year, KMC received Ms. Natalie Long, a field work supervisor of Curtin University, Australia as an Australian Volunteer for International Development for two years. Having an experienced field work supervisor on board, KMC changed its field work practicum pedagogy from an AB to CB framework, incorporating Curtin University's learning plan. Along with Ms. Long, the field work department developed the KMC Field Work Learning Plan in 2016, incorporating all ten competencies of the CSWE aligned with the revised curriculum. This learning plan drove the student learning dimension towards competency-specific observation, integration, and practice and guided students to demonstrate their theoretical knowledge and skills as per the listed competencies. This development shifted the centrality of the learning approach from activity to the demonstrability of competencies. With this the looseness of AB knowledge and skills development got tightened with defined competencies and clearer guidance as to a student's role, task, and learning. A process of integration of the competencies came to fruition and was seen in student action and behaviour. This followed the three-step process of the field work practicum: preplacement interview, on-placement supervision, and post-placement consolidation, providing space for sequential instruction and guidance from field work supervisors.

Evaluation Context

The effect of the CB pedagogy was assessed continuously by the field work department from the individual student's performance. KMC waited to complete a full circle of the four-year study programme in order to evaluate the impact of the new pedagogy on the first cohort. This study population of the students is from the batch of 2015 who completed seven placements as per the new Learning Plan and as graduates of KMC.

Latest Developments

Universities are at the centre of preparing human resources for the global market. In the early 21st century, along with economic development processes and the rapid development of new technologies, competition between educational institutes accelerated (Butova, 2015). Such rivalry was to prepare their graduates for the employment market with not only knowledge but also with the applicability of this knowledge, referred to as competence. Following the idealisation of the concept of CB education from the late 1960s, the development of this theory in the modern era has been actualised by higher education academia adapting not only to the evolving needs of students but also to those of society. In this regard, social workers are recognised as professionals engaged with people and structures to address life challenges and enhance the well-being of people and the planet (IFSW, 2020). CB education became the pedagogy for the preparation of such graduates with an outcome-oriented curriculum. CB learning enhances integration of knowledge and skills systematically and teaches students to master and apply skills (Larsen & Hepworth, 1982). It ensures that students are able to demonstrate the integration and application of competencies in practice, grounded by the social work knowledge, values, and skills in a purposeful, intentional, and professional manner to promote human and community well-being (CSWE, 2015). This process features elements of personalisation and self-pacing of students with comprehensive supervision. During this process, the students learn to think themselves as practising social workers, perform various tasks, adopt roles, and engage with diverse people; thus students have a rich set of learning with different competencies (Hodgson & Walford, 2007). Understanding the value of competency testing and development, the revised KMC field work pedagogy adheres to the norms of CB learning throughout its three steps process flow. In this flow, it prepares students for the placement, guides and assesses mastery of the competencies from their practice, and measures outcomes from their ability to demonstrably link theoretical knowledge to their behaviour.

Concept

The study intends to examine the effectiveness of the CB field work pedagogy of KMC. For that, it assesses students' performance in terms of skills, abilities, and knowledge combinations in a specific context and sees how students have mastered the competencies (Fain, 2019). This study follows a conceptual framework to guide data gathering and analysis. The framework is based on the CB learning model of the National Postsecondary Education Cooperative's report from the United States (US) Department of Education (US Department of Education, 2002) and Kolbe's experiential learning cycle (Cherry, 2019). Both models are integrated to prepare a four-tiered pyramid, matching the KMC field work practicum process and purpose.

Foundation – Setting Competency-Based Learning Placement (Student – Agency Matching)

CB education emphasises focusing on learner development by considering the individual student's trait and characteristics to be the foundation of learning experiences (US Department of Education, 2002). This helps supervisors to guide and select students as per their interest and readiness. This enables students to accommodate themselves in the practice situation with their innate ability and knowledge and develop their capacity from the concrete experiences they receive in the process of experiential learning. Information collected from field work supervisors and students provides the effectiveness of this foundational base of the learning process.

Developing Learning Experiences – Integration of Skills and Knowledge (Identification of SW Competencies and Linkage to Theoretical Knowledge)

This tier of the pyramid is experiential as students engage in their field practice in agency, participating in activities with diverse clients. Students understand the practical aspects of their classroom learning and build their ability to link to the theoretical knowledge. This process of integration happens with the guided learning plan and students' supervisions enabling learners to conceptualise and concretise the meaning of competencies and experiences during practice and engagement. The weekly individual conference and skill lab classes foster the experiential developmental process. Field work supervisors and student reflections provide insights into this developmental learning experience.

Acquisition of Ability to Practise Skills and Knowledge (Competency-Based Practice and Behaviour)

The integrative learning experiences enable students to use their skills, abilities, and knowledge during their interaction and actions, shaping their practice and behaviour as trainee social workers. It leads to the application of the competencies when they practise active experimentation. The weekly report, individual conference, and group conferences show the ability of students to be competency-specific in their tasks and the effectiveness of the students' ability is assessed from the supervisors and student reflection.

Measurement of Performance (Demonstration of Competency)

The application of the competencies is measured to assess the outcome. The assessment of the student's ability to link the learning of the two systems – theoretical knowledge and practice – are reflected in their behaviours and reports. A continuous assessment of the demonstrability is carried out by the supervisors and the university external examination. Supervisors' observation, internal assessments, and final year score of the grade measure the outcome.

Method

The research design of this study is qualitative and exploratory in nature. A triangulation method with three levelled data sources was used to collect and analyse information to validate the outcome and impact. Convenience sampling was applied in a sample selection of the participants. This sampling method was chosen to avoid judgments of, selectiveness, and bias towards the participants. A mail was sent to the total population of the students of batch 2015, informing them about the study and seeking their interest as participants. The first 13 students (both male and female) – representing 50% of the total population – who responded first were considered as a first level data source as participants. All the three field work supervisors representing the total population of the field work team at KMC were considered as the second level data source since trainers' and students' final year practicum examination grading was considered as the third level data source as a result. In-depth interviews were conducted to collect the lived experience of field work from the supervisors and students. Before the in-depth interview of the students, a rapport was established to make them feel comfortable. This helped them open up and talk freely about their experience of field work, which helped in generating insightful responses for valuable findings. Interviews with both the field work supervisors and the students were recorded with their verbal consent and then later transcribed, organised, analysed, and reported as per the conceptual framework of the impact pyramid. The cross reference of the three sources of data helped in establishing the validity and reliability of this study. However, this study is limited to only one batch of students who were the first to adopt and complete the CB field work practicum. There was no data of AB field work from graduates. The information of the AB field practicum was collected from the supervisors only.

Substantive Discussion

The social work field practicum facilitates the process of thinking to doing, translating the philosophy into actions (Social Work Education: Fieldwork Practicum, n.d). In this process, students learn both the functional and technical aspects of social work as they gain competency. When the CB approach is applied, it provides positive outcomes over less structured methods of internship (Ali & Muhamad, 2018). CB provides well-organised instructions, clear learning outcomes, and expected performance (Woggins & McToghe, 2005 in Voorhees & Voorhees, 2014). The same has been applied in the KMC field practicum to develop competencies to perform as professionals.

The following are the outcomes and impacts on students as they move to the different tiers of the CB learning pyramid.

Foundation – Setting Competency-Based Learning Placement (Student – Agency Matching)

The three field work supervisors including the field work coordinator who supervised the students for four years acknowledged the importance of the preplacement process where they collect and verify the agencies for the best interest of their students.

> 'As social work supervisor we focus on the best interest of students' learning. In this process student's interest and the quality of field work agency also plays vital role' (Supervisor A).

> 'We make agency visit, call or email, making sure that the agencies are also ready to take our students which creates social work friendly environment in the agencies' (Field work coordinator).

This shows that the preparedness is not only limited to students, but that the working environment is also equally important to set the foundation of the CB learning. Students come from different backgrounds with diverse personal experiences. Respecting their diversity and acknowledging their characteristics and interest was important. Supervisors practise social work values and principles in guiding students. The process sometimes gets intense, as students share their personal events or issues such as domestic violence, self-harm, history of substance abuse etc. and were not ready to go to agencies like a correctional home or rehabilitation centre etc. Supervisors took consideration of these facts when finding a best match with an agency.

> We know students' understanding of different settings in pre placement interviews. Students not only share their challenges and difficulties of their past internship; they also share their personal issues which might become a barrier in certain settings. This procedure helps us to consider the professional aspect of students' learning along with their personal status and readiness.
>
> *(Supervisor A)*

> 'As all the individuals are unique in their own way, we believe that students also have their own innate character or traits'.
>
> *(Supervisor B)*

CB education places emphasis on considering an individual student's trait and characteristics as the foundation of their learning experiences. It serves as the first step to a ladder of learning, upon which further experiences are built (Voorhees & Vorhees, 2014). The earlier experiences of students help field supervisors to understand how these different experiences can be utilised to coach students in acquiring competencies. Larsen and Hepworth (1982) mentioned the nature of CB instruction as a systematic way of achieving specific educational objectives in observable and measurable terms. The field supervisors also mentioned systematic coaching and collaborative strategies to help students achieve the objectives. They assess students' progress continuously and evaluate their degree of achievements. This allows students to gradually fully gain competence. KMC supervisors' narratives confirmed the understanding of this foundational rung of CB and valued the students' interest, their choices, and their challenges, setting the base of experiential learning (Voorhees, 2001).

The students also acknowledged the guided freedom, choice, and collaborative approach in matching them with an agency.

> 'The best part of the KMC field work was the space given to us for field work as we could choose our own organization' (KMC student).

> 'when I joined, I found that the placement wasn't up to my expectation. I consulted my supervisor. She advised and encouraged me not to leave immediately but to search my area of interest there. After few days, I decided not to continue. Then my supervisor made an arrangement in another organization where I completed my placement successfully' (KMC student).

This reflects the fact that students' interests and status are prioritised and respected. A collaborative strategy and effort were carried out to achieve the objectives of the placement. This helped students to understand the setting that they had chosen or placed, setting the primary step on the ladder of experiential learning. This created a positive momentum to the gradual process of mastering skills, advancing students from single to more complex tasks and expanding the sense of competence gain (Larsen & Hepworth, 1982).

Developing Learning Experiences – Integration of Skills and Knowledge (Identification of SW Competencies and Linkage to Theoretical Knowledge)

As students move to the second tier of the learning pyramid, they are exposed to real-life situations in their profession. The dimension of time and space plays an important role in experiential learning, emphasising how experience, including cognition, environmental factors, and emotions influence the learning process (Cherry, 2019). The CB learning provides a path of action and sets the direction of learning in terms of goal attainment articulated clearly in different sections, aiming to capture as many aspects of experiences and outcomes as possible (Hodgson Walford H, 2007) and accommodate the features of experiential learning. The well-articulated learning plan and process of KMC field practicum provides the same direction and actions for the attainment of the ten core competencies over the period of seven internships.

Students participate in their fieldwork agencies as a new experience. As per Kolbe's experiential learning, the first process is the grasping of the fundamentals of the intended new knowledge and skills, starting with their engagement with the actual social work practice environment and hands-on activities providing them with active experimentation in the social workers' role and interaction with clients and the agency (Cheung & Delavega, 2014). They observe and apply the knowledge of classroom and their own past experiences. Every week, all students sit with their respective supervisor, individually, reflecting, sharing, and asking queries about their experiences. They receive guidance and learn the process of concretisation of their experience with understanding the meaning of their experiences in terms of defined competency. In this stage, both aspects of experiential learning – concretisation and conceptualisation – take place.

> Experiencing learning plan is interesting to students as it guides them to the ten competences of social work. One student shared me how she was judged by her agency supervisor as not committed internee. It was good to see how she could recognize the judgmental attitude from the remarks she received. When she recognized the principal of social work ethics in action, she also built her competency of critical thinking. Instead of judging supervisor negatively, she searched for the reason behind his remark.
>
> *(Supervisor A)*

> The AB reporting students used to describe the action or observation first, then reflected what they felt, understood/ build queries. Then they linked their understanding to the theoretical knowledge of social work, its values, principles and theories. Now the CB learning plan has a discrete section of competencies and its illustrations. The action/activities and experience students had, are critically analyzed to link to the competency. The competence demands students to go back to theoretical knowledge continuously. The process of making sense of actions and observation, building connection and present evidences, help them to conceptualize the experiences. It is a subjective process to achieve the objectivity of the learning plan. The experiences were quite captivating and complex to this batch at the beginning. Gradually they learnt to understand the applicability of the plan, guided closely in individual conference and group conference. They were given skill lab class in first four semesters to understand their experiences and make sense of the actions from theoretical perspectives.
>
> *(Supervisor B)*

These narratives present how experiences fostered the cognitive activities of students to observe, reflect, question, and relate to their theoretical knowledge. The KMC students were seen grasping the fundamentals of the agency environment and their own role to start their engagement with the actual social work practice environment in this crucial step. The supervisor outlining the complexity of the process at the beginning depicts the comprehensiveness of the learning plan. Unlike the AB field practicum, the learning plan demanded evidence of the skills that students applied or observed in the placement. Instead of acting and reflecting, it guided them to reflect on their experiences through the lenses of competency attainment, orienting them to the achievement of goals or outcomes. During this, a spectrum of experiences were concretised with the supervision, illustration, and linkage to the theoretical knowledge of social work. The supervisors said that above 90% of the students of the batch were very good in linking theoretical knowledge to their practice. However, the first two semesters were very important in crafting this learning style in students.

'90% of the students were good in linking theoretical knowledge to practice by the end of their final placement. Many students received letter of appreciation from their agency highlighting their professional behaviour and the knowledge of social work' (Field work Supervisor).

> In report, students wrote their observation and learning with examples. when they were not clear on linking to competency, I used to discuss individually coaching them to link the experience to the competency and to their theoretical knowledge. I encouraged them to use theory, principal and values in their personal and professional life. The first two semesters were little harder for this batch.
>
> *(Supervisor B)*

> In individual conference, I was keen on knowing how did they approach their field educator and how did they build the rapport. How was their reaction to the activities and professional behaviour of the agency and agency professionals? Had they been able to see any linkage to their knowledge of IASSW code of ethics, social work principles, values or theories? Earlier in AB field work, the competency development was limited to what activity they did. Some skills could be missed out when activity did not have any link to the desired competence. Now with the competencies on the top, students have to find them in placement. It had made students more explorative and deepened their learning. When they came to fourth semester, majority of the students were very good integrating theories into their observation and practice.
>
> *(Supervisor A)*

The majority of students did show satisfactory progress with integrating knowledge to skills and became impressive by the end of the final placement, providing a positive impact on their learning and receiving appreciation as an outcome. When students were interviewed about what the Learning Plan meant to them, they reported:

> It encompassed competencies, tasks, skills, knowledge, values and ethics required to pass social work field practicum. The guiding questions had helped me to critically analyse the activities, manage time and know organisation in detail. It aware me on the values, ethics and theories of social work. It made me more observant and analytical.
>
> *(KMC student)*

> 'Learning plan was a guide to understand fieldwork. It helped me to observe, learn and understand the process of organization from policies of organization, norms and values, organizational structures, work of organization. It guided me to act professionally'
>
> *(KMC student).*

> Learning plan helped me to record tasks, skills, knowledge, values and ethics and theories applied in field work. It facilitated me in addressing my personal and professional learning and helped me with skills for self-care'
>
> *(KMC student).*

This indicates the efficiency of the learning plan in guiding students to attain competency as a positive effect. The students also built a connection between the classroom knowledge and field practice.

> During my internship at school, I could see the behavioural theory in student's behaviour. I saw how classical conditioning and operant conditioning shaped the behaviour of children. I also understood how re-enforcement plays a crucial role in changing behaviour of students.
>
> *(KMC student)*

> I met a 19 years' girl who was struggling to get national citizenship card. Her mother was a single mother. Due to this the girl did not have her father name in her birth certificate. This took me to my classes on human rights and social justice and helped me understand the importance of legal procedures that I studied.
>
> *(KMC student)*

This reflects the students' understanding of professional identity, values and ethics, critical thinking, social and economic justice, human behaviour and the environment, engagement, and social policy. In terms of research as competency, most of the students were found to understand the importance of engaging in research-informed practice as well as practise informing research.

> I think the social worker should engage in both 'research informed practice and practice to inform research'. We have to rely upon research to identify best practices, evaluate the effectiveness of programmes for well-being of our clients. The practice when guided by research, helped us to prepare a new framework, evaluate and use findings to improve social service and delivery.
>
> *(KMC student)*

Voorhees R, (2014) highlighted the specificity of CB by the use of distinct units of learning with close monitoring of student performance in mastering competencies. The AB field practicum of KMC did not have those discrete units of learning. However, it was also shaped by experiential learning pedagogy. The CB field work has well-organised guided direction for the core competency achievements. Each action or observation was reported with a link to competencies. Though AB learning is a strategy of demonstrating realistic challenges and providing practical life opportunities to develop a student's personality and professional capabilities (Ali & Muhammad, 2018), it had limitations regarding skill attainment activities in the case of KMC. One field supervisor mentioned the students potentially missing some skills. On the contrary, in CB-based learning, the competencies led to the attainment of skills from an activity or observation. Having competence in the centrality of the fieldwork, provided students with the ability to define themselves as social workers eliminating personal choice (Voorhees, 2014). This was articulated by students when they talked about the learning plan. Students also depicted the conceptualisation of the abstract experiences they had, connecting them to theories of social work, and making sense of the action and observation. With this conceptualisation, the students built appropriateness while practising with a solid theoretical and practical grounding (Cheung & Delavega, 2014).

Acquisition of Ability to Practise Skills and Knowledge (Competency-Based Practice and Behaviour):

> The first two semesters placements are observatory as students are learning to equip themselves. The same happened with this batch too. However, I have noted the change in their behaviour and attitude aligning with the social work values, principles, and code of ethics from the first semester. The third and fourth semesters were very interesting when they brought complains or appreciation of their practicum experience. The fifth, sixth and seventh semesters were more performance oriented. Ten students in fifth semester conducted a puppet show on awareness of child cyber abuse in 18 schools for one agency. Their programme became so good that UNICEF Nepal asked them to present this in their national level programme in Kathmandu.
>
> (Field supervisor)

The ability to perform happens as a result of learning. From the supervisors' interview, this was what happened to KMC students when in fifth placements. The individual conference turned out to be short and effective. The agenda that the students set out to discuss with their supervisors became more concrete. Their knowledge in research also played a good role in shaping their behaviour and practice. One group of students conducted their project on environmental protection and prepared a policy for KMC and two schools. Another group conducted a needs assessment of a community tuition centre. The students enhanced their abilities each semester. They held a community café, a focus group discussion, an awareness campaign, and a data gathering for their agencies. Most of the students went on to have a one-month international placement in India where 90% of them finished with appreciation.

The students were also satisfied with their performance in the field. They followed the KMC Learning Plan strictly which helped them to build their abilities and gain competencies.

> 'I always applied ecological system theory which suited best in understanding the development of a child and design activities accordingly' (KMC student).

> 'When I came to know that we had to design a puppet show for the agency, we collected information on the age of children, type of school, the use of mobile phone etc. from two schools. The act had to be amicable and also informative. It turned out to be very effective project for us. We were highly appreciated by UNICEF for our ability to convey the message effectively' (KMC student).

> 'There were times when my supervisor was flexible in terms of changing some plan of action in field but we never lost focus from the learning plan. I believe KMC learning plan is a goal-oriented plan and drives us toward developing the competency in each section. I was offered a job from my last placement agency' (KMC student).

'In fifth semester, I did a training on self-care and stress management to engineers working in disaster management. Then did one-month internship there again. I collected data from community on hazard mapping of artificial big water pond made by municipality as water sources. I found some families excluded from taking water from there. I shared this to municipality meeting. The mayor said he was not aware of the exclusion. He assured me for immediate measures to get them to access the water' (KMC student).

The students adopted the Learning Plan in earnest. With the guidance of the supervisors they inculcated the core competencies of social work which were reflected in their practice as trainee social workers.

There was a family in a rural area of my agency. They had not received any monitory support from government after the earthquake. They were poor, illiterate and not in position to access that service. No one from the community was helping them. I interviewed the family, prepared a report and submitted to my agency. My report was included in plan to reach out to these marginalized families.

(KMC student)

The experiential learning cycle of Kolbe (Schmidt & Rautenbach, 2015) points to transforming experiences into knowledge, reflecting observation, and engaging in active experimentation. This happened in KMC with the active participation of students and the effective facilitation of the supervisors. This dyadic relationship of the trainee and trainers increased the impact of the CB learning plan. The conceptualisation and concretisation of experiences to gain the ability to perform led many students to appreciate the active experimentation.

Measurement of Performance (Demonstration of Competency)

The measurement of the performance or the demonstration of the students' competency was assessed continuously as internal assessments in individual conferences, group conferences, internal examinations, and external examinations. As competency is the combination of skills, abilities, and knowledge needed to perform a specific task (Voorhees, 2001), the publicity regarding the awareness programme, the self-care training, and reporting to address marginalisation, show the demonstration of students' strengths. This outcome aligns with the explanation of how rubric facilitates a student's movement from a lower level of 'identify and explain' to a high level of 'apply, analyse, and evaluate' in social work (McGuire & Majeswski, 2011). The inadequacy of the guideline to specify competencies results in the loss of an invaluable learning opportunity for students (Larsen & Hepworth, 1982). Contrary to this, the CB field practicum with an adequate specification of the competencies in the learning plan fulfilled the attainment of KMC students' competencies. This emerged as a major feature of the CB practicum, with its distinct organisation of competencies. The reporting system of illustrating the competency attainment also helped to conceptualise and concretise students' experiences and make them perform efficiently. The chances of missing out on the prerequisite competencies were ruled out. Instead it reversed the learning gear to competency regarding activities. Students were found to explore the activities or observation related to the ascribed skills.

Since the practicum is an academic course, the outcome of the CB field practicum must also align with the students' grades. In the final grading, 12 (46%) of the students scored 90% and above, 10 (38.5%) scored 85% and above, and the rest who numbered 4 (15.3%) scored 80% and above in their two consequent final field work practicums. Unlike the supervisors' observation that students who attained 90% or more were good at demonstrating their competencies and effective internship, only 46% of students were able to project this in their grades. However, the lowest level of performance was 80%. The range of demonstrability was 80% to 90% and more. This indicates the positive impact of the CB practicum on building competencies amongst learners. Among the 26 students, five are already working in the same agencies where they had undertaken their internship and, at the time of writing, two more positions are in process for the outgoing students. In spite of the completion of university examinations and completing their research, the job offers for the students show the readiness of the newly graduated for employability.

Conclusion

This study highlights the positive impact of KMC's CB field work practicum on student learning. The adaptation of this pedagogy has not only fulfilled the evolving need of students but also showed these learners' evolving capacity to demonstrate competencies during their training. The CB learning plan has created a process of goal attainment as development of the ten-part specific core competence of CSWE which has shifted the approach of learning from one of activity to competency. When the latter led the practicum, students were directed accordingly to engage, observe, or explore the activities in term of specified competencies. The same was found in KMC students who were impressive in reflecting, conceptualising, and demonstrating their competencies in action in their practicum, grounded and guided by the theories and principles of social work. They demonstrated ethical and professional behaviour in their agencies. They identified the cultural structure, the power to oppress, and used their knowledge and skill to advocate. Many students have adopted the process to assess, intervene, and evaluate the practice of their agency, along with their own. Some of them have also received job offers before completing their graduation course.

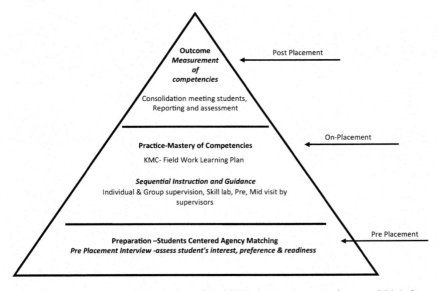

Figure 3.1 KMC Competency-Based Field Work Practicum Pedagogy 2016. Source: Authors

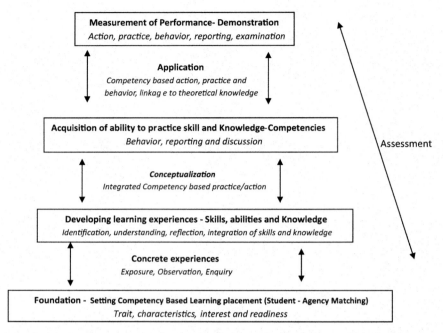

Figure 3.2 Conceptual Framework: Impact Pyramid of the Competency-Based Field Work Practicum in Student Learning. Source: Authors

This shows the outcome of the CB pedagogy at KMC. It also recognises the value of the supervisor–student relationship and how insightful supervision may transform the subjectivity of the social work attributes with demonstrable competence. The field work supervisor's knowledge, experience, and guidance are important for a quality field work practicum, as is having a distinct competency-organised learning plan. The continuous involvement of the supervisors in the three tiers of the pyramid (shown in Figure 3.1) of the field work practicum contributed highly to the experiential learning process and increased the efficiency of the learning plan. Since CB education is a dynamic process, it needs time and space to make the learner a performer. Each tier of the impact pyramid supported this process by allowing students to establish a foundation, understand the link between knowledge and practice, conceptualise learning, and finally, to perform.

The students recognised the importance of the KMC learning plan for their growth and achievement. But some students did not acknowledge the CSWE ten core competencies as the foundation of the KMC learning plan – rather they related the competencies as the learning plan competencies. KMC needs to find out why students did not highlight the core competencies of CSWE as KMC reference competencies.

The triangulation method applied in the study helps to validate the results from different data sources. The result of the positive impact was seen in the students' ability to demonstrate competence, as seen with the students' answers, supervisors' narratives, the letter of appreciation received from agencies, along with the job offers. There is a slight contrast with the figures produced: those of the supervisors' remarks and the university grades. Unlike the supervisors' mention of 90% and more students showing the highest performance, only 46% of students' grades show 90% plus while 54% scored 80% and above. However, the achievement of 80% to 90% grades and the job offers show the high efficacy of the learning process.

In conclusion, the goal that KMC has set from the CB field work practicum to ensure students' ability to demonstrate the integration and application of competencies in practice is impactful and moving in the right direction. There are a few areas where studies are necessary to maximise the impact in future.

References

Ali, A., & Muhammad, A. K. (2018). Understanding the role of internship as an activity based learning: A case study. *Journal of Education and Educational Development, 5*(2), 92–106.

Butova, Y. (2015). The history of development of competency-based education. *European Scientific Journal, 1,* 250–255.

Cherry, K. (2019). *The Experiential Learning Theory of David Kolb.* Retrieved March 2020, from Very Well Mind: https://www.verywellmind.com/experiential-learning-2795154

Cheung, M., & Delavega, E. (2014). Five-way experiential learning model for social work education. *Social Work Education, 33*(8), 1070–1087. https://doi.org/10.1080/02615479.2014.925538

Council on Social Work Education. (2012). *Educational Policy and Accreditation Standards.* Retrieved March 6,2020 from https://www.cswe.org/getattachment/Accreditation/Accreditation-Process/2008-EPAS/Candidacy/2008EDUCATIONALPOLICYANDACCREDITATIONSTANDARDS(EPAS)-08-24-2012.pdf.aspx

Council on Social Work Education. (2015). *Educational Policy and Accreditation Standards.* Retrieved March 6,2022 from https://www.cswe.org/getattachment/Accreditation/Standards-and-Policies/2015-EPAS/2015EPASandGlossary.pdf.aspx

Fain, P. (28 January 2019). *Slow and Steady for Competency-Based Education.* Retrieved February 10,2020 from https://www.insidehighered.com/news/2019/01/28/slow-growth-competency-based-education-survey-finds-interest-and-optimism-about-it

Hodgson, D., & Walford, H. (2007). Planning for learning and learning about planning in social work fieldwork. *Journal of Practice& Learning, 7*(1), 2006–2007, pp.50–66.

International Federation of Social Work. (2020). *Global Definition of Social Work.* Retrieved February 10, 2020 from https://www.ifsw.org/what-is-social-work/global-definition-of-social-work/

Larsen, J. A., & Hepworth, D. H. (1982). Enhancing the effectiveness of practicum instruction: An empirical study. *Journal of Education for Social Work, 18*(2), 50–58. Retrieved March 10,2020 from https://doi.org/10.1080/00220612.1982.10778575

McGuire, L. E., & Majewski, V. (2011). Social work and service-learning in the age of competency-based education. *Advances in Social Work, 12*(1), i–vii.

Nikku, B. R. (2012). Building social work education and the profession in a transition country: Case of Nepal. *Asian Social Work and Policy Review, 6*(2012), 256–264. Retrieved March 10,2020 from https://doi.org/10.1111/aswp.12001

Schmidt, K., & Rautenbach J.V. (2015). Field instruction: Is the heart of social work education still beating in the Eastern Cape? *Social Work, 52*(4), 589–610. Retrieved March 15,2020 from https://doi.org/10.15270/52-2-532

Social Work Education: Fieldwork Practicum. Chapter 3. Retrieved February 6, 2020 from http://14.139.116.20:8080/jspui/bitstream/10603/16128/10/10_chapter%203.pdf

U.S. Department of Education, National Center for Education Statistics. (2002). *Defining and Assessing Learning: Exploring Competency-Based Initiatives, NCES 2002–159.* Washington, DC. Retrieved March 12,2020 https://nces.ed.gov/pubs2002/2002159.pdf

Voorhees, R. A. (2001). Competency-based learning models: A necessary future. In. R.A. Voorhees (Ed.), *Measuring What Matters: Competency-Based Learning Models in Higher Education. New Directions for Institutional Research: No. 110.* San Francisco, CA: Jossey-Bass.

Voorhees, R., & Voorhees, B. A. (2014). *Working with Competency-Based Learning Models.* Retrieved from Retrieved March 12,2020 from www.researchgate.net/publication/341354875_Working_with_Competency-Based_Learning_Models

4
Challenges Faced in Field Work
An Indian Perspective

Deepshikha Carpenter

Fieldwork education is still a challenge in India due to a wide range of ideologies and types of work engaged in by various schools of social work. The community initiative in the field is more than 80 years old. Reynolds (1961) mentions how modern professional classroom teaching involves a relationship between field work and the classroom setting. The social work courses taught in class have a direct implication on the type of work that students consider doing in the field. In a week of five to six working days, either two or three days are meant for field work. That is again dependent on the type of work and the placement agencies too. There are tools and techniques of field work which have limited uses. According to the needs of the agency, specific tools are utilised for the cases involved within a specific period of time.

There are seven tools of field work such as Visits and observations, Interviews, Study of reports, records, pamphlets; actual participation in work situation; recording; reporting of these experiences in class seminars and participation in seminar and criticism depending upon physical, social and cultural' (Moorthy 1953, p.63–64).

Matthew (1975) indicates various dimensions to facilitate learning through motivating the capacity for learning, learning by doing, and field work supervision with up to date knowledge to face variety of situations. Living in a multicultural country, social work students should be equipped to work in various environments. The settings for field work agencies are mostly of a community, medical, or labour welfare context that have again specialised in further development.

The mushrooming of social work institutes in India poses a challenge with regard to incorporating students in different types of agencies. Also, the teacher-student ratio in institutions is even more testing as it affects the teaching quality. Lalwani (2009) views that there are challenges of settings, recording of field work reports, justification of marks in field work, number of days and work done in agencies. The guideline of working for a minimum of 30 days or 14–15 hours a week can be demanding with regard to the parameters that students are assessed with both by the department field work supervisor and the agency supervisor. Hence, it is necessary to understand the different kinds of issues raised in the field work setting.

Challenges in the Indian Setting

India, due to its multifarious identity, also opens a plethora of structural issues in the community setting linked to poverty, caste, class, ethnicity, and gender. Students who come from various backgrounds to the classroom setting stumble to adjust if placed under the same agencies. The very principles of social work on empathy, acceptance, and non-discrimination are jeopardised due to lack of experience. Teachers as well as assigned supervisors need competency to observe such situations. Field work lacks curricular thrust, opportunities in the field, and adequate educational focus. The need to review and improve the need of students' field assignments was felt long ago when promoting the involvement of students in field work and improving the quality of field instructions to make professionals (Desai 1987, p.164). There are other field work issues related to maintaining a case diary and writing it regularly. Another issue is that practices in most of the internships are undertaken in an urban setting, whereas students should familiarise themselves with both rural and urban environments. The majority of institutions are located in urban areas. In the case of research, there is a lack of rigour with regard to leaving the comfort zone and with structural issues. There is also a paucity of neighbourhood community support where field work students could be placed or practice indigenous methods in that surrounding.

Indigenisation in India

Social work, as a movement of indigenisation, started in the 1970s as a major challenge. Even after 40 years, the concrete practice in India is still bleak. According to Midgley (1983), the challenge is with diverse cultural ideologies. Only with specific models and contextual theories is intervention at a grassroots level possible. Yip (2003) also mentions that indigenisation is about awareness and local culture which comprises intervention, ideologies, and cultural contexts. It is a phase of transition of putting an imported knowledge, one that is western, through a process of authentication to make it relevant to the local social, cultural, political, and economic characteristics (Walton and Abo El Nasr, 1988). The International Federation of Social Workers (IFSW) aims at recognising and respecting the ethnic and cultural diversity in which they practise (IFSW, 2004). It rises above the various differences in which social workers can help. Countries who are a part of the IFSW regions of Africa, Asia and Pacific, Europe, North America, Latin America, and the Caribbean have more or less felt the need for indigenisation in 141 nations to have different ways of being understood and dealt with in the social work agenda and transformation.

In India, Dr. Clifford Manschardt, through the efforts of the American Marathi Mission in 1925 and later the Nagpada Neighbourhood House, blended the methods of professional social work to suit the locality in the way a 'professional has to marry with the indigenous' (Desai, 1985; Kulkarni, 1993). To date, this is seen in village adoptions and community practice around social work institutions where students and interns practise the methods of community organisation through development initiatives. Veneracion (2003) also discusses the distinguishing terms of authentisation; that is, identifying genuine and authentic roots in the local system and de-westernisation, a capacity to break away from the original borrowed knowledge of the west. Lalwani (2009, p.23) highlights the issues of social work education being taught in English. There is no social work literature in Indian regional languages nor are teachers trained to teach in regional language at a postgraduate level. There is a lack of universality in social work education. The profession of social work lacks uniformity across universities in India and the teaching community is small as it is an emerging discipline which is built on local ethos. Buenviaje and Leyson (2015) mention the ways field instructions are maintained in social work schools. It is

Table 4.1 A sample of field work guidelines as observed from the course of study.

1.	A total of 21 days of field work is mandatory.
2.	A total of 8–15 hours of field work in a week is mandatory.
3.	Field work diaries should be maintained with the dates and activities.
4.	Checked reports are discussed during individual/group counselling every week.
5.	Field work reports should be submitted immediately after the field visit.
6.	If a field work visit is missed, it has to be made up for on the consecutive days.
7.	Prior permission for any field work related activity should be communicated at least 15 days before.
8.	Field work reports are checked by the concerned supervisor.
9.	Integrity will be practised while maintaining the field work timing.
10.	Disciplinary action will be taken if any student is found absent during the field work day without any prior notice.
11.	Tools and techniques of social work to be used on defining the relationships and reinforcing better relationships.
12.	Dress code is adhered to due to diverse cultural communities.
13.	All the six methods of social work are taught in the respective community or office setting.

Source: Author

to provide maximum opportunities to put all the social work values, theories, knowledge, and principles as articulated in the Table 4.1 Field Work Guideline.

> Although field work is more or less conducted according to the Field Work Manual, fieldwork reports are written with a proper format time log, using an activity sheet. Importance is given to student learning and evaluation. Various techniques such as interviewing, listening, observing, questioning, supporting, counselling, and explaining hence are instructed. However, a limited range of methods is used due to frequent placement in the same type of organisations. Field work instructions might be uniform across India, nevertheless the context and demand for various specialised services might limit the client and social work students due to lack of training with the limited range of organisations at hand. There are other factors associated with it such as is the student well equipped? How do they appear on field work days? What type of approach is adopted? Are they immersed in *gnothi seauton* or experiential learning? The methodology while dealing with grassroots issues should be based on a needs-based process. Effective implementation of participatory rural or learning mechanisms can help to identify social problems.

Conceptual Articulation and Methodology

According to Boroujerdi (2002), theories based on indigenous intellectual traditions, history, and culture should be developed to build indigenous social sciences. This is a challenge as social work knowledge and inquiry in India has mostly relied on western theories. Hence, a postmodern approach allows for introspection and reflexivity of positionality. The standpoint of the students is important as postmodern thinking allows for awareness that different forms of knowledge can be counted differently which may generate new knowledge (Fook 2012, p.41). Chang (2005) mentions that grounded research with careful field work asks indigenous scholars to develop their own problems, techniques, and research agendas relevant to indigenous societies. This chapter examines the challenges that students face in the field work setting looking for indigenous practices.

Atal (1981, p.193) indicated four forms of indigenisation of the social sciences in Asia: '(a) teaching in the national language and use of local materials; (b) research by insiders; (c) determination of research priorities; and (d) theoretical and methodological reorientation'. This raises a major question of how many local materials are developed or research carried out by the teaching community, field agencies, students, and research scholars. Most of the works cited are from western writers. Huang and Zhang (2008) elaborated on how almost all proponents of indigenisation in social work insisted that social problems and people's needs should be understood and addressed in the unique locality-specific social, cultural, historical, and political contexts. It is almost as if most western social workers do not pay attention to it.

This chapter is an effort to bring the universality to specificity (Yip, 2006), looking at various locations in the field work setting, in a socioeconomic context through social work in a North East Indian setting. The research aims to uncover the various challenges posed due to the diverse settings in which students practise social work. It also tries to understand the areas which need to be developed for future possibilities in social work development.

Social Work and Field Work Practices in North East India

The North East of India is comprised of Assam, Meghalaya, Manipur, Mizoram, Tripura, Nagaland, Arunachal Pradesh, and Sikkim. It is an amalgamation of myriad cultures and ethnic diversity. The education system was modernised by missionaries from different parts of the world. Social work education in the North East came into being in the late 1990s in Assam University Silchar and Mizoram University, Aizawl in late 2008. The Department of Psychiatric Social Work was established at the Lokopriya Gopinath Bordoloi Regional Institute Mental Health (LGBRIMH) in 1998. Due to demand for social work as a source of potential employment, this area has witnessed growth in competitive private and public universities. Now there are about 24 institutes in North East India (Riamei 2015). The state of Sikkim is yet to have functional social work education. Indigenous knowledge places emphasis on inclusion, interconnectivity, and a holistic way of being (Dumbrill and Green 2008). There are reputed organisations which cater for the needs of indigenous communities in all the eight states of North East India like the IDeA (The Ant), Promotion and Advancement of Justice, Harmony and Rights of Adivasis (PAJHRA), North East Network (NEN), Aaranyak, Ashadeep, NEDAN Foundation, Committee On Socio Economic and Health Development Assam (COSEHDA), Indo-Global Social Service Society (IGSSS), North East Research and Social Work Networking (NERSWN), Kripa Foundation, Rashtriya Gramin Vikas Nidhi (RGVN), Growing Seed, SHALOM, Shishu Sarothi, National Youth Project, Ramakrishna Mission, Seneh, Bethany Society, NEFSA. Issues are mainly related to cultural variation, ethnicity, customary practices, and social institutions of indigenous communities. In recent times, issues with immigrants and refugees have drawn a stir in North East India. The scope in field work is related to microfinance and microcredit, corporate social responsibility, school social work, medical psychiatric social work, child rescue. Due to the rising number of social work institutions, there is a dearth of organisations for concurrent field work and block placements. It means going through a transformative process of empowerment and strengthening of people's traditional natural capabilities and resources.

Methodology

The study is qualitative in nature. A purposive sampling method has been used for the research as it allows us to choose the subjects who are useful for delineating the specific features which we are interested in (Silverman 2001). The investigation is in the form of case studies as the primary research method. It shows an in-depth analysis of the practical challenges in field work to investigate. Case study research also can excel in accommodating a relativist perspective (e.g., Boblin, Ireland, Kirkpatrick, & Robertson, 2013; Leppäaho, Plakoyiannaki, & Dimitratos, 2015). A pilot case study was done to determine the feasibility of the study. The basic inclusion criteria was that the student was working for more than a semester in the field work setting. Flyvbjerg (2011, p.301) shares 'if we decide to use a case study in our research, this does not mean the selection of a method, but rather a selection of what will be explored'. The position of the researcher is neutral. The questions were on challenges or limitations that were felt in the field by students in three settings: 1. urban community setting, 2. psychiatric and medical setting, 3. corporate setting. Three students shared their experience and the challenges they faced in the field setting through unstructured interviews. According to Polit and Beck (2008), unstructured interviews are useful in allowing participants to relate aspects of phenomena of interest with an emphasis on matters of greatest importance to each individual to exchange free ideas for a rich description of experience. QDA Miner Lite (Version 4), qualitative data analysis software, was used to thematise the cases for cross case analysis to find commonalities. Also through the direct observation method in individual counselling, 12 students were placed under the researcher's supervision and shared the field work challenges whenever the sessions for individual counselling were arranged. Themes that emerged were on the role of the agency supervisor and schedules, learning and communication issues, risky people and areas while conducting surveys, difficult terrains, the relationship between employers and the employed, non-maintenance of laws, leave rules, time management, health hazards, confusion with roles and responsibilities in the setting, controlling emotional involvement, indigenisation, limitations in exploration, difficulties in understanding terminologies, and culmination of theory into practice. Direct observation helped to acknowledge the multiple realities and meanings. Hence, presenting the data from a relativist orientation was important to share the several perspectives of students. Confidentiality was maintained with the names of the students for ethical reasons. The data collection for secondary resources was based on books, reports, articles, and websites.

Reflexivity and Positionality

The entire process of field work is an experiential learning and evolving of one's personality as a social worker. It shapes the identity to identify the reality of society. The researcher is constantly struggling with her multiple identities coming as a woman from a specific socio-religious identity belonging to North-East India. However, with previous experience working in all three types of setting as a trainee, be it medical, urban, and corporate, it is comforting to share with the students to discuss the issue through the medium of individual and group conferences. Hence, the students involved in this study are from different gender, socio-religious, and ethnic identities. Their body language and dress codes are guided beforehand due to direct field contact in different settings and they are encouraged to use local dialects and languages to make them feel like insiders as the study aimed only to identify the challenges in field work as a student. The constant engagement and involvement in field work practice from more than ten years following the basic principles of social work such as 'acceptance', 'non-judgemental attitude', 'individualisation', and 'self-determination' and challenging ethical dilemmas help to position oneself as a researcher in a neutral manner.

Discussion

The methods of observation and case studies enabled examining the nature of the challenges, bringing a reflexive approach with it due to the students' various backgrounds.

The observation of the 12 (trainee) students, which was recorded through note-taking, revealed the challenges throughout their experience. The students were assigned concurrent placements in NGOs working with issues of substance abuse, HIV/AIDS, child rescue projects, surveys on livelihood, solid waste management, transport department (water and land), old age homes. Through the process of reflexivity, students could point out the baggage they carry and also how to deal with the challenges. According to Myerhoff and Ruby (1982), reflexivity is the process by which a field worker understands how his/her social background influences and shapes his/her beliefs and how this self-awareness pertains to what and how he/she observes, attributes meanings, and interprets action and dialogues with his/her informants. Reflexivity is very important in identifying indigenous ways to break down challenges. According to Roy (2012, p.199), a study conducted among 300 respondents across 15 schools revealed that 36.3 percent opted for industrial relations and personal management, 22.3 percent opted for urban and rural community development, 8.3 percent opted for medical and psychiatric work, 15.3 percent opted for family and child welfare, 4 percent opted for criminal and correctional administration, 2.7 opted for other specialisations such as social work with the elderly, HIV/AIDS, and counselling. The case studies in this chapter occurred in an urban community setting, medical and psychiatric context, and a corporate or industrial environment. They took place in concurrent placement for two days a week. The time for two days was roughly between 8 and 15 hours.

The observations for the 12 students are as follows:

1. In the case of working in a community setting for Oral Substitution Centres (OSTs) to monitor the pandemic of HIV/AIDS, the students revealed that they had to wait for the injecting drug users (IDU) as they do not come on time. The employees of OSTs had busy schedules so there was a lack of time as a trainee to understand the whole process.
2. There was a violation of the 'principle of controlled emotional involvement' as working with children for a rescue mission was emotional for the trainees, sometimes looking at the apathy that occurred when parents encouraged children to be involved in child labour. The parents also made the children avoid communicating with the trainees. Hence, poverty is a vicious circle and child labour is an integral part of it.
3. In organisations related to retirement homes, there was a blur between social work as a professional service and as a general social service. Trainees were subjected to household chores and marketing. It was due to a lack of understanding of the organisation's role in professional social work education.
4. Retirement homes also needed experienced trainees as first semester students found it difficult to practise methods, skills, or techniques due to the temperamental nature of those in care. Hence more gerontological practice should be undertaken as a part of the course curriculum.
5. Students who were placed from other North East states experienced a language barrier as more than three languages are spoken in addition to local dialects. Hence, placement in certain settings was sometimes a limitation.
6. While working with high-risk groups, the trainees' fear of contracting a communicable disease was an issue that requires vigorous work.
7. Rescue programmes are risky, yet the trainees cooperated with the police in a professional manner. North East India is a hub for traffickers. The trainees were motivated by their mission.
8. Teaching children who have dropped out of school is difficult due to the work the children are involved with.

9. There is a dearth of human resource managers and a conflict of curriculum was seen in the organisations as most of them are not proper industries.
10. If placed under a government office, the designated holidays on second and fourth Saturdays affected the working days. Hence the trainees have to extend their days in order to compensate for the official holidays and there is limited guidance from the organisational supervisors.
11. Some of the NGOs charged money for placement due to maintenance issues. It has become more difficult for social work institutions to grow.
12. The trainees working with children's organisations had limited time with the children as the latter need to attend school, hence constraints regarding the duration spent with the trainee.
13. The trainees were charged around 500–1000 Indian rupees for maintenance charges in some NGOs.

Payne (1998) views about reflexivity share how thoughts affect actions and a given situation provides various forms of feedback through observation and individual counselling. The next discussion on case studies also reflects the challenges the students faced in field work agency.

Case Study Based on Intrinsic Situations

1. Urban Community Setting

    TD aged 22 was working in a community setting. She was working as a part of the research team in an NGO that mainly works for children, in order to understand educational issues through a survey. She shared that when she went to border areas,

    'it is a challenge for me to talk with them … for the first time. As a social worker we had go various area, some of the very remote area and some of them are very hilly areas. Some are slum areas and some are very backward area. And when the organisation supervisors advise us to go then I go to every area. And it is a big challenge for me.' TD being a local speaker within a span of limited time, met indigenous communities such as Khasi, Garo, Mishing, and Bodo and learnt their traditional culture and living conditions. TD also faced respondents who processed alcohol in their home as a part of their culture. Alcohol is a part of everyday life. It is both culturally and ritually significant for some communities. However, TD had a fear of talking to them, 'we actually did not know how we could behave which was a big challenge to me'.

2. Psychiatric and Medical Setting

    RD aged 24 was working in a medical and psychiatric institution. Due to strict guidelines, there were professional challenges. She said, 'Orientation for each and everything was not possible for the supervisors since they also had clinical duties for this I faced difficulty to know who is from which department'. There are limitations in this setting such as-

    I was not directly allowed to do intervention like case work and group work but I was asked to observe only which restricted me to explore more about the cases. Following the protocol made me anxious every time I take a new step. I was anxious to initiate things like interacting with the patients.' There was a restriction of things she could explore; she was asked to be careful. There was also difficulty in understanding language and terminologies.

Challenges Faced in Field Work

> She mentioned, 'I had to struggle to know the new terms and catching up during the academic sessions and rounds'. There was also difficulty as the trainee went for two days of field work – 'Since I used to go twice a week so it was difficult for me to follow the intervention done by the supervisors or the M.Phil trainees'. There was confusion with the roles and duties of the staff and whom to approach since everyone was usually busy either with academics or the clinical duties. But later on she got to know the system: how it works and how to manage time. There were other fears related to reading file records as they were treated with confidentiality – 'Once I was told to seek permission from the ward sister ... then it became easier for me to read the files of the patients'. Regarding indigenisation practices, she mentioned,
>
> Getting a chance to be posted in a health as well as mental health set up as an intern gives an exposure to the health conditions of the people. It is indigenous in the sense that getting direct link with the people and using traditional ways of interacting to know about the patients, knowing their cultural practices and traditions. For this, knowledge about the local language and background knowledge about the cultural practices is equally important.
>
> It is also global in the sense that that the professors use scientific terms and treatment processes. There was observation of ongoing research findings and trends in medication, new machines, and test kits.
>
> 3. Corporate Setting
>
> LD aged 22 was working in a manufacturing company looking from the perspectives of human resource management. The first challenge that was faced was the difficult terrain. She mentioned 'When we go to the factories and also to the main area, we do not have much access to the bus services'. Looking at the theoretical teaching of what is taught on industrial laws and workers right, the trainee identified lot of issues in field work. There were health hazards identified which the workers face, 'in manufacturing process, there is dust and fume or other impurity of such a nature. So effective measures should be taken to prevent its inhalation and accumulation in workplace. There is no sufficient drinking water. Effective and suitable arrangements shall be made in every factory for securing and maintaining in every worker. Proper and adequate ventilation system is most important of fresh air and lights. But in one factory there is no proper ventilation and windows system. Therefore, the factories do not have clarity on workers' rights. Also, the leave policies are not according to the rules and regulations. Most of the workers leave the organisation due to leave issues'''.

'Workers are not aware of the maternity benefit or the benefits that are listed in the Industrial Relations'. Although the trainee shares a cordial relationship with the HR Manager, training is given on some rules and regulations and the concept and scope of human resources management. However, there is a discrepancy between what is taught and the reality of labour laws. It was mentioned that the Maternity Benefit Act was followed, but in practice it is missing. It is mentioned, 'When the women worker are pregnant, they leave the job'. The workload is very high in the factories. Because of the high workload some of the employees quit the job.

In the process of identifying the challenges in the light of indigenisation, it is still in an exploration phase in North East India. The community setting has the biggest potential for research enquiry in local language, that is, from an insider practice. The problems are mostly to do with terrain and language as students work in different environments and cultures. All of them work for two days a week for concurrent field work. Communication is not a problem with supervisors or other staff. However, the system in which the process of organisation works is lacking professional skills. The limitation is how to explore theoretically with local skills and theoretical improvement? The corporate or industrial setting is still juggling between exploitation and rules. The medical and psychiatric setting with its protocols and strict rules and regulations is still working according to the western style of practice. The North East of India has a lot of work opportunities in various specialised community-based organisations among indigenous communities. Some of them have been mentioned already. Nevertheless, it is important to learn and record how each society reacts and acts to a certain problem in the community. Social work research as a method has lot of potential for exploration. Roy (2012, p.8) has rightly pointed out the challenges facing the internationalisation of social work education in Asia:

(1) insufficient professional identity or recognition; (2) inability to secure jobs in social work; (3) a public perception that social work is a voluntary vocation requiring no professional training; and (4) the necessity of creating textbooks written in indigenized languages. Such a challenge is truly reflected in the case of North East India. In order to move away from 'academic colonisation', there is a requirement for a maximum integration of theory into practice in specialisations such as human resource management and medical and psychiatric social work. Driven by the strong values of cultural heterogeneity, there is a potential to draw from multiple realities and reflective practices. Also, a case diary should be maintained by teachers, students, and scholars to write all the observations rigorously made in the field work. The commercialisation of NGOs can be stopped when more independent community initiatives are brought through village and local adaptation and block placement in rural areas to build partnerships.

The fixed mentality that deems that social work in India to be only a service should be questioned. It is because social work has not been able to be at its professional best that people have reduced it to just a service to humankind. Due to lack of work associations, platforms for exposure, and protection of interests at a regional level, professional social work is difficult to practise independently. The notion of unconditional service is rooted in religious and cultural movements as well as political ideology in India. Hence, more field level intervention by social workers is needed with a localised approach to lessen the challenges over a period of time.

Conclusion

The challenges in field work can be summarised in two parts: A. The creation of complete indigenous knowledge and more involvement of students in the community setting to harness the rich localised practices to deal with social problems or issues. For instance, the traditional knowledge systems in preserving flora and fauna creating sustainable efforts or women's groups fighting for their men drawn in insurgency and violence. The local perspectives can then be incorporated as a part of literature, theoretical orientations, and techniques. B. To make social work education based on generic ideas rather than specialisation. Generic nature widens the ambit for more indigenous knowledge first and later can be collaborated for specialisation. According to Lasan (1997), the Philippians' idea of 'creative literature' dealing with the themes of human interest and relationships are a way of working on indigenous practice. The idea that people have of reality is important not the reality itself (Vogrinc, 2008, p.27). The reality through reflexive practices should be representatives of marginalised people. The role of a social worker according to Fook (2012, p.47) is to be more than a cog in the wheel. It has to be a reflective practice of how knowledge (the power structure and relations) is maintained and how it can be emancipatory. The curriculum across India should be examined every three to five years to determine if indigenous knowledge has been mainstreamed. The priorities of research in different parts of India should be based on the demands of ground realities. If ethnic violence and mitigation is an issue for one zone, for others it could be about farmers' land rights or lack of credit facilities. Research on public distribution systems, implementation of government special schemes on women, children, and persons with disability is scarce. The purpose of field work should be about filling the gap between public policies and grassroots work. Other research areas where field work plays an important role is the identification and work of local governing bodies, autonomous councils, and customary practices. The easiest way is when organisations involve students for surveys. There are education and health surveys in generic terms. No specificity is there to understand the indigenous dynamics.

According to Desai (1987), competence is required to do need-based assessment, policy analysis, advocacy, project identification, preparation administration, and evaluation. This is to enable field workers to function as development workers. The beauty of multicultural identity has to be reflected and appreciated due to its diversity that localised social work practice can be highlighted in various forums. More social work research is needed to cut across localised issues. The purpose of indigenisation, therefore, is to make social work education, research and practice fit local contexts. Huang and Zhang (2018) also mention the 're-engineering of skills and techniques'. This will be possible only when a detailed exploration of all four zones of India is initiated. It is no longer about the western humanist ideas of liberalism or rationalisation but community ownership and sustainability that indigenisation can bring about in India.

References

Atal, Y. (1981). The call for indigenization. *International Social Science Journal, 33*(1), 189–97.
Boblin, S. L., Ireland, S., Kirkpatrick, H., & Robertson, K. (2013). Using Stake's qualitative case study approach to explore implementation of evidence-based practice. *Qualitative Health Research, 23*(9), 1267–1275. https://doi.org/10.1177/1049732313502128
Boroujerdi, M. (2002). Subduing globalization: The challenge of the indigenization movement. In R. Grant & J. R. Short (Eds.), *Globalization and the Margins* (pp. 39–49). New York: Palgrave Macmillan.
Chang, M. (2005). The Movement to Indigenize the Social Sciences in Taiwan: Origin and Predicaments. In J. Makeham & A. C. Hsiau (Eds.), *Cultural, Ethnic, and Political Nationalism in Contemporary Taiwan: Bentuhua* (pp. 221–60). New York: Palgrave Macmillan.
Desai, A. (1987). Development of social work education. *Encyclopedia of Social Work in India*. New Delhi: Ministry of Welfare.
Desai, A. S. (1985). The foundations of social work in India. *The Indian Journal of Social Work, 46*(1).
Dumbrill, G. C., & Green, J. (2008). Indigenous knowledge in the social work academy. *Social Work Education. The International Journal, 27*(5), 489–503. Retrieved May 2020 fromhttps://www.semanticscholar.org/paper/Indigenous-Knowledge-in-the-Social-Work-Academy-Dumbrill-Green/640c97eee69caf88969d4c467b32775ec9bcb8e2
Flyvbjerg, B. (2011). Case study. In: N. K. Denzin & Y. S. Lincoln (Eds.), *The Sage Handbook of Qualitative Research* (4th ed., pp. 301–316). Thousand Oaks, CA: Sage.
Fook, J. (2012). *Social Work: A Critical Approach to Practice* (pp. 3–197) Thousand Oaks, CA: Sage.
Huang, Y. & Zhang X. (2008) A reflection on the indigenization discourse in social work. *International Social Work*, Sage, *51*(5) 611–622 Retrieved June 2020 from https://doi.org/10.1177/0020872808093340
International Federation of Social Work (IFSW). (n.d.). https://www.ifsw.org/social-work-action/the-global-agenda/
International Federation of Social Workers (IFSW). (2004). *Ethics in Social Work, Statement of Principles*. Retrieved June 2020, from http://www.ifsw.org/en/p38000324.
Kulkarni, P. D. (1993). The indigenous base of social work profession In India. *The Indian Journal of Social Work, 54*(4), 555–565.
Lawani, B. T. (2009). *Social Work Education & Field Instructions*. Agra: Current Publications.

Leppäaho, T., Plakoyiannaki, E., & Dimitratos, P. (2015). The case study in family business: An analysis of current research practices and recommendations. *Family Business Review, 29*(2), 1–15.

Mathew, G. (1975) Educational and helping aspects of field work supervision. *The Indian Journal of Social Work, 35*(4), 325–31.

Midgley, J. (1981). In Whitaker, W. H. (1983). *Professional Imperialism: Social Work in the Third World.* London, UK: Wm. Heinemann Educational Books. 191 *Social Work, 28*(1). Retrieved June 2020, from https://doi.org/10.1093/sw/28.1.85

Moorthy, M.V. (1953). Scientific approach to field work. *The Indian Journal of Social Work,* 144–59.

Myerhoff, B., & Ruby, J. (1982). Introduction: A crack in the mirror: Reflexive perspectives. In J. Ruby (Ed.), *Anthropology.* Philadelphia, PA: University of Pennsylvania Press.

Payne, M (1998). Social work theories and reflective practice. In R Adam, L Dominelli, M. Payne, & J Campling (Eds.), *Social Work* (119–137). London: Palgrave.

Polit, D.F. and Beck, C.T. (2008). *Nursing Research: Generating and Assessing Evidence for Nursing Practice.* 8th Edition, Philadelphia: Wolters Kluwer Health/Lippincott Williams & Wilkins, p. 796.

Raimai, J. (2015). Social work education in Northeast India: Some reflections. *The Sangai Express.* Retrieved June 2020, from http://epao.net/epPageExtractor.asp?src=education.Social_Work_Education_in_Northeast_India_Some_reflections_By_Joseph_Riamei.html.

Reynolds, R. R. (1961). The relationship of field placement to classroom teaching. Teaching of students and staff. *Supervision,*

Roy, S. (2012). *Fieldwork in Social Work.* Jaipur: Rawat Publication.

Silverman, D. (2001). *Interpreting Qualitative Data: Methods for Analysing Talk, Text and Interaction (second edition).* London / Thousand Oaks / New Delhi: Sage, p. 325.

Tatsuru, A., & Matsuo, K (2013). *Internationalization of Social Work Education in Asia. Social Work Research Institute Asian Center for Welfare Society (ACWelS).* Japan: Japan College of Social Work. Retrieved on March 2020, from https://pdfs.semanticscholar.org/9e4c/cf1a1479f4933647d8a151782ece59e3969c.pdf

The Second Review Committee Report by UGC Review of Social Education in India. Retrieved April, 2020, from http://www.pswa.org.in/download/2%20review%20committee-SW%20edn-UGC-tiss%20doc.pdf044

Veneracion, M. C. J. (2003). *Social Work in the Philippine Tradition and Profession.* Quezon City: Philippines Association of Social Workers.

Vogrinc, J. (2008). *Kvalitativno raziskovanje na pedagoškem področju.* Ljubljana: Pedagoška fakulteta.

Walton, R. G., & Abo El Nasr, M. M. (1988). Indigenization and Authentization in terms of Social Work in Egypt. Retrieved March, 2022 from http://citeseerx.ist.psu.edu/viewdoc/download?doi=10.1.1.978.6176&rep=rep1&type=pdf

Yip, K. (2006) Indigenization of social work: An international perspective and conceptualization. *Asia Pacific Journal of Social Work and Development, 16*(1), 43–55. https://doi.org/10.1080/21650993.2006.9755991

5
Concurrent Fieldwork in Macro Practice
Cases from the South Indian Context

S. Kanagaraj

Field education is an essential component for professional practice where students develop skill sets to translate theory into practice and test their professional social work practice (Fortune, Mccarthy, and Abramson 2001) (Chen and Fortune 2017). Due to the low availability of professional social work supervisors, there is a lack of proper fieldwork training (Devi 1997) .). Hence efforts are necessary in the creation of field projects at university departments – through that fieldwork placement is enabled. Supervised fieldwork is an essential part of the field and one which carries the highest weightage in assessing students (Chandrapa and Saxena 2017; Andharia 2011). In particular, field instructors require a comprehensive guide and field instruction manual to guide the students appropriately, especially in the context of the growing number of students joining social work (Nair, Juva, & Nadkarni V. 2020). Moreover, in most situations students do not have enough fieldwork exposure in organisational settings (Andharia 2011). It is also one of the reasons for the author's creation of field projects. It provides an opportunity for the teachers to work, show leadership, and paves the way for students to contribute their energies (Andharia 2007). Practical wisdom is crucial to translate theory into practice (Baum 2011). This chapter attempts to give effective concurrent fieldwork exposure to the open setting community fieldwork in the Indian context. This is based on the author's live field contact and is imparted among the students as part of the department's field project.

Macro Practice of Social Work

Community development students require open setting fieldwork[1] for adequate exposure on macro practice in the social work context. Exposure is better in community-based open setting field work because it prepares the student better for dealing with macro level problems. It's highly challenging to practise professional social work in India, especially in rural areas because of the obvious fact that it is still a growing profession there. Moreover, the trainees also have a greater responsibility to take part in a clearly established role whilst establishing their identity not as a service provider but in the practice of professional social work.

Concurrent Fieldwork

Concurrent fieldwork happens alongside classroom education. It is usually two days of fieldwork on a weekly basis in a community practice or agency setting (Anand & Adusumalli 2019), and approximately 15 hours per week in the field (National Assessment and Accreditation Council 2005). In our fieldwork we covered more than the specified time. In this study, I will provide an explanation of guided concurrent field work assigned to four fieldwork students at the Department of Social Work, Amrita Vishwa Vidyapeetham (deemed to be university) during the year 2015. The field work was created as part of the department's field project. (Figure 5.1)

The context of concurrent field work at the university consists of community members, social work trainees,[2] and faculty supervisors[3] as the stakeholders. Unlike the regular fieldwork system where stakeholders include the agency supervisor, in this field work setting the agency supervisor was not there as a part of the field project. The students visited the field every Tuesday and Thursday for a minimum of 6.5 hours under the guidance of the faculty supervisor. But the students spent more than the required time based on outcome-oriented aspects. The trainees were given independent tasks and the freedom to complete the assigned individual tasks as part of the fieldwork. They were provided an adequate learning environment to enrich their knowledge, skills, and experience for professional social work practice. Further field work practice provides the next level of learning from the basic understanding to independent practice of social work with the acquired classroom learnings (Dhemba 2012).

Making the Field Ready

In agriculture, before we do farming we prepare the field such as ploughing the land, fertilising the land etc., which enables better growth of the crop. In a similar way, before we send the students to community settings, we need to prepare the students for appropriate exposure. Moreover, students will only receive appropriate and quality learning if they have a basic understanding of the field placement (Knight 2001). Hence community orientation explaining the process clearly is a necessity. After the orientation, the following steps may be adhered to in creating a field ready for the students.

Figure 5.1 Stakeholders of community open setting fieldwork as part of departmental fieldwork (Source: Author)

Selecting the Field

We needed to choose a community which was suitable for the students to commute to and with a sufficient number of issues requiring intervention. Also necessary was a community of diverse people for exposure to and an understanding of the diverse ways of resolving various issues. There had to be adequate public transport facilities to enable them to visit the field on their own: within a radius of around 16 kilometres of the institution would be ideal for appropriate fieldwork exposure.

About the village: Valukkuparai is a village in Madukkarai Taluk, Coimbatore District, Tamil Nadu State (10.8554° N, 76.9256° E). The population is 2474 in which there are 1192 men and 1282 women. There are a total of 600 families, out of which 250 are living below the poverty line approximately, its average size of the family members is 1 to 5. The following castes are in the village: Arundhathiyar, Boyar, Konguvellalar, Maathati, Christian, Kaligar. The total area of the village is approximately 1500 acres and the nearest town is Coimbatore, which is around 19 kilometres away; the nearest railway station is Madukkarai, which is about 12 kilometres from the village. Tamil, Kannada, and Telugu are the spoken languages in this village. There is a functioning Anganwadi (Child Development centre) and primary and high schools in this village. The regular transport facilities and road conditions are good for reaching the village. A post office, bank, ration shop, and village library are to be found in this village. The social work trainees need to travel at least two hours by public transport to reach the village. It was highly challenging to reach the village itself but the trainees managed to visit without fail.

Rapport Building

This important step – as part of the initial process – is to create a rapport with the community. It is considered to be the most essential part of community open setting fieldwork.

I) Meeting Key People
The author had a key contact person in the village – through him it was possible to create a rapport with many other people in the community. The author interacted with Oor Goundar (village leader), Panchayat President, ward members, other key people such as SHG members, local Panchayat officials, and other important members in the community. However, he is from an upper caste and he was not comfortable visiting the lower caste community. As a social worker, we cannot conveniently exclude the community in need. Hence the author made an effort to visit the scheduled caste community on his own. Initially the author started interaction with people in the tea shop which enabled interaction with community members.

II) Frequency of the Field Visit
The author made a visit to the village on alternate days to meet people for creating a rapport and gaining an understanding of the village. It would take roughly three to six months to make the field ready for the students to visit. During this period, we undertook a number of activities such as meeting individual key persons, hence increasing our presence in the village. Sometimes there was confusion as to the schedule when going to the village but at times we visited the village without any agenda. But this was beneficial, allowing us to be closer to the community members and yielding positive results later.

III) Entry Point Activities
Once the initial meetings and rapport building with key persons were over, the next step was creating useful awareness programmes on various issues. The author conducted

an awareness programme on health and hygiene for the children and general public; this was handled by a public health expert. An awareness programme on various government schemes was available for the farmers, and vocational training opportunities for women were conducted by the employment training institute and with officers from the Tamilnadu Women Development Corporation, Coimbatore. Simultaneously, a baseline survey was conducted to understand the basics about the village.

Opportunities for Concurrent Fieldwork Community in an Open Setting

The initial level of rapport building and the basic level of information was collected within a three-month time period which included identifying key persons in the community and orientation there. The field was now ready for the students' level of exposure and possible intervention. The following are accounts of the four students' intervention in the field.

Orienting the Trainees before the Fieldwork

It is necessary that the trainees be oriented properly before they enter the community. This makes clear to the trainees as well as to the supervisor on what exactly they can do in the field. Firstly they should be given clarity as to what field work is and its objectives, its values of social work, and professional social work practice. The following are some of the points which were given by the faculty supervisor in the field which helped achieve the objectives more successfully.

- No false promises to be made: One of the common mistakes made by earlier trainees was to give the community members false promises. This was basically to satisfy the community members and to get the work done using shortcuts. For instance one of the trainees was assigned to arrange a bank account for all the community members but initially without understanding the situation, the trainee started giving false promises that all the members would be given a bank account without checking their valid documents. Also, the trainee left it them to process all the documents. Instead the faculty supervisor suggested identifying suitable volunteers to fill in the documents and arrange the required documentation to open a bank account. In that process we empower the community as well learn the process of opening a bank account.
- Role clarity: Most of the time community members would always expect something to be free whenever outsiders visited the village. The expectations would be high especially when called for a meeting or discussion. In such conditions the community members need to be oriented clearly: trainees come to the community just for learning and to know more about the people, so such a clear role should be explained to the community members. It is most important to carry out community level intervention in a better way. Moreover, it helps to build sustainable local level solutions and the community members become independent. Though the trainees arrange certain social welfare services for those in need, it should be made clear that the trainee is just a facilitator provided by the government. Also the community members should be oriented to understand the process of availing such facilities which provides clarity of the role to the members. The trainees should not be portrayed as givers but that they can work amongst them in order to achieve certain things in the community.

- Dress code: In India, judgements are made based on someone's dress due to cultural traditions followed in remote villages. However, the scenario is slowly changing in most urban areas for various reasons. Hence it is highly important to orient the trainees to wear clothing that is considered respectable and accepted generally in the community. For girls, *salwarkameez, chudidar,* saree, and for boys generally formal attire are considered appropriate ways of dressing. Clothing assists when connecting to the local community. Personal rapport is very important to build relationships and for further intervention at various levels. So the trainees should be oriented to wear the appropriate clothing and hence forge a bond easily during practice at a macro level.
- Health: Open setting fieldwork is considered to be more challenging than other situations because the trainees need to be in the field irrespective of the climatic conditions of the area. Therefore, there is a high risk of contracting an illness if there is no proper orientation before the fieldwork. Usually during day time trainees need to visit the community where they are exposed to direct sunlight which might be harmful to their health because it may lead to dehydration, tiredness, and other issues. Hence the trainees need to be oriented to take an umbrella, water can, a small bag, food, and healthy snack items. Water is the main source of many diseases, so the trainees needed to arrange their own clean drinking water facilities which helped them to overcome most health issues. The majority of the time the supervisor noted that field work students had stomach issues the day following placement, due to intake of unhealthy food the previous day. It is the responsibility of the individual to take nourishing food. Based on the conditions of the open setting fieldwork area the supervisor should provide them with such information and precautionary measures to avoid health issues.
- Introduction of key contacts in the community: The faculty supervisor should ensure to establish key contact persons in the community. This is to ensure the safety and security of the trainees. In some cases, there are high chances that some members in the community react in different ways, some of which might be harmful to the trainees if they do not have anyone from the community to support them in a positive way. In the case of discussion of fieldwork, the supervisor made key contacts in the community which made them comfortable and secure during all the time in their fieldwork. This is crucial because trainees will have initial inhibitions when interacting with the community – in such circumstances these key contacts help them to feel at ease during interventions.
- Basic discipline: The trainees need to be clearly explained that they are seen as representatives of the institution and that their non-appropriate behaviour in the community would spoil the name of the institution. Also, it would limit future entry into the community and further interventions. Hence, they should interact with the community with the utmost care and respect. Moreover, the children in the community observe the trainees' way of interaction during activities in the community and they might also consider them as role models. During the process of interaction among the trainees and whenever entering the community, they should be conscious of talking very respectfully. Sometimes the trainees might chat between themselves in an informal manner, forgetting their situation. This could give the trainees a bad name if they do not converse appropriately.
- Punctuality: It is very important to visit the community at appropriate times and also to maintain punctuality for meetings. Even if there is tardiness for one or two meetings from students then the community members may also start to come late, hence spoiling the entire progress of the intervention. Also, the trainees should inform the community members as to every visit. It should not be a surprise to the community members when they receive a visit.

Confidentiality: There will be different kinds of people in the community. In the process of interaction there could be certain information about the individuals in the community. In that situation, whatever information about the individual's sensitive cases should not be discussed with everyone in the locality. Later, if they come to know about such a thing it would create a bad impression and it could damage the entire process of intervention.

First Day at the Community Open Setting

The faculty supervisor and author guided the students to meet the key persons in the community. Firstly, the farmer and contact person in the village showed them the field office: where to keep their belongings, use of the restroom, where to have their lunch, and the importance of taking some rest in between the fieldwork. In every open setting the faculty supervisor should establish such contacts in the village which will make the setting comfortable for the students. We observed how the farmer also welcomed the students and showed his happiness in assisting the students.

Humanity Adds Fieldwork Success

Sometimes there is an issue in bonding with the community members due to student attitudes towards undertaking the fieldwork in an earnest manner in the field. But an interesting incident happened on the second field visit. All four students reached the farmhouse around 10.00 am, and only the farmer's wife was there. Unfortunately, she had sustained an injury and was bleeding, so immediately one of the students took her to the nearby dispensary and treatment was given to her. It created a very positive opinion of the students from the farmers and those in the locality. This provided a very strong base for further interventions in the open setting community.

Regular Visits to the Community

As the students were introduced to the field, it was not necessary to accompany the students all the time. But it was important to know how the students were able to connect to the field for further interventions. After two visits, there was an individual conference (IC) to gain an understanding of progress made. The students were asked to list down their difficulties in the field. Though they studied the basics of community organisation in the class, applying it in the field was always a challenging task. The following were the questions asked by the students:

- What to do in the community?
- Where to start?
- How will the community react?

These were some of the common questions among the students. The author guided the students to clarify each of the questions in a professional way. The students needed to relate to the community in a better way – for which they had to visit the community every alternate day, initially without any agenda. They could undertake a number of activities in the community such as sit in the tea shop in order to talk to visitors and from those people they connected with other people in the village. Students could start talking to the women group leaders and members to understand the functioning of the groups, in addition to playing cricket with the local community in order to break the ice with the village youth. An appealing characteristic of Indian villagers is the respect for outsiders, whoever comes and talks with them is welcomed with a smile and reply. These factors helped them gain the confidence to work in the community. They followed all the strategies specific to this village and it worked out well. Meanwhile the students were assigned individual tasks to be completed as part of their fieldwork. It identified four important areas for intervention in the village on the part of the four students. All students had around 20 fieldwork days to complete their possible intervention. Hence, they were asked to restrict their intervention within the time period to avoid the following related issues:

i) Health and hygiene
ii) Women's empowerment
iii) Agriculture
iv) Linking the government schemes

i) *Health and Hygiene*

There was a spread of dengue during the year 2015 in the community. A trainee was assigned to deal with the issue and provide any possible intervention. Fieldwork trainees planned to conduct an awareness programme in the community. Planning was done to instil knowledge among the people in the community. Initially the rapport building process was carried out through meeting the key people in the community and playing cricket with the local youths. It helped for interaction with many people in the community. A common meeting was arranged to conduct an awareness programme. A trainee was assigned to find the resource person. A senior nurse from the local PHC was arranged to undertake the training. Further planning was done with the participation of the people in carrying out the programme. A sound system, electric power, chairs for the resource persons etc. were organised, with the programme being held on 19 March 2015. The programme started with a prayer song by Ms. P. Sasikala (I MSW). Ms. Kalpana (Puthuvalvu project, Vazhukkuparai village) gave a welcome address and introduced the village people. After that nine students from Madukkarai Panchayat Union Middle School, Ettimadai sang a folk song (Villu paattu) about Dengue fever, how it spreads, preventive measures, and its effects on the human body. It allowed everyone to understand clearly – in an accessible way – through folk songs. One of the resource persons for the programme was Mrs. Ponnu Sirumbayi, village health nurse at the Primary Health Centre, Arisipalayam who explained swine flu: how it spreads, how it causes health problems in the human body, and various preventive measures. She also explained the various services available at PHC, Aricipalayam and requested people contact the PHC and avail of the services if there were any health problems. After that 11 methods of 'safe hand washing techniques' were explained by Madukkarai Panchayat Union Middle School, Ettimadai students, and Mrs. Ponnu Sirumbayi, VHN.

Villagers were encouraged to participate, learning practically about the hand washing techniques. Following that, social work students performed a skit on the issues and ill effects of open defecation. It was possible to sensitise many people to know about the seriousness of the issue. Videos were shown regarding hookworm, roundworm, importance of toilet usage, and the ill effects and causes of health problems due to open defecation. In between there was interaction with the people and questions were asked and prizes were given to the participants. Overall, more than 100 people witnessed the programme including the students, many areas were covered, these being hot topics in society. After gaining an understanding of the issues, it was a great opportunity to sensitise the youth to create a group to renovate the unused toilet in their area. Finally, the social work trainee proposed a vote of thanks.

ii) Women's Empowerment

One of the trainees was assigned to take up the intervention with women in the community. Earlier itself the rapport building process had been started by the author, and in continuation with the process the trainee started interacting with the women's group. There are lots of tomato growers in this community, and during the peak season many tomatoes are grown and so the farmers do not receive a fair price. In such conditions, they throw away the tomatoes in the local markets as they cannot even justify paying the transport costs. The trainee took up the issue and planned to conduct a meeting with the women. It was decided by all the members to initiate a household level tomato processing unit. The trainee and women group members planned to conduct a training programme on tomato processing. The trainee approached Dr. P.R. Janci Rani, Head of Food and Nutrition Lab, Amrita Vishwa Vidyapeetham, Coimbatore campus. She agreed to provide training in her laboratory. A one-day training programme on 'Empowering Rural Women on food processing and preservation' was conducted on 30 April 2015. Around 16 women attended the training programme. Dr. Janci Rani and Dr. Tharani Devi were the resource persons.

The trainee made it possible to conduct the training programmes for the women which helped to win their trust. In the beginning, it was a challenging task to unite these women because of caste issues; however, the trainee was able to unite them through strong determination and regular visits to the community.

iii) *Agriculture*

Agriculture is one of the important sources of work in this community. Some of the farmers have already shown interest and joined some programmes. Mainly the author conducted many programmes in the villages for the farmers due to which the participation was active for the further programmes. Earlier, the trainee visited individual farmer's households to understand agriculture and the key issues for those concerned. It was observed that the farmers did not have proper occupational ID for availing of various government schemes. Hence the trainee explored the possibility of obtaining identity cards for them. Farmers needed to test the soil, then results were submitted to the Block Agriculture office – in turn they prepared the farmers' identity card for them. In the initial process the trainee collected the soil samples of around 16 farmers and handed them over to the soil testing lab in Coimbatore. After the test the results were added to the farmers' identity cards.

iv) *Linking the Government Schemes*

Experience of helping connect the community to governmental systems is an essential component in fieldwork (Andharia 2011). And so an effort was made by the trainees to do this. One of the important concerns in the community is that most people are not aware of the government schemes. A trainee was assigned to take up the issue and help connect the state system to the people. The Prime Minister announced a banking-for-all scheme called 'Pradhan Mantri Jan Dhan Yojana' (PMJDY). Banking is essential for everyone – some of the governmental social welfare systems are directly transferred to beneficiary bank accounts. However, it's not easy for everyone to go to the bank and go through the process of opening a bank account. Trainees found two illiterate women struggling with this, so they were taken to the bank with all the required documents and assisted with setting up their accounts. It was actually an uphill task for the poor but the trainees made it easy for them. This helps to show empathy with the village and it helps with further plans for assistance in the village.

Unique Supervision

Fieldwork supervision seems to be challenging in the realms of social work practice, especially as there is infrequent contact with the faculty and students, which limits a deeper understanding of the various dimensions of professional and personal development (Sukhramani 2019). In order to fill this gap the faculty supervisor spent the entire time with the social work trainees in the field. It was a unique practice where trainees received full-fledged training exposure from the beginning. The interactive process helped the trainees as well as the supervisor to resolve the nitty-gritty of the fieldwork. The trainees had the luxury and confidence to approach and interact with the community for any level of intervention. It is highly essential to avoid initial inhibitions when starting fieldwork – it is important to step into the community. On the other hand, if the faculty supervisor meets the trainees in between or only during the individual conference, there could be a delay in progress.

Community development professionals require intensive fieldwork to interact with community members. It is a process which requires initial support to start the interaction process. The trainees were given necessary support in the field on the spot – a supervisor encouraged the trainees to initiate community practice in a better way for professional social work practice. It required a conscious use of self, and supervisory notes contributed towards promoting self-awareness. In particular, the faculty supervisor should ensure the students acquire such technical skills as observation, interviewing, home visits, report writing, communication, rapport building, awareness generation etc.

Real-Time Feedback

The social work trainees' initial level practice of professional social work was evaluated and given to the trainees by the supervisor. Usually, it happened in a separate location post-fieldwork but in this concurrent fieldwork setting feedback was given in real time, i.e. on the spot. Based on the experience from the field it was observed that the students struggled in the initial phase hence appropriate guidance was given to them on the spot.

Individual Conference (IC)

The trainees went every Tuesday and Thursday for their fieldwork and IC was held every Wednesday and Friday at the department. In our case IC was conducted live at the community itself. There are higher chances of interaction and clarification as the supervisor knows the entire case as both parties are in the community all the time. The trainees hence gain confidence and are immediately ready for the next step: they go to the community with clear aims on their subsequent visit. On the other hand, in other cases there is information overload which limits the learning process in many ways.

Group Conference (GC)

All the trainees were given individual assignments to carry out; the interventions were discussed during IC but GC helped to examine many aspects, with every single trainee sharing their experience. This assisted in other areas of intervention and mistakes were corrected as a part of the learning process, thus helping prevent similar kinds of mistakes in future practice. GC was also conducted at the field live in the community. The atmosphere brought lots of energy and enthusiasm to help move forward with interventions.

Advantages and Disadvantages of Own Fieldwork Setting

The main advantage of the department's own field project was in the provision of better fieldwork opportunities. This priority was given to learning and professional development opportunities rather than administrative functions (Chui 2009). In our experience, it was found that some of the organisations engage the social work trainees in administrative functions due to a lack of professionals in the field. Though they gain some exposure at an administrative level with projects, still they lack professional social work training. Also, if there is a need for more supervision in the organisations, there is less help given to acquire the required training (Deal et al. 2007). Yet, the main disadvantage of own fieldwork settings is that it takes two to three years to have complete interventions and funded projects, so students do not get complete exposure to intervention. It was also observed that the students did not get attention in some cases as the organisation settings were filled with many students from other institutions which resulted in unproductive fieldwork training (Wayne, Bogo, & Raskin 2006).

Conclusion

There is always an initial inhibition when a team enters the community for the first time – for the faculty supervisor as well as the students. Authors have narrated in this chapter the possible scope of social work intervention in the community open setting concurrent fieldwork. It was observed that the trainees received first-rate exposure in the open setting fieldwork in terms of acquiring the required skills such as rapport building, assessing community needs, planning for interventions, solving individual problems, use of social work tools, applying classroom practice, and practising community level practice etc. The students expressed their satisfaction and felt each of the trainees had done something in the field. The continuous interaction with the trainee and follow-up with the community would yield fruitful social work intervention. At the end of the concurrent field work, the students were able to have a holistic understanding of the issues and its root causes. This was in addition to initiating social work intervention and finally intervening in areas of concern, and was possible because of the open setting field work of the department's field project. Moreover, the faculty supervisor was with the students all the time. The constant presence of the faculty with the student increased the scope of field projects which helped solve many social issues in the community. Further, it provided greater opportunities for the social work trainees to acquire fruitful hands-on experience in a community setting.

Notes

1. Open setting fieldwork refers to fieldwork in the village Vazhukkuparai, Madukkarai block, Coimbatore district, Southern India.
2. Social Work trainees are meant as the II MSW students of Department of Social Work, Amrita Vishwa Vidyapeetham.
3. Faculty Supervisor could be a social worker employed at the Department of Social Work, Amrita Vishwa Vidyapeetham.

References

Anand, M., & Adusumalli, M., (2019). Towards standardization of field work practicum: Experiential reflections from Delhi, India. *Social Work Education* 39(4)

Andharia, J. (2007). Reconceptualizing community organization in India: A transdisciplinary perspective. *Journal of Community Practice*, *15*(1–2), 91–119.

Andharia, J. (2011). Fieldwork education in community organization: Privileging the process of political engagement. *Community Development Journal 46*(SUPPL. 1), i96–i116.

Baum, N. (2011). Social work students' feelings and concerns about the ending of their fieldwork supervision. *Social Work Education*, *30*(1), 83–97.

Chandrapa, S., & Saxena, A. (2017) Social work: A practice based profession. *Research on Humanities and Social Sciences*, 7(17), 4.

Chen, Q., & Fortune, A. E. (2017). Student perceptions of the learning process during undergraduate field practicum: A qualitative study. *Social Work Education*, *36*(5), 467–80.

Chui, W. H. (2009). First practice placement: Great expectation and anxiety of a cohort of social work students. *Journal of Practice Teaching and Learning*, *9*(2), 10–32.

Deal, K. H., Hopkins, K. M., Fisher, L., & Hartin, J. (2007). Field practicum experiences of macro-oriented graduate students: Are we doing them justice? *Administration in Social Work*, *31*(4), 41–58.

Devi, Prasad B, (1997). Field Instruction In Social Work Education In India: Some Issues. *Indian Journal of Social Work,* 58(1), 74–77.

Dhemba, J. (2012). Fieldwork in social work education and training: Issues and challenges in the case of Eastern and Southern Africa. *Social Work & Society*, *10*(1), 1–16.

Fortune, A. E., Mccarthy, M., & Abramson, J. S. (2001). Student learning processes in field education. *Journal of Social Work Education*, *37*(1), 111–24.

Knight, C. (2001). The process of field instruction: BSW and MSW students' views of effective field supervision. *Journal of Social Work Education*, *37*(2), 357–79.

NAAC: National Assessment and Accreditation Council. (2005). *A Manual for Self-Study Of Social Work Institutions*. Bangalore: The National Assessment and Accreditation Council.

Nair, R., Juva, S., & Vimala Nadkarni, V. (2020). *Field Instruction in Social Work Education: The Indian Experience. First.* India, London: Routledge.

Sukhramani, N. (2019). Fieldwork supervision. In R. Nair, S. Juvva, & V.V. Nadkarni (Eds.), *Field Instruction in Social Work Education: The Indian Experience* (pp. 68–86). India: Routledge.

Wayne, J., Bogo, M., & Raskin, M. (2006). Field notes: The need for radical change in field education. *Journal of Social Work Education*, *42*(1), 161–69.

6
Field Work in Social Work Education
An Account of the Sri Lankan Experience

Shamila Sivakumaran and S. Jeevasuthan

Introduction to the National Institute of Social Development (NISD)

This chapter begins with a brief introduction to the Sri Lankan welfare system and the National Institute of Social Development (NISD) which is a premier institute in social work education and training in Sri Lanka. Sri Lanka has witnessed stable progress in human development since the middle of the last century and is far ahead of her South Asian neighbours. Sri Lanka's social service net, which was established in the latter part of the 1940s, has been relentlessly striving to enhance literacy and life expectancy in order to place the country among the Medium Human Development group (UNDP 2010). Pledging to execute sound educational policies, extensive and effective health programmes and medical facilities for all citizens led the country to adopt a successful welfare state. Amidst these endeavours, with other educational programme initiatives, an institution for social work education was also launched in 1952 through the collective effort of some leading non-governmental individuals, a few non-governmental institutions, and some leading personalities from government departments. However, unlike other countries, in Sri Lanka, the government and its service apparatuses act independently to ensure uninterrupted provision of advanced welfare facilities.

The NISD has three main components which involve different activities: the Sri Lanka School of Social Work is responsible for conducting academic programmes in social work; the Research and Publication Division is committed to carrying out research and its dissemination; and the Training Division is assigned to the design and implementation of training programmes in counselling and other relevant social welfare projects such as offering higher diploma, diploma, and certificate programmes in the fields of gerontology, child protection, sign language. However, their training programmes are not limited to the areas mentioned above.

The Sri Lanka School of Social Work under the auspices of the NISD has been committed to nurturing professional social workers to meet the higher demand for trained staff in social work and social development, nationally and internationally. It offers diploma programmes, higher diplomas, Bachelors, and Master's degree courses in social work. These courses are designed to entice adult learners and persons with considerable experience in social work (Ranaweera 2012). The institute also needs to be competent and dynamic to compete with traditional universities, university colleges, and private educational entities to maintain its professional status and the quality of its programmes. Furthermore, the social work profession ordinance is awaiting its legal approval from the state legislature. In Sri Lanka, although social work programmes pave the way for employment opportunities and professional status for trained practitioners, the discipline is not celebrated like others such as science and Information Technology. It is also worth considering that the institute needs to maintain its uniqueness and autonomy by offering an efficient and advanced field practicum.

Background to the Study

Social work is a profession which comprises both educational and field practicum elements. It involves direct classroom teaching and field education which aims at integrating theoretical and conceptual aspects into field work education. Therefore, integrating theoretical aspects into real life experience is the prime objective of the field practicum in any social work programme.

The definition of social work, jointly developed by the International Federation of Social Workers (IFSW) and International Association of Schools of Social Work (IASSW) in 2004, states that the social work profession promotes social changes, problem-solving in human behaviour and social systems, and that social work is the point where people interact with their environment. Principles of human rights and social justice are fundamental to social work. This definition shows us that social work intervention has a typical approach to support the needy and help them manage day-to-day challenges (Dhemba 2012). This involves promoting the inner ability of its clients to deal with their problems more efficiently and professional rapport assists in linking with appropriate resources to manage challenges, whilst extending its support in dealing with the challenging environment (Wisner 1943).

Social work is grounded on a unique curriculum consisting of both theory and fieldwork components. Consequently, as Hall (1990) asserts, a generally accepted view is that field instruction and education is of equal importance as theoretical academic instructions. Other concepts used to refer to fieldwork include field practicum, field placement, field instruction, fieldwork placement, internship, and field practice education (Dhemba 2012 p. 1). All these denote one feature in common; that is, the concept of linking theory to practice.

The following are some of the general objectives of fieldwork stipulated in the BSW Handbook of the NISD:

a. Strengthen the link between social work theory and practice
b. Foster collaboration between the School of Social Work and social administration and human service agencies
c. Crystallise the international recognition of the programmes and enhance the confidence of students enrolled in the accredited programmes

The field practicum is an inevitable element in the social work programmes and theoretical learning into practice is a central goal for all social work programmes taught at the NISD. However, the authors were able to evaluate how the number of social work students at the NISD encountered challenges in their concurrent field placements and how they faced many challenges while conducting social case work and social group work in their field placements. It was also found that there is no proper evaluation which has been conducted on the field practicum activities by the Field Work Unit at the NISD as it completed four years of service. And no official reports or research are available on the challenges and issues encountered by social work students and supervisors. Therefore, it is high time for a study of the nature of existing practice and for recommendations for future consideration.

A Brief History of Social Work Field Practice in Sri Lanka

According to Ranaweera (2013), the historical development of field practicum at the NISD can be traced through different stages of curriculum development for the entire period of social work education in Sri Lanka starting from 1954 to the present day. This can be divided into four stages:

1. Formative stage from 1954 to 1964
2. Development of the diploma courses based on western models from 1965 to 1982
3. Attempts to modify the curricula to suit local social situations from 1983 to 1993
4. Graduate level curriculum development

The Sri Lanka Institute of Social Work started providing short-term training soon after its establishment in 1954. The first certificate course in Child and Youth Welfare for a duration of six months was designed with a field component and the students were sent to 12 organisations for orientation field visits. In addition, a rural camp was also held under the field component. In the second term the students were sent to two residential agencies for the field practicum. In 1960, a certificate course in social work commenced at the Institute of Social Work, where students were offered three field placements to practice social case work, social group work, and community work. Three months were allocated for social case work and social groups while four months were allocated to community organisation (Ranaweera 2013).

After the establishment of the Ceylon School of Social Work under the Government's patronage, a two year diploma programme in Social Work was introduced. The programme of professional social work was designed to prepare students for professional practice in social work (De Silva 2002). The first year of this particular Social Work Diploma programme consisted of two semesters of class room teaching and one field instruction course unit. In the second year, they were attached to ongoing projects for the field placements which were implemented either by government or non-government organisations. Basically, the objective of this second year was to assist the students to transfer their learning from the classroom to their own practice.

The students were taken on an observation trip to various social welfare organisations for six days. This provided them with an opportunity to develop an understanding of remedial and development services provided in the country. After being given information on working with individuals and families, they were placed in the communities for field practice for a duration of six weeks. At the end of the field placement, a common session was organised to share their experience. Then the students learnt about working with groups and communities for practice. Students were placed in communities for practice. Students had to follow courses on social policy and project planning and implementation before they were assigned final field placements for a duration of eight months.

Most of the students were attached to development projects such as integrated *Mahaweli* Development programmes. This was an ongoing long term development programme which was designed to promote the agriculture sector and provide settlements for landless and homeless people (Ariyathunga et al. 2019), in addition to resettlement schemes implemented by both government and non-government organisations.

Method of Selecting the Sample and Justification

A qualitative approach was used by the authors to complete the sampling and data collection. For the primary data collection purpose, a semi-structured interview was administered with the selected participants. With primary data collected, authors carried out a brief desk review to locate relevant literature to construct the introduction and background to the study. A thematic analysis was done using the data collected from the participants. The authors preferred to have discussions with some of the participants when they realised it was necessary to clarify or confirm some information with the participants. Before starting the gathering of information, the authors shared the data collection tool with at least three persons to obtain their comments on the subject and structure of the device. And the tool was modified based on the comments received accordingly.

Ethical Considerations

The ethical considerations of this study are constructed based on the following three basic principles: respect for participants, the principle of beneficence, and justice. These principles implied that the authors not only respect the participant's individual autonomy, but also the health and well-being of participants. Before and during the development of data collection tools, the authors carefully considered if the research activities were not likely to cause any harm to the participants.

Firstly, the participants were sensitised to the whole research. The authors detailed the objectives and nature of the study to the participants before they were recruited for the interview. The participation was optional and the participants were not given the impression that their taking part was compulsory.

The participants' anonymity and personal identification were kept confidential and the information which was disclosed by them was used only for research purposes. The authors made it clear to the participants that they were permitted to amend or restrict the disclosure of information after it had been given in interviews.

Sampling Criteria and Size

The sample size was decided to be kept small as a majority of the participants are attached to a particular education institute – the National Institute of Social Development – and the number of educators was also relatively small. However, the social work educators who expressed their willingness to contribute to this study were only considered for the sampling purposes. Those who were newly recruited to faculty were not invited and therefore the total number of participants was 20. This included faculty supervisors (4), BSW degree students (4), Diploma Students (4), MSW students (4), agency supervisors (2), and field supervisors (2). The authors encountered some limitations when collecting data. For instance, initially it was decided to conduct the study with a sizeable proportion of samples, totalling 40. However, the authors restricted the sample size to 20 due to various practical reasons such as unavailability of time for supervisors due to tight work schedules, students' unwillingness to openly discuss the field activities and issues, and lack of response from the field and the agency supervisors. The semi-structured interview schedule which was administered to garner information consisted of the following domains. They were respondents' perception on the efficiency of the field practicum, challenges faced by the respondents in the field practicum, gap between the expectation and the application of the field placement, opportunities for improving the field practicum, and recommendations for future research potentials.

Existing Field Education Programmes

Orientation Field Placement: DipSW/BSW 111

This placement is designed to provide a comprehensive understanding of the social welfare services available and their delivery system in the Sri Lankan context. This course unit consists of two parts. Part one concentrates on conceptual explanation and information on the service delivery in Sri Lanka while part two provides the opportunity to be given the required orientation of field settings in social work practice. It attempts to inculcate the appropriate attitude and values for working with different categories of people in need by providing necessary exposure through study tours and hands-on exercises in social welfare organisations (BSW Handbook 2017/2021).

Concurrent Placements: DipSW/BSW 124 – Field Placement I

With the commencement of the revised social work degree programme in alignment with Sri Lanka Qualifications Framework (University Grants Commission 2015) block field placement starts in the first semester of level 4 and ends with the inter-semester break. The placement takes a period of 13 weeks. Students are expected to work for two days a week and a minimum of four hours each day. This implies that throughout the semester students are required to be undergoing field work concurrently with lectures. Unlike the block field placement during the long vacation which exposes students to methods of working with individuals and communities, the purpose of the concurrent field is to expose students to working with therapeutic groups. They are expected to attend group meetings, observations, and discussions, as well as interview members and assist them to achieve their objectives or goals (BSW Handbook 2017/2021).

The concurrent field placement was firstly introduced to the BSW (2013–2017) batch by the NISD, which was scheduled to run concurrently for two days a week in the second year of the degree programme hence covering 405 hours of practice; thus the purpose of the concurrent placement is to expose the students to work with individuals, families, and groups (BSW Handbook 2017/2021).

Concurrent Placement: HDipSW/BSW 211 – Field Placement II

The field practice II schedules implementation throughout both semesters in the second year of the Higher National Diploma in Social Work programme (HDipSW). It covers a minimum of 405 hours of practice in ten months. Students are expected to work 12 hours per week. The focus of the practice is on working with individuals, families, groups, and communities. The students are prepared to work in selected field settings/communities. They are encouraged to work in collaboration with government and non-governmental agencies (BSW Handbook 2017/2021).

Human Settlements and Service Delivery: BSW 324 – Rural Camp

This provides students with an exposure to rural life, problems and issues related to social development, and enables them to organise a camp for the study of the community needs, implementing selected programmes with the Divisional Secretariat. The rural camp exposure helps students' participative, reflective, and analytical skills in learning. This course has two parts. The first part explains the important concepts related to human settlements and provides an overview of the causative factors that have determined the evolution of such settlements in Sri Lanka. The second part is a practical immersion related to service delivery systems in Sri Lanka and aims to enable the students to develop the skills required for the evaluation of actual service delivery situations in a selected divisional area and in organising the Rural Camp (BSW Handbook 2017/2021).

Challenges Experienced by Social Work Students and Supervisors in Field Practicum

This section presents the challenges relating to the current context in which learning of social world field occurs in the Sri Lankan social work arena. The study focused on challenges encountered by social work students and supervisors during field placements at different settings. The crucial findings from a qualitative study with 20 participants on their perceptions and experiences of field work practicum learning are reported with recommendations for the enhancement of existing field work practice at the NISD.

Orientation to Field Placements: Challenges and Opportunities

Under field learning, the students are placed at different social welfare organisations with small groups based on the availability of welfare agencies. They are expected to visit the respective organisation for ten days. Students are provided with an opportunity to give a group presentation and share their experiences with the other groups at the end of the placement. However, the study found that the students encountered various challenges during the placement. They are:

a. Developed sympathy for the clients

The students and supervisors accepted that most of the students developed sympathy for their clients during the orientation placements. They would visit the agencies with the purpose of developing a perspective on the nature of the organisations and the services rendered by them. They also would use this opportunity to choose an organisation for the purpose of future placement. Developing this sort of feeling may give them a negative view about the organisation and the services rendered to their clients. The students who are generally placed in national and local level organisations and government departments often have this feeling.

A diploma student accepted that:

My orientation field placement was at an orphanage. The agency and the orphans had lots of problems including lack of money, trained manpower, and counsellors. Some orphans suffered some sort of severe emotional pain but no one was prepared to listen to them and find remedies for them. I talked to the head of the orphanage who ignored my worries and acted as if they were busy with their routine. At the end of the field practicum, I wanted to write a complaint letter to the Probation Department but one of my faculty staff consoled me and said these are very fundamental issues and each organisation has its own problems to be fixed. We were sent there just to observe the activities and gain some understanding about the prevailing service system.

A faculty member with a similar view opined that:

When students are sent to observe activities and the structure of a particular organisation such as an orphanage, elderly home, or rehabilitation centre, they are emotionally attached with the problems the inmates encountered and they wanted to find immediate solutions for them. They also have a feeling that they are worthless if they are not allowed to do something immediately for the clients on their own.

The orientation of field placements does not give space to the students to think about sustainable solutions for the problems they identify or what the organisation shares with them. Some students are unable to adapt to the agency's existing situation due to various reasons. For example, students who are attached to an organisation which provides care for persons with spinal cord injury would find it difficult to adjust to the severe psychological problems that are faced by the orphans. The students take the issues personally and suffer a lot. They are not prepared enough to face reality and develop the qualities needed for a professional and neutral person. This is a highly required attitude for a good social worker.

An agency facilitator disclosed that:

Some students really do not know what professionalism is. They confuse their personal qualities with professional commitments and suffer mentally. This resulted in increased students dropping out from the field activities.

A faculty supervisor agreed with this view saying that:

Some students do not know how to cope with the pain of the real world. We are unable to develop such qualities in the beginning of the programme. This puts the students in peril and sometimes compels them to leave the field practicum before they complete. Finding a placement and an agency facilitator to assist the students to catch up with the field learning also would be an additional burden to us.

Faculty supervisors find it difficult to visit their students at least once during the orientation placement due to tight work schedules, lack of logistical facilities such as transport or travelling allowance, or both. Paying visits becomes more challenging when a student is placed far away from the NISD.

Benefits of Orientation to Field Practicum

Challenges, apart from the orientation of field practicum, have some benefits as follows: a. Students are able to develop a mental map about the nature and scope of the social welfare organisations and services provided by them. b. Students get an opportunity to build rapport with organisations prior to their concurrent and block field placements. Therefore, students are able to decide the suitability of their future placements. c. Students' confidence level would increase before they are sent for the field practicum. d. Some students are hired by the organisations as part-time members of staff if they are willing to work. e. Some organisations strive to promote a passion for social work among the students.

Challenges for Supervision

Supervision refers to those planned, regular periods of time that student and supervisor spend together discussing the student's work in the placement and reviewing the learning progress (Ford 1987). This is defined as a continuous relationship in which a qualified and experienced supervisor monitors the professional development and competency of social work students and provides guidance to improve the appropriate qualities needed for the profession (Shokane, Nemutandani, and Budeli 2016). Supervision is an important part of the training of competent and effective professional social workers. However, most of the participants agreed that supervision is a crucial issue for both students and supervisors.

A faculty supervisor assented that:

Some first year and second year students are irregular with their field practicum. This may create problems to the service users and to the particular agency where the students placed for field placement. Therefore, periodical and close faculty supervision is more important when it comes to concurrent field work practice.

The results show that most of the social work students did not receive sufficient field supervision and they are disappointed when they realise that the agencies depend more on the students to learn because of lack of trained social workers in the agencies. Further, they stated that students feel discouraged when they find that some of the agencies do not exercise or apply the basic social work practices that they have learnt (Shaffie and Baba 2013).

One student stated that:

I felt extremely disappointed when I learnt that the agency facilitator whom I work with was not adequately familiar with the social work profession. The agency facilitator did not know much about proper social work supervision or field mentoring. He plainly admitted that he is not trained in providing social work supervision.

Poor Student–Supervisor Relationship

Supervision is a collaborative relationship which allows the supervisor to make desirable changes in the supervisee based on mutual agreement on the goals and tasks of supervision as well as a strong emotional bond. The process of fieldwork training involves many distinctive characteristics that are not typical of a classroom and the most distinctive are the supervisory relationship between fieldwork supervisor and social work students. The quality of the student–supervisor relationship is an important factor in mediating outcomes of social work fieldwork practice. This connection is the cornerstone and the heart of fieldwork training in social work education (White and Queener 2003). The significance and the quality of this rapport are paramount in achieving the goals of fieldwork practice. Such undertakings in social work take place within the context of a relationship (Ghitiu and Mago-Maghiar 2011). The findings indicated that social work students and all supervisors had a similar perception regarding the unhealthy relationship in the field supervision.

A supervisor mentioned that:

I am not happy with the quality time which I spend with my supervisees and we are unable to maintain a cordial relationship with them due to the lack of student commitment to their field activities. Sometimes I force my supervisees to make an appointment with me for supervision.

A concerned student said that:

Getting an appointment with my supervisor over the phone or email is hectic and they do not even have time to send us a short message to convey their inability to contact us at that moment.

An agency supervisor expressed that:

Students meet me to get my signature to submit their assignments but they do not talk about the real issues and support needed to sort out the issues. They think that we are signing authority and they would get negative grades if they do not get our signature and submit their field assignments on time.

The faculty supervisors explained that:

Before 2013, there was no concurrent placement and students were attached to social welfare organisations for block field placements. Typically, field practice occurs concurrently with classroom courses. A block placement represents an exception rather than an option. It differs from the concurrent arrangement in two major respects: 1) It is concentrated within a shorter timeframe, and 2) It is not taken concurrently with related academic course work. This block placement also had many practical difficulties. The participants expressed different perceptions on the challenges of field placement. From the students' point of view, there were some considerable challenges encountered by them during the block field practicum, as follows:

1. The students were unable to receive regular supervision as they were on block field placement for six months at a stretch. This did not allow them to meet their faculty supervisors to discuss the field issues and get their doubts clarified.
2. The faculty supervisors found it difficult to have regular supervision and discuss the block placement issues.
3. The relationship and coordination between all the supervisors (faculty, field, and agency) was not beneficial and this led to a communication gap among the agencies and the NISD.
4. Some students who were sent by the agencies to work with their service users directly in the field lost contact with their respective faculty supervisors. This created a communication vacuum between the agency and faculty.
5. Some students and faculty supervisors were concerned that the social welfare agencies used the field work trainees to complete their official responsibilities and administrative work such as drafting letters, writing reports, and computer work. This seriously curtailed the purpose of the field practicum.

After the revision of curriculum to incorporate the SLQF recommendations in 2013, students were placed in social welfare agencies for concurrent placements. The faculty supervisors and students accepted that concurrent field placements are relatively beneficial compared to block placements.

One faculty supervisor contented that:

We have less problems now compared to the previous situation. We had lots of practical issues and burdens when our students were on block placements. We were unable to control the field trainees previously but now the situation has changed favourably.

Some of the students had the collective view on the concurrent field work and said that:

Now, we are being supervised regularly and peer supervision is also arranged by the faculty field coordinator. Some experience sharing is arranged on regular basis by the field coordinators with the support of faculty supervisors, occurring every month. We are provided with ample opportunities to share our learning experiences such as theoretical and conceptual applications in the field practicum, problem management, and building rapport with agency employees and clients. We also listen to some best practices and innovative ideas from the students.

Rural Camp in Human Settlements: Challenges and Opportunities

Students are provided with an entirely different field learning opportunity during this practicum. They are sent to a rural village and stay with the local communities for ten days to study the existing service delivery system and relevant issues. A needs assessment is done by students with the assistance of different stakeholders including the village headman, economic development officer, probation officer, women development officer, and divisional secretary. A presentation is arranged for the government stakeholders to discuss the pros and cons of the service delivery system in the jurisdiction of the particular administrative area. Students are expected to submit a project proposal to the relevant stakeholders to enhance the existing service delivery system based on the needs assessment done by them.

Challenges for Rural Camps

Students find it difficult to adapt to the unfamiliar situation and suffer various physical and psychological challenges such as food allergies, fever, loose motion, and homesickness as they are away from their families for ten days at a stretch. The effectiveness of the assigned task, which is preparing a proposal based on the needs assessment, is always questionable and there is no mechanism in place to ensure the submission of the proposal after they get back to their routine academic activities. It really challenges the sustained relationship with the rural communities. It was accepted by the faculty and the students that this would be just an opportunity to learn about the community but does not ensure that something is given back to the community in return. Furthermore, it creates an expectation among the community members and the government stakeholder on students to fulfill the community needs without acknowledging their role and responsibility in fulfilling them.

Opportunities for Rural Camps

It was found that the students gain some advantages from the field placements. They are: a. They get an opportunity to closely work with senior government sector employees during their entire four-year learning period. Perhaps this is a remarkable opportunity to interact with government sector employees at all levels, b. they can utilise this period to make some positive changes in their personal and professional life – and c. adaptability becomes a most important positive professional quality which they garner during rural camps.

Opportunities and Challenges for the Field Practicum for Master of Social Work (MSW)

Most of the MSW students are attached to the organisations where they work during the field practicum. Under this practicum, the individual is placed on a regular service provision and learns the skills and attitudes necessary to deliver their services in an effective manner. The trainee social worker learns under the supervision and guidance of a qualified agency supervisor who is employed in the same organisation. These kinds of field placements have the advantages of giving first-hand knowledge and experience under actual working conditions. While the social work trainee learns how to deliver his/her services more effectively than earlier, he/she is also a regular member of staff providing the services for which he/she is paid. Emphasis is placed on applying the theoretical aspects and conceptual knowledge in the most effective manner during the service provision rather than learning how to perform routine tasks. However, the social work students, faculty, agency, and field supervisors acknowledged the following opportunities and challenges for the field activities conducted by the NISD.

Opportunities for the Field Practicum

The NISD does not need to bear an additional burden and undertake the commitment to find placements for its students as they are already employed either at a government or non-government organisation.

a. Most of the students are believed to have considerable prior experience in the field of service they are attached to. Therefore, they can perform their field activities with minimum supervision.
b. It is mandatory for the social work trainees to work at least for eight hours a day to cover the stipulated field work hours without much challenge.
c. The social work trainees can be easily monitored and mentored by the agency supervisor as they function in the vicinity and guidance can be given there if need be (in case there is a trained and qualified social worker employed at the same institute).
d. The faculty or field supervisor can always communicate to the social work trainee or the agency supervisor via phone or any available online communication mode to have discussion over the performance or the challenges he/she faces during the field practicum.

Challenges concerning the MSW Field Practicum

Though there are perceived benefits in the MSW field practicum, the social work trainees and supervisors also accepted that they encountered some challenges during the field practicum process as follows: a. Though the social work trainees are experienced and mature enough, b. they faced difficulties in finding sufficient time to obtain supervision from their respective supervisors, c. The social work trainees were occupied with their official commitments and field practice during weekdays and had to attend the classroom lectures at the NISD on Friday evenings and all day Saturdays, d. though the social work trainees are expected to allocate at least one hour weekly for supervision, this tight schedule restricted them from obtaining regular supervision at least once in a week. It was acknowledged by the field supervisors that some social work trainees are not really committed to their professional development and they just like to add a qualification to their profile and this degree may help them to apply for their promotion or just a salary increment.

The faculty supervisors also struggled to find suitable time to supervise their students amidst their tight work schedule. Some of them are involved in out-reach training programmes. The interviewed field supervisors and agency facilitators speculated that inculcating professional qualities and right attitudes into social work trainees would be always challenging since most of them are placed in an organisation where they are employed as permanent staff. This privilege would definitely influence their field practice activities and prevent them from delivering their tasks with a genuine interest. Therefore, the prime objective of nurturing true professional qualities through field practicum is always questionable.

A social work trainee agreed that:

The lack of supervision often challenges our morale. The field activities are not only expected to improve our skills and attitudes but also enhance our morale, thereby making a student contented and leading to a sustain professional development.

A field supervisor said that:

Apart from breaking the boredom in the workplace, field supervision offers social work students a learning platform where they are able to master new skills and to become more efficient. This is possible where there is a constant and constructive supervision available but, unfortunately, we are unable to provide them with good quality supervision due to various practical reasons such as lack of time and work overload.

An agency facilitator admitted that:

I am not sure how far the students would practise the code of conduct and familiarise themselves with social work principles and core values with minimum or no supervision. We have to make sure of access to a timely supervision in order to facilitate the students' experience, with a professional transformation from ordinary service provision.

Some agency supervisors and social work trainees agreed that they are unable to engage in meaningful supervision process as a considerable number of students come from faraway places including Down South, and the Northern and Eastern Provinces of Sri Lanka. They are granted one day study leave only on Fridays and it would be administratively challenging for them to obtain additional leave other than the one officially allocated. Therefore, making additional appointments with faculty supervisors for supplementary supervision is not feasible. Also, the School of Social Work is closed on weekends – even if they try to obtain supervision on Sundays.

A student expressed the concern that:

I am employed in the Northern Province of Sri Lanka which is some 400 kilometres away from Colombo. It would be extremely challenging for me to obtain leave from my office as I am granted study leave on Fridays. Travelling to Colombo is hectic and means having to bear an extra cost in addition to the course fee and other expenses. Therefore, getting quality supervision and getting my doubts cleared make me really worried. I am unable to sort out this issue. I am also extremely concerned about a fruitful learning relationship during my field practicum.

Both supervisors and students conceded that some of the senior members are reluctant to translate their mode of field supervision to the electronic platform which is becoming mandatory in modern education practice in Sri Lanka. Though some supervisors are prepared to deliver their expertise to students via online mode, the students are not occupied with the relevant skills to use the devices appropriately. This makes using online supervision more challenging and uncertain.

A field supervisor stated that:

It is important to introduce a new mode of knowledge sharing in this situation due to various practical reasons. However, students seem to be unprepared to switch the mode of supervision to the alternative method which is the electronic platform. All the leading

NGOs and social work education providers should work together to formulate a policy to introduce the electronic or online interactive supervision mode – which seems to be inevitable nowadays to reduce our work stress and enjoy an alternative and innovative mode of supervision.

A student also expressed a similar view regarding this aspect saying that:

I wish my supervisor would guide me using the electronic platform. Then I could use the devices available in my office during my duty hours. However, he is not willing to do so as he is not familiar with these modern communication vehicles. Otherwise, I could make use of my free time for the supervision purpose meaningfully.

A student should maintain a minimum of 80% attendance for all the course units including field work in order to become eligible to attend examinations and be assessed. Full appearance at field practicum sessions and participation in observation visits, field visits, and block field placements are compulsory. A student who is absent from field work for more than two days in a semester, for any reason, will have to fully compensate in accordance with the instructions of the supervisor concerned, and in consultation with the field work coordinator. The field attendance sheets provided to the students should be duly signed by the field supervisor and submitted to the Director of School of Social Work through the Field Coordinator at the stipulated time (MSW Handbook of NISD, 2018/2019). However, the challenges with regard to the attendance of the field work practicum are considered to be a prime concern of the faculty and field supervisors. For instance, irregular attendance and agency facilitators' inability to distinguish between the field work tasks and the routine activities appeared to be major issues during the discussions.

A field supervisor referred to these issues:

I know some agency supervisors are incompetent recognising the actual field activities and often confuse them with the routine activities. They fail to examine the field work activities with due attention. Some social work trainees manipulate this opportunity to complete their field work hours unethically. We have to give proper guidance to the agency facilitators on this issue. However, supervisors are not equipped with professional qualities.

A social work student also had a parallel view that:

I get confused at times and I am unable to differentiate my official work from the field work responsibilities due to lack of guidance and supervision from my superiors. They keep quite when I do something wrong and do not try to give me guidance to improve my work. Therefore, I think whatever I do is never good enough.

Lack of training for agency and faculty supervisors is also acknowledged as another crucial issue in the field practicum training. The faculty, field supervisors, and agency supervisors were really concerned that they are not provided with adequate and relevant refresher trainings or opportunities for experience sharing to be effective in their supervisory role.

A faculty supervisor consented that:

The lack of funding and absence of stable policy on the provision of training programmes are the main causes which prevent us from receiving good training on supervision. I am sure that I am not well equipped with the necessary skills and attitude to provide a good professional supervision to my supervisees. And, I am also unable to adopt creative strategies to sort out any crucial or unfamiliar issues in the field practicum.

Some supervisors are appointed for field supervision without sufficient qualification or relevant experience. Supervising students without relevant qualifications and sufficient experience puts both students and supervisors in peril.

A field supervisor conceded that:

> My bachelor's degree is a general degree this is not adequate to guide my supervisees effectively. I also need a postgraduate qualification in social work with a strong field training. Now, I feel inadequate at my supervision which gives me a sense of inferiority.

In summary, the study showed that the skills acquired in an educational institute vary from those required for the work or field placement. The field practicum helps the students and educational institutions to look beyond classroom learning and offer students practical experiences, where they are able to acquire first-hand exposure in the real world. Such a practicum can assist students in developing a sense of the actual professional world and help them establish a network with relevant experts. However, it is the field practicum or field placements that can enable social work students to acquire new and definite skills for a specific role, increase their contribution for better service delivery, and build their self-esteem.

The following table gives the details of field practicum subjects which are expected to be completed by social work students at different levels of study programmes taught at the NISD.

Table 6.1 Field work practicum subjects offered at the NISD at a glance

Course Unit	Course Level	Placement Type	Duration	Credit
Diploma SW/BSW 111	First year first semester	Orientation to social welfare organisations (Orientation field placement)	90 Hours	02
Diploma SW/BSW 124	First year second Semester	Field placement I (Concurrent)	315 Hours	07
Higher Diploma SW/ BSW 211	Second year first semester	Field placement II (Concurrent) (continuing from first semester)	405 Hours	09
BSW 324	Third year second semester	Human settlements and & service delivery (Rural Camp)	90 Hours 15Hours	02 01
BSW 421	Fourth year second semester	Community work (Block field placement)	765 Hours	17
MSW-513	Foundation field practicum	Concurrent field work	700 Hours	08
MSW-514	Advanced field practicum	Concurrent field work	500 Hours	10

Source: DipSW/BSW 2017/21 and MSW Handbook, 2018/2019.

Recommendations for Improvement of Field Practicum at the NISD

Based on the major findings of the study, the following recommendations are made, to be taken into consideration for the future enhancement of field work practicum conducted by the NISD.

a. A systematic and periodical evaluation needs to be carried out to upgrade the quality of field practice. For this purpose, the field work unit of the NISD, faculty supervisors, field and agency facilitators should work together and should revisit the existing field practices.
b. Faculty, field supervisors, and agency facilitators should be provided with ample opportunities to refresh their skills and knowledge in the field practicum.
c. Building a strong network among the above stakeholders is pivotal.
d. It is the responsibility of the NISD to create opportunities to develop a meaningful relationship between faculty, field supervisors and agency supervisors, and students to make the field practicum more professional and effective.
e. Framing a specific policy driven by the scientific research to exclusively promote field practicum is crucial.
f. Reducing the workload of the faculty supervisors is very important when they are allocated students for supervision.
g. Mobilising the existing logistic facilities and potential resources for field work practicum would be more beneficial.
h. The NISD should constantly insist on quality supervision through workshops and motivational activities. Tapping relevant local and international resources and expertise would be an appropriate approach for this purpose.
i. Consideration of using the available alternative interaction platforms such as electronic modes of communication and online devices would result in increasing the frequency of interaction between the supervisors and social work students.
j. Field agencies need to be educated on social work education and the purpose of field placement in the manner of appreciation and acknowledgement of their contribution.
k. Periodical agency visits need to be arranged in an effective and systematic way.
l. Appointing graduate students as mentors in the field would help the NISD to ease the burden of faculty supervisors.

Conclusion

This study was carried out using a qualitative approach to investigate the existing situation of the field practicum at the NISD. In the view of the foregoing analysis and discussion it is evident that students and the supervisors are facing numerous challenges related to field placements since it is newly introduced in the BSW curriculum. Due to a lack of welfare agencies and agency supervisors who are qualified in professional social work, concurrent field placement has become a burden for the students and the faculty. The allocated days for field work are not effective in many of the agency settings where students struggle to accomplish their field work requirements such as social case work and group work.

Furthermore, it is acknowledged that supervision plays a crucial role in field work, and supervisors are not able to provide effective supervision due to their administrative and academic-related burden. Since it is an initial stage, there are innovative changes according to the Sri Lankan context need to be carried out by the field work unit of the School of Social Work at the NISD. The field work unit is more responsible for developing and implementing field work education at the NISD.

With training and skills development, social work trainees and supervisors are able to think outside the box and widen their professional abilities and qualities, and enhance their skills and attitudes that can improve an organisation's quality welfare service delivery. Such field practicum programmes are the best way to promote innovation and improve social workers' and supervisors' involvement. They are likely to feel valued if they are being invested in, and would work harder to exceed expectations on their profession. However, the NISD should adopt stronger and more successful field practice training strategies and policies that assist it to build its professional brand name and enable it to emerge as a hub in social work education among social work educational institutes in Sri Lanka.

References

Ariyathunga, K., Ruberu, J., Dayananda, P. G., & Wehella, V. (Eds.) 2019. *Mahaweli: sanhidiyawa gangawa. [Mahaweli: The River of Reconciliation]* (p.641p). Colombo, Sri Lanka: Mahaweli Authority of Sri Lanka.

De Silva, G. (2002). *Memories of the Past: Recalling the Early Years of Social Work Education in Sri Lanka.* Colombo, Sri Lanka: NISD.

Dhemba, J. (2012). Fieldwork in social work education and training: Issues and challenges in the case of Eastern and Southern Africa. *Social Work & Society, 10*(1), 1–16

Ford, K. (1987). *Student Supervision.* New York: Macmillan International Higher Education.

Ghitiu, M. E., & Mago-Maghiar, A. (2011). Field instructors on key issues in social work education: A comparative approach. *Revista de Asistenta Sociala, 4,* 73.

Hall, N. (1990). *Social work training in Africa: A fieldwork manual.* Harare: Journal of Social Development in Africa.

Ranaweera, A. (2012). *Professionalization of Social Work in Sri Lanka. 60th Anniversary 1952–2012.* Rajagirya, Sri Lanka: National Institute of Social Development.

Ranaweera, A (2013). *Review and Record of the History of Social Work Education in Sri Lanka.* Research project funded and implemented by Social Work Research Institute, Asian Center for Welfare in Society (ACWelS), Japan College of Social Work and cosponsored by Asia Pacific Association for Social Work Education).

Shaffie, F., & Baba, I. (2013). Internationalization of social work education in Malaysia. *Internationalization of Social Work Education in Asia,* 79–116.

Shokane, A. L., Nemutandani, V., & Budeli, N. J. (2016). Challenges faced by fourth year social work students during fieldwork practice at a rural-based university. *AFFRIKA Journal of Politics, Economics and Society, 6*(1), 133–163.

Student's Handbook. (2017–2021). *The Bachelor of Social Work 2017–2021: Incorporating Diploma In Social Work/Higher Diploma in Social Work.* Rajagiriya, Sri Lanka: National Institute of Social Development.

Student's Handbook. (2018/2019). *The Master of Social Work 2018/2018.* Rajagiriya, Sri Lanka: National Institute of Social Development.

UNDP. (2010). *Sri Lanka Has Progressively Improved in Human Development.* Colombo, Sri Lanka: UNDP.

University Grants Commission. (2015). *Sri Lanka Qualifications Framework.* Sri Lanka: Higher Education for Twenty First Century (HETC) Project of the Ministry of Higher Education.

White, V. E., & Queener, J. (2003). Supervisor and supervisee attachments and social provisions related to the supervisory working alliance. *Counselor Education and Supervision, 42*(3), 203–218.

Wisner, E. (1943). Helen Leland Witmer, Social work: An analysis of a social institution (book review). *Social Service Review, 17*(1), 103.

7
The Need for Decolonising Field Work Training in Social Work in India

Bishnu Mohan Dash

The social work curriculum introduced in India in 1936 was based on western values and ideologies based on individualism. With the introduction of social work courses by the Tata Institute of Social Sciences (TISS) in Mumbai, the West-centric values and ideologies permeated into Indian social work educational institutions which were further reinforced by Indo-USA social work education exchange programmes after India's independence. Still in India social work institutions continue to propagate the western values, ethics, methodologies, and pedagogies as received from the West. According to Midgley (1981, p. 72), studies of the curricula of schools of social work in developing countries in the 1960s revealed that the contents conformed with western, particularly American, approaches. The overall social work curriculum and particularly theories in social work in many of these institutions of social work have lots of similarities with western countries (Roy & Dash, 2019; Mupedziswa, 2005). The syllabus in most of the universities in India has more or less remained the same and unchanged. Whatever minor revisions made in the curriculum, they were also within the Eurocentric western framework.

The ideological orientations based on western values are contrary to Indian traditions, beliefs, and practices. The imported research methodologies, field work practice methods, and lack of application in Indian settings have not only halted the professional journey of social work in India but also could not bring any desired result in the process of social change and development. Without any kind of needs assessment, the social work discipline and field work methods, including western bibliographies, were introduced in India without testing its relevance for suitability, relevance, appropriateness, and effectiveness in Indian settings. In order to realise the effectiveness of the social work discipline as a profession in India, there is a need to employ appropriate strategies and methodologies. Without the use of such appropriate strategies and methods, the goals of relevance and appropriateness would almost certainly remain a pipe dream (Mupedziswa & Sinkamba, 2014). The social work profession is primarily influenced by the liberal values of America and the western countries which are either of very little relevance or entirely irrelevant in our Indian society. Jones (1978, p. 32) said that Asian social work has been hindered due to its reliance on European and American models of social work for which its progress towards indigenisation is unstable. Of course, a few social work educators have triggered a debate for the need for an indigenous model of social work education, in India, but sadly the majority of social work educators have continued to maintain the status quo and followed

DOI: 10.4324/9781003270119-9

western curricula and field work methods either knowingly or unknowingly with regard to its irrelevance and ineffectiveness in the Indian context. After more than eight decades of social work education, a few social work educators in India have started critiquing the obsolete curriculum and field work training in social work based on western universalism. These scholars are devotedly working towards the Indianisation of social work in India across universities by organising seminars, conferences, and refresher courses for faculty members as well as developing an indigenised social work curriculum and accompanying literature. It has created a ray of hope for the Indian social work fraternity and consequently Indian social work has entered a new era of social work; recently the Masters in Social Work programme obtained the Bharatiya Curriculum[1], implemented partially in selected universities in India.

Since the introduction of western social work curricula and alien western field work techniques/ models in Indian universities, there have been debates in some quarters regarding the universality and validity of western curricula and field work practicum/models in the Indian context. This paper also argues why American and British patterns of field work modules are not compatible in the Indian context and why there is such a need to decolonise the field work practicum in India and develop an Indianised model of field work practicum. The arguments for an indigenisation of field work practicum are gaining momentum in various countries because the values, nature of reality, and traditions in India are entirely different than the USA. Social workers across the globe do not agree on the universalisation of social work values (Mabvurira, 2018). Titmuss (1974, p. 45) argued 'that one cannot theorize or generalize in any universal sense from American values and experience'. Cossom (1990) also argues that in the developing world, social work should free itself from the inbuilt assumptions and cultural biases of first world theories and models of practice and come up with indigenous education and practice. Social work practice must be contextually oriented, i.e. it must be suitable for and relevant to the local conditions. An indigenous base of social work education or indigenisation of social work education in India demands a cultural competence on the part of the professionals. Understanding about cultural diversity and knowledge of different cultural groups are a prerequisite for developing cultural competence. It is important to know that diversity also exists within ethnic or cultural groups (Jaswal & Pandya, 2015).

In the current Indian context, a group of social work educators under the banner 'Bharatiyakaran'[2] of social work education have recently started contesting and challenging the effectiveness of western social work education because they argue that western curricula is not fit for all societies. Besides that, the continuation of the western curricula continues to marginalise indigenous social work education. The obsolete social work curriculum and ineffective field work practice modules have halted the growth of the social work profession in India.

Dissenting voices are growing towards American and British curricula in various print media. Due to the movement for Indianisation of social work education, social work education in India is now gaining a new perspective, new identity, and new vision and more recently the development of the 'Bharatiyakaran of Social work curriculum'[3] which is rooted in its rich traditions, culture, heritage, and ancient wisdom, as well as philosophical texts. Even the social work fraternity has accepted the new curriculum based on Indic wisdom. Some of the universities in India have also adopted sizeable components from the Bharatiyakaran of Social Work Curriculum. The social work discipline as an imported and borrowed profession had always been dependent on western wisdom and knowledge which was either irrelevant or less relevant to Indian society as the nature of reality in the country varies from western nations. Due to the initiatives and interventions of the pro-Indianisation scholars of social work, the social work curriculum in India has been reconstructed, redefined, and reformulated and is fully and partially implemented in a few native schools of social work.

Field Work Practices in Social Work

Field work practice is an integral part of the social work curriculum, providing learners with opportunities to apply social work theories, principles, methods, and techniques in institutional and non-institutional community settings. Different terminologies are used for 'field work training' in social work, such as integrated learning, (Humphrey, 2011), field education, field instruction, (CSWE, 2008), social work placements (Lomax et al., 2010; Mathews et al., 2014), social work field practicum (Holden et al., 2011; Parker, 2007), and internship (Anastas, 2010). The Council on Social Work Education (CSWE, 2008, p. 8) has described field work as the 'signature pedagogy' that represents the central form of instruction and learning in which a profession socialises its students to perform the role of practitioner. Field work is an important and essential component of social work education. Like other professions, social workers also need pedagogical norms through which they can connect and integrate theory and field work practice. The importance of field work training in social work as a medium for combining theoretical knowledge and practice skills has been highlighted in many studies (Agnimitra, 2018; Roy & Dash, 2019; Adsule, 2005; Dhemba, 2012; D'Souza, 2012; Johnson et al., 2012; Westerfelt & Dietz, 2001; Royse et al., 2007). The goal of field work training is to acquaint students with actual social work situations and problems and prepare them for professional social work practice through which students enter the profession through inculcation and assimilation of social work ethics, principles, and values (Sunirose, 2020). Jeyarani and Jebaseelan (2017) describe it as 'a consciously planned set of experiences occurring in a practice setting designed to move students from their initial level of understanding, skills and attitudes to levels associated with autonomous social work practice'. (Kasake, 1986) also states that 'Fieldwork is an instrument of socialization since it prepares the students for a future role as a social work practitioner'. During field work students acquire a positive attitude and create a value frame under the supervision of expert academicians and practitioners (Agnimitra, 2018, p. 18). Therefore field work training in social work presents a variety of opportunities for the students to understand social problems and to develop professional skills to address these problems through observation, analysis, and intervention under the guidance and supervision of a trained faculty supervisor and field work supervisor. Field work training in social work engages the student in supervised social work practice and offers opportunities to marry theory and practice. It is an instrument that is used to initiate students into the profession through inculcation and assimilation of social work ethics and the principles and values of social work (Hepworth et al., 2002).

Field work in the area refers to a setting which is a real-life situation such as a social welfare/development organisation, or an open community that provides avenues for the students to interact with clients and the client systems. In the field, the students are given opportunities to apply theoretical learnings in social work – basically social work methods, principles, skills, and techniques under the supervision and guidance of a professionally qualified supervisor/teacher in the respective schools of social work as well as a trained practioner based in the particular settings. As a mode of teaching, field instruction uses pedagogical norms to train students in the role of practitioner while providing a professional platform to integrate theory into practice (Barker et al., 2011). Schiff and Katz (2007, p. 794) state that field work practice has long been acknowledged as a major component of social work. It is in field practice that knowledge learned in the classroom is assimilated in real-life situations, which concurrently and eventually shape the professional identity of the student social worker. In the social work field work placement, students can put into practice what they learned in the classroom, which is to integrate theory with practice. Field learning through social work practicum enables students to develop specific skills using individual approaches and socio cultural learning approaches (Papouli, 2014). It enables the students to obtain hands-on working experience within a diverse range of human service organisations (Royse et al., 1999; Wilson, 1981). The field work training provides the students with first-hand experience of using various practical skills such as interviewing, needs assessments, negotiation skills, mediation, advocacy, managing professional boundaries, and utilising reflective and effective practice skills (Trevithick, 2008). Due to its importance in social work education, field work placement has been described by Doel and Shardlow (1996) [cited in J Dhemba (2012) as the 'heartbeat of social work".

Field training for social work students plays a vital role in preparing professionals for high-quality practice, stressing the importance of integrating theory with practice in social work and higher-education systems (Sarhan, 2005; Al-Latif, 2007; Shaw, 2011). This brings to the fore the importance of field work training for social work students, as it places them in the context of their work environment and gives them the opportunity to capitalise on skills required during their professional careers. This includes problem-solving, teamwork, and communication skills, as well as reflexivity (Regehr et al., 2007). Furthermore, it places students in contexts that require them to deal with different stakeholders involved in community development. Through such experiences, students are able to apply skills to address individual and community needs and participate in social change.

Because the integration of learning into practice is a central goal for all professions, the question of how to bridge the gap between theory and practice and between the classroom and the field work practice is one which has preoccupied social work education since its very beginnings in universities (Clapton et al., 2008, p. 334). So field work learning in social work is considered as the missing link between theory and professional practice (Parker, 2007). In social work education, both theoretical class room learning and field work training are equally important. However, in reality field work is marginalised when compared to its academic counterpart in many training institutions (Dhemba, 2012; D'Souza, 2012; Mallick, 2007;). Kaseke (1986) [7] reported that due to a lack of literature in field work, educators, students, and field supervisors are deprived of getting meaningful and comprehensive guidance for field instruction. Field work in social work education in contemporary India is facing many challenges and requires addressing (Baikady et al., 2014). Various studies in India show that field work training given in Indian schools of social work is badly designed and ineffective. Bhanti (1996) has highlighted the irrelevance of the field work education in the existing social system in India. Subedar (2001) highlights the lack of literature on concurrent field work training and pointed out the lacuna existing in the education field in some universities and has suggested devising modalities for field practicum for social work students. Chaugale (2010) and Botcha (2012) also mention the problems and challenges of social work education and practice in India. Roy & Dash (2019) list various problems relating to field work training in India such as unchanging patterns of field work, lack of supervision and visitation by the supervisors; absence of field work manuals; lack of uniformity among various schools of social work in regard to field work training; lack of suitable agencies, lack of competent agency supervisors; and inadequate field work methods to address contemporary social problems have hampered field work training in India. Most importantly, in Indian schools of social work there is a complete disconnect between theories taught in the classroom and whatever is practised in the field settings, hence field work training remains as a 'ritual'.

> The point where social work theory meets practice is a tenuous link and spanning the bridge between abstract theorising and concrete action requires tangible and practical remedies. The rift between theory and practice perpetuates the status quo of a continuing

> culture of silence and a culture of complacency and denial within the social work professional with respect to issues of racism and oppression.
>
> *(Sinclair & Albert, 2008, p. 2)*

All partners in field education including students, faculty, field work coordinators, and field supervisors need to interrogate the oppressive policies and practices that continue to perpetuate Eurocentric practices (Clark et al., 2020). So, it is highly imperative to explore and design Indic field work manuals and practices for effective field work training in the Indian context.

Why Is Decolonising Field Work Training in Social Work Essential?

Decolonisation basically refers to the 'undoing' of colonisation. Decolonisation aims at changing the Eurocentric dominant landscape of academia (Pickering, 2010). According to Fanon (1963), it is a violent phenomenon because it calls into question the colonial situation as it seeks to overturn the order of the colonial situation. Decolonising social work requires returning to one's cultural roots for direction and it entails resistance to social work's 'West to the Rest' movement, which seeks to 'internationalise' and 'standardise' the profession (Ibrahima & Mattaini, 2018). Decolonisation also refers to coming out of collective oppression of the West and asserting their right to self-determination (McNabb, 2017). In the context of decolonising social work it involves destroying irrelevant practices and reviving the traditional as well as institutionalising the latter in social institutions.

The western hegemony and imported social work curriculum as well as field work practices from the West continue to dominate since the introduction of social work education in India. There have been vigorous debates and discussions raging on the applicability and suitability of imported western social work content in Indian settings. Midgley (1992) says that the exportation of knowledge and technology shows the complex process of colonialism and professional imperialism. In the context of field work training it refers to replacing the western models and paradigms of social work with the Indic indigenous methods of social work practice. Indigenisation is one of the processes of decolonisation and it refers to the extent to which social work fits local contexts (Gray, 2005). According to Shawky (1972), indigenisation refers to adapting imported ideas to fit the local needs. Endogenous indigenisation, on the other hand, focuses on the contemporary relevance of cultural heritage and native theories. Sinha (2002) has termed this kind of indigenisation as a 'purist trend' that relies primarily on the native wisdom and knowledge derived from Indian scriptures and philosophical texts. Indigenisation is the process of making the discipline sensitive to cultural nuances and social reality (Dalal, 2011). Sinha (1993) mentions two types of indigenisation – endogenous and exogenous. Endogenous indigenisation is the product of culture and native concepts whereas exogenous indigenisation is the product of the interaction of cultural variables with concepts, theories, and methods introduced from outside. He says that it is a gradual process when alien concepts and theories are adapted to a different culture. On the other hand, imperialism refers to the dominance of western worldviews over diverse local and indigenous cultural perspectives (Gray, 2005). According to Wong (2002), indigenisation challenges universal knowledge and the cultural hegemony of the dominant discourses locally and globally. In order to formulate the Indic modules of field work practicum in social work there is a need for applying Indic modules of social work interventions through intensive practice and reflective learning. Besides that there is a need for testing the utility and applicability of western social work methods that will fit into the Indian sociocultural context. Therefore the transferability and import of western field work techniques need to be examined empirically for their effectiveness. The socioeconomic, political, as well as cultural context of India is not similar to an American setting. India is characterised by a diversity of languages, culture, values, ethnicity, and religions. There is widespread diversity in beliefs as well as ethics. The social problems of India are quite different than those of European and American countries. In India there are various socioeconomic problems like poverty, illiteracy, superstitions, natural disasters, communalism, female infanticide, dowry, casteism, low per capita income, and other such problems. In view of these unique socioeconomic problems, India requires its own social work interventions models and field work techniques for its social work professionals. It is quite unfortunate that the ancient Indic wisdom, knowledge, and best practices which were quite relevant to our Indian context have been completely sidelined due to colonisation but also are considered as inferior in comparison to western practices. As Makhubele (2011) notes, due to the emergence of western systems of knowledge, indigenous knowledge systems are considered as inferior and even relegated to lower levels. Several studies also highlight the inappropriateness of western methods (Ragab, 1982; Muzzale, 1987; Mupedziswa, 2001; Mwansa, 2010). In this context, Nagpaul, 1972 cited in Mupedziswa and Sinkamba, 2014 said 'it was unfortunate the schools of social work in that part of the world were dependent on Western literature. He admonished that the western textbooks used had been written with a Western audience in mind'. Weil (2008) and Kadushin (2008) have highlighted the importance of contextualising social work practice and community-based development, as well as recognising interventions as adaptable and 'critical tools [that] frame thinking and action' (Weil, 2008, p. 6). So there is a need to revamp the field work training in the Indian context.

Need for Revamping Social Work Models/Practices

During field work training students were given training on various social work methods to solve the problems of the individuals, groups, and communities. During the training programme they had to rely only on western therapeutic interventions. However, the Indic models of treatment were practised before the introduction of social courses in Indian universities. For example, social case work is a method of helping individuals to solve their individual problems. Various ancient psychological treatments like *Daivayaparsya* (spiritual or faith therapy), *Yuktivyapasrya* (rational therapy), *Satvavajaya* (psychotherapy) are extremely useful in dealing with the psychological problems of individuals (Nagar, 2018) and have become obsolete during field work training and practices. *Daivayaparsya* is a kind of faith-based treatment mentioned in Ayurveda which describes that if the patient chants religious mantras, the process of cure will be much faster. *Yuktivyapasrya* is also based on the Ayurveda principles of Pancha Mahabhoota, *tridosa, samanya,* and *vishesha* which are very much effective for treating psychological problems. *Sattvavajaya* therapy founded by Charak helps in controlling the mind. It is a very effective method to bring better coordination and harmony between intellect, memory, and patience.

Yoga is extremely useful in helping cancer patients and survivors improve their quality of life, as well as reducing stress and cancer-related symptoms such as nausea and pain. Numerous studies also show that yoga therapy is beneficial for dealing with clients with chronic pain, hypertension, and injuries. Besides that several studies also mention use in attention-deficit/hyperactivity disorder, anxiety, stress, depression, chronic insomnia, and addiction (Büssing et al. (2012), Nayak & Panda, 2012). Yoga can be used as a potent therapy for the treatment of drug addicts (Sedlmeier, 2019). Besides that yoga can also be very helpful for social workers in relieving their own stress. Yoga is not only a physical exercise but an important medium of integrating body, mind, and soul. An ancient Indian theory of personality – *Guna* theory – is also a very relevant technique for addressing the psychological problems of individuals. The traditional Indic method *Japa* is also an important therapeutic technique to address smoking-related problems.

Meditation and *Japa* are effective Indic therapeutic techniques for the treatment of psychological problems, drug addiction, smoking, and depression. *Pranayama* not only produces delightful settling influence on mind and body, but also helps in enlivening certain levels of 'subtle energy' within the tissues (Sharma et al., 2014). Numerous studies also show that it helps in test anxiety reduction, and improving test performance (Nemati, 2013). *Pranayama* is extremely useful in addressing high levels of stress among students (Shastri et al., 2017). Patanjali's astanga yoga, yogic therapies, ancient system of naturopathy, and use of hydrotherapy are also very useful techniques and need to be included in field work training manuals. But unfortunately these Indic intervention practices are neither taught nor practised among the social work fraternity in India. The ancient Indian practices for solving mental health problems are quite holistic and have been completely sidelined by the social work educators in India. If they were to be incorporated in field work training manuals, it would certainly be of great advantage to the social workers. The Indic community development practices of low-cost housing and the sanitation model of L. Baker and B. Pathak, rural development practices like natural farming, organic consumption models of Dhabolkar, Palekar, Shiva, and Nammazhvar, the water harvesting and renewable energy model of Anna Hazare and Rajendra Singh should be taught to children and would be more relevant in Indian settings.

Social workers should also be trained on Indic social work values[4] such as *dharma*, *ahimsa*, *satya*, *nishtha*, and *upeksha*. These values are very important for social workers as they imbibe among them the feeling of love, moral duty and responsibility, non-violence and moreover it will socialise them to work for clients in a more responsible, compassionate, selfless, and devoted way.

Notes

1 Masters in Social work gets Bharatiya Curriculum, retrieved from https://duexpress.in/masters-in-social-work-gets-bharatiya-curriculum/ on 30 July 2018.
2 The concept of 'Bharatiyakaran of Social Work' is based on three major premises – Indianisation, Indigenisation, and Decolonization. retrieved from https://www.newdelhitimes.com/bharatiyakaran-of-social-work-understanding-the-meaning-and-concept/ on 7 December 2018.
3 The Bharatiyakaran of Social Work Curriculum was developed in the National Workshop on Bharatiyakaran of Social Work Education, retrieved from https://www.newdelhitimes.com/social-work-curriculum-in-india-moving-towards-bharatiyakaran/ on 2 October 2018.
4 Indic social work values, published in *New Delhi Times* on 22 April 2019 and can be retrieved from https://www.newdelhitimes.com/indic-social-work-values/, retrieved on 30 April, 2019.

References

Adsule, J. (2005). Fieldwork training for radical settings. *Perspectives in Social Work, 20* (2), 18–24.
Agnimitra, N. (2018). Field work in the contemporary context: Vision and engagement. *Journal of Social Work Education, Research and Action, 1*(1), 28–49.
Al-Latif, R. A. A. (2007). *The Environment and the Human*. Alexandria: Alwafa for Printing and Publications.
Anastas, J. W. (2010). *Teaching in social work: An educator's guide to theory and practice*. New York: Columbia University Press.
Baikady, R., Pulla, V., & Channaveer R. M. (2014). Social work education in India and Australia. *International Journal of Social Work and Human Services Practice Horizon Research Publishing, 2*(6), December 2014, 311–318.
Bhanti, R. (1996). *Field work in social work perspective*. Delhi: Himanshu Publications.
Botcha, R. (2012). Problems and challenges for social work education in India: Some recommendations. *International Journal of Multidisciplinary Educational Research, 1*(3), 201–212.

Büssing, A., Michalsen, A., Khalsa, S. B. S., Telles, S., & Sherman, K. J. (2012). Effects of yoga on mental and physical health: A short summary of reviews. *Evid. Based Complement*. Alternat, Vol. 12, retrieved from https://www.hindawi.com/journals/ecam/2012/165410/ on 26 March 2020.

Clapton, G., Cree, V. E., Allan, M., Edwards, R. R., Irwin, I. M., MacGregor, W., Perre, R. (2008). Thinking outside the box: New approach to integration of learning practice. *Social Work Education, 27*(3), 334–340.

Clark, N., Drolet, J., Mathews, N., Walton, P., Tamburro, P.R., Derrick, J., Michaud, V. Armstrong, J., & Arnouse, M. (2020). Retrieved from https://ojs.uwindsor.ca/index.php/csw/article/download/5812/4743?inline=1 on 31 March 2020.

Cossom, J. (1990). Increasing relevance and authentisation in social work curricula by writing and teaching from indigenous cases. Paper Presented at the 25th International Congress of the International Association of Schools of Social Work, Lima, Peru.

Council on Social Work Education. (2008). Purpose: Social work practice, education, and educational policy and accreditation standards. Retrieved 1 December 2016, from www.cswe.org/File.aspx?id=13780

Dalal, A. K. (2011). Indigenization of psychology in India. *Psychology Teaching Review, 17*(2), 2–9.

Dhemba, J. (2012). Fieldwork in social work education and training: issues and challenges in the case of eastern and Southern Africa. *Social Work & Society, 10*(1), 464–80.

D'Souza, A., & Sebastin, K. (2012). Field practicum: Need for evolving best practices. *Deeksha, 10*(2), 33–42.

Fanon, F. (1963). *The wretched of the earth*. Broadway, NY: Grove Press.

Gray, M. (2005). Dilemmas of International social work: Paradoxical processes in indigenisation, universalism and imperialism. *International Journal of Social Welfare, 14*(2), 230–7.

Hepworth, D. H., Rooney, R., & Larsen, J. A. (2002). *Direct social work practice: Theory and Skills*. Salt Lake City, UT: Brooks/Cole.

Holden, G., Barker, K., Rosenberg, G., Kuppens, S., & Ferrell, L. W. (2011). The signature pedagogy of social work? An investigation of the evidence. *Research on Social Work Practice, 21*(3), 363–372.

Holden, G., Barker, K., Rosenberg, G., Kuppens, S., & Ferrell, L. W. (2011). The signature pedagogy of social work? An investigation of the evidence. *Research on Social Work Practice, 21*(3), 363–372.

Humphrey, C. (2011). *Becoming a social worker: A guide for students*. London: SAGE.

Ibrahima, A. B., & Mattaini, M. A. (2018). Social work in Africa: Decolonizing methodologies and approaches. *International Social Work, 62*(2), 799–813.

Jaswal, S., & Pandya, S. (2015). Social work education in India: Discussions on indigenization. *The Indian Journal of Social Work, 76*(1), 139–158.

Jeyarani, S. J., , & Jebaseelan, A. U. S. (2017). Fieldwork practicum as perceived by social work students with special reference to Madurai. *Research on Humanities and Social Sciences, 7*(17), 1–5.

Johnson, E, Bailey, R, & Padmore, J. (2012). Issues and challenges of social work practicum in Trinidad and Tobago and India. *Caribbean Teaching Scholar, 2*(1), 19–29.

Jones, J. F. (1978). *Human well-being: Challenges for the 80's*. Bombay.

Kadushin, A. (2008). What's wrong, what's right with social work supervision. *The Clinical Supervisor, 10*(1), 3–19.

Kaseke, E. (1986). The role of fieldwork in social work training. In Social Development and Rural Fieldwork. Proceedings of a Workshop held in Harare (pp. 52–62), Harare: Journal of Social Development in Africa.

Lomax, R., Jones, K., Leigh, S., & Gay, C. (2010). *Surviving your social work placement*. New York: Palgrave Macmillan.

Mabvurira, V., (2018). Making sense of African thought in social work practice in Zimbabwe: Towards professional decolonization. *International Social Work, 63*, 1–12.

Makhubele, J. C. (2011). The effectiveness of indigenous knowledge in the prevention and treatment of infertility in a rural community of Limpopo Province: A social work perspective. *Journal of Community and Health Sciences, 6*(1), 9–20.

Mallick, A. (2007). Fieldwork training in social work curriculum. *The Indian Journal of Social Work, 68*(4), 573–80.

Mathews, I., Simpson, D., & Crawford, K. (2014). *Your social work practice placement from start to finish*. London: SAGE.

McNabb, D. (2017). Democratising and decolonising social work education: Opportunities for leadership. *Advances in Social Work and Social Welfare, 19*(1), 121–6.

Midgley, J. (1981). *Professional imperialism: Social work in the Third World*. London: Heinemann.

Midgley, J. (1992). The Challenges of International Social Work. In M.C. Hokenstad, S. Kinduka, & J. Midgley (Eds.), *Profiles in International social work* (pp. 13–28). Washington, DC: NASW Press.

Mupedziswa, R. (2001). The quest for relevance towards a conceptual model of development social work education and training in Africa. *International Social Work, 44*(3), 285–300.

Mupedziswa, R. (2005). Challenges and prospects of social work services in Africa. In J. C. Akeibunor & E. E. Anugwom (Eds.), *The social sciences and socio-economic transformation in Africa* (pp. 271–317). Nsukka: Great AP Express Publishing.

Mupedziswa, R., & Sinkamba, R. P. (2014). Social work education and training in southern and east Africa: Yesterday, today and tomorrow in 'Global social work Book: Crossing borders, blurring boundaries'. In C. Noble (Eds.), *Helle Strauss, Brian little child* (pp. 1–15). Sydney University Press.

Muzaale, P. (1987). Rural poverty, social development and their implications for fieldwork practice. *Journal of Social Development in Africa, 2*(1), 75–87.

Mwansa, L. K. (2010). Challenges facing social work in Africa. *International Social Work, 53*(1), 129–36.

Nagar, A. (2018). Making case work treatment Indian: An indigenous remedy for psycho social problems. *International Journal of Social Science and Economic Research, 3*(7), 1–8.

Nagpaul, H. (1972). The diffusion of America social work education to India: Problems and issues. *International Social Work, 15*(3), 13–17.

Nayak, L. M., & Panda, B. (2012). Yoga, meditation in social work: A journey from edges to the mainstream. *Marian Journal of Social Work, 4*, 45–58.

Nemati, A. (2013). The effect of pranayama on test anxiety and test performance. *International Journal of Yoga, 6*(1), 55–60.

Papouli, E. (2014). Field learning in social work education: Implications for educators and instructors. *Field Educator, 4*(2, Fall), 1–15.

Parker, J. (2007). Developing effective practice learning for tomorrow's social workers. *Social Work Education, 26*(8), 763–779.

Pickering, T. M. M., (2010). *Decolonization as a social change framework and its impact on the development of Indigenous-based curricula for Helping Professionals in mainstream Tertiary Education Organisations*, Doctoral Thesis submitted in University of Waikato, Waikato. Retrieved from https://researchcommons.waikato.ac.nz/handle/10289/4148 on 25 March 2020.

Ragab, I. A. (1982). *Authentization of social work in developing countries*. Tanta: Integrated Social Services Project.

Regehr, G., Bogo, M., Regehr, C., & Power, R. (2007). Can we build a better mousetrap? Improving the measures of practice performance in the field practicum. *Journal of Social Work Education, 43*(2), 327–44.

Roy, S., & Dash, B. M. (2019). Eight decades of field work training in India: Identifying the gaps and missing links. In B. M. Dash & S. Roy (Eds.), *Field work training in social work*. London: Routledge, Taylor and Francis.

Royse, D., Dhooper, S. Royse, D., Dhooper, S. S., & Rompf, E. L. (1999). *Field instruction: A guide for social work students* (3rd ed.). New York: Longman.

Sarhan, N. A. M. (2005). *The social work curriculum for the protection from pollution curriculum*. Cairo: Dar el-Fikr el-Arabi.

Schiff, M., & Katz, P. (2007). The impact of ethnicity and phase in training on Israeli Social Work Students' satisfaction with the field instruction. *Social Work Education, 26*(8), 794–809.

Sedlmeier, P., (2019). Indian psychology and the scientific method. Retrieved from https://ipi.org.in/texts/others/petersedlmeier-ip-sm.php on 30 March 2020.

Sedlmeier, P., & Srinivas, K. (15 March 2016). How do theories of cognition and consciousness in ancient Indian thought systems relate to current Western theorizing and research? *Frontiers in Psychology*. https://doi.org/10.3389/fpsyg.2016.00343 retrieved on 31 March 2020.

Sharma, V. K., Rajajeyakumar, M., Velkumary, S., Subramanian, S. K., Bhavanani, A. B., & Madanmohan, T. D. (2014). Effect of fast and slow pranayama practice on cognitive functions in healthy volunteers. *Journal of Clinical and Diagnostic Research, 8*(1), 10–13.

Shastri, V. V., Hankery, A., Sharma, B., & Patra, S. (2017). Impact of pranayama and vedic mathematics on math anxiety and cognitive skills, *Yoga Mimamsa, 49*, 53–62.

Shaw, T. V. (2011). Is social work a green profession? An examination of environmental beliefs. *Journal of Social Work, 13*(1), 3–29.

Shawky, A. (1972). Social work education in Africa. *International Social Work, 15*, 3–16.

Sinclair, R. & Albert, J. retrieved from https://ojs.uwindsor.ca/index.php/csw/article/download/5756/4698?inline=1 on 30 March 2020.

Sinha, D. (1993). Indigenisation of psychology in India and its relevance. In U. Kim & J. W. Berry (Eds.), *Indigenous psychologies* (pp. 30–43). London: Sage.

Sinha, J. B. P. (2002). Towards indigenization of psychology in India. In G. Misra & A. K. Mohanty (Eds.), *Perspectives on indigenous psychology* (pp. 440–457). New Delhi: Concept.

Subedar, I. S. (2001). *Field work training in Social Work*. Rawat Publications.

Sunirose I.P. (2000). Fieldwork in social work education: Challenges, issues and best practices, retrieved from file:///C:/Users/Win7/Downloads/147-Article%20Text-431-1-10-20180704%20(2).pdf on 28 March 2020.

Titmuss, R. M. (1974). *Social Policy, An Introduction*. London: George Allen & Unwin.

Trevithick, P. (2008). Revisiting the knowledge base of social work: A framework for practice. *British Journal of Social Work, 38*(6), 1212–1237.

Wilson, S. J. (1981). *Field instruction: Techniques for supervisors*. London: Collier MacMillan Publishers.

Weil, M. (2008). Introduction: Models of community practice in action. *Journal of Community Practice, 4*(1), 1–9.

Westerfelt, A., & Dietz, T. (2001). *Planning & conducting agency-based research: A workbook for social work students in field placements* (2nd ed.). Needham Heights, MA: Allyn and Bacon.

Wong, Y.-L. R. (2002). Reclaiming Chinese women's subjectivities: Indigenizing social work with women in China through postcolonial ethnography. *Women's Studies International Forum, 25*(1), 67–77.

8
A Critical Reading of Community Social Work Methods and Practices Employed within Urban Underserved Communities in Sri Lanka

H. Unnathi S. Samaraweera

Introduction

Community social work specifically focuses on communities who may need social, economic, political, cultural, and ecological support to enjoy their well-being and achieve social justice (Delgado 1999; Teater et al. 2012). Historically, community work was mainly based on social welfare-related community organisations and agencies, community action for community development, and advocacy of equal rights and social justice for politically disadvantaged communities (York 1984). On the one hand community social work investigates various communities or social groups without being limited to underserved, challenged, or other disenfranchised groups such as gated, LGBTQI+, fishing, caste-based, ethnicity-based, religion-based, and income-based groups. On the other hand, community social work engages deeply with a particular community, addressing needs arising from different layers from individuals to groups and larger institutional levels thereby providing a platform to engage with the micro, mezzo, and macro level needs of a particular community (Delgado 1999; Payne 1995; Teater et al. 2012).

One of the hardest tasks carried out by a social worker is engaging with communities who require social work support to achieve social justice (Delgado 1999; Teater et al. 2012). This can be identified as a form of transformation from institutional-based social work to community social work. Instead of undermining the role of a social worker stationed in an institution, this chapter attempts to highlight the difficulties and complexities involved within community social work in the field and to critically engage with community social work methods such as community mapping, SWOT analysis, risk analysis, and empowerment which are often exercised in the urban underserved communities in the Sri Lankan context. Since the author has engaged with different urban underserved communities in Colombo for nearly ten years as a social work academic, this chapter uses examples from those experiences as ground-level realities. Further, the fieldwork diaries maintained by the author while working as a community social worker in underserved communities in Colombo are also used appropriately. Available relevant literature is also used as secondary material to develop the analysis sections in the chapter.

In addition, the purpose behind selecting community mapping, SWOT analysis, risk analysis, and empowerment is the author's attempt to select the most suitable yet distinct and relevant four methods often practised in community social work. Generally, as the entry point to the communities and in order to recognise the nature of the particular community, community social workers often start their methodological interventions using community mapping as a tool. Borrowing from the industrial sciences, SWOT analysis in community social work provides an opportunity to recognise and deeply engage with the ground-level realities of the community. Moreover, community mapping and SWOT analysis not only provide a platform to understand the spectrum of behaviours in underserved communities, but also direct community social workers to identify community needs, the required positive changes, and necessary interventions to achieve social justice. While the above-mentioned two methods help provide a larger picture of the underserved communities, risk analysis and empowerment as community social work methods allow community social workers to engage with multiple levels of a community from the micro, mezzo, to the macro as both can be used at all individual, group, and community levels without restricting the community social worker's interventions to one level. Even though later these two methods may often be utilised at individual levels within institutionalised social work, this chapter attempts to emphasise their significance even within the community setting itself. Further, the lack of literature regarding these methods and their application in community social work (York 1984) led the author to specifically focus on these four methods in this chapter.

The chapter attempts to contextualise the nature and characteristics of urban underserved communities first and then focus on social work interventions at micro, mezzo, and macro levels specifically investigating the various roles played by community social workers as informants, coordinators, and empowering agents to develop communities with more empowered resilient citizens by applying the above-mentioned methods. It brings attention to the importance of adapting these methods particularly on the basis of geographical setting, environment, and context accordingly. Finally, the chapter seeks to bridge the gaps between these community social work methods and ground-level realities in order to raise practical concerns for future community social work practitioners in countries like Sri Lanka that are often shaped by specific sociocultural and socioeconomic patterns and behaviours.

'Slums and Shanties' to 'Low-Income Settlements' to 'Urban Underserved Communities': The Road to Better Terminology

Before moving to the main focus of the chapter, at this point it is important to provide a clear view regarding the usage of the terminology 'underserved community' from a social work perspective as the chapter specifically deals with urban underserved communities in Sri Lanka. In general, ghettos, underclass, slums, shanties, urban poor, low-income urban neighbourhoods are a few terms used in different contexts in different time periods to identify vulnerable, underprivileged, and oppressed communities all over the world (Eisenhauer 2001; Fry et al. 2002; Hussain et al. 1999; Kumar 1996; Rogers 1970; Wilson 1988). These were the groups of disenfranchised people who did not equally enjoy rights as citizens mainly on the basis of their gender, ethnic, religious, social, cultural, political, and economic identities (Eisenhauer 2001; Fry et al. 2002; Hussain et al. 1999; Kumar 1996; Rogers 1970; Wilson 1988).

In the Sri Lankan context, the local language usage of the term *mudukku* which can be translated as 'slums' was common to identify such underserved communities since the 1930s

(Sevanatha 2003). Due to the social exclusion they faced as slum dwellers, they themselves started using the term 'row houses' (*peli gewal* in Sinhalese) to identify their dwellings. Meantime the term 'shanties' – called *pelpath* in Sinhalese – also became a part of the linguistic identification of underserved communities (Sevanatha 2003). Given how social exclusion and marginalisation are intrinsically embedded in these terms, such common language use has been avoided mostly in academic contexts and policy documents to instead adopt more 'socially acceptable' terms such as 'low-income settlements'.

According to the Urban Development Authority (UDA) (year of publication is not mentioned) today more than 50 percent of the Colombo city population lives in underserved communities occupying nine percent of the total land extent of the city Colombo. The UDA (year of publication is not mentioned) statistics further highlight that a total number of 68,812 families are living in 1,499 underserved communities within the city of Colombo. These underserved settlements mostly illegally occupied state-owned lands, often did not have regular water and electricity supplies, and were built with non-durable materials (Silva & Athukorala 1991). Given the economic incapability and vulnerability of these illegal dwellers, they were mostly identified as deprived, disadvantaged, and underprivileged (Sueyoshi & Ohtsuka 1999). The earlier terms used to represent their dwellings such as ghetto, slum, and shanty were often mingled with a notion of social stigma. However, even the term 'low-income settlements' was subsequently critiqued as a negative term on account of its direct focus on poor economic status. In this backdrop, today the term 'underserved communities' is used to highlight the socioeconomic disadvantaged and unequal position as opposed to individual incapability.

Analysing these linguistic and discourse changes from a social work perspective, it is important to note that they highlight the significance of not ascribing incapability at an individual level. Rather than focusing on people who are in need as a 'problem', it therefore brings attention to the 'solution' and encourages us to consider people who are in need as solution-oriented human beings faced with socioeconomic disadvantages. This shift of the view point from a 'problem' to a 'solution' exemplifies the significant changes which have occurred in social work as a discipline, encouraging us to understand service users as social beings with capabilities and capacities. It is for this reason that this approach is important even in community social work practices in order to better understand members in a community having various capabilities, capacities, and strengths not only at an individual level but also at that of the community.

The Term 'Community' and Community Social Work Methods

Next it is equally important to discuss the complexity involved with the term 'community' as it includes various components with different nuanced meanings. As evident in the literature, 'community' may commonly be defined on the basis of its geographical settings or common characteristics among particular members. Therefore, the term 'community' can be defined in numerous ways such as a geographical and/or physical space; as a group who share common characteristics on the basis of culture, identity, values and norms, social status, and social networks; as a social system with various horizontal and vertical boundaries; and as a common identity and a common set of issues (Butcher 2007; Cohen 1985; Hardcastle et al. 2011; Willie et al. 2008). Explicating multidimensionality involved in the term 'community' Cohen (1985) brings an emotional aspect, personal identification, and symbolic construction to the term. Butcher (2007) outlines the spatial, interactional, and emotional components of community dimensions while Willie et al. (2008) describe vertical and horizontal hierarchical orders within communities further capturing the important dimensions of the word. While identifying the complexity involved with the label, the current chapter specifically engages with urban underserved communities without limiting its meaning to geographical space and symbolic construction but instead expanding the term 'community' to encompass interactional and emotional dimensions with common ties and shared sentiments.

The lacuna of academic literature focused specifically on community social work methods may lead to misapplication of methods, misinterpretation of mere welfare programmes as community social work interventions, and misidentification of anybody who merely works in a community as a social worker. In an attempt to bridge the methodological gap, this chapter next discusses community mapping, SWOT analysis, risk analysis, and empowerment as community social work methods and examines how these have been used in urban underserved communities in order to create positive change despite the challenges in practical community social work contexts. In addition, the lack of community social work-based academic literature specifically focused on the Sri Lankan context adds further significance to the chapter.

Community Mapping

Since there is a lack of literature on community mapping as a method in the community social work discipline it is challenging to trace its inception and establishment within social work. Community mapping has mainly been used for planning purposes in geography, cartography, and urban planning (Kurniawati et al. 2018). Despite its interdisciplinary usage community mapping in community social work has its unique characteristics. Further, it is evident in the literature that social networks and social support were the main focus of mainstream social work discipline during the 1970s and 1980s (Baker 1977; Collins & Pancoast 1976). Therefore, presumably with the focus on social networks and social support the community mapping method has been established in the practice of community social work.

However, as Corbett and Lydon (2014:113) explain,

> we each have our own stories and geographies, as well as different physical, mental, and social landscapes that we experience and inhabit every day. How we spatially and visually represent such stories and geographies is, in effect, cartography. When we do this with other people, we are 'community mapping'.

There is no one form of mapping in social work and this flexibility allows community social workers to adapt the tools according to the context. However, community social work employs community mapping as a method not only to outline the present nature of a particular community but also to sketch the issues and concerns, strengths and limitations, and available and necessary resources in order to bring a positive change in that particular community and hence achieve social justice.

According to Delgado (1999) there are six goals in any form of mapping: (1) To allow participation of community members in the process; (2) To recognise new ideas to bring changes in the community; (3) To empower the community; (4) To direct how to expand their local capital; (5) To allow their experience to transform into any other form of mapping in the future; (6) To allow their experience in engaging with mapping to transform into their life experiences in a necessary manner. In this light it proves that the method leads to knowledge production, reflective learning, and empowerment action among community members (Corbett & Lydon 2014).

Two techniques can be identified to develop the community map within underserved urban communities. After visiting the particular community for a reasonable time, (1) Community social workers who work in the particular community draw the map with their knowledge and receive feedback from selected members in the community or (2) Community social workers and community members draw the map together with the help and guidance of the community members. While one could argue this method is similar to Participatory Rural Appraisal (PRA), the main difference can be manifested vis-à-vis the aim of utilising community mapping as a method in community social work. This aim entails understanding the present nature of the community and identifying the key areas required to bring positive change as identified most importantly by the community members themselves. Further, through community mapping community social workers collaboratively work with the community members who are also identified as service users in order to bring positive change and social justice. This direct intervention in the community and involvement in the process of achieving positive change and social justice collaboratively are not the aims of the PRA method (Chambers 1994). Bringing positive change with the identification of the community map as outlined by community members themselves is the main objective of the method. In this manner, a piece of art or a set of visual images can be used to summarise the present nature, basic needs, issues, resources, and the necessary changes in a particular community as expressed primarily by the community members themselves.

The main challenge of employing this method in urban underserved communities is linked with the trust between community members and the community social worker. Most underserved communities in Colombo, Sri Lanka face a number of social issues such as poverty, substance abuse, alcohol addiction, school dropouts, unemployment, limited or no sanitary facilities, broken families, stigma, and social exclusion characterising their existence in an underserved community. Therefore, the preliminary days of entering and building a rapport with the underserved community consume more time than anybody expects. Most of the community members do not wish to share their stories with community social workers as there is often a power gap and unequal social relationship where community members are seen as 'insiders' and community social workers as 'outsiders'. Therefore, opening up about the reality of the community is closely associated with building trust with them.

The strengths of the method as it is used in urban underserved communities are: it leads us to recognise the present nature of a community including both its positive and negative aspects that directly identify the genuine needs of the community; its emphasis on social work studies which examines both positive and negative aspects while attempting to recognise required changes; it provides a summary of the present status of the community in an art form; both community social workers and community members have equal power relations as they develop the community map together; the flexibility of developing the map according to the choices of community members as there is no agreed structure of the map; and the information still remains anonymous.

The limitations as described earlier are: it may take considerable time to develop social trust between community social workers and community members in order to identify genuine needs; the negative and positive aspects of the particular community; the contradictory narratives may lead to confusion and since there are ongoing developments there could be daily changes in the map that may affect the long-term plans and goals of both the parties. Since social work students work in one particular community for maximum three months per semester, it takes nearly an entire semester to build the precise community map with the community members which reflects the time-consuming nature. However, that does not reduce the overall price paid for the developed community map in each underserved community as it can be treated as a starting point to engage with underserved communities to bring positive change and social justice.

SWOT Analysis

Earlier SWOT analysis method has mostly been used within industry-based research work for the strategic planning purpose subsequently expanding its horizons to various other disciplines without being limited to the industrial sciences (Helms & Nixon 2010). Therefore, today the method has extended its directions towards the development sciences, results-oriented strategic planning, and the social sciences including social work.

The starting point of the SWOT analysis would simply emerge from the community map as it deeply engages with identifying the strengths, weaknesses, opportunities, and threats involved with the particular community. The main difference between community mapping and SWOT analysis springs from the presentation of their results where community mapping is developed in an art form while SWOT analysis lists out each category with words. Further, SWOT analysis focuses only on four main areas while community mapping is flexible by including a wide spectrum of fields visible in the particular community. Using SWOT analysis community social workers categorise all positive and negative aspects related to the community. Significantly, following the rationale of service users not being 'problems' but being positive vibrant involved humans who may have challenging issues and circumstances, the method first attempts to recognise a positive aspect which is that of the strengths in the community. The strengths may be material capacities and resources, human capacities and resources, local capitals etc. Following the positive aspects then the method focuses on the negative aspects that are the weaknesses involved in the community. These may spring from the lack of materials and resources to human incapability. Next the technique pays attention to the opportunities involved in the community which provide a platform not only to recognise the positive aspects in the locale but also to render the notion that still there are certain possibilities and openings that are available for underserved communities. Finally, this method emphasises the threats involved in the community covering economic, social, and cultural dimensions (Table 8.1).

Table 8.1 Example of SWOT analysis method conducted in an underserved fishing community

Strengths	Weaknesses
• Multi-religious, multi-ethnic, and multi-cultural backgrounds • Bilingual speaking abilities • Close neighbourhood setting • Close to sea • Fishing market	• Early school dropouts • Poverty • Unemployment • Lack of skilled labour force • Early-age marriages
Opportunities	Threats
• Easy access to city centre • Out-sourced business opportunities • Close to government schools • Tourism • High land price	• Alcohol addiction • Drugs • Crimes • Lack of control over urban development plans • Social exclusion and stigma

Source: (Fieldwork diaries 2017).

The strengths of the method are: it focuses on both positive and negative elements inherent within a community; provides a platform for both parties to collaboratively work and delineate required changes; and allows for the development of a critical analysis of the present nature of the community. The limitations again include developing trust between both parties, certain threats requiring larger scale political and governmental interventions beyond the control of community social workers, the reluctant attitude of officials during the process of positive change etc. In academic scholarship various scholars have used SWOT analysis in a cross-disciplinary manner including in health care practices (Wazir et al. 2013), in social work interventions to improve interactions among parents and their children (Kiamanesh et al. 2018), and planning purposes to build sustainable settlements including housing, urban spaces, and economy (Azami et al. 2017). Since community social work interventions may take a different path from other disciplines, employing the SWOT analysis method in urban underserved communities often leads to developing broader but specific and deep understandings of communities allowing the identification of necessary interventions. However, community social workers should recognise that each underserved community has its own strengths, weaknesses, opportunities, and threats which are often context-, environment-, and time-dependent.

Risk Analysis

Similar to earlier methods discussed in this chapter, risk analysis too has been used in other disciplines including in statistics, the natural sciences, and social sciences (Aven 2018). Further, literature is available on risk analysis itself as a science (Aven 2018). Nevertheless, the specific risk analysis method discussed in this chapter is often used in social work for institutionalised service users, for instance, from elderly homes, children's homes, recovery and rehabilitation centres etc. It does not, however, mean this method cannot be employed for urban underserved communities. The central strength of this method is it can be used to analyse risk not only at an individual level but also paving the way to expand its horizons to group and community levels. In this light, the method allows growth from short-term positive changes to long-term and sustainable positive changes through the course of the method. The basic steps in the risk analysis method are: (1) Identifying the risk, (2) Analysing the risk, (3) Looking for minimisation of risk, (4) Implementation, (5) Reflection of changes. At the initial stage members in the community should be able to identify the risk involved in their lives. This risk may be at an individual level, community level, or at both levels with negative outcomes.

The following example is related to a common issue identified in underserved communities in urban Sri Lanka and this chapter specifically deals with only one service user the author has worked with. Sarath[1] is a male, daily labourer in a factory in Colombo and had identified himself as an alcohol addict by the time the author met him in the underserved community in which he lived. After some time was spent building trust between both parties, he requested working with a community social worker to minimise the impact of certain issues that prevailed in his life. The narrative explored many issues intertwined with his life such as his actions leading to domestic violence, his wife and children in the process of ignoring him, the possibility of this leading to unemployment and poverty etc. After a few discussions it was revealed that the main cause of a number of issues in his personal life was closely related to his alcohol addiction. Therefore, both parties agreed to conduct a risk analysis mainly on his dependence and find a way to minimise some risks involved in his life. His concern was that on the way back home from work there was a liquor store which did not prevent him from buying alcohol. He also added that there was a group of friends at work with whom he frequented the bar on a daily basis. So, he wanted to cut off ties with his friends and with the liquor store on the way back home. After looking at possible changes which could be added to his behaviour, he agreed to use a different route from work to home which was more distant therefore leading to time consumption. While the author was in the community, Sarath was able to use the lengthy route to avoid the bar and come home without using alcohol, despite it not being a sustainable change. While considering long-term plans to minimise alcohol addiction, the working semester came to an end and the author has stopped visiting the community (Figure 8.1).

Community Social Work in Sri Lanka

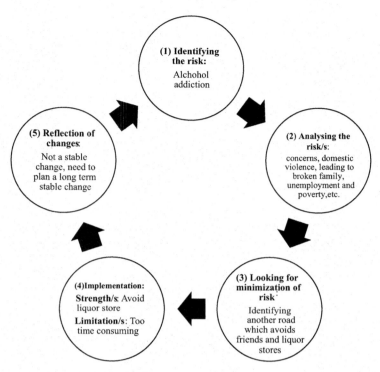

Figure 8.1 Example of risk analysis method. Source: (Fieldwork diaries 2018)

The concerns that arose from this example were numerous. What would have happened if he chose a path which contained more bars and more accompanying friends? What would have happened if he could not stop consuming alcohol after returning home in the new route and start drinking illegal alcohol available in the community which is cheaper with easy access? And what would have happened if he did not receive support from his family to minimise this addiction? The significant aspect of the risk analysis method is that it advises both parties to closely consider all the risks involved with the issue from individual to other wider levels and analyse all the risks before making a move. This approach of examining all the risks involved with the issue and changing actions is a necessary step which allows the community social worker to concentrate on the larger picture and its circumstances.

In addition, social work students often visiting one community for nearly three months without follow-up renders the notion that social workers are faced with a dilemma of not knowing what happened to the client afterwards. Unfortunately, as described earlier, the social worker was only able to be involved with the community member during the short first phase of the risk analysis method – which highlights the limitation of the methods in the practical context due to the limited time availability. It is therefore evident that there is a need for conducting a risk analysis method which not only targets short-term plans but also prepares a long-term plan developed through a process of identifying a number of short-term plans and interventions.

Empowerment

Today empowerment-oriented social work is not exclusive to community social work as it has gained significant currency in social work discipline at large. The act of oppressed individuals or groups attempting to achieve their rights can be simply defined as 'empowerment' (Lee 2001). Empowerment can be that of the individual or community. In underserved districts it is evident there are a number of segments such as children, women, men, elderly, disabled who can be identified as vulnerable groups looking for empowerment due to different social issues. According to Lee (2001) empowerment as a method focuses on three interrelated dimensions: (1) Building a positive, potential self, (2) The knowledge construction of real social and political environment and (3) Guiding and educating on resources, strategies, competence, capacities, personal achievements, and capabilities.

In addition, Lee (2001) points out eight principles in empowerment: (1) Challenging the distruption by both service users and social workers, (2) Maintaining a holistic perspective about the situation, (3) While encouraging self-empowerment for the service users, the social worker should advise on a service user's rights and responsibilities, (4) Collective common ground among service users and social workers, (5) Establishing a mutual and reciprocal relationship between the two parties, (6) Allowing service users to use their own language to explain the situation, (7) Maintaining the focus on service user as a victor/survivor not as a victim and (8) Continuing the focus towards positive change as empowerment.

It is important to note that community social work not only focuses on individual empowerment but also encourages community empowerment at large. Understanding the range of issues within underserved communities that request support for empowerment, the author has worked with various individuals in underserved communities including school students with education needs, school students with identity-related issues due to social stigma and social exclusion, youth facing unemployment, women facing domestic violence, men with alcohol addiction and substance abuse, elderly people without proper care and health facilities, people with disabilities without economic support, people with mental health-related issues etc. During the period of three months in each underserved community it was identified that these individuals were a part of larger and complex social settings where their disempowerment was often linked with certain other social identities and social standings. While community social workers successfully collaborated in some study workshops, job fair workshops, and self-employment opportunities to achieve empowerment for some individuals in the community, it is significant to note that there were a number of unsuccessful stories in underserved communities too.

However, without being limited to individual empowerment, during community social work practices, social workers utilised the method as a form of community empowerment. For instance, the unavailability of proper garbage collection was a major issue in one of the underserved communities where social work students worked. When one dug deep into the issue, it was revealed that social stigma and exclusion were also part of the larger issue of local authorities not coming to collect garbage in the community. The social work students identified the situation as a process which required community empowerment interventions. With the support of the community, the social work student group developed a short-term plan leading to long-term empowerment. During the process both parties collaboratively worked, starting with raising awareness on waste management in the community through leaflets and street theatre. Then they developed communication with community leaders to take leadership in developing written requests within the community neighbourhood and coordinating and submitting these requests to the relevant officials in the municipal council which was the responsible authority for garbage collection. At the end of the three-month period the underserved community was able to exercise their right to access waste management facilities provided by the local authority such as periodic collection of garbage. This remarkable outcome was the lesson learnt by community members: to act as responsible citizens supporting systematic garbage collection. The sustainability of the programme was also evident (Fieldwork diaries 2016).

However, during another attempt towards community empowerment in a different resettled underserved community, the uncooperative official responses and humiliation of community social work students led to a failure of the process. The project attempted to provide a sticker approved by the relevant authorities for the vehicles owned by the members in the particular community as it was evident through community mapping and SWOT analysis that the community faced a number of difficulties due to limited parking space and non-residents using the same parking space in the community (Fieldwork diaries 2018).

Future Scope for Community Social Work Students

A globally accepted definition of social work denotes

> the social work profession promotes social change, problem solving in human relationships, and the empowerment and liberation of people to enhance well-being. Utilizing theories of human behaviour and social systems, social work intervenes at the points where people interact with their environments. Principles of human rights and social justice are fundamental to social work.
>
> *(Hare 2004:409)*

In line with this definition, community social work methods discussed in this chapter primarily attempt to achieve positive social change and well-being at different levels while working with various oppressed communities.

At this point it is important to note that though the history of social work's establishment goes back to 1952 professional social work (including community social work) is relatively new and yet to be professionally established in the Sri Lankan context (Dissanayake 2003; NISD year is not mentioned; Zaviršek & Herath 2010). Even though community-based social support systems such as *shramadana* (donating labour), *dansel* (distributing cooked meals and food to anybody who are willing to come and eat) during the Poya Days, almsgiving not only for Buddhist monks but also for people who are in need and blood donation programmes are embedded within sociocultural practices, professional community social work is somewhat new to the Sri Lankan context which reduces it to charity and philanthropy. Therefore, community social workers may face a number of issues and challenges while working in the underserved communities in Colombo city.

When working with underserved communities one of the major concerns was to develop trust among community members to work with community social workers. Often these people were socially excluded and stigmatised under the title of underserved communities therefore not allowing them to trust outsiders. Underserved communities cannot be viewed as a monolith as each underserved community has its own characteristics. Hence the formulation of a common singular mechanism to develop rapport, social trust, and necessary interventions needs to be preempted. In this light, it can be argued that community social workers have to act upon context-specific practical concerns which may not necessarily be covered in social work classrooms.

Furthermore, language plays a significant role in social work communication (Dominelli 2002). It is advantageous for community social workers to be at least bilingual especially if they are working with Sri Lankan urban underserved communities which are often multi-lingual, multi-ethnic, and multi-religious in nature. The style of speech, usage of colloquial words and local vernacular or dialect during the communication often lead to building social trust with community members. Community social workers should recognise how community members develop collectivity which is actually a part of larger sociocultural constructions and socialisation processes (Teater et al. 2012). Community social workers' understanding of sociocultural constructions behind their collective nature can certainly help develop social trust and in turn bring social justice to them.

Specifically, in relation to underserved communities in urban Sri Lanka, the notion of equal power relations appears to be a myth, as half of the community members as service users take longer to accept it and act accordingly. The other half often attempts to remain powerless – depending on and expecting community social workers to act as advocates and guardians. In fact, issues pertaining to power imbalances are often evident in various community settings (Foster 2017). Certain unsupportive officials in a community setting can exacerbate the circumstances. When community social work students first enter an underserved community, they realise how hard it is to build social trust and perhaps get discouraged with negative responses from the community members. Then during the second phase of working with relevant officials their lack of support could potentially lead the students to remain discouraged, hopeless, helpless, and unenthusiastic. Therefore, it is noteworthy that working with underserved communities in which the community members face challenging and difficult circumstances, community social work students may not always be successful as they expect.

To overcome the above-mentioned barriers community social work students can employ a 'Strengths Perspective' which often prioritises and highlights strengths and resources available at individual, group, and community levels to achieve positive changes and social justice (Teater et al. 2012). Every individual, group, and community has their own strengths which may not have been identified or may have been blocked or not used. These unidentified strengths are acknowledged through the strength's perspective (Sallebey 2009). Community social workers can acknowledge and assess their strengths facilitating underserved communities to bring the solicited change.

The next concern is linked with first and second discouragement. The methods used in community social work such as SWOT analysis, risk analysis, and empowerment are often utilised within institutional spheres where the outcome may be more progressive and positive. The attempt to apply the same methods in the field with underserved communities is a challenge in itself. It is therefore essential to note that challenges are distinct and mostly context-dependent requiring community social workers to adjust accordingly.

In addition, it is ambiguous whose goal community social work needs to achieve in the underserved community: whether it is social workers' goal or community members' goal (York 1984). Therefore, during the community social work process it is important for community social workers to emphasise how both parties need to collaboratively work towards a common goal which is derived and owned by service users. It is equally important for community social workers to remind themselves that their role is only intervening in the process where the goal is owned by (a) service user/s in the community. Overwhelmed, overenthusiastic, and unexperienced community social workers may treat the process as their own and experience false outcomes.

Further, when applying earlier described community social work methods they tap in to all individual, group, and community levels as opposed to social work with institutionalised individuals. After identifying areas which require positive changes through community mapping and SWOT analysis, when developing collaborative programmes, a number of concerns need to be addressed such as short-term positive changes leading to long-term positive changes, sustainability of the positive change/s, minimising unplanned negative risks and changes, delivering services to all individual, group, and community level requirements etc.

Sustainability is yet another major concern faced by community social workers as they work with social beings in a community. In one of the communities, the identified community empowerment project established a library for school students in the community which was successfully carried out by social work students. In order to maintain sustainability of the functioning of the library, during the process both parties collaboratively identified and established a children's society in the community. Subsequently, however, when another batch of community social work students visited the same community after a year, they found that the children's society had stopped functioning properly. Even the door keys of the community hall which had been renovated as the library were misplaced and functioning of the library had come to an end (Fieldwork diaries 2017). The author gives this example to illustrate not only the significance of sustainability of the positive changes occurred in the community but also to point out the need for a critical approach to community social work methods capturing ground-level realities in underserved communities. Thus, community social workers may need to play multiple roles in underserved communities such as that of an enabler, broker, advocate, guardian, activist, mediator, informant, instructor, coordinator, facilitator, organiser, manager, evaluator, and supervisor etc. (Grosser 1965; Hardcastle et al. 2011; Hardina 2013).

Conclusion

Community social work constitutes its own methodological interventions and practices to bring positive changes in different communities. However, the lack of specific literature on community social work methods and the application of larger social work methods within community settings raise valid concerns in academic scholarship. This chapter specifically discussed four different methods often taught in the community social work discipline as well as practised within urban underserved communities in Colombo, Sri Lanka. While critically engaging with methods this chapter highlighted the need to revisit and rethink community social work methods within the particular context. Social work academics may teach highly Western-oriented theoretical concepts and methods in social work classrooms yet overlook how such scholarship may require adaptation with regard to community social work in terms of the context, environment, time, and other sociocultural and socioeconomic constituents. Community social workers may perhaps tend to forget that community social work fundamentally deals with members in a particular community who are also social beings.

Considering community social work methods as tools with both pros and cons when used to engage with a particular community could lead to adopting those methods in a more accurate and pragmatic manner. Each community social work approach discussed in this chapter has its own strengths and limitations which are also largely influenced by a community social worker's professional skills, attitudes, social behaviours, and capabilities. Hence it is vital to identify community social work experience as a unique professional socialisation process as outlined by Cohen and Shenaar-Golan (2018).

Note

1 In order to maintain ethical concerns, pseudonyms are used in the entire chapter.

References

Aven, T. (2018). An emerging new risk analysis science: Foundations and implications. *Risk Analysis, 38*(5), 876–888. doi:10.1111/risa.12899 (Last accessed 5 February 2020).

Azami, M., Azami, M., Tavallaei, R., Tavallaei, R., Mohammadi, A., & Mohammadi, A. 2017. The challenge of sustainability in informal settlements of Iran (case study: Sanandaj city). *Environment, Development and Sustainability, 19*(4), 1523–1537. doi:10.1007/s10668-016-9817-4 (Last accessed 7 March 2020).

Baker, F. (1977). The interface between professional and natural support systems. *Clinical Social Work Journal*, *5*(2), 139–148. doi:10.1007/BF02144239 (Last accessed 2 March 2020).
Butcher, H. (2007). *Critical community practice*. Bristol: Policy Press.
Chambers, R. (1994). The origins and practice of participatory rural appraisal. *World Development*, *22*(7), 953–969. doi:10.1016/0305-750X(94)90141-4 (Last accessed 12 February 2020).
Cohen, A., & Shenaar-Golan, V. (2018). What are social work students' perceptions of the community practice method? *Journal of Community Practice*, *26*(1), 23–40. doi:10.1080/10705422.2017.1413022 (Last accessed 2 March 2020).
Cohen, A. P. (1985). *The symbolic construction of community*. London: Ellis Horwood Ltd. and Tavistock Publications Ltd. doi:10.4324/9780203131688 (Last accessed 2 March 2020).
Collins, A. H., & Pancoast, D. L. (1976). *Natural helping networks: A strategy for prevention*. Washington, DC: National Association of Social Workers.
Corbett, J., & Lydon, M. (2014). Community-based mapping. In C. Etmanski, B. L. Hall, T. Dawson (Eds.), *Learning and teaching community-based research: Linking pedagogy to practice*. Toronto: University of Toronto Press (pp. 113–134).
Delgado, M. (1999). *Community social work practice in an urban context: The potential of a capacity-enhancement perspective*. Oxford: Oxford University Press.
Dissanayake, D. (2003). The Sri Lanka school of social work: My life and times. In A. Ranaweera (Ed.), *Mathaka Satahan, Ninaiveduhal, memories of the past: 1952–2002*. (pp. 57–111). Colombo: National Institute of Social Development.
Dominelli, L. (2002). *Anti-oppressive social work theory and practice*. New York: Palgrave Macmillan.
Eisenhauer, E. (2001). In poor health: Supermarket redlining and urban nutrition. *GeoJournal*, *53*(2), 125–133. doi:10.1023/A:1015772503007 (Last accessed 1 March 2020).
Foster, J. W. (2017). *Building effective social work teams*. New York: Routledge.
Fry, S., Cousins, B., & Olivola, K. (2002). *Health of children living in urban slums in Asia and the near east: Review of existing literature and data*. Washington, DC: Environmental Health Project, US Agency for International Development.
Grosser, C. F. (1965). Community development programs serving the urban poor. *Social Work*, *10*(3), 15–21. doi:10.1093/sw/10.3.15 (Last accessed 2 March 2020).
Hardcastle, D. A., Powers, P. R., & Wenocur, S. (2011). *Community practice: Theories and skills for social workers* (3rd ed.). Oxford: Oxford University Press.
Hardina, D. (2013). *Interpersonal social work skills for community practice*. New York: Springer Publishing Company.
Hare, I. (2004). Defining social work for the 21st century: The international federation of social workers' revised definition of social work. *International Social Work*, *47*(3), 407–424. doi:10.1177/0020872804043973 (Last accessed 1 March 2020).
Helms, M. M., & Nixon, J. (2010). Exploring SWOT analysis: Where are we now?: A review of academic research from the last decade. *Journal of Strategy and Management*, *3*(3), 215. doi:10.1108/17554251011064837 (Last accessed 4 March 2020).
Hussain, A., Ali, S. K., & Kvale, G. (1999). Determinants of mortality among children in the urban slums of Dhaka city, Bangladesh. *Tropical Medicine & International Health*, *4*(11), 758–764.
Kiamanesh, P., Olaßen, K. S., & Drozd, F. (2018). Understanding factors that promote and limit the use of video guidance in child protection services: A SWOT analysis. *Child & Family Social Work*, *23*(4), 582–589. doi:10.1111/cfs.12447 (Last accessed 8 March 2020).
Kumar, S. (1996). Subsistence and petty capitalist landlords: A theoretical framework for the analysis of landlordism in third world urban low income settlements. *International Journal of Urban and Regional Research*, *20*(2), 317–329. doi:10.1111/j.1468-2427.1996.tb00318.x (Last accessed 11 February 2020).
Kurniawati, U. F., Idajati, H., Susetyo, C., Firmansyah, F., & Pratomoatmodjo, N. A. (2018). Community mapping condition of settlements in kelurahan keputih. *IOP Conference Series: Earth and Environmental Science*, *202*, 12072. doi:10.1088/1755-1315/202/1/012072 (Last accessed 1 March 2020).
Lee, J. A. (2001). *The empowerment approach to social work practice: Building the beloved community* (2nd ed.). New York: Columbia University Press.
NISD Official Webpage (n.d.). http://www.nisd.lk/web/ (Last accessed 25 October 2018).
Payne, M., (1995). *Social work and community care*. London: Macmillan International Higher Education.
Rogers, T. W. (1970). Ulf Hannerz, Soulside: Inquiries into ghetto culture and community. *The Journal of Negro History*, *55*(3), 239–240. Doi:10.2307/2716426 (Last accessed 8 February 2020).
Saleebey, D. (2009). *The strengths perspective in social work practice* (5th ed.). Boston, MA: Pearson Education.

Sevanatha. (2003). *The case of Colombo*. Sri Lanka: Urban Resource Centre, Rajagiriya.
Silva, K. T., & Athukorala, K. (1991). *The Watta Dwellers: A sociological study of selected low-income communities in Sri Lanka*. Lanham, MD: University Press of America.
Sueyoshi, S., & Ohtsuka, R. (1999). Growth and residential conditions of a slum community in Colombo, Sri Lanka. *Journal of Human Ergology, 28*(1–2), 55.
Teater, B., Baldwin, M., Dr, & British Association of Social Workers. (2012). *Social work in the community: Making a difference*. Chicago, IL: Policy Press.
Urban Development Authority. (n.d.). https://www.uda.gov.lk/urban-regeneration-programme.html (Last accessed 5 July 2020).
Wazir, M. S., Shaikh, B. T., & Ahmed, A. (2013). National program for family planning and primary health care pakistan: A SWOT analysis. *Reproductive Health, 10*(1), 60. doi:10.1186/1742-4755-10-60 (Last accessed 5 March 2020).
Willie, C.V., Ridini, S. P., & Willard, D. A., (2008). Theoretical and conceptual issues in effective community action. In C.V. Willie, S.P. Ridini, & D.A. Willard (Eds.), *Grassroots social action: Lessons in power movement* (pp. 3–20). New York: Rowman & Littlefield.
Wilson, W. J. (1988). The ghetto underclass and the social transformation of the inner city. *The Black Scholar: Theory Or Fact? The Black Underclass, 19*(3), 10–17. doi:10.1080/00064246.1988.11412818 (Last accessed 15 February 2020).
York, A. S. (1984). Towards a conceptual model of community social work. *The British Journal of Social Work, 14*(3), 241–255. doi:10.1093/oxfordjournals.bjsw.a054957 (Last accessed 5 March 2020).
Zaviršek, D., & Herath, S.M.K. (2010). 'I Want to Have My Future, I Have a Dialogue': Social work in Sri Lanka between neo-capitalism and human rights. *Social Work Education, 29*(8), 831–842. doi:10.1080/02615479.2010.516987 (Last accessed 25 October 2018).

9
Social Work Education and Practice in Pakistan
Mapping the Terrain and Missing Links

Sakina Riaz

An Introduction to Social Work and Social Welfare in Pakistan

Pakistan is the second largest Islamic state in the world. The beginning of a modern concept of social work in Pakistan can be traced back to its colonial heritage, the pre-partition period through many forms of voluntary work by religious and cultural institutions. Social work was hosted in Pakistan as a response to a challenging situation after the emergence of freedom in 1947.

Pakistan, as a Muslim state, has most people helping others based on spirituality and for the sake of humanity. As Pakistan hosts the sixth largest population and second largest Muslim entity within the world, the country has a rich history and has a geographical location of international interest. Pakistan, along with other developing countries, depends on an agrarian economy. As a result of low productivity and an alarming population growth (Report, 2005) and being a country in which one-third of people live below the poverty level, it requires an organised social welfare system to assess the fight against poverty. It is ranked 152 out of 189 countries (UNDP, 2020).

Around the world, social work is currently emerging as a demanding profession that requires considerable knowledge and expertise in human relations. The unique characteristic of social work is that it is a service-oriented occupation. Doing service for someone once in a lifetime in a certain way is one thing that can be done for the sake of kindness but the assistance of others as an occupation requires a specific set of personal attitudes and attributes. It is studied as 'the applied science of helping people achieve an effective level of psychosocial functioning and effecting societal changes to enhance the well-being of all people' (Barker, 2003).Social work is value-laden because it is directed towards the upliftment of human being in addition to the more technical accomplishment of skilled practice' (Hugman, 1998).

Historically, since its inception, social work has always been the consequence of humanitarian actions by governments and non-governmental organisations (NGOs) in many countries. In this context, the United Nations has played a crucial role at an international level in promoting the advancement of education and professional development in the area of social work worldwide. International collaboration for the advancement of social work is not only critical but also necessary in this new period of globalisation. It must be remembered that scholars, students, and target audiences would practice their indigenous social work based on their theoretical knowledge, particular socio-economic and cultural features of the respective communities. It is not just a career that allows people to solve challenges, instead, more accurately, it is an approach that ensues in wider communities to create an enabling environment and play a positive role in preventing the society from malfeasance and provide awareness, guidance, and motivation towards better and brighter future for the entire communities so that people can function effectively. When it comes to social work in Pakistan, the field encounters numerous social and structural problems. The legacy of western-based theories and concepts continues to affect education and practice. The profession is under-resourced and consequently holds only limited influence on social policies.

The education system in Pakistan has been identified as a negative factor as marginalised groups have been eliminated and it contains low significance for native knowledge. Social work education (SWE) has been identified as an emerging profession as it lacks a connection between classroom learning and field activities. The current scenario of SWE in Pakistan is that it faces a few problems that should be addressed quickly for the smooth flow of this system. For instance, there is a lack of public and government identification of SWE when recognising it as a profession. Also, there are limited resources in properly conducting the SWE in the country; a lack of local literature is another problem that is present in the current situation (Shah, 2018). Besides this, there were 22.8 million children in 2016 that were not attending school (aged 5–16 years) and Pakistan has been termed the second worst country and there is no proper presence of social work education and its professional association. Similarly, there are no proper principles and strategies that can help people to engage in educational activities (Zaidi, 2021).

Also, in 2017 it was shown that degree-seeking students grew by 70 percent from the previous decade but were from neighbouring countries. People in Pakistan go abroad for completion of their degrees as the country lacks educational and social work activities for attracting people (Hunter, 2020). Similarly, since its creation, Pakistan has faced social work and education problems. For instance, the presence of strong educational strucutre and a high literacy rate are both lacking in Pakistan as people are moving abroad to study as well as building their lives in those countries. There are no proper educational facilities in the country (Rehman & Farooq, 2020) and under these circumstances, social work is also lacking due to a lack of sociopolitical and financial resources that could provide SWE.

Social Work in Pakistan: From Charity to Social Development

Pakistan was established in 1947 due to the division of the Indian subcontinent into two independent states, those of India and Pakistan. Scholars recognise that social security and social policy have remained a legacy of colonial days in many developed countries (Chitereka, 2009). Such social policy and welfare services reflected the rulers' concern with public order and a very narrow interpretation of social welfare (Boyden, 2015). The profession's growth has been portrayed as 'academic colonisation', mirroring political and scientific colonisation (Clews, 1999; Ragab, 1990). The separation of the subcontinent led to one of the most significant trans-border migrations in the history of the world. The newly created state was expected to host millions of refugees, resulting in organised social protection activities involving both voluntary and state actors (Ghafur & Mollah, 1968).

Globally, social work grew up within a social service infrastructure (Gray, 2002), whereas in Pakistan the professional journey of social work was attached to the rehabilitation of the people of a newly established country. However, the roots of professional social work reach back to the early 1950s when as per the government request, the first UN group of social welfare consultants came, and a temporary agency called 'The Social Welfare Project' was founded in 1952. The project served as an operation base for imparting elementary training in the field of social work. Besides instruction, the consultants advised the government to take on the responsibility of encouraging the growth of voluntary social welfare organisations and to initiate community development programmes, both in urban and rural areas (Akber, 1965). Yet, the social work profession in Pakistan struggled with a continuous conflict with the ideological adjustment between different ideas of human well-being – stretching from traditional concepts of social well-being, Islamic values, indigenous customs, and emerging concepts such as social development. For instance, the archives of the National Workshop on 'Meaning of Social Welfare in Pakistan (as a developing country)', held in 1976, stated that:

> *Pakistan's ideology is based on Islam which believes in social interdependence and enjoins upon all to help the distressed. It stands for equality, personal liberty, freedom of thought and belief, and rights and responsibilities of every individual ... Social welfare is inherent in our religion, and when viewed closely, it is also found to be basic to the theory and practice of scientific social work.*
> (National Council of Social Welfare, 1976)

Amazingly, about the same time, in the 'developing world' the welfare paradigm shifted into the emergent concept of 'social development', which became a political mantra throughout the developing world (Healy & Thomas, 2020; Jabeen, 2013; Midgley, 1999). This divergence of thought at the policy formation level spawned a gap between social work with and without a profession in the country. Consequently, both social work education and social welfare policy had to deal with problems related to the identity of the profession (like Islamic, traditional social welfare, and social development ideologies), purpose (such as welfare services for the most vulnerable, marginalised, and excluded or socioeconomic development of the masses) and direction (such as curative, preemptive, or progressive social welfare), which remains to date (Jabeen, 2013).

The Ministry of Social Welfare was established late in the 1980s. It is evident from government allocations that social welfare has always been given the lowest level of priority in government-organised social sector programmes during the last 40 years. Government budgets have seen considerable cuts, cutbacks, and reductions in public services.

The low budget given is proof of the low importance and recognition of social welfare at the policy and planning level. As a result, due to the weak human and financial capacity of the Ministry of Social Welfare, social welfare provisions have been limited. They often respond only to the most serious and public situations, such as the missing, the homeless, or street children, and this too is restricted to urban communities (Boyden, 2015; Jabeen, 2013). In turn, this results in a lack of due recognition of the Ministry of Social Welfare, its progress, contiguous momentum, and buoyancy, which have strong repercussions on both an educational and a professional level.

As Neville (2002) described, decision-making rules and structures regulating the wider political arena can affect sector-specific policymaking, as is the case of social welfare in Pakistan, as both the federal and provincial governments tend to leave social welfare to the other party. Similarly, Jabeen (2013) found that the Federal Ministry of Social Welfare concluded that accountability and funding for the social sector remain predominantly with provincial governments in Pakistan's government structure; thus, they should play a proactive role in resolving these problems. In contrast, the provincial governments looked towards the Federal Ministry of Social Welfare for any initiative (Jabeen, 2013; Jillani & Jillani, 2000), which has neither the capacity nor the resources to act appropriately.

Birth of Social Work Education in Pakistan: A Glimmer of Hope

Historically, social work education in Pakistan was initiated by UN technical assistance and the Government of Pakistan in Karachi in 1952 through a short-term in-service training course. Later, in 1954, formal social education began with a two-year diploma programme, introduced in the Punjab University, Lahore, which was established and headed for many years by Arthur Livingstone, the UN special representative of Social Welfare (Elliott & Segal, 2008). From 1957 the same university started a two-year course leading to an MA in Social Work. Soon after, schools of social work were established in different parts of the country. Likewise, the University of Karachi in 1961, followed by the University of Sindh in 1967, started courses on social work (Khalid, 2008). More importantly, international factors have shaped the development of social work as a profession and a service system. So, the syllabi and teachers had a western orientation with a worldview that was shaped and fashioned by a western perspective. Now, social work in Pakistan is not the same as in western countries. Indeed, the development of the profession of social work is always grounded in a society which, with its specific cultural and social context, can be different from one place to another.

For the last seven decades in Pakistan, social work education has been offered at graduate and postgraduate levels in different colleges and universities. The social work discipline has been proposed in 20 public sector universities in Pakistan and has also been extended as an elective course at graduate level in different colleges. These universities impart social work as a bachelor's degree (BS), Master's Degree in social work (MA), Master's in Philosophy (MPhil) and Doctor of Philosophy (Ph.D.). too. No doubt in Pakistan, the schools of social work have tendered quality education by using mixed methods of teaching i.e., case studies, face-to-face interactive classroom lectures, group forums, panel discussions, extensive research work, and field observatory visits for onsite learning and supportive group sessions specifically constructed to build interrelational skills and reflectivity (Moss et al., 2007) and this produces professional social workers, who serve the oppressed community with knowledge, skills, zeal, and enthusiasm. But there is not a single private university available to present social work as a discipline.

Social Work Practice and Voluntary Social Work: Nexus between Public and Private Sector

Social work as a practice-based profession (IFSW, 2014) entails a unique blend of theoretical and practical learning. Yet, social work as an internationally recognised professional discipline has its methods and theories as an academic discourse oriented towards the welfare of the clients. Even now in Pakistan, the professional recognition of this profession is in a transition stage. It is a more effective job but remains less visible, less recognised, and less compensated. Nevertheless, the government sector has played a significant role in offering jobs and acknowledging the services of professional social workers.

Pakistan, having a population of 220,892,340 according to UN data and ranking number five in the list of world populations, is a country where inequalities in the provision of welfare resources have not been ignored ironed out (Worldometer, 2020). The social work client tends to be located at the bottom end of the prevalent structure of inequalities and oppression. In every underdeveloped country like Pakistan, public and private sectors are the two main sectors supposed to cater to the needs of individuals as well as society. The public sector is ineffective, and the private sector is a monopolist. Under this scenario, the third sector – the NGOs – have entered to serve the people. As per Malena (1995), the 'NGO sector has become increasingly professionalized over the last two decades, principles of altruism and voluntarism remain key defining characteristics'.

No doubt, the NGO sector has to fulfil the gaps by providing the desired services where the state has abandoned its duty. But there is a vast gap between the work approach of the government sector and the NGO sector. The latter currently practises in a context of growing competition between different providers associated with the trend of commercialisation. In this sector, there is a fast and dynamic competition between for-profit enterprises and not-for-profit providers. But the private sector does not follow any recruitment strategy for the appointment of any social programme. Consequently, many professional social workers employed in the non-governmental sector have faced various multidimensional problems.

Pakistan has a multitude of visionary people who have always done great work by providing selfless services by catering for and serving humanity in such a way that they have become a beacon of hope to those in need. For example, Abdul of Edhi Foundation, Dr. Ruth Pfau of the Marie Adelaide Leprosy Centre, Dr. Amjad Saqib of Akhuwat, Ansar Burney of Ansar Burney Trust, Imran Khan of Shaukat Khanum Hospital, Shehzad Roy of Zindagi Trust, Abrar ul Haq of the Sahara for Life Trust, Dr. Abdul Bari Khan of the Indus Hospital, Dr. Adeeb Rizvi of SIUT, Muhammad Ramzan Chhipa of Chhipa Welfare Organisation, Mushtaq Chhapra of The Citizens Foundation, Dr. Akhter Hameed Khan of Orangi Pilot Project (OPP), All Pakistan Women's Association (APWA), Young Men's Christian Association (YMCA), and the Pakistan Red Crescent Society. These are a few examples of the voluntary social workers in Pakistan who have plunged wholeheartedly into welfare work to uplift the vulnerable person in the country. But it is important to mention here that all the above-mentioned personalities do not have any professional degree in the social work profession, nor do they appoint professional social workers in their organisations except the Sindh Institute of Urology (SIUT), where social workers are commendably working for the welfare of deserving patients.

Pakistan's current welfare policies are insufficient to address the needs of the poor. Despite welfare legislation and social policies, poverty levels continue to rise. Is the increase in poverty just a result of population growth in Pakistan? The notion of well-being in Pakistan needs to be revisited to improve the quality of life for poor citizens. A few queries have arisen regarding the implementation of the above-noted programmes; for instance, does the extent of these programmes not accurately address the needs of the targeted beneficiaries, or is there an absence of any quantitative measurement of the impact of these government schemes to scrutinise the effects on poverty alleviation? Under such circumstances, the greatest responsibility lies with the management of the social welfare system. A tailor-made, purposefully designed structural set-up of professionals who can address the needs of the destitute in the country is the need of the hour. In Pakistan, there is rarely any scholarly work done on the needs and importance of social work. In this study, an effort has been made to identify the missing link between theory and practice, as neither can be separated from the wider context within the professional periphery of this discipline. The main purpose of this study is to discuss the challenges associated with this discipline in the professional development in Pakistan.

Moreover, there are various challenges faced in the proper use and implementation of social work as this process is a debatable issue (Rehman & Farooq, 2020). Likewise, there are issues regarding career guidance as the educational and social challenges that are present include high unemployment and lack of resources. Also, the country faces challenges that include cultural, social, and political questions that hinder the process of basic education – of which people are unaware (Zahid, Hooley, & Neary, 2020). Social work has not yet achieved general recognition as a distinctive professional subject. Although social work training was launched by the government itself in the early days and the need for such training is recognised by the Public Services Commission as still this discipline is not listed in the category of Central Superior Services (CSS),[1] as an optimal subject which restricted the professional growth of the holds social work as discipline, and also created a feeling of hopelessness for many social workers to demonstrate their 'technical competence' is. The professional de-recognition as a subject is primarily accountable for the non-acceptance of social work as profession by the general public especially from those prospective students who are planning to select the discipline for their graduation. Perhaps, it is just because of this weakness that trained social workers still have not been able to be acknowledged and make a place for themselves, even after nearly 70 years of university education. A well-organised professional body to safeguard the professional interest is not operational. Besides, the presence of the COVID-19 pandemic has created an enhanced number of challenges for social workers, policymakers, and social users as well. The major challenge is ethical, raising questions like What is society doing in these tough times? and, Is the state of the economy more important than the population's health? The country is going through difficulties regarding the provision of proper SWE as the presence of a pandemic has hindered the process of providing basic needs and education for the people (Banks et al., 2020)

Methods

This section aims to concisely explain the sequence of steps of how this study was conducted. In this chapter, the study used a critical content analysis with a mixed-methods approach. The questions for which qualitative comments were taken, were scrutinised, categorised, and represented in tables. Empirical evidence is also reviewed in terms of the development and indigenisation of social work in the country. From a review of the literature and experience of the authors, this chapter explores emerging issues where the practice of social work should be a promising alternative to sustainable social development in Pakistan. Drawing on interviews mixed with personal experience and in some cases personal communication with appropriate personnel form the basis of the writing. The author's involvement as a social work pedagogue, working in Pakistan for the last 23 years, was also made use of where deemed appropriate. Hence, to review the professional status of social workers and social work education and practice as a profession in Pakistan, I asked a few questions from the stakeholders of social work in Pakistan at different forums like conferences, seminars, and other interactive meetings, where I got a chance to ask the following questions: 1) What tasks need to be accomplished for improving the existing human conditions and meeting the welfare needs in Pakistan? 2) What kinds of personnel are required to accomplish these tasks in NGOs and public sectors? 3) How are social work education and training programmes offered and perceived in our society? 4) How can we bridge the gap between existing social problems and the welfare service delivery system in Pakistan? 5) How is the status of the social worker professionally recognised in Pakistan, and what needs to be done?

This study was designed based on the responses to the above questions and in discussing the pitfalls of the past that reflect the current and future scope of the social work profession in Pakistan's pedagogical context. However, with the help of the available literature (books, journals, conference papers, etc.) the methodology was designed to carry out the body of this study and derive the stipulated outcome of the study.

For a comprehensive analysis to provide an in-depth assessment of existing situations, I did my best effort to collect the data across Pakistan. I used four key sources (stakeholders' input) for data collection as outlined below:

1. The first source consists of faculty members who have also served as educationists in the department of social work.
2. The second source consists of several social work professionals who worked in different NGOs, GOs, and have master's degrees in social work.
3. The third source represents the students.
4. The fourth source is based on the alumnae of social work (who were unable to join the SW as a profession or have left the profession for better job attainment) in Pakistan.

Keeping in mind the research questions as mentioned above, I asked some questions about professional challenges, job availability, field work concerns, and administrative issues in detail. Data were collected from January 2020 to July 2020. Interviews were taken in natural settings, some in offices, some during the first international social work conference held at Peshawar city in March 2020, where I got the opportunity to meet all representatives personally. I used the interview protocol and observation protocol for the recording of the interview with permission.

From Figure 9.1, among the 122 faculty members/social work educationists, 26 were from Sindh province, 38 were from Punjab province, 33 respondents were from KPK province, 13 were from Baluchistan province, and only 12 respondents were from Gilgit-Baltistan (GB). Similarly, 41 respondents were social professionals working in NGOs from Sindh province while 34 were from Punjab province, 21 respondents were from KPK province, 19 were from Baluchistan province, and only 7 were from GB. With regards to the social work students, 37 respondents were from Sindh province, 15 were from Punjab province, 33 respondents were from KPK province, 16 respondents were from Baluchistan province, and 21 were from GB. Lastly, 40 social work alumnae were from Sindh province that are not engaged in the social work profession, 35 social work alumnae were from Punjab province that are not engaged in the social work profession, 25 social work alumnae were from KPK province that are not engaged in the social work profession, 17 social work alumnae were from Baluchistan province that are not engaged in the social work profession and only 5 social work alumnae were from GB that are not engaged in the social work profession.

Study Objectives

- To discuss the social work programme that has been designed and implemented in Pakistan since its inception.

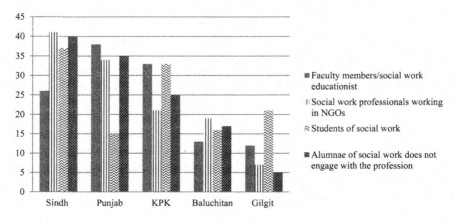

Figure 9.1 Geographical distribution of the respondents (n = 122). Source: Author's Estimation.

Social Work Education in Pakistan

- To explore the social workers' experiences, difficulties, challenges, and future opportunities of the social work profession in Pakistan.
- To identify the rift between theory and practice of social work in Pakistan.

Research Questions

Taking into consideration the challenges of pursuing social work as a profession, the author aimed to address the following questions:

1. What is the role of the social work programme that has been designed and implemented in Pakistan since its inception?
2. What is the role of social workers' experiences, difficulties, challenges, and future opportunities of the social work profession in Pakistan?
3. What is the rift/gap between theory and practice of social work in Pakistan?

Results

In seeking to answer the study questions, 122 respondents participated in this study. The sample of the study is taken from 16 universities of Pakistan offering social work education in the five provinces i.e., Sindh, Punjab, Baluchistan, Khyber Pakhtunkhwa, and Gilgit-Baltistan, for national representation. Due to the wide variety of cultural backgrounds, religious beliefs, preferences, and practices represented within this diverse group of social workers, I used the qualitative method as a research strategy and used the nonprobability, purposive sampling technique.

From Figure 9.2, 73 percent of social work students were between 16 years to 25 years old, comprising the largest section of this age group while respondents between 26 years to 35 years of age comprised 26 percent of social work professionals working in NGOs and 25 percent of students. However, 45 percent of the respondents were alumnae of social work with the age group between 46 years to 55 years and 12 percent of the respondents were also the alumnae of social work with the age of 56 years and above. A total of 53 percent of the male respondents

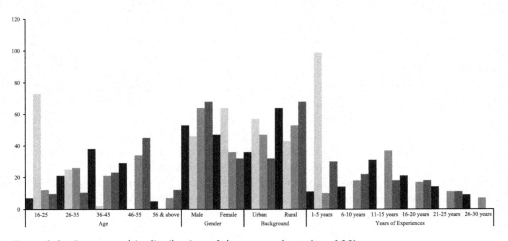

Figure 9.2 Demographic distribution of the respondents (n = 122)

were faculty members, 46 percent were students, 64 percent were professionals working in NGOs, and 68 percent were social work alumnae. With regards to female respondents, 47 percent were faculty members, 64 percent were students, 36 percent were professionals and 32 percent were alumnae. With regards to respondents with an urban background, 36 percent were faculty members, 57 percent were students, 47 percent were professionals working in NGOs, and 32 percent were social work alumnae. However, with regards to a rural background, 64 percent were faculty members, 43 percent were students, 53 percent were professionals working in NGOs, and 68 percent were alumnae. It can be observed that most of the respondents belong to the middle management cadre in the public or NGO sector. Also from this table, it is evident that more than 60 percent of the respondents are experienced and have an experience of more than five years. Also, the majority of our samples belong to a rural background. It is important to mention here that alumnae of the social work department from various universities are still working in a field other than social work but the researcher has included them here to have their opinion regarding leaving the profession.

Challenges for the Social Work Profession towards Social Development in Pakistan

The Common Perceived Perception of Social Workers

Social work focuses on social issues that restrict the progress of a community. However, social work practice is striving to deal effectively with development challenges. In Pakistan, the professional recognition of this profession is in a transition stage. At present, Pakistani social welfare is not in good shape. Many social workers, employed in the non-governmental sector, have faced various multidimensional problems. As a result, progress is paralysed. So, the quest to raise social work to a higher position and gain identity as a profession remains a monumental challenge (Figure 9.3).

To explain and validate objective number 2 of this research, 67.3 percent of faculty members that participated in the study have high respect in society, whereas this is the case for 44 percent of students, 48 percent of professionals working in NGOs, and 44.2 percent of social work alumnae. Moreover, 32.7 percent of the respondents that have low respect in society were faculty members, 56 percent were students, 52 percent were social work professionals employed in NGOs, and 55.8 percent were alumnae. In addition, respondents that agreed with the opinion that social workers are not accepted as professionals by society were largely alumnae (79 percent), followed by students (71 percent), professionals (69 percent), and the least in agreement were faculty members (62 percent). On the other hand, 38 percent of the respondents disagreeing with the opinion that social workers are not accepted as professionals by society were faculty members, 29 percent were students, 31 percent were professionals working in NGOs, and 21 percent were alumnae. Regarding the exchange visit of faculty and students for training purposes, 84 percent of faculty members were in favour, 94 percent of students, 88 percent of professionals, and 74.4 percent of alumnae. However, 16 percent of faculty members, 6 percent of students, 12 percent of professionals and 25.6 percent of alumnae disagreed with this opinion. Lastly, with regards to the lack of uniformity in the social work curriculum, 69 percent faculty agreed while 31 percent faculty disagreed with the perspective. A total of 87 percent of students agreed while 13 percent of students disagreed with the opinion. Of the professionals, 78 percent agreed while 22 percent disagreed with the perspective. However, 92 percent of alumnae agreed while only 8 percent of alumnae disagreed with the viewpoint.

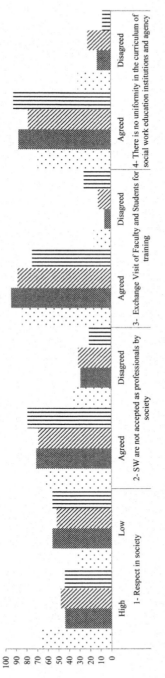

Figure 9.3 Professional challenges (n = 122). Source: Author's Estimation.

Quest for Ideology and Identity

The term 'social work' has been widely debated in Pakistan's pedagogy. It is tempting to assume that social work is not even a discipline. And whether it should be understood solely in professional terms or whether it is necessary to include aspects like the profession, this debate has opened a door of confusion. It can be traced back and connected with culture and religion at a grass-roots level. Historically, Pakistan served as a 'gateway' for Greek invaders to Central Asians, Arabs, Iranians, and the British who all left many of their cultural practices behind (Mumtaz et al., 2003). This situation influenced and hybridised a set of customs, values, and cultural practices in Pakistan's culture that are difficult to trace. Simultaneously, in Pakistan, most of the population has neither treated social work as a professional subject that is based on scientific knowledge nor known the difference between professional and non-professional social workers.

Subsequently, the term 'social work' maintains a very vast domain and is considered as a helping activity for generously giving time or money to deserving people around the world. The social worker always deals with these two dimensions of society: social structure and the cultural climate. So, the common perception is that assessing the deprived is not rocket science, thus not requiring any professional degree. Hence, under these circumstances, growth has always been restricted and the profession has not been nurtured as compared to other disciplines of the social sciences – particularly in the case of Pakistan. As a consequence, many non-professional, non-academic personnel have joined this field without any proper credentials. One of the social workers shared with us what he hears daily – somewhat like this:

> **Nobody in my family considers that my work is scientific, whenever I told them that my work is technical, I get the feedback "What! Social work or ha-ha a scientific charity", I have to bear their criticism as they think that this is only limited to charity collection and its distribution mechanism.**

The study confirms that the common man's knowledge regarding social work is extremely limited. The majority of the respondents complained about societal attitudes towards the profession, when informed that people do not recognise social work as a professional job.

Professional Challenges

Low Recognition

Even with its significant contribution to the welfare of underprivileged and vulnerable populations, still social work has not gained its due recognition as a profession in Pakistan. This mindset runs through communities and is mirrored in social workers' employment status, work environment, compensation, authority, and lack of rights. The discipline still suffers from a lack of merit when compared to other fields, such as architecture, pharmacy, education, and nursing. Moreover, non-social workers often occupy local and even provincial positions requiring social work qualifications because of the erroneous notion that nearly everyone should practise in this area of endeavour. Consequently, the ideals, beliefs, expectations, ethics, and, above all, the mission and purpose of the social work profession have been widely forgotten and neglected by those who accept these positions. Thus, the future of social work in Pakistan is in the hands of universities and associated colleges and the few graduates and educators in social work, leading to a lack of institutional attention and engagement by both state and non-state actors. Their commitment, strategies, and passion are crucial to the survival and growth of social work in Pakistan, an important country in South Asia.

Causes of Ineffective Professional Growth and Recognition of Social Work Practice

Crafting the Social work Association

Referring to the item related to professional liaison, it was revealed as a felt need among all the stakeholders in the study. With regard to the debate, the discourse about the development of a professional association of social work in Pakistan, it was unanimously recommended and proposed by the entire respondents as a necessity for professional recognition and further alliances with the global community with unanimity, usefulness, and suitability. The lack of counselling on social work education as a central coordinating body creates a lot of imbalance in the professional approach at a provincial level in the country. Currently, academia is working to determine ways to unite various social activities into an overarching collective social work response so that these activities will become part of a bigger campaign and ultimately turn into a movement for social work that will lead to its professional recognition in Pakistan. Nevertheless, this is not an easy task as it requires social workers to have up-to-date knowledge, skills, leadership, and passion (Figure 9.4).

Tragically, on a higher scale, this misconception and delusion connected with the discipline has created – both in the public and private sector – a sense of identity crisis at the individual as well as the institutional level (Cohen, 2002). The future growth and development of social work practice are reliant on the commitment and performance of social workers. As reflected in table number 4, it is confirmed to establish the Professional National Association for the standardisation of the policies, procedures, and future growth. Furthermore, social workers ought to be trained with new methods and practice tools, as well as the historical aspects and the essence of the issues, hence enabling them to play an important part in solving problems in the future. They need to be more committed to addressing their consumers' basic needs and helping them combat the present and potential challenges that will occur in the years to come. So, a well-organised professional body is needed for safeguarding the qualified social workers, professional recognition, and for resistance against current recruitment practices of converting social work jobs into another professional domain in Pakistan.

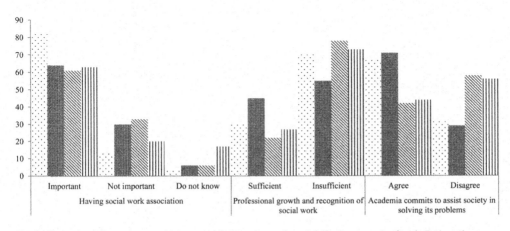

Figure 9.4 Social work association and importance (n = 122). Source: Author's Estimation.

Discussion

Almost all the participants showed their concerns regarding redefining their role. A lot of confusion was observed regarding the term 'social worker'. Nearly all the respondents noticed that there is a missing link between social work education and practice and national development goals in Pakistan. The social services are always considered as a key instrument of social policy and a cornerstone of social protection systems. It was also highlighted – with great concern – that the higher levels of academia engaged in research activities in different universities in Pakistan have had their contribution completely ignored in addressing the social problems of Pakistan.

The research which has been taught and conducted in the universities as per the requirement of the social work curricula is overlooked and sidelined by the government and policymakers. There is a need for academic and policy collaboration to resolve the social problems of people in Pakistan. More importantly, it was also confirmed from the respondents that NGOs are always trying to work as per the requirements and the agenda of their international donors or financial supporters and often they miss the ground realities. This result confirms the statement of Parks (2008), and this is the reason for often experienced fluctuations in NGOs in Asian countries.

Administrative Issues

Job Market

The majority of the respondents were dissatisfied with the job titles of social workers and stressed that the government should recognise and utilise their professional competency for the benefit of the deprived. Although the overall employee performance and the quality of the work done by a social worker – employed in a public or private set-up – is satisfactory still there is a need for improvement in the approach towards the standard of professional service.

Furthermore, the job market for the social worker in the private sector has dwindled and, therefore, trained social workers have to accept lower wages or low-status jobs in the private sector. In this context, the working environment for NGOs in Pakistan has become more commercial in many areas such as social services, healthcare, and the educational and cultural services. This working approach has led to a reduction in the recruitment process for social workers in NGOs. The government recruitment process is also seen as a ray of hope whenever the government makes an announcement. But it is not an easy task to obtain government jobs without any difficulty due to numerous hurdles and red tape. Hence, this vacuum amongst social work jobs in public and private organisations has deprived the status of social work in all segments of society. The missing connection between the theoretical approach and field practices of the profession is not linked with the country's existing job market, which is the reason for professional de-recognition.

Another social worker shared his concerns that:

> *I was working in a rural support programme as a front-line field worker in an NGO, the working environment was very friendly, had gained a lot of learning there but I left the organisation due to the low salary package. I worked there for more than three years but there was only a very small increase in my salary even though I had attended many pieces of training and obtained several letters of recommendation.*

(Figure 9.5)

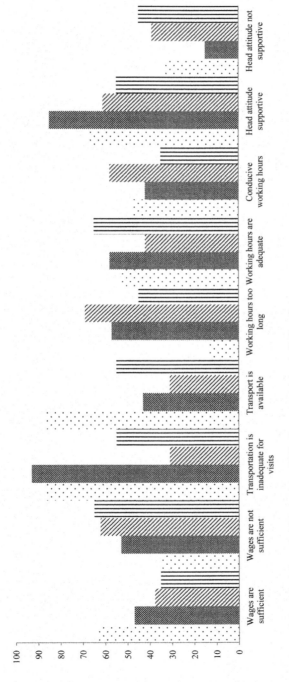

Figure 9.5 Administrative issues (n = 122). Source: Author's Estimation.

Another one was of the view that

The future of my family lies in my decision, so I left this field for my family's prosperity. Because I do not find a bright future in this field and I wonder how many of my fellows have survived with this situation with lower wages and prolonged working hours and how are they going to save the future of their families?

In short, the proper job market is an important aspect for social work recognition and future growth of the discipline.

Field Work Concerns

Field work was an important component of the curriculum and students were required to do it:

Field work is an instrument of socialization since it prepares the student for a future role as a social work practitioner ... a meaningful field work placement enhances the students understanding of the social work profession and the nature of the problems the profession addresses itself to.

(Kaseke, 1986: 55)

Field work connects the student in supervised social work practice and offers opportunities to integrate theory and practice. The field work opportunities take the students to an enormous variety of ground realities of the world around. Hence, it is seriously important for social work students to incorporate the acquired knowledge, practice principles, values and ethics, and the scientific basis for practice. There are two types of field work that are offered in different universities in Pakistan. The University of Karachi offers two days of field placement, 40 percent of the curriculum, whereas the University of Punjab and the University of Sindh offer ten weeks of block placement in the third and final years, respectively. The field placement programmes in universities have used a variety of agencies where casework, group work, and community organisations are the main methods of intervention in urban and rural settings. This exposure equips students to understand real-life situations. Of course, field work is a unique component of the social work discipline, but periodic and specialised training courses should also be planned for the faculty.

Besides this, it was also pointed out by the students across the country to redesign the social welfare model that best fits within the context of Pakistan's societal problems and needs. The students reported the complaint about the outdated curriculum of social work and the entire training programme of field work placements and suggest that it is time to rethink the scope of social work teaching and the future of our students in the field. Moreover, it was also highlighted by the respondents that there is a pressing need for well-trained professionals in social work in the international arena of human development for national representation and the development of minimal standards of ethical social work practice to be accepted at an international level.

Almost 70 years ago, the UN advisor and their Pakistani colleagues initiated field work in Pakistan. In 1952, the urban community development programmes were started as experimental learning at 'Haji Dilboth Goth', Malir, and at 'Lyri community development project' in Karachi city. Afterwards, the government also launched the Village Aid (V-Aid) programme. These lofty ideals (projects) are not functional now. It can be said that the pioneers built for us a lighthouse to beacon us forward to such a path. The lights of this lighthouse have now become very dim. The task of revitalising these lights is the task of the future (Figure 9.6).

Social Work Education in Pakistan

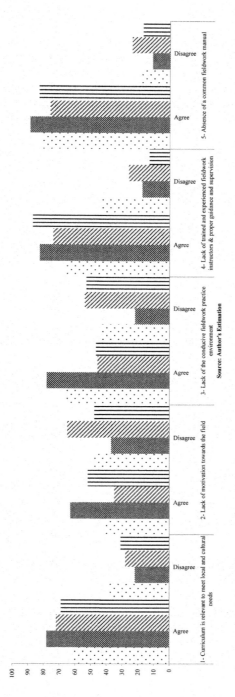

Figure 9.6 Field work practice (n = 122). Source: Author's Estimation.

I remember that whenever I used to go to field work, I was accompanied by my father or brother for community work as the door-to-door field work was a great challenge for young girls especially in urban slums where people do not consider social work a discipline. I am thankful to my family members who supported me in continuing my social work education.
(Stated by a female respondent, working as an Assistant Professor)

I want to plan rigorous field exposure for my students, but I have to curtail the field trips because there is not any financial provision available for facilitating the field trip expenses, often we have to produce the money from our pocket! University management does not consider it an important piece of work and refuses our requests due to financial obstacles.
(Stated by a male respondent, working as an Assistant Professor)

Field work is very good, but I do not find any particular manual or programme which reflects Pakistani society and its complex social system for student training'.
(Stated by a female respondent, working as a lecturer)

'Field work is interesting but a cost-consuming activity and I had to face a lot of difficulties in collecting the amount from students for the food, transportation, and other expenses'.
(Stated by a student respondent, working as a Class Representative)

I love field visits, we used to enjoy long-distance trips with our class fellows and used to meet with culturally diversified people. We gained a lot of experience and used to thank Allah, the All Mighty whenever we met with less privileged, uneducated people suffering from diseases or other social inequalities.
(Stated by a student respondent)

'field work is very good but I have not found any particular manual or programme for the training'.
(Stated by a faculty member form University of Punjab, Lahore)

Field work was very hectic and often long-distance travelling coupled with a low salary; all these factors forced me to switch jobs. I obtained good results and positive feedback from my clients but I was unable to continue it.
(Stated by a respondent, who left the field of social work)

After completion of my Master's in Social Work, I tried my level best to get a government job but failed. Finally, I received a job offer as a field officer in a CBO based in the countryside. The organisation tries to work for the improvement of women's reproductive health work without community involvement in this process, they raised funds, perhaps not transferred the benefits at the grass-root level. I was fed up with this malpractice, hypocrisy, and the field.
(Stated by a respondent, who left the field of social work during the interview with the author)

During the discussions, a common issue related to the agency and the student perspective was pointed out by the participants across the country. Students raised their concerns related to the selection of the agency: a shortage of seating places and their work environment was criticised. Moreover, a lack of professional social work leadership and agency environment was also highlighted by the respondents. In this context, it was stated by many agency supervisors that they are proving the supervisory services are 'cost-free' and neither government nor the university has provided any financial benefit to them. They also expressed the feeling of being overburdened during field work. In contrary to them, the students, though being mostly satisfied with field practices, held the view that the supervisor often treated them 'as a servant or subordinate'. Furthermore, a lack of indigenous literature, professional supervision, filed work curriculum and its content, in addition to the field evaluation process, all need to be reexamined. Based on the above-mentioned feedback, some key points were raised by the stakeholders, for instance: lack of appropriate agencies for field work training, lack of trained social work manpower in most of the NGOs, semi-trained persons either as the head or as a supervisor, lack of professional subject-oriented field supervisors, absence of suitable content of field work training, lack of a field work manual. Also there was mentioned a shortage of literature on field work, lack of public understanding of field work, lack of financial support or budget allocation for field training, absence of maintenance of standard for field work training in social work education. There is a need for a Memorandum of Understanding (MOU) or a contract between the agency management and university is required with governmental legal support for the university academia, especially the social welfare department has to offer legal protection for field placement and may restrict the reputable agencies i.e., the NGOs for the acceptance of a student's field placement and facilitation in urban and rural settings along with some monetary benefits.

In general, there is a lack of awareness about the nature of jobs among the Pakistani people, and students are regarded as unfortunate ones who were not intelligent enough to obtain their admissions in other disciplines. Women were criticised as being stupid during the field work at the community level, as reported by many female students during their discussions.

Availability of Social Work Literature

Up till now, very little social work literature has been produced considering Pakistan's perspective. The departure of UN experts left a vacuum in terms of qualified teaching faculty, which, in turn, led to a lack of research and publications based on indigenous experiences. It can be said that it is the lack of expertise in transforming social inclusion into the country's social welfare structures. According to Rehmatullah (2002), "at the outset of social work in Pakistan, United Nations advisers who helped form social welfare legislation

> recognized the Islamic values and injunctions about social welfare in the lifestyle of the people, but they did not see any of these concepts translated into a policy document which would guide the development of the programmes or plans in any scientific manner, nor did they see any practical implementation machinery for dealing with the pressing problems which the country was facing then
>
> *((Rehmatullah, 2002: 177) cited by Graham et al., 2007: 628)*

In 2002, the University Grants Commission called a series of meeting comprising of representatives from social work departments in various universities and their affiliated colleges across the country to revise the curriculum for both bachelor and master's levels. This resulted in minor changes only, such as an addition of an optional course or a more updated bibliography in another course, leaving the basic structure and content untouched.

Additionally, in this era of globalisation, it is anticipated that social work will have to produce indigenous expertise along with western knowledge that reflects the professional identity in national and international contexts. The transformation of social work requires a reorientation of curricula and teaching methods that facilitate and support holistic interventions reflecting local needs and values while abiding by the accepted global standards. So, a comprehensive formulation of the social work national curriculum is immediately required to become more responsive and revised following the growing demands of the profession. Currently, data reveals that there is a lack of coherence in social work curriculum contents, code, teaching, and practice standards in Pakistan. The profession has a long way to go, and academia has to work hard to recognise it as an occupation. By identifying the global, regional, and local strengths that influence social work teaching and professional practice, standardisation in practice is needed. Otherwise, this would be a loss of opportunity for social work education in the country if not accustomed soon to societal demands. Thus, the professional development and expansion of social work practice are reliant on the commitment and performance of social workers. One of the respondents said that:

> *Social work is not mature in Pakistan and has to face structural problems a lot than casual problems. It is related to the structure of the government and related to problems at the family and community, which condones the oppression of social work. We have to tolerate the red-tapism, nepotism under political pressure for job continuation, personal security, and mind peacefulness.*
>
> Source: Auhtor's interview

Another respondent who is not affiliated with the profession said:

> *I used to work with different NGOs, where I learned a lot about professionalism and work presentation skills, but I left the field due to internal office politics which is everywhere in NGOs and now I am running my own estate agency.*

New fields New Avenue Need to be Opened: Concerns for Consideration

The respondents belonged to different parts of the country. When summing up, they suggested some potential topics that are needed to be incorporated in the future for expansion of social services and social work education which are: developing mechanisms for reducing tribal rivalries and peacebuilding, collaboration and cooperation with international organisations and NGOs for poverty eradication, social work and public health, social work with children and child protection, developmental social work, social work with extremism. Similarly, social work with minorities, strengthening the School of Social Work, professional courses on capacity building, negotiation, counselling, skills, and Disaster Management. So, in the modern complex society there is a growing need for social work to emerge as a modern discipline.

We do criticise the internal professional shortcomings that hinder professional development. Also, we do consider external factors like the sociopolitical environment filled with corruption and inefficiency and dogged by failed policies dreamt up by incompetent governments (sometimes), poverty, illiteracy, economic instability, cross border terrorism: all these elements have coupled to move towards the dismal failure of the profession.

Surprisingly enough, as far as the credibility of the profession is concerned, it is widely accepted that there is not any other occupation that has evolved to do the job as social workers do in the country and around the globe. Social workers do their work with passion, are ready to work with people with special needs, and are used to doing work with insufficient resources. In fact, no other profession would work on humanitarian grounds as a social worker has done and this gives it a professional edge that elevates its status above other occupations. However, there is a dire need to improve the deteriorating standing of social work in Pakistan. The School of Social Work and urban community development projects which flourished in the profession are not functional in many areas in the country. Similarly, the fields of group work and school social works have been neglected. For public interpretation on the subject, we need to train, educate, re-deploy and employ a new category of workers in social development to respond to the realities of social services and to review the training and reorientation programs for social service workers. Through this transformation, I believe that developmental challenges can be addressed.

Conclusion

It is concluded that the professional journey of social work practice in the world evolves with each passing day. Whereas the field practice of social work in Pakistan has shown no significant change. Based on the opinion of stakeholders in evaluating the existing challenges, this study has identified the main reasons that make the practice of social work in Pakistan somewhat complex as compared to other professions. First, the absence of a professionally designed curriculum which produces the gap between theory and field practice is lacking. Now it is time to take steps to address the problem. The curricula must be updated and revised following the needs of our local and international communities. It is important to resolve the field work-related concerns as placements act as the lifeline of a social work degree. A separate budget allocation is also needed for field work. Second, it is even more troubling that sometimes trainees do not accomplish professional expertise. As a result, many other disciplines and professions have been progressively displaced them from areas that were considered specific areas of social work field practice. Third, there is a dire need for a professional association or government agency to examine the qualified knowledge and skills of a candidate for using a recognised professional 'title'. Fourth, the professional needs a service 'licence' – one granted by the State for these professional services in Pakistan – which would also be useful for close alignment with universal standards. Fifth, the 'Professional Registration of Social Work and Welfare Agencies' – which could be further separated into 'voluntary registration' and 'obligatory registration' for recognising the services support of NGOs, business sectors, volunteers, and the general public's participation in social welfare arrangements. Sixth, the job market has limited positions as there are few opportunities for social workers to continue in service delivery positions. It is time to redesign its professional status by enhancing professional standards, setting up job specifications. The state must ensure that no other professional can be hired as a social worker practitioner at a national level when performing social welfare services. Seventh, social work education accreditation is needed at an international level to strengthen the national social work set-up. Due to the absence of professional recognition in terms of a licence, universally recognised degree credit hours, the development of indigenous literature covering local issues, books, the practice of a code of ethics, and a professional association are all needed to ensure professional progress. In this regard, technical and financial support are needed for active and professional networks among social work schools around the world (Graham, 2002). In a nutshell, to improve the current state of the profession in Pakistan the following are needed: uniform curricula, strong links and collaboration of academia with international funding agencies and local NGOs regarding the job market, as well as a market-oriented, local needs-based revision of the curriculum, with meticulous and comprehensive international level faculty training, converting the professional degrees and services into a professional licence.

To address the above-noted critical issues certain initiatives should be taken in terms of organising local, regional, national, and international conferences, seminars, workshops, short-term academic exchange programmes of faculty and students, incorporation of more international perspectives into the social work curricula, and a scheme of distance learning as options of reaching out and bridge-building cooperation. More importantly social work as a profession is considered a lighthouse within Pakistani socioeconomic problems, one that offers a variety of solutions for the underprivileged but now it has become very dim. It is time to recharge its energy through structural uplifting and overhauling so that the profession does not remain unaffected or limited by time. I believe that social workers are primarily superhuman because they are always on the frontlines of every social problem in the country. Despite the confrontation of all challenges, still, they are optimistic, still, students are getting admissions in Social workers, still, they are serving humanity, and this is the ray of hope for a bright future. Let us move forward to embrace change and develop new professional development expertise to speed up the professional proficiency at local, national, and international levels.

Note

1 Central Superior Service (CSS) Exam, a recruitment test conducted for bureaucrats by the Federal Public Service Commission (FPSC) in Islamabad. The successful candidates are appointed as gazetted government officers holding BPS-17 under the Federal Government of Pakistan.

References

Akber, M. A. (1965). *Elements of social welfare* (3rd ed.). Dhaka University. https://www.worldcat.org/title/elements-of-social-welfare/oclc/55542

Banks, S., Cai, T., de Jonge, E., Shears, J., Shum, M., Sobočan, A. M., Strom, K., Truell, R., Úriz, M. J., & Weinberg, M. (2020). Practising ethically during COVID-19: Social work challenges and responses. *International Social Work*, 63(5), 569–583. https://journals.sagepub.com/doi/pdf/10.1177/0020872820949614

Barker, R. L. (2003). *The social work dictionary* (6th ed., Vol. 1). NASW Press.

Boyden, J. (2015). Childhood and the policy makers: A comparative perspective on the globalization of childhood. In *Constructing and reconstructing childhood: Contemporary issues in the sociological study of childhood* (2nd ed., Vol. 2, pp. 190–229). Rouledge Taylor and Francies Group. https://books.google.com.pk/books?hl=en&lr=&id=q_EjCQAAQBAJ&oi=fnd&pg=PP1&dq=Constructing+and+reconstructing+childhood:+Contemporary+issues+in+the+sociological+study+of+childhood&ots=EjPM5ZNIXJ&sig=9_xA-H6weR_SCT3HYq7O1yCTsdM#v=onepage&q=Constructingpercent20andpercent20reconstructingpercent20childhoodpercent3Apercent20Contemporarypercent20issuespercent20inpercent20thepercent20sociologicalpercent20studypercent20ofpercent20childhood&f=false

Chitereka, C. (2009). Social work in a developing continent: The case of Africa. *Advances in Social Work*, 10(2), 144–156.

Clews, R. (1999). Cross-cultural research in Aboriginal rural communities: A Canadian case study of ethical challenges and dilemmas. *Rural Social Work*, 4(1), 26–32.

Cohen, S. P. (2002). The nation and the state of Pakistan. *Washington Quarterly*, 25(3), 109–122.

Elliott, D., & Segal, U. A. (2008). International social work. In K. M. Sowers & Catherine N. Dulmus (Eds.), *Comprehensive handbook of social work and social welfare* (2nd ed., Vol. 2, pp. 343–348). The Profession of Social Work. https://onlinelibrary.wiley.com/doi/epdf/10.1002/9780470373705.chsw001020

Ghafur, M. A., & Mollah, A. K. M. (1968). *Social welfare* (1st ed., Vol. 1). Pubali Prakashani.

Graham, J. R. (2002). All our futures: Principles and resources for social work practice in a global era. *Families in Society, 83*(1), 105–109.

Graham, J. R., Al-Krenawi, A., & Zaidi, S. (2007). Social work in Pakistan: Preliminary insights. *International Social Work, 50*(5), 627–640.

Gray, M. (2002). Developmental social work: A strengths' praxis for social development. *Social Development Issues, 24*(1), 4–14.

Healy, L. M., & Thomas, R. L. (2020). *International social work: Professional action in an interdependent world* (2nd ed., Vol. 2). Oxford University Press.

Hugman, R. (1998). *Social welfare and social value: The role of caring professions* (1998 ed., Vol. 3). Macmillan International Higher Education.

Hunter, R. (2020). *Education in Pakistan*. World Education Services. Retrieved May from https://wenr.wes.org/2020/02/education-in-pakistan

IFSW, I. (2014). Global definition of social work. Retrieved https://www.ifsw.org/global-definition-of-social-work/

Jabeen, T. (2013). Social work and social welfare in Pakistan: For the society but not from the society. *Journal of Law and Society, 44*(63), 43–57.

Jillani, A., & Jillani, Z. (2000). *Child rights in Pakistan* (1st ed., Vol. 1). SPARC (Society for the Protection of the Rights of the Child).

Kaseke, E. (1986). The Role of Field work in Social Work Training", Social Development and Rural Field work. Journal of Social Development in Africa, Harare. P:55

Khalid, M. (2008). *Social work theory and practice with special reference to Pakistan, Karachi* (2nd ed., Vol. 5). Kifayat Publishers.

Malena, C. (1995). *Working with NGOs: A practical guide to operational collaboration between the World Bank and nongovernmental organizations*. World Bank.

Midgley, J. (1999). Social development in social work: Learning from global dialogue. *All Our Futures: Principles and Resources for Social Work Practice in a Global Era, 1*(1), 193–205.

Moss, B. R., Dunkerly, M., Price, B., Sullivan, W., Reynolds, M., & Yates, B. (2007). Skills laboratories and the new social work degree: one small step towards best practice? Service users' and careers' perspectives. *Social Work Education, 26*(7), 708–722.

Mumtaz, K., Mitha, Y., & Tahira, B. (2003). *Pakistan: Tradition and change* (2nd ed., Vol. 1). Oxfam.

Neville, A. (2002). Analytical Framework. In *Policy choices in a globalized world* (1st ed., Vol. 1). Nova Science.

Parks, T. (2008). The rise and fall of donor funding for advocacy NGOs: Understanding the impact. *Development in Practice, 18*(2), 213–222.

Ragab, I. (1990). How social work can take root in developing countries. *Social Development Issues, 12*(3), 38–51.

Rehman, A., & Farooq, A. (2020). Social and political dynamics of higher education in Pakistan. *Pakistan Vision, 21*(1), 184–198.

Rehmatullah, S. (2002). *Social welfare in Pakistan* (2nd ed., Vol. 1). Oxford University Press.

World Bank. 2004. World Development Report (2005). A Better Investment Climate for Everyone. World Bank. © World Bank. https://openknowledge.worldbank.org/handle/10986/5987 License: CC BY 3.0 IGO.

Worldometer. (2020). *Pakistan: Country profile*. Department of Economic and Social Affairs, Population Division.

Zahid, G., Hooley, T., & Neary, S. (2020). Careers work in higher education in Pakistan: current practice and options for the future. *British Journal of Guidance & Counselling, 48*(4), 443–453.

Zaidi, A. (2021). *Education: Giving every child the right to education*. UNICEF. Retrieved May from https://www.unicef.org/pakistan/education

10
Social Work Practice in India
In Search of a New Direction

Poonam Gulalia and Chittaranjan Subudhi

Social work education requires incorporating new arenas for education while simultaneously emphasising e-learning modalities, e-communication, and rethinking on delivering education while highlighting critical thinking (Gilliland & Anderson, 2011). Undoubtedly, the rigour and effectiveness of social work practice has been questioned, leading to these uncertain times and unanswered questions on the curriculum and professional training. With the draft of the National Council for Social Work Education Bill, 2021, new insights are being addressed to meet the needs of the 'new normal', which require deliberation, acceptance, and dialogue. Professional practice requires continuous learning, while Baikady, Pulla, and Channaveer (2014) reiterated that the social work curriculum in India remains westernised. It seems to be missing the indigenised social work components (Botcha, 2012). It has not adequately modified western social work to meet local cultural contexts. There is a dearth of indigenous knowledge and literature for social work education and practice in the Indian context (Desai, 1994, 1997; Desai, Jaswal, & Ganapathi, 2004).

Fieldwork is known as the vein system and signature pedagogy of social work education. It (fieldwork) provides opportunities for students to take responsibility for addressing peoples' issues and is an instrument of socialisation by preparing student learners for future roles as social work practitioners. The work can be any act of a social worker that emanates from a conscious and purposeful use of self, directed towards ameliorative and structured change within a context (Bodhi, 2012). Thus, fieldwork in social work education can be defined as the process of enabling a student to acquire skills, values, and attitudes in the backdrop of knowledge covering a specific practice setting, with social work principles and ethics being integral to learning.

Objective of the Chapter

The chapter explores the current social work education, including fieldwork practicum in India.

Review Protocol/Methodology

As this chapter is a review of reviews, the researcher collected the articles from different online databases like ResearchGate and Google Scholar using the keywords of 'social work', 'field work', 'indigenous social work', 'virtual field work', 'social work education', 'field work supervision' 'e-learning' along with the terms 'principle', 'practice', 'profession', 'spirituality', 'importance', and 'India'. This was inclusive of other relevant literature from print journals, books, chapters in edited books, and conference presentations through an iterative process for strengthening the chapter's objective.

Journey of Social Work in India: The Last Two Decades

There has been a spate of writings in the Indian context from the beginning of 2000, including the emergence of professional bodies and journals, which began taking rather seriously the need for documenting and consolidating the profession in varied ways. The Indian Journal of Social Work (IJSW), Tata Institute of Social Sciences (TISS) released a special issue in its platinum jubilee year (2011). However, it has now been over decades that this documentation was undertaken which included the potential role of social work education institutions towards indigenous knowledge building. Field Action Projects (FAPs) were initiated thus helping in strengthening social work knowledge and education in the Indian context through reflection, dissemination of learnings from the field. Subsequently, these FAPs became field placements for first-year and second-year students of the Masters' programme of Social Work at TISS and a few other colleges of social work, including Nirmala Niketan, Mumbai, India. The trends and terminology, of course, changed over time from 'beneficiary' to 'client' to 'people', from 'treatment' to 'therapy' to 'healing' and 'well-being', and from 'welfare' to 'developmental' to 'rights-based' and 'empowerment'. This has had implications for the role of supervision and the stakeholders too, namely, the student, the supervisor, the placement agency and of course, the 'people' with whom we work.

A review of the literature with a focus on the past two decades revealed the learning experience in social work as including four broad areas, namely knowledge, attitudes, skills, and perspective (Mallick, 2007) but also had a futuristic approach in stating that the training programme should prepare the students for professional practice as it exists today and also as it might develop in the near future. His emphasis on the spiritual dimension of social work (Mallick, 2007) was about the first mention of this aspect in the context of supervision that was taken ahead by speaking of the value-based profession and engaging with it through various discourses (Thomas, 2010). Pawar (2000) examined the relevance and adequacy of the profession by addressing the current needs and challenges in North East India and identified the significance of the models, methods, and techniques by searching for answers on the adequacy of the current social work training. The profession has direct implications for the supervisory spaces currently constructed across institutes of social work and these need redefining. Dash (2018) highlighted his concerns related to distance education and the issues related to fieldwork. It may get diluted with the possibility of exploring virtual field placements, video-based field experiences, and ensuring that professional growth can be promoted across a developmental continuum. New Frontiers in Social Work Education continued the much-needed debate on the indigenisation of the profession despite facing odds from various quarters. Desai (2016), in her very own progressive approach, highlighted the importance of training of social work educators at various levels and through multiple modes while reemphasising curriculum and resource development on social work education and its methodology for institutions, educators, and students as an essential prerequisite for social work education and training.

Indigenous Literature in Social Work

The paucity of indigenous material and literature has highlighted that the problem arose as social work educators are not practitioners and that primarily no activity is undertaken for continuous professional development (CPD) (Botcha, 2012). The experiences of academicians and practitioners began to set the path for others to be more explicit about their learnings. The westernised model of social work has highly predominated the Indian professional social work practicum and fieldwork practice, which led authors to conclude that social work practice is ineffective in the local cultural context (Baikady, Pulla, & Channaveer, 2014).

Bodhi (2011) had begun questioning the predominant discourses by saying that traditional dominant discourses have become irrelevant. And that comprehensive alternative discourses are to acquire factual content. He discussed the status of social work education in India, identifying the contours of contemporary debates within and proposed a movement towards indigenous liberatory social work education and practice. The use of indigenous knowledge in teaching and, by extension, supervision is a dire need (Jadhav & Rana, 2020). Through their doctoral thesis, she flagged that 'social work educators' developed contextual knowledge through their fieldwork experiences which included being mentors and supervisors to students of the graduate programme of social work in the country. 'Social Work bases its methodology on a systematic body of evidence-based knowledge derived from research and practise evaluation, including local and indigenous knowledge specific to its context' (IASSW/IFSW, 2000 in Trevithick, 2011).

Importance of Supervision in Fieldwork

In a keynote address at a national seminar on fieldwork practicum, Singh (2012) stated that 'it is closely supervised fieldwork practice in the schools' social work programme that differs from any of the many courses in other social sciences. It establishes the professional character of our training'. Sharma (2015) simultaneously shared her experiences in an international journal article highlighting that the process of supervision aims to develop critical thinking amongst students by deliberately creating spaces for them. It also attempts to create a dialogue for review and reflection. She emphasised the need to develop a dialogue for review and reflection besides attempting a constructive evaluation of the role of supervision in the context of third world countries, which face the problem of structural inequality in their societies. She opined that fieldwork is crucial to both the supervisor and students to assess and evaluate each other as co-travellers in the process of learning.

Other researchers stated that there is limited debate and discussion on the different fieldwork components, including supervision (Nusrat, 2020). Literature and experiential learning reveal that barring a few schools of social work, there is no capacity building initiative for being a fieldwork supervisor. There is an inadequate discussion on how fieldwork supervisors could respond to the altered context. The fieldwork supervisor appears to be competing with the other curricular components for time, resulting in infrequent faculty-student contact. The reinforcement of task accomplishment is the result of the supervisor's role getting reduced to a vigilante ensuring action of different fieldwork components without necessarily being able to nurture the potential of the student. Supervisors need to move beyond vigilantism. The current situation calls for a need to reiterate the purpose, ethos, and functions of supervision and design and debate on mechanisms to deal with the altered contextual realities.

Adaikalam (2014) stated that concurrent fieldwork supervision is neither structured nor supervised as per University Grant Commission (UGC) guidelines and regulations (UGC, 2001). There are no agreed-upon standard guidelines on fieldwork practice and recording among schools, by twisting hours of work to suit intuitional needs, appointing teaching staff without calculating fieldwork in the curriculum. Supervisors need to understand their roles and responsibilities and initiate different actions towards developing alternative discourse on the self, field, and the social context (Sonar, 2013). NASW (2013) understood that supervision needs to provide direction to the supervisee so that the latter can apply theories, standardise knowledge, skills, and competencies and understand the use of ethical obligation in practice.

Gangadhar (2017) argued that educating students to analyse their selves critically is a gradual process that takes patience, perseverance, and acceptance of students' thoughts and beliefs on the side of the supervisor. Throughout the supervisory process, the supervisor must constantly critique the current discourse on community work. Bodhi (2013, 2017) and others have been flagging this through their discourses, writings, and dialogues. Minimol (2016) conducted a workshop on open dialogue between practitioners and social work educators concerning their experience in supervising students for field practicum. The interactions with practitioners revealed many apprehensions and expectations about field practicum and its effectiveness in developing social work competencies. Johnson, Bailey, and Padmore (2012), dealing with the issues and challenges of social work practicum, concluded that a significant emphasis is to enable trainees to apply critical thinking skills in social work practice (Nadesan, 2020a, b). To help them to encourage citizen participation in addressing issues of socioeconomic justice, mainly among the disadvantaged.

Strengthening Fieldwork Practicum

Fieldwork in social work education is a guided interactive process between a student and a social life situation (Tippa & Mane, 2018). They also described fieldwork training as a supervised practice of student social workers under a trained social work educator or field personnel. Jeyarani and Jebaseelan (2017) studied field practicum learnings of students in a small town in Madurai, India, by adopting an explanatory research design. Examining the themes that emerged from the focus group discussion on student perception towards training in the fieldwork agency (placement), student perception towards faculty guidance obtained through individual conference, and student perception towards application of theory into practice – all of which throw light on the elements – and which became part of review and reflection for supervisory practice behaviours.

Gulalia (2014) seemed to question the supervisory practice behaviour in the light of her experiential learning from student groups. She explored four primary aspects of student learning, namely, a) Fieldwork as an essential learning environment, b) Building and maintaining relationships, c) Making learning a conscious process, d) The role of fieldwork for student learning. She flagged the asymmetrical power equations among stakeholders, thereby also implying the lack of a shared understanding of supervision. The need for focussing on the review and reflection process of other researchers (Rae, 2012; Labaree, 2002; Campbell & Baikie, 2012) have said about 'recovery and repair' and sought to reinforce Narayan's Samagrata approach of recognising 'inter-connectedness, interdependence … well-being of all' (Narayan, 2020; Narayan & Pandit, 2017).

In an attempt to strengthen fieldwork, Panda and Nayak (2012), highlighted 'further need for developing professional skills through practical learning, apply acquired knowledge for the study of relevant facts, analysis of the problem and focus on the concurrent opportunity for the integration of classroom learning into field practice and vice-versa'. Paracka (2014) highlighted the integration of theory and practice at the practicum that shapes and reshapes the professionals in social work; shapes and reshapes the professionals in social work where field practicum becomes the sole venue where professional social workers are carved out.

The concept 'bringing back the field' was highlighted by Vijaya Lakshmi (2014). She mentioned that one of the hallmarks of the profession is the transfer of knowledge and skills under supervisory guidance to its entrants. The supervisory conference, she wrote, defeats its purpose by becoming ritualistic and a lifeless routine activity, defeating the very purpose for which fieldwork is made a mandatory curricular activity in social work education.

The country is lacking a common and standard fieldwork manual in terms of quality of supervision. But, needless to add the Indian Journal of Social Work (IJSW) and other social work journals have consistently documented the experiences and research findings of field-related activities. Including supervision, supervisory spaces related to student learning besides the four-decade-old journeys of FAPs have 'helped upgrade practice-based knowledge' (Narayan, 2008). As a result of this mammoth effort, it has helped develop a framework for social work education and practice in the given context.

Challenges to Social Work Practice and Future Prospects

Against this backdrop, social work educators find it challenging to inculcate and strengthen a rights-based approach among students of social work in culturally constrained spaces in the social work practice of India. It has been observed that students and trainees of social work often face challenges in adopting the human rights framework in juxtaposition to their values of conformity to authority. Consequently, during fieldwork practice, instances of human rights violations go unnoticed. Often unintentionally, social work trainees overlook discriminations based on caste, gender, age, economic status, and view them as usual ways of life. Sometimes, social work educators, too, are unable to practice the rights-based approach themselves and subtly and subconsciously expect complete obedience and compliance to their words from their students. This creates a gap in praxis and practice of social work values. It is also a dimension that has not received attention from social work research.

No doubt there has been criticism as social work education and social work practice in India for its lack of relevance to the Indian context (Adaikalam, 2014; Jaswal & Kshetrimayum, 2015; Anscombe & Pawar, 2015; Thomas & Varghese, 2012). But it is within this space that one begins to understand that indigenous social work education and practice is being advocated within cultural, social, and political contexts. What researchers (Balakrishnan, 2011; Bodhi, 2013; Dash, & Roy, 2020; Baikady et al., 2014) have all been in consonance with is that social work is a profession in India that has been significantly influenced by the western models of practice that are grounded in supporting the status quo and advocacy for reforms within the existing societal structures.

Supervisory Processes and Mentoring

A new paradigm 'can be built on the growing acceptance and concern to value interdependence, partnership, co-operation, sharing of power and use of strengths, respect for nature and a belief in the unity of all things that are emerging in the society' (Mosher, 2010) which is also echoed by Graham, Coholic, and Coates 2006, Narayan, 2000; Bodhi and Tirupura, 2013; Dash and Gulalia, 2020. It implies the need for acceptance through research, ethnography, and experiential learning as a mentor that a collaborative model of social work practice is in consonance with an indigenous world view of respect and gratitude to nature, resulting in a sustainable and co-existing demonstration of collective consciousness by all stakeholders in due course of time (Gulalia, 2020). There is no doubt that sustainable collaborations develop over time, language, norms, signs, and practices which symbolise the 'we-ness' of the group (Hardy et al., 2005; Mansur et al., 2011).

It also leads one to examine the approaches essential for developing students' learning capabilities, skills, and competencies. In enabling a mentor to plan fieldwork opportunities for students in their hometowns, vicinity of stay and neighbourhood, supervisors and mentors have had to plan differently and think differently, too, thus challenging their own experience and skills, including those of communication, networking, and collaboration. The structured tasks which help focus on metacognitive strategies emerge from detailed transactions between the student and the supervisor, which in this revised space changes the meaning. When a student-centred approach is discussed, an emphasis is placed on internal motivation and learning is achieved by experimentation and exploration.

Additionally, in a collaborative environment provided by virtual peer learning opportunities, choices need to be made amongst trainees as to how to manage time, set their own learning goals, find resources, and try out new tools and make them work. Undoubtedly, stepping into a supervisory role in social work involves shifting status, perspective, and identity. In these challenging times, not to forget that supervisors bring skills and experience, which can be both an asset and hindrance, the transition can be made by creating an interpersonal environment and by being proactive in the process of change. The quality of fieldwork practice can be used more effectively for student learning and revised learning of the mentor as well. In fact, group learning is an integral part of enquiry-based learning and needs to be incorporated into the Indian context (Lee et al., 2004). By being prepared for lifelong learning, one is necessarily encompassing an ecological, spiritual evolution, which has been a hallmark of learnings from other professionals who are also engaged in meaningful ways of change and transformation (Myss, 2019; Brown, 2013;) and enables students to arrive at their own conclusions (Smith & McCray, 2007).

The purpose of including these aspects as the core aspects of experiential learning is based on 'experience-based learning within a constructivist, strengths-based, social justice framework' (Gibbons & Gray, 2004, p. 279). Within this framework, critical and reflective thinking remains at the core of self-directed learning. In fact, dialogue, collaborative exercises, and small group work tasks become primary so that the new incumbents are not 'constrained conformists' (Fook, 2002). More interdisciplinary spaces can enhance the fieldwork curriculum with an emphasis on interpersonal interactions. The students can explore the field realities and the practice within the global context. Given that human beings are fundamentally open to transformation and that the educator needs to prepare themselves with time and overtime, one would need to dwell a little on implementing blended supervision, including remote supervision, as is being tested these days in the virtual world of social work practice. It is happening these days.

Incorporating Virtual Placements and e-Learning

The world is going largely virtual these days due to the pandemic and related social contexts in play. One would need to revisit literature wherein discussions and various researchers have explored the pros and cons of virtual field placements and online field-based learning. Kulkin, Williams, and Ahn (2008) describe students' comfort levels in choosing online courses and their perceptions of what they considered the best learning forums in these courses. It is interesting to note that evaluation reports suggest that 'e-learners met the learning outcomes of the module to the same extent as the classroom group and were highly satisfied with the mode of delivery' (Webber et al., 2010, p. 44). Studies over the past decade across continents seem to suggest that the flexibility and autonomy provided by the online fieldwork method enable students to bridge physical hemispheres and differences whether they are related to culture, class, race, ethnicity, language, or socioeconomic background.

Research reveals that e-learning spaces can have a constructive long-term impact on social work students and create a general sense of multicultural issues. Cornelius and Greif (2005) have stated the most pertinent issue by flagging that 'social workers throughout the world are part of one profession and have common goals regardless of where practice occurs' (p. 32) and, therefore the need to think and act both locally and globally. It needs to be acknowledged that social workers have limited knowledge of developmental social work (Lombard & Wairire, 2010). As suggested, there is a need for training and retraining in this approach which has implications for social work practice across borders, specifically in the Indian context.

In the given context, Virtual Field Placements (VFP) could be considered an alternative approach in which congruous with blended learning can hope to revisit the field through a new lens. Since all courses, curriculum, and programmes are going online, it becomes essential that video-based field experience and other online learning platforms be tapped based on supervisor and student reflection. In the given circumstances, it is suggested that student learners learn professional vocabulary, gain exposure to models of reflection, engage in self-reflection, and undertake a high order assignment. It involves applying, analysing, and reflecting, besides getting a risk-free learning environment for objective, critical analysis by promoting professional growth across a developmental continuum.

Having understood the pressing need, it becomes essential to enable students to move beyond binary thinking in this digital age and continue to remind themselves that as young learners, they are constantly trying to make meaning of new information. In the supervisory space, the mandate for enabling students to move beyond binary thinking through conversations and turn to critical thinking is on the mentor. It has been proven that critical thinking skills enable students to become more informed and responsive decision-makers (Reid, 2019). A *Harvard Business Review* article by Baldoni (2011) stated that in a world of ongoing uncertainty, there is an exceptional value in having critical thinkers who help people move forward in a way that brings cohesion and constancy to the way one works.

Social Work Practice, Supervision, and Spirituality

Social work practice has been changing and more so in the past year, which has kind of helped practitioners, researchers, and academicians relook at and reexamine the outlook and approach to supervision and supervisory spaces. One fundamental feature which remains constant, though, is networking and understanding the perplexing spaces of human experience. While being a highly skilled space, there are 'no easy remedies in social work, especially when dealing with oppression and deprivation'. The complexity is highlighted in the international definition of social work coupled with Pawson et al. (2003, p. 40) when they flag the 'utility' in relevance to the concerns being encountered in practice. Reamer (2019) appropriately stated that technology has transformed the nature of social work education. Traditional face-to-face interaction and instruction have somewhat taken a back seat. New benchmarks must be created (NASW, CSWE, ASWE, and CSWA 2017) to explore and accept social work education and social work practice in this digital age and in these changing times. The fact remains that a supervisory alliance forms the basis of a relationship (Nelson et al., 2008).

Communication in practice is equally important and therefore, a relationship-based approach in social work forms the foundation of practice (Munro, 2011, p. 136). The relationship-based method is also linked to capacity building, not to undermine, of course, the importance of spiritual values and techniques, which can influence daily lives, routines, and the meaning we make of it (Egan & Swedesky, 2003; Dash & Gulalia, 2020). By focusing on spirituality, Ferreira (2010) ascertained that it helps support and encourages interdependence for people, society, and the environment per se. Researchers have highlighted the importance of practising the 'inner self' of spirituality being an ally in social work practice (Besthorn, 2003, Baikady et al., 2014; Mosher, 2010; Ferreira, 2010). Including eco-spiritual consciousness in social work, researchers have echoed discourse across the globe (Nadesan, 2019, 2020a; Narayan, 2000; Gray, Coates & Hetherington, 2007). Jones, Topping, Wattis and Smith (2016) had been studying the concept as 'a key dimension of person-centeredness but how to address it in everyday practice remains a challenge ... spirituality in occupational therapy practice was found to be associated with a holistic person-centred approach to care. It aimed to restore a sense of well-being and to recognise individual coping strategies'. An outline was also developed for the same in other helping professions like occupational therapy which could be studied for the purpose of social work.

Spiritual values and practices impact daily life, routine activities, and the experience of meaning in everyday life (Egan & Swedersky, 2003). Moreover, everyday discourse between social work educators, mentors, and students can help legitimise the importance of spirituality as an essential element in the lives of those being served. The fieldwork curriculum concerning spirituality will need to clarify how theory is translated into practice: so that as professionals, one gets finally prepared for a pluralistic society. It is essential to be exploring the spiritual element of people's lives, for one would not wish to miss opportunities to help people construct holistic narratives that accurately fit their experiences. With the creation of the Canadian Association for Spirituality and Social Work (2013) and with the initiation of Centre for Dalit and Tribal Studies and Action in the School of Social Work, TISS (2011) at two ends of the globe, with conferences on Spirituality and Social Work, the discussion and merger of spirituality in the profession have begun gaining ground. Although the literature highlights the potential place of spirituality in the helping professions, including social work and occupational therapy (Egan & Swedersky, 2003; Baikady et al., 2014), still there is a need also to be mindful of what is being termed 'contextual adaptation'. The need of this hour is defined as a 'biopsychosocial process allowing for an integrated focus on the influence and management of the overlapping contexts of self, interpersonal experience and sociocultural demands' (Pollock, 2013).

Concluding Thoughts

In an attempt to enhance the cycle of connection and interweaving innovation in social work practice and education, there is an element that becomes essential. There is also a part wherein one can contribute to the advances in knowledge development while retaining the primary need for spiritual growth. It is also necessary to meet the current requirements in field education during this pandemic's fallouts – if it may be said so – in terms of the enhanced need for tranquillity, peace, and connectivity. The expansion of collaborations, as well as new ways of delivering field education opportunities through alternate placement models or partnerships, show some of the creative reactions of field education programme staff to deal with placement shortages. This is not necessarily a new development as similar strategies for innovative field education have been explored and implemented and document students' satisfaction with varied models of field placement (Cleak & Smith, 2012)

The literature review and over three decades of experiential learning as an ethnographer have revealed that in working collaboratively, students can reflect on and assess their strengths and weaknesses in the collaborative effort being made by them. One has questioned and deliberated as to how collaboration can be taught. We have learnt that students need to be taught collaboration theory and its application (Five Dimensions – autonomy, mutuality, administration, governance, and trust-reciprocity) (Thomson, Perry, & Miller, 2009). Social constructivism theory stated that the inspiration for learning and constructing meaning is contextual and is guided by interaction with significant others. In this context, mentors must develop the skills students require to participate within a constructivist framework. It is good to revisit Vygotsky's work which defines scaffolding as part of the education concept of the 'zone of proximal development (ZPD)' (1980). The ZPD is the set of skills or knowledge a student can't do independently but can do with the help or guidance of someone else. It's the skill level just above where the student currently is. Ponnuswami and Francis (2012) discussed the need for strengthening inclusive perspective and approach and by extension, suggested that while we are 'on the job', in the field and of the field, practitioners and academicians liaise on unpacking the nuances of the above by and by in the Indian context. The importance of interdisciplinary practicum learning and a parallel curriculum integration model need studying in this digital context of remote supervision and mentoring. Moreover, it would require thought and reflection within Husserl's admonition that the lived experience is a dimension of 'being' that has yet to be discovered.

More study, specifically on teaching and learning critical thinking in social work education and practice, is highly required (Banks & Faul, 2007; Miller, Hall, & Tice, 2009). The implications for social work education are significant as more and more courses and field and social realities are being shared in an online environment. No doubt technology promotes critical thinking in social work by ensuring consistency in curriculum and techniques, encouraging interactive dialogue when adequately enabled, and creating an active, insightful learning environment (Banks & Faul, 2007). Utilising multiple methods to engage students and develop critical thinking in the online environment can further enhance student and mentor learning and help open up learning spaces that so far remain unexplored in the Indian context.

References

Adaikalam, F. (2014). Contextualising social work education in India. *Alternativas. Cuadernos de Trabajo Social*, 21, pp. 215–232.
Anscombe, B. & Pawar, M. (2015). *Reflective social worker practice: Thinking, doing and being*. Cambridge University Press.
Baikady, R., Pulla, V., & Channaveer, R. M. (2014). Social work education in India and Australia. *International Journal of Social Work and Human Services Practice*, 2(6), 311–318.
Balakrishnan, G. (2011). Field work supervision: A review of literature with specific reference to the supervisor–student relationship. *College of Social Work Nirmala Niketan*, 26(2), 42–70.
Baldoni, J. (2011). How a good leader reacts to a crisis. *Harvard Business Review*. Jan. Retrieved from https://hbr.org/2011/01/how-a-good-leader-reacts-to-a
Banks, A. C., & Faul, A. C. (2007). Reduction of face-to-face contact hours in foundation research courses: Impact on students' knowledge gained and course satisfaction. *Social Work Education*, 26(8), 780–793.
Besthorn, F. H. (2003). Radical ecologisms: Insights for educating social workers in ecological activism and social justice. *Critical Social Work*, 4(1), 66–106.
Bodhi, S. R. (2011). Professional social work education in India: A critical view from the periphery (discussion note). *Indian Journal of Social Work*, 72(2), 289–300. https://journals.tiss.edu/archive/index.php/ijswarchive/issue/view/338
Bodhi, S. R. (2012). Reassembling content and pedagogical processes in fieldwork supervision-reflections from a critical social work episteme. *Indian Journal of Dalit and Tribal Social Work*, 1(1), 1–13.
Bodhi, S. R. (2013). Theorizing the 'Field' in social work education and practice: Reassembling conceptions from a critical perspective. *Indian Journal of Dalit and Tribal Social Work*, 1(2), 1–22.
Bodhi, S. R. (2017). Protected: De-familiarizing content and pedagogical processes in fieldwork supervision. *Journal of Tribal Intellectual Collective India*, 1(1), 1–13. Retrieved from http://www.ticijournals.org/reassembling-content-and-pedagogical-processes-in-fieldwork-supervision-reflections-from-a-critical-social-work-episteme/
Bodhi, S. R., & Tirupura, B. (2013). International social work: An Indian experience. *Indian Journal of Dalit and Tribal Social Work*, 3(1), 1–24.
Botcha, R. (2012). Problems and challenges for social work education in India: Some recommendations. *International Journal of Multidisciplinary Educational Research*, 1(3), 201–12.
Brown, Brene. (2013, December 10). Brené Brown on empathy [Video]. *YouTube*. https://www.youtube.com/watch?v=1Evwgu369Jw, accessed on October 2021.

Campbell, C., & Baikie, G. (2012). Beginning at the beginning: An exploration of critical social work. *Critical Social Work, 13*(1), 67–81.

Canadian Association for Social Work Education. (2013). Standards for accreditation. Retrieved on 18 October 2014 from http://caswe-acfts.ca/wp- content/uploads/2013/03/CASWE.ACFTS. Standards.Oct2013.pdf.

Cleak, H., & Smith, D. (2012). Student satisfaction with models of field placement supervision. *Australian Social Work, 65*(2), 243–258.

Cornelius, L. J., & Greif, G. L. (2005). Schools of social work and the nature of their foreign collaborations. *International Social Work, 48*(6), 823–833.

Dash, B. M. (2018). Social work education through open and distance learning in India: opportunities and challenges. *Social Work Education, 37*(6), 813–820.

Dash, B. M., & Gulalia, P. (2020, June 19). Revamping field work practicum in social work education during covid-19: Need to develop indigenous model of field work in India. *New Delhi Times*. Retrieved from https://www.newdelhitimes.com/revamping-field-work-practicum-in-social-work-education-during-covid-19-need-to-develop-indigenous-model-of-field-work-in-india/

Dash, B. M., & Roy, S. (2020). *Fieldwork training in social work* (1st ed.). Routledge Chapman & Hall.

Desai, A. S. (1994). A study of social work education in India: Student, the Educator and the educational process (mimeo). In K. S. Kendall (Ed.) (2000), *SWE: Its origin in Europe*. CSWE Tata Institute of Social Sciences, Bombay.

Desai, M. M. (1997). Literature on social work profession in India, 1936–1996: An overview. *Indian Journal of Social Work, 58*, 149–160.

Desai, M. M. (2016). Training for family and child welfare. *The Indian Journal of Social Work, 28*(1), 115–119.

Desai, M. M, Jaswal, S., & Ganapathi, S. (2004). Issues and directions for promoting relevant social work knowledge. *The Indian Journal of Social Work, 65*(1), 151–170.

Ferreira, S. B. (2010). Eco-spiritual social work as a precondition for social development. *Ethics and Social Welfare, 4*(1), 3–23.

Egan, M., & Swedersky, J. (2003). Spirituality as experienced by occupational therapists in practice. *American Journal of Occupational Therapy, 57*(5), 525–533.

Fook, J. (2002). *Social work: Critical theory and practice*. Sage.

Gangadhar, B. S. (2017). Teaching social work practice through intervention fieldwork. *Social Work Foot Print*. Retrieved from https://www.socialworkfootprints.org/articles/teaching-social-work-practice-through-intervention-fieldwork, Accessed on October. 2021

Gibbons, J., & Gray, M. (2004). Critical thinking as integral to social work practice. *Journal of Teaching in Social Work, 24*(1–2), 19–38.

Gilliland, S. W., & Anderson, J. S. (2011). Perceptions of greed: A distributive injustice model. In Gilliland et al (Eds.) *Emerging Perspectives on Organizational Justice and Ethics*, 137–166.

Graham, J., Coholic, D., & Coates, J. (2006). Spirituality as a guiding construct in the development of Canadian social work: Past and present considerations. *Critical Social Work, 7*(1), 1–17.

Gray, M., Coates, J., & Hetherington, T. (2007). Hearing indigenous voices in mainstream social work. *Families in Society, 88*(1), 55–66.

Gulalia, P. (2014). Empowerment of student social worker: Reading between the lines. *International Journal of Social Work and Human Services Practice, 2*(6), 303–310.

Gulalia, P. (2020). The Buddhist experience of an ethnographer: Reporting from field experience. In B. B. Dash et al. (Eds.), *Indian Social Work* (1st ed., pp. 148–164). Taylor & Francis.

Hardy, C., Lawrence, T. B., & Grant, D. (2005). Discourse and collaboration: The role of conversations and collective identity. *Academy of Management Review, 30*(1), 58–77.

Jadhav, J., & Rana, S. (2020). Indigenous and Indianized social work education in India: A way forward. In *Indian social work* (pp. 37–53). Routledge.

Jaswal, S., & Kshetrimayum, M. (2015). Social work research and its methodological vicissitudes in the Tata Institute of Social Sciences. *Social Work Journal, 6*(1), 6–21

Jeyarani, J. S., & Jebaseelan, U. S. (2017). Fieldwork practicum as perceived by social work students with special reference to Madurai. *International Journal of Humanities and Social Science, 7*(17), 1–5.

Johnson, E. J., Bailey, K. R., & Padmore, J. (2012). Issues and challenges of social work practicum in Trinidad and Tobago and India. *The Caribbean Teaching Scholar, 2*(1), 19–29

Jones, J., Topping, A., Wattis, J., & Smith, J. (2016). A concept analysis of spirituality in occupational therapy practice. *Journal for the Study of Spirituality, 6*(1), 38–57.

Kulkin, H., Williams, J., & Ahn, B. (2008). Exploring baccalaureate social work students and Web-based learning. *Journal of Baccalaureate Social Work, 13*(2), 97–113.

Labaree, R. V. (2002). The risk of 'going observationalist': Negotiating the hidden dilemmas of being an insider participant observer. *Qualitative Research, 2*(1), 97–122.

Lee, V. S., Greene, D. B., Odom, J., Schechter, E., & Slatta, R. W. (2004). What is inquiry-guided learning? In V. S. Lee (Ed.), *Teaching and learning through inquiry: A guidebook for institutions and instructors* (pp. 3–15). Stylus Publishing.

Lombard, A., & Wairire, G. (2010). Developmental social work in South Africa and Kenya: Some lessons for Africa, The Social Work Practitioner-Researcher, Special Issue, April 2010 https://repository.up.ac.za/bitstream/handle/2263/16241/Lombard_Developmental%282010%29.pdf?sequence=1&isAllowed=y.

Mallick, A. (2007). Field work training in social work curriculum: Reflections on learning and teaching. *The Indian Journal of Social Work, 68*(4), 573–580.

Mansur, R., Tuval, S., Barak, J., Turniansky, B., Gidron, A., & Weinberger, T. (2011). Storying curriculum making in a collaborative research and teaching landscape. In *Narrative inquiries into curriculum making in teacher education*. Emerald Group Publishing Limited.

Miller, S., Harnek Hall D., & Tice, C. (2009). Assessing critical thinking: The use of literature in a policy course. *Journal of Baccalaureate Social Work, 14*(2), 89–104.

Minimol. (2016). *Social work academicians-field educators interface: A best practice in social work education.*

Mosher, C. (2010). A wholistic paradigm for sustainability: Are social workers experts or partners. *Critical Social Work, 11*(3), 102–121.

Munro, E. (2011). *The Munro review of child protection*. Stationery Office.

Myss, C. (2019, May 17). Why we search for personal power & self esteem: Sofia Institute 2018 [Video]. YouTube. https://www.youtube.com/watch?v=rgr7GQQL-ww, accessed on November, 2021

Nadesan, V. (2019). *A system analysis of field instruction in social work education*. University of Johannesburg.

Nadesan, V. (2020a). Challenges of social work students from historically disadvantaged universities during placements in semi-rural areas in South Africa. *Southern African Journal of Social Work and Social Development, 32*(3), 17.

Nadesan, V. (2020b). Social Work Supervision in a Developing Country: Experiences of students. *The Indian Journal of Social Work, 81*(3), 263–282.

Narayan, L. (2000). Freire and Gandhi: Their relevance for social work education. *International Social Work, 43*(2), 193–204.

Narayan, L. (2008). Contextualising social work practice in India: Some explorations. *The Indian Journal of Social Work, 69*(2), 107–110.

Narayan, L. (2020). The relevance of Gandhi for social work education and practice. In *The Routledge Handbook of Critical Pedagogies for Social Work* (pp. 424–436). Routledge.

Narayan, L., & Pandit, M. (2017). Samagratā Framework for Social Work. *The Indian Journal of Social Work, 78*(3), 533–560.

National Association of Social Workers [NASW]. (2013). Best practice standards in social work supervision. National Association of Social Workers.

National Association of Social Workers, Association of Social Work Boards, Council on Social Work Education, & Clinical Social Work Association. (2017). NASW, ASWB, CSWE, & CSWA Standards for Technology in Social Work Practice

Nelson, M. L., Barnes, K. L., Evans, A. L., & Triggiano, P. J. (2008). Working with conflict in clinical supervision: Wise supervisors' perspectives. *Journal of Counseling Psychology, 55*(2), 172.

Nusrat, R. (2020). Indigenization of Indian social work: A critical curriculum analysis for knowledge building. In *Indian social work* (pp. 73–83). Routledge.

Panda, B., & Nayak, L. M. (2012). Strengthening field work practicum in social work education. *Social Work, 1*(2), 14–30.

Paracka, S. (2014). Field practicum: The venue for competence development in social work. *Indian Journal of Research, 3*(1), 195–196.

Pawar, M. (2000). Social work education through distance mode in India: A proposal. *Indian Journal of Social Work, 61*, 196–211.

Pawson, R., Boaz, A., Grayson, L., Long, A., & Barnes, C. (2003). *Types and quality of knowledge in social care*. Social Care Institute for Excellence.

Pollock, N. B. F. (2013). *Contextual adaptation. Human functioning as dynamic interaction: A social work perspective*. Doctorate in Social Work (DSW) Dissertations. 35. Accessed on October 2021, https://repository.upenn.edu/edissertations_sp2/3

Ponnuswami, I., & Francis, A. P. (2012). *Professional social work: Research perspectives*. Authors Press.
Rae, R. (2012). *A study of service user and carer involvement in social work admissions in one UK University-power, professionalism and trust*. In: 2nd International Conference on Practice Research, 30-31st May 2012, University of Helsinki, Finland. (Unpublished)
Reamer, F. G. (2019). Social work education in a digital world: Technology standards for education and practice. *Journal of Social Work Education, 55*(3), 420–432.
Reid, L., Judith, K. P., Barbara, M., Margie, E.-B. (2019). *The Routledge Companion to Career Studies (1st Eds.)*. Routledge
Sharma, S. (2015). Fieldwork supervision: Meeting requirements of social work education through critical thinking. *The Hong Kong Journal of Social Work, 49*(1–2), 3–14.
Singh, R. R. (2012). *Key note addressed in a national seminar on social work field practicum: Opportunities and challenges*. Department of Social Work: Jain Vishva Bharati University.
Smith, N., & McCray, R. (2007). Shell-shocked diffusion model for the light curve of SN 2006gy. *The Astrophysical Journal Letters, 671*(1), L17.
Sonar, G. B. (2013). Teaching Social Work Practice through Intervention of Field Work. *Social Work Foot Prints, 7*(3), 345–360.
Thomas, G. (2010a). *Professional social work in Indian perspectives*. IGNOU.
Thomas, G. (2010b). *Resilient social work: The gracious way*. Ane Books.
Thomas, G., & Varghese, J. (2012). Social work education around the world. *Encyclopaedia of Social Work, 4*, 1385–96.
Thomson, A. M., Perry, J. L., & Miller, T. K. (2009). Conceptualizing and measuring collaboration. *Journal of Public Administration Research and Theory, 19*(1), 23–56.
Tippa, N. G., & Mane, S. R. (2018). Problems and prospects of field work training in social work education: A Review. *Innovare Journal of Social Sciences, 6*(1), 1–2.
TISS. (2011). *Standards for assessment of quality in social work education: seminar report*. TISS.
Trevithick, P. (2011). *Social work skills and knowledge: A practice handbook*. McGraw-Hill Education.
University Grant Commission (UGC). (2001, December). *UGC model curriculum: Social work education*. Retrieved February 10, 2020, from University Grants Commission.
Vijaya Lakshmi, B. (2014). Let us bring back 'field' to fieldwork: An overview of the current scenario of fieldwork in social work education in India. *Social Work Foot Prints, 4*(4), 17–40.
Vygotsky, L. S. (1980). *Mind in society: The development of higher psychological processes*. Harvard University Press.
Webber, M., Currin, L., Groves, N., Hay, D., & Fernando, N. (2010). Social workers can e-learn: Evaluation of a pilot post-qualifying e-learning course in research methods and critical appraisal skills for social workers. *Social Work Education, 29*(1), 48–66.

Part II
New Insights into Social Work Field Education in Developing Asia

11
Practice Teaching in the Social Work Master's Degree Programme
Fostering the Third Mission of Universities: The Case of Georgia

Shorena Sadzaglishvili

This study analyses the current status of field education of the Master of Social Work Programme at Ilia State University. The problems revealed are as follows: the field education is not systematised, there are not enough relevant practice placements with qualified supervision available, there is no fixed minimum number of practice hours, limited participation of field instructors involved in the assessment of students' practice, there is no position for a university-based Practice Coordinator in charge of monitoring student's practice, lack of motivated professional field instructors, and so on. The study findings also showed a positive feature of field education in Georgia. This is an original idea of social projects that enhance civic engagement of students and fulfil the third mission of the university. Social projects can be seen as a service-learning component, which is a modern educational strategy introduced at many European universities.

Establishment of Social Work in Georgia

Georgia is an ancient country in the Caucasus region of Eurasia. Located at the crossroads of Western Asia and Eastern Europe, the population of the country is about 3.7 million, around 300,000 of which were been internally displaced due to the occupation of 20% of the Georgian territories. After regaining independence in 1991, Georgia engaged in diverse reform initiatives, aiming to overcome the legacy inherited from the socialist regime. The Government of Georgia (GoG) embarked on large-scale reforms, many of which demonstrated an urgency in introducing the profession of social worker (Partskhaladze, Sadzaglishvili, and Gigineishvili, 2020).

Macro-level reforms in Georgia, including new legislative frameworks, strategies, and action plans, and reorganisation of major social welfare institutions, evoked exo-systemic exchanges at both mezzo and micro levels. On the mezzo level, new state bodies such as the Social Service Agency, the Guardianship and Care Panels, the Psycho-Social and Rehabilitation Programmes Division of the National Agency of the Execution of Non-Custodial Sentences and Probation, and others were established and the role of social worker was recognised. Micro-level impacts were thus felt in terms of the availability of more home-based services, safer conditions for children, prisoners and other vulnerable groups, improved access to welfare benefits, etc. The two major fields of child welfare and criminal justice were prioritised and well developed in Georgia by the coordination and active participation of international, local state, and non-governmental organisations (Sadzaglishvili, 2017b).

The establishment of the Georgian Association of Social Workers (GASW) in 2004 was one of the key steps in increasing the awareness and profile of social work in the country. GASW heavily influenced the development of the social work profession and education in Georgia. In close collaboration with international (International Federation of Social Workers, UNICEF, Open Society Foundation (OSI), the Global Social Service Workforce Alliance, International Council on Social Welfare) and local stakeholders (Social Service Agency, Parliament of Georgia, etc.), GASW promoted the role of social work at the policy level and instigated reforms that affected the legislative framework, supporting new social work establishments in the country (Sadzaglishvili, 2017b).

Currently the Georgian Association of Social Workers has over 600 members and is a part of the global social work professional community. Besides providing professional expertise and support to the GoG, social service providers, and social workers, GASW is also active in responding to challenges facing the country and requiring social work expertise (Partskhaladze, Sadzaglishvili, and Gigineishvili, 2020).

Policy Documents Affecting Social Work Education

There are two major policy documents greatly affecting the current status of social work education and profession in Georgia.

(1) The first document is the Law of Higher Education approved in 2004 by the Parliament of Georgia. In this document social work was included as new interdisciplinary profession, listed among the other professions. In 2019 the revised National Qualifications Framework and Classifiers of Fields of Study were approved by Order of the Minister of Education, Science, Culture, and Sport of Georgia. According to the new amendments, social work became a welfare field (092) instead of being an interdisciplinary field. Within the welfare field there are different specialisations like (1) Care of elderly and of disabled adults (0921), Child care and youth services (0922), Social work and counselling (0923). This last area is concentrated on the study of the welfare needs of communities, specific groups and individuals, and the appropriate ways of meeting these needs. The focus is on social welfare with emphasis on social policy and practice.

The new National Qualifications Framework considers the requirements of the European Qualifications Framework (EQF LLL) and European Higher Education Area Qualifications Framework (QF-EHEA) (National Center for Educational Quality Enhancement, 2019). The EU-funded Twinning project started in July 2019 and its overall objective is to contribute to human capital development by improving quality assurance, transparency, and governance of skills and qualifications in a lifelong learning (LLL) perspective. The Twinning project is implemented by the German Academic Exchange Service (DAAD) in partnership with the Estonian Quality Agency for Higher and Vocational Education (EKKA). Within the above project, international experts from Germany and Estonia in collaboration with local experts developed 'Sector Benchmark for Social work: Levels VI and VII' that defines what can be expected of a graduate, at bachelor's and master's level, in the subject, and in terms of learning outcomes at the end of their studies. This document sets out the principal qualities, abilities, and attributes that are to be expected of a graduate in social work at bachelor's and master's levels. The goal of the sector benchmark for social work is to support the design of bachelor's (VI level) and master's (VII level) degree education programmes, student mobility, international recognition of graduate qualification, and entry into the social work profession and employment. This document states that in social work, supervised professional practice and field placements are a crucial part of study programmes. However, it does not specify the required number of hours for field placement.

(2) The second document that greatly influencing social work education is the Law on Social Work approved by the Parliament of Georgia in 2018. The legislation established the uniform social worker system and determined the key principles of social work profession obliging the social worker to adhere to the fundamental aspects upon the official duties which are: a respect for human rights, social justice, equality, sector competence, proportionality, honesty, and professional ethics. It specifies rights and obligations to ensure maximal protection of the beneficiaries and social servants as well as defining the professional qualification of the worker and the competences (Parliament of Georgia, 2018). This is a first step for advancing the professionalisation of social work in Georgia, as it ensures the development of professional expertise and the individual accountability of social workers and social work practitioners in Georgia.

However, the Law on Social Work creates new challenges for social work education and training to be planned in ways that support the formation of a professional workforce acquired with skills and expertise and adapting to new job roles, career structures, and local and international professional discourses. In this context the role of social workers reaches a critical importance in terms of connecting high quality education and training to service needs and ensuring that social workers develop the expertise necessary to improve outcomes for service users and create effective services by using research and evidence to inform their practice decisions to meet rapid socioeconomical changes and complex needs of transitional societies.

The legislation refers to the development of the social welfare system of Georgia as well as emphasising the social workers' role. The law also states the need for specialisation of social work e.g., health care social worker, municipal social worker, school social worker, social worker in the criminal justice system, etc. This means that soon the demand for social workers in each system/sector will rise. In addition, according to the legislation, the current caseload of social workers must be decreased to 50 per specialist (Chapter 47). Moreover, after 2021 a person without an academic education will not be able to enter the social work profession. Thus, the Law on Social Work increases the demand on academia, especially regarding the creation of new social work programmes, well-developed specialised courses, and field education at the universities to increase the number of graduates from Social Work Programmes (Parliament of Georgia, 2018).

Social Work Education and Social Work Workforce

Social work education has a very short history in Georgia. In 2006 the first social work programmes (BA, MA, and Doctoral Programmes in Social Work) were created at two major state universities: Ilia State University and Tbilisi State University. Social work education development in Georgia is influenced by two social work models of social work: American (Columbia University and California State University) and UK/European schools (Sheffield Hallam University (UK), Kiev Mohyla-Academy Ukraine, University of Ljubljana Slovenia, Tallinn

University Estonia, and Vilnius Pedagogical University Lithuania). The first graduate social work programmes were developed with the financial support of the Tempus/Tacis Programme of Europe (2006–2012) and the Open Society Foundation Academic Fellowship Programme/ Higher Education Support Programme (2003–2007). Thus, Georgian schools of higher education can be described as a mixed model of American and British/European universities.

There are more than 300 generalist practice social workers graduated from the local academic (bachelor and master degree) social work programmes, specialised mostly in two concentrations – child welfare and criminal justice. Their ranks are increasing at the rate of about 50 graduates per year.

It has been estimated that approximately 334 (60%) are employed by state agencies, while the remainder are employed by non-state (NGO) agencies. While many of the latter work in child protection, a comparatively large subgroup works in substance abuse and others are found in a range of fields from health care to human rights and community mobilisation (Partskhaladze, 2014).

In general, social workers in the NGO sector consider themselves to be less qualified than state social workers (Shatberashvili, 2012). In both state and non-state agencies, social workers mostly play the role of case manager. Roles such as supervisor, mediator, advocate, and broker are also practised. However, the roles of clinical counsellor, social researcher, policy analyst and planner, social activist, program developer and evaluator, educator, facilitator, and community mobiliser are very rarely practised and when they are, it is only in the non-statutory sector (Namicheishvili, 2014).

Social Work Educators and Opportunities for Development of Scientific Social Work

Local social work professors are qualified social workers graduated from western universities who are directing and leading social work programmes and courses at two major state universities in Georgia (Ilia State University and Tbilisi State University). Social work doctoral education has been introduced to prepare social work professionals to teach in higher education settings; however, social work profession is significantly challenged within academia and is not readily seen as a science and research field.

There are limited university research centres and grant opportunities for the advancement of social work professional practice and creating and implementing social work interventions. Georgia is a fertile climate for integrative social work expansion. However, Georgian social work is still lacking scientific shape. It is critical to promote an idea of social work as science worldwide and especially in the countries where social work is a newly emerging discipline. In this case, social work will be raised as a global profession and will meet ongoing globalisation discourse and global political and economic processes (Penna, Paylor, and Washington, 2000). At the same time, scientific social work will be able to answer national challenges considering its ecological contexts based on evidence-based practices and scientific innovations to shape effective and responsive educational programmes in transitional countries (Ashley et al., 2017).

Thus, social work educators can be seen as the main agents in developing evidence-based practices of field education for BA and MA Social Work programmes that will be adapted to the Georgian context.

International Standards of Field Education

The current status of social work education and profession can be described as very dynamic and rapidly growing. There is a high need for the development of quality social work educational programmes and an increase in the number of professionals who are graduates from social work MA and BA programmes. Social work educational programmes need to be developed in accordance with international standards. In particular, it is crucial to develop social work fieldwork that is directly related to the positive outcomes of the social work programme. The benefit of well-organised fieldwork is the formation of competitive social work professionals enabled to become change agents at their workplaces and maintain professional standards of practice. The graduates of social work programmes should fight for their place in the social welfare field despite facing competition from the other helping professionals (psychologists, mental health specialists, etc.) by adding more scientific basis and professionalism in dealing with their beneficiaries (Sadzaglishvili, 2017a).

The philosophy of the field education programme is that field practice supplements and reinforces classroom instruction through the utilisation of a field practicum site. The practicum offers students an opportunity to come in contact with a variety of populations that have various types of needs and problems reflective of the population the student would encounter in future practice. In the practicum, the student is able to go where the client population is located, provide a service, and assist in meeting the individual, families, groups, organisations, communities, and societal needs. The practicum plays a vital role in the preparation of competent future social work professional practitioners. In addition to the skills and theoretical knowledge needed for direct service with various client systems, students also gain a hands-on understanding of the social work profession's value base, its expectations in terms of practice, and its codes of conduct, communication, and protocols (Sadzaglishvili, 2017a).

In order to identify the main concepts for analysing a social work programme, two major documents are discussed below.

(1) The Global Standards for Social Work Education and Training

The International Federation of Social Workers (IFSW) and the International Association of Schools of Social Work (IASSW) updated the Global Standards for Social Work Education and Training (GSSWET) in 2014. This document is an aspirational guide setting out the requirements for excellence in social work education for many countries (Global Standards for Social Work Education and Training, 2019). This updated version of Global Standards supports creating platforms for indigenous social workers to shape curricula and relevant courses. The Global Standards for Social Work Education and Training take into consideration the most recent global developments in the social work profession while appreciating the diverse political, historical, and cultural contexts as well as maintaining a delicate balance between detailing unifying themes and allowing sufficient flexibility to ensure relevance to local-level social work education and practice. This document underlines the standards of field education.

(2) Educational Policy and Accreditation Standards for Baccalaureate and Master's Social Work Programmes

The other more detailed document that can be used for setting international standards for Social Work Education is 'Educational Policy and Accreditation Standards for Baccalaureate and Master's Social Work Programmes' introduced by the Council on Social Work Education (CSWE) Commission on Educational Policy and the CSWE Commission on Accreditation. This educational policy was approved by the CSWE Board of Directors on 20 March 2015 and Accreditation Standards were approved by the CSWE Commission on Accreditation on 11 June 2015. In particular, the Council on Social Work Education introduced a new framework for the accreditation of social work education programmes, emphasising the responsibility to educate for nine specific professional competencies. As a result, the curriculum design now includes an integration of a programme's mission and goals, explicit curriculum, implicit curriculum, and assessment of educational outcomes (Council on Social Work Education, 2015).

Similar to the Global Standards for Social Work Education and Training, it intends to encourage flexibility and programmes have the opportunity to develop innovative approaches for preparing students for contemporary and emerging social work practice relevant to the context and mission of the school. The Educational Policy and Accreditation Standards (EPAS) describe four features of an integrated curriculum design: (1) Programme mission and goals, (2) Explicit curriculum, (3) Implicit curriculum, and (4) Assessment. Below explicit and implicit curriculum will be discussed in the context of field education.

The explicit curriculum is the programme's formal education and includes the courses and field education. Using a competency-based education framework, the explicit curriculum prepares students for professional practice at the baccalaureate and master's levels. Baccalaureate programmes prepare students for generalist practice while Master's programmes prepare students for advanced generalist practice and specialised practice. Specialised practice builds on generalist practice and extends the Social Work Competencies for practice with a specific population, problem area, method of intervention, perspective, or approach to practice.

Field education is the signature pedagogy for social work, which includes elements of instruction and socialisation of students. Signature pedagogy teaches future practitioners the fundamental dimensions of professional work, which is 'to think, to perform, and to act ethically and with integrity' (Council on Social Work Education, 2015, p. 12). Field education intends to integrate the theoretical and conceptual contribution of the classroom with the practice. Classroom and field are the two interrelated components of curriculum having equal importance within the curriculum. Field education needs to be 'systematically designed, supervised, coordinated, and evaluated based on criteria by which students demonstrate the Social Work Competencies' (Council on Social Work Education, 2015, p. 12). The field education programme provides generalist and specialised practice opportunities for students to demonstrate social work competencies with individuals, families, groups, organisations, and communities as well as within an area of specialised practice and illustrates how this is accomplished in field settings. It also specifies that the field education programme provides a minimum of 400 hours of field education for baccalaureate programmes and a minimum of 900 hours for master's programmes (Council on Social Work Education, 2015).

The programme explains how on-site contacts or other methods are used to monitor student learning and field setting effectiveness. Field instructors should have credentials and practice experience to be able to supervise a student's practice. For instance, field instructors for master's students hold a master's degree in social work from a CSWE-accredited programme and have two years post-master's social work practice experience. For cases in which a field instructor does not hold a CSWE-accredited social work degree or does not have the required experience, the programme assumes responsibility for reinforcing a social work perspective and describes how this is accomplished. The programme should also state how its field education programme provides orientation, field instruction training, and continuing dialogue with field education settings and field instructors. The programme also should describe how its field education programme develops policies regarding field placements in an organisation in which the student is also employed.

The implicit curriculum refers to the learning environment in which the explicit curriculum is presented. The implicit curriculum in social work education includes 'policies that are fair and transparent in substance and implementation, the qualifications of the faculty, and the adequacy and fair distribution of resources' (Council on Social Work Education, 2015, p. 14). It informs the student's learning and development through the culture of human interchange, the spirit of inquiry, support for difference and diversity, and values and priorities in the educational environment, including the field practicum and inform the student's learning and development (Bogo & Wayne, 2013, p. 3). The learning environment consists of the programme's institutional setting; selection of field education settings and their clientele; composition of programme advisory or field committees; educational and social resources; resource allocation; programme leadership; seminars, and so on.

According to EPAS (Council on Social Work Education, 2015), in recognition of the importance of field education as the signature pedagogy, programmes must provide an administrative structure and adequate resources for systematically designing, supervising, coordinating, and evaluating field education across all programme options. The programme should identify the field education director and describe the field director's ability to provide leadership in the field education programme through practice experience, field instruction experience, administrative and other relevant academic/professional activities in social work. To carry out the administrative functions of the field education programme at least 50% assigned time is required for master's programmes. The programme should describe its administrative structure for field education and explain how its resources (personnel, time, and technological support) are sufficient to administer its field education programme to meet its mission and goals. In addition, implicit, or hidden, curriculum refers to lessons that students take from teachers' and especially, practice teachers' (field instructors) attitudes and the practice environment. It refers to the transmission of norms, values, and beliefs conveyed in the social work classrooms as well as in practice placements, which should be congruent with the values of the profession and the mission, goals, and context of the programme. Thus, the implicit curriculum is as important as the explicit curriculum in shaping the professional competences of the students.

To summarise, here are the main criteria regarding the organisation of field education identified in above documents that can be used for assessment of social work field education of the Master's of Social Work programme.

This matrix is used for assessment of the field education of Master's of Social Work Programme at Ilia State University.

MSW Programme as Assessed by the International Standards of Social Work Field Education

The social work master's programme at Ilia State University is the first master's programme in Georgia. It has both theory and practice components. The programme has its practice conception that includes all details of organisation of fieldwork for students. The primary goal of the practice component is to offer a quality of practical experience through intensive field placements.

The social work programme administers field education consistent with programme goals and objectives that emphasise the importance of a multicultural focus on human systems and the helping process. The fieldwork experience is an extension of the classroom. It is designed to provide a challenge to the student, exposing them to the myriad of social work practice opportunities. The fieldwork experience is designed to engage students in a supervised direct service at the macro, mezzo, and micro levels. The fieldwork experience provides students with the opportunity, under supervised conditions, to apply theories and knowledge learned in both the foundation and concentration courses of social work practice. Additionally, the fieldwork experience provides students with an opportunity to reflect on their learning and to experiment and develop confidence in the skills they are developing during the experience. It is an integral

Table 11.1 Assessment criteria for field education of MSW programmes

1	The programme provides a rationale for its formal curriculum design for specialised practice demonstrating how the design is used to develop a coherent and integrated curriculum for both classroom and field.
2	The programme explains how its field education programme connects the theoretical and conceptual contributions of the classroom and field settings.
3	The programme explains how its field education programme provides generalist practice opportunities for students to demonstrate social work competencies with individuals, families, groups, organisations, and communities and illustrates how this is accomplished in field settings.
4	The programme explains how its field education programme provides specialised practice opportunities for students to demonstrate social work competencies within an area of specialised practice and illustrates how this is accomplished in field settings.
5	The programme explains how students across all programme options in its field education programme demonstrate social work competencies through in-person contact with clients and constituencies.
6	The programme describes how its field education programme provides a minimum of 900 hours for master's programmes. The programme's field education is sufficient in duration and complexity of tasks and learning opportunities to ensure that students are prepared for professional practice.
7	The programme provides its criteria for admission into field education and explains how its field education programme admits only those students who have met the programme's specified criteria.
8	The programme describes how its field education programme specifies policies, criteria, and procedures for selecting field settings; placing and monitoring students; supporting student safety; and evaluating student learning and field setting effectiveness congruent with the social work competencies. The programme has clear plans for the organisation, implementation, and evaluation of the theory and field education components of the programme.
9	The programme describes how its field education programme maintains contact with field settings across all program options. The programme explains how on-site contact or other methods are used to monitor student learning and field setting effectiveness. The school and the agency/field placement setting have planned co-ordination and linkages.
10	The programme describes how its field education programme specifies the credentials and practice experience of its field instructors necessary to design field learning opportunities for students to demonstrate social work programme competencies. Field instructors for master's students hold a master's degree in social work from a CSWE-accredited program and have two years post-master's social work practice experience. For cases in which a field instructor does not hold a CSWE-accredited social work degree or does not have the required experience, the programme assumes responsibility for reinforcing a social work perspective and describes how this is accomplished. The programme appoints field supervisors or instructors who are qualified and experienced, as determined by the development status of the social work profession in any given country.
11	The programme describes how its field education programme provides orientation, field instruction training, and continuing dialogue with field education settings and field instructors. The school supports provision of orientation for fieldwork supervisors or instructors.
12	The programme describes how its field education programme develops policies regarding field placements in an organisation in which the student is also employed. To ensure the role of student as learner, student assignments and field education supervision are not the same as those of the student's employment.

(Continued)

Table 11.1 Continued

13	The programme describes the specific and continuous efforts it makes to provide a learning environment that models affirmation and respect for diversity and difference.
14	The programme explains how these efforts provide a supportive and inclusive learning environment.
15	The programme describes specific plans to continually improve the learning environment to affirm and support persons with diverse identities.
16	The programme identifies the field education director. The programme describes the field director's ability to provide leadership in the field education programme through practice experience, field instruction experience, and administrative and other relevant academic and professional activities in social work. The programme describes the procedures for calculating the field director's assigned time to provide educational and administrative leadership for field education. To carry out the administrative functions of the field education programme, at least 50% assigned time is required for master's programmes. The programme demonstrates how this time is sufficient.
17	The programme describes its administrative structure for field education and explains how its resources (personnel, time, and technological support) are sufficient to administer its field education programme to meet its mission and goals. The programme ensures that adequate and appropriate resources are available to meet the needs of the fieldwork component of the programme.
18	The programme presents its plan for ongoing assessment of student outcomes in the generalist and specialised levels of practice (master's social work programmes). Assessment of competence is done by programme-designated faculty or field personnel. The plan includes a description of the assessment procedures that detail when, where, and how each competency is assessed for each programme option. At least two measures assess each competency. One of the assessment measures is based on demonstration of the competency in real or simulated practice situations. Benchmarks for each competency, a rationale for each benchmark, and a description of how it is determined that a student's performance meets the benchmark. An explanation of how the programme determines the percentage of students achieving the benchmark. Copies of all assessment measures used to assess all identified competencies.
19	The programme involves service users in the planning and delivery of programmes.
20	Fieldwork supervisors or instructors are included in curriculum development.
21	The educational institution, the agency, and service users promote a partnership in decision-making regarding field education and the evaluation of a student's fieldwork performance.
22	The students as well as field instructors and supervisors are provided with a field instruction manual that details its fieldwork standards, procedures, assessment standards/criteria, and expectations.

Source: Author

part of the preparation process for students for entry into the social work profession and allows them to develop a range of intervention techniques and strategies suitable for use in diverse practice settings, with a variety of cultural, ethnic, and racial groups.

Criteria#1

The practice component is accomplished through two formats: (1) Practice assignments that are built in the core and specialised courses. Courses require assignments that can be done only by using real practice cases from field placements; (2) Independent practice component in which social work practice courses are offered to students.

Criteria#2

Practice assignments that are built in the core and specialised courses are focused on topics that are implied in proposed courses. On the other hand, the practice component itself is comprised of four practice courses. It is different from international social work programmes, where mostly practice placement is an independent practice component and it does not include practice seminars that are provided at university classrooms.

At the Social Work Programme at Ilia State University, practice courses are practice seminars that are provided to students in parallel with practice placements. During the two years of study, a student undergoes two different practice placements. The practice placements are in six different directions. These directions are: (1) Child Protection Services (Social Service Agency, SOS Children's Village, Caritas–Georgia, Foundation – Youth House, Child and Environment, etc.); (2) Penitentiary System (National Probation Agency, The Georgian Center for Psychosocial and Medical Rehabilitation of Torture Victims (GCRT), Rehabilitative Initiative for Vulnerable Groups, etc.); (3) Human Rights: cultural, religious and etc. victims of violence (Georgian Association of Social Workers, Anti Violence Network Georgia, Civic Development Agency, Partnership for Human Rights – PHR, The State Fund for Protection and Assistance of (statutory) Victims of Human Trafficking is a Legal Entity of Public Law (LEPL), Women Initiative Support Group, etc.); (4) Mental Health, Addiction, Alcohol use (Center for Information for Information and Counseling on Reproductive Health, ISU Mental Health Resource Center, ISU Center of Addiction, GIP – Global Initiative on Psychiatry – Tbilisi Office, etc.); (5) Disability, Developmental Problems (Child Development Institute (ISU), The First Step, Social Therapy House; School Social Work (Buckswood International School, Tbilisi Free Waldorf School, Orbeliani Georgia, etc.); (6) Homelessness, poverty, unemployment (Tbilisi Shelter-Lilo, Georgian Library Association, etc.). In total, there are about 30 organisations. All the abovementioned state and non-governmental agencies signed the memorandum of understandings with the university that covers details of practice teaching and learning, the agencies' and university's responsibilities towards practice teaching. There are no fees to be paid by the students or university. All students are obliged to undergo practice placements and there is no recognition of prior learning. In fact, prior learning of the prospective student is one of the selection criteria for enrollment in the MSW programme (Master of Social Work Programme, 2019).

The first year (two semesters) students undergo one practice placement, and in the second year of study, students are supposed to undergo a different practice placement. The main idea is to spend a longer time with the service agency so she/he can gain a better and deeper understanding and expertise in working with the specific vulnerable populations.

In addition to practice placements (118 academic hours per semester), students undergo practice seminars. Each practice seminar is 32 academic hours per semester. The first practice course named 'Social Work Practice Seminar 1' is a general practice course, taught in the first semester and aims to develop students' practice skills in real contexts in direct contact with individuals. The second semester students are obliged to take the second practice course named practice Social Work Practice Seminar 2 'Homelessness, social housing and poverty'. In this course students are given theories and methods that are concentrated on homelessness. In addition, they continue their practice work that is focused on working with individuals and their families. Emphasis in the first year of fieldwork is placed upon developing appropriate foundation social work practice skills and knowledge (Master of Social Work Programme, 2019).

Social Work Practice Seminar Three 'Children Rights, Harm Reduction and Reproductive Health' is concentrated on issues of addiction, reproductive health, and harm reduction. The student starts her/his second practice placement. Social Work Practice seminar 4 'Violence in the family: justice and social perspective' is concentrated on issues of gender-based violence, women issues, and domestic violence. During the second year, the student is expected to develop increased insight in and depth of understanding of agency and/or client systems and social work practice skills via exposure to a variety of experiences. Another area of emphasis is the students' ability to develop diagnostic, leadership, and administrative skills, as well as increase their competency of their foundation practice skills.

Criteria#3, #4, #5, #7

The focus of the first-year field practicum (so-called Foundation Year) is to provide the students with generalist social work practice/hands-on skills. In the foundation year, students are placed in an identified social work agency which has met the MSW programme placement requirements (see below Criteria #8–#17, #22).

In general, students' placements are based on faculty assessment of prior experience and entry-level learning needs. In order for the field staff to ensure the most appropriate field placement for students, students are asked to fill out a Foundation-Year Field Application and attend a pre-placement field interview at the beginning of the practice programme. The students are provided with the field manual that has all the information about field teaching and agencies that are included in the programme. A student selects an agency from the list of agencies (agencies that signed the Memorandum of Understanding with Ilia State University) and then prepares for the pre-placement field interview. If she/he is not selected by the agency and pre-placement interview is not successful, then the other agency is chosen and the student undergoes the same procedures until she/he is placed in an agency. In addition to the field practicum placement, students participate in a field seminar that offers support, offers feedback, and input from peers regarding challenges, positive and negative situations, etc. occurring in their field settings. (The specific schedule is determined at the beginning of each academic year).

In the first semester students initiate their assignments by becoming oriented with the agency placement. Students initially observe professionals in practice and later in the semester may begin to carry caseloads, case assignments, and participate in client, agency, and community activities. If students are assigned caseloads, they are expected to carry and manage them with the guidance of the field instructor. The first-year placement focuses on generalist social work practice skills (Master of Social Work Programme, 2019).

In the Advanced Year of Field Education, students continue to build upon the micro and macro knowledge and skills gained during the Foundation Year, and through advanced coursework, continue to expand their application of new skills in micro, macro, and mezzo settings. Some of these advanced practice skills consist of increased self-analysis and reflection, autonomy, constructive utilisation of supervision, management of more complex caseload assignments, and legal and ethical issues. In the Advanced Year of Field Education

students have more input on their selection of a placement site. The focus of the advanced-year field practicum is to provide the student with more advanced social work practice/hands-on skills. The focus of this concentration year encompasses helping the student develop more advanced interventions and strategies that will help them work more effectively with all populations.

Criteria #6

The students are supposed to take 6 ECTS credits of fieldwork in each semester, which equals 118 hours in the field and 32 hours at the university classrooms – at the social work practice seminars. The 118 hours of filed placement are distributed in the following manner:

Table 11.2 Distribution of filed hours per semester

Topic	Hours
Supervision	14
Practice assignment	78
Practice recordings	13
Seminars, trainings, conference, multidisciplinary meetings, other activities	13
Total	118

Source: Authors

Table 11.3 32 hours of university classroom field seminar conducted by a Practice Coordinator

Topic	Hours
Active participation in discussions, role plays, and class practice assignments	26
Midterm e-portfolio	2
Social project	2
Final e-portfolio	2
Total	32

Source: Author

In total, students are required to get 24 credits (600 hours). During the two years of study, a student undergoes two different practice placements (two semesters for each placement). The main idea is to spend longer time with the service agency so she/he can gain a better and deeper understanding and expertise in working with the specific vulnerable populations.

Criteria #8–#17, #22

The selection of agencies for field education is an important part of the Master of Social Work Programme. It is the responsibility of the Director of Master of Social Work Programme (Practice Coordinator) to determine an agency's suitability for student training and to work closely with interested agencies in this process. The Practice Coordinator is responsible for the creation, revision, and all forms of the Field Manual.

Potential field education sites may be identified in a number of ways. Agencies may request students or may be suggested by a student, faculty member, alumnus, or community representative. An agency assessment is conducted by the Director of Master of Social Work Programme. There is no paid position for the Director of Field Education, Field Liaison, or Field Education Coordinator. The evaluation of agencies covers topics such as: the function and service of the agency; possible student assignments and availability of resources for the student; level of practice competence; and special requirements for student placement. The agency is also provided information pertaining to curriculum, field requirements, and expectations regarding assignments, supervision, and evaluation.

The following general criteria are used in selection of agencies:

1. The agency's philosophy, goals, programmes, and policies are compatible with professional social work standards and the agency practices are consistent with the GASW (Georgian Association of Social Workers) Code of Ethics.
2. The agency maintains a working and learning environment free from discrimination and harassment of students and employees.
3. The agency is in good standing in the community.
4. The agency is large enough to maintain and develop its basic programme without reliance on students.
5. The agency's training programme must be compatible with the MSW programme's educational objectives.
6. There should be a correlation between the agency and the programme's practice perspective so as to provide an integrated class/field curriculum and a consistent learning experience for the student.
7. The agency is committed to the field instruction programme, its goals and objectives, and due process protection of the student.
8. The agency will support staff time availability for effective supervision and professional learning, including participation in the MSW programme's orientation, field instruction training, and field coordinator's (Master of Social Work Programme Director) visits. It is expected that students receive a minimum of one (1) hour of weekly supervision for foundation and concentration-year students.
9. The agency should provide a range of practice assignments on an ongoing basis that are appropriate to the student's educational needs. The student work load should reflect opportunity for involvement in varying modalities of service as well as exposure to diverse populations.
10. The agency must provide the necessary space and facilities, including privacy for interviewing.

The following criteria are used in the selection of field instructors:

1. Field instructors must hold an MSW degree from an accredited programme of social work or related programmes such as Psychology, Sociology, Health, Mental Health, etc.
2. Field instructors must be committed to the teaching function of social work field education.
3. Field instructors must have an interest in, and time to fulfil, the responsibility of teaching social work students.

In fact, there are not enough qualified field instructors who are motivated to supervise students. Generally, field instructors think that this is 'a waste of their time'; they do not see any benefit of being a field instructor. All prospective field instructors must complete: A Field Instructor information form; A résumé which includes education and work experience; Field Instructor orientation/training (at beginning of academic year).

    The director of the MSW programme (Practice Coordinator) reviews this information in order to ensure that all selected field instructors meet the selection requirements listed above. The geographic location of field placements encompasses the regions closer to Tbilisi, the capital of Georgia. Each student is placed at two different agencies (private, non-profit, or public) during their two-year programme.

Students who are working in the same agency where they have internships must submit assignments. However, they are not required to change the agency.

The Practice Coordinator is responsible for site visits once a semester to assess students' performance and meet the field instructors.

Criteria #18, 21

At the beginning of the field placements a student, a Practice Coordinator (course teacher/the director of the MSW programme) and a field instructor at a practice placement elaborate an educational plan, which includes practice assignments that are assigned to the student during the semester. At the end of the semester the student is assessed by both the field instructor (10% of assessment) by using a special practice assessment form and practice coordinator/course teacher (90%). The Practice Coordinator who is a practice seminar course leader at the same time provides student's assessment based on students' mid-semester and final assignments. The student presents her/his e-portfolio of practice work as middle and final assessment. E-portfolios should include the following sections: Practice Journal (Self-Reflection Diary), Process Recordings, Bio-Psycho-Social Assessments, and an attendance form signed by their field instructors. All assignments are designed to measure students' by the following fundamental social work competencies:

Competency 1: Demonstrate Ethical and Professional Behaviour
Competency 2: Engage Diversity and Difference in Practice
Competency 3: Advance Human Rights and Social, Economic, and Environmental Justice
Competency 4: Engage In Practice-informed Research and Research-informed Practice
Competency 5: Engage in Policy Practice
Competency 6: Engage with Individuals, Families, Groups, Organisations, and Communities
Competency 7: Assess Individuals, Families, Groups, Organisations, and Communities
Competency 8: Intervene with Individuals, Families, Groups, Organisations, and Communities
Competency 9: Evaluate Practice with Individuals, Families, Groups, Organisations, and Communities

Criteria #19

The students are also required at the second, third, and fourth semesters to submit a social project/initiative activity that is concentrated on the specific topics of the social work practice seminars: Homelessness, Children's Rights, Harm Reduction, Reproductive Health, Family Violence. These social projects serve to accomplish the third mission of the university, which is to engage with society and address growing socioeconomic challenges. In addition, students involve service users in their assignments e.g., specific social projects involved co-teaching with service users.

Criteria #20

field instructors are involved in some aspects of curriculum development, in particular, development of practice assignments.

Conclusions

Field education is the 'signature pedagogy' for social work programmes. Thus, it's highly important to develop field education for academic social work programmes according to international standards. Especially, this is true for the former Soviet Union countries with no prior history of social work education. The present study analysed the current status of field education of the Master of Social Work Programme at Ilia State University, Georgia, the former Soviet Union country in accordance with the international standards such as the Global Standards for Social Work Education and Training and the Educational Policy and Accreditation Standards.

It is revealed that there are several challenges for the developing of field education within the social work programmes. In fact, field education is not systematised as expected from an accredited social work programme. In particular, practice placements are lacking qualified supervisors (field instructors) who have relevant education as required by international regulations.

Consequently, field instructors do not have relevant SW qualifications to supervise students' practice. In order to minimise this latter factor, a compensation mechanism is in place. In particular, students are required to be enrolled in the practice seminars of 32 hours in parallel to their practice placements. Practice seminars are taught by the Master of Social Work Programme Director who also provides additional supervision for students. At the practice seminars students discuss their practice cases in the classroom through social work practice e-portfolios. Field educators participate in student's assessment only on a minimal level (10%). There is no separate field education department which will recruit and monitor all social work agencies participating in practice teaching.

The Master of Social Work Programme Director is obliged to be responsible for organising practice activities. This is an additional responsibility that is not paid by the university separately. It complicates provision of many responsibilities such as meetings and practice orientations for field instructors on a regular basis. There is a high need for a well-organised university field education department with qualified field liaisons and a university-based practice coordinator in charge of organising and monitoring field education. It is also very noticeable that field instructors are not motivated enough and the university does not put any effort towards increasing their motivation by different possible methods (hiring field instructors, providing minimal incentives, and so on).

Another important issue is regulation of practice teaching by imposing a minimum number of practice teaching hours for social work study programmes. As was mentioned, the practice hours at Ilia State University are not relevant to the international standards for MSW programmes (600 hours instead of 900) and this criterion is not regulated by the revised National Qualifications Framework and Classifiers of Fields of Study. This is a critical issue in terms of compromising graduates ability to find work internationally, especially in the United States where MSW is a terminal degree for social work practice. However, the European standards of social work education do not specify the number of hours for field placement either. Moreover, the new document 'Sector Benchmark for Social work: Levels VI and VII' of Georgia that was developed with the support of European colleagues from Estonia and Germany with the mission of assisting Georgia's higher educational system and social work development in particular, only highlighted the importance of social work supervised professional practices and field placements for social work study programmes. This unclear notion could even worsen the existing situation as new schools of social work will follow the standard and may not include field education at all.

In fact, there is no agreement between different European schools of social work regarding the status of the profession in general. As indicated by some European authors, the status of social work can be described as poor and struggling for acknowledgement (Sommerfeld, 2014, Erath and Littlechild, 2010). Despite the different approaches of the European nations towards social work nothing has considerably contributed to an improvement of the status of social work on the continent (Erath and Littlechild, 2010).

For instance, in Germany, Austria, and Switzerland, social work does not have a strong position as a science nor as a practice while in the United Kingdom and France social work is merely understood as a practice and in the Czech Republic and Slovakia, social work is only seen as a science (Erath and Littlechild, 2010). Thus, it is not surprising that there are no clear standards for social work practice and it differs country by country. In fact, history shows that social work practice developed disparately in separate countries and is idiosyncratic to the cultures in those separate countries (Penna et al., 2000). Georgia as a country which is in the process of becoming a close neighbour of Europe and willing to become a member of the EU, gives more credentials to the European experts rather than local requirements and needs which will result in an imbalanced development of social work (Sadzaglishvili, 2017a).

The positive side of practice teaching at Ilia State University is its innovative idea of providing social projects by students that are accomplished at social work practice seminar classes. Through social projects the students are involved in service-learning activities. Service learning itself is an educational strategy which has been successfully developed at many European universities. Service learning has a rich history and there are many examples and documented benefits of its implementation in the education of social workers. Thanks to it, universities fulfil their basic mission in a complex way and prepare a new generation of social workers able to integrate academic qualities, social responsibility, and civic engagement. Moreover, the service-learning component is increasing the importance of practice teaching and visibility of field education among the faculty and university administration. Through service-learning, clients/beneficiaries participate as co-teachers and co-researchers in social work classes. All of these are directly connected to the third mission of the university, which is fulfilling its function of social responsibility by enhancing civic engagement of students. For this purpose, it is planned to use service learning as concurrent practice for the other social work courses as well.

References

Ashley, W., Decker, J. T, Sadzaglishvili, Sh., & Priebe, N. (2017). Enhancing the science of social work and expanding social work research in transitional Countries. *Journal of Sociology and Social Work*, ISSN: 2333-5807 (Print), 2333-5815 (Online), 5(2), 20–28, DOI: 10.15640/jssw.v5n2a3. URL: http://dx.doi.org/10.15640/jssw.v5n2a3.

Bogo, M., & Wayne, J. (2013). The implicit curriculum in social work education: The culture of human interchange. *Journal of Teaching in Social Work*, 33(1), 2–14, DOI: 10.1080/08841233.2012.746951

Council on Social Work Education. (2015). Educational policy and accreditation standards (EPAS) for baccalaureate and master's social work programs. Retrieved January 2020, http://www.socialservicewo rkforce.org/system/files/resource/files/Accredidation%20Standards.pdf

Erath, P., & Littlechild, B. (Eds.). (2010) *Social work across Europe. Accounts from 16 countries*. Ostrava: ERIS with Albert.

Global Standards for Social Work Education and Training. (2019). Retrieved January 2020, from The International Federation of Social Workers (IFSW) and the International Association of Schools of Social Work (IASSW): https://www.iassw-aiets.org/global-standards-for-social-work-education-and-training/

Master of Social Work Program, Ilia State University, Tbilisi. (2019). *Fieldwork manual*. Tbilisi: Ilia State University Printing Press.

Namicheishvili, S. (2014). Effects and impacts of research on participants. In *Summer school: MA in advanced development in social work (advances)*. Paris, France: University Paris Ouest La Defense Nanterre, July 2014.

National Center for Educational Quality Enhancement. (2019). *The national qualifications framework and learning fields classifier*. Retrieved January 2020: https://eqe.ge/eng/parent/787

Partskhaladze, N. (2014). *History of social work in Georgia*. New York: Unpublished Internal Document for Open Society Foundations.

Partskhalaladze, N., Sadzaglishvili, Sh., & Gigineishvili, K. (2020). Role of the Georgian association of social workers in supporting the Covid-19 response in Georgia. *Scottish Journal of Residential Child Care SJRCC Special Feature: Reflections on COVID-19*. ISSN 1478-1840, CELCIS.ORG.

Penna, S., Paylor, I., & Washington J. (2000). Globalization, social exclusion and the possibilities for global social work and welfare. *European Journal of Social Work, 3*, 109–122, DOI: 10.1080/714052818

Sadzaglishvili, Sh. (2017a). The current status of social work science and research: A review of the literature and its implications for post-communist countries. *International Journal of Social Work*, ISSN 2332-7278, 4(1), 22–38 . DOI: 10.5296/v4i1.11157

Sadzaglishvili, S. (2017b). Reconstructing social welfare institutions and building a professional social work workforce in post-Soviet Georgia: An ecological systems framework. *International Social Work, 61*(6), 1198–1208. DOI: 10.1177/0020872816674790

Shatebrashvili, N., Sadzaglishvili, Sh., Gotsiridze, T., Demetreashvili, N., Namicheishvili, S, & Cherkezishvili, E. (2012). *Child rights situation analysis of children at risk of losing parental care and children who have lost parental care*. Report, Georgia: SOS Children's Village.

Sommerfeld, P. (2014). Social work as an action science: A perspective from Europe. *Research on Social Work Practice, 24*, 586–600. https://doi.org/10.1177/1049731514538523

12
Field Work as a 'Crucible of Practice' in the Pursuit of Social Justice and Defence of Human Rights

The Philippine Context

Gil 'Jake' I. Espenido

The social work profession in the Philippines requires a four-year Bachelor of Science course. Field instruction was institutionalised with the Republic Act no. 4373 of 1965. This law required the completion of a minimum period of one thousand hours of practical training under the direct supervision of fully trained and qualified social workers before a student can take the social work board examinations and become a registered social worker. Thus, the four-year Bachelor of Science in Social Work course incorporates in its curriculum 1000 hours of field work practicum in the different social work practice areas – casework, groupwork, and community organising. To give focus, the field work practicum is done separately at different times. Often, the students stay and live in their respective field work areas, immersing themselves in actual practice. The only difference is that they still go back to school to process their experiences with their teachers and classmates. Field supervisors are assigned to each student.

The field instruction programme in a social work course is one of the most anticipated practice subjects before graduation. For most senior social work students, responses vary; for some it can be the most feared part of their education, for others excitement to put into practice their knowledge and develop their core competencies. The transition from classroom setting to the field instruction programme naturally creates tensions. It triggers anxiety that comes from the fear of the unknown. It pushes students to question or doubt their capacity to engage in such a pedagogical practice. For some, the fear of non-completion is rooted in their personal constraints like non-adaptability to live with non-relatives or individuals they have just met, resistance to leave their closeted life and comfort zones, unresolved insecurities and issues that lead to many forms of rationalisation. On the other hand, it might be the opposite.

Fundamentally, the field instruction programme is the umbilical cord that binds classroom learned theories to the lives of the ordinary Filipino people. Social work students are expected to create their own practice together with the service users during the field instruction. Using this wide array of theories, they are expected to consciously make use of these theories to guide their field instruction practice. And based on the practice, the field work students can engage in a new level of theorising where their previous grasp of the theories is further deepened and appreciated.

Beyond the compliance with the academic requirements for the social work students to graduate, field instruction serves as an arena to learn and establish one's unique brand of practice. Therefore, it is crucial for universities and colleges to ensure that the selection of agency and community partners presents opportunities aligned to the overall goals and objectives of the academic curriculum, putting forward the dire need for critical social work practice. Our academic curriculum makes us partner with non-government organisations, local government units (LGUs), or people's organisations. Through these partnerships, the field work students are presented with opportunities that bring out the core belief and function of social work going beyond the traditional problem-solving but towards deliberate pursuance of social justice and human rights.

Field instruction is an opportunity to remould and temper oneself for the sole purpose of cultivating love for the people and making one selfless in the realisation of people's tactical and strategic interests. From our experience, partnering with apolitical non-government organisations and local government units (which exhibits reactionary traits at its various levels of programmes and services) at the onset can be a big hindering factor in cultivating critical consciousness. On the other hand, fielding critically minded field work students in these institutions can uncover the different modes of cooptation employed and systematically practised by these partners using well-funded programmes and services.

Furthermore, we should start and sustain partnership with people's organisations that are doing political organising, conducting educational activities with progressive and radical contents, and engaging in tactical battles to defend their rights and assert their strategic interests amidst the massive poverty brought about by the neoliberal policies implemented since the 1970s. Under President Duterte's 'war on drugs' and 'war against terrorism', these neoliberal policies have swept the human rights discourse and advocacy under the rag.

Of utmost importance is the concept of commitment. This can neither be taught or demanded. Commitment is steeled in practice together with the people. It comes from a relatively higher level of political consciousness and continuous integration with the people amidst their poverty and struggle. The resolve to act on these problems comes after. These field work practices provide the conditions to deepen the commitment of the social work students to serve the people.

The success in cultivating and deepening the commitment of the field work students hinges on the premise that both the faculty adviser and the partner organisation/agency supervisor are in sync. Accordingly, it is imperative for the academic institution to ensure that all its faculty supervisors for the field work practice are convinced and committed to pursue social justice and human rights whatever may be the risks involved. Field work instruction is one effective way of shattering the university as a comfort zone for the faculty. Moreover, the academic institution should also be conscious of partnering with institutions whose mandates and personnel/staff are truly promoting people's empowerment within the ambit of building a genuine people's movement and resistance.

At the end of the field instruction programme, most of the students would claim that such practice has qualitatively changed them and made them better future social work practitioners. Social work students also regard the field experience as the most critical time in their professional preparation (Havig, 2010, citing Mallick, 2007).

Social Justice and Human Rights as Ideological Moorings of Social Work

Social work field work in the Philippines as a 'crucible of practice' in the pursuit for social justice and defence of human rights, firmly stands on the ideological moorings of global social work practice.

Social justice and human rights are central to the social work course, profession, and practice. The 2014 International Federation of Social Work (IFSW) definition of social work states that

> it is a practice-based profession and an academic discipline that promotes social change and development, social cohesion, and the empowerment and liberation of people. Principles of social justice, human rights, collective responsibility and respect for diversities are central to Social Work. Underpinned by theories of Social Work, social sciences, humanities and indigenous knowledge, social work engages people and structures to address life challenges and enhance well-being. The Social Work profession promotes social change, problem solving in human relationships and the empowerment and liberation of people to enhance well-being.
>
> *(IFSW, 2014)*

Social work is the only helping profession that has a rich history of social justice as its fundamental value and concern (Lundy, 2011).

Earlier in 1988, the International Federation of Social Workers declared that historically social work has been a human rights profession.

> The profession's focus on human needs shapes its conviction that the fundamental nature of these needs requires that they be met not as a matter of choice but as an imperative of basic justice ... Thus, social work moves to a consideration of human rights as the other organizational principle for its professional practice...The transition from needs orientation to rights affirmation has been made necessary because of tangible substantive needs that have to be met...A substantive need can be translated into an equivalent positive right, and entitlement to the benefits of that right is sought from the State and beyond
>
> *(UNCHR, 1994).*

> Social workers by their very positions and commitment are human rights workers, advocating for individual and collective rights everyday ... Human rights are intrinsic to social work and these rights are closely connected to economic, political environmental, and social forces
>
> *(Lundy, 2011).*

The Locus of Field Instruction in Social Work Education

Field instruction in social work education reinforces the role of the academe in serving the people, especially in pursuit of social justice and human rights.

The relationship between university and society is dialectical, one of dynamic interaction (Nemenzo, 1977). Since the university must adapt to the resources and capabilities and constructively respond to the needs of society, it must necessarily reflect the character of that society in its instructional programmes; but on the other hand, the university, as a reservoir of creative energy, also has the latent power to transform society that shaped it (Nemenzo, 1977). The highest contribution a university can offer to the national community is precisely to actualise this transformative power without debasing itself into a handmaiden of state and corporate bureaucracies (Nemenzo, 1977).

> The scholarship of engagement is about connecting the rich resources of the university to our most pressing social, civic, and ethical problems … What is also needed is not just more programs, but a larger purpose, a larger sense of mission, a larger clarity of direction in the nation's life.
>
> *(Brackmann, 2015, citing Boyer, 1996)*

Among the colleges of the University of the Philippines (UP) System, the College of Social Work and Community Development (CSWCD) stands unique as having an academic life closely immersed in the lives of the ordinary and struggling people, closely combining theory and practice and integrating them into the value system and standpoints of the students, especially the fieldwork students. Fieldwork likewise enriches social work education in its teaching content and spirit, research advocacies, and extension opportunities.

Accordingly, the Department of Social Work (DSW) of the CSWCD conducted an undergraduate curriculum revision in 2018. It institutionalised four new courses. Among them was Social Work 110 (Critical Social Work). SW 110 is designed to teach students that social work is not a neutral profession and it can both function as an apologist to the ruling class or be a liberating profession with the people. Not to be a doomed profession is to emphasise and rebut the exploitative and oppressive system. To be a liberating profession and become more relevant to the 'needs of the times', it must pursue a transformative practice. This becomes one of the foundations of the students' journey of field instruction.

With the intent of trailblazing the practice of transformative social work in the country, it is incumbent on those who finish SW 110 to eventually use their classroom-based learned theories in the field while doing their field work.

The objectives of field instruction in the undergraduate level are directly related to the general objective of the Bachelor of Science in Social Work (BSSW) curriculum. In more specific terms, the teaching-learning experience in field instruction should help the students (Department of Social Work, 2008):

- Identify, relate and apply relevant theory to practice, as well as consider possible theory development from practice.
- Develop a critical awareness of Philippine reality from exposure to existing economic, political and socio-cultural reality situations.
- Develop commitment to the people served (individuals, groups, communities) and to the creation of a just society.
- Develop beginning skills in social work practice with all types of clientele – individuals, groups, families, and communities.
- Acquire specific skills and techniques essential to all social work practices, e.g., communication, interaction, diagnostic intervention, and documentation skills.
- Develop identification with the social work profession.
- Prepare a community profile/case study reflecting adequate knowledge of the community, i.e., demographic characteristics, economic and political structures socio-cultural values and practices.
- Understand the power structure in the community in order to identify and develop leaders.
- Enable community residents to express/identify common needs/problems.

- Stimulate people with the same needs/problems/issues to unite, plan and act together and then reflect/evaluate on the actions they have undertaken related to these needs and problems.
- Document the problem-solving process, focusing on significant learning points on the experience in relation to the objectives of the fieldwork.

The Awakening of Fieldwork Students on Socio-political Realities

Fieldwork is just part of the whole educational journey of the social work student. Like other schools offering social work courses, CSWCD, particularly the DSW, promotes an integrated model in its field education.

Even before the field instruction placement, students already engage in various exposure and immersion activities designed to give life to their theoretical studies. Although the students immerse themselves in the field and in the lives, problems, and needs of the people and communities where they are placed, they continue their active role in the university as part of the studentry. In a way, their fieldwork experiences sharpen their own views on the issues of their own sector and how the student sector relates with society.

Social work students vary according to the community, sector, and organisation they are placed in, the type of services provided more specifically their programmes, projects, and activities, and their organisational culture.

For the casework and groupwork practicum, CSWCD's current model is primarily agency-based and focused on service delivery. As an agency-based model, field education primarily occurs in agencies that provide individualised and group-based services, through programmes, projects, and activities (PPAs). These PPAs are often directed towards specific client individuals and/or their families, and or by particular clusters of people, i.e., the elderly, youth, and persons with disabilities (PWDs). Services are very focused on the psycho-social interventions or simple provision of material needs.

Given the agency-based model, it is assumed that problems can be effectively addressed through programmes and services (Preston, George, & Silver, 2013, citing Baines, 2004). Hence, the latter within this model become an end in themselves, and not as a means toward social transformation (Preston, George, & Silver, 2013, citing Fisher & Shragge, 2000; Leighninger, 1999; Mullay, 2001; Razack, 2002). Programmes are more on livelihood, income generation, capacity-building, training on courses like cooking, gardening, etc. There are hardly any discussions on the what, why, and how of their poverty and abject situation. Even if they are organised, it is along specific livelihood and market possibilities. There is an acceptance of oppression and exclusion. What is being taught is how to best adapt to the situation, and not question, root out, and change the status quo.

This approach to field education tends to decontextualise and depoliticise practice, ignoring historical relations of power and processes of marginalisation (Preston, George, and Silver, 2013). Depoliticisation is when the political content and consideration of any problem, individual, phenomenon, and process is being glossed over, hidden, and even robbed. This is in sharp contrast to the critical social work perspective students get exposed to in the classroom (Preston, George, and Silver, 2013). Within this context, field education prepares students for depoliticised practice (Preston, George, and Silver, 2013).

Students feel the disconnect of their theoretical foundations and actual societal conditions.

After imbibing critical social work perspectives in the classroom, students come face-to-face with depoliticised social work practice, where apart from having a very individualised outlook detached from socioeconomic and cultural relations and structures, people are viewed from a disempowered position, highlighting their powerlessness and helplessness on the situation. The causes often cited for their abject poverty is destiny, laziness, and lack of opportunity. Hence, the solutions provided are livelihood programmes, skills development, and psycho-social counselling. Nothing on community or sector organising that questions power relations, policies, and the whole socioeconomic/-political/-cultural roots of the problem.

Tension is felt when there is a disconnect between what is taught in class and what the students are doing in their field work. Some of my former students under previous undergraduate programmes felt frustrated and shortchanged when what they were required by putting into motion the processes and parameters of the mainstream social work practice. In the classroom discussions earlier, akin to what Bernasconi (2016) earlier asserted, they have come to realise that

> the mainstream of social work, especially the one embedded in state welfare organisations, has only one answer to the suffering and problems of the described individuals and groups, namely control and repression according to a top-down mono-mandate of help as control.

Moreover, these students are also convinced that mainstream social work perceives individuals from a deficit stance, requiring service to help them adapt to the norms and practices of society. Furthermore, they fully understood that mainstream social work tends to view social problems in a depoliticised way that emphasises individual shortcomings, pathology, and inadequacy (Campbell & Baikie, 2012). Practically all interventions are aimed largely at the individual with little or no analysis or intent to challenge power, structures, social relations, culture, and economic forces (Campbell & Baikie, 2012).

As the students encounter individuals, groups, and communities in the mainstream depoliticised social work practice, the students recognise that their presence is by itself a political act because then they realise their role in how to become better and more effective change agents – being part of the forces of change or the forces of reaction. Again, tensions occur. The students appreciate that social work and field practice is simply neither an academic nor a neutral activity. As per Baines (2001), 'Social Work, together with its field practicum courses is a contested and highly politicized practice'. Realities on the ground awaken the fieldwork students and make them question the services and limitations of their partner agencies.

Field Instruction as the Crucible of Practice of Future Social Workers

Student evaluation and supervisor assessment plus feedback from the agency and community synthesise and put into context the fieldwork experience. Since this is based on actual practice, this assessment is a validation of some assumptions of a guide to teaching social justice for social work.

The students come face-to-face with people and their relations, with the different structures of society, the various relations and structures of oppression and exploitation, and the machinations of these structures. As the students immerse themselves, they get to question things, even their own belief systems, get to know themselves better and define their standpoints and social work practice.

Both the agency and the community become the crucible of practice because it is where these relationships unfold. As these relationships are sustained, class relations and class contradictions can easily be understood through the various forms of exploitation and oppression that are part of the daily lives of the people. This is where social workers 'face the human result of all the contradictions and inefficiencies of a neo-colonial and semi-feudal society as well as the sheer pain and suffering that is part of life' (Lundy, 2011, citing Withorn, 1984).

The Role of Theory

The sole purpose of theory is to guide the practice. In the field, there is theory to inform and theory to intervene (Collingwood, 2005). Certainly, there are theories that can help the students to make a relatively comprehensive assessment and theories that guide the students on what is the most appropriate form of intervention after making the assessment. Moreover, field work students will be making assumptions about a range of factors (the nature and causes of human behaviour; how society works; the nature and causes of social problems; how best to communicate; how to recognise emotional reactions) and so on (Thompson, 2010).

A good theory carries with it some good description (Thompson, 2010). It points to a way of life; is socially relevant; optimistic and affirms the possibility of social betterment; increases our political awareness; adds to our understanding of the particular obstacles that impede human development and underscores inclusive and participatory community life; and lastly, contributes to the empowerment of all of society's members.

Applying theory to practice is not a one-way approach. In reality, it is better to see the relationship between theory and practice as a two-way street, in the sense that history should inform practice, but practice should also inform and test theory (Thompson, 2010). This is the theorising part since the practice provides the conditions to further clarify, enrich, and fully appreciate theory, or on the other hand, debunk the theory. The prerequisite for this is doing an assessment of the practice. Consultations between the faculty supervisor and the student should be essentially an assessment of the breadth and depth of practice of the student. In this way, the grasp on the theory is qualitatively raised to a new level leading to the development of new knowledge. Consultations are more productive with assessments rather than consultations alone.

The generalist practice of social work has the inherent character of bringing within the social work practice the phenomenon of eclecticism. Eclecticism is often used as a catch-all to refer to an uncritical approach to theory that just takes often unconnected concepts and muddles them together. To avoid this is to pursue critical reflective practice. This involves drawing on theoretical insights from a wide range of sources but having the ability to integrate them into a meaningful whole that makes sense in relation to the particular practice scenario. This reflects the aspect of reflective practice epitomised by the notion of a knowledge base to produce a closely tailored solution to the practice challenge being faced, rather than looking for a ready-made, off-the-peg solution (Thompson, 2010).

Yet, the 'closely tailored solution to the practice' has also its ideological undertones. Thus, our theorising proceeds from the belief that social work exists to serve people in need (Reynolds, 1946). 'If it serves other classes who have other purposes, it becomes too dishonest to be capable of other theoretical or practical development'. (Reynolds, 1946). This demands that we immediately discard reactionary theories and embrace those of a progressive and even revolutionary nature: for instance, our understanding of the history of human rights movement.

The history of this movement, including the struggle for the right to vote, the right to form a union, women's rights, the right to political self-determination, the right to education, the right to economic development, and the right to a clean environment are part of humankind's history. History is very important for any social worker who identifies as a human rights worker, and it can thus be a central component of social work education (Efi, 2008).

If people are not aware of the historical and contextual nature of human rights and are not aware that human rights become realised only by the struggles of real people experiencing real instances of domination, then human rights are all too easily used as symbolic legitimisers for instruments of that very domination (Stammer, 1999).

Raising Political Consciousness

The discourse and practice of human rights and social justice are basically political.

Field practice is about developing our political sense and sensibility. At first encounter with individuals, groups, and communities, the students should recognise that their presence is by itself a political act because it is assumed that they want to help in tilting the balance of forces between the forces of reaction (represented by the ruling class together with the sophisticated arsenal of the whole government bureaucracy) and the forces for change (the oppressed and exploitation sections of the society).

Accordingly, the field practice is not simply an academic nor a neutral activity. Social work, together with its field practicum courses is a contested and highly politicised practice (Baines, 2011). According to Baines,

> everything is political despite the relatively widespread sentiment that most of everyday life is completely apolitical. For the holders of power, social problems are conventionally understood to be results of individual difficulties and poor decision making rather than unequal distribution of power, resources and affirming identities. They seek solutions by tinkering with the existing social system, applying managerial techniques to most or all social questions, or encouraging individuals to seek medical or psychological interventions for the problems they experience.

As we try to bridge practice and social activism, it is important to ask who benefits from the way things operate at any given point in time, who can help make the changes we want, how we can help ourselves and others see the many ways in which issues are political, and how multiple strands of power are operating in any given scenario (Baines, 2011). At the very core of social work's existence are conflicts amongst competing social political groups, forces, and classes over defining needs and how to interpret and meet them (Baines, 2011).

During the second semester of the academic year 2018–2019, two UP CSWCD-supervised students were placed in a mixed urban community in southern Metro Manila. In this mixed community, dominant groups were the informal settlers, contractual and regular workers, odd-jobbers like ambulant vendors, drivers of passenger jeepneys and tricycles. However, there were also some middle-class subdivisions within the limited land area.

In their integrated paper, they wrote the following narrative (Pascua & Barrameda, 2019):

> Law enforcement officers continue to control and take advantage of civilians, particularly those who belong to the youth, by improperly implementing their City Ordinance on Curfew – having minors brought to the precinct and are asked for monetary compensation. Moreover, matters on extra-judicial killings (EJKs) have been accounted for in the area. The war on drugs becoming a bloodshed of the poor demonstrates how the political situation at the national level is being translated at the local. With the situation being encountered by people, the instance of fear and keeping their voices to a minimum was the initial response. This, then, signifies that the need to engage people in political discussions and make them reflect on their realities (to hopefully heighten their desire to actually move and express their stance on issues) is a priority to be handled in the area.

This assessment is a validation of some assumptions of a guide to teaching social justice for social work. Some of these assumptions are that all forms of oppression are interrelated; we are socialised into oppressive structures; challenging oppression benefits everyone while assigning blame helps no one; enhanced self-awareness allows us to be more effective change agents; and, that we learn most from exploring lived experiences of ourselves and others (Havig, 2010).

Commitment Is a Standpoint

Our standpoint is decidedly pro-people. Our interests as social workers are inextricably linked with the people. In our field practice, we should be able to situate ourselves in relation to the people, not above nor below, not ahead nor at the rear. We are not only for the people but with the people. We believe in people and their invincible strength, once united, to effect social transformation.

As students in practicum having this standpoint, we reject the counter culture and mindset propagated by exploiters, who, to protect their interests, thrive on spreading falsehood (i.e., pathologising the individual's problems), inculcating passivity (heavy reliance on social services) and decadence, and maintaining the backward belief of people. Consequently, we must adopt an outlook of society and the world that is the paragon of truth as opposed to the sophisticated use of deception by the few who need to preserve their power and wealth.

Many formulations of social work are still constructed within an apolitical context, with the assumption that social workers may occupy a full range of ideological positions, or indeed may have no articulated political position at all (Ife, 2008). A human rights perspective rejects this (Ife, 2008). It is about power relations and is therefore inevitably political (Ife, 2008). Further, it to some extent determines what political positions are compatible with social work and it identifies individualism and a pure reliance on the free market as being incompatible with human rights-based practice (Ife, 2008). Human rights workers are political workers, and human rights, in the broad sense, require a political commitment (Ife, 2008). Politics and ideological critique therefore need to be part and parcel of social work practice (Ife, 2008).

As always, experience is the best teacher. Again, the two supervised students had this to share (Pascua & Barrameda, 2019):

> The experienced human rights violations further depict how community members are faced with structural violence wherein legal institutions that enforce marginalization such as laws and programs that essentially renders a neo-colonial status of the country and that legitimizes neoliberalism in the country since the 1970s is felt. The neoliberal policies and anti-humane administration intensify the oppression and exploitation of the marginalized, making them occupied with their survival means – having them silenced and neglecting them the opportunity to take a step back and look at their situation. This punitive system remains an influential part of blurring of truths.
>
> Realizing how facets (directly and indirectly) affect them and allowing them to recognize their capacities to make a difference definitely starts with the discourse of exchanging ideas, experiences, and instances in order for the people to come up with a decision on how to go about the situation. Through this, political movements and mobilizations would truly respond to their needs and issues as their inputs and decisions are discussed among them. In relation to this, a sense of ownership with such goals and projects is felt considering that they are the actual ones who are affected by the problem and are collectively working with one another to come up with the solution.
>
> In such discussions, the manner in analyzing the matters that concern them is already considered a political move as education is not a neutral affair. With such discourse, encouraging the people to see the underlying implications and problems is central to the learning process as the need to look at matters with a critical eye is emphasized. From this aspect

alone, the political nature of the community organizing work is featured. The need to let people realize – through their sharing of main points and insights – that their active role and influence is in the whole picture, is imperative to the tilting of the economic and sociopolitical balance and must be kept at all times to provide the platform of true systemic change.

Creating Sites for Dissent and Spaces for Resistance

The faculty supervisor may be thought of as a model of lived empowerment (Having, 2010, citing Brownstein-Evans, 2006.) Elemental to his discussion of field education as the path to liberation is an understanding of the nature of oppression and of the potential of the oppressed to challenge and dismantle it (Havig, 2010).

> The role of the educator ... is the permanent transformation of the world .... toward the creation, the invention, of a society without injustice .... the social worker uncovers and makes explicit a certain dream about social relations, which is a political dream.
> *(Havig, 2010, citing Freiri, 1970)*

It is about the idea that social work education is about creating vision, asking questions about one another and society, and empowerment for those made powerless by society (Having, 2010). This model is helpful not only in thinking about social work education, but social work practice for transformation and liberation of others (Havig, 2010).

Faculty supervisors should have the sharpest political sense. Understandably, social services settings, constricted by bureaucratic policies and funding sources, hinder critical practice (Preston, George, and Silver, 2014). The faculty supervisor should anticipate that students may model the practices they see in those settings, and supervisors may reinforce this more traditional approach that minimises, denies, discursive influences, and evades the challenge to dominance (Preston, George and Silver, 2014). In effect, students become trained in social service rather being prepared for critical practice (Preston, George and Silver, 2014). This is the reason why the social work curriculum theoretical courses includes Critical Social Work, Philippine Realities, and Development Perspectives. Both faculty and students constantly immerse themselves in communities and issues even before the full semester fieldwork.

To counter the purely social service paradigm, the faculty supervisor, agency supervisor, and the student should transform the field instruction as also training for social work activists. To be an activist means to possess a deep-rooted sense of empathy. The field instruction offers the best opportunity where the faculty supervisor, agency supervisor, and the student can partake in the joy and suffering of the ordinary lives; to listen, to respect, and to be involved in the historical process of the people. In order to develop a genuine concern for the people, an activist must strive to understand the complexities of human interactions. All must understand the mechanics of society and the processes of social change. An activist cannot adopt a simplistic and naïve viewpoint in addressing the issues of the people. We cannot impute social problems to individual failings. There are structural issues that activists need to contend with (Taib, 2006). These assumptions are highlighted in the fundamental premise of assessing the cause of social dysfunction, wherein external factors of lack of opportunities, resources, and other similar external influencers that require to be critically assessed to uproot the core problem that often link to the current political, economic, and social strata existing in the country and not reduce it to failure of the individual to cope and manage one's problems and issues.

However short the field instruction, the experience should help in sowing the seeds of resistance so as to confront the multi-faceted problems of the people. Its relation-based helping process should help in building the 'infrastructure of dissent'.

One way of building this 'infrastructure of dissent' is cultivating again the concept of social cohesion. This proves to be pressing since the neoliberal hegemony has produced individuals whose lives exhibited what they call the 'neoliberal self'. What is now systematically promoted is the individual responsibility rather than collective responsibility. People now find it politically expedient to become an activist without having to be with the people. This is outrightly wrong.

The field instruction can again significantly help along this line.

Conclusion: Creating Liberating Practice with the People at the Community Level

The field instruction has always been a contested practice: tailor-fitting the practicum to the requirements of the traditional social service delivery system or disrupting the well-entrenched apologist orientation and practice and pursuing a critical and radical practice.

Overall, what is forwarded is a more radical transformation of field education – drawing on a new understanding of the realm of collaboration between academics, social workers, students, and service users, in constructing new knowledge that is grounded in the experience of service (Preston, George, and Silver, 2014, citing Healy, 2005). The transformation being considered involves a shift from field placements that are focused mainly on agency-based service-delivery with limited critical analysis and social justice focus, to placement communities and larger social issues are the focus of the field placement (Preston, George, and Silver, 2014). It is a shift from the traditional service agency-based education to a community/issue-based model (Preston, George, and Silver, 2014). With this shift, field education potentially bridges both service delivery and activism (Preston, George, and Silver, 2014). Field supervisors may shift from individual student responsibility to broader roles in advancing activist strategies in the field and the faculty may find ways to bridge the gap between classrooms and practice by becoming more engaged in field settings, and integrating teaching, research, and practice (Preston, George, and Silver, 2014).

There is a need to reimage field education creatively, thinking out of the box in a way that exposes and unsettles current practices (Preston, George, and Silver, 2014). This unsettling is not to abandon the agency, but to support their activist intentions that become veiled and constrained within the current context (Preston, George, and Silver, 2014).

Overall, the field education should be reconceptualised in ways that link agencies and sectors to the issues that are most relevant to marginalised communities (Preston, George, and Silver, 2014). With the need for field education to become organised around issues and communities, the focus of the placement shifts accordingly and unveils opportunities for alliance building (Preston, George, and Silver, 2014).

While we recognise the difficulty of shifting the historical model of field education, the current situation obligates radical responses (Preston, George, and Silver, 2014). The intensity of our response must at least match the intensity of the neoliberal assault on the lives of the people (Preston, George, and Silver, 2014). To do otherwise risks submission to the dominant discourse and practice – to the detriment of social work's vision and intent (Preston, George, and Silver, 2014). As earlier discussed, 'Social work exists to serve people in need' (Reynolds, 1946). If it serves other classes who have other purposes, it becomes too dishonest to be capable of other theoretical or practical development (Reynolds, 1946).

As human rights and social justice form the foundations of social work and become deeply instilled in the students, the field work becomes an arena for them to assess firsthand how these lofty ideals are uplifted or violated and fought for. Interventions go along these lines. Social workers and social work field work students become champions and defenders of human rights and social justice.

References

Baines, D. (2011). *Doing anti-oppressive practice, social justice social work.* (J. Kearns, & B. Turner, Eds.). Manitoba, Canada: Fernwood Publishing.
Bernasconi, S.S.. (2016). *Social work and human rights: Linking two traditions of human rights in social work.* International Journal of Human Rights in Social Work, Volume 1. (pp. 40–49). New York: Springer International Publishing.
Brackmann, S. M. (2015). Community engagement in a neoliberal paradigm. *Journal of Higher Education, Outreach, and Engagement*, 19(4), 115–146
Campbell, C., & Baikie, G. (2012). Beginning at the beginning: An exploration of critical social work. *Critical Social Work*, 13(1), 67–81. Ontario, Canada: University of Windsor.
Collingwood, P. (2005). Integrating theory and practice: The three-stage theory framework. *Journal of Practice Teaching*, 6(1), 6–23.
Department of Social Work. (2008). *Field instruction manual for undergraduate and graduate programs of social work* (Vol. 1). Quezon CIty, National Capital Region, Philippines: Department of Social Work.
Havig, K. K. (2010). *Empowerment for social justice: A grounded theory study of social work field instruction strategies.* A Doctoral Dissertation Presented to the Graduate School at the University of Missouri-Columbia.
George, P., Silver, S., & Preston, S. (2013). Reimagining field education in social work: The promise unveiled. *Advances in Social Work*, 14(2), 642–657.
Ife, J. (2008). *Human rights and social work: Towards human rights practice.* Cambridge: Cambridge University Press.
International Federation of Social Work. (2014, August 6). *Global definition of social work.* Retrieved from ifsw.org: https://www.ifsw.org/global-definition-of-social-work/
Lundy, C. (2011). *Social work, social justice & human rights: A structural approach to practice* (2nd ed.). Toronto: University of Toronto Press.
Nemenzo, F. (1977). The continuing relevance of academic freedom. *The University of the Philippines Gazette, VIII*(1). 15–20.
Pascua, P. M., & Barrameda, M. J. (2019). *Carrying the cross of today: The struggle for human rights with the youth of our lady of the most holy rosary.* Department of Social Work. Quezon City: College of Social work and Community Development.
Preston, S., George, P., & Silver, S. (2014). Field education in social work: The need for reimagining. *Critical Social Work*, 15(1), 57–72
Reynolds, B. (1946). *Re-thinking social case work.* New York: Social Work Today, Inc
Stammer, N.. (1999). Social movements and the social construction of human rights. *Human Rights Quarterly*, 21(4), 980–1008. University of Sussex.
Taib, M. I. M. (2006). The (de)meaning of social activism. *Karyawan Magazine*, 7(1).
Thompson, N. (2010). *Theorizing social work practice.* London: Palgrave Macmillan.
United Nations Centre for Human Rights. (1994). Human rights and social work. In *A manual for schools of social work and the social work profession.* Geneva: United Nations Centre for Human Rights.

13
Social Work Field Education in Turkey

Eda Beydili Gürbüz, İlkay Başak Adıgüzel, and Sinan Akçay

As agreed by IFSW and IASSW in 2014, social work is a profession based on scientific practices as well as being an academic discipline to support social change and development, social integration, empowerment, and the liberation of people. Being an integral part of social work, field practice is part of the education where students learn social work through on-the-job practices in social welfare institutions (Bogo, 2006).

As is known, the history of field education in social work dates back to the Charity Organization Society – in the last quarter of the 19th century – when students learned social work on-the-job. Field education helped students acquire knowledge on the impact of poverty and adverse social conditions on human life. In the National Conference of Charities and Corrections dated 1915, the significance of educational field practice experience was emphasised – of which social work schools influence students' learning assignments (Abbott, 1915).

Council on Social Work Education (2015) refers to field practice as 'signature pedagogy'. Field education – that is 'signature pedagogy' – aims to combine the theoretical and conceptual contribution of the classroom with the practical benefits of application. The basic principle of social work is that two interrelated components of the curriculum (classroom and fieldwork) have equal emphasis, each contributing to acquiring the necessary competencies related to the professional practice. Field education is systematically designed, supervised, coordinated, and evaluated according to the criteria which shows whether students have acquired the necessary programme qualifications.

Standardisation of professional practice is as important as improving professional practice competencies. Standardisation of professional practice ensures all beneficiaries are provided with the services on an equal basis, in line with respective principles and values. The standardisation in question refers to the provision of social services based on differences and human rights, social state understanding on equality and social justice – not uniformity of social services. As Çalış (2016) stated, parallel to many other professions, with the adoption of the new public administration approach and the rise of accountability, the phenomenon of standardisation of social work as a profession and a discipline has become an important agenda. Since the early 2000s, many countries have attempted to set professional standards of social work, including Turkey. A number of competency and qualification matrices have been introduced together with academicians and practitioners from the social work field, based on the European Qualifications

Framework. Thence, the infrastructure of applied education in Turkey is also in line with the flexible nature of social work. Training programmes constitute a fundamental infrastructure in this sense, thus, supporting the authenticity of the social worker in practice. At the core of this approach lies the fact that all needs, developmental features, problems and ways to tackle with, strengths, ways to relate to others, etc. are unique issues; therefore, professional intervention should be context-specific. This assumption applies to all levels of client groups.

Linking Asian and European continents and having 84 million inhabitants (Turkey Statistical Institute [TurkStat], 2021), the history of social work education in Turkey dates back to the 1960s. In 2002 social work education was merely delivered in a single school; thus, increasing rapidly after 2006. As an integral part of social work, the significance of field education has maintained its importance over time. Today, in the vast majority of social work schools, in the senior year students spend three days a week in field practice and take lessons at school in the remaining days for the autumn semester, and spend all weekdays in field practice for the spring semester. Still, as will be mentioned in the following sections, practices have differed with the increase in the number of schools providing social work education.

In social work education, it is frequently emphasised that this profession is based on knowledge, skill, and values; thus, any lack thereof leads to unsuccessful practice. Therefore, to ensure the integrity of theory and practice, students receive training at individual, group, and societal levels; hence, they are expected to reflect their acquisitions to the field practice. All three levels of social work education programmes in Turkey constitute a broad framework of knowledge, where practice influences the weight of curricula (Cılga, 2004).

The historical background of social work education in Turkey is closely related to the field education. In this context, this section will initially provide background information on the history of social work education, then the field education will be dealt with in line with the accompanying problems in social work education.

Background on Social Work in Turkey as a Profession and a Discipline

Initially, social welfare practices emerged towards the end of the 19th century, by providing voluntary assistance to the problems caused by the Industrial Revolution in England and Europe; thus, in time, it was necessary to form a discipline and a profession through realising the importance of professionalisation in this field. Two significant developements in this field were: the courses that emerged for volunteers in the UK constituted the foundations of social work education, and then the first social work school established in Amsterdam in 1899. Until 1910, 14 social work schools were established in Europe and the United States (USA), and then initial social work schools were opened in Bombay in 1936, in South Africa in 1924, and in Egypt in 1924. It is known that social work education began in the 1960s in Turkey (Koşar & Tufan, 1999)

As a profession and discipline, social work in Turkey originates in social welfare and social assistance practices which date back to the Ottoman period. Similar to Western practices, social work emerged from the concepts of aid and philanthropy. In Ottoman society where people with different ethnic backgrounds lived together, many foundations were established to meet the needs of all segments of the society, including but not limited to the poor, forlorn, war survivors – especially women and children. Constitutions such as the *Himaye-i Etfal* Cemiyeti (Society for The Protection of Children which formed the basis of the contemporary Ministry of Family and Social Services) and the *Hilali-Ahmer* Cemiyeti (The Red Crescent), which still exists today, also met the needs of people in need. With the declaration of the Republic in 1923, the state became the main actor to provide such services (Karataş & Erkan, 2002).

In Turkey, external factors have played a significant role in the initiation of social work education. In particular, the United Nations, which was established after the Second World War, is known to have influenced undeveloped or developing countries, including Turkey (Karataş & Erkan, 2002). Known as the Social Services Academy, the school was founded in 1961 in line with the Law on the Establishment of the Social Services Institute affiliated to the Ministry of Health and Social Aids. The core reason to establish such an academy was to find a solution based on scientific knowledge to the emerging global social problems in Turkey. Tomanbay (2002) pointed to the tole of the United States to trigger social work education in Turkey; thus, social work practices, the problems, and related discussion in the United States in the 1940s were translated into Turkish in 1960, to fulfil the needs of first social work students. Further, the first group of social work scholars received a Fulbright Scholarship in America. Additionally, nationals from the Netherlands, Pakistan, and India were also listed in the academy's primary education staff.

Twenty-two years after the establishment of the first social work school in Turkey, the Department of Social Work and Social Services was established in 1967 within Hacettepe University. However, with the Higher Education Council Law, numbered 2547, this school was closed, and then in 1981 the Social Services Academy, which was established in 1961, was transformed into the College of Social Work, affiliated to Hacettepe University, and the staff of the Department of Social Work and Social Services were transferred accordingly (Tomanbay, 2002). The College of Social Work at Hacettepe University was affiliated to the Faculty of Economics and Administrative Sciences in 2006. From 1961 until 2002 it was the only school in Turkey to deliver social work education; then in 2002, two faculty members left Hacettepe University to establish the same department at a private university, Başkent University. According to the 2019 Yükseköğretim Program Atlası (Higher Education Programme Atlas) [2019], there are a total of 33 state and 15 private universities in Turkey that have undergraduate social work programmes available. Additionally, some universities also offer distance social education. There are also social work associate degree programmes, where students hold the right to enrol in undergraduate study, with the endorsement of the Student Selection and Placement Center (ÖSYM).

The Structure and Content of Social Work Education in Turkey

In Turkey, having completed high school education, students take the Higher Education Institutions Examination (YKS) provided by the Student Selection and Placement Center (ÖSYM) in order to attend university education. Students who get eligible scores may prefer to enrol in the departments and universities of their choice. They are entitled to attend departments with regard to their placement scores. Therefore, there is no separate test to take in order to enrol in the social work profession.

In Turkey, the generalist perspective is adopted in social work education, which requires students to make multiple interventions in multiple problem areas at the undergraduate level. To ensure that, students are offered courses such as human behaviour and social environment, social work theories and intervention methods, social problems, research, ethics, social policy, and social work management. More detailed information about the courses will be provided in the section below.

Social work education in Turkey is given at undergraduate, graduate, and Ph.D. levels. However, graduate and Ph.D. programmes are quite limited. The undergraduate programme is a total of four years, each year consists of two semesters – autumn and spring. The undergraduate programmes aim to equip students with working with individual groups and communities, to ensure problems in the society are eliminated, social justice, human rights in accordance with the international definition of social work introduced by IFSW. Field practice is a fundamental part of the training. Regarding the courses offered in social work education in universities in Turkey, the courses delivered in the first two years tend to reinforce the informative background of social work and are basic theoretical courses, such as sociology, law, economics, anthropology, public administration; whereas, in the final two years courses tend to focus more on professional intervention methods as well as applied practices. Course delivery methods include but are not limited to lecture, case study, role-playing, and brainstorming.

A university degree is required to become a social worker in Turkey. Social work undergraduate education mostly consists of six semesters (three years) of theoretical and three years of theoretical education, as well as field practice in the fourth year. In some universities, field practice can be involved earlier on, and for shorter periods. Graduate and Ph.D. programmes welcome graduates of any undergraduate programme, especially disciplines with similar backgrounds such as sociology and psychology. Social work curriculum and content vary by institution, both for undergraduate and graduate programmes; and there is no single guidebook available. For instance, at the undergraduate level some institutions reserve the entire eighth semester to applied training, whereas in other institutions, field practice is done on certain days in the sixth, seventh, and eighth semesters.

The Social Services Academy was the only school to offer social work education until 2002; after 2006 it went into a period of rapid growth and expansion. Alptekin (2016) states that the departments lacking the necessary infrastructure, which are unplanned, unscheduled, and opened in the framework of power relations introduced dispersed social work education as well as an identity crisis. While undergraduate social work education started in 1961, it took many years for graduate education to follow. This has led graduates to continue their graduate and Ph.D. studies mostly in other fields. The same reasons led to a late start for social work education in various universities. Again, for the same reason, people from various backgrounds such as sociology, psychology, family and consumer sciences, theology were enrolled in most of the social international programmes listed in the previous section, rather than those who receive socialwork education.

In terms of employment opportunities, despite the ever decreasing numbers, public institutions are still among the places where a large number of social workers are densely employed. Moreover, social workers are also placed in the private sector or in their own private organisations. The Ministry of Family and Social Services, the Ministry of Health, and the Ministry of Justice are among the places to employ the highest number of social workers. According to the figures published by the Türkiye Sosyal Hizmet Uzmanları Derneği (SHUDER- Turkey Association of Social Workers) as of May 2015 there are a total of 6150 social services graduates; 2381 of which are employed in the Ministry of Family and Social Policies (now the Ministry of Family and Social Services); 938 of which in the Ministry of Health; and 449 of which in the Ministry of Justice. It is estimated that approximately 350 people work in non-governmental organisations or individual private organisations. It is estimated that approximately 1175 of them are retired, deceased or not working (SHUDER, 2017, as cited in Bolgün & Şahin, 2019).

In Turkey graduates of sociology, psychology, family and consumer sciences, guidance and psychological counselling and child development, and teaching professions are also employed under the name of social workers as well as social services professionals. In practice, the job descriptions of these professions are not specified separately; yet, all of these occupations also fulfil duties of a social worker, such as interviewing, counselling, house visits, and writing a bio-psycho-social report.

Although the first social work school was founded in 1961, social work – as a profession – is not well recognised in society. Thus, in their research dated 2015 Bolgün and Şahin (2019) rendered that 53% of the participants have never heard of the social work profession before. Social workers do not have a professional code yet, and are organised under the umbrella of SHUDER. SHUDER has become a member of IFSW in 2002, and has ongoing activities in 23 branches with a total of approximately 2200 social workers (SHUDER, n.d).

In Turkey, social work education field practices started with the onset of social work education in 1961, with the establishment of the Social Services Academy. Social work education was offered under a single university until 2002, both theoretically and practically. Based on the principles of human rights and social justice, and structured in line with international standards as well as with social structure and needs, the educational content has been regularly restructured over the years to meet evolving conditions and needs.

The number of educational institutions to provide field education started to increase as of 2006, and as of 2012 a rapid acceleration took place. In Turkey, as of March 2020, there are a total of 66 social work programmes to enrol students in formal education, dual education, and distance education programmes affiliated to the state or various associations. The uncontrolled increase in the number of departments has raised concerns about whether social work education can be delivered in line with universal principles and norms. One of the most important reasons for this situation is the insufficient number of academicians who possess the necessary theoretical and practical knowledge on social work in order to meet the educational and research needs of the academy. To ensure these requirements are met, hundreds of faculty members from more than 45 disciplines including medicine, sociology, theology, public administration, family and consumer sciences, various engineering branches, etc. (Alptekin, 2015) are enrolled in the social work departments of universities, to deliver social work education, and are still holding these places. Since education is delivered by experts who are qualified in transforming knowledge to intervention – which is the basis of successful practice – but do not have sufficient expertise in the knowledge-skill-value base of social work, this raises the concern of the increasing number of unqualified professionals and academicians due to the decrease in the quality of field education on a national level. Besides, academic cooperation ensured between departments until 2012 could not be maintained with many departments established as of that year. Which, all together, raised the question as to whether social work education is provided according to national and international standards. The establishment of the Association of Schools of Social Work in 2015 has been promising in this sense. The association ensures that social work education programmes are configured in line with the universal social principles and norms, as well as national needs, thus further ensuring improved quality and high efficiency of social work education in Turkey through the provision of standardisation, evaluation, and accreditation of educational programmes. Such practices are also determinant over applied practices of social work education. Under the leadership of the aforestated association, with the participation of faculty members from various social work departments and social work experts from the Association of Schools of Social Workers, the seventh Social Work Education Workshop was held in 2017, which significantly contributed to setting the national standards of social work education. National standards are also related to educational methods and field practice. In the workshop, the ideal education and training methods are highlighted, emphasising the need to improve; role-playing, group working, inviting guests, discussion, presentations, watching movies, literature analysis, field and institutional examination etc. skills. The need to follow the methods to improve the application skills is highlighted. The following decisions are rendered regarding the field practice:

- The department explains the necessary conditions for the student to enrol in field practice courses
- The department establishes the administrative structure (such as field practice coordination) necessary for the management of field practice
- The instructor to bear the responsibility for coordination of field practice should have received undergraduate and/or graduate level social services education, and be a faculty member; should have at least two years of field experience
- The department covers what is necessary for human resources (field practice educational and institutional consultants), bureaucratic procedures (official permissions, protocols etc.) and technical support for field practice
- Field practice conducted in collaboration with the student, educational counsellor, institutional counsellor (students carry out field practice under the dual supervision of their educational counsellor at the university who are social work academicians and their institutional counsellor at the host institution who are social services professionals) and the hosting institution. How to implement such collaboration in the education programme is explained
- Field practice provides students with the necessary insight and basic skills to apply social work methods and techniques in the field in line with the characteristics of client systems
- Field practice is a minimum of 500 hours
- The principles of field practice (educational counsellor, institutional advisor and student's duties and responsibilities, calendar, procedures followed, record keeping, field education supervision, etc.) are determined by a regulation or directive (Sosyal Hizmet Okulları Derneği, 2017)

In social work education, educational practices that involve implementing the theoretical knowledge have an important role. The generalist perspective is adopted in social work education in Turkey. Utilising the eclectic background of practitioners, it is aimed to equip them with the necessary skills to work with individuals, families, groups, and communities, as well as becoming competent in responding to various subject areas, such as poverty, disease, violence, neglect and abuse, addiction, homelessness, disaster, unemployment, etc. Educational practices are functional to fulfil this aim.

Parallel with many other countries, the generalist perspective in Turkey is built upon human diversity. Every situation, problem, and need is important and unique to that specific person. Still, the determining role of environmental and social impacts in the formation of individual problems is stressed as well. In practice, the structural causes of problems as well as the functioning of the destructive power mechanisms that create pressure-control are recognised, and the client system for personal-interpersonal-political empowerment is supported. This, in fact, points to the inseparability of micro and macro interventions. Therefore, it is important to adopt a versatile and holistic approach in the intervention; to conduct planned intervention processes with client systems of all levels; to consider different systems and their interactions; and to utilise a rich knowledge and skill accumulation in parallel. Education programmes are structured in a way to ensure practitioners are raised accordingly.

One of the three pillars of educational practice is knowledge. The contents of the knowledge base are as difficult as revealing the mysteries of the complex existence of human beings; as it contains information on all dimensions of human life – the bio-psycho-social-cultural-economic-spiritual dimensions, etc. Consequently, this means that in addition to the scientific knowledge produced by social work, the basis of knowledge includes information on sociology, psychiatry, psychology, social anthropology, law, economics, etc. Thus, it is important to ensure the evaluation of the client systems and environmental systems in a needs-oriented and rights-based manner; fully understanding the need to eliminate the problem at hand; utilisation of the eclectic knowledge base to mobilise the necessary resources and to plan an effective intervention. Ignoring the information produced by different disciplines guarantees a failed application. Social work departments in Turkey have foreseen these risks, and included basic courses on the aforestated discipline in their curricula. These courses include but are not limited to: general economics, introduction to law, basic mathematics, introduction to sociology, use of basic information and communication technologies, basic English skills, introduction to philosophy, introduction to psychology, introduction to statistics, public administration, social-cultural anthropology, introduction to statistics.

Lessons that include scientific knowledge on social work can be dealt with in two parts: learning *theoretical information* (information on human behaviour and social environment, theory-based information on understanding and intervention, information on problem areas and research) and developing *practical skills*.

Although it is not easy to render a respective distinction on the courses delivered because each theory is derived from practice, the following lessons on intervention, intervention methods and techniques taught at micro-mezzo-macro levels are planned separately. Although different names are given to these courses in available curricula, their essence is similar. These courses, which are generally called 'the theory of social work', consist of a number of prerequisite courses. The course structure is designed to teach micro, mezzo, and macro level interventions, and course credits (as well as course duration) are higher than usual. These courses are delivered through in-class practices and extracurricular homework and projects. The primary objectives of these courses involve, specifically, developing intervention skills, teaching the use of methods and techniques in line with the requirements of the client system.

At the individual, family, group, community-level: Applied research courses and practical courses (as to *focus on developing practical skills*) that are designed for the social work departments that teach how to produce scientific knowledge and conduct science-oriented interventions in line with the liberating values of social work, tailored for the different needs and risk groups have a significant role.

Applied research courses: introduce field information and the essence of the field work to the student. One of the functions borne by the social worker is a researcher, where he/she produces information on social work. Such a role requires steering professional practices; thus, students learn to conduct research on specific problem areas in which further information is required. Before taking applied research courses they are expected to take prerequisite field courses (on human behaviour and social environment, social problems, etc.), a statistics course and research on social work courses (usually two prerequisite courses, where information of both positivist-oriented and interpretive paradigms are dealt with).

In social work research courses, students learn to design research by preparing a research proposal, to collect or create data in line with the research design, to analyse the findings, and to produce a research report. These compulsory courses constitute the necessary ground for applied research courses (similar to research on social work courses, they consist of two prerequisite courses delivered in two semesters). Prior to reaching this stage, students observe their client systems in almost every subject area in line with the requirements of the course; however, they do not contact them directly for the purposes of social work practice. The first true encounter with the client system in social work practice happens in applied research courses when students get in contact with subjects. Besides that, the following dimensions come to the forefront, regarding of the functionality of social work practice related to the research process:

- Establish a link between theoretical knowledge and life experience
- Acquire necessary skills to design, implement, and manage the possible problems that may arise during the research process
- Acquire the most important functions of a social worker; that is, find and activate resources, and link them with those in need
- Learn how to produce a report
- Develop sophisticated (multi-dimensional) evaluation skills
- Experience in teamwork, peer supervision and working under supervision (Hacettepe Üniversitesi Sosyal Hizmet Bölümü, no date)

A group of students carry out research under educational supervision. At the end of the second semester, students share their social work knowledge with the professional and scientific community. Some departments organise poster presentation activities to disseminate the research results.

Field practice courses on social work are among the most important courses to develop practical skills. In this process, students learn how to practise the theoretical knowledge they have acquired so far. Moreover, they also have opportunities to improve self-knowledge; identify personal limits as well as that of others, and act accordingly; ensure effective communication with clients and colleagues; learn the institutional structure and functioning; understand the corporate culture; acquire information on available services; take professional responsibility; conduct precise observation, evaluation, planning, implementation and monitoring of activities, etc. (Hacettepe Üniversitesi Sosyal Hizmet Bölümü, 2014). One may suggest that social work field practice is an area where students may test their acquisitions at the end of a long theoretical and semi-applied learning period, and in which practical learning is significant.

As mentioned before, Turkish scholars in social work departments have differing views on how to teach social work field practices. Unfortunately, the efforts put in place to bring together the scholars to take joint decisions have not been successful so far. Still, although the method of delivery differs, formal education institutions adopt similar processes. As in all other courses, practical training is designed in line with global standards set by IFSW and IASSW (2004). The international code of conduct on social work as well as professional ethic codes and responsibility identified by Turkish Association of Social Workers is honoured at all levels (undergraduate, graduate, Ph.D.) throughout the process of social work field practice education.

In Turkey, social work field practice is compulsory in social work departments. To be eligible to take field practice courses, one must take and pass prerequisite courses. In general, students are assumed to be ready to perform professional interventions only after establishing a solid understanding of the respective field of knowledge, skills, and values.

Each department that accepts students for the formal undergraduate programme provides a specific curriculum on the theoretical and practical scope of social work field practice. Teaching methods, how to practise and assess theoretical knowledge, class attendance, and student acquisitions in the process, etc. – such pieces of information are clearly stated in the curriculum. Social work field practice coordination centres/coordinators established in the social work departments organise all processes related to the field practice, including but not limited to the field practice preferences of the students; obtaining permissions from hosting institutions; informing consultants in hosting institutions, as well as students and educational counsellors; follow-up and evaluation of the implementation process, etc. The coordinators are all social work academicians. Coordination centres produce guide books that provide information on possible requirements of field practice. Hence, they ensure field practice is carried out effectively during the whole course of education.

Several issues are considered when placing students in hosting social services institutions, such as, lessons taken so far, former field practice experiences, total GPA, and willingness to focus on a particular problem area. Field practice coordination centres in the departments conduct initial assessments, get in contact with various private/public social services institutions, and place students in hosting institutions. Next, coordination centres help students identify the educational counsellor, under supervision of whom they will work. Matching is done in line with the field of expertise of the educational counsellors. Unfortunately, it is not possible to follow this process in the departments that do not have enough academic human resources.

The social work field practice process has three main actors: the student, educational counsellor, and institutional counsellor. The academic-educational coordination and contact between these three parties are rather important to ensure a fully functioning process. Departments play an intermediary and encouraging role in establishing and maintaining this relationship.

Field education starts with an orientation meeting held in many social work departments during the first weeks of the field education period (in general, starts in the first semester of the fourth grade and lasts two semesters). Educational counsellors and institutional counsellors are also invited to this meeting. Various issues are discussed at the orientation meeting, including but not limited to the weekly field practice schedule – how many days and hours a week; the observations, the quality of the observations, evaluations and practices expected to be carried out by the students on a micro-mezzo-macro scale; expectations from academic and educational cooperation, operational details of the supervision process. In addition, information is given on the field subject areas as well as hosting social welfare institutions to be applied. After the orientation meeting, students, educational counsellors, and institution counsellors are expected to come together to prepare a work plan, and to sign a contract to fulfil the agreed responsibilities. After this point, the bilateral counselling process is conducted with meetings that are planned separately with each consultant, and the tripartite team meets at regular intervals (usually at least three times during the period) and to assess the field practice. Students have a supervision meeting with their educational advisor at least once a week. The role of institutional consultants is particularly important in the implementation process. All interventions carried out throughout the day are under the supervision of the institutional consultant. By doing so, students may reflect on the field practice process thoroughly, learn from their own experience as well as the advisors. Unfortunately, in practice it is not always possible to follow this order as designed. As will be discussed in detail in the next section, the lack of competence and qualifications of professionals in the field influences the success of field practices; thus, whether all the students benefit from field education is questionable.

The first weeks of field education are dedicated to acquiring information on the problem area in question, forming an understanding of the mission and organisation of the hosting institution, grasping the essence of the corporate culture, mastering the respective legislation on the subject area, recognising and observing the client systems as well as its requirements. The next step is accompanying the institutional advisor in the field practices to make observations. At the end of a couple of months of the observation period, if agreed by the counsellors and if the student feels comfortable, he/she may take a more active role in the intervention. In the following stages, the level of professional practices (in line with the service structure of the hosting institution) expands from micro to macro, and students may work more independently as they gain experience in the field.

Record keeping is one of the most important parts of the learning process as well as being a fundamental role of a social worker. Students record the whole course of the field practice starting from the observation process. The proper collection, evaluation, and sharing of information with relevant authorities may have a direct influence on the life of our client system(s).

In addition, special emphasis is put on keeping records as it affects issues such as conducting effective teamwork, steering new services to be offered by the institution, revealing the needs of the employees and counsellor systems in the institution, referral systems for the client, and identifying the need for further consultation. The reports (process report, activity report, group introduction report, community review report, project report, etc.) produced may vary with regard to the nature of the professional intervention.

Self-reflection is particularly valuable in social work field practice training, as the process mirrors the extent of the information, skills and values acquired, internalised by the student and reflected on their own life as well as professional interventions. Such a reflection process taking place under the supervision of the counsellor supports the student in improving self-awareness, while ensuring to keep up with the pace. Here, it might be necessary to question performance evaluation processes. Both counsellors contribute to a student's performance evaluation process. Meetings held during the process are necessary to make assessments. At the end of the field practice, students are expected to become proficient and competent practitioners who can fulfil their professional responsibilities in line with national and international professional standards. At the end of the training, a social work practice workshop is organised. Students who have participated in similar subject areas come together under the leadership of an educational counsellor to organise a workshop, where they evaluate and report the micro-mezzo-macro-scale problems they have identified in the hosting institutions, as well as their needs and solution offers from a rights-based perspective. After the workshops are conducted, all department students, educational counsellors and institutional counsellors, all professional bodies working in the field and academy, public authorities delivering social services are invited to an event where students present their reports and respective actions at different levels of intervention.

Once again it is necessary to underline the fact that these processes might be implemented differently in various departments. In addition, the implementation process is planned quite differently in remote education system. In the formal open education system hosting institutions for field education are limited with those affiliated to the Ministry of Family and Social Services. Those who enrol in the programme to complete undergraduate courses in the health sector or those work in institutions and organisations affiliated to the Ministry of Health are required to perform their practices in the social work units of these organisations. The implementation process takes place under the supervision of the provincial counsellor and covers two academic years in the seventh and eighth semesters. In both semesters students spare one full day of the week to field practice. Compared with the departments providing formal education, obviously, the time spared for applied training is insufficient. (i.e., Hacettepe University is the first university where social work field education is carried out. Here, social work field practices are carried out three full days a week in the first semester and five full days a week in the second semester). Students upload the reports they produced in the field practice to the national system of distance education faculty. Provincial counsellors review these reports to make student assessments. There is no face-to-face interaction in this process (Anadolu Üniversitesi, 2020).

Social work field education in graduate programmes is structured on national and international standards similar to that of the undergraduate programme. The time spent in practice being less (in general, half a day for both semesters half a week per week) and emphasis being placed on indirect applications rather than direct application are where it differs from the structure of undergraduate programmes. During the implementation process, students are expected to plan and carry out direct and indirect interventions in order to meet the requirements, to improve their well-being, and to create the desired change by utilising the theoretical approaches related to the situation. (These expectations may vary according to the structure of the graduate programme. For example, in clinical social work programmes, working with individuals, families, and groups is at the centre of the practice). Understanding and information on the subject area, reflecting on the research results, and presenting evaluations from a critical perspective are required to ensure successful results.

Postgraduate social work field education – namely advanced professional practice –is carried out with dual supervision, similar to that of the undergraduate applied training. Working under the dual supervision of the institutional counsellor and educational counsellor is believed to improve learning opportunities.

This chapter provides information on social work field education in Turkey. The next section will provide an in-depth analysis of the existing problems.

Discussion

Social work being a practice-oriented profession indicates the importance of field education in social work education. Parallel to global practices, social work education in Turkey is based on a curriculum involving theoretical and practical courses; thus, the aim is to design the theoretical and applied training in line with the field practice.

One of the most fundamental problems of social work education in Turkey is the increase in the number of human resources and training institutions providing social work education without the necessary infrastructure in place. The rapid increase in the number of universities providing social work education is an indicator of the unplanned growth in this sense. Although the increase in the number of institutions providing social work education is an important development, the quality of the education provided is also a matter to be taken into account. Many problems such as insufficient physical conditions, different backgrounds of scholars, high numbers of student enrolment in social work departments of universities, and the tendency to increase are the barriers to providing qualified social work education. While these problems are experienced intensely in the social work departments of various universities, in some others these are less and less experienced. Consequently, one may suggest that the quality of social work departments in Turkey have significant differences. This situation affects both theoretical education in social work departments as well as in applied education. For example, in the research conducted with 117 students studying in the third grade of Hacettepe University Social Work Department with the qualitative research method, it was revealed that 61.5% of the students who participated in the study (Erbay, Adıgüzel and Akçay, 2013) did not feel ready for the field practice. The students indicated that the courses delivered are purely theory-oriented and that they experience knowledge, skill, and value deficiencies, which is why they did not feel ready for the practice.

Social work field education has three basic components: student, educational counsellor, and institutional counsellor. In this context, it is possible to say that social work field education is not independent from these three aforementioned elements as well as available social policies. One of the main problems in terms of social work field practice in Turkey is the heavy workload of social workers. A study examining the professional practices and working conditions of social workers (Zengin & Çalış, 2017) pointed out the high amount of work undertaken by social workers and intense stress factors borne by the work environment. Another study (Berkün, 2010) revealed the inadequate number of and overburdened caseloads of social workers. The excessive number of clients assigned to social workers will have an inevitable impact on the social work students in field education. This situation may lead to not allocating enough time to the social work students, and even involving the student in activities outside the professional boundaries.

One of the main problems faced in the delivery of social work education in Turkey is social work students having difficulty in finding eligible hosting institutions. Eligibility of the institution for social work field education is determined based on features such as the presence of a social worker actively working in the hosting institution, different social work methods in practice in the hosting institution, the perception of the institution towards the student in field education, and the support provided in the learning process. Especially, the presence of a social worker actively working in the institution is important for the development of professional identity in social work students through observation and modelling processes, etc.

Considering the inadequate number of social workers working in the public, private, or non-governmental organisations in Turkey, the difficulty of finding eligible training institutions comes to the forefront. This is even a bigger problem in cities where there are more than one social work department. Considering the increasing number of students, the existing institutions cannot fulfil the needs of field education –which leads to social work students undergoing field education in institutions ineligible for field practice. The absence of social workers and an established social work practice culture in the institution is a challenge for social work students who undergo field practice for the first time.

In social work field practice locations, in addition to social workers, there are workers with various backgrounds – such as sociology, psychology, guidance and psychological counselling, child development, and teaching. All of these professional groups are appointed under the name of social services professionals and all of them fulfil duties such as interviewing, counselling, making home visits, producing bio-psycho-social reports, etc. Therefore in field practice, not all institutional consultants are social workers. Moreover, there are even no social workers in some institutions. Unlike careers on the global level, social work provided in schools is not a widely implemented practice in Turkey. In contrast, in line with the need for social workers in schools, within the scope of the field education schools are provided with social work students. Therefore, the institutional counsellors in such locations are either psychological counsellors, or in their absence, teachers. Accordingly, students may have problems acquiring the necessary professional perspective. Moreover, even if the institutional consultant is a social worker, each and every individual possess different skills. Not every social worker is able to participate, or participate to the same extent. Hence, an educational counsellor's contribution is unquestionable. As Strydom (2011) puts it, without collaboration, field practices cannot be successful.

Standardisation has become an issue in social work education with the increasing number of institutions providing social work education in Turkey. The standardisation problem in question manifests itself in field education courses as well as that of theoretical. For instance, some social work departments have internship programmes in summer, while others do not. Or, in some departments, field education starts in the third grade, while in other departments only starts in the fourth grade. Another example is that the number of days spent in practice differs for students. Some departments offer continued field education four days a week, whereas others offer five days a week. In addition to these, many other differences in social work field education can directly influence the quality of the field practice.

Supervision is of great importance in social work field education. Still, there are no standards or corporate supervision system in place in Turkey. In social work field education, each student has an institutional and educational counsellor. In the absence of a social worker or social worker available in the hosting institution who is responsible for the student's learning process, another practitioner with a different background fulfils the institutional counsellor position. The educational counsellor is any scholar working in the social work department where the social work student is attending. However, there are no minimum criteria for both consultants. For instance, the academic staff in the social work department may have a background in psychology or sociology, and may not necessarily have any social work education background. This does not constitute any obstacle for the scholar in question to provide educational counselling within the scope of social work education. Another example is the fact that a social worker who is new in practice and does not have enough professional experience can become an institutional consultant. Both examples are common in social work field education and training that adversely affects a student's practical capability in Turkey. On the other hand, the fact that the educational counsellor and institutional consultant are competent and experienced in the field of social work is not in itself sufficient in terms of field education. Social work field education training is an important process that requires certain knowledge and skills. In Turkey there are no training programmes in place for educational and institutional consultants, who are integral components of the orientation process.

In the history of social work education in Turkey, one of the major turning points seems to be the introduction of social work education in open education faculties of universities. Social work being an applied profession and academic discipline, delivering undergraduate education through open education faculties does not coincide with the nature of social work. Social work education provided through open education faculties cannot provide the necessary knowledge, skills, and values to build the professional competencies of students. In fact, in the study of Sehman and Yolcuoğlu (2020) conducted social workers working at open education faculties, only 13.1% of the participants felt themselves professionally competent, whereas 41.7% felt partly sufficient, and 45.2% felt professionally insufficient. Considering the practical training of social work departments affiliated to the open education faculties, it is seen that social work students practise one day a week for each semester for 14 weeks in the seventh and eighth semesters. The time spent in field practice, which is compulsory in the social work departments of Open Education Faculty, is extremely lacking compared to that of formal education. In addition, supervision support is highly limited and the mechanisms to support the professional development of students are almost nonexistent compared to formal education.

Social work field education has an important place both in undergraduate and graduate education. Thus, in social work, graduate education facilities are not as widespread as undergraduate education in Turkey. The Hacettepe University Department of Social Work, one of the leading providers of social work education in Turkey, stands as an example of graduate education in social work field education. Two field practice courses are offered in the undergraduate degree and two in the postgraduate (Ph.D.) programmes at the Hacettepe University Department of Social Work. A guideline on advanced professional practice has been created for supervision in these courses, and courses are implemented accordingly. The guideline points to the obligation for students to perform supervised professional practice in various institutions and organisations for at least five hours a week, and the institutional counsellor and the educational counsellor are responsible for supporting the learning process. The guideline also stresses three main development areas; namely, utilise knowledge, values, and skills to the full in applied education for graduate degree; conduct research based on critical policy analysis, evaluation of services and practices in the subject area; efficient utilisation of the supervision process (Hacettepe Üniversitesi Sosyal Hizmet Bölümü , 2015).

Conclusion

This study focuses on the scope of and problems in social work field education, in line with the history of social work education in Turkey. Although as a discipline and profession social work has been globally recognised for over a century, it does not have a very long life story in Turkey. However, Turkey being a country which has had to tackle many major social issues such as unemployment, poverty, and violence against women has recently paved the road in emphasising the need for social work professions.

Having human rights and social justice as core principles brings great responsibilities to the social work profession and its members. Fulfilling these responsibilities is dependent on the acquisition of necessary professional qualifications. From this perspective, it is possible to say that social work education is determinant. Although the rapid increase in the number of universities to offer social work education in Turkey is an important opportunity for the development of social work profession, the unplanned growth has also revealed many problems. Since theoretical and applied education should be considered a whole in social work education, one may suggest that the problems experienced in social work education directly affect the field practice. In this context, Turkey needs to undertake the necessary steps to transform crisis into opportunity in the field of social work education. Among these steps are increasing the number of scholars trained in the field of social work, keeping student enrolment quotas at a minimum level, and providing the necessary infrastructure for providing qualified education.

Social work field education is based on ensuring an efficient supervision relationship. Unfortunately, not all departments have a full understanding of its necessity. Along with the uncontrolled growth, there has been a deviation from the basic standards of field education improving the well-being of the clients, whose lives we touch, raising concerns about the realisation of rights-based and needs-oriented micro-mezzo-macro level professional practices. The open education system, which is especially operational in the country and has hundreds of graduates every year, stands as a threat in this sense. It is clear that establishing a new department, which started as a way of closing the labour gap in the country, will raise the problem of the dequalification of open education studies. Therefore, the nature of social work as an applied science, one that requires a long practice period under supervision to improve practical skills on the basis of knowledge and values, should be understood, and accordingly be addressed by all departments with a collective effort.

References

Abbott, E. (1915). Field work and the Training of the Social Worker. In *National Conference of Charities and Corrections, Proceedings of the National Conference of Charities and Corrections*. Chicago: Hildmann.

Alptekin, K. (2015). *Sosyal Hizmetin Eğitiminin Geleceği:Düşünceler ve Öneriler*. Sosyal Hizmet Sempozyumu:İnsan Değer ve Onurunu Yüceltmek, Manisa.

Alptekin, K. (2016). *Başlangıçtan Bugüne ve Yarına Türkiye'de Sosyal Hizmet Eğitimi*. Konya: Atlas Yayınevi

Anadolu Üniversitesi. (2020). Açıköğretim duyuruları. 8 Nisan 2020 tarihinde https://www.anadolu.edu.tr/acikogretim/aof-duyurular/sosyal-hizmet-lisans-programi-ogrencilerinin-sosyal-hizmet-uygulamasi-i-dersi-1570451264 adresinden alınmıştır.

Berkün, S. (2010). Sosyal hizmet uzmanlarının çalışma hayatında karşılaştığı mesleki sorunlar:Bursa örneği. *Toplum ve Sosyal Hizmet*, 21(1), 99–109.

Bogo, M. (2006). Field instruction in social work: A review of the research literature. *The Clinical Supervisor*, 24 (1–2), 163–193.

Bolgün, C., & Şahin, F. (2019). Public perception and attitudes about social work in Turkey. *International Social Work*, 62 (5), 1329–1342.

Çalış, N. (2016). Sosyal Hizmet Uygulamasında Standartlaşma. İ., Cılga E., Erkul, B. Yıldırım, & İ. B. Adıgüzel (Ed.) içinde, *Sosyal Çalışma ve Sosyal Politika Yazıları* (ss. 83–102). Ankara: Bellek Yayınları.

Cılga, İ. (2004). *Bilim ve Meslek Olarak Türkiye'de Sosyal Hizmet*. Ankara: Hacettepe Üniversitesi Sosyal Hizmetler Yüksekokulu.

Council of Social Work Education. (2015). Educational policy and accreditation standarts for baccalaureate and master's social work programs. Taken from the following address on April 8, 2020, https://www.cswe.org/Accreditation/Standards-and-Policies/2015-EPAS

Erbay, E., Adıgüzel, İ. B., & Akçay, S. (2013). Sosyal hizmet öğrencilerinin sosyal hizmet uygulaması dersleri kapsamında uygulama yürütecekleri kurumları tercih etme süreçleri. *Toplum ve Sosyal Hizmet,* 24(2), 95–107.

Hacettepe Üniversitesi Sosyal Hizmet Bölümü. (2014). Uygulama Yönergesi. Ankara. 3 Mart 2020 tarihinde http://fs.hacettepe.edu.tr/shy/2015/Lisans/417-418/417_uygulama_yonergesi_15.09.2014 .pdf adresinden alınmıştır.

Hacettepe Üniversitesi Sosyal Hizmet Bölümü. (2015). Süpervizyona dayalı ileri mesleki uygulama yönergesi. 8 Nisan 2020 tarihinde http://fs.hacettepe.edu.tr/shy/2016/Lisans%C3%BCst%C3%BC/Uygulama/H.U._IIBF_SHB_ileri_uygulama_yonergesi_09.12.2015.pdf adresinden alınmıştır.

Hacettepe Üniversitesi Sosyal Hizmet Bölümü (no date). Uygulamalı Araştırma Kılavuzu. 14 Mart 2020 tarihinde http://fs.hacettepe.edu.tr/shy/2019/Lisans/316-319/Yeni-UYGULAMALI%20ARA%C5%9ETIRMA%20KILAVUZU.pdf adresinden alınmıştır.

IASSW, & IFSW. (2004). Global standards for the education and training of the social work profession. Adelaide Australia. Taken from the following address on March 3, 2020, http://cdn.ifsw.org/assets/ifsw _65044-3.pdf.

Karataş, K., & Erkan, G. (2002). Türkiye'de Sosyal Hizmet Eğitiminin Tarihçesi. Ü. O. (Yay.Haz.) içinde, *Sosyal Hizmet Sempozyumu 2002: Sosyal Hizmet Eğitiminde Yeni Yaklaşımlar* (s. 112–134). Ankara: Hacettepe Üniversitesi Sosyal Hizmetler Yüksekokulu.

Koşar, N., & Tufan, B. (1999). Sosyal Hizmetler Yüksekokulu Tarihçesine Genel Bir Bakış. N. G. (Ed.) içinde, *Prof. Dr. Sema Kut'a Armağan:Yaşam Boyu Sosyal Hizmet* (s. 1–21). Ankara: Hacettepe Üniversitesi Sosyal Hizmetler Yüksekokulu.

Sehman, H. & Yolcuoğlu, İ.(2019). Açıköğretim sosyal hizmet bölümü mezunlarının gözünden Türkiye'de sosyal hizmet eğitiminin işlevselliği. *Toplumsal Politika Dergisi,* 1(1), 12-26.

Sosyal Hizmet Okulları Derneği. (2017). Türkiye'de Sosyal Hizmet Eğitiminde Ulusal Standartların Değerlendirilmesi ve Geliştirilmesi. 7. Sosyal Hizmet Eğitim Çalıştayı . İstanbul

Tomanbay, İ. (2002). 1960'lı Yıllardan 2000'li Yıllara Sosyal Hizmet Eğitimi. Ü. O. (Yay. Haz.) içinde, *Sosyal Hizmet Sempozyumu 2002: Sosyal Hizmet Eğitiminde Yeni Yaklaşımlar* (ss. 59–73). Ankara: Hacettepe Üniversitesi Sosyal Hizmetler Yüksekokulu.

Turkey Statistical Institute [TurkStat]. (2021). The Results of Address Based Population Registration System, 2021. Taken from the following address on March 7, 2021, https://data.tuik.gov.tr/Kategori/GetKategori?p=Nufus-ve-Demografi-109.

SHUDER [Sosyal Hizmet Uzmanları Derneği]. (n.d.). Türkiye'de sosyal hizmet uzmanları derneğinin tarihsel gelişimi. 10 Nisan 2020 tarihinde http://shuder.org/Sayfa/sosyal-hizmet-uzmanlari-derneginin -tarihcesi1656 adresinden alınmıştır.

Yükseköğretim Program Atlası. (2019). *Sosyal Hizmet (Fakülte) Programı Bulunan Tüm Üniversiteler.* 10 Nisan 2020 tarihinde https://yokatlas.yok.gov.tr/lisans-bolum.php?b=10193 adresinden alınmıştır.

Zengin, O., & Çalış, N. (2017). Sosyal hizmet uzmanlarının mesleki uygulamaları ve çalışma koşulları. *Toplum ve Sosyal Hizmet,* 28(1), 47–67.

14
Social Work Field Education in India and China
A Comparison

Rajendra Baikady and Varoshini Nadesan

Social work is an internationally recognised human service profession committed to achieving social justice, equality, and human development in contemporary society. Responding to social evils, poverty eradication, human development, and establishing an equitable society are the guiding principles of this helping profession. Social work education is offered at universities, colleges, and institutes of higher learning across the globe with an intention to prepare a professionally trained workforce to address the social issues and problems experienced in various parts of the world. Different countries follow a range of methods of education and training for social work graduates with greater differences in the curriculum, teaching learning methods, and the practice education. Reportedly social work education and practice are well-established and well-recognised – more so in the western world than in the developing and underdeveloped countries. The International Association of Schools of Social Work (IASSW) and the International Federation of Professional Social Workers (IFSW) have developed the global standards for social work education and training that address many issues related to the development of social work education and training, while offering insightful guidelines for the educators and schools of social work in formulating and delivering social work education and practice training. The development of global standards for social work education and training along with the global agenda for social work and social development in recent decades is expected to contribute considerably to the professionalisation, internationalisation, and indigenisation of social work education, practice, and research in many countries across the globe (ICSW-IFSW-IASSW, 2020). This chapter addresses the challenges faced by social work field education in two Asian countries i.e., India and China, while discussing the development and growth of social work as a profession and educational discipline in these two countries.

Field work is considered to be an integral part of the social work education. Graduate students are expected to undertake independent, supervised field practicum during their social work programme, which in a way is testing the applicability of theories and methods learnt in the classroom (Nadesan, 2020). Arguably, theoretical learning without practice is empty and practice learning without theory is meaningless. Field work practicum in social work is considered as the heart and soul of the professional learning (Homonoff, 2008; Schmidt & Rautenbach, 2016). It is believed that any successful intervention in social work with individuals, groups, and the community depends on a strong foundation of field practice learning. Field work education also plays a very important role in graduating ethically competent social workers and preparing them for professional practice (Bogo, 2010). Field work education provides an opportunity for students to transform their experiential learning into professional knowledge and then apply it in their practice with individuals, groups, or communities. It is also during the field work practicum that students experience and understand social realities in different societies and communities.

In this chapter we compare social work field education in India and China. Social, political, and economic conditions experienced by both countries are different and so are the problems faced. However, social issues such as poverty, overpopulation, corruption, gross income, and social inequality are similar in both India and China. Hence social work as a human service profession plays a major role in rebuilding societies with the values of equality, social justice, and human rights.

Development of Social Work Education in India

Professional social work education in India was introduced in 1936 with the establishment of the first school of social work, now called Tata Institute of Social Sciences. Similar to other parts of the world, the introduction of professional social work in India is attributed to western initiatives and, moreover, an immediate response to the social problems that were experienced by pre-independent India. Poverty, inequality, illiteracy, caste, class, and gender discriminations were rampant in Indian society. Social work's origin as a response to these social inadequacies alongside the principles of establishing social justice, equality, and a just society, attempts to address these social ills. The first social work courses in India were developed and delivered with the help of western academic institutions mostly from the United States. As a result, even after 84 years of teaching, practice, and research, social work education and practice in India are largely western-centric. Even today western models and literature are used to teach graduate and postgraduate students in contemporary India. Nevertheless, social work in India has achieved several millstones such as establishing its professional association, setting up approximately 600 schools of social work for undergraduate and postgraduate teaching as well as doctoral research, and the foundation of several regional and local social workers associations across the country. However, despite an increasing number of social work teaching programmes and student enrolment, the professional status of social work in the country remains unchanged. Social work as a human service profession is still struggling to establish its identity in the country (Baikady et al., 2014, 2020). The current challenge for social work education in India is to establish its identity and get an accrediting body for education and practice alongside developing more context-specific educational programmes.

Development of Social Work Education in China

The introduction of social work education to China occurred in the 1920s, here again possibly due to western influence. However, professional social work education and practice were suspended by the Chinese government for 30 years, between the 1950s and 1980s. The reintroduction of social work education and practice in the 1980s saw China's plan to produce one and a half million social workers by 2020 (Guo 2017; Mo et al., 2019). However, the development and professionalisation of social work education in China is influenced largely by the Chinese government's plan to develop social governance, social welfare delivery, and to maintain social stability in Chinese society (Guo, 2017; Li et al., 2012). Over the years, the Chinese government promoted social work education across the country and as a result the number of social work educational institutions increased considerably. However, one factor that had prevailed previously continued i.e., the quality of education and field work placements for students, remained unchanged. Many scholars have discussed the importance of enhancing the quality of social work education and professional identity of the discipline (Lei et al., 2019; Baikady & Cheng, 2020). Notably, the professional status of social work in China is given little significance. Other professions are afforded more status, career opportunities, and remuneration when compared to social work (Blumenthal & Hsiao, 2015). This chapter elaborates on the challenges faced by social work field education in China and its impact on the professionalisation and standardisation of social work education and practice in contemporary China.

Structure and Content of Field Education: India

The implementation of the social work practicum in India occurs on many levels. There are varied placements for students to obtain practical experience during the two years of the master's programme. The types of placement agencies, hours at placement agencies, and the experiences at different placements differ from one training institution to the next. The nature of the field work practicum in Indian schools of social work can be categorised into four types: (i) Concurrent field work, (ii) Summer placement/internships, (iii) Block placement, (iv) Rural practicum/camp. The concurrent field work is an ongoing fieldwork programme where students go for practicum and simultaneously attend class when not in the field. In the summer placements, students are set for one month block internships in organisations in and around the country. The summer placements take place in between the end of the first year and the beginning of the second year of study. The block placement is based on a specialised interest of students and takes place during the second year of study, largely in the third semester of the academic programme. The rural camp is a unique component which is implemented by every school of social work in the country. The aim of the rural camp is to give a rural exposure to students, and to enable urban students to understand the difficulties of rural people. The majority of social work educational institutions in India are established and functioning in the urban centres and thus students would have had little exposure to working in rural areas.

A student in the master's level social work programme is expected to complete a minimum of 30 days of fieldwork practicum in a semester to qualify in the programme. Usually, a student is expected to attend 15 hours of fieldwork training in a week, and at the time of graduation would have gained 1800 hours of field experience including all the placements, across the summer, block placement, and rural camp. As noted by Baikady (2017) overall objectives of the fieldwork practicum across the schools differed but to some extent the objectives are:

(i) To help students understand the socioeconomic, cultural, and political issues and develop critical examination skills among the students
(ii) Providing the students an opportunity to apply theory in practical situations
(iii) Help the students to identify, plan, and implement social work intervention
(iv) To make student social workers understand the role of the social work profession in empowering individuals, groups, and communities
(v) To help students develop skills and appropriate personality traits required for professional social work practice
(vi) To provide opportunities for working with and responding to varied situations and challenging circumstances

The evaluation of practical learning happens in many ways. Students are expected to submit their weekly reports of concurrent fieldwork.

Structure and Content of Field Education: China

Social work in China is offered at both undergraduate and postgraduate levels. Students in China experience varied fieldwork practicums in their course curriculum at both bachelor's and master's levels. Yet the fieldwork education requirement is not the same across the schools of social work in China. As one author observes, some schools of social work take into account the background of students at admission and then review and structure the fieldwork practicum credits or hour requirements accordingly. On average, the fieldwork practicum in Chinese schools of social work can be categorised as either:

(i) Being placed in the concurrent placement where students go for their field practicum during the weekends and holidays to do their activities
(ii) Being placed in the block placement where students are sent to the field practicum for a full semester.

Many schools follow the second method of field work placement (point ii above) so that students obtain a fulfilling, varied, and beneficial fieldwork experience. The total required hours of fieldwork per student differs from university to university and is dependent on the educational background of the student. A student who has a bachelor's degree in social work is required to complete 600 hours of compulsory supervised fieldwork. On the other hand, a student from a discipline other than social work degree at their undergraduate level is required to undergo 800 to 900 hours of supervised fieldwork practicum. The distribution of the credit hours in each semester depends on the faculty or the department; thus, each university department predetermines its field placement requirements and the distribution of the credits and notional and practice hours in a semester. The nature of the placement also changes from university to university.

Challenges for Field Work Education

In this part of the chapter, we discuss the relevant challenges faced in social work field education in both India and China. While doing so we attempt to present a comparative understanding of two different social work educational settings, whilst discussing their similarities and differences. Some of the common threads that were noted from the data were (a) Lost focus on practice teaching, (ii) Lack of available agencies for field practice, (iii) Lack of practice standards, (iv) Lack of a social work education council, (v) Lack of trained educators and supervisors for student field practice, (vi) A general lack of trained supervisors at placement agencies.

(a) Lost Focus on Practice Teaching

The fieldwork component within the social work programme is crucial in developing students with skill and knowledge. Importantly this component of training also presents students with realistic situations and develops their responsiveness to social realities and problems that are experienced in contemporary society. However, in many schools of social work in both India and China, the fieldwork practicum has been relegated to a mere formality or requirement of the programme, whereas theoretical or classroom teaching takes dominance in the academic timetable. Much of the social work curricula in China has a clear focus on theoretical learning, whereas an emphasis on the practice component is largely absent. In addition to this, the fieldwork practice requirements, curriculum, and standards vary across China (Li et al, 2012). The existing gap between the theory and practice learning across the schools of social work in China is evident of a neglected fieldwork education in social work (Liu, Sun, & Anderson, 2013; Wang & Huang, 2013).

Further, scholars have continuously criticised the theory-centric nature of social work education where students are denied practice experiences and thereby their skills and competences are shrinking. Consequently, students' abilities to practise in diverse contexts are questioned by many scholars. However, in spite of its remarkable success in a short period of 30 years after its reestablishment, the social work programme in China continues to be criticised for its 'theory-centric' nature. Even after three decades of return to social work, Chinese education continues to neglect the field education training in social work. Similar to the findings in earlier studies (Xiong & Wang, 2007; Yan et al., 2012; Shi, 2004; Ting & Zhang, 2012; Tong, 2006), the present study also found that field education training was widely neglected in Chinese social work education and that many students were not satisfied with their practical learning. All the 33 students interviewed for the study reported that the curriculum of social work in master's level is very theoretical, with little opportunity for acquiring practical knowledge.

Further, debates in academia are also centred around the issues of building skillful social work communities that can contribute to nation-building. However, despite hours of field work practice, both in India and China, skills, competencies, and the ability to contribute to social development is always questioned by academics and the public; thus, affecting the professional identity of social workers in both of these Asian countries. Social work graduates have acquired a registered degree in social work yet remain ill-equipped and have little confidence in conducting social work interventions at the community, group, and individual levels. It appears that such teaching programmes in social work are focused on equipping students with theoretical knowledge rather than allowing them to test that knowledge in the practical setting. The schools of social work in both India and China need to concentrate more on developing practice-oriented social work programmes in order to produce practitioners who are informed by the needs and requirements of their respective societies. It is also important that social work educators and school administrators understand the need for combining theory and practice; simply learning theories and the theory of social work practice will not achieve the objective of social work education. Only a combination of these teaching practices can achieve these goals and should therefore be relevant.

Further there is also an imbalance in the credit allotment for the social work practice and theoretical paper. In some schools the practical courses are grouped under the elective courses or even under the other courses instead of compulsory courses. Nevertheless, for graduating with a master's degree in social work it requires a student to undergo a minimum 600 to 800 hours of practicum under supervision. But what student should do in the practicum and what are the learning outcomes are not specifically defined as there are no field work manuals or curriculum that guides students' field practicum.

(b) Lack of Available Practice Placement Agencies

Another associated problem with respect to the field practicum is the limited availability of placement agencies, together with the collaboration of the agency and the social work department at the university This collaboration is crucial in imparting quality learning and making social work students competent practitioners in their field of expertise. However, the most common challenge faced by the schools of social work in both India and China is finding an agency that is well-equipped with supervisory support, projects serving the verity of population in which students can get involved and gain hands-on experience, agencies with community outreach programmes, and agencies within the reach of the schools or departments. Schools of social work in China follow different approaches in providing fieldwork experiences to students. Literature predominantly notes two types of placements followed by these schools of social work i.e., a concurrent session model and a block fieldwork model (Cai, Bo, & Hsiao, 2018; Liu, Sun, & Anderson, 2013). However, due to the unavailability of well-resourced placement agencies with trained social work supervisors in schools in both India and China, some training institutions redirect their students to the available agencies irrespective of preference of specialisation or geographical locations. Thus, the availability and development of projects that are relevant to the community needs aligned with the students' expertise and its contribution to the students learning is questioned. Moreover, schools located in outlying regions make the prospect of finding agencies with the social workers as supervisors for their students an impossible task. The lack of agencies with good practice opportunities, resources, and provisions consumed a lot of students' energies in sorting out the requirements expected to learn during their field practicum.

Another relevant finding of the study is that unfortunately, both in India and China, the schools of social work were not able to build sufficient networks among the social service agencies in and around the country. Yet, such a network would support students' placements, practice learning opportunities, students' research and project assignments, alongside contributing to the curriculum planning and community outreach programmes. However, because of the unavailability of such agencies, students were sent to agencies located within cities and very rarely had opportunities to gain an international placement experience. Further funding constraints, administrative reasons, and students' personal inadequacies also impact on their field practice learning.

(c) Lack of Practice Standards

The components of fieldwork training in India are different than that of China. More often than not, fieldwork education in Indian schools of social work is a combination of rural camps, concurrent field work, study visits, agency visits and block, summer, winter placements. However, most of these activities are conducted as a sheer requirement rather than giving an enriching experience to the students. During the rural camp students were expected to spend time visiting the homes in the community conducting surveys and needs analyses, rather than learning core aspects of community and rural development, dynamics in the rural governance, and experiencing the countryside lifestyle. However, the implementation of the rural camp as a means of training in Indian social work is an important component within the social work practicum as it provides a unique learning experience. However, in some cases the provision of the bare minimum of supervisory support during the rural camp has hindered students learning instead of bringing out the potentials in students. Further literature notes that despite developments in Chinese social work in line with national standards, the qualifications and requirements of social work supervisors are not specified (Wu & Peng, 2018).

(d) Lack of a Social Work Education Council

As previously indicated, with India's approximate 600 schools of social work across the country, these schools vary in structure, student enrolment, availability of resources such as educators, administrative support, and the location of the institutions. Further, Nithi Ayog (previously known as UGC) is the sole higher education governing authority in India: an organisation that formulates the rules and regulations for all the educational programmes offered in the country. Social work is a practice-based education; practical learning is the core of students' learning that is intended to reshape learners as humane practitioners in their field of expertise. However due to the high number of institutions and diversity in terms of geography, population groups, problems experienced, and interventions required the social work education, curriculum, practice teaching, and practice standards differ greatly across the country. Each school follows its own curriculum, practice hours, and practice requirements, which in turn results in a great variety of differences in students' learning – even in the core curriculum and training.

Understanding these issues, social work educators and practitioners alike – as well as the community – have demanded a regulatory body for the social work profession and education. The existence of a social work education council in the country would mandate the basic standards to be followed by each educational institutions in terms of core curriculum, fieldwork practice, and practice hours required for the completion of social work graduate learning and research requirements. It is also observed by the literature that many schools take the fieldwork lightly and students were not sent to the fieldwork practicum on a regular basis despite the availability of agencies and the other resources. The lack of awareness among social work educators and the absence of a regulatory body appear to be the reasons behind these irregularities in the Indian context.

(e) Lack of Trained Educators and Supervisors

Social work education literature (Liu, Sun, & Anderson, 2013; Ting & Zhang, 2012; Xiong & Wang, 2007) reflects that a common problem of social work education in China is the lack of trained social work educators and supervisors for student field practice. While the origins of the supervision of social work trainees is traced back to the late nineteenth century (Magnussen, 2018), the importance of supervision in social work continues to reign supreme by many scholars internationally (O'Donoghue, 2015; Nadesan, 2020). Further, such supervision was the only source of learning during the early nineteenth century (Kadushin & Harkness, 2002; Tsui, 2005). The majority of the social work current educators in the departments of social work in China are from different academic backgrounds with minimal or no field work experience (Ting & Zhang, 2012; Xiong & Wang, 2007). This may be the reason why students in their master's level of study have supposedly been neglected in fieldwork supervision, with many not satisfied with the practical skills that they gained from their social work training. Students face many challenges during their field work practicum which has a negative impact on their learning. Further, literature has also documented (Wu & Peng, 2018; Caspi & Reid, 2002; Davys & Beddoe, 2010; Kadushin & Harkness, 2002) the shortage of practice educators, clear supervision structures, and the clear availability of supervisory time in Chinese social work. These hindrances affect the students' professional learning as well as the development of the profession of the social work in China.

(f) Lack of Trained Supervisors at the Placement Agency

The lack of trained social workers on-site at the placement agency where students are sent for field practicum is the major issue that Chinese social work communities face. Literature notes a minimal number of agency staff with training in fieldwork supervision (Wu & Peng, 2018). Finding an agency with trained social workers as supervisors is a current challenge in China (Ting & Zhang, 2012). Because of the lack of supervisors with social work background, students are expected to do a lot of administrative work such as maintaining the documents of the agency and tending to phone calls. These activities are largely unrelated to their social work training and students are therefore denied the opportunity to apply the theory they learn in the classroom to practice. It is noted that administrative tasks as listed bear little relevance to social work training and knowledge. When analysed, this behaviour by placement agencies demonstrate the abuse of social work students as cheap labour instead of training them as future social work staff. Furthermore, this trend is also visible in Indian social work and documented in literature (Baikady, 2017). Though students are sent to agencies working on a variety of issues such as the aged population, poverty, and hospitals, the fieldwork practice hours are minimal and leaves students perplexed about their learning objectives and goals. Because of the lack of supervision in the agency with social work education and the lack of or minimal supervision in the departments some students experience limited or no field work experience, and become frustrated during and at the end of their fieldwork practicum. While supervision is an integral part of quality learning, the relationship between a supervisor and supervisee has been termed a 'working alliance' (Mackrill, 2011 cited in Magnussen, 2018) and a 'working relationship' based on rapport, trust, and caring (Schulman, 2005 cited in Magnussen, 2018). Such working alliances and relationships seem absent in many schools of social work in India and China.

Conclusion

The fieldwork education and practice learning in the placement agency is intended to provide a combined, realistic learning opportunity to the students, hence the importance of field learning is crucial. Supervised, guided, and monitored field work and other practical learning activities form the basis of social work education and practice (Baikady et.al. 2022). It is also important that the quality of future social work professionals depends on the quality of fieldwork practicums undertaken during their study. Further it is also well noted that theory with practical learning in social work makes social workers more human-centric and responsive to social problems. In other words, theory-centric learning without guided or supervised practice is just like other social science subject. In summary, it is observed that the field work component within social work is becoming largely a neglected concept whereas the theoretical teaching and other assignments take precedence over the fieldwork practicum. Such poor practices within social work training institutions do not understand the importance of a guided, supervised field work placement in social work training.

To conclude, schools of social work in both India and China need to strengthen their respective fieldwork practice settings and emphasise equally theory and practice within teaching and learning. Perhaps these schools should initiate the formation of mutual bodies of interest to guide and make uniform the training requirements. Furthermore, students' fieldwork experiences must be taken into consideration during the theoretical teaching, so that it helps students to better understand the theoretical concepts and apply it in their practice. Schools of social work should find alternative methods in finding well-established, social work-oriented, and supervisory support available agencies for the students' placements alongside establishing minimum standards for social work practice and field practicum at the national level. Social work academia in India should seriously work towards establishing the national council or authority for social work education to mandate the education and practice learning of students in the country.

References

Baikady, R. (2017). *Comparing social work education in a parliamentary democracy and in a communist regime: A study of India and China* (unpublished doctoral thesis) Central University of Karnataka, Gulbarga.

Baikady, R., & Sheng-Li, C. (2020). Challenges for social work education in China: findings from three metropolises. *Social Work Education*. 41(1), 34–49. doi: 10.1080/02615479.2020.1795109

Baikady, R., Pulla, V., & Channaveer, R. M. (2014). Social work education in India and Australia. *International Journal of Social Work and Human Services Practice*, 2(6), 311–8.

Baikady, R., Sheng-Li, C., & Channaveer, R. M. (2020). Eight decades of existence and search for an identity: Educators' perspectives on social work education in contemporary India. *Social Work Education*. 40(8), 994–1009. doi: 10.1080/02615479.2020.1773780

Baikady, R., Nadesan, V., Sajid, S.M & Islam, M.R. (2022). Introduction Signature Pedagogy – A Practice Laboratory of Social Work Education. In: R. Baikady, S.M. Sajid, V. Nadesan, & M.R. Islam. (eds) The Routledge Handbook of Field Work Education in Social Work (1st ed.). Routledge India. https://doi.org/10.4324/9781032164946-1

Blumenthal, David, and William Hsiao. 2015. Lessons from the East—China's rapidly evolving health care system. *New England Journal of Medicine* 372: 1281–85.

Bogo, M. (2010). *Achieving competence in social work through field education*. Toronto: University of Toronto Press.

Cai, Y., Bo, A., & Hsiao, S. C. (2018). Emerging social work field education trends in China. *Journal of Social Work Education*, 54(2), 336–42. doi: 10.1080/10437797.2017.1350233.

Caspi, J., & Reid, W. J. (2002). *Educational supervision in social work: A task-centered model for field instruction and staff development*. New York: Columbia University Press. doi: 10.7312/casp10852

Davys, A., & Beddoe, L. (2010). *Best practice in professional supervision: A guide for the helping professions*. London: Jessica Kingsley Publishers.

Guo, Y. (2017). Career barriers for social work students in China. *Journal of Social Work*, 17, 732–48.

Homonoff, E. (2008). The heart of social work: Best practitioners rise to challenges in field instruction. *The Clinical Supervisor*, 27(2), 135–69.

ICSW/IASSW/IFSW. (2020): 2020 to 2030 global agenda for social work and social development framework: 'Co-building inclusive social transformation. Retrieved from https://www.ifsw.org/2020-to-2030-global-agenda-for-social-work-and-social-development-framework-co-building-inclusive-social-transformation/

Kadushin, A., & Harkness, D. (2002a). *Supervision in social work*. New York: Columbia University Press.

Kadushin, A. E., & Harkness, D. (2002b). *Supervision in social work* (4th ed.). New York: Columbia University Press.

Lei, Jie, Luo, M. Chui, E., & Lu, W. (2019). Whether professional training matters: Attitudinal antecedents to the turnover intentions of social workers in Guangzhou, China. *Journal of Social Service Research*, 45, 444–54.

Li, Y., Han, W.-J., & Huang, C.-C. (2012). Development of social work education in China: Background, current status and prospects. *Journal of Social Work Education*, 48, 635–53.

Liu, M., Sun, F., & Anderson, S. G. (2013). Challenges in social work field education in China: Lessons from the Western experience. *Social Work Education*, 32(2), 179–96. doi: 10.1080/02615479.2012.723682.

Magnussen, J. (2018). Supervision in Denmark: An empirical account of experiences and practices. *European Journal of Social Work*, 21(3), 359–73. doi: 10.1080/13691457.2018.1451827.

Mo, Y. H., Tong Lit, L., & Sum Tsui, M. (2019). Chaos in order: The evolution of social work supervision practice in the Chinese Mainland. *The Clinical Supervisor*, 38(2), 345–365.

Nadesan, V. S. (2020). Challenges of social work students from historically disadvantaged universities during placements in semi-rural areas in South Africa. *Southern African Journal of Social Work and Social Development*, 32(3), 17. https://upjournals.co.za/index.php/SWPR/index. New York.

O'Donoghue, K. (2015). Issues and challenges facing social work supervision in the twenty-first century. *China Journal of Social Work*, 8(2), 136–49. doi: 10.1080/17525098.2015.1039172

Schmidt, K., & Rautenbach, J. V. (2016). Field instruction: Is the heart of social work still beating in the Eastern Cape? *Social Work* (Stellenbosch.Online), 52(4), 589–610

Ting, W., & Zhang, H. (2012). Flourishing in the spring? Social work, social work education and field education in China. *China Journal of Social Work*, 5, 201–22. doi:10.1080/17525098.2012.721172

Tsui, M. (2005). *Social work supervision: Context and concepts*. London: Sage Publications.

Wang, Z. H., & L. Q. Huang. (2013). Exploring models for indigenizing social work education in China. *Chinese Education & Society* 46(6), 42–9. doi:10.2753/CED1061-1932460605.

Wu Qiang Chen Lei, & Tingting Peng (2018) Exploring gaps between MSW students' experiences and expectations of field supervision in a Chinese setting, Social Work Education, 37:2, 265–276, DOI: 10.1080/02615479.2017.1395406

Xiong, Y., & Wang, S. B. (2007). Development of social work education in China in the context of new policy initiatives: Issues and challenges. *Social Work Education*, 26(6), 560–72. doi:10.1080/02615470701456210.

Yan, M. C., Gao, J. G., & Lam, C. M. (2012). The dawn is too Ddistant: The experience of 28 social work graduates entering the social work field in China. *Social Work Education*, 32(4), 538–551. https://doi.org/10.1080/02615479.2012.688097

Yingsheng Li, Wen-Jui Han & Chien-Chung Huang (2012) Development of Social Work Education in China: Background, Current Status, and Prospects, Journal of Social Work Education, 48:4, 635–653, DOI: 10.5175/JSWE.2012.201100049

Part III
Field Work Education in the Latin American and the Caribbean Context

15
Clinical Social Work in Chile

*Carolina Muñoz-Guzmán, María Olaya Grau,
Karla González Suitt, and Valentina Garrido López*

This chapter argues the need of a broader understanding of social work practice for Latin American countries, that, including the traditional goal of pursuing social change, acknowledges the relevance of attending to subjective wellbeing and social unrest, especially in vulnerable populations. To do that, social workers need a formal training in clinical social work. We focus on Chile as a case of study, to describe the difficulties and opportunities the profession has faced to meet that need.

We will claim that the contributions clinical social work can make to reach social justice in Latin America, specifically in Chile, would need a specialised professional training in clinical social work which acknowledges critical social work perspective, to avoid reductionism in understanding social problems.

Social work in Latin America has been framed by an ethical-political dimension committed with democracy, as well as changes in social structures to ensure social justice. This pre-eminence has put under dispute the possibilities of clinical social work, which is seen as a narrow understanding of social problems in Latin America.

The increasing complexity of people's life, related not only to poverty but the convergence of many difficulties across life's course, provides a disciplinary opportunity for social workers to apply effective tools and skills to cope with violence, addictions, mental health problems, discrimination, and exclusion. Clinical social work comprehends a set of tools through which practitioners establish a relational process that aims to help individuals to cope with such psychosocial problems, and enhance their interpersonal relationships, using their personal capabilities and strengths, and contextual resources (Ituarte, 2017).

The chapter is organised as follows. Firstly, a glance at the reconceptualisation process of social work in Latin America is presented. This will explain the predominance of macro practice and the political ethos of the profession. Additionally, it will delineate the influences of theoretical developments such as structural and radical social work. Later, the limitations of social services underpinned by the neoliberal principles drawing public policies within the region, as well as a broader understanding of social problems that embrace the intersectionality characterising them, is explained. All of which result in a renewed comprehension of radical social work, such as anti-oppressive perspectives demanding the interplay of private and public views, and subjective and objective understandings to advance social change. Under this transformation,

DOI: 10.4324/9781003270119-19

clinical social work emerges as an alternative to offer more effective solutions to more complex problems.

Chile is a good example of the myriad effects of living in more complex societies marked by commodification. Therefore, the chapter illustrates the need for clinical social work using Chile as a case study. Likewise, demographics of social problems are presented together with its effects on people's wellbeing. Consequently, evidencing the need for including in social work interventions individuals' resources or strengths, the independence and ability to seek his or her individual and collective projects, connecting their personal trajectories.

From this set of relationships, social workers distinguish clinical and political dimensions that need to be supported.

Once justifying the need for clinical social work, the chapter advances proposing specific components of a clinical social work specialisation that maintains the public commitment of social work and acknowledges the roots of the profession on social transformation towards a more egalitarian society; and, at the same time, takes into account the complexities of society, where gender, race, class, and other forms of oppression are the result of how society is organised, and produces effects not only at societal levels, but also at personal levels. It is in this intersection where clinical social work has as an important role to play.

Lastly, we present final remarks that summarise main aspects discussed towards the chapter and the challenges Latin American social work is facing nowadays.

Latin American Social Work

Reconceptualisation and Predominance of Traditional Critical Perspectives

Social work in Latin America faced a process of reconceptualisation in the 1970s, aimed at the acknowledgement of the value to understand the position of oppressed people in the context of the social and economic structures they lived in. Thus, reconceptualisation challenged the traditional professional perspective that supported the ruling-class hegemony, and argued that social work should assist people to understand their alienation in terms of their oppression and build up their self-esteem (Bailey et al., 1975, pp. 9–10). Reconceptualisation tenets emphasised that social workers and service users should avoid experiencing their social world from an individualised perspective. Instead, they supported collective action based on solidarity between social workers and service users through group action. It sought to build on strengths of the existing working-class movement by bringing together community political activity with collective class action through the working-class movement, including trade unionism, to achieve growth.

The social context then prevailing in Latin America was one of the general crises affecting the economic, social, political, and ideological spheres. The region was becoming an object of development for industrialised countries. Latin American people became concerned with the levels of exploitation and marginalisation that they were living in, because development was being achieved at the expense of poor people while benefitting traditional elites and partners of international companies (Smith & Smith, 1991; Boff, 1985). There was awareness about the contradictions produced by political and economic policies. On one side, there was capitalist development, and on the other, there were several populist measures involving marginalised groups which suffered failures similar to those of the Alliance for Progress (Taffet, 2012). These capitalist initiatives impoverished a high proportion of the Latin American population who became doubly affected by tragedy through repression exercised under the emergency powers of military dictatorships which assumed control in many countries (Dodson, 1979; Boff, 1985;

Gutiérrez & Sobrino, 1984; Silva, 2009). These issues had an enduring legacy on developing forms of social involvement and political engagement.

Thus, in Latin America in general, social work is associated with a field of knowledge influenced by critical social work and inspired by Marxist interpretations of social relations, a perspective which was particularly emphasised in the development of social work as an academic field (Iamamoto & De Carvalho,1982; Saracostti et al., 2012; Molina, 2015). Brazil has had a huge influence on Latin American social work education, where it promoted that social work, in addition to being a profession, become a field of knowledge (Mota, 2013). This contrasts with the situation in other realities dominated by a concept of the profession that has a strongly (but not exclusively) technical-interventionist and at times therapeutic inspiration.

There are several influences from sources coming from international social work, such as Structural Social Work in Canada (Lundy, 2004 ; Moreau & Leonard, 1989; Mullaly, 2007), and Radical Social Work in Britain (Bailey et al., 1975) which brought social workers close to service users through action-research and attempted to create alliances with them to develop new forms of practice. Although this quickly moved to Marxist Social Work (Corrigan & Leonard, 1978), this approach was found to be insufficient because it ignored crucial social divisions, such as 'race' and gender, giving rise to alternative theories and paradigms for practice. Decisive among these were the Antiracist Social Work (Dominelli, 2017; Dominelli, 1996), Feminist Social Work (Dominelli & McLeod, 1989), and Anti-Oppressive Practice (Dominelli & Campling, 2002). In Australia, these critiques were elaborated further through postmodernism and were named as Critical Social Work (Fook, 2002).

In Latin America yet there was a trend to follow Corrigan and Leonard (1978) who tried to promote Marxist Social Work and emphasised a collective approach avoiding the individualisation of problems. Overall, there is a controversy about the reductionism of the individual and its social relations in psychologisation, and the recognition of social work solely as actions oriented towards sociopolitical ends.

Therefore, macro practice of social work has been in dispute with clinical social work, since reconceptualisation time. This split between 'adjusting the individual to society or society to the individual' (p. 27) posed a tension between 'traditional' and 'critical' approaches that remains embedded in social work today (Chambon, 1999).

Fook (2002) recognised the tendency to avoid individualising the problems of service users and to instead connect these problems with larger social structures, facing them through political actions. These early critical social work theorists saw clinical modalities at best as providing 'symptomatic relief' (Mullaly, 2007, p. 307).

In Latin America persists the vision of social workers as political agents, exclusively related to practices which serve public problems from a macro perspective, intervening social programmes, budgets, and public policies, most of it from a critical perspective. Elaine Behring, a Brazilian intellectual of social work in 2014 stated that clinical social work produces 'exotic interventions when plays with subjective interpretations – in a very individual sphere – ending up in processes based on insufficient interventions' (Behring, 2014)

These rooted visions in Latin American social work, that take distance from decontextualised, person-focused actions, have been challenged within current critical social work theorists, who pursue to overcome, both in theory and in practice, this division between the structural and sociopolitical levels on the one hand, and the personal and interpersonal levels on the other (Fook, 2002; Mullaly, 2007)

From this renewed vision, the anti-oppressive perspective stresses an intersectionality of diverse types of coercions that take place, not only on structural levels but also on personal, interpersonal, and cultural levels. Trevelyan (2008, p. 9) indicated that earlier critical social workers' emphases on large-scale structural change have shifted to include a focus on also effecting changes on more micro levels.

Updated critical social work questions current hegemonies of Latin American social work, especially when there is a common agreement about the inefficacies of the profession's performance in the public sphere.

Social Work and State

According to Sonia Fleury (Fleury, 2017), even though the emergence in Latin American region of a mixture of social protection measures has increased coverage and reduced poverty, these have been unable to guarantee universal citizens' rights and longevity. The role of social work in facing this tension has been complex. For example, social workers face several constraints as they must respond to competing loyalties when playing dual roles as helper and controller. In addition, they experience permanent institutional demands, frameworks, and situations that require highly ethical awareness to implement high quality professional interventions (Strier, 2007).

The achievement of social justice aims requires defeating the structures of power relations, and routine practices, underpinning radical social change and participatory models of action. This explains Fook's claim that consciousness of a social context informed by the experience of service users becomes one of the earliest principles of critical social work (2002).

Estalayo and Sáez (2017) emphasise the importance that the professional relationship be based on the defence of social rights and the provision of economic resources and benefits, preserving essentialist visions of social work. The authors reinforce the notion of going beyond discourses that establish an antagonism between intervention based on rationality or emotionality; on the objective or the subjective; on material help or psychosocial support; on bureaucracy or adhocracy.

Based on the fact that daily work in social services is increasingly complex and brings social unrest because there is a predominance of commodification and neo-philanthropy, Estalayo and Sáez. (2017) appeal to a relational social work woven within the management of social benefits and attending subjective rights. Social work carried out in the public system of social services needs to be rethought in today's reality, because, as Bourdieu (1999) warned us, it seems that some of the discourses that favour the withdrawal of the State and impairment of public affairs are winning the battle in our minds. And far from resisting or fighting, we adopt forms of resignation or collaboration.

Therefore, Latin American social work needs to be revisited, not to abandon its mission of social justice and transformation, but to broaden the understanding of social problems, where different levels of the social world – the private and the public spheres – are considered to complexly co-constitute one another (Pozzuto et al., 2005). It implies bringing to discussion emancipatory approaches to social work (feminist, structural, and anti-racist, anti-oppression) to address issues of gender, race, class, and other forms of oppression. The understanding of these issues requires the blending of interdependent spheres: the individual and the social, the personal and the political, and it supposes that changing the social order requires more than a focus on structural levels of society. Considering this ampler understanding, larger forms of social change should include personal and interpersonal levels, which drives to practising clinically with individuals. Fook (2002) warns about how clinical social work practice remains a relatively undeveloped area, and there is a need for research and a way of teaching clinical social work that intends intervention framed by dialectical processes such as has been described here, to a commitment with structural change.

Emergency of Clinical Social Work, Chile as a Case Study

Increasing Complex Needs

The complexity of modern life has created over the years a challenging scenario for social work in Latin America. The impact of social injustice and oppression has dramatically increased not only inequality and inequity, but also the incidence of mental health problems, associated not only with poverty, but with complex barriers connected within different stages of the life span. This represents a greater challenge for Latin American social work that lacks training in clinical skills.

Incorporating subjective wellbeing in the discussion of social development, is an urgent task that not only responds to international organisations' debate but also to academic and educational reflections. Over the past years, global conversation on development has gone hand in hand with growing expressions of discomfort with society, which have highlighted that today, more than ever, they incorporate what people feel and think into the discussion of development as an inescapable task (PNUD, 2012).

These arguments are relevant to understand the emergency of clinical social work as a bastion of critical social work, since reaching human development is a milestone for social justice. And today, human development cannot be indifferent to subjectivity notions. The conceptualisation of a broader social work practice that searches for human development should incorporate the following premises.

First, integral subjective wellbeing should be understood considering individual and social dimensions, which includes social unrest. Second, both individual wellbeing and social unrest, are socially conditioned; in this regard the 2012 PNUD report clearly showed that social conditions are key to achieve Chilean subjective wellbeing. Third, the report has established that this relationship between development and subjectivity is not linear, not only because it must operate on social relationships and practices, but because there is an inevitable difference and tension between the diversity of individual ends (what each person wants for their lives) and the ends of society (the common horizons under which society decides its regulatory order and the distribution of its resources). In a democratic society, mediation between the ends of individuals and the ends of society can only be produced and legitimised through institutionalised deliberation.

Fourth, the promotion of capacity building must be done with the understanding that society can increase the probability that people achieve subjective wellbeing if it endows them with capacities – that is, with real liberties for the realisation of their lifetime projects. Capacities are socially constructed opportunities that make sense to people depending on their purposes, which can be appropriate thanks to adequate mechanisms of social distribution, and that can be put into movement in social settings provided with regulations, relationships, and basic resources. This is a central and empirically grounded fact in the report: the greater the endowment of capacities offered by a society, the greater the probability that its members have of achieving subjective wellbeing. Wellbeing levels and subjective discomfort of the Chilean population can be explained to a large extent by the specific and differentiated combinations of abilities that people possess. This is the key to understanding some of the apparent paradoxes of subjectivity in Chile.

Once the notion of subjective wellbeing is included as part of human development, then all the measure variables about people wellbeing become part of the goals of social work practice. The following panorama is critical about one of the core dimensions of subjective wellbeing: mental health.

As reported by the World Health Organization (World Health Organization, 2017), the Chilean population experiences high levels of depression. According to the report 'Depression and Other Common Mental Disorders', in Chile 844.253 people over 15 suffer from depression, that is, 5% of the population and more than a million suffer from anxiety (6.5%) – this ranks us in fourth place in the Americas region among the countries with prevalence of this disease.

One of the issues raised by the WHO is that even though there are effective treatments available for depression, more than half of those affected worldwide do not have access to them, indicating that 'barriers to effective care include: lack of resources and trained health personnel, in addition to the stigmatization of mental disorders and inaccurate clinical evaluation' (World Health Organization, 2017). Additionally, the national survey of employment, work, health, and quality of life indicated the main symptoms and health problems reported by workers are strictly related to mental health. Highlighting the recurrent feeling of tiredness with 30.3% feeling melancholic, sad, or depressed for two weeks during the past 12 months with 21%. These numbers show important disparities when analysed according to gender, occupation, and occupational hierarchy, where women working in domestic services, unpaid family occupations, those who work in informal jobs, and women working within the public sector are the most affected population (World Health Organization, 2017).

According to the Division of Disease Prevention and Control (Guajardo, 2017) (Minoletti et al., 2014), in Chile mental health problems are the main source of disease burden. According to the latest study of Burden of Disease and Attributable Burden carried out in our country, 23.2% of the years of life lost due to disability or death (DALY) are determined by neuropsychiatric conditions. For children between one and nine years of age, 30.3% of DALYs can be attributed to these conditions, a proportion that increases to 38.3% between 10 and 19 years of age. Among women, unipolar depressive disorders and anxiety disorders are among the top five causes of DALY (Minoletti et al., 2014). In contrast to men, alcohol consumption disorders play a predominant role, along with accidents and violence. When comparing different risk factors, alcohol consumption encompasses the highest attributable risk, explaining 12% of the total disease burden – even doubling high blood pressure (hypertension) and obesity (Guajardo, 2017)

On the other hand, the same author indicates that the most vulnerable groups are most affected: people with a lower educational level, younger population, women, and people with indigenous backgrounds. In addition, mental health problems begin early in life: among children from 4 to 11 years old, 27.8% have some of these disorders (Guajardo, 2017)

According to the World Health Organization (WHO), rising suicide rates globally have seen suicide declared a public health problem. Almost a million people die from suicide every year and about 250,000 are under the age of 25 (World Health Organization, 2014). In Chile as presented by the Health Department (Ministerio de Salud, 2017) the suicide rate in the general population doubled between 1990 and 2011, from 5.6 to 11.8, which means that if in 1990 5.6 people committed suicide for every 100,000 inhabitants, in 2011 11.8 people per 100,000 inhabitants took their lives. (Echávarri et al., 2015; Guajardo, 2017)

Research developed by Valdivia and Pihá (Vicente et al., 2016; Vicente et al., 2012), shows that lifetime prevalence of psychiatric disorders in Chile represents a third of the total population. Similarly, anxiety disorders have the highest prevalence, closely followed by major depression. Likewise, alcohol and drug-related disorders are also highly prevalent (11% and 8.1%, respectively).

Furthermore, increased social vulnerability enhances risk factors associated with suicide. Therefore, WHO distributes risk factors in five different dimensions: individual components, human relationships, community component, society, and the health system. This allows us to identify a space for intervention of clinical social work, since the incidence in communities and its relationship with social vulnerability is a specific area of social work intervention. With these statistics into account, the scope of intervention in social work research and intervention becomes an urgent need in the development of our discipline.

The field of mental health is an interdisciplinary field of intervention, therefore it is a place where different professionals, theoretical models, diverse ways of looking at reality, different institutions and even different political and social ideologies intertwine to propose multiple ways in which attention and services should be provided. As presented by García, interdisciplinary work characterises the functioning of mental health intervention because it needs to provide integration, coherence, and articulation of services as key to securing effective and quality actions (García, 2004).

Social workers specialised in mental health issues need to be integrated into interdisciplinary teams, understanding as such a set of professionals with a common purpose whose insights are equally important, how to offer contributions for problem-solving while providing different types of information and assessments that are integrated and considered according to the characteristics and priorities of the problem in place.

Therefore, the development of a clinical social work specialisation in Latin America and in Chile would be an opportunity to improve the work that social workers are already doing in the field without the specific tools and skills needed.

Professional Landscape: Type of State Organisation, Lack of Specialisation in Workforce, Lack of Programmes

This section refers to challenges social workers must overcome to promote social justice in Chile, where both state organization and social policies implementation are a constant struggle. It briefly describes the distance between social programming and its implementation and how this directly impacts social workers and their clients.

Following that, it presents a discussion about the need for specialised training in clinical skills to improve the impact of social workers on social justice, in consideration of both the increasing complexity of social life but also the impact of the distance of social programming and its implementation. The need for specialised training is supported by diverse evidence gathered by the School of Social Work at the Pontificia Universidad Católica de Chile.

Social policy implementation in Chile, even though it is underpinned by a rights perspective, does not only depend for its failure or success on the autonomous action of social forces, or on the effects of organisational structures, but also deeply depends on the role of implementers. In Chile, government organisational structures have affected resources and actions, but the agency (or lack thereof) of organisational actors has also undermined structural properties. To attend to the current needs of the population in a more complex social landscape, social workers are required to defeat the structures of power and routine practices, underpinning radical social change and participatory models of action.

The distance between social programme design and its effective implementation are examples of the challenges that social workers must confront regularly. Social programme design is led by a centralised structure that lacks formalisation, resources, and effective communication. It is one which does not fit the characteristics of the agencies implementing the policies, as agencies do not have the capacity to make authoritative decisions or encourage meaningful staff participation.

This mismatch has an impact on staff running the programmes, decreasing their commitment and productivity, and turning policy outcomes into failure.

This kind of formal power distribution which only allows decision-making to occur at the top of the hierarchy, and an inflexible centralisation in programme implementation which does not foster an efficient process when judgements are made, combines with passive and powerless staff, causing programmes to neglect the basic rights expected by policy outcomes. Centralisation, then, emerges as a key component of the organisational dimension enabling progress toward rights-based policies.

It is commonly understood in matters of social policy design and among policy-makers that in order to move forward towards policy outcomes, policy design must acknowledge that agencies implementing social programmes and their human resources ought to enjoy a certain amount of autonomy enabling them to exercise discretion and criteria to decide about best courses of action in the local milieu. If policy-makers do not involve implementers and their staff members in decision-making, they may not perform adequately in concordance with policy goals.

The key problem described above represents the first challenge for social workers, as they are to defeat structures that limit their discretion and to fill implementation with solutions that accurately represent people's needs, and not those defined in a decontextualised manner. For that to happen, social workers need to be able to properly assess those needs and design efficient solutions. When achieving both actions, social work serves its *macro* and *micro* mission described earlier. Next, we will discuss how to approach to the *micro* responsibility.

As presented before, social workers in Latin America have historically attended to the underserved population from a systemic, ecological, political, and social programming perspective, but now need to incorporate the complexity of working both at the intersection of subjectivity and social context in addressing interpersonal problems that are closely connected with social context. Therefore, creating a specialised master's programme that aims to fill the gap of clinical tools and skills needed by professionals that are already doing clinical work without the currently required specialisation becomes an urgent task.

To develop a clinical area of research and intervention in the region we must first face the challenge of conceptualising this new field of knowledge in line with the particular needs of specialisation.

According to Ituarte and Regalado, clinical social intervention is a professional exercise in which social work has historically been carried out from a central connection of human subjectivity and moved towards social transformation, since the central aim of our professional work is in the problems related to oppression and social discrimination (Idareta, 2018; Ituarte, 2017). In this sense, we would define clinical social work as a

> specialised practice of social work and a psychotherapeutic relational process that aims to help a client face their psychosocial conflicts, overcome their psychosocial discomfort and achieve more satisfactory interpersonal relationships, using their personal capacities and the resources of its socio-relational context
>
> *(Ituarte, 2017, p. 20).*

Clinical social workers intervene in different spaces, with an emphasis on the interactions of subjectivity and its environment. Subjectivity is the space and process in which individuals construct an image of themselves, others, and the world in context of their social experiences. Subjectivity is made by someone's emotions, images, perceptions, desires, motivations and evaluations, among other elements (PNUD, 2012).

As mentioned before, offers of training in Latin America and particularly at the national level are non-existent at master's level in clinical social work. In Chile, the Master of Social Work (MSW) programmes are usually disciplinary which means that their aim is to contribute to the creation of disciplinary knowledge and to the pursuit of an academic career and do not necessarily provide specialised training on advanced professional skills.

Instruction developed for a specific purpose in clinical social work is based on the need for public and private services that implement different social programmes. To have professionals specialised in treating psychosocial problems, where the intersection of precarious structural conditions and situations of emotional, affective, relational, and social instability constraints and stresses social groups in an intersectional manner (age, gender, race, class) and a need from professionals to promote innovative complex interventions that required therapeutic skills that are not included in the bachelor programmes of social work.

The growing social crisis is manifested by the increase in suicides rates in older adults, growing neglect and violence rates against children and youth, high levels of depression in adolescents, family violence and against women, discrimination and social isolation of migrant groups, violence and mental health in prisons and future problems that this pandemic will create in the near future are evidence of the inability of social services to provide an effective response to these issues and stand out the urgent need to train professionals capable of promoting and implementing integral interventions to mitigate these problems.

Social work addresses the intersection between social precariousness and its impact on mental health and wellbeing of these populations. Organisations and public services have recognised an urgency to improve interventions in these fields, therefore the creation of a clinical social work master's programme to responds to a public problem in Chile today.

Considering this, the School of Social Work at the Pontificia Universidad Católica de Chile has developed a Clinical Master's Programme that would allow social workers and professionals from different disciplines such as nurses and occupational therapists, to develop these skills that are urgently needed. In Chile, master's programmes with an emphasis in the clinical field are mostly located in schools of psychology and are usually available for students that already hold an undergraduate degree in psychology, but psychotherapy does not necessarily aim to social transformation or social justice, nor does usually address problems related to oppression and social discrimination. In this sense, the fundamental difference between disciplines such as psychology is based on attending to human subjectivity with a contextual and systemic view; that is, working for psychosocial wellbeing focusing on the person, but also paying attention to the context and its social functioning, from a systemic approach, including systemic family therapy and narrative approach.

In an effort to identify the particular training needs for a clinical social work programme, in 2019, the School of Social Work at the Pontificia Universidad Católica de Chile (SSWPUC) conducted a study to identify social workers' needs of specialisation to face the current demands from the field.

Different sources of information were used, and complementary evidence was gathered:

1. A survey was applied to social workers who were SSWPUC alumni, to identify both the kind of problems they worked with, requiring clinical interventions, and specific competencies valued in a specialised professional training. Results showed that alumni dealt mainly with children's neglect, substance addiction, parenting stress, family relationships, intimate partner violence, and gender violence. Other issues were LGBTI families, elderly neglect, migrant discrimination. Among the competencies professionals would value to tackle the mentioned phenomena, the following were mentioned: therapeutic intervention strategies, assessment, evaluation strategies, people's mental health assessment and intervention strategies with various mental health problems, strategies for dealing with violence, competencies such as building a therapeutic relationship, clinical supervision, and intervention strategies to work with children and adolescents.

2. A survey applied to ten representatives of the seven schools of social work in the country that integrate the national council of Chilean universities, with the purpose of problematising the need for a clinical social work master's. Results indicated the need to establish a professional field independent but complementary to the field of intervention of a psychologist, that would provide academic and professional training in specific problems associated with mental health and wellbeing. Alongside this, this consultation would allow for the identification of multiple working spaces for clinical social workers, including hospitals, health care centres, schools, women's care centres, programmes that work with homeless persons, and of particular relevance the child welfare system – Servicio Nacional de Menores – was mentioned.
3. Further, the Direction of Institutional Analysis and Planning of the Pontificia Universidad Católica de Chile (DAIP) carried out interviews with professionals who lead hiring processes in diverse social programmes. The aim of this process was to explore in this occupational field the needs of qualified social workers regarding clinical skills. The most valued professional skills were 'to contribute to the solution of the needs and problems that affect people', and the ability 'to design and implement clinical interventions and promote dignity and social justice to ensure effective and humane interventions'. As was shown, the capacity to link clinical interventions with a broader impact in social justice is always a demand.
4. Lastly, the School of Social Work UC carried out a comparative analysis between national programmes that offer training associated with clinical skills. The programme analysis was focused on training professionals capable of designing, implementing, and evaluating clinical interventions that contribute to problem-solving related to quality of life and mental health of individuals, families, and diverse groups, but none of those were offered by schools of social work, and more importantly, none of those states a commitment to impacting on social justice.

Summarising, different voices from the social work field, academia and professional, agreed with the need for specialising in social work interventions, with clinical skills, in order to face the current social problems associated with mental health and human relationships. Added to this, there is an absence of programmes addressing the dependency of subjective wellbeing from societal conditioning.

With all the previously mentioned including a wide collection of information from diverse sources, we next present the main components that a specialisation in clinical social work should cover.

Previous Findings Conduct to the Following Conclusions

The kind of specialisation required has a professional orientation, different from a disciplinary approach, thus it should be characterised by applying the latest updates of the field into practice.

Specialised clinical education in social work should respond to the challenges identified earlier, with the use of teaching specific tools to approach mental health from a holistic view that integrates the micro and macro elements of social work, while understanding that both individual and social environmental factors have a shared influence. This permanent interaction affects individuals' subjectivity when experiencing suffering, depression, parenting complications, violence in the family, and chronic grief (Ituarte, 2017). As illustrated above, former students, scholars, and employers highlight that those specific skills are necessary when attending to these issues in the specialised training of clinical social workers.

The main competences for any clinical social work specialisation programme should be designing, evaluating, and implementing clinical interventions. For Latin American countries, a programme like this should also ensure the capability of reflective practice and a critical perspective, emphasising an ethical-political commitment to promote dignity and social justice from an intercultural and gender perspective.

Given that collected data about mental health problems showed that these are the main sources of disease burden in Chile, and that the vulnerable population is not receiving the services it rightly deserves, this specialised training should be oriented to social workers assisting primary care in excluded neighbourhoods, child protective services, public schools, municipalities, or agencies who assist clients directly.

Within our profession we have a body of knowledge about the social value for the whole of society when there is investment and construction of services for children, for people with learning disabilities and psychiatric problems, and for migrants and several other groups of people facing complex and diverse needs. We must emphasise, using the reputation of our work, that we cannot render invisible these whole new expressions of inequality. We should fight the tendency to blame these for their own burden, denouncing victims of domestic violence for the violence they suffer and people with mental health problems for their maladjustment. Social workers are called to be a part of the solution.

The solution should show the discrepancies between how disadvantaged groups perceive their ways of living and how the establishment judges them. The solution must acknowledge and fight discursive marginalisation, and power and control relations sustaining exclusionary practices that leave all the responsibilities of life's difficulties to those who suffer them. To unveil these practices, social work must understand people's narratives, their explanations of their life trajectories, and together find strategies to cope with their life complexities. In doing that, social workers must deploy clinical skills and critical thinking.

Final Remarks

In this chapter, Clinical Social Work in Chile, we have identified two key spheres that challenge social workers to comply with a renewed understanding of radical social work. These two spheres refer to private and public perspectives, subjective and objective understandings, and both will allow contemporary social work to advance towards social change and social justice.

Regarding the relation to the public sphere, we have seen a predominance of commodification and neo-philanthropy in social services provided by the public system in which social workers haven't been able to resist and change structures and have taken a resignation or collaboration stand. This clearly is a good picture of the current Chilean welfare state direction, turning a critical term to reflect upon the political effects of delegating welfare state responsibilities to non-state agents. Lack of resistance brings lack of interrogating the kind of influence shareholders have over the public wellbeing, the identity of current shareholders, and even more, the role of government.

Especially in times when the effect of inequity and inequality are manifested with even greater intensity in there is a particular need to resist a hierarchical policy process that endures through the different layers of the administrative state apparatus, acting as a barrier for the needed participation of public policy implementors and stakeholders to improve social services and social programming. In order to be consistent with and loyal to its mission to not only promote but actually secure social justice and social transformation, social work has to constantly resist structural power in organisational arrangements and actively propose and advocate for improvements in social policy that aim to develop a fairer society. To do that, social workers should engage in the fight to defend best practices brought by the old welfare state, refusing to act as neoliberal subjects, and in that process develop the capacity to rebuild a new form of democratic and compassionate welfare.

Taking this stand, we will resist the idea that those who experience poverty, depression, poor housing, or dysfunctional relationships are people who have failed to empower themselves and solve their 'own' problems. Conversely, social workers must be prepared to offer services from a collaborative stance, and not from a punitive one, to impede the triumph of the state denying its historic responsibilities of addressing social problems. Being available to tackle those problems, social workers should fight the approach of defining people as 'responsible' enough to be recognised as 'deserving' citizens.

In addition to these deeply needed upbringing of social work voice in public policy-making, conveying a perspective towards subjective and interpersonal understanding to advance in social change. We noted in this chapter a large field in need of intervention in Latin America, which is that of the subjective wellbeing, including the mental health arena. Evidence showed the increment of mental health problems associated not only with poverty, as well as complex barriers connected within different stages of the life span, representing a greater challenge for Chilean social work, rigged with a lack of training in clinical skills.

Justifications for these statements were found in the assessment carried out by the School of Social Work at the Pontificia Universidad Católica de Chile, which raised main social problems being faced by its graduates, all of them related to people´s subjective wellbeing; and the skills graduates claimed as needed to effectively tackle those problems, which are represented by clinical abilities and knowledge. These skills should fill the gap of clinical tools, abilities, and assessment needed to complement their traditional professional education.

Additionally, the assessment through several Chilean social work schools showed that main working spaces lacking professionals with the skills mentioned above were public services for excluded population. Therefore, if professionals can contribute to subjective wellbeing of this population, then their work would also have an impact in social justice.

In this regard, social work has historically been concerned for those who are most poor, marginalised, oppressed, or vulnerable i.e., who are socially excluded. In doing that, cultural competency and clinical skills help the understanding of exclusion, as well as the processes that accompany it, allowing support this population without pathologising their ways of life. Thus, these abilities can be regarded as critical to work with marginalised groups and communities.

Lastly, the comparing process of different clinical training programmes, showed a lack of social work programmes providing the specific required teaching, were professionals develop the capabilities of attending underserved population intersecting subjectivity and social context, to address interpersonal problems that are closely connected with the social status quo. The required programmes should be grounded in the principles of respect, dignity, and compassion, emphasising the universality of human rights for the highest attainable standard of freedom, health, and wellbeing.

Schools of social work must give answer to new social requirements and be responsible for developing training projects that are sensitive to emerging trends. We have given account of specific areas of skills and knowledge requiring greater educational and training emphasis. Curricula planning and development needs to be responsive as social work roles and responsibilities are changing in a more complex world, in addition to more sophisticated ways to understand human development.

Therefore, a clinical social work practice for our region should be like as defined by Pakman (1997) a therapeutic practice as social criticism, which does not follow the preestablished guidelines of a social policy that aims to maintain a status quo and a supposed neutrality depoliticising the social body through a linguistic normalisation of subjectivity. Recovering the history, whether disciplinary, that of our peoples and of each person who compose it, is a daily task, and our actions performed into practices, should honour the singularity, the collective, and the people with whom we work. All of these constitute the transversal axis to make of social justice a principle, and not only a discourse.

The challenge of developing that sort of social work practice must avoid the neglect of spatial and social inequalities, all of which constitute important political dimensions to social wellbeing. Keeping a relational and comprehensive perspective will act as a protection from the extreme individualisation of social problems.

Thus, developing a specialised clinical social work practice will provide answers to move forward an area or specialisation needed not only in Chile, but in the entire region. We must train clinical social workers that are aware of a political system that lacks participation and representation of local needs and are ready to resist it and create new strategies to transform it as well as rigorously trained professionals that are prepared to assist people to healthy cope with the suffering that inequality and inequity brings to the private sphere of their lives. In doing that, social work will be faithful to its mission of ensuring social justice.

References

Bailey, R., Bailey, R. V., & Brake, M. (1975). *Radical social work*. Edward Arnold. https://books.google.cl/books?id=2kBHAAAAMAAJ

Behring, E. R. (2014). The ethical-political project of social work in Brazil. *Critical and Radical Social Work*, *1*(1), 87–94. https://doi.org/10.1332/204986013x665983

Boff, L. (1985). *Teología del cautiverio y de la liberación* (L. Boff (ed.), 3rd ed.). Ed. Paulinas.

Bourdieu, P. (1999). Scattered remarks. *European Journal of Social Theory*. https://doi.org/doi.org/10.1177/13684319922224563

Chambon, A. S. (1999). *Reading Foucault for social work*. In Allan Irving and Laura Epstein (Eds.), Columbia University Press. ISBN 023110717X, 9780231107174.

Corrigan, P., & Leonard, P. (1978). *Social work practice under capitalism: A Marxist approach*. Springer.

Dodson, M. (1979). Liberation theology and Christian radicalism in contemporary Latin America. *Journal of Latin American Studies*, *11*(1), 203–222. https://doi.org/10.1017/S0022216X00022367

Dominelli, L. (1996). Deprofessionalizing social work: Anti-oppressive practice, competencies and postmodernism. *British Journal of Social Work*, *26*(2), 153–175. https://doi.org/10.1093/oxfordjournals.bjsw.a011077

Dominelli, L. (2017). *Anti-racist social work*. Macmillan International Higher Education.

Dominelli, L., & Campling, J. (2002). *Anti-oppressive social work theory and practice*. Macmillan International Higher Education.

Dominelli, L., & McLeod, E. (1989). *Feminist social work*. Macmillan International Higher Education.

Echávarri, O., Maino, P., Fischman, R., Morales, S., & Barros, J. (2015). Aumento sostenido del suicidio en Chile: un tema pendiente. *Temas de La Agenda Pública*, *10*(79), 3–14.

Estalayo, M. M., & Sáez, L. N. (2017). El trabajo social en los aparatos del Estado y su posicionamiento ético-político en la garantía de los derechos sociales. *Revista Katálysis*, *20*(3), 335–343. https://doi.org/10.1590/1982-02592017v20n3p335

Fleury, S. (2017). The Welfare State in Latin America: reform, innovation and fatigue. *Cadernos de Saúde Pública*, *33*, e00058116.

Fook, J. (2002). *Social work: Critical theory and practice*. Sage.

García, R. (2004). Salud mental comunitaria ¿Una tarea interdisciplinar? *Cuadernos de Trabajo Social*, *17*(2004), 273–287.

Guajardo, G. (2017). *Serie Libros Flacso-Chile Suicidios Contemporáneos : Transformaciones Socioculturales*. Flacso Ecuador.

Gutiérrez, G., & Sobrino, J. (1984). *Beber en su propio pozo*. Latinoamérica Libros SRL.

Iamamoto, M.V., & De Carvalho, R. (1982). *Relações Sociais e Serviço Social no Brasil: esboço de uma interpretação histórico-metodológica*. Cortez.

Idareta, F. (2018). Ituarte, A. I. (coord.) (2017). Prácticas del Trabajo Social Clínico [Clinical Social work practice]. Valencia: Nau Llibres. 252 pp. ISBN: 8416926131. *Cuadernos de Trabajo Social, 31*. https://doi.org/10.5209/CUTS.55555

Ituarte, A. I. (2017). Prácticas del Trabajo Social ClínicoTY - JOUR AU - Ferguson, Iain AU - Lavalette, Michael PY - 2013/04/01 SP −3 EP - 14 T1 - Critical and radical social work: an introduction VL - 1 DO - 10.1332/204986013X665938 JO - Critical and Radical Social Work ER -. Nau Llibres.

Lundy, C. (2004). *Social work and social justice: A structural approach to practice*. University of Toronto Press.

Minoletti, A., Alvarado, R., Rayo, X., & Minoletti, M. (2014). Evaluación del Sistema de Salud Mental de en Chile. *Sistema De Salud Mental De Chile Segundo Informe*, 1–122. https://doi.org/10.1021/ja049648s

Molina, P. V. (2015). Pensamiento Crítico del Trabajo Social en América Latina. *Conversación con Elaine*, 59–68.

Moreau, M., & Leonard, L. (1989). *Empowerment through a structural approach to social work: A report from practice*. Montreal and Ottawa: École de service sociale, Université de Montréal.

Mota, A. E. (2013). Brazilian Social Work: profession and field of knowledge. *Revista Katálysis*, *16*(SPE), 28–38. https://doi.org/10.1590/S1414-49802013000300003

Mullaly, R. P. (2007). *The new structural social work*. Oxford University Press.

PNUD. (2012). Bienestar subjetivo: el desafío de repensar el desarrollo Santiago. *Desarrollo Humano En Chile*, November 2014.

Pozzuto, R., Angell, G., & Dezendorf, P. (2005). *Therapeutic critique: Traditional versus critical perspectives* (pp. 25–38).

Salud, M. de. (2017). Plan Nacional de Salud Mental 2017–2025. *Ministerio de Salud de Chile*. Subsecretaría de Salud Pública.

Saracostti, M., Reininger, T., & Parada, H. (2012). Social work in Latin America. *The Sage Handbook of International Social Work* (pp. 466–479).

Silva, S. (2009). La Teología de la Liberación. *Teología y Vida*, *50*(1–2), 93–116. https://doi.org/10.4067/S0049-34492009000100008

Smith, C., & Smith, W. R. K. J. P. S. D. C. (1991). *The Emergence of Liberation Theology: Radical Religion and Social Movement Theory*. University of Chicago Press. https://books.google.cl/books?id=I_XnJF4aYOgC

Strier, R. (2007). Anti-oppressive research in social work: A preliminary definition. *British Journal of Social Work*, *37*(5), 857–871. https://doi.org/10.1093/bjsw/bcl062

Taffet, J. (2012). *Foreign aid as foreign policy: The Alliance for Progress in Latin America*. Routledge.

Trevelyan, C. (2008). Critical approaches to clinical social work practice: Considerations from contemporary relational psychoanalytic theory. In *ProQuest Dissertations and Theses* (Vol. MR46142).

Vicente, B., Saldivia, S., De La Barra, F., Kohn, R., Pihan, R., Valdivia, M., Rioseco, P., & Melipillan, R. (2012). Prevalence of child and adolescent mental disorders in Chile: A community epidemiological study. *Journal of Child Psychology and Psychiatry and Allied Disciplines*, *53*(10), 1026–1035. https://doi.org/10.1111/j.1469-7610.2012.02566.x

Vicente, B., Saldivia, S., & Pihán, R. (2016). Prevalencias y brechas hoy: salud mental mañana. *Acta Bioethica*, *22*(1), 51–61. https://doi.org/10.4067/s1726-569x2016000100006

World Health Organization. (2014). *Preventing suicide: A global imperative*. WHO Press.

World Health Organization. (2017). Depression and other common mental disorders: global health estimates. genev. *Obstetrics and Gynecology*, *48*(1), 56–60.

16
Cultural Practices in Indigenous Chilean Communities
New Findings for Social Work Practice

Lorena P. Gallardo-Peralta, Julio Tereucán Angulo, Abel Soto-Higuera, and Esteban Sánchez-Moreno

Ethnic-cultural diversity is a topic that is widely present in social work, with one of the most developed areas of training being that of cultural competencies in professional work (Abrams & Moio, 2009; Nadan, 2017; Sue, 2013). In this regard, there have been notable advances in the development of skills of social workers who interact with indigenous ethnic minorities (Australian Association of Social Workers, 2015; Bennett, Redfern, & Zubrzyck, 2018; Gray, Coates, & Yellow Bird, 2008; Laitinen & Väyrynen, 2016).

In this chapter we will analyse the social dynamics and characteristics of two Latin American indigenous peoples, Mapuche and Aymara, their historical and social antecedents, with an emphasis on the maintenance of their indigenous cultural practices; how they perceive various domains of subjective wellbeing; and the differences in wellbeing when they maintain such cultural practices. We will then discuss how this knowledge can be incorporated into social work practice.

In this context we would like to start with the concept of ethnicity, which will undoubtedly guide this presentation. Thus, when we speak of ethnicity, we are referring to a category associated with 'expressions of collective identity or feeling of belonging to a group' (Pujadas, 2011:25). Together with the feeling of belonging to a specific group, ethnicity makes sense with the maintenance of cultural practices, that is, 'it refers to how individual and collective subjects conceive and rate their cultural traditions in relation to that of other social groups' (Gavilán et al., 2018:326).

The elements that commonly define ethnic groups are language, political organisation, territorial contiguity, distribution of particular features, ecological adjustment, and the structure of the local community. It is important to point out that ethnic groups do not constitute fixed or predetermined units. In fact, its classification is not necessarily given by the presence of observable cultural features; rather, ethnic groups are entities that emerge from processes of cultural differentiation, are socially established, and subjectively perceived among groups that interact in specific inter-ethnic contexts (Pujadas, 2011; Wade, 2010).

Indigenous Peoples in Chile: Historical and Socio-Demographic Aspects

The most recent data indicates that 9.5% of the population in Chile are indigenous, which means that 1,694,870 people declare they belong to some indigenous people or they are of indigenous descendent. In this sense, nine indigenous ethnic groups are recognised: Mapuche (84.8%), Aymara (6.6%), Diaguita (4%), and the remaining percentage is distributed among the Atacameño, Quechua, Colla, Kaweshkar, Rapa Nui, and Yamana (Ministry of Social Development and Family, 2017). As mentioned previously, in this chapter we will focus on the two peoples that are most representative in terms of population.

Mapuche means 'people of the earth', and the Mapuche people were indeed originally hunter-gatherers. Their territorial identity emerges from the territories in which their population has historically been located: *nagche* are the northern people, *wenteche* are the people of central valleys, *lafkenche* are the coastal people, *pewenche* are the people from the foothill and *huilliche* are the southern people, which would include urban Mapuche identity. They live in rural areas that are connected to large cities, having experienced significant migration to urban settings.

The Mapuche people occupied the central and southern territories of present-day Chile until the arrival of the Spanish. They were subsequently confined to south of the Bío-Bío Region as a result of the so-called Pacification of La Araucanía by the Chilean State towards the end of the nineteenth century. The Chilean State then imposed settlement and division processes on communities, breaking up the territory into small communities that today form a fundamental part of the social, cultural, economic, and identity dynamic of their population. Changes in urban/rural composition from the 1980s and 1990s onwards meant structural shifts in terms of location in addition to new economic, social, and intercultural relationship dynamics, since owing to migration the Mapuche population is now located more in urban sectors of the country in percentage terms (Briceño et al., 2020).

The social organisation of the Mapuche people is based on territorial components, religiousness, cultural structures of patrilineal kinship, and the dynamics of marriage, inheritance, residence, and identity-based components framed by two basic principles: *tuwün* (place of origin) and *Küpan* (kinship bonds) (Tereucán, 2008; Course, 2011). In the urban context, Mapuche people live together in traditionally organised structures made up of at least four levels: *rukache*, referring to the domestic group residing in a particular dwelling; *xokinche*, which is the kinship group with patrilinear bonds in a single residential territory; *lof*, which includes a territorial delineation referring to the old Mapuche community; and *rewe*, which is a religious territorial authority for highly important rituals such as *gijatün* (Tereucán, 2008). Added to this is an organisational dynamic that has preferential links to the instrumental relationship of the Mapuche communities with State authorities such as committees and indigenous communities related to indigenous law, among others.

Their economic basis remains subsistence agriculture, but this has been changing with various agricultural developments such as commercial horticulture, the production of berries and cheeses, and recently tourism, to name some of the main areas. Income is supplemented through salaried positions that are increasingly commonplace owing to the new configurations of territorial spaces and boundaries, with urban life increasing influencing rural life. There is accelerating mobility and new access to educational environments, for example, which also has repercussions for family structures within communities that are today heavily dominated by adults and older people.

In response to an extensive process of discrimination, acculturation, and loss of rights over three decades, spaces of cultural resistance have been reinforced. This has involved the recovery of language (*mapudungun*), the practice of family rituals such as *eluwün* (burial), *mafutün* (matrimony), *we xipantu* (new year), rites of passage such as *katawün* (ear piercings); rituals associated with economic cycles such as *mingako, aretün, trafkintu, kakunün*, and *wulatün*, all linked to support and relationships of reciprocity and exchange; healing rituals (*machitun)* and territorial religious rituals (*gijatün*) (Tereucán-Ángulo, Briceño-Olivera, & Gálvez-Nieto, 2016).

The Aymara people form part of the 'Andean'" conceptualisation in Chile. This term synthesises spatial, topographic, and religious elements from pre-Hispanic and pre-colonial tradition with identity markers such as the Aymara language, relationships with the supernatural world (for example, *malkus*), the patrilinear social system, the political concept of settlement or *marka*, the economic practice of interfamily cooperation or *ayni*, and other sociocultural structures that have persisted and resisted interference from the State and Pentecostalism. The current Aymara territory traces its origins to the reduction in population and territory effected by the Kingdom of Spain in the Andes by means of the creation of 'Indian villages' and agricultural and mining transformation, involving the dismantling of indigenous communities through smallholdings in the Republican period. During this lengthy process, two types of communities have taken shape: those in agricultural valleys and canyons in foothill areas, clustered in small villages and surrounded by consolidated areas; and farming communities in the high Andes, whose dwelling and ownership unit is the *estancia*, consisting of rural grasslands on plains and wetlands. This is organised based on patrilinear inheritance of land or the system of succession of ownership (Romero-Toledo & Sambolín, 2019).

Changes resulting from processes involving migration to cities since the 1980s have generated a fall in the population living in rural areas, with increasing ageing, but this has not led to the disintegration of the Aymara. Aymara families and communities are not only reproduced in the historical territories; they also go beyond their old boundaries, and where relationships with the original rural community are central for life in the city and migrant families are decisively inclined towards the area in economic and political terms (Gavilán, 2020). Along the same lines, Cortes and Gundermman (2020) state that these are not domestic units aiming at living solely off their produce and animal rearing, but rather a new type of subject that comes from and goes into other economic categories. As well as small agricultural and fishing producers, these may also include salaried employees, artisans, traders and transporters, as well as those who move through different spaces.

Aymara cultural dynamics continue to be reproduced in both urban and rural settings, in which maternal kinship remains a significant matter in cultural identification. Cerna and Muñoz (2019) state that this has permitted the production of a repertory of collective and local identifications referring to different settlements, where the link between the parental (surname) and geographic (settlement) points of reference has been significant. Current religiosity incorporates into the principles of cosmovision elements of syncretism of various religious expressions (Gavilán & Carrasco, 2009; Mansilla & Muñoz, 2017), with the most important ceremonies being those that emphasise changes in climate in terms of space-time, and which interlink the meanings associated with *inti, Pachamama*, and the patron saints (Gavilán & Carrasco, 2009). The basic traditional social organisation continues to be the *Ayllu*, which is involved in both social and economic issues. However, the complexity of the new dynamics has led to changes whereby, according to Gundermann and Vergara (2009), three forms of organisation can be identified: the Andean community, local territorial community-based organisations, and the indigenous organisation supported by the Chilean State. In addition to these visible structures, Aymara social organisation must also be understood through elements of kinship, religiosity, inheritance, marriage, and economic components that add complexity and dynamics involving constant change.

Chilean indigenous people generally face unfavourable social prospects. The National Survey of Socioeconomic Characterisation, through the Ministry of Social Development and Family (2017), in its section on indigenous peoples, confirms this complex situation. In terms of education, they have a higher illiteracy rate, 4.5% versus 3.5% in the non-indigenous population. This value reaches 8% in rural areas and 13.6% in the population above 60 years of age. In terms of economy, the average income for indigenous households is $582,819 (693 USD), well below the average of non-indigenous households ($794,396, which is 945 USD). There is also a gap in equality in terms of internet access; 69.4% of indigenous people use the internet versus 72.2% of non-indigenous people. Finally, there is also a greater history of poverty and social exclusion in the indigenous population.

As shown in Figure 16.1, figures related to income poverty double in the indigenous population and significant differences can be observed in the dimensions of social exclusion – education, health, work, and social security, housing and environment, social networks and cohesion – confirming that indigenous people are in a situation of greater social exclusion.

Although social policies in Chile have positive discrimination towards indigenous peoples, the gap in historical social inequality that these groups have experienced has not yet been reduced (Gavilán et al., 2018).

Social Work and Latin American Indigenous People: The Case of Chile

In Latin America there are more than 500 indigenous peoples, representing a significant percentage of the population in the different Latin American countries. However, the advance of an Indigenous Social Work or a social work with specific cultural ethnic sensitivity is still a pending challenge (Gallardo-Peralta, Sánchez-Moreno, & Rodríguez-Rodríguez, 2019; Guzmán, 2011). It seems that assimilationist social policies, which tend to the acculturation and homogenisation of the population, have also had an impact on social intervention. As stated by Law and Lee (2016), the tendency to the import of western values and practices in indigenous minorities has led to the construction of a multicultural social work.

Indeed, authors like Guzmán (2011) point out that a specific theoretical-practical framework has not been created in Latin America in order to address Latin American ethnic minorities, specifically indigenous people. The tendency is usually towards the export of Anglo-Saxon models, with an emphasis on models based on multiculturalism. Social work positions itself on the basis of dominant paradigms and does not manage to give a voice to indigenous ones (Coates, Gray, & Hetherington, 2006).

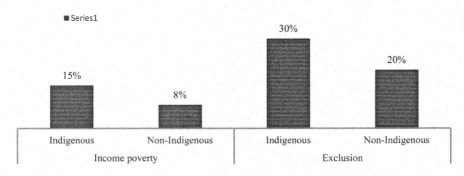

Figure 16.1 Percentage of population in poverty and social exclusion in indigenous population. Source: Own elaboration.

Objectives

Few studies specifically analyse indigenous cultural practices in Latin American Social Work, especially in Chile. In this sense, this chapter tries to give visibility to the most representative indigenous peoples of Chile through their current cultural practices by proposing the following aims:

1. To compare potential differences between the Aymara and the Mapuche people in terms of maintenance of cultural practices in the areas of language, ceremonies, medicine, and cultural transmission.
2. To analyse potential differences between the Aymara and the Mapuche people in the domains of subjective wellbeing: standard of living, health, achieving in life, relationships, safety, community-connectedness, future security, and spirituality/religion.
3. To determine the impact of maintaining (or not) indigenous cultural practices on perceived subjective wellbeing.

In order to do so, we start from the premise that maintaining cultural practices such as language, ceremonies and rituals, indigenous medicine and cultural transmission, would have an effect on their wellbeing. Furthermore, in this work we offer cultural competencies that emerge from knowing the cultural practices of indigenous peoples – Mapuche and Aymara – which can be considered in the training of social workers.

Methodology

Participants

The sample was made up of 569 indigenous Mapuche and Aymara older adults living in the north and south of Chile. Convenience sampling was used. Criteria for inclusion were being aged 60 or over, belonging to an indigenous ethnicity, and not suffering from serious cognitive deterioration. In order to obtain an appropriate level of structural representativeness in the selected sample in each of these territories, it was designed and stratified by sex, age, ethnicity, and place of residence. One socioeconomic feature common to indigenous older adults is their low level of education. In quantitative terms, the main difference is whether they have completed primary school. We hence found a population with a low general literacy level, which was considered when designing the questionnaire and was decisive in choosing how to administer it. The features of the sample are set out in Table 16.1. These features are a faithful reflection of the population distribution according to the aforementioned variables.

Procedure

A face-to-face interview method was used to collect the data, taking an approximate time of 45 minutes. The questionnaire – comprising various scales as described in the following section – was read out loud to interviewees. Qualified social work and psychology professionals administered the questionnaire. The main language used for the scales was Spanish, since it is the binding language in Chile. However, they were also included in indigenous languages (*Mapundungun* and *Aymara*) specifically for the different cultural practices.

The Ethics Committee of Tarapacá University and the National Council for Science and Technology of Chile approved and monitored the ethical aspects of the study. All procedures

Table 16.1 Participant's characteristics

	Categories	Aymara (n=201)	Mapuche (n=368)	Overall Sample (n=569)
Gender	Women	106 (53%)	180 (49%)	286 (50%)
	Men	95 (47%)	188 (51%)	283 (50%)
Age groups	60–69 years	97 (48%)	162 (44%)	259 (46%)
	70–79 years	75 (37%)	134 (36%)	209 (37%)
	80+ years	29 (15%)	72 (20%)	101 (17%)
Marital status	Married or cohabiting	120 (60%)	202 (55%)	322 (57%)
	Single	23 (11%)	54 (15%)	77 (13%)
	Widow	45 (22%)	96 (26%)	141 (25%)
	Divorced or separated	13 (7%)	16 (4%)	29 (5%)
Education	Primary school incomplete	127 (63%)	250 (68%)	377 (66%)
	Primary school	49 (24%)	76 (21%)	125 (22%)
	High school or vocational education	21 (10%)	39 (10%)	60 (11%)
	Higher education	4 (3%)	3 (1%)	7 (1%)
Residence	North (region of Arica y Parinacota)	201 (100%)	0	201 (35%)
	South (region of the Araucanía)	0	368 (100%)	368 (65%)

Source: Own elaboration

performed in studies involving human participants were in accordance with the 1964 Helsinki declaration and its amendments or comparable ethical standards. Having first obtained the informed consent of participants, the data were processed confidentially and anonymously.

Measures

Indigenous cultural practices. A questionnaire about the maintenance of certain indigenous cultural practices, in terms of frequency, was created. These practices can be divided in the following sections:

(a) Understanding and use of native languages and transmission to close relatives through teaching. The response categories were 1 = Yes, 2 = No.
(b) Participation in religious festivities or indigenous ceremonies, such as: indigenous New Year, weddings, and funerals. Besides, they were asked if they had exercised leadership or participated in the organisation of such festivities. Responses were evaluated based on the frequency with which these activities were carried out: 1 = never; 2 = rarely, 3 = sometimes, 4 = often, and 5 = always.
(c) They were asked if in case of illness, they resort to either going to the indigenous doctor (health cultural agent) or to herbal medicines for ointments, massages, and preparation of indigenous infusions (1 = never; 2 = rarely, 3 = sometimes, 4 = often, and 5 = always). They were also asked if they have influenced the decision of any woman in the family to give birth with an indigenous traditional midwife (1 = Yes, 2 = No).
(d) Finally, we assessed to what extent the elders transmit these indigenous cultural practices to close relatives such as children and grandchildren (1 = Yes, 2 = No).

Subjective wellbeing. The personal wellbeing index (PWI) was created from the comprehensive Quality of Life Scale (Cummins et al., 2003). A nine-item scale was used to evaluate satisfaction across the following factors: standard of living, health, achieving in life, relationships, safety, community-connectedness, future security, and spirituality/religion, with a question also included on the ninth item of overall life satisfaction. There are Likert-scale responses to the questions, with a range from 0 to 10 points where 0 represents *totally unsatisfied* and 10 means *totally satisfied*. In order to calculate the global scale, the general averages are obtained per item and on a general level. This questionnaire has been validated in the Chilean population, including indigenous elderly people (Gallardo-Peralta, Molina, & Schettini del Moral, 2019).

Analysis

Firstly, in order to assess the differences per indigenous group in the different cultural practices that were analysed (indigenous language, indigenous ceremonies, indigenous medicine, and cultural transmission), the χ^2 was calculated. Secondly, a comparison of the means (student's *t* test for independent samples) was performed for the subjective wellbeing domains (standard of living, health, life achievements, relationships, safety, community-connectedness, future security, and spirituality or religiousness) between indigenous Mapuche and indigenous Aymara. Finally, ANOVA was used to assess statistical significance of the difference between maintaining or not maintaining cultural practices and the perception of subjective wellbeing (SWB). The results were considered significant when p<.05. Data analysis was performed through the IMB-SPSS programme, version 25.

Findings

The results show a high maintenance of cultural practices in both indigenous communities in general terms, highlighting the use or understanding of the native language in most of the interviewees (>75%). More than half of the interviewees have taught or are teaching their language within their family (children, grandchildren) and celebrate the indigenous New Year (*Wue Tripantu* or *Machac Mara*). A significant percentage of them also see the indigenous doctor if they are feeling sick (*Machi* or *Yatiri*). However, there are some statistically significant differences between the two indigenous peoples regarding practices in indigenous rituals or ceremonies, in indigenous medical practices, and in cultural transmission. In general, the Mapuche people maintain cultural practices to a greater extent. Thus, 39% participate in indigenous marriage rituals, 73% attend more indigenous funerals, and 44% have a greater chance of leading or organising an indigenous ceremony.

Regarding health practices, it can be observed that the Aymara people maintain more health practices in the event of an illness: 69% consume medicinal herbs and 68% prepare traditional teas. However, the Mapuche show a greater preference (28%) for traditional childbirth with an indigenous midwife (*pvñeñelche*), for the women in their families. It is observed that the Mapuche tend to maintain the transmission of their cultural practices within their families to a greater extent: 66% pass them on to their children and 56% to their grandchildren (Table 16.2).

Regarding the SWB in the studied sample, it is observed that in general, most of the domains would establish adequate levels of satisfaction with the quality of life. Again, differences that are statistically significant can be observed between the studied indigenous groups. In general, the Aymara elders show better results in subjective wellbeing in the following domains: general assessment of life, health, achievements, social relations, security, and community connection (Table 16.3).

Table 16.2 Chi-square analysis with respect to indigenous cultural practice

Variable	Mapuche %(n)	Aymara %(n)	X^2	df
Native language (Mapudungun and Aymara)				
Speaks or understands indigenous language	75% (276)	75.6% (152)	.027	1
Teaches or has taught the indigenous language	48.1% (177)	52.7% (106)	1.119	1
Indigenous celebrations or ceremonies				
Indigenous new year	64.7% (283)	56.7% (114)	3.489	1
Weddings with indigenous ritual	39.1% (144)	25.3% (104)	8.408**	1
Funerals with indigenous ritual	72.6% (267)	58.7% (118)	11.393***	1
Has led or organised an indigenous ceremony	43.5% (160)	35.3% (71)	3.585*	1
Indigenous health practices				
Going to the indigenous doctor	35.1% (129)	41.3% (83)	2.165	1
Herbal medicines for ointments, massages	39.1% (144)	69.2% (139)	46.874***	1
Preparation of indigenous infusions	53.3% (196)	69.2% (137)	11.887***	1
Has influenced relatives to have indigenous childbirth	28.3% (104)	18.3% (83)	10.007**	1
Cultural transmission				
Has transmitted cultural practices to children	66.3% (244)	42.9% (114)	5.122*	1
Has transmitted cultural practices to grandchildren	56.3% (207)	44.3% (89)	7.464**	1

Source: Own elaboration
* p< 0.05; ** p< 0.01; *** p< 0.001

Table 16.3 Differences between ethnic groups for the domains of subjective wellbeing

Domains for the personal wellbeing index	Mapuche M(SE)	Aymara M(SE)	t
Standard of living	7.26(2.06)	8.27(1.72)	-6.278***
Health	6.38(2.27)	7.08(2.51)	-3.324***
Achieving in life	7.53(195)	8.09(1.94)	-3.293***
Relationships	7.57(2.07)	8.28(1.73)	-4.397***
Safety	7.31(2.17)	7.67(1.91)	-2.011*
Community-connectedness	7.39(2.12)	8.38(1.80)	-5.833***
Future security	7.06(2.20)	7.18(2.30)	-.633
Spirituality or religiousness	7.97(2.14)	8.25(2.23)	-1.472

Source: Own elaboration
* p< 0.05; ** p< 0.01; *** p< 0.001

Finally, we analyse the difference between indigenous elderly people that maintain and those who do not maintain cultural practices in the general assessment of subjective wellbeing. In general terms, maintaining cultural practices is related to better SWB results. Specifically, the cultural practices that show a higher average of SWB are: speaking the native language, teaching relatives the language, participating in indigenous funerals, leading or participating in the

Table 16.4 Differences in SWB depending on the maintenance of cultural practices

Cultural Practice	Yes	No	F
	M(SE)	M(SE)	
Speaks or understands indigenous language	60.14(12.42)	57.08(14.53)	9.122**
Teaches or has taught the indigenous language	61.19 (12.64)	59.10 (13.41)	3.642*
Indigenous new year	59.61(12.95)	61.01 (13.22)	1.549
Weddings with indigenous ritual	59.31 (13.23)	60.79 (12.92)	1.799
Funerals with indigenous ritual	61.10 (12.65)	59.14 (13.70)	6.425**
Has led or organised an indigenous ceremony	63.82 (12.67)	57.63 (12.74)	32.573***
Going to the indigenous doctor	61.08 (13.51)	59.59 (12.78)	1.730
Herbal medicines for ointments, massages	62.41 (12.86)	57.90 (12.89)	17.445***
Preparation of indigenous infusions	62.29 (12.16)	57.11 (13.71)	22.460***
Has influenced relatives to have indigenous childbirth	6105 (12.41)	59.69 (13.36)	1.360
Has transmitted cultural practices to children	62.70 (11.39)	55.80 (14.53)	39.596***
Has transmitted cultural practices to grandchildren	62.50 (11.26)	57.58 (14.36)	20.84***

Source: Own elaboration
* p< 0.05; ** p< 0.01; *** p< 0.001

organisation of indigenous ceremonies, using herbs and medicinal infusions in case of illness, and transmission of indigenous cultural practices to children and grandchildren (Table 16.4).

Discussion

Social work has seen significant processes in theoretical and social intervention models from an ethnic perspective (Sue, 2013), which recognise that cultural and ethnic differences are central factors for professional practice. The current approach affirms that '[s]ocial work is a practice-based profession (…). Principles of social justice, human rights, collective responsibility and respect for diversities are central to social work. Underpinned by theories of social work, social sciences, humanities and indigenous knowledge' (International Federation of Social Workers). Ethnic diversity is thus identified as a transversal element of our discipline.

Interculturality proposes an action framework that is consistent with the basic principles of social work, in that it encourages the development of communication, knowledge, and recognition of the Other, valuing people's contributions, negotiation, and establishing common goals (Vásquez, 2002). But additionally, and from the critical perspective of interculturality, it involves attempting to reduce injustices and inequalities, for which purpose there is a need for transformations in structures, institutions, and social relationships, and the construction of different conditions of being, thinking, knowing, learning, feeling, and living (Walsh, 2010). In this context, intercultural competence can be understood as a relationship that is established among different subjects that means professionals can relate to different Others, so that the meanings of shared elements can be captured; this implies understanding the behaviour of the Other (Díaz, 2007).

UNESCO (2017:5) states that 'intercultural competences are abilities to adeptly navigate complex environments marked by a growing diversity of peoples, cultures and lifestyles'. They represent a tool for recognising and integrating the Other. These intercultural competencies must be taught and learned, as '[i]ndividuals are not born interculturally competent, they become competent through education and life experiences' (UNESCO, 2017: 38).

Intercultural competence is a key element in professional practice and forms the basis for the exercise of citizenship by individuals who find themselves in cultural contexts other than their own (Aneas, 2005). There are many benefits of possessing intercultural competences, including that it helps in cultural integration and social adaptation, facilitates relationships among people of different origins and cultures, permits conciliatory interaction in the context of conflicts and disputes that arise, and promotes peaceful and harmonious coexistence among different cultural groups (UNESCO, 2017). In this context, Byram and Cain (2001: 43) state that intercultural competences facilitate:

- Acquisition of the ability to interpret social phenomena that professionals may encounter during their contact with other cultures.
- Development of flexibility and the ability to respect other interpretative systems and compare and contrast them with one's own.
- Rethinking of one's own culture and practices in comparison with those of other communities.
- Becoming aware of one's own cultural practices.
- Acquisition of knowledge regarding other social groups and their cultural practices.

Cultural competence in social work practice entails increased awareness of how culturally diverse populations experience their specificity and address their differences and similarities within a broader social context (NASW, 2015). It also requires social workers to recognise their own positions of power, and how these impacts on their professional activity and on the reproduction of institutionalised practices that are not necessarily consistent with intercultural approaches. In this regard, the ongoing process of seeking knowledge, abilities, and values is a necessary requirement for the intercultural practice of social work, particularly with indigenous populations in the case of Latin America.

The cultural competencies that a social worker should acquire in their educational training go through different levels of action: 1) *awareness* of one's attitudes and beliefs, 2) *knowledge* about cultural differences between different groups, in which human diversity is manifested, 3) *skills* to work with these diverse groups, 4) the need for effective interaction with members of other groups in specific *cultural events*. In this regard, a cultural competence would go through a dynamic process of consciously recognising that we are different, towards a process of becoming interested in knowing the different *other*, to then get involved in the development of culturally appropriate professional practices and thus finally achieve a cultural encounter in a close relationship, where respect, tolerance, active empathy, and the desire for an equitable cultural exchange prevail (Campinha-Bacote, 1998; Martínez, Martínez, & Calzado, 2006; Sue, Arredondo, & McDavis, 1992).

Following this classic proposal of cultural competencies, in this work we have focused on the knowledge of the cultural practices that make up the worldview of two Andean indigenous peoples: Mapuche and Aymara, and then propose how these can be transformed into intrinsic knowledge of social intervention. In other words, move on to the skills that should be developed in social workers.

Understanding Their Practices: We Approach Their Cultural Identity

Indigenous peoples in Chile are under the protection of Indigenous Law No. 19253. Progress towards social inclusion policies with an intercultural perspective in the area of health is recognised (Ministry of Health, 2013). However, its application in areas such as education, justice, social welfare, housing, and other social benefits, is still scarce. Therefore, there is a general lack of knowledge of how indigenous practices are reproduced and, furthermore, how they could be incorporated into the different fields of action of social policies.

The only study of national and public nature that differentiates native peoples introduces a question about the knowledge and use of the native language in its latest version (Ministry of Social Development and Family, 2017). The data in this survey is devastating from the point of view of indigenous ethnic groups, since only 9.9% of the population understands and speaks their language. However, this improves if we analyse the group of indigenous elders, reaching 20.5%. In our findings, the results are very positive, showing that the majority of the interviewees use and understand their native language (≥ 75% of the 569 interviewees). This data has to be addressed in the specificity of the interviewees, who are indigenous elderly people that reside in rural areas that are geographically native, many of them isolated and peripheral (Gundermann, Vergara, & Díaz, 2011; Lagos, 2012). The figures confirm that maintaining *Mapundungung* or *Aymara* and being able to transmit or teach it is associated with better results in subjective wellbeing. This data makes sense as it refers to places of family and community reproduction where language has its use; hence the indigenous identity of Mapuches and Aymara is mediated by the maintenance of the native language (Gundermann, González, & Vergara, 2007; Lagos, 2012; Salas, 1985).

Cultural practices are another relevant space to understand the worldview of the indigenous people. According to the data that we have analysed, many religious ceremonies are maintained as a result of cultural syncretism (Catholicism and Indigenism) such as marriages and funerals. The rituals typical of the Andean indigenous communities are the celebration of the New Year on the winter solstice (June) through *We Tripantu* or *Machac Mara*. It is a sacred celebration that symbolises the return of the sun, the beginning of a new agricultural cycle, and the beginning of a new cycle of life. Of all these ceremonial practices, only the participation in indigenous funerals would be linked to subjective wellbeing.

The ceremony of burying the dead constitutes a key element in the analysis of the cultural identity of indigenous peoples. For these communities death is a positive experience since it involves the extension of earthly life, therefore, it is a process linked to transcendence (Andrade et al., 2018; Carrasco, 1998). The term 'death' does not even exist in Mapuche language, *mapulugün* is used instead, which means that the person will return to earth, their spirit will return to remain in their territory. The realisation of the *eluwün* (burial of the dead) is not only an act that is performed in the cemetery, but the most relevant part of this process is that it articulates the cycle of life (Rojas, 2016):

1 Activation of the *kiñe eluwün*, which is the specific organisation for these cases. It is made up of all the patrilineal relatives and it is part of the identity complex that implies *küpan* (kinship) and *tuwün* (place of birth). Every person is born and dies in a *kiñe eluwün*, and they have a cultural obligation to participate.
2 Psychosocial support for the family of the dead person from patrilineal relatives and the network of kinship and friendship that is built through the mechanisms of reciprocity and exchange.
3 Financial support for the family to conduct the ritual.
4 Help the family of the dead person to effectively leave without leaving pending matters, so that the family continuity dynamics are not altered. If it occurred through dreams or otherwise, a specific ritual must be performed.
5 Contributing to the social prestige of the family in the community, since the more people participating in the ritual, the greater the relevant and social consideration of the family

in the territory. Obviously, this implies contributing significantly to the economic costs involved in assisting 200, 300, or up to 2000 people in the event of the death of a *lonko* (chief of a community).

6 Granting subjective wellbeing to the family by saying goodbye to a family member according to the importance that they have.

Similarly, in the Aymara indigenous people, death means the renewal of life, that is, 'life that comes from death', which applies to the world of man and nature in general (van Kessel, 2001).

Indigenous health and medical practices are also central cultural aspects for the understanding of the Andean worldview, health being understood as the harmony between the physical, mental, and spiritual aspects of a person. This harmony encompasses environment, social, and cultural aspects. For an Andean person, being healthy (*monguelen* or *thani*) is a state of wellbeing, moral tranquillity, and physical integrity (Flores-Guerrero, 2004). The findings would indicate that the number of visits to the indigenous doctor (*Machi* or *Yatiri*) is high; however, high frequency in the use of herbs and natural infusions to relieve pain is observed in the Aymara people (Madaleno & Delatorre-Herrera, 2013). Perhaps promoting childbirth with indigenous traditions and under the responsibility of an indigenous midwife (*pvñeñelche* or *q'olliri*) is the area that has undergone an accelerated process of acculturation. This tendency to the disappearance of this cultural practice is due to a series of public benefits that are granted to the mother and the new-born when the childbirth takes place in public hospitals in Chile. Specifically, medical practices, such as the use of natural herbs for massages or infusions, would be linked to subjective wellbeing, which would confirm that indigenous people maintain a natural lifestyle in situations of illness. Finally, the reproduction and maintenance of cultural identity requires processes of intergenerational transfer of knowledge. In the case of indigenous elderly people, they are the ones who carry the wisdom and experiences, and they have social recognition in their community as conveyors of culture (Gavilán, 2002). The findings of this study show high implication in the transmission of cultural practices to children and grandchildren. In addition, they are both related to subjective wellbeing.

In Chile, important advances in intercultural public health have been recognised (Ministry of Health, 2013). For example, medical treatment is carried out by both a doctor and an indigenous cultural agent (*Machi* or *Yatiri*) simultaneously, which translates into the revitalisation of cultural and ecological resources for health care and greater intercultural skills of professionals in this fields, which leads to the revaluation and knowledge of culture. This implies a greater set of intercultural competences of social workers who work in the health sector or in local development programmes.

Having said that, taking into account the importance of native language, mortuary rites, herbal medicinal practices, and cultural transmission to family members in the subjective wellbeing of indigenous communities, how does this translate into cultural competencies for social work?

Cultural Competencies: Social Work and Andean Indigenous Minorities

When we speak of social competence in social work, reference is made to:

> The process by which individuals and systems respond respectfully and effectively to people of all cultures, languages, classes, races, ethnic backgrounds, religions, spiritual traditions,

immigration status, and other diversity factors in a manner that recognizes, affirms, and values the worth of individuals, families, and communities and protects and preserves the dignity of each

(Nacional Association of Social Worker, 2015, p. 13)

Social workers acquire their competencies through academic training and they are reinforced in professional practice. It is important to consider the cultural context in which they are developed. In this paper, we have focused on analysing cultural elements related to wellbeing in two indigenous Andean communities. This has unquestionable practical implications for social work in Chile and Latin America. Based on our findings, we can identify the following cultural competencies:

1. It is important for social workers to acquire *native indigenous language* skills or to include some terms in indigenous language in the process of social intervention. It is also important to consider the use of intercultural intermediaries – translators that are native and culturally competent – to stimulate communication that is close, smooth, culturally appropriate, and trustworthy.
2. Promoting community activities related to their *religious ceremonies and indigenous rites*. It is a community space in which the social worker acquires the role of organiser, facilitator of cultural practices, and community promoter.
3. Social workers must understand the *significance of death as a cyclical process* and the beginning of life, which would imply facing death as a natural process. Social workers intervene in many crisis situations due to grief, which is why this competence can transcend other social groups.
4. *Health as a process that involves the harmony of the physical, mental and spiritual dimensions.* Social workers may include the indigenous worldview in the design of social intervention with sick people, which would imply having a holistic vision of the situation to intervene as opposed to one that is only focused on the specific problem.
5. Social workers can promote, empower, and boost the elderly *to pass on their ancestral knowledge* in their indigenous communities. In order to do so, different activities and spaces for intergenerational and intercultural meetings can be designed.
6. Giving relevance to social *interventions focused on the community*, not on the individual, the effectiveness of the transformation that the intervention seeks in collectivist or community societies must understand that the axis of change is the community.

This work offers preliminary results for the construction of specific cultural competencies to intervene in Andean indigenous communities. However, it is necessary to delve into the practices and their impact on the wellbeing of the communities. One of the areas that should be strengthened in the intervention with indigenous communities is the empowerment that entails a transition process from their condition of oppression, inequality, discrimination, exploitation, and exclusion to a state of awareness, self-determination, and autonomy, so that they can enjoy a free exercise of their rights (Sosme and Casado, 2016). It is necessary to insist on the importance of designing empowerment processes from community spaces (*lovche* and *ayllu*) where the social worker fulfils the role of community manager that integrates individuals, their families, and their significant environments. Another competence in social work practice with indigenous communities is therefore the *promotion of community empowerment* rather than individually based empowerment.

Finally, a central element in the development of intercultural competencies for social work is the comprehensive understanding of wellbeing that is present in indigenous communities. For Latin American indigenous communities, 'living well', which corresponds to the terms *suma qamaña* in Aymara and *küme mongen* in Mapuche, is related to an approach to living that involves balance between the individual, community, and nature and encompasses a series of values and principles, including fairness, identity, and sustainability (Ribadeneira, 2020). The indigenous cosmovision seeks harmony between nature and the individual, mediated by spiritual elements. This is incorporated into the approach of Coates, Gray, and Hetherington (2006) through what is labelled the 'ecospiritual perspective' in social work. A final proposed competence arises in this regard: the need for *a holistic understanding of wellbeing in indigenous communities*.

In light of all the forementioned, the design of social interventions with and for indigenous older people must include the more sensitive cultural elements of the Aymara and Mapuche people. These include their indigenous language, ceremonies and rites, the meaning of death, a comprehensive understanding of health, and the importance of intergenerational transmission. From the perspective of social work, there is a need to strategically design interventions that include the community and thereby allow for community empowerment, but also include a holistic view of wellbeing that transcends the personal and reflects an ecospiritual approach.

A competent social work professional must take into account the knowledge and information specific to the ethnic-cultural group. In this work we have approached the worldview, through Mapuche and Aumara indigenous cultural practices, to then propose a series of competencies in which social workers that intervene with these collectives should be trained.

Acknowledgement

This work was supported by the Government of Chile ('Proyecto FONDECYT 1170493').

References

Abrams, L.S. & Moio, J.A. (2009) Critical race theory and the cultural competence dilemma in social work education. *Journal of Social Work Education, 45*(2), 245–261.

Andrade, P., Fonseca, K., Leyton, L., López, A., Pacheco, A., Dalenz, J., & Martínez, M. (2018). Funeral patterns and colonial encroachment in the Biobío region: the case of the San José de la mocha mission in concepción from the seventeenth to nineteenth century. *Atenea, 518*, 133–149.

Aneas, A. (2005). *Competencia intercultural, conceptos, efectos e implicaciones en el ejercicio de la ciudadanía*. Barcelona: Universidad de Barcelona

Australian Association of Social Workers (AASW). (2015). *Preparing for culturally responsive and inclusive social work practice in Australia: Working with Aboriginal and Torres Strait Islander peoples*. http://www.aasw.asn.au/document/item/7006

Bennett, B., Redfern, H., & Zubrzycki, J. (2018). Cultural responsiveness in action: Co-constructing social work curriculum resources with aboriginal communities. *The British Journal of Social Work, 48*(3), 808–825.

Briceño, C., Tereucán, J., Galván, M., & Miranda, H. (2020). Evaluación de la Escala de Identidad Étnica en adolescentes mapuche de Chile. *Revista Latinoamericana de Ciencias Sociales, Niñez y Juventud, 18*(3), 1–25.

Byram, M., & Cain, A. (2001). Civilisation/estudios culturales: un experimento en escuelas francesas e inglesas. In M. Byram & M. Fleming (Eds.), *Perspectivas interculturales en el aprendizaje de idiomas. Enfoques a través del teatro y la etnografía* (pp. 38–50). Madrid: Cambridge University Press.

Campinha-Bacote, J. (1998). *The process of cultural competence in the delivery of healthcare services*. Cincinnati, OH: Transcultural C.A.R.E. Associate Press.

Carrasco, A.M. (1998). Constitución de género y ciclo vital entre los aymarás contemporáneos del norte de Chile. *Chungará, 30*(1), 87–103.

Cerna, C., & Muñoz, W. (2019). Movilidad, parentesco e identificación en el valle de Codpa, norte de Chile. *Chungará, 51*(4), 661–674.

Coates, J., Gray, M., & Hetherington, T. (2006). An 'Ecospiritual' perspective: Finally, a place for indigenous approaches. *The British Journal of Social Work, 36*(3), 381–399.

Cortes, H., & Gundermman, H. (2020). La realidad económica actual de la comunidad aimara del norte de Chile. *Interciencia, 45*(10), 475–479.

Course, M. (2011). *Becoming Mapuche: Person and ritual in indigenous Chile.* Chicago, IL: University of Illinois Press.

Cummins, R., Eckersley, R., Pallant, J., Van Vugt, J., & Misajon, R. (2003). Developing a national index of subjective wellbeing: the Australian unity wellbeing index. *Social Indicators Research, 64,* 159–190.

Díaz, R. L. (2007). Trabajo social intercultural: algunas reflexiones a propósito de la intervención con una Comunidad Indígena del Trapecio Amazónico Colombiano. *Palobra: Palabra que obra, 8,* 154–171.

Flores-Guerrero, R. (2004). Salud, enfermedad y muerte: lecturas desde la antropología sociocultural. *Revista Mad, 10,* 1–8.

Gallardo-Peralta, L.P., Molina, M.A. & Schettini del Moral, R. (2019a) Validation of the personal wellbeing index (PWI) for older Chilean adults. *International Psychogeriatrics, 31*(11), 1679–1680.

Gallardo-Peralta, L.P., Sánchez-Moreno, E, & Rodríguez- Rodríguez, V. (2019b). Strangers in their own world: Exploring the relation between cultural practices and the health of older adults in native communities in Chile. *The British Journal of Social Work, 49*(4), 920–942.

Gavilán, V. (2002). Seeking for life: Towards a theory on Aymara gender labor division. *Chungará, 34*(1), 101–117.

Gavilán, V. (2020). Prácticas matrimoniales y relaciones de género en dos comunidades aymaras del altiplano del norte de Chile. *Estudios Atacameños,* 65, 339–362. http://dx.doi.org/10.22199/issn.0718-1043-2020-0037.

Gavilán, V., & Carrasco, A.M. (2009). Festividades andinas y religiosidad en el norte chileno. *Chungará, 41*(1), 101–112.

Gavilán, V., Vigueras, P. C., Madariaga, E., & Parra, M. G. (2018). Intercultural aspects of health. A critical analysis of health policies aimed at the Aymara people of northern Chile. *Interciencia, 43*(5), 322–328.

Gray, M., Coates, J., & Yellow Bird, M. (2008). *Indigenous social work around the world: Towards culturally relevant social work education and practice.* London: Ashgate Publishing.

Gundermann, H., & Vergara, J.I. (2009). Comunidad, organización y complejidad social andinas en el norte de Chile. *Estudios Atacameños, 38,* 107–126.

Gundermann, H., González, H., & Vergara, J.I. (2007). Currency and displacement of the Aymara language in Chile. *Estudios filológicos, 42,* 123–140.

Gundermann, H., Vergara, J.I., & Díaz, A. (2011). Historia moderna de una lengua originaria: el *jaqi aru* en Chile. *Revista de lingüística teórica y aplicada, 49*(1), 69–108.

Guzmán, O. (2011). Ethnic diversity as a variable in social work interventions. *Trabajo Social, 13,* 171–180, 2011.

International Federation of Social Workers (IFSW). (n.d.). Global definition of the social work profession. https://www.ifsw.org/what-is-social-work/global-definition-of-social-work/

Lagos, C. (2012). Mapudungun in Santiago de Chile: Vitality and social representation among urban mapuche people. *Revista de Lingüística Teórica y Aplicada, 50*(1), 161–184.

Laitinen, M., & Väyrynen, S. (2016). Social work practices and research with Sámi people and communities in the frame of indigenous social work. *International Social Work, 59*(5), 583–586.

Law, K., & Lee, K. (2016). Importing Western values versus indigenization: Social work practice with ethnic minorities in Hong Kong. *International Social Work, 59*(1), 60–72.

Madaleno, I.M., & Delatorre-Herrera, J. (2013). Popular medicine of Iquique, Tarapaca. *IDESIA, 31*(1), 67–78.

Mansilla, M., & Muñoz, W. (2017). ¿Evangélicos o aymaras?: dinámicas de las representaciones culturales de los evangélicos aymaras (Chile). *Estudios Atacameños, 54,* 239–258.

Martínez, M.F., Martínez, J., & Calzado, V. (2006). The cultural competence and the human diversity on the social intervention and the provision of services. *Psychosocial Intervention, 15*(3), 331–350.

Ministry of Health (2013). *Special program for health and indigenous peoples. Methodological guide for the management of the program [Programa especial de salud y pueblos indígenas. Guía metodológica para la gestión del programa]*. Santiago of Chile: Ministry of Health. Retrieved from: http://www.bibliotecaminsal.cl/wp/wp-content/uploads/2018/01/030.OT-y-Guia-Pueblos-indigenas.pdf

Ministry of Social Development and Family. (2017). *Encuesta Nacional de Caracterización Socioeconómica, CASEN [National Socioeconomic Characterization Survey]*. Santiago of Chile: Ministry of Social Development.

Nacional Association of Social Worker (NASW). (2015). *Standards and indicators of Cultural Competence in Social Work Practice*. Washington, DC: National Association of Social Workers.

Nadan, Y. (2017). Rethinking 'cultural competence' in international social work. *International Social Work*, 60(1), 74–83.

National Association of Social Workers (NASW). *NASW standards for cultural competence in social work practice*. Washington, DC: NASW.

Pujadas, J.J. (2011). Los claroscuros de la etnicidad. El culturalismo evaluado desde la óptica de la cohesión social y la ciudadanía. In P. Palenzuela, & A. Olivi (Eds.), *Etnicidad y desarrollo en los andes* (pp. 223–254). Sevilla: Universidad de Sevilla.

Ribadeneira, K. (2020). Buen vivir (Living Well): Reviewing the balance sheet of a social paradigm under construction. *Diálogo andino, 62*, 41–51.

Rojas, P. (2016). The Mapuche funeral rite of descanso (repose): From the ontological change to the tree of ancestors. *Chungará, 48*(4), 657–678.

Romero-Toledo, H., & Sambolín, A. (2019). 611. Indigeneidad y territorio: los aymaras y quechuas en el Norte de Chile. *Scripta Nova. Revista Electrónica de Geografía y Ciencias Sociales, 23*, 1–32.

Salas, A. (1985). Hablar en mapudungún es vivir en mapuche. Especificidad de la relación lengua-cultura, *Revista de Lingüística Teórica y Aplicada, 25*, 27–35.

Sosme, M.A, & Casado, E. (2016). Etnia y empoderamiento: elementos para el análisis de la transformación de identidades femeninas en la Sierra de Zongolica, Veracruz. *Sociológica, 31*(87), 143–173.

Sue, D.W. (2013). *Multicultural Social Work Practice*. New York: Wiley.

Sue, D.W., Arredondo, P., & Mcdavis, R.J. (1992). Multicultural counselling competencies and standards: A call to the profession. *Journal of Counseling & Development, 70*, 477–486.

Tereucán, J. (2008) *Reciprocidad e intercambio entre los mapuches. Organización social y económica en comunidades rurales del sur de Chile*. Tesis Doctoral. Universidad Iberoamericana, México.

Tereucán-Angulo, J., Briceño-Olivera, C., & Gálvez-Nieto, J. (2016). Equivalencia y valor en procesos de reciprocidad e intercambio entre los mapuches. *Convergencia, 23*(72), 199–220.

UNESCO. (2017). *Diálogo intercultural, Competencias Interculturales: marco conceptual y operativo*. Bogotá: Universidad Nacional de Colombia.

van Kessel, J. (2001). El ritual mortuorio de los aymara de Tarapacá como vivencia y crianza de la vida. *Chungará, 33*(2), 221–234.

Vázquez, O. (2002). Trabajo social y competencia intercultural. *Portularia, 2*, 125–138.

Wade, P. (2010). *Race and ethnicity in Latin America*. Retrieved from: https://ebookcentral.proquest.com

Walsh, C. (2010). Interculturalidad crítica y educación intercultural. *Construyendo interculturalidad crítica, 75*, 96.

17
Social and Field Work Abilities of Teaching Professors

Claudia Reyes-Quilodran, Paula Miranda, and Liliana Guerra-Aburto

Social Work in Latin America and Chile

Latin American social work has been influenced by a path of critical discussion (Rozas, 2006) in such a way that the professional profile has been developed on the basis of the discussions and effects of the social question. The macro-historical contexts and their influences on political, social, cultural, and economic nature have shaped Latin American social work. The discursive-argumentative statements about equity, social justice, democratic processes, human rights, and poverty become more important than methodical, procedural, and bureaucratic issues. These issues are perceived as oppressive and barriers that oppose necessary social transformation.

The various authors who have analysed Latin American social work have observed that professional practice and social intervention are influenced by state centralism and by an excessively ideologised practice. Moreover, the notable differences between regions that support and build up theoretical approaches are limited in developing a deep comprehension of social reality. This fact favours the incongruence between the research and social intervention. Social work intervention becomes relevant when it responds to the demands of the social dynamics and social complexity of Latin American people (Galeana, 2008).

In Chile, social work was established as a career in 1925 with the creation of undergraduate training. This discipline has developed specialised knowledge to address emerging social issues. Today, the undergraduate programme lasts five years on average. Owing to the extended educational period required for this career, most of the professionals do not have master's degrees, and they do not have clinical training. Instead, these professionals focus on social problems and develop an intervention plan based on the context, methodological tools, and case features. In other words, social workers move along a continuum between professional knowledge and an intuitive method based on the environment and the case's characteristics. This tendency has gradually changed in a group of Chilean workers who investigate technical tools and intervention models to develop social interventions.

The School of Social Work at the Pontifical Catholic University of Chile (ETSUC) is one of the older schools in the country. The programme was implemented in 1929 and has been uninterruptedly conducted until today. The long history of this school allows one to see the different social changes in the culture and the socio-political scenario and how they impact teaching. In

DOI: 10.4324/9781003270119-21

this study, we examined a model of professional practice to understand the professional abilities that an undergraduate professor should actually develop among social work students.

School of Social Work and the Professional Practice Model

The professional practicum has a central role in the Social Work School at the ETSUC. This aspect has motivated the ETSUC to make efforts in developing a professional practicum model proposal, which is built on the basis of the professional experience of the academics and field organisations and the sociohistorical context of the country. In Latin America, research on this issue is very limited. Therefore, this model includes other international literature reviews to recall the international experience, which gives some information on how the professional practicum is implemented at the international level. These elements define the professional practicum in terms of an active learning process in which the practicum experience is a period that allows students to acquire specialised knowledge and social work abilities (Lee & Fortune, 2013; Teigiser, 2009; Bogo, 2006; in Proposal for a Professional Practice model ETSUC, 2016).

The professional practicum is a learning experience in which the students are able to be involved in the professional work of field organisations. The practicum is an opportunity to learn while doing the work. As Munson (2002) states, the ETSUC established that the professional practicum is a stage in which the students gradually begin to leave the classroom, apply the lectures to their involvement in the professional world, and finally make the link between theory and practice. For this purpose, the students should apply general principles about organisations' procedures that allow them to acquire knowledge.

Thus, through professional practice, the students must develop professional social work skills. For such purposes, the ETSUC has established two semesters for the development of professional practice. In the first semester, students have two courses. The courses are the following: first, decentralisation and national development; second, an optative course. The objectives of the decentralisation and national development course are that the student understands the different notions of development, local development, and decentralisation and establishes relationships between these concepts. In this semester, the students work in agencies three times per week for an equivalent of 24 hours per week. The ETSUC provides the students with different agencies from which they can choose according to their personal interests, which will be the agency where they will conduct their professional practicum. The agencies can be public or private, and they cover diverse social problems related to vulnerable families, child protection services, juvenile offenders, the elderly, community service, and company wellness. The group of students is separated into smaller groups according to the theme of each agency (each group has approximately ten students). Each group has a professor in charge of supervising their professional practicum. In addition, each agency has a supervisor who is a social worker that works in the agency. The field supervisor guides the students in their roles in the agency. Meanwhile, the professor in charge of each group and the field supervisor establish the roles of the students in the agency and the assessment criteria. Their agreement clearly indicates what is expected from the student, the agency, and the professor.

In the second semester of the professional practicum, the students stay in the same agency, but they reduce their time at the agency to two periods a week or 16 hours per week. The students reduce their time in the agency since they have to take three courses this semester. Those courses include the following: Ethics, Public Policy, and Contemporary Proposals in Social Work. The professional ethics course reviews the ethical dilemmas that have emerged in professional practice. The Public Policy course addresses conceptual approaches about public policy and analyses the cycle of the design, implementation, management, and evaluation of public policy. The course on contemporary proposals addresses the configuration of new complex intervention models.

Despite the fact that the students should register for courses during their professional practicum, in this instance, they are offered a closer approach to social reality and daily organisational functioning, provided tools that allow them to 'deal' early with organisational contexts (Zeira & Schiff, 2014 in Proposal for a Professional Practice Model ETSUC, 2016), and allowed to participate in the organisation's activities.

The courses contents of the undergraduate programme should permit the students to identify the problems and processes in the clients and organisations and understand the relationships between them. In other words, the content must contribute to the training of the social worker in the exercise of their professional practicum. Owing to this fact, the other disciplines that contribute to the formation of social workers are relevant, such as sociology, psychology, statistics, and economics. This relevance is observed because they contribute to understanding the societal complexity and improving social intervention, particularly in areas that today emerge as new fields of social intervention that use interdisciplinary work to understand their complexity. This principle requires that students, before undertaking professional practice, complete each of the courses required by the programme, which shows that they have acquired the necessary knowledge to carry out professional practice. Therefore, the proposal for the ETSUC professional practice model is based on a training component supported by the curriculum of a social work career.

The proposal of the professional practice model highlights the importance of the reflection about social work practices to develop effective professional interventions (Puig, 2010; Papouli, 2014; Lee & Fortune, 2013 in Proposal for a Professional Practice Model ETSUC, 2016). Reflective practice is identified as a process of reflection that students and professionals carry out in their own professional practice (Sánchez, 2013 in Proposal for a Professional Practice Model ETSUC, 2016). This reflection is undertaken in such a way that students and professionals are able to explain the relationship between their knowledge and their practice in a coherent, exhaustive, and convincing way (Trevithick, 2002 in Proposal for a Professional Practice Model ETSUC, 2016). Professional practice is then a set of actions that a student performs in a real context of intervention related to professional practice, where professional learning is consolidated in an organisational context. Here, the educational programme occurs in the field practicum, where field instruction provides the students opportunities for teaching and learning about social work practice (Bogo & McKnight, 2006). Therefore, the proposed model of professional practice is aligned with the student's graduation profile, the ultimate goal of which is as follows: Training excellent quality social workers with a solid base in theory that is capable of understanding contemporary society and providing input through innovative ideas for social intervention for complex realities and that can contribute to the creation of knowledge through intervention and research of social phenomena with a capacity to analyse policies and design and manage programmes and social projects with the abilities to work with diverse teams. The professionals act in an ethical manner, are committed to human development and their own professional development, recognize and accept diversity, promote participation and citizenship and work towards the defence and promotion of human rights with a clear option for social justice.

(http://trabajosocial.uc.cl/pregrado/perfil-de-egreso, 2020, p. 1)

The development of social work activities requires the performance of competences, which the student begins to acquire through theoretical training and subsequently consolidate with practical exercises. In this sense, the practice enables students to complete their training so that they are in a position to begin their professional careers. To achieve this goal, the proposal of the ETSUC professional practice model establishes that the professional training of the students is composed of the interaction between the field supervisor and the professor.

Since the professional practice programme encourages students to achieve deep theoretical, methodological, and ethical knowledge about social intervention, the programme strengths include the development of general skills in social work practices, such as the following: self-awareness and the ability to perform a critical self-assessment; commitment to their own training and professional development; developing autonomous, creative, and innovative performance; making appropriate and responsible use of social and public resources; assessing an agency's records of processes and outputs that provide evidence of the actions undertaken; maintaining adequate interpersonal relationships and facilitating teamwork; developing ethical values consistent with the professional exercise of social work, such as social justice, dialogue, reliability, individualisation, self-determination, acceptance, respect for differences and professional secrecy; and deploying social research skills and techniques to strengthen social intervention.

Problem Statement

The proposed professional practice model provides a clear definition of what actions are expected to be taken in the student training process. However, when examining what specific professional skills students are expected to develop, they are presented ambiguously. In other words, the model refers to 'soft' skills, which include conflict management, emotional containment, and interdisciplinary work. In addition, these skills are ascribed to the skills proposed by the British Association of Social Workers (BASW), such as leadership, culture, ethical professionalism, rights and justice, diversity, knowledge, and critical reflection. However, each of these skills is not reflected in how they are implemented in students and subsequently evaluated.

The model proposal places special emphasis on written and oral communication skills, where the subject communicates the results and conclusions of the diagnosis and research. Effective and empathetic communication is expected to generate spaces for mutual collaboration in the organisational framework. At this level, it is also observed that the student ethically argues for their decisions considering the diversity of social interventions and social policies. Another expected skill is the ability to efficiently manage available resources and develop collaborative work with interdisciplinary work teams. Then, the following questions arise. What are the specific skills that a professional practice professor should have to transfer and identify them in students? In addition, how does a practice professor determine whether these skills are installed in the student? To answer these questions, the objective of this study was to examine the professional abilities developed during the professional practicum.

Professional Skills and Technical Knowledge

On the basis of the ETSUC concept of professional practicum, this study defines professional practice as a stage in which students gradually begin to leave courses and classrooms to gradually enter the professional field. In this instance, the students are able to make the link between theory and practice and are able to apply the general principles of the procedures (Munson, 2002), which enables them to acquire knowledge. Through the professional practicum, the student must develop professional social work skills. According to Cournoyer (2018), these skills are related to cognitive articulation and consistent behavioural performance. The students have to use scientific knowledge based on research, including values, principles, and ethical obligations.

The student has to develop the facilitator abilities utilised in social work and promote the necessary social legitimation of social work's purposes. In this way, the ETSUC model points out that the practice process has the following stages. The first stage refers to the preparation and beginning of the professional practicum. At this stage, the student must be introduced to the agency and become familiar with the organisational context. In the second stage, the tasks that the student has carried out in the agency are evaluated, and the student designs an intervention plan of action. In a third phase, the intervention plan is implemented at the same time that the results of the work are evaluated.

In this practicum process, supervision plays an important role because it becomes a process through which the professor and the student are able to discuss professional practicum issues and where questions, concerns, weaknesses, failures, observations, skill gaps, and expectations are examined to help the student to select techniques to apply in practice. The supervision is a process of collaboration, facilitation, and mutual understanding between the student and the professor; hence, it requires mutual trust (Munson, 2002).

In this scenario, the professor who supervises the professional practicum must consider the following five basic aspects that are useful to generate effective supervision where the expected skills are transferred to the student (Munson 2002). The first aspect is a *clear and formal structure* for supervision. This structure implies having a format for conducting supervision, either for individual supervision, group supervision, or a combination of both. Next is *regularity*. Regardless of the structure used, supervision must be carried out regularly. *Consistency* is where the supervisor must work to ensure that the style and approach used with the student are consistent. There must be a connection between the style and pattern for decision-making such that the student can have clear expectations regarding the supervision. Next is *case orientation*. For the supervision to be effective and efficient, it must always be case-oriented. The administrative aspects, personal matters and learning should be connected to the case under discussion. The goal is to keep the focus on supervision. If monitoring is not performed on a case-by-case basis, monitoring can lose its primary focus. Finally, we have the *Supervision Assessment* itself. Munson (2002) argues that it is the responsibility of the supervisor (professor) to periodically request formal and informal feedback about the supervision. Based on these concepts, it is essential to be able to determine the abilities that a supervising practicum professor should have. To answer this question, the competency approach is used because it provides guidance on how skills should be defined.

The competency approach is a theoretical concept, which claims that the acquisition of competences is achieved through an educational process that includes acquiring certain knowledge, consolidating certain attitudes and training in specific skills. The tools to achieve competency are the following: teaching, orientation, and training (Ugarte & Naval, 2010). In this sense, competencies are defined as those habitual observable behaviours that enable a person to succeed in his or her activity or function (Ugarte & Naval, 2010). Knowledge, values, attitudes, and skills are components of competencies (Ringstad, 2013; Salazar, & Chiang, 2007). A skill is demonstrated when a capacity manifests itself and allows the application of knowledge about a specific reality for its transformation. Skill refers to the ease, aptitude, and speed of carrying out any task or activity. Skills are processes seeking efficiency and effectiveness that are put into action, but they also integrate the understanding of the situation, the spirit of the challenge and responsibility. The importance of skills is based on the fact that to transmit knowledge related to competencies, it is necessary to promote the acquisition of skills that encourage the consolidation of habits through training.

Skills are highly important for professional practice. Some of the skills required to be a social worker relate to interpersonal and professional skills. For this reason, an exploratory study on this matter becomes essential, as qualitative research allows one to understand the skills developed in the professional practicum from the students and professors.

Methodology

The research objective is to characterise the professional abilities that a professor who conducted a field practicum to contribute to the social work curriculum may have. To accomplish this objective, exploratory and qualitative research was conducted, with the aim of gathering information from the actors involved in the professional field practicum: the professors of the field practicum and the social work graduate students.

To accomplish the objective, in-depth interviews were conducted with six field practicum professors who served in this role from 2014 to 2019. The professors have at least two years of experience doing this work. In addition, an online questionnaire with open-ended questions was sent to 19 graduated students who graduated during the same time period from 2014 to 2019. This number is due to the low number of responses that these types of surveys usually have. However, because this is a qualitative study, this number will enable sufficient information to be collected to achieve the objectives of this investigation.

The data analysis was carried out through content analysis because it permits the construction of models of codes, categories, and relationships that account for the opinions and motivations of the actors (Paillé, 2006; Albarello et al., 1995). This qualitative approach identifies the basic units of meaning of the actors and the relations of opposition and equivalence that structure the meanings. Once the information was collected, the categories of professional skills that favoured student learning were created. At this stage, the study identified how the field practicum professors transferred professional skills and technical-professional knowledge, how they evaluated the installation of technical-professional knowledge in students, and, finally, the characteristics that a field practicum professor should have to contribute to the installation of professional skills in social work students. The research was approved by the ethics board of the Pontifical Catholic University of Chile (N°191219004).

Results

In the following section, the results from the interviews with the professors who supervise the professional practicum and the findings from the graduate students' online questionnaire with open-ended questions are presented. The results are analysed and compared with those of different authors to investigate how the professor transfers the professional skills and technical knowledge to the students and evaluates the students' technical-professional knowledge and abilities during the field practicum compared with the international experience. The comparative approach will allow us to identify the differences between the local and international experience and improve the professional practice model proposal.

The interviewed professors argue that a professor who supervises students' professional practicum must have skills similar to those that are being demanded from the students. The professors must possess the knowledge and skills required for the students because they work under the logic of transferring skills. The professor should act primarily as an example through modelling. In this sense, the professor must be able to transmit not only technical knowledge but also professional and soft skills through active examples. This argument is identified by Cournoyer (2018), who explains that social work is a profession that is learned by doing. The professional practicum is the first instance where students leave the classroom and are linked to work. Then, the students must be guided by a professional who knows the field and has acquired the skills through constant exposure to the environment. The professor's professional experience would be able to better guide the practice instances. This importance is especially relevant if we consider that the interviewees emphasise professional and soft skills more than technical knowledge. In this sense, knowledge not only is a unique feature of social workers but also is the adaptive capacity offered by the soft and professional skills that determine the social worker's practice.

Soft and Professional Skills

The interviewed professors identified two types of skills: soft skills and professional skills. Soft skills are described by the professors in terms of the abilities that a social work student must develop to promote positive interaction with their social environment, such as users, teamwork, and authorities. Meanwhile, the professional skills refer to the ability to apply professional techniques according to the situation and case. The interviewed professors tended to highlight professional skills over soft skills. They argued that social work practice will depend on the abilities to handle the agency's practices. Therefore, soft skills support the development of professional skills.

As Papouli (2014) states, the professors agree with the fact that the professional practicum's purpose is learning by doing, as the professor wants to transfer the professional and soft skills that help this process to the students. The relationship between the professional skills and social work practice is tied in such a way that the student must acquire these skills to become a social worker. The successful process will depend on the professor's skills, as the student can perceive these abilities in and trust the professor.

The professors use soft skills to take care of the relationship between the professor and student. One of these skills is the capacity to emotionally support the student because the agency requires constant emotional commitment. The professors state that mutual trust is the basis for the relationship with the student and helps to transfer professional abilities. Therefore, one of the first tasks of professors is to gain the trust of the students and empathise with their needs.

The interviewed professors, such as Munson (2002), point out that effective communication, the capacity to lead teams, and problem-solving are the soft skills the students are expected to possess. The professors highlight the importance of communication skills, rather than creative skills, in professional practice. The professors believe that communication skills should be emphasised, reinforcing the fluidity of the student-professor relationship, rather than the transmission of knowledge. This emphasis may be placed because the professional practicum emotionally challenges students; therefore, the professors prioritise giving them emotional support. Even though the professors encourage the students to develop knowledge and creative contexts, professional knowledge is a priority over creative skills. This important point suggests that creativity is a rarely considered dimension within the supervision of a professional practicum.

Another aspect observed is the fact that the interviewed professors do not clearly and concretely identify the educational and training skills. Indeed, there is no agreement between them concerning these abilities. This aspect can be explained by the fact that a group of interviewed professors claim that they must have training in social work, whether at the undergraduate or postgraduate levels. These professors believe that having studied social work necessarily brings students closer to achieving the necessary professional skills. Meanwhile, another group of professors believes that it is more important that the supervisor is strongly linked to social intervention. This last group believes that it is enough to be involved with social transformation through field practicum. Despite the differences between professors, they agree that some professional skills should be developed by the students, and it is necessary that they have these professional skills to achieve this goal.

At this point, it is possible to observe that some of the skills identified by professors are similar to those proposed by Puig (2010). Nevertheless, the author offers a more complex and complete list of skills that a professor should possess. Puig (2010) explains that the professors' skills should align with three areas: communication, education and training, and knowledge and creation of creative contexts. The following table presents each of the skills that a professor should develop (Table 17.1).

The success of introducing skills in the students also implies that the professor must consider other aspects. In other words, Munson (2002) emphasises that structure, regularity, consistency, a case-oriented approach, and assessment are the basic elements that a professor should develop to achieve good supervision, as these skills are the same as those that will be demanded by field supervisors. Moreover, these elements will support the student's agency collocation and the use of technical tools. In this sense, the professors interviewed agree with Munson's definitions, which are presented in the following table (Table 17.2).

The assessment is one of the elements that the author and the interviewed professors agree is necessary to assess the students' progress and successes. Nevertheless, the professors say that they do not have a common methodology or tools to assess the students, and they wonder whether each identified skill is fully evaluated. Indeed, the professors suggested that this oversight occurs because they have not thought about this aspect yet, and one of them says that 'evaluation is one of the weakest aspects of student supervision'. However, the case-oriented intervention is one of the best covered elements because the students are trained and supervised on how to give users emotional support, and they create true engagement in the intervention. To achieve this goal, the professors should be very familiar with the students' needs, weaknesses, and strengths. Indeed, when graduate students are asked about the abilities they developed during their professional practicum, they mention that they were able to learn about group management and frustration management, and they became more flexible in the intervention. The students developed professional autonomy and a proactive attitude. The emotional support, active listening, and rapport with the user were other abilities learned during this time. In this instance, it is observed that both teachers and students have a consensus on the learning achieved via soft skills.

The professors argue that they are able to establish the soft skills in students, which is accomplished because they are aware of the students' complexity. Furthermore, establishing soft skills is a necessary skill of a professor that does not require an evaluative model. The professor used a similar argument to explain the lack of skills related to the structure and consistency areas. In other words, the absence of an evaluative model in the professional practicum does not offer guidelines to the professors, and they tend to follow their own common sense based on their professional expertise. These results coincide with those expressed by the graduate students, who argue that they do not have access to clear evaluation criteria. Some of the graduates indicate that they did not know how they were evaluated; moreover, another group of graduates refers to the evaluation form. Despite this difference, they agree that it is necessary to evaluate not only the final results but also the learning process by using progressive evaluations. The progressive evaluation would give the students the opportunity to see their weaknesses and have the chance to improve them.

Munson (2002) explains that the supervisors should be familiar with five activities to work with the students, namely, reading, writing, observing, listening, and speaking. Among the skills identified by the interviewed professors, some of them are consistent with the activities proposed by Munson. These skills are identified in the following table (Table 17.3).

The professors identified that it is necessary to know intervention models and that they should have expertise in this area. The graduate students agree with this argument and point out this aspect as a weakness of some professors who do not have training in intervention. Another criticism of students is that some professors do not have expertise in the specific issues of the

Table 17.1 Professor skills

Areas	Skills
Communication	• Express non-verbal language according to the context. • Engage in affectivity. • Develop a bond of trust with students. • Provide psychological support. • Give interpersonal balance. • Generate spaces of emotional support in the face of difficult situations. • Develop an attitude-space to support professional care. • Promote the development of empathetic human relations that are respectful of diversity. • Participate in strategic conversations with the student that provide direction. • Perform adequate management of power. • Develop a relationship of responsibility with the student. • Provide flexibility in the context of the situation. • Diagnose situations of professional stress. • Maintain permanent communication with the student.
Education and training	• Develop a critical view of the students about the work that they perform. • Provide clarity regarding the professional practicum's objectives. • Provide training in the supervision model. • Identify intervention models and apply them based on the context features. • Analyse and make decisions based on the information offered by the student, the field supervisor, and their own observations.
Knowledge and creation of creative contexts	• Link field work with professional experience. • Encourage student resources without focusing on their weaknesses. • Grant skills through modelling. • Encourage collaborative work. • Promote an objective-oriented attitude in the student. • Develop a self-evaluation attitude in the student. • Provide technical support. • Establish the ethical dimension of the intervention. • Instil the empowerment of the subjects in the student. • Carry out reflexive exercises. • Strengthen the technical content used by the students. • Establish a close co-trainer relationship with the field supervisor. • Implement performance indicators. • Have clear standards of disapproval and approval, which are accompanied by expected profiles and protocols. • Develop and set limits in the relationship with the student. • Develop and implement the normative-bureaucratic status.

Source: Adapted from Puig, 2010

users, such as the elderly, child services, or migration. This fact made them not feel confident about their learning process. However, the graduates value the soft skills taught by their professors, which permitted them to establish close relationships with their professor or supervisor.

The professors who led the professional practicum included Munson's activities, but it is necessary to deeply develop each of these activities and offer the students the opportunity to understand the abilities that they will need to develop during their professional practicum. Moreover,

Table 17.2 Basic elements of successful supervision and professor skills

Basic elements of successful supervision	Skills identified by the professor
Structure	• Being objective-oriented. • Establishing and developing clear limits.
Regularity	• Developing a responsible relationship between the student, the professor, and field supervisor. • Developing strategies for self-care.
Consistency	• Displaying consistency between what is expected from the student and agency. • Being explicit about the professional practice and the expected student behaviour.
Case-oriented	• Distinguishing the differences between students. • Providing psychological support. • Having the flexibility to understand the agency context. • Encouraging students' strengths and avoiding focusing on their weaknesses. • Developing self-appraisal in the student. • Providing technical support.
Assessment	• Having supervision from others.

Source: Adapted from Munson, 2002

Table 17.3 Munson's activities and skills identified by professors

Munson´s activities	Skills identified by professors
Reading	• Identifying and understanding intervention models
Writing	• Recording the students' evolutionary process • Developing qualified tasks, activities, and reports about the students' performance.
Observing	• Having the ability to analyse and make decisions based on information from the student, the field supervisor, and their own judgement.
Listening	• Establishing a close co-trainer relationship with the field supervisor.
Speaking	• Achieving interpersonal balance.

Source: Authors

the students need to know how these abilities will be evaluated. In order words, professors and students should be clear about what is expected from them.

Brief Discussion of the Results and Contributions to the Social Work Curriculum

Although the findings show that there are gaps between the area of management (specifically in evaluation) and supervision, the ETSUC has made important efforts to advance the consolidation of a practice model which is aligned with the graduation profile and the requirements of the labour market. The model is theoretically based on three essential axes. Although not yet perfectly delineated, it is possible to recognise some elements according to their most relevant characteristics, but they are presented unclearly. To propose an improvement to the ETSUC's model, in this section, we describe the three axes and how they should be focused on while teaching social work skills to students. The suggestions are based on the ETSUC's model and the findings of this study. The axes are the following: training, supervision, and management.

Axis of Training

The axis of training refers to the theoretical and conceptual knowledge that the student must have acquired during their academic training throughout their career. These theoretical-conceptual concepts are observed in the way the student understands the social phenomena in the intervention and how they respond to the requirements that these phenomena demand. This dimension also includes the use of techniques and instruments specific to the organisation and the subject of care. In the professional practicum, the student must develop interpersonal skills that allow her/him to work with different disciplines at the same time that s/he develops communication skills, both with the subjects of care and with the different intra- and extra-organisational instances. Professors and students highlighted the features of the axis of training, but they do not identify it as a specific axis of the professional practicum. Then, it appears to be highly relevant that the skills expected in the students and professors are established using clear and evident descriptions such that each of the involved individuals is able to identify their role in students´ learning. These definitions should also be aligned with the field instructor in such a way that professors and field instructors can encourage the development of the skills in the students. Therefore, this axis is bounded by the axis of supervision.

Axis of Supervision

In supervision, it is expected that both the professor who guides the professional practicum and the field instructor can observe the professional behaviour based on the training elements. Supervision facilitates the students' organisational insertion and diagnosis, as well as monitoring of the impeding and facilitating aspects of the students' expected performance. In this axis, self-care tools are provided and reflect the ethical elements typical of social interventions in an institutional context led by a legal framework. In this axis, it is possible to also distinguish the presence of skills, such as the use of ethical elements and self-care skills, which are not frequently mentioned by the participants but are fundamentals of social work intervention, especially the ethical issues. Successful supervision and training require a structure that favours the adequate performance of the professional practicum, and this structure is offered by the axis of management.

Axis of Management

Management establishes the procedures, standards, and forms of evaluation that will be carried out during professional practice. For this purpose, agreements are established with the agency and the field instructor regarding the tasks that the student will carry out and the actions and commitments that the organisation must assume. The schedule and number of weekly hours that the student must meet are established. The supervising professors should monitor these agreements. This axis is considered transverse to the previous axes. One of the main weaknesses argued by the participants is that the absence of evaluation procedures and standards does not enable the students and professors to distinguish the expectations regarding the students' performance. This axis establishes the evaluation methods and requirements in such a way that students can see how they are evaluated, their progress, and the expected skills. Even though the ETSUC in the last two years has implemented assessment forms to evaluate the students' results, these assessment forms appear to be insufficient to measure the skills developed by the students, and the assessment forms do not reflect how the students progressively reach specific achievements.

The results show the need to clearly define the social work skills that should be developed by the students. The professors who supervise the professional practicum should share these definitions, the techniques to teach the skills, and common assessment forms to evaluate the gradual learning progress and final results obtained by the students. Furthermore, for the professors who supervise a professional practicum, they should have the skills required of students. Therefore, reaching a clear definition of professional skills could also help to establish the ideal profile of a professor who supervises a professional practicum.

References

Albarello F., Digneffe, F., Hiernaux, J. P., Maroy, C. & Ruquoy, D. (1995). *Pratiques et méthodes de recherche en sciences sociales*. Paris. Armand Colin.
Bogo, M. (2006). Social Work Practice: Concepts, Processes, and Interviewing. Columbia University Press. In *Proposal for a Professional Practice Model, 2016. Propuesta de un modelo para la práctica profesional*. New York. USA: Escuela de Trabajo Social. Pontificia Universidad Católica de Chile.
Bogo. M. & McKnight, K. (2006). Clinical Supervision in Social Work. *The Clinical Supervisor, 24*(1–2), 49–67. https://doi.org/10.1300/J001v24n01_04
Cournoyer, B. R. (2018). *The social work skills workbook* (8th ed.). Boston, MA: Cengage Learning.
Galeana, S. (2008). *La centralidad de la intervención social: Un análisis para su redefinición en el contexto mexicano actual. Informe de investigación*. México: ents-unam.
Lee, M., & Fortune, A. E. (2013). Do we need more 'doing' activities or 'thinking' activities in the field of practicum? *Journal of Social Work Education, 49*(4), 646–660. https://doi.org/10.1080/10437797.2013.812851. In *Proposal for a professional practice model*, 2016. Propuesta de un modelo para la práctica profesional. Escuela de Trabajo Social. Pontificia Universidad Católica de Chile.
Munson, C. E. (2002). *Handbook of clinical social work supervision* (3rd ed.). New York: Hawthorn Press.
Paillé, P. (2006). *La méthologie qualitative: Postures de recherche et travail de terrain*. Paris: Armand Colin.
Papouli, E. (2014). Field Learning in Social Work Education: Implications for Educators and Instructors. *The Field Educator: A Scholarly Journal from the Simmons College School of Social Work, 4*(2), 1–15. Available at http://fieldeducator.simmons.edu/article/field-learning-in-social-work-educationimplications-for-educators-and-instructors/ [Accessed 15 January 2020].
Puig, C. (2010). *La supervisión en la intervención social: Un instrumento para la calidad de los servicios y el bienestar de los profesionales*. Universitat Rovira i Virgili. Available at https://www.tdx.cat/bitstream/handle/10803/8438/Tesi.pdfCarmina?sequence=1 [Accessed 10 December 2019].
Ringstad, R. L. (n.d.). Competency Level versus Level of Competency: The Field Evaluation Dilemma. *The Field Educator: A Scholarly Journal from the Simmons College School of Social Work, 4*(2), 1–16. Available at http://www2.simmons.edu/ssw/fe/i/Ringstad.pdf [Accessed 15 January 2020].
Rozas, M. P. (2006). *La formación y la intervención profesional: Hacia la construcción de proyectos ético políticos en trabajo social* (1st ed.). Buenos Aires: Editorial Espacio.
Salazar, C. & Chiang, M. (2007). Competencias y Educación Superior. Un estudio empírico. *Horizontes Educacionales, 12*(2), 23–35. Available at http://www.redalyc.org/pdf/979/97917592003.pdf [Accessed 15 January 2020].
Sánchez, A. (2013). Prácticas de resistencia y alternativas para el cambio. Una defensa del Trabajo Social con colectivos y comunidades. Trabajo Social Global. *Revista de Investigaciones en Intervención Social, 3*(4), 157–176. In *Proposal for a Professional Practice Model*, 2016. Propuesta de un modelo para la práctica profesional. Escuela de Trabajo Social. Pontificia Universidad Católica de Chile.
Teigiser, K. S. (2009). Field Note: New Approaches to Generalist Field Education. *Journal of Social Work Education, 45*(1), 139–146. https://doi.org/10.5175/JSWE.2009.200600056. In *Proposal for a Professional*

Practice Model, 2016. Propuesta de un modelo para la práctica profesional. Escuela de Trabajo Social. Pontificia Universidad Católica de Chile.

Trevithick, P. (2002) *Social work skills: A practice handbook* (1st ed.). Maidenhead, UK: University Press In *Proposal for a Professional Practice Model*, 2016. Propuesta de un modelo para la práctica profesional. Escuela de Trabajo Social. Pontificia Universidad Católica de Chile.

Ugarte, C. & Naval, C. (2010). Desarrollo de competencias profesionales en la educación superior. Un caso docente concreto. *Revista Electrónica de Investigación Educativa* [Número Especial]. 1–14. Available at https://core.ac.uk/download/pdf/83571478.pdf [Accessed 10 December 2019].

Zeira, A. & Schiff, M. (2014). Field Education: A Comparison of Students' and Novice Social Workers' Perspectives. *The British Journal of Social Work*, 44 (7), 1950–1966. https://doi.org/10.1093/bjsw/bct038

18

The Block Placement in Social Work Field Education

A Barbados Case Study

Thérèse Odle-James and Letnie F. Rock

The chapter discusses the field education component of the final year BSc Social Work at the University of the West Indies (UWI), Cave Hill Campus, Barbados. Field education is a fundamental ingredient of the curriculum of social work programmes globally. It is 'the hallmark of any good social work programme, whether graduate or baccalaureate' (Rock, 2015, p. 104). The Council on Social Work Education (CSWE) (2015) considers it to be the signature pedagogy of the profession (p. 12). It is 'designed to support the integration of empirical and practiced–based knowledge and promote professional competence' (Hepworth, Rooney & Larsen, 2006, p. 15) for students, and therefore it allows them through supervised social work practice the opportunity to combine theory and practice (Ibid).

Students need to have experiences that are 'integral to their learning how to practice as responsible professionals' (Ibid). Therefore, while pursuing their course of study students need opportunities to apply their knowledge, values, and skills in the field and receive modelling and appropriate feedback from experienced social workers who act as their field instructors/supervisors (Ibid). Shardlow and Doel (1996) opine that practice through fieldwork and class attendance are two contexts for learning and 'need to be integrated … the challenge is for the student and agency supervisor, to make this a reality' (p. 6). The practicum experience is an integral aspect of social work education, few disciplines apart from social work, particularly at the undergraduate level, 'devote the time and energy to field practice education that social work does' (Csiernik & Karley, 2004, p. 2). The field placement period in a real working environment provides unique opportunities for social work students to have first-hand experiences of applying and developing knowledge and skills regarding the values and ethics of the profession (Papouli 2014, 2016).

Kirst Ashman and Hull (2012) view the field education experience for students as challenging but valuable. Research also suggests that students find their practicum experiences to be the most important element in their preparation for competent practice (Bogo, 2015) and that students are particularly satisfied with their placement experience when their supervisor is adequately prepared, renders strong input and support, and where learning goals and linkages between theory and practice can be realistically attained (Fortune & Abramson, 1993). On completion of study, social work graduates need to be able to practice competently which is an ethical requirement of the social work profession. Bogo (2006) notes that 'through academic courses and field education students develop into professional practitioners, having learned professional knowledge, values, and skills and integrated these components of practice into their personal self' (p. 7).

The internship within the undergraduate social work programme at the Cave Hill Campus Barbados is delivered as a one-time block and not in concurrent format. This model is not common within baccalaureate programmes and has not been adopted by other social work programmes in the Caribbean region. However, it has been successful to date at the Cave Hill Campus, in preparing students for practice. Some social work scholars are of the view that recent traditional models of field education have become a less tenable way to accommodate student practice within social work education programmes in the 21st century (Gursanky & Le Sueur, 2012; Lager & Robbins, 2004; Morley & Dunstan, 2013; Noble & Irwin, 2009; Preston et al., 2014). This is a view that is worth exploring.

The Cave Hill programme uses the Global Standards as a benchmark for programme development and renewal (Rock, 2015; Rock & Buchanan, 2014). The Global Standards for the Education and Training of the Social Work Profession (International Association of Schools of Social Work (IASSW) & International Federation of Social Workers (IFSW), 2004) address social work standards with regard to programme curricula including field education. Clear guidelines are given in the Global Standards, for example, Standard 2.4 states that the social work programme should reflect 'the core knowledge, processes, values and skills of the social work profession, as applied in context-specific realities'. Standard 3.7 states that 'field education should be sufficient in duration and complexity of tasks and learning opportunities to ensure that students are prepared for professional practice', while Standard 3.8 states that there should be 'planned co-ordination and links between the school and the agency/field placement setting'.

Social work in the Caribbean must be grounded in the identity of the region. Thus, it is important to embrace not only the conventional settings such as social service organisations but the unconventional that involve traditional practitioners and indigenous forms of helping that are found in communities (Maxwell 2002). The social work students of the Cave Hill Campus on internship are able to benefit from conventional placements (such as placements within social service agencies, schools, and hospitals and unconventional placement opportunities (such as placement with churches, NGOs, and in communities to work with community leaders). However, unconventional placements are increasingly being pursued by the university as traditional social service agencies in Barbados have become overburdened with student internships from the disciplines of social work, psychology, and sociology. Faculty is aware that they must provide opportunities for students to improve the quality of their professional practice by developing effective partnerships with governmental, non-government, and community organisations with goals consistent with those of the placement (Johnson et al., 2012).

The Context

The Cave Hill Campus, Barbados is one of the five campuses of the University of the West Indies and was opened in 1966. The University of the West Indies is the leading tertiary level institution of learning in the Caribbean and was the first institution in the region to offer social work education. Social work programmes are currently offered by the UWI campuses and other universities and community colleges in the region. At the UWI the social work programmes have institutional accreditation (Rock, 2015) and are located in multidisciplinary departments (Rock, 2015; Maxwell, 2002).

The Mona Campus located in Jamaica was the first to offer social work training with the delivery of a certificate programme in 1961. The Cave Hill Campus in Barbados followed suit in 1988 and the St. Augustine Campus in the Republic of Trinidad and Tobago started a programme in 1990. These programmes when established tended to follow the Mona Campus model (Maxwell, 2002) and delivered field education as a concurrent placement; that is, having students engaged in field education at every level of the programme and concurrent with the delivery of the theory and methods courses. Internships were secured for students mainly in social service agencies, local communities, health facilities, and probation services through liaising with the heads of the various agencies and community leaders.

The Cave Hill Campus' social work programme was introduced first as a certificate programme but later evolved into the undergraduate degree programme in social work, namely, the BSc Social Work (Rock, 2013). The certificate programme enrolled a small number of students as a cohort every two years. In 1997 the Campus introduced the BSc Social Work (Special) degree for those students who had completed the certificate programme. Students were required to complete an additional year of full-time study, post certification to receive the degree.

Rae Rambally, who coordinated the field education component of the social work programme at the Cave Hill Campus during the early years of the certificate programme writes that 'field education in a developing country has many of the same features as in countries of the developed world' (2002, p. 170). She also notes that there were several challenges the Cave Hill Campus' programme faced in implementing the field education component in the early days. These included the fact that non-social work faculty misunderstood the nature of the practicum and often scheduled courses in which social work students were enrolled, to take place at the same time that students were to be at practicum sites and that furthermore faculty 'were reluctant to alter the time scheduled for their courses' (p. 169) to accommodate the social work student. Also, with social work being a new discipline at the campus and its placement in a multidisciplinary department, few administrators 'appeared to have more than a superficial understanding of the multifaceted nature of the programme or its demands' (Rambally, 2002, p. 170). This lack of understanding was reflected in the weighting of the practicum 'as any other three-credit classroom-based course in terms of the resources allocated to it' (Ibid. p. 171). In terms of the practicum sites there were not many at the time and there were few qualified social work professionals within agencies to supervise the students. This led to the added task of having to train social workers in the agencies in aspects of supervision to 'ensure consistent standards of students' supervision throughout the field' (Ibid. p. 172). Rambally (2002), points out that:

> in a developing country such as Barbados, where social work education is new, a disproportionate amount of time, energy and skills had to be invested to open up new placements and to train supervisors so as not to compromise standards in the practicum.
>
> *(p. 171).*

Rambally (2002) further notes that many supervisors at that time were also confused in terms of the role of the field supervisor vis-à-vis the field coordinator. However, over time field education was strengthened and expanded through curriculum development, the recruitment of additional agencies for placement of students, peer learning, and the training of supervisors.

In 1998, ten years after it was started, the certificate programme was terminated and in 2000 a newly structured baccalaureate degree in social work, with a generic focus, was fully implemented. This new programme allowed for an annual intake of students and the number of students recruited and enrolled in the programme substantially increased. It was at this juncture that the concurrent placement was replaced with a block placement to be conducted during the final year of the programme (Rock & Ring, 2010). The Cave Hill Campus became the only UWI campus to deliver the block placement. Rock and Ring (2010), the crafters of the one-year block placement at the Cave Hill Campus, acknowledge that 'the extended field block placement model of one year duration is not the norm in baccalaureate programs and is somewhat atypical of social work programs at the Masters level' (p. 178).

The Block Placement

Within the block placement structure, students have the opportunity to engage in one or maybe two placements for an entire academic year within the same agency/organisation or at the least in two different agencies, which has the advantage of providing students with an intensive learning experience that includes application of theory to practice, continuity with clients and supervisors, and exposure to varied learning opportunities. These placements also allow for a more even client transition and provide students engaged in macro projects sufficient time to conduct need assessments, implement projects, and evaluate them. Therefore, within the one-year block placement students learn more about practice because of long-term exposure to their clients and supervisors (Rock & Ring, 2010).

Rock and Ring (2010) opine that:

> extended continuous time experienced on placement such as a semester long placement provides the opportunity for much learning to take place and for the student to gain adequate knowledge and insight into the functioning of the organization in which he/she is placed ... the block placement of three months' duration allows the student to become more meaningfully involved in placement activities that can result in a transformational experience for the student
>
> *(p. 177).*

Overall, the block placement allows for greater skill development, more intense supervision and learning, and research opportunities on relevant social issues within the Caribbean societies.

Students and faculty are guided by the campus' *Social Work Field Education Manual* that identifies the expectations, protocols, learning and teaching components of field education. This resource guide is available to students and field supervisors on the campus' website. The use of the manual allows for some consistency across the local, regional, and international placement of students enrolled in the field education programme.

The general goals of social work field education include expanding placement experiences; developing, integrating, and applying practice knowledge, skills, and values; providing opportunities for the integration of theory with practice, identification with and commitment to the social work profession (Kirst Ashman & Hull 2002). According CSWE (2012) "Field education is systematically designed, supervised, coordinated, and evaluated based on criteria by which students demonstrate the Social Work Competencies" (p. 8). *The Social Work Field Education Manual* for the Cave Hill Campus documents the objectives that are incorporated into the student's learning goals once the student is placed within the agency setting. These include the following:

1. The ability of the student to demonstrate how to assess and understand the impact of psychosocial, political, cultural, racial and economic systems on the lives of people.
2. The ability of the student to understand and apply theory into practice.
3. Student to demonstrate the ability to engage in a process of self-reflection.

4. Student to demonstrate knowledge of various strategies of social work intervention with community and institutional systems, small groups, families and individuals and the theoretical bases of these strategies.
5. Student to demonstrate the ability to conduct culturally sensitive interviews, give and receive information and communicate clearly, both verbally and in writing.
6. Student to demonstrate knowledge and understanding of the human resource and service network to facilitate appropriate referrals and understand policy and practice implications.
7. Student to demonstrate an understanding of the policies of the agency and the skills required to practice in a human service organization.
8. Student to demonstrate the ability to document client interviews.
9. Student to demonstrate the ability to write policy papers and reports.

Organisation of the Block Placement

All students enrolled in the baccalaureate programme must complete the field placement consisting of 835 mandatory contact hours and the mandatory field integrative seminar consisting of a total of 84 hours per academic year. The integrative seminar is held once weekly for three hours. These two components are administered concurrently each semester.

The field education component is evaluated by a midterm and final assessment of the student each semester. This evaluation is conducted by the field coordinator with input from the agency supervisor and the student. The grade for the field component constitutes one hundred percent. Over the course of the year the field coordinator regularly keeps in contact with field supervisors by telephone and electronically via email, *WhatsApp*, and *Zoom* and conducts regular visits to placement sites. It is mandatory for the field coordinator to visit those students who are engaging in their field placements in other Caribbean countries, once per semester, in order to successfully evaluate their progress. These students are also expected to participate in the integrative seminar either face to face or virtually via Skype or Zoom. All students on placement are required to submit an integrative paper and a reflective journal at the end of each semester. These two assignments provide the field supervisor and field coordinator with much insight into the student's personal and professional development and they factor into the grade for the integrative seminar which constitutes one hundred percent of the final grade. Students receive therefore a grade for the block placement (nine credits) and a separate grade for the integrative seminar (three credits) each semester.

Before being considered for the internship, students must complete two years of classroom work focusing on theory, methods, and practice. They must complete the core courses within the social work programme together with electives and the required university courses. Field education is a core requirement for full completion of the Bachelor of Social Work degree. Therefore, all students must complete the placement in order to satisfy graduation requirements. Within the block placement structure, the two-semester placement is actually one course with a value of 12 credits per semester or 24 credits per academic year. The field coordinator is responsible for training and liaising with the field supervisors around issues relating to the students' performance.

Students are generally required to engage in some micro, mezzo, and macro practice activities during their tenure on placement under the supervision of the field supervisor. They may engage in these three levels of practice as they work with various client groups. Most students gain exposure to macro practice through their involvement in policy development and implementation; programme planning, implementation, and evaluation; public education initiatives; proposal writing; research; advocacy; and community mobilisation. The field coordinator and the agency field supervisor assist students in developing their practice skills in applying a critical social work perspective to the context in which they are practicing. Honing these skills is essential for students to plan and implement strategies for change that will address structural and other barriers present in their practice environment and that can become a transforming experience.

A recommendation of a Quality Assurance Review of the Social Work programme that was conducted in 2017 is that the students on internship benefit from more community placements. This is fortuitous because the block placement has been providing the ideal opportunity for students to be engaged in practice with communities. The benefits of the one-year block placement structure in working with communities is highlighted by the following case study.

> During the academic year 2018–2019 two final year social work undergraduate students completed their internship of two semesters in an inner-city community in Barbados. They conducted a needs assessment that identified that the community was grappling with negative stigma due to high unemployment and crime. The students got to work and assisted the community in establishing a local committee to tackle the issues. The members of this committee included leaders of local schools, businesses, churches, and other NGOs within the community. The committee explored and created solutions to unemployment and the perpetration of criminal activity through the creation of job opportunities for the young residents of the community, with the overarching goal of eradicating the negative stigma of the community. The committee developed community job fairs, partnerships between the community and national training programmes, mentorship programmes for school children with local business owners, local and national employment opportunities for the unemployed youth.
>
> The initial needs assessment and the recruitment of local leadership was critical in sustaining commitment and continued momentum to fulfilling the objectives of the committee. The student's ability to remain on practicum for an academic year provided the necessary support, resources, and expertise to the committee as they were available exclusively in the formative stage of the committee's development and shared a commitment to assist the community in achieving its objectives.
>
> The students were able to work on a consistent basis with the Committee and the residents of the community to bring about change and the experience was quite transformational for the students themselves. Although the students have graduated, the committee has remained active and committed to the initial goal of creating job opportunities for the youth of the community and eroding the negative stigma.

Field placements are chosen after a thoughtful process which includes relevant feedback from social work faculty who would have taught the students. In order to qualify for placement (Level III of the programme), the student must pass all of the Level I and Level II courses in the programme. Maxwell (1999), one of the leading social work educators in the Caribbean, opines that preparation is imperative to the optimal benefit of the field placement. Students and supervisors participate in an annual orientation which educates about the protocols, policy, legal matters, and expectations of the placement. At the start of the placement the field supervisor provides an orientation for the student which includes opportunities for the student to gain knowledge of the functioning of the agency or practice setting. As the placement progresses the student is provided opportunities to apply knowledge obtained in the classroom setting, and develop skills fundamental to the achievement of the core competencies of social work. Bogo (2006) states that:

once students begin their field education they report arriving at a new understanding of the links between knowledge and practice, recognizing that connections often are not linear, simple, or direct. Skills and techniques are important but not enough … practitioners need a variety of theories or models and the opportunity to use them as potential or temporary lens to guide practice

(p. 15–16).

Within the placement structure, peer learning opportunities are encouraged. Geng et al. 2017 note that although peer learning cannot replace guidance from lecturers, it does provide supportive systems. The programme at Cave Hill introduced an optional student support element in 2019. The objective is to afford new students the opportunity to be supported by past graduates of the programme. The mentoring allows current students to learn from those who have been in a similar placement setting (Aberbigbe et al.), for example, the field coordinator encourages past graduates of the programme to assist students who are currently undertaking their placements within the same local community where the graduate had been placed. The programme selects the graduates as brokers in order to provide support to the students currently in the field. Although this is not a structured supervisory relationship, the graduates offer support by grooming present students for the profession, and by discussing placement related issues and career development goals. It is envisioned that graduate student support along with structured professional supervision will aid students in their professional growth.

Rock (2013) notes that social work field education in the Caribbean is challenged by the lack of qualified social workers to perform the role of field supervisors, the increase in younger more inexperienced students engaging in field placement, and the competition for scarce field placement sites due to students in other disciplines clamouring for the same opportunities. That is, the field placement opportunities have proved challenging with other tertiary institutions (universities and community colleges) vying for the placement of their students in the same organisations/agencies. In such a competitive climate many agencies have not been reserving spaces for social work students but have been extending placement opportunities to non-social work students, including students from institutions overseas. This has impacted the availability of internship sites for the university students for whom faculty are increasingly pursuing placements in non-traditional settings (Rock & Buchanan, 2014). In these settings suitably qualified social worker professionals may not be available to provide supervision, therefore the field coordinator supervises the students directly. These non-traditional placements as well as international placements have proven to be very valuable in addressing the need for internship sites (Rock, 2013) as the number of students requiring placement opportunities have increased.

The Field Integrative Seminar

Rock and Buchanan (2014) inform that:

A strong component of the internship at The UWI is a weekly field integrative seminar which allows students to process and assess their level of engagement in the agency, their success in applying the theory learned in the classroom to their work with clients, their own suitability for the social work profession and [to] benefit from peer support

(p. 135).

In order for students to develop critical consciousness and learning from their field experience, the practicum should include student-centred dialogue and teaching that is classroom-based

(Johnson et al., 2012). As stated earlier, students are given the opportunity through the weekly field integrative seminar (usually conducted face to face), to benefit from peer support and guidance from the field coordinator. The goal of the field integrative seminar is to provide students with a forum to discuss the connection between theory and practice and their feelings and experiences of the internship and engage in peer support. 'Through this dialogue greater understanding of others can be achieved as well as insights into self revealed' (Bogo, 2006, p. 19). The seminar is also a mechanism for evaluation of the students' acquisition of programme objectives and the honing of their critical thinking skills.

The marriage of field placement and the integrative seminar in social work programmes is deliberate. Feedback from field to class and vice versa reinforces both learning environments. The goal is to help the student critically examine their own progress and to make professional use of the critical analysis of peers. A non-threatening environment is created and maintained throughout the seminar since 'classroom dynamics and interactions between the instructor and students and between students can affect student learning … Contemporary social work classrooms can model valued professional interpersonal processes such as respect and collaboration' (Bogo, 2006, p. 19). Students are also afforded individual confidential sessions with the field coordinator each week to discuss any challenges and concerns that they may be encountering during their placement experience.

Preparation of Students for Internship and Support to Field Supervisors

In a concurrent placement students enter the field after the first year of coursework so that they may learn to integrate theory with practice. However, in the block placement as delivered at Cave Hill, students are initially prepared for field work through two academic years of coursework that include role plays and simulations relating to the integration of practice and theory and that involve critical social work issues. At level two they take part in a mandatory interpersonal skills laboratory, engage in group work with special populations within an agency setting or in a community as the practice assignment for the group work course, and conduct a community project based on a needs assessment as the major assignment for the community organisation course. Through these assignments students are able to learn to integrate theory with practice. The undergraduate programme is generic in focus and therefore prepares students not only to work at every level of practice but in diverse fields of practice. These include government and non-profit sectors to work with various populations such as people with disabilities, LGBTQAI people, children and the youth, battered women, the elderly, persons recovering from substance abuse, persons living with HIV, youth in conflict with the law, the poor, prisoners, homeless people, and people with mental health challenges. Students receive grounding in systems theory, the ecological-systemic perspective, the empowerment model, and the strengths perspective, and select psychological theories as foundation for practice. When the student qualifies for the internship, the student is given the opportunity to choose possible placement sites in tandem with his/her professional interests. However, finding an appropriate placement for a student is at times challenging, particularly with younger and younger students enrolling in the programme. Therefore, there are times when students are not given the placement of choice if the field coordinator believes that a particular practice/agency setting will augur better for the student's professional development.

Once placements are assigned and before the students begin practice with clients students participate in an orientation seminar. Bogo (2015) opines that when students begin their practice with clients 'there is a strong desire to learn new skills: what to do and how to do it' (p. 15). **The students gain practice skills and knowledge from their placement**

experience, but they are also expected to have knowledge and skills to bring to the placement setting. In this way faculty and field supervisors have found that students can expose their supervisors and other agency professionals to current trends in social work practice. Such exchanges between students and agency staff mean that agency staff also learn from the students. Students directly assist with the work of the agency in which they are placed, whether it is through conducting agency based research, developing and evaluating new agency programme or engaging in direct practice.

The field supervisor plays a vital role in field education. The National Association of Social Workers (2013) defines professional supervision as:

> the relationship between supervisor and supervisee in which the responsibility and accountability for the development of competence, demeanor, and ethical practice take place. The field supervisor is responsible for providing direction to the supervisee, who applies social work theory, standardized knowledge, skills, competency, and applicable ethical content in the practice setting. The supervisor and the supervisee both share responsibility for carrying out their role in this collaborative process
>
> *(p. 6)*.

The UWI generally sources and seeks to retain field supervisors who have obtained a Bachelors and/or Master's degree in Social Work and who have at least three years postgraduate practice experience. Professional supervision within the agency is central to the success of the placement and therefore it is essential that supervisors are qualified and knowledgeable. An annual field supervisor orientation training seminar is held for field supervisors, both new and continuing, with the objective of preparing them for the field experience with students. The areas that are covered during the training seminar include the goal of field education, the core competencies and practice behaviours in social work, learning goals, orientation and supervision requirements for students, use of the social work practicum manual, protocols, boundaries, the role of the student, the role of the field supervisor, ethical issues, and the grading system for field education.

Field education relies on a model of externalising learning beyond the university and into the workplace, delivered by social workers in the field, who 'educate' through professional supervision (Bloomfield et al., 2013). The willingness of many agencies to support social work field education is important to the survival and sustainability of the field placements. Over time there has been an increase in qualified social workers in Barbados and this has led to the concomitant increase in agency placements. However, the field supervisors who are involved with the Cave Hill Campus social work programme are not paid for their services due to the lack of funds to remunerate them. This is unfortunate. The critical need for the services of the agency staff as supervisors means that the university must explore ways through which they can be compensated for the time invested in the supervision of social work students.

International and Regional Field Placements

Lager et al. (2010) note that international field placements and student exchanges are a part of a 'burgeoning field of practice' (p. 59). The field education component of the social work programme at UWI has taken advantage of the several memoranda of understanding signed between UWI and international universities to engage in international student exchange, that provides various placement opportunities in Canada, Finland, the USA, the UK, and South Africa. The international exchange programme prepares students to practise not only in the region but also in a world of 'global interdependence' (Healy, 2008) and allows students the opportunity to participate in cross-cultural exchange through shared experiences. Students develop skills in ethnic sensitive social work while combining theoretical knowledge with relevant social, economic, environmental, and cultural nuances of the host country. Since 2012 students from the Cave Hill programme have benefitted annually from internships in Canada and the programme has been accepting social work students from universities in Canada to engage in internships in Barbados. This programme has been working effectively in part due to the block placement which affords students from the Cave Hill Campus the opportunity to conduct their field internship internationally during the second semester of their field experience. Students have also completed internships within schools of social work in the USA. All students enrolled in the student exchange programme are supervised by experienced social workers or field supervisors within the agency where they are placed internationally. The role of the field supervisor in the host country under the student exchange arrangement is to provide feedback, guidance, and support to the student, conduct student evaluations, and liaise directly with the field coordinator at the Cave Hill Campus. Anecdotal evidence has shown that the students from the Cave Hill Campus have adequate grounding in their preparation for the internship because they generally demonstrate very high performance in their international placement environments.

After completing their internship at the Cave Hill Campus, students are also granted the opportunity to participate in the Caribbean Internship Programme (CIP) (a regional programme providing internships for students from various disciplines). The CIP aims to assist regional partner institutions through the provision of voluntary social work and other services by university students/graduates. The goal is twofold, to provide human resources and indigenous skill transfer across the region that will enhance coverage to agencies in diverse settings while providing interns with practical learning and cultural experiences. On successful completion of the block placement, the field coordinator recommends students for this programme through the CIP liaison officer located at the Cave Hill Campus. Students are interviewed to determine their eligibility. Once selected to participate in the internship they are placed within a governmental or non-governmental agency in the Caribbean region for a duration of three months. Students are provided with airfare, accommodation, and a stipend. The programme is well-structured and students are provided with supervision by experienced social workers within the agencies where they are placed. The Field Supervisor keeps in contact with the CIP liaison officer at the Cave Hill Campus.

Advantages and Disadvantages of the Block Placement

Every social work internship arrangement will have advantages and disadvantages. Rock and Ring (2010) report several advantages and disadvantages of the block placement as delivered at the Cave Hill Campus. In terms of advantages, these include the following: (a) students are able to spend an entire semester or an academic year within the same agency setting to establish relationships with clients and agency staff, apply practice skills and integrate their knowledge of theory, and to experience the placement as meaningful; (b) the termination and follow-up of client cases by students, and their completion of projects are much more possible because they have sufficient time to complete tasks; (c) field supervisors gain a better understanding of their students' growth and their challenges as they are with them for a longer period. That is, the block placement provides students and field supervisors with adequate time to accomplish the placement objectives and the acquisition of relevant social work skills by the student; (d) students who reside abroad may choose to pursue their internship within their country of residence rather than Barbados which allows them to save on accommodation and living expenses; (e) the block placement also allows for greater flexibility within non-traditional placements where students can engage in projects over a duration of an entire semester; (f) it provides the opportunity for students to engage in an international field internship if they qualify for such a placement; (g) after graduation many students are able to find employment in agencies where they interned based on their demonstration of competence in the placement setting.

Rock and Ring (2010) found that some disadvantages of the block placement experience were also reported by students and field supervisors. These include (a) some students face financial difficulties while studying full-time given the lack of provision of a stipend (and there is the lack of a stipend for students while on two semesters of internship); (b) lack of exposure to the agency setting during the first two years of the social work programme means that younger students and those who lack confidence in their abilities begin the block placement in their final year with timidity; (c) there is lack of opportunity for students to learn how to effectively integrate theory and practice before they reach the final year of study; (d) students have to complete two course electives while on internship which some find burdensome; (e) the inability of students who need financial support to be employed during the final year of the programme since the block placement demands full-time engagement; (f) the lack of a stipend for field supervisors who invest an inordinate amount of time in the supervision of the students. While the block placement may be beset with some disadvantages the block placement arrangement has been able to develop the professional competencies of the undergraduate social work students at the Cave Hill Campus and ground them in the nuances of the social work profession through their immersion in practice activities. Through continuous monitoring of students in the field, faculty and field supervisors have been able to discern significant growth in students both personally and professionally by the end of their placement experience.

Conclusion

The field education component continues to be an integral part of social work education. The intent is for the student 'to integrate the theoretical and conceptual contribution of the classroom with the practical world of the practice setting' (CSWE, 2015, p. 12). The block placement in the social work programme at the Cave Hill Campus has achieved this objective. It continues to be 'the mechanism for introducing students to the profession of social work and the world of work' (Rock & Ring, 2010, p. 180). It has been ten years since the evaluation of the block placement by faculty, students, and agency/field supervisors. It is therefore critical that the structure be reviewed to determine if it is still effectively and efficiently meeting the needs of all stakeholders in these times when local communities, government agencies, local and regional institutions and societies, and the global environment are experiencing significant change. In the meantime, students entering the social work programme are exposed to the structure and culture of various agencies and communities during the first two years of study as a means of helping to prepare them for the block placement.

With the advent of the COVID-19 pandemic in 2020 the delivery of field education in social work has responded to meet the emerging changes. Many social service agencies have and continue to grapple with structural social distancing and the attendant protocols. Many have also resorted to flextime which is impacting consistent student supervision. The need for social action, social justice, and policy development is also critical at this time so that vulnerable groups and communities will not be overlooked in the provision of services. Bright (2020) notes that due to the COVID-19 pandemic there is an opportunity for social workers to advocate for policy development on behalf of the vulnerable clients they serve. The social work curriculum of the Cave Hill Campus, including the field education component, is responding to these new and emerging social development needs of the Caribbean region.

References

Aderibigbe, S., Antiado, D., & Sta Anna, A. (2015). Issues in peer mentoring for undergraduate students in a private university in the United Arab Emirates. *International Journal of Evidence Based Coaching and Mentoring, 13*(2), 64–80.

Bloomfield, D., Chambers, B., Egan, S., Goulding, J., Reimann, P., Waugh, F., & White, S. (2013). *Authentic assessment in practice settings: A participatory design approach*. Sydney: Office of Learning and Teaching, Australian Government.

Bogo, M. (2006). *Social work practice: Concepts, processes, and interviewing*. New York: Columbia University Press.

Bogo, M. (2015). Field education for clinical social work practice: Best practices and contemporary challenges. *Clinical Social Work Journal, 43*(3), 317–324. doi: 10.1007/s10615-015-0526-5

Bright, C. (2020). Social work in the age of a global pandemic. *Social Work Research, 44*(2), 83–86. https://doi-org.ezproxy.lib.uconn.edu/10.1093/swr/svaa006

Council on Social Work Education (CSWE). (2012). Educational Policy and Accreditation Standards. https://www.cswe.org/getattachment/Accreditation/Accreditation-Process/2008-EPAS/Candidacy/2008EDUCATIONALPOLICYANDACCREDITATIONSTANDARDS(EPAS)-08-24-2012.pdf.aspx [Accessed 6 March 2022]

Council on social Work Education (CSWE). (2015). Educational policy and accreditation standards for baccalaureate and master's social work programs. https://www.cswe.org/getattachment/Accreditation/Accreditation-Process/2015-EPAS/2015EPAS_Web_FINAL.pdf.aspx [accessed 23 April 2020]

Csiernik, R. & Karley, M. (2004). *Experience of social work practicum activities in the field. New Scholarship in the Human Services*. The University of Calgary Press. https://www.researchgate.net/publication/256082523_The_experience_of_social_work_practicum_activities_in_the_field [accessed 20 April 2020].

Doel, M., Shardlow, S., & Sawdon, D. (1996). *Teaching social work practice*. London: Routledge. https://doi.org/10.4324/9781315241739

Fortune, A. E., & Abramson, J. S. (1993). Predictors of satisfaction with field practicum among social work students. *Clinical Supervisor, 2*, 95–110.

Geng, G., Midford, R., Buckworth, J., & Kersten, T. (2017). Tapping into the teaching experiences of final year education students to increase support for students in their first year. *Student Success, 8*(1), 13–23. doi: 10.5204/ssj.v8i1.363

Gursansky, D., & Le Sueur, E. (2012). Conceptualizing field education in the twenty-first century: Contradictions, challenges and opportunities. *Social Work Education, 31*(7), 914–931. doi: 10.1080/026/5479.2011.595784

Healy, L. M. (2008). Exploring the history of social work as a human rights profession. *International Social Work, 51*(6), 735–748. https://doi.org/10.1177/0020872808095247

Hepworth, D. H., Roney, R. H., Rooney, G. D., Strom-Gottfried, K., & Larsen, J. A. (2006). *Direct social work practice: Theory and skills* (7th ed.). Belmont, CA: Brooks/Cole.

Hepworth, D.H, Rooney, R. & Larsen, J. A. (2002) *Direct social work practice: Theory and skills*. Belmont, CA: Brooks/Cole.

International Association of Schools of Social Work (IASSW) & International Federation of Social workers (IFSW). (2004). *The Global Standards for Education and Training for the Social Work Profession*. Retrieved from: https://www.iassw-aiets.org/wp-content/uploads/2018/08/Global-standards-for-the-education-and-training-of-the-social-work-profession.pdf [Accessed 25 April 2022].

Johnson, J, Rose, K; Bailey, B. & Padmore, J. (April 2012). Issues and challenges of social work practicum in Trinidad and Tobago and India. *Caribbean Teaching Scholar, 2*(1),19–29. Retrieved from: https://www.researchgate.net/publication/228058126_Issues_and_challenges_of_social_work_practicum_in_Trinidad_and_Tobago_and_India [Accessed 25 April 2020].

Kirst-Ashman, K. K., & Hull Jr, G. H. (2012). *Understanding generalist practice* (3rd.). Pacific Grove, CA. Brooks/Cole.

Kirst-Ashman, K. K., & Hull Jr , G. H. (2012). *Understanding generalist practice* (6th ed.). Pacific Grove, CA. Brooks/Cole.

Lager, P. B., & Robbins, V. C. (2004). Guest editorial: Field education: Exploring the future, expanding the vision. *Journal of Social Work Education*, 40(1), 3–12. doi: 10.1080/10437797.2004.10778475

Lager, P. B.; Mathiesen, S. G.; Rodgers, M. E., & Cox, S. E. (2010). *Guidebook for international field placements and student exchanges: Planning, implementation and sustainability.* Alexandria, VA: CSWE Press.

Maxwell, J. (1999). Student assessment of supervision in social work field practice in Trinidad and Southern Africa: A comparative study and commentary. *Journal of Social Development in Africa*, 14(1), 85–100.

Maxwell, J. (2002). The evolution of social welfare services and social work in the English-speaking Caribbean (with reference to Jamaica). *Caribbean Journal of Social Work*, 1(March), 11–31.

Morley, C. & Dunstan, J. (2013). Critical reflection: A response to neoliberal challenges to field education? *Social Work Education*, 32(2), 141–156. doi: 10.1080/02615479.2012.730141http://opencommons.uconn.edu/sw_intlconf/4

National Association of Social Workers (NASW). (2013). *Best practice standards in social work supervision.* Washington, DC: NASW Press.

Noble, J., & Irwin, J. (2009). Social work supervision: An exploration of the current challenges in a rapidly changing social, economic and political environment. *Journal of Social Work*, 9(3), 345–358. doi: 10.1177/1468017309334848

Papouli, E. (2014). Field learning in social work education: Implications for educators and instructors. *The Field Educator: A Scholarly Journal from the Simmons College School of Social Work*, 4(2)/Fall, 388. Ethical issues in Practice, 2014: 1–15. Retrieved from http://fieldeducator.simmons.edu/article/field-learningin-socialwork-education-implications-for-educators-and-instructors/ [Accessed 15 November 2014].

Papouli, E. (2016). Teaching and learning for ethical practice in social work education. In I. Taylor, M. Bogo, M. Lefevre, and B. Teater (Eds.), *Routledge International Handbook of Social Work Education* (pp. 157–170). Abingdon, Oxon: Routledge.

Preston, S., George, P., & Silver, S. (2014). Field education in social work: The need for reimagining. *Critical Social Work*, 15(1). Retrieved from http://www1.uwindsor.ca/criticalsocialwork [Accessed 15 November 2020]

Rambally, R. T. (2002). *Practice imperfect: Reflections on a career in social work.* Quebec, Canada: Shoreline.

Rock, L. (2015) Social work education: The Caribbean experience. *The Indian Journal of Social Work*, 76(1), 95–114.

Rock, L. F. (2013). The role of social work education in advancing social development in the English-speaking Caribbean. *Social Work Education*, 32(6), 734–747. Retrieved from https://doi.org/10.1080/02615479.2013.809201 [Accessed 23 April 2020].

Rock, L. F., & Buchanan, C. (2014). Social work education in the Caribbean: Charting pathways to growth and globalization. In C. Noble, H. Strauss, & B. Littlechild (Eds.), *Published in Global Social Work: Crossing Borders, Blurring Boundaries.* Sydney University Press. ISBN: 9781743324042.

Rock, L. F., & Ring, K. A. (2010). Evaluating the one-year block placement in field instruction. *Social Work Review*, 9(4), 175–184.

Shardlow, S. and Doel, M. (1996) *Practice learning and teaching.* Basingstoke: Macmillan.

19
Constructing a Culturally Relevant Social Work Curriculum in Papua New Guinea
Connecting the Local and Global in Field Education

Dunstan Lawihin

The history of social work dates back to the late 19th century, a period manifested with the Industrial Revolution. The Industrial Revolution, the Great Depression, and the Second World War and subsequent adversities are the significant factors in the development and application of social work. Social work began during these periods in Europe and North America through volunteer efforts to address ensuing poverty and inequalities. By the 1900s, social work practice became an occupation and achieved professional status in the 1930s. This social work approach to practice continued to expand into schools, hospitals, child and family welfare, and housing agencies. Further expansion in social work was based on the need to conceptualise its approach and develop a knowledge base. Social work educational institutions and programmes were introduced and funded in the 1930s. This marks the period where contemporary social work education was 'born'. The first academic institution in the Asia Pacific region was the Tata School of Social Work in India, established in 1936.

Contemporary social work education was introduced in Papua New Guinea (PNG) in the early 1970s, as the result of both internal political developments and external factors. Social work in PNG is still developing. Subsequently, there is limited knowledge about the relevant type and form of social work practice and education model to address PNG's specific social development needs in the context of globalisation. PNG needs a culturally relevant and globally consistent social work model.

This chapter presents and discusses the findings from the study conducted as part of my Master's of Social Work (Research) thesis at Monash University. Two main themes emerged from this study: the field education components and the attention on global standards. The focus of the chapter is on the local and global knowledge identified by participants as necessary for culturally relevant social work education in fieldwork. Having these field education components spelt out clearly would allow for a better understanding of dominant perspectives on localisation of social work field education standards and curriculum in PNG. The chapter begins with providing the social work context in PNG, followed by the literature review. The following section presents the methodology employed in the study and then the findings. The final section is on the discussion of study results. The conclusion highlights strategic recommendations for developing culturally relevant social work curriculum in PNG.

Papua New Guinea: Context and Challenges

PNG achieved its political independence on the 16 September 1975 from Australia and has a constitutional democratic government. Contemporary PNG is rich in natural resources and continues to develop, yet many challenges remain. Poverty is high in PNG is ranked 155th of 189 countries in the 2019 United Nations Human Development Index; existing wealth is unevenly distributed, despite considerable developments in mining, petroleum, oil, and gas; and service provision is hindered by the rugged terrain, land tenure issues, and the high cost of developing infrastructure. Given these conditions, it is perhaps not surprising that life expectancy is the lowest in the region and less than two-thirds of the population is literate (CIA, 2016). There are also concerns about the welfare of children, including child labour, rates of school participation, and the needs and priorities of children with disabilities, which are often neglected. The rate of school enrolment in PNG is the lowest in the Asia Pacific region at 63% (MacPherson, 1996; Hayward-Jones, 2013). General violence against persons and property is notable in PNG. The worst of such forms of violence are those related to sorcery-related killings and the ongoing problem of violence against women. According to government reports (GoPNG, 2016), two-thirds of women have experience violence.

Domestically, the complex cultural and linguistic diversity of PNG is not well understood by natives or outsiders. PNG is one of the most diverse countries culturally and linguistically, with over 830 different languages spoken and tribes often having their own specific localised decision-making, organisation, and role distribution systems. For example, Hayward-Jones (2013) asserts that models and systems that work in one part of the country do not work in other parts. There are significant differences in culture and practices in doing business and functioning daily, and in learning styles and approaches across urban and rural settings and in formal and informal systems. These differences are viewed as key barriers to effective government, doing business, and learning from and repeating success (Hayward-Jones, 2013). According to the World Health Organization (WHO), health outcomes have stalled over the last quarter century and the country failed to meet any of the United Nations' Millennium Development Goals in 2015.

Urbanisation is a problem in larger cities in PNG. Although there is a national urbanisation policy, Hayward-Jones (2013) notes that the government is struggling with urban planning processes to keep up with the consequences of high population growth. Part of this population growth is due to uncontrolled rural-urban migration and cross-national movement of people. This also reflects earlier colonial interventions, where administrators built towns and separated them from villages, resulting in rural and urban divisions, and perpetuating imbalances between rural and urban areas. This trend continues today as successive governments have paid more attention to urban development. Such inequalities have not been fully addressed and this has implications for social work practice. A further challenge is how to address the needs of refugees and asylum seekers of different cultures, races, and ethnicities.

Global issues like climate change, environmental and social injustice, human rights abuse, and others present PNG's government and its people with considerable challenges. Although the country's human facilities and resources capacities are limited, it is essential to take on these challenges and address them effectively. It is at this point, where developing human capital is paramount, that social work education and training can contribute to these solutions. However, national efforts often fall short of addressing global issues, and solutions through cooperation and collaboration across the globe are necessary (Nikku, 2010).

Although social work is needed and has played an important role in PNG's contemporary development, it remains a product of colonisation, now reinforced by the process of globalisation. This study acknowledges the development of professional social work in PNG as a significant contribution from colonisation and intends to add value to this by utilising local knowledge to inform contemporary social work education and practice.

Social Work Practice and Education in PNG

The social work education programme at UPNG is the only social work school in PNG. The programme offers a generalist social work curriculum reflecting the diverse practice settings and changing social development needs of PNG communities. Courses offered at UPNG covers community development/empowerment, social development and planning, NGOs and Community Work, Social Policy and Administration, Family Welfare, Social Research, and Field Education.

UPNG graduates have numbered between 20 to 30 social work graduates annually since the 2000s. Most of these graduates are employed by government and non-government organisations, although some of them are successful in the corporate and business sector as well. Except in academia and hospitals where social work graduates are employed as academic researchers and medical social workers, most are employed as welfare officers, case workers, counsellors, policy advisors in monitoring and evaluation roles, and as community relation officers.

In fact, social work in PNG has evolved overtime, given the social, political, and economic conditions noted earlier. At the time of its introduction and after independence, social work education responded to emerging social issues and changes. For example, the focus was on urban community development when there was increased rural-to-urban migration in the 1960s. In the 1970s, social work focused on contributing to government's social policy developments and planning. Reflections from Lovai (2015) highlight that the problem of school leavers in the 1980s directed the focus on youth work, social services, and community work. By the mid-1990s, social work education emphasised the study of how to work with people, and its primary focus was to meet the social needs and improve the social lives of the people in both rural and urban communities. Towards the late 1990s, a restructure at UPNG set the context for the social work programme and its role in higher education as being:

> concerned with social welfare aspects of development and aims to enhance the quality of life of people in both rural and urban communities using appropriate social work practices. It is also concerned with the application of social sciences to develop and to promote the wellbeing of the society (Social Work Strand, 1995, p. 5).

The focus of social work education as reflected above has not changed, but the challenges continually exert pressure on its practice to adequately respond to social, family, and community needs and the needs of the marginalised, disadvantaged, and vulnerable. Ensuring the appropriate application of relevant social work models supported by best practices is challenging. Therefore, the preparation of future social workers is critical, and such preparation must be harnessed through tested knowledge and applied skills. This makes field education an appropriate ground for researching social work training.

Flynn, Kamasua, and Lawihin (2016) describe social work in PNG as challenged in recent years, due to limited academic and professional oversight. For example, although the Papua New Guinea Social Workers Association (PNGSWA) was established in the mid-1980s, it has remained less active. Similarly, the UPNG Social Work programme was given international accreditation in 1974 by IASSW. While the IFSW still lists UPNG Social Work as a member organisation, Flynn, Kamasua, and Lawihin (2016) indicate that its accreditation status is unknown. These are two of the primary reasons PNG social work is yet to have its local standards developed to guide social work education and practice.

Literature on Indigenisation and Localisation of Social Work

As globalisation spreads across the world, it affects people and communities in varying degrees. Non-Western societies are responding to these effects through indigenisation and localisation. According to Samad and Hossain (2014) *indigenisation* describes a process where locals take something from a society or community outside of their own, and make it their own. This involves the transformation of ideas, discourse, and services to suit local people and culture. Similarly, in social work education and practice, indigenisation means imparting and applying adapted knowledge and skill in a modified manner from Western social work instead of replication of the same (Gray & Coates, 2010). *Localisation* on the other hand is an aspect of indigenisation, a process of translating global social work standards to fit specific sociopolitical, cultural, and educational contexts. Localisation in this paper is defined as the process of adapting something global for a true understanding by locals of a specific country context and population.

Localisation involves an appreciative enquiry through 'integration, creative synthesis, adaptation, realignment, appropriateness, genuineness and authentication, cultural appropriateness and relevance, and balancing the local and the foreign' (Gray et al., 2008, pp. 15–18). The argument is that indigenisation and localisation present similar perspectives that emphasise the need to develop locally relevant social work that promotes local knowledge and strategies, as well as using these to inform broader social work profession. Indigenising and localising a social work education curriculum means a fair level of prominence is given to local knowledge such as the Melanesian Way and methods of teaching and learning to promote professional identity and cultural competence. This is important for PNG because the current curriculum and the teaching approaches are largely Western.

Almost all the social work academics and students at UPNG are Melanesians. Therefore, it is appropriate that teaching and learning is localised to a PNG-Melanesian context. In this way, our lecturers and students can easily relate to and connect course content directly to practical examples in the local practice settings and communities. In my recent publication (Lawihin, 2018), I argued for PNG-Melenesian culturally relevant pedagogies to be integrated into formal teaching and learning in social work at UPNG. This is where PNG communities can provide excellent opportunities for social work learning, practice and research to social work students, graduates, and researchers. Ensuring this is likely to advance social work in PNG that is culturally relevant and globally consistent with professional social work education and practice standards.

The concept of indigenisation was first introduced into the social work discussion by the United Nations in 1971 with reference to the inappropriateness of American social work theory in other societies (Yunong & Xiong, 2008). Gray (2005), for instance, refers to indigenisation as the extent to which social work practice fits the local context and how this context is shaped by local social, political, economic, and cultural factors, which mould and define local social work responses. In addition, indigenisation emphasises that

> social work knowledge should arise from within the culture, reflect local behaviours and practices, be interpreted within a local frame of reference and thus be locally relevant to effectively address culturally relevant and context specific problems' (Gray & Coates, 2010, p. 3).

Indigenisation therefore refers to a process where indigenous ways of knowing, being, doing, and relating are integrated into the formal educational, organisational, cultural, and social structures. As such, the purpose of indigenisation in this paper is to (re)develop and make social work education, research, and practice fit the local context, bearing in mind that the 'local' coexists with the global community. Conversely, localisation is the process of adapting and modifying universally acceptable values and principles to fit specific local contexts as well as guide local action.

In a scholarly discussion, Yip (2006) provides an international perspective on the indigenisation of social work discourse. According to Yip 'indigenisation of social work practice is challenged by the globalisation of economies, technologies, diversity of cultures, traditions and religions across the world', (p. 45). This argument indicates tensions in social work practice, where globalisation of the economy and Western and migrant cultures clash with indigenised needs, and indigenous local culture and traditions. Yip's assertion is for social work professionals to be aware when practising in non-Western cultural contexts that these have their own specific indigenised values and interventions.

Furthermore, social work education needs to emphasise both international and contextual content and intervention models to develop students' abilities to recognise, respect, and practice within their clients' indigenised cultures. Although these are scholarly ideas and opinions, the observations and informed reflections highlighted important complexities and issues in the local-global social work knowledge. For example, as shown by Crisp's (2015) reflection on how to achieve the right balance between the local-global is now well understood and creates tensions.

According to Yunong and Xiong (2008) indigenisation acts against the dominance of Western social work philosophies and education and research and practice must be shaped by the local context. Lawihin (2018) addressed the issues of localisation of social work education and discussed the process for implementing indigenisation of social work education in PNG. The key argument for indigenising social work curriculum in PNG is the centrality of community as the centre for learning and the local Melanesian culture and history as the basis for social work globally and locally. For example, Yunong and Xiong (2008) emphasise that 'indigenisation in social work criticises professional imperialism, questions Western values and theories and affirms the importance of indigenous social and cultural structures' (p. 616). The researchers then conclude, based on their literature review, that social work should be made to fit local contexts, which is an implicit requirement of the profession. This perspective is summarised as:

> the inherent expectation as social workers is to integrate social and cultural knowledge and sensitivity with skills for appropriate and effective helping practice. This would mean emphasising social work as an achievement of human civilisation to improve social work practice, education and research (Yunong & Xiong 2008, p. 620)

Gray and Coates (2010) extend the debate on indigenisation, not just as a movement as alluded to in Yunong and Xiong (2008), but as a field of knowledge. They argue for the development of truly indigenised and culturally appropriate social work knowledge, unrestricted by positivistic Western worldviews. They further argue that indigenisation is a movement that promotes research and practices of cultural and local relevance to develop respected indigenised social work knowledge. In their view, indigenisation is a way to develop indigenous social work knowledge based on culturally and locally relevant and problem-oriented research. Furthermore, indigenisation is viewed as being a naturally occurring process in social work knowledge development. Yunong and Xiong (2011) supported this argument because in their view, local cultures and contexts are everywhere; indigenisation is therefore inherent in the social work profession.

Methodology

This research investigates how participants frame local and global issues, ultimately aiming to localise global social work education standards in PNG. It explores participants' subjective views on global standards and local knowledge necessary for developing a culturally relevant social work curriculum, using the UPNG field education programme as a case study. The case study uses a mixed methods approach with a strong qualitative and interpretive element.

The Participants

The recruitment of the research participants was through open invitation via public social media and emailed communication from the UPNG Social Work Strand, allowing prospective participants to opt in; thus, their participation was free and voluntary. All these participants were de-identified using pseudonyms and their views kept confidential. The primary population samples for the study mostly resided in the vicinity of Port Moresby except for one former academic. The multiple data sources and data collection approaches are helpful for comparative analyses and triangulation of participants' views and experiences regarding the development and delivery of field education curriculum by groups.

The initial strategy was to recruit 15 participants from each stakeholder group. However, the returned results showed that 20 students and 11 educators participated in the study. The main factors determining this level of participation were accessibility and time. The main reason for selecting these samples is that they play a significant role in the UPNG fieldwork programme. There are important factors considered in the selection of the sample population and these include accessibility, time, and resources.

According to Bryman (2012), purposive sampling illustrates a 'typical case' where the sample chosen has some dimensions of interest in the study that will necessitate some level of commitment and honest participation. With the study being dominantly qualitative, a purposive sampling (Barbbie 2002) of the non-probability method was used. This is because the research questions required specific information from key stakeholders of the UPNG fieldwork programme that have had some fieldwork experiences in their respective roles as supervisors, students, and academics.

Data Collection Methods and Analysis

This research aims to reform the social work field education curriculum at UPNG to reflect greater compatibility with international standards and flexibility to suit locally relevant industry and development practice needs in PNG. Given that the social work practice and training base in PNG has been striving to maintain professional credibility amidst a dearth of national professional standards or guidance (Lawihin & Brydon, 2013; Lawihin, 2012), this study examines local PNG stakeholders' knowledge and application of global fieldwork standards, as well as seeking their views on the necessary local knowledge to guide the curriculum and practice. These aims have provided the platform by which the research question objectives and question were developed. The main question for the study is: *What do key stakeholders identify as the necessary components of social work field education in PNG to respond to local and global challenges?*

A range of methods for collecting data was utilised. These methods are linked to the interpretivist research ideology and the cultural issues and approaches to knowledge development. Whilst some data were gathered through a survey asking both closed and open-ended questions, further qualitative data were gathered via semi-structured interviews with individuals and focus groups. The interviews were based on a hypothetical case study of a student on placement. The case study was used to encourage participants to explain what knowledge, skills, and attributes social work students should attain in fieldwork and the key components of a culturally relevant field education. Data was also sought using metaphors.

The selection of data collection tools was based on factors such as limited prior research conducted on this subject. At the same time, having regard for cultural norms in PNG about time allowed for a flexible approach to data collection as the researcher worked with the availability and timing of the participants for interviews. Similarly, participants were allowed to complete questionnaires in their own time. Importantly, as the study is one of the first on the subject in PNG, a flexible response strategy was needed to 'dig out' new information and to be prepared for the unexpected. Table 19.1 shows the different methods of data collection used to answer the research question.

To answer the research question, raw data from different data sources and responses were recorded using an Excel spread sheet and Word document. This was later imported into the NVivo Analysis Software for coding and sorting purposes. Coded responses were then teased out to link views and ideas collectively, according to different categories of data sources and data collection techniques regarding fieldwork, standards, and strategies for integration and localisation.

Thematic, text, and descriptive content analyses were used to evaluate data from the interviews and questionnaires. The flexibility of these methods of analyses allows for data to be analysed in different ways and across the whole data set or a single aspect of the data in great depth. This means that data was read, re-read, and coded in order to identify emerging themes and their relationship to the study objectives. The thematic content analysis method was used to identify the major themes emerging from the transcriptions which represented the views and perspectives of the study participants. To enable easy analysis, information was coded according to years of experience, knowledge of global standards, useful local knowledge and practices in fieldwork, participant groups, and data collection approaches.

The study was supported by the UPNG Postgraduate Research Committee by giving permission to access the participants and complying with UPNG's institutional protocols for a safe and responsible conduct of research with humans. The design and methodology of this research met Monash University's ethical conduct of research standards. Subsequently, the study received ethics approval from the Monash University Human Research Ethics Committee (MUHREC), and the Project Number for the research is CF15/4475 – 201500193.

Table 19.1 The data collection methods and number participants for this study

Method	Question types	Data analysis method
Survey questionnaire	Predetermined/closed: global standards Open-ended	Descriptive Likert scale Content
Individual interview	Semi-structured and emerging: integration of standards and local knowledge Hypothetical case study	Content and thematic
Focus group	Semi-structured and emerging: integration of standards and local knowledge Hypothetical case study	Content and thematic

Source: Author

Study Limitations

There are several limitations, posing potential questions regarding the validity and trustworthiness of findings. The first weakness is that very little has been written on social work education and none regarding its fieldwork component in PNG. Most literature reviewed was on social work education outside of PNG, which may facilitate a situation of unsubstantiated claims. Secondly, the study sample was small, and the findings may be questionable for this reason alone. There is limited voice from the field education supervisors because less than half of that representative sample participated in the interviews and questionnaires, which further limits the effectiveness of comparison, replicability, and adequacy of the findings. Furthermore, the study is also limited due to the lack of participation of fieldwork clients as important stakeholders of the UPNG Social Work programme.

However, the sampling technique used gives this study some strong advantages. Firstly,

> with purposive sampling, it was easy to identify and select supervisors who were currently working with fieldwork students and academics that had experience in delivering fieldwork courses. Secondly, very experienced fieldwork supervisors participated so that their views on culturally relevant fieldwork are representative of the current curriculum.

Findings

The findings presented here reflect the perspectives of key players in social work education in the context of the UPNG programme. From the data collected, there is focus on knowledge required for developing culturally relevant social work education – specifically fieldwork in PNG.

A Focus on Melanesian Knowledge and Wisdom

The primary themes that emerged from the data include knowledge of local culture and practices, local authorities and institutions, and local issues and social support models – the Melanesian Way. The most discussed aspect of the Melanesian Way among educators reflects Melanesian dominant communal and oral culture. Whilst the students prefer supportive learning through direct lectures, teaching materials, and practical examples, educators as facilitators of learning viewed participation and teamwork as effective learning approaches for social work in PNG. Almost all educators expressed the need for students to learn about teamwork and participation in groups to enhance their learning. Educators also identified observation and narrative therapy as being helpful, where stories are utilised as tools for healing. Understanding the family values system in PNG was argued by educators to be the primary basis for understanding wider PNG society. This argument was captured in the SWEQ3 response:

> we must have value in the reciprocity of caring and sharing among family and extended family lines, respect for elders and the community and utilise observation as the key to work well with communities.

Like Confucian (East Asia) and Ubuntu (Africa) cultures, PNG has a rich communal and oral tradition that social work can draw on to enable culturally relevant teaching and learning. The value of PNG's rich oral tradition was evident in this research. Two educators advocate for the inclusion and integration of oral expressions of ideas and learning through stories into classroom teaching at UPNG. For example, narrative therapy or theories, which focus on people's stories about their strengths and weaknesses. [These illustrate] family systems and theory and how households' function in villages, towns and cities. Having these story sessions in classrooms, where supervisors and community leaders are invited to share their living experiences is ideal for students to stay connected with communities and families in PNG.

(Educator SWEQ2, 3)

Social work functions globally but also in specific cultural contexts such as in PNG's Melanesian culture. Across both educators and students, the key aspect of Melanesian content identified in this study is that local culture should feature more in the fieldwork courses. This was reflected in discussions surrounding customs and traditions, language and the use of metaphors and parables. The aspects of local Melanesian culture that were identified include learning about local authority and leadership, institutions, and structures. One of the educators (SWEQ8) argues that Melanesian approaches to learning and practice are important and UPNG should include 'approaches of community relations, knowledge of PNG community institutions and structures, leadership and decision-making procedures and processes for ceremonies and rituals' in the field education content. Furthermore, reflecting the general state of social development in PNG, educators highlight specific local issues that students need knowledge of to practise locally, the most dominant of these being gender inequalities, land disputes, and polygamy. Having these issues identified as major local concerns requires competent social work graduates with appropriate and relevant skills to address them.

Developing Graduates with Culturally Relevant Skills

In terms of desirable social work graduate attributes, the findings point to communication and cultural competence as highly regarded skills. All participants highlight these skills as critical in social work. It was noted in the results that communication skills intersect with cultural competence, such that communication also includes the related skills of advocacy, facilitation, and negotiation, while cultural competence covers Melanesian counselling and cultural sensitivity in the context of conflict resolution and domestic issues. For example, a fieldwork supervisor expresses this clearly: 'communication must be conducted with greater cultural awareness and sensitivity ... (and) thus should be adaptive and flexible ... which is susceptible to change with various contexts and audiences across PNG'.

(Multicultural) communication, organisation and planning, networking, and counselling are equally, essential skills. Time management and planning in the Melanesian PNG context accepts flexibility and focuses on the result and the agreed deadline of the outcome. Melanesian counselling is applicable in PNG in the context of group counselling. In the cases of individual focus, the place and space of counselling determines the cultural and ethical boundaries between the client and counsellor. The example given was when a male talks with a female. In this case they do not make eye contact during the conversation, which is in conflict with the Western definition of effective communication. One of the educators expresses this difference explicitly.

> Our Melanesian approach to communication or counselling for that matter is different. They must not sit face-to-face or talk face-to-face but must be sideways to each other or a distance away from each other.

This culturally acceptable distance is defined by those involved and others within the proximity of engagement.

Programme management skill is important for social work graduates. Most educators and students identify management functions of planning, monitoring, and evaluation as valuable skills in social work. However, the development of monitoring and evaluation skills in the Melanesian context can have varying connotations. For example, educator SWEQ10 reports that,

> everything has to start with a story and getting supervisors and students to understand the purpose and what good planning and evaluation will bring to what we do in fieldwork. [This means] initially starting with networking and interactions, which then makes planning and evaluating research easy.

Further results indicated the need to incorporate global/generic skills, such as research into field education. According to SWEQ5, 'our students when graduating should have good research and writing skills and must be competent in both generic and specialised social work skills such as counselling and working with communities and individuals'.

Networking and collaboration were also identified by many educators and more than ten students as essential skills. Such skills are important because field education involves multiple organisations and people playing significant and complementary roles, thus the need for constant collaboration. In fact, both local and global social work knowledge are important and warrant integration.

Aspects of Local-Global Knowledge for Integration in Field Education

Connecting Global and Local Social Issues

Both educators and students had considerable amount of discussion on the need for knowledge about social issues and intervention strategies. Social work student must demonstrate acceptable knowledge of broad global issues concerning human rights, migration, violence and war, refugees, global warming and climate change, child abuse, health, and hygiene. Similarly, most educators and half of the student participants highlight awareness of local issues and related social policies that students must be taught in order to have effective and quality learning experiences during placement. In a focus group, one participant emphasised the intertwined nature of local-global issues affecting local communities: 'I see environmental issues, global warming and climate change and gender issues as critical in this day and age'.

International social work issues were viewed as international development challenges across a range of countries.

> Knowledge of international social work standards and social work code of ethics, guidelines for practice and teaching are essential. International social work issues like mental health, refugees, and human trafficking apart from gender-based violence and child abuse must be taught to students. (Educator SWEQ2)

The students also shared similar views. 'I am keen to learn about the current issues of climate change, environmental degradation, violence against women and children, domestic violence and HIV/AIDS and its effects on communities'. While this research exposed these local knowledge gaps, there is limited research and literature that provide a locally sound knowledge 'bank' to draw from.

The development of a more nuanced understanding of the 'local' environment is important. Interview data indicates that the course content should also focus on cultural diversity and Melanesian communities. The summarised views of educators SWEIV2, SWEIV3, and a student focus group indicate that there should be a subject on cultural diversity in PNG and/or Melanesia and the integration of cultures that contribute to empowering communities. Students from the second focus group suggested that skills in multicultural practice should be included in fieldwork tasks. In doing so, it enables equal attention to the teaching of specific cultural knowledge and issues in the context of broader external issues.

Connecting Global Expectations and Standards

Connecting the global and local social work guidelines and policies signifies a balanced curriculum. This is evident as seven educators and six students suggested for the inclusion of the specific topics on the IFSW social work code of ethics (Statement of Ethical Principles), national social policies, and international conventions. SWEIV2 said, 'we need to do more on linking global conventions and local social policies and laws like the CRC [Convention on the Rights of Children] and Lukautim Pikinini Act [National Children's Act], even relating these to our Vision 2050'.

However, there are practical challenges to implement this integration. Data from educators reveal this ongoing challenge for social work in PNG, where the local and global knowledge are separated, and their relationship is vague. SWEIV3 illustrated this knowledge gap:

> I think it is both the local social development knowledge and international social work knowledge that must be brought together, compared and analysed and then imparted to our students so that they are culturally competent to practice in any context.

This finding highlights the need for educating social work students to respond to global and local issues appropriately from a specific context regardless of place, time, and institutional culture.

On the other hand, students' survey data highlight that the integration of local-global social work knowledge is limited in the current field education curriculum. For example, SWSQ3 described her understanding: 'I feel that I should learn about ... international standards such as social work code of ethics, values and principles, including placement agencies and their guidelines and the international social work practice models'.

The IFSW International Social Work Code of Ethics appeared to be highly significant for most participants. The main finding from students on the issue of developing culturally relevant field education curriculum, is by integrating local and global knowledge, issues, and standards. For example, Student SWSQ1 mentioned, 'integration of common Melanesian cultures, values, norms and practices into the standards' ... 'knowledge of people, customs and traditional belief systems needs to be included in the standards'.

Moreover, SWSQ12 held the view that 'knowledge of what constitutes patrilineal and matrilineal societies in defining people's identities, gender roles and gender related issues is critical'. Students' views were further supported by an educator who proposed that, 'the standards should promote PNG's social safety net as an important part of Melanesian culture' and the communal outlook of many PNG communities that requires a group approach to working with communities.

To achieve effective integration and build a culturally relevant social work curriculum, support for locally driven research is essential.

Research for Knowledge Building

Research is seen as a key skill for social work graduates. Some participants also viewed research as an approach whose purpose was to develop a local knowledge base. With their professional academic role and experience in social work, educators highlighted the significance of culturally relevant research for knowledge development. SWEIV3 emphasises teaching research methods and enabling students to engage in research, 'it is critical that we teach our students to do research so that we develop our own local knowledge base' for localisation to thrive. For culturally relevant research, 'we need to do research and write about standards. To make sure that the standards remain connected to local practice settings, we must teach the standards in the fieldwork courses and emphasise these during placement with students and supervisors'.

This indicates that participants regarded research as both knowledge and activity that can help raise our awareness and understanding of the rich social support systems that are strong in PNG.

Social Care and Support Models

Attention to teaching PNG's community support models necessary as social work practice in PNG is encouraging this informal social support system. Family and kinship play a central role in providing social care that meets the welfare needs of members. Although this is a key area to integrate for culturally relevant social work in PNG, it functions in a context where contemporary Western welfare systems are increasingly favoured in formalised urban communities. This view was mostly expressed by educators: 'this is our social care system, and it is working well in our rural communities, but unfortunately the major urban population is becoming individualistic and competitive, a common feature of an introduced western model,' (Educator SWEIV2).

The results showed community sharing and social support, casework, and group work, cultural and gender sensitive approaches, and integrated social policy models as relevant to PNG context. The knowledge and understanding of these models of social work practice will help facilitate preparations for students' placements and professional practice after graduation. Both educators and students indicated that the fieldwork curriculum should take a bottom–up approach in its design and delivery. These views are consistent with the emerging theme of linking local knowledge and the Melanesian Way of helping and the contemporary welfare models. SWEIV3 expressed this clearly,

> 'we really need to look at integration in all stages and components of fieldwork – that is in the process, models and content. In the content we have to specify the models and processes of that connection'.

Specific practice models suggested for integration into fieldwork were the reciprocity/residual model and community social work.

Connecting with Practice Settings

In the context of the local, data shows some significance placed on participants' knowledge of practice settings in PNG, although are also aware of the work of international NGOs in the country. Such knowledge is necessary to enable students to understand different practice contexts. SWEIV3 educator said, 'we must train our students to practice in diverse contexts reflecting both internal and international diversity'.

Another educator emphasised that knowledge about diverse settings locally is critical for students during fieldwork. reported that, the fieldwork coordinator has to work with supervisors to identify what programs and issues are addressed by the agencies. In this way supervisors will provide relevant information on the programs and activities of the agencies. What is important here is cultural integration – engage supervisors as guest lecturers on specific topics,

(Educator SWEIV4)

Communication was identified as a culturally relevant skill, especially multicultural communication to be taught as a topic. Teaching communication will advance other complementary skills highlighted earlier. To practice effectively in diverse contexts locally and globally, fieldwork students must embrace greater flexibility and cultural sensitivity.

Governance and Policy Systems for Localisation

An effective system of governance and policy administration is critical for localisation to thrive. In this study, participants identify the impact of governance systems as essential for localisation to evolve. Administration and management aspects of field education concerned resources for fieldwork, skills, and processes of planning, evaluation, and reporting, and supervision. The text analyses of interviews generated multiple discussions on governance and policy components of fieldwork, with 16 from students and 12 from educators. A consensus of 16 and 12 references from students and educators noted that the localisation process should begin with the review of global standards in a learning forum for stakeholders to give their input and develop a localised version that fits the PNG context. Student SWSQ8 contends that: 'Workshopping of the fieldwork standards to get the stakeholders to review and add value and acceptability to the standards'. Educator SWEQ2 also advocates to 'provide a fieldwork manual and communicate standards to partner agencies which will also acknowledge their contributions to fieldwork'.

Similar views were expressed in the interview data. Educator SWEIV4, adds that: 'I would be happy to see PNG Social Workers Association taking the lead in this review of standards and I bet this is the most important issue right now'.

The other four educators highlight that one way to localise global standards was to review the social work programme in order to integrate global standards and agency policies into the field education curriculum. In their view, this would allow for correlating linkages between the global standards and local agency specific operational guidelines.

Among many educators and student participants, their data show that global standards could be used in teaching and learning and for the development of programme policies and guidelines. The educators specifically refer to global standards as guidelines to develop national standards including a code of ethics for international benchmarking and programme evaluation. SWEQ6 survey data suggests a blend of the two approaches, firstly is to 'review international standards and develop national and localised standards … then use these standards for planning and evaluating fieldwork', including curriculum review and development to guide supervision and coordination.

Discussion

How to Achieve Global-Local Connectedness in Field Education

This study finds that strong oversight by both a professional local organisation and the social work school is necessary to cultivate culturally relevant field education as illustrated in Figure 19.1. This educational development is relevant when there is effective integration of global issues and standards with local knowledge and processes.

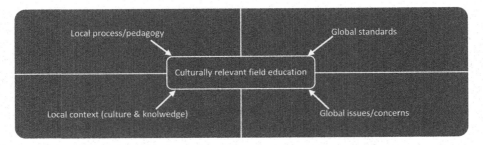

Figure 19.1 How to integrate the local and the global aspects of field education. Source: Author

The current study offers important preliminary ideas on how to address localisation with specific strategies presented in the data for a strong local-global connectedness. The key theme emerging is *pasin wok bung*, achieving connectedness between local and global social work ideals as a primary factor for the development of culturally relevant field education.

Effectively integrating the global Western ideals of social work and the locally specific cultural and social norms in specific locations remains a convoluted task. Connectedness and commonalities have been reported in the literature as associated with internationalisation (Crisp, 2015; Dominelli, 2014; Weiss-Gal & Welbourne, 2008; Gray & Coates, 2010; Yip, 2006). However, this study presents an interesting case for a strong connection that can only be achieved when localisation and internationalisation are effectively integrated to complement each other. Localisation is given more weight in this research because participants believe this will lead the way to achieve cultural relevance in social work education. While Gray and Coates (2010) advocated for indigenous knowledge and systems, findings from this study highlight the need for connectedness and for such connections to include local and culturally relevant organisations, systems, beliefs, and practices to be actively made in field education.

There is a strong indication for a balance between internationalisation and localisation for their connections to be complementary. This theorisation is consistent with claims that local cultures and contexts exist everywhere (Yunong & Xiong, 2011) and it relates to the ideals of glocalisation (Nikku & Pulla, 2014), a recent concept that describes a harmonious intersection of local-global aspects of social work. However, in this study, 'localisation' is chosen because it is a user-friendly term commonly used in the context of Melanesian and Pacific communities with dominant oral and observatory local cultures and population. Localisation in this discussion is therefore taken to replace the term 'glocalisation', providing a framework of balanced complementarity between internationalisation and indigenisation for the development of a culturally relevant social work field education curriculum.

This study contributes several aspects of connectedness, relevant for effectively linking the global and local aspects of social work education: global and local issues, global and local expectations and policies, connections between university and the community, global and local approaches to practice, and the local application of global standards as guidelines.

Connecting the Global and Local Issues

PNG, like other countries, is faced with many development challenges including social problems of different types and of various magnitudes. Some of these problems cut across national boundaries, while others are specific to PNG. Social work has been seen over many years to be taking a central role in the efforts to help people and communities address such social injustices in society, both in specific localities and across the globe, through joint action and collaboration. It is at this point that the centrality of knowledge on social issues should be an important component of social work education.

In a similar study in the Swedish context, Christensen (2016) argues for 'acting locally and thinking globally' as a way of internationalising social work education. However, his arguments reinforce the ideals of globalisation which undermines the vision to build culturally relevant social work education globally. My research highlights the desire for the teaching of both local and global content in the social work (field) education curriculum. One of the key areas for integration into the curriculum is that of global and local issues. These are critical for students' understanding to prepare them for fieldwork and independent professional practice afterward. Therefore, teaching field education must cover social issues in the broader external context as well as internally.

Another significant finding is the value of local knowledge regarding the Melanesian Way and culturally relevant practice models. There is a strong push for Melanesian models of learning to be included as primary teaching topics for fieldwork. As noted in the participants' views, these topics must include local culture and practices, local authorities and institutions, and local issues and social support models. While there is a call for the teaching of social work to reflect both local and global issues and social policies, it is more important to teach these in the context of local practice.

The need for social work students to acquire knowledge of the broad global social issues of human rights, climate change, migration, and health and education is equally significant. It is important to be aware of the implications that some of these issues have for local communities. That is the reason attention must be given to both the related local issues and social policies. The results from this research indicated that when students are taught the relationship between issues like local and international migration, and local and international NGOs, it brings about effective and quality learning experiences for them. This is where the emphasis on the interconnectedness of local and global issues affecting local communities helps with devising locally appropriate intervention strategies and accepted global joint actions. In doing so, this enables equal attention to be paid to the teaching of specific cultural knowledge and issues in the context of broader external issues and vice versa.

Connecting the Global Expectations and Local Policies

It is common that national social policies and strategies also reflect international conventions and guidelines. Given the significance of international relations embraced by globalised systems of government, local needs must be linked to global aspirations and development goals such as the United Nations Sustainable Development Goals. Therefore, teaching knowledge of global expectations and standards and applying them locally is the act of making links between the global and local, which further positions teaching as the central aspect for locating local knowledge in the professional social work framework. IFSW's (2012) Statement of Ethical Principles, national social policies, and international conventions provide the basis for this linkage.

However, the connecting of local and global policy aspirations and expectations is a challenge. This challenge concerns avenues where the relationship between the local and global knowledge is vague. This is evident when connections are strictly based on differences and commonalities apart. To filter these differences and advance cultural competence among students in practising in any context, this study argues for social work education to equip students to respond to global and local issues appropriately from a specific context regardless of place, time, and institutional culture. This is where Lawihin (2018) and Nikku and Pulla (2014) advocate for balanced attention to be given to global and local knowledge in the teaching and practice of social work.

Integrating the global and local knowledge into social work curriculum has been at the core of this research, which from the perspectives of participants consulted, provides the basis for the establishment of a culturally relevant field education programme. Such integration in the Melanesian PNG context covers common Melanesian cultures, values, norms, and practices to inform the global standards. The logical preference for incorporating international social work expectations is to frame the local issues and understand local social policies often developed to address these issues, which allows for active participation in a global dialogue. The IFSW's standards and code of ethics (IFSW, 2012) continue to emerge in the data as content worthy of being taught in fieldwork courses, although contribution to this involved multiple stakeholders. Subsequently, integrating this important knowledge content to enrich students' learning is a huge challenge, and thus requires a combined effort by the university, professional social work organisation and community at large to stay connected and work collaboratively.

The Link Between the University and the Community

Local knowledge is essential in social work education and practice to inform social work professionals' behaviour and approach with the communities and people they are engaged with. Without this knowledge of local cultures, social work interventions, and educational approaches can lead to unfavourable outcomes and insensitivity to local cultures and values. Faleolo (2013) has identified useful principles for incorporating local knowledge to achieve indigenised social work education in Samoa: knowledge of culture and local practices for cultural competence, and a philosophical authentication should be systematically incorporated and applied to suit local contexts. Similarly, this research has found evidentiary support for this argument. Localisation of the standards and field education curriculum is seen to acknowledge the value of local knowledge and experiences to inform the development of national standards and culturally relevant field education.

The input from the local community and leaders in the development and teaching of social work is important for adding quality and relevance to the curriculum. In doing so, this act of inclusion acknowledges the place and culture in which social work functions. For example, the *Wantok* system – family and kinship relationships in PNG are significant helping and sharing virtues that need to be drawn on to complement Western theories and models of assistance and welfare. The link between the university and the community is also demonstrated through knowledge of local practice settings, such as local institutions, including international organisations operating in a country. Knowledge of such community settings is necessary to equip students to work in diverse contexts as these settings reflect both internal and international diversity. The research data indicated this as important in the process of cultural integration and can be achieved by engaging fieldwork supervisors as guest lecturers on specific topics.

In countries like PNG where there is greater internal diversity, embracing greater flexibility and cultural sensitivity is recommended. Local input is also essential in holding social work accountable to the local population and its needs in contexts where practice standards are lacking, as well as for practising across diverse cultures, as alluded to in the research of Fouché and colleagues (2016) about migrant social workers in New Zealand. The study also indicates soliciting local input from community leaders to strengthen social work's local connections to the field. Echoing findings from earlier research (Lawihin, 2012), research collaboration between social work academics and fieldwork supervisors adds quality to the academic content and recognises the role of field educators to effectively contribute to the development of knowledge in social work and its human resources.

This study provides some understanding of how important local knowledge is, in our efforts to localise globally focused knowledge discourse and social policy standards. The task for localisation in PNG is made difficult by our cultural diversity and dominant oral cultures, in which much is unwritten and thus close links to the local community are required to connect with the local people, their environment, rituals, and traditional ancestral wisdom.

Local knowledge encapsulates an understanding of the local social, cultural, economic, political, and environmental characteristics and how local people relate and function within these contexts. Scholars such as Faleolo (2013), Gray and Coates (2010), Mungai, Wairire, and Rush (2014), and Costello and Aung (2015) have argued for local knowledge as being important to define responses and interventions to address local issues and indeed international issues as manifested in a local context. Furthermore, Costello and Aung (2015) and Mungai and colleagues (2014), discussed local knowledge in the context of a collective society, like that of PNG but in a different geographical, historical, and political context. However, these scholars did not provide pragmatic approaches to integrate local knowledge systematically into social work curriculum. Yet there is a common social work identity in the sense that professional social work in these contexts originated from the West. As such there are similar challenges regarding the limited number of professional local social work teachers and lack of resources for social work training (Costello & Aung, 2015).

In PNG, local knowledge is dominantly about the Melanesian Way, the community orientation of support and problem-solving and the notion of *Wantok* (relative) for accessibility to social services. However, Lawihin (2012) and Brydon and Lawihin (2014) uncovered some less helpful aspects of *Wantok* that denote corruption and unfair access to services. The conclusion drawn from that study was that local realities favour the application of the Melanesian Way, resulting in less attention to international social work education standards. According to Brydon and Lawihin (2014), some Melanesian approaches to fieldwork have undermined the professional tenets of social work. To enrich this picture, the current research identifies meaningful and positive aspects of the Melanesian Way and the *Wantok* system for incorporation into social work teaching, to counter those negative areas. Teaching these topics will allow for closer examination and alignment with related contemporary social work models, principles, and values common across other settings.

Linking Global and Local Approaches to Practice

Local knowledge and practices occupy a position from within a specific context looking outward and upward, often referred to as a bottom–up approach to knowledge development. Educators and practitioners particularly favour this approach. Given their forte in practice experiences, they could utilise it to inform theoretical discussions. The bottom–up approach in social work encourages active local participation and community empowerment (Ife, 2002), which both ultimately inform higher-level policies at the government and global levels. Such local approaches to practice in specific contexts thus minimise the challenges of internationalisation that were seen to limit local participation at some level (Dominelli, 2014). Domielli's research addresses local participation in internationally supported humanitarian community projects, where long-term community empowerment and sustainability is nebulous. In contrast, my research emphasises integrating local knowledge and applied approaches by local practitioners and educators thus likely to achieve long-term sustainable and culturally relevant social work education in PNG.

Building connections between the Western narrative therapy and a family-oriented storytelling approach, both in problem-solving and in teaching and learning, is a relevant example for connecting global and local approaches. This was evident in the study results where respondents were advocating for the teaching of PNG's community support models as important for social work practice. This informal support is a key area for practising culturally relevant social work in PNG. For example, SWEIV2 stated, 'this is our social care system, and it is working well in our rural communities, but unfortunately the major urban population is becoming individualistic and competitive, a common feature of an introduced western model'. Proposed practice models for linking with social work locally include reciprocity/residual model of care, bottom–up planning, family therapy, and community social work. Understanding these models of social work practice can help facilitate preparations for students' placements effectively.

One of the key findings from the data recommends stories and storytelling to be incorporated into classroom teaching pedagogies (Lawihin, 2018). This can involve the engagement of community leaders in classroom discussion sessions, as suggested earlier, or participant observation and simulation, which has always been how learning happens in the village. This method of learning helps student to understand and know about the communities we are working in.

Nikku and Pulla (2014) identify localisation as a significant connection to the broader global goals. Their views are confirmed by this study, where localisation is perceived as promoting a 'balanced' approach (global with local) in social work education and practice. Yet, we also know from Crisp's (2015) reflections on a project aiming to develop an international curriculum that this is difficult to enact in practice. Some of these challenges have been addressed by this research by recommending strong and equal attention to both the global and local social work knowledge and standards.

Yunong and Xiong (2008) argue that contemporary approaches reflecting a Western orientation to teaching and learning have become dominant in educational institutions at all levels. Conversely, Faleolo (2013) and Mungai, Wairire, and Rush (2014) defended the use of local indigenous knowledge and approaches for teaching and learning in specific contexts – decolonising social work education and practice. For example, Faleolo (2013) describes the effectiveness of using metaphor and story for learning in the Samoan context, a pedagogy that was given similar significance in this study. Gray, Kreitzer, and Mupedziswa (2014) also recommend these culturally relevant pedagogies for contemporary classroom and field-based learning from the African Ubuntu cultural perspectives in an increasingly globalised context.

Local Application of Global Standards

One of the biggest questions regarding the relevance of global social work education and practice standards is the application of these in different and rather diverse contexts. Advocates of the IASSW and the IFSW expect individual countries to adapt and apply these standards to suit their local social and political contexts with utmost freedom. Such an expectation is impractical without some enforcement mechanisms and an accepted level of desirability regarding what needs to be done in translating the standards into practice. Mungai et al. (2014) confirm this struggle from the Kenyan experience where efforts have been trialled to apply these standards, as in the case of maintaining social work ethics. Research on the application of global standards is therefore necessary in the development and sharing of the local knowledge base. This can then inform the localisation of global standards in specific country contexts. Therefore, the good link between research and standards at the local context is at the point of researching standards as they apply locally, and teaching about this research, to contribute to a culturally relevant social work education.

Another avenue where links are created between standards and local application is during the development of national social work education and practice standards. Strong evidence from this study shows that the development of national social work standards is informed both by global standards and local social work knowledge and practices. An example illustrating this is the actual translation of global standards into local languages, such as Tok Pisin in PNG. This finding is consistent with the scholarly views of Faleolo (2013) in the Samoan context and empirical evidence from Ethiopia (Yishak & Gumbo, 2014), Jordan (Sullivan et al., 2010), and PNG (Lawihin & Brydon, 2013), where the utilisation of local language is seen as key to localising social work curriculum and practices.

As identified in my previous study (Lawihin, 2012), global standards are often used by social work schools to review their curricula and general programmes. This study highlights the value of global standards to maintain consistency of the local programme with the other social work programmes in other countries, given the increasing professionalisation of social work globally. The local schools also play an important role in promoting the global social work standards. For example, participants suggested incorporating global standards into the fieldwork manual, for the purposes of teaching and learning and distribution to partner agencies involved in field education. In this way, the local programme, regardless of context, would still maintain some level of connection to the broader social work profession. Such connections are unclear in cases where there is weak social work professional leadership through a professional association and a lack of established national social work standards.

The framing of a new standard, which stresses a commitment to local knowledge in a globalised world and acknowledging local voices and aspirations everywhere, is a key argument of this chapter. Having a statement on local knowledge inserted in the current global standards will provide the basis for countries to address global issues locally, instead of going through the struggle of incorporating various aspects of local knowledge and practices. For example, participants proposed the utilisation of local knowledge (the *Wantok* system) to inform the localisation of certain aspects of global standards in PNG.

It follows also that national social workers' associations play a critical role in the 'translation' of both local and global needs and expectations into workable strategies in specific contexts. Results from this study acknowledge the challenges of localising standards in PNG, given the less active role of the professional association in promoting global standards and developing PNG specific standards. Subsequently, social work education at UPNG is functioning within the jurisdictions of the university and not through the standards set by a professional social work body. While national social work associations are responsible for setting guidelines and standards for the education and practice of social work in respective countries, PNGSWA is far from assuming that role in PNG. This study has revealed that PNGSWA must take the leading role in the localisation of global social work standards and begin the process for the development of culturally relevant social work education in PNG.

Conclusion

Social work is argued to be a global profession and is practiced in many countries but there is ongoing debates particularly in non-Western contexts where social work is less developed regarding the application of social work concepts and strategies. What seems to be unclear is knowing what type and form of social work and social work education is relevant to PNG, and how this connects with the globally accepted social work definition, standards, and general professional identity. This hints at the need for an 'interconnecting hub' in which the local and global can intersect harmoniously for the development of culturally relevant and globally consistent social work.

This study examined social work field education in PNG, including the role of global social work field education standards, from the perspectives of social work educators and students in PNG. With the current social work curriculum generally being a replicate of the Western model, the provision of social work education is likely to reflect general concepts and theories not firmly rooted in the local setting. The utilisation of global standards and a case study approach with a mixed methods paradigm allowed for the examination of a factual and descriptive knowledge base. The study findings show that a culturally relevant social work curriculum is strongly linked to a notion of localisation that focuses on global-local connectedness.

The literature review underpinning this study discovered that there is limited research on localisation, particularly on how this can be operationalised. The current study sought to generate some understanding of localisation as the key approach to developing culturally relevant social work education in PNG context. The study focuses specifically on field education as both the 'front line' of social work education and its 'signature pedagogy'. The central theme of the importance of connectedness emerged from the data, highlighting four key areas to address to ensure the development of a culturally relevant field education curriculum. These are: through connecting global-local issues; connecting global-local policies and standards; connecting universities and local communities; and connecting contemporary and local teaching and learning approaches. In general, the study found that we stand a greater chance to create a culturally relevant social work curriculum in PNG, if we pay balanced attention to both the local and global aspects of social work. It is this kind of social work that is likely to prepare social work professionals to practise globally.

Strategic Recommendations

In terms of advancing the development of a culturally relevant social work curriculum in PNG, options for building networks and collaboration locally and internationally are available. This research generates new knowledge, which shows that the process of localising field education must occur by actively making connections at theoretical and practical levels. These connections will be built through teaching content and approaches, and through framing standards and policies, with strong input from the local community and the professional associations.

Connecting Curriculum

Commitment to local knowledge acknowledges the living patterns and aspirations of the local population, which can be hidden inside existing globalised standards including IFSW's Statement of Ethical Principles (IFSW, 2012). Therefore, a *balanced* attention must be given to both local and global issues in the teaching of social work. The need to actively focus on the local was emphasised, incorporating culturally relevant learning approaches (including addressing the language of instruction) and local content, remaining connected to the local practice context, and soliciting local input to achieve this. UPNG is strategically placed in conducting culturally relevant research to generate a local knowledge base and participate actively in the global social work knowledge economy.

Connecting Organisationally

Having strong and effective social work governance mechanisms for the development and delivery of social work education in PNG provides a favourable space to begin the process of localisation, setting up a basis from which culturally relevant field education may be built. This might mean work to address the localisation of global standards and the incorporation of local knowledge to inform the development of national standards and the curriculum, a keyway of giving local people a voice in curriculum development. This can begin with reactivating the professional social work association that will lead the process for the development of national social work education and practice standards including the code of ethics.

The Role of the PNG Social Workers Association

One of the key recommendations from this study is for local social work organisations such as PNGSWA to play a central role in providing guidance and oversight in the ongoing review and development of social work training and practice. In this way, the professional association can both 'translate' and represent the global standards for the local context as well as representing local needs and perspectives in the broader arena.

References

Barbbie, E. (2002). *The Basics of Social Research* (2nd ed.). Belmont: Wadsworth.
Brydon, K., & Lawihin, D. (2014). Melanesian visions: Some preliminary thoughts about social work education and practice in Papua New Guinea. *International Social Work, 59*(2), 192–204.
Bryman, A. (2012). *Social Research Methods* (4th ed.). Oxford University Press.
Central Intelligence Agency (CIA). (2016). *World Factbook. East and Southeast Asia: Papua New Guinea*. Retrieved from: https://www.cia.gov/library/publications/the-world-factbook/geos/pp.html
Costello, S., & Aung, U.T. (2015). Developing social work education in Myanmar. *International Social Work, 58*(4), 582–594.
Crisp, B. R. (2015). The challenges of developing cross-national social work curricula. *International Social Work*, 1–13. DOI: 10.1177/002087281557413.
Christensen, J. M. (2016). Acting locally and thinking globally in social work education. *International Journal of Social Sciences and Education Research, 2*(3), 938–948.
Dominelli, L. (2014). Internationalizing professional practices: The place of social work in the international arena. *International Social Work, 57*(3), 58–267.
Faleolo, M. (2013). Authentication in social work education: The balancing act. In C. Noble, M. Henrickson, & I.Y. Han (Eds.), *Social work education, voices from the Asia Pacific* (2nd ed., pp. 105–132). Sydney: Sydney University Press.
Flynn, C., Kamasua, K., & Lawihin, D. (2016). Aspirations and realities in delivering field education in a developing country context: Learning from Papua New Guinea. In I. Taylor , M.Bogo , M.Lefevre , & B. Teater (Eds.), *Routledge International Handbook of Social Work Education* (pp. 209–219).
Fouché, C., Beddoe, L., Bartley, A., & Parkes, E. (2016). Are we ready for them? Overseas-qualified social workers' professional cultural transition. *European Journal of Social Work, 19*(1), 106–119. doi:10.1080/13691457.2015.1022858
Government of Papua New Guinea (GOPNG). (2016). *Papua New Guinea national strategy to prevent and respond to gender based violence*. Retrieved from Papua New Guinea: Government of Papua New Guinea.
Gray, M. (2005). Dilemmas of international social work: Paradoxical processes in indigenization, universalism and imperialism. *International Journal of Social Welfare, 14*(2), 230–237.
Gray, M., & Coates, J. (2010). Indigenization and knowledge development: Extending the debate. *International Social Work, 53*(5), 1–15.
Gray, M., Coates, J., & Bird, M.Y. (2008). Introduction. In M. Coates, J. M.Y. Bird, (Eds.), *Indigenous Social Work Around the World* (pp. 1–10). Burlington, VT: Ashgate.
Gray, M., Kreitzer, L., & Mupedziswa, R. (2014). The enduring relevance of indigenization in African Social Work: A critical reflection on ASWEA's Legacy. *Ethics and Social Welfare, 8*(2), 101–116.
Hayward-Jones, J. (2013). Violence: PNG's women face a crisis. The Lowy Institute. Accessed at: http://www.lowyinterpreter.org/post/2013/03/08/Sorcery-killing-draws-attention-to-treatment-of-women-in-PNG.aspx
Ife, J. (2002). *Community development: Community-based alternatives in an age of globalisation* (2nd ed.). Australia: Pearson Education.

IFSW. (2012). *Statement of ethical principles*. Retrieved August 18, 2020, from http://ifsw.org/policies/statement-of-ethical-principles/

Lawihin, D. (2012). *Shaping the future of student fieldwork in social work education at UPNG, Papua New Guinea, Applied Research Study Report*. Melbourne: Department of Social Work, Monash University.

Lawihin, D. (2018). Culturally relevant pedagogy for social work learning in Papua New Guinea: Perspectives from the University of Papua New Guinea's fieldwork program. *Aotearoa New Zealand Social Work, 30*(4), 40–55.

Lawihin, D., & Brydon, K. (2013). The current situation in social work education in Papua New Guinea. *Advances in Social Work and Welfare Education, 15*(2), 69–83.

Lovai, B. (2015). *Social work and society*. University of Papua New Guinea.

MacPherson, S. (1996). Social work and economic development in Papua New Guinea. *International Social Work, 39*, 55–67.

Mungai, N., Wairire, G. G., & Rush, E. (2014). The challenges of maintaining social work ethics in Kenya. *Ethics and Social Welfare, 8*(2), 170–186.

Nikku, R. B. (2010). Social work education in Nepal: Major opportunities and abundant challenge. *Social Work Education: The International Journal, 29*(8), 818–830.

Nikku, R. B., & Pulla, V. (2014). Global agenda for social work and social development: Voices of the social work educators from Asia. *International Social Work, 57*(4), 373–385.

Samad, A., & Hossain M. A. (2014). Indigenization of social work education in Bangladesh: Knowledge, perception and realities. In A. Tatsuru (Ed.), *Internationalization and Indigenization of social work education in Asia*. Kiyose, Japan: Japan College of Social Work.

Social Work Strand. (1995). *Social Development Information and Course for 1995*. Port Moresby: School of Humanities and Social Sciences, University of Papua New Guinea.

Sullivan, M. P., Forrester, D., & Al-Makhamreh, S. (2010). Transnational collaboration: Evaluation of a social work training workshop in Jordan. *International Social Work, 53*(2), 217–232.

Weiss-Gal, I., & Welbourne, P. (2008). The professionalization of social work: A cross national exploration. *International Journal of Social Welfare, 17*(4), 281–290.

Yip, K. (2006). Indigenization of social work An international perspective and conceptualization. *Asia Pacific Journal of Social Work and Development, 16*(1), 43–55.

Yishak, D. M., & Gumbo, M. T. (2014). Indigenising the curricula in Ethiopia from a gamo ethnic group perspective: The case of constitutional, policy and strategy provisions. *Mediterranean Journal of Social Sciences, 5*(10), 185–197.

Yunong, H., & Xiong, Z. (2008). A reflection on the indigenization discourse in social work. *The International Social Work, 51*(5), 611–622.

Yunong, H., & Xiong, Z. (2011). Further discussion of indigenisation in social work: A response to Gray and Coates. *International Social Work, 55*(1), 40–52.

20

Social Work Practicum in Chile

The Role of Field Supervisors in a Neoliberal Context

Daniela Díaz-Bórquez, Magdalena Calderón-Orellana, and Rafael Araya-Bugueño

Analysing social work education in Chile, especially that of interns, inevitably implies understanding the sociopolitical scenario in which social work is taught. This, then, the economic, political, and social context of the country, affects the practice and teaching of the profession (Miranda et al., 2018; Vidal, 2011). In this sense, ever since neoliberal reforms were installed under Pinochet's dictatorship during the 1980s, social work in Chile is practised in a precarious institutional setting, where the State, instead of guaranteeing rights, outsources services in a logic of economy of scale. This implies the delivery of services mainly in urban and highly populated areas, with social services tendered for limited periods. Consequently, this situation generates high personnel turnover, labour instability, and difficulties for the specialisation of professionals and programmes.

In this way, this context has implied the deterioration of social services and the precarisation of the professional practice of social work. As well it strengthens the idea that although professional practice is the optimal scenario for teaching and learning social work (Petrila et al., 2015), it is necessary to develop reflective processes to face the complexity of the phenomena involved. This means that it is not only necessary for students to face reality but also to reflect on it and its lessons constantly, both in the classroom and in the field (Caspi & Reid, 2002).

In the professional practice of social work, the space that guarantees the accompaniment and reflection of students is supervision, which is defined as the process of reflection focused on the student, their professional development and welfare, encouraging the improvement of their interventions and the promotion of their learning (O'Donoghue, 2010).

Thus, recognising that strengthening learning requires reflection on the practice and that the key space for this is supervision, the question arises regarding the case of Chile and how student practice and supervision is developed in a context characterised by a focused, privatised social policy based on welfare subsidies (Aguayo et al., 2018). This implies investigating the actual possibilities of practice spaces for supervision, highlighting the role of the professionals who accompany students in the field.

Thus, this chapter analyses internship training in Chile, highlighting the role of internship supervisors, in a context of weakened social services, stemming from the installation of a neoliberal development model.

Addressing these issues is of primary importance, since the practice of social work involves the insertion of students and supervising professionals in institutions with poor work conditions. Therefore, there is an urgent need to analyse this situation and plan actions that will help strengthen the role of supervisors in order to enhance the training of social work students.

It is important to note that at the time of writing this chapter, the prevailing model in Chile, characterised by a neoliberal development model and social policies, is being challenged by the Chilean citizenry through a process of social mobilisation, driven by days of protests that began in October 2019 and have resulted in the beginning of a process that seeks to create a new constitution.

For this reason, this chapter is politically relevant, as it discusses the current state of social services and social work education and allows for reflections on the new scenario demanded by citizens in Chile.

In order to meet this objective, firstly, a description of the situation of social work in Chile will be provided, focusing on the current state of internship training. Then, the model of development of the last 40 years will be described, to then review the challenges of professional supervision in this scenario through an exhaustive bibliographic review.

Social Work Education in Chile

Social work education in Chile has its origin in the foundation of the school of Social Service of Santiago de Chile belonging to the Central Board of Charity, in 1925. This became the first school of social work in Latin America (Castañeda & Salome, 2010) and the first project to train social workers in Spanish. As in Europe, the nascent schools of social work emerged in Chile at the eaves of the state in the midst of the particular social issue that was developing in the country (Vivero, 2017) and as a discipline in the service of medicine and public health (Illanes, 2001).

Four years later, the Catholic Church, through a private foundation annexed to Universidad Católica de Chile, created the Elvira Matte de Cruchaga School of Social Service, which sought to train Catholic social workers, in contrast to the lay formation of the first school (González, 2014). Regardless of the orientation of these schools and recognising the innovation that they represented, both schools stood out for the role they played in the development of other formation projects in Latin America (Manrique, 1982; Quiroz, 1998).

Since the origin of social work in Chile and for 50 years, social work education was challenged by the sociopolitical context of the country, such as the economic crisis of 1929 and the subsequent Chilean political crisis of 1931 (Universidad Catolica de Chile, 1933); the reform process of universities towards the end of the 1960s and the installation of a socialist government, to name a few milestones (Castañeda & Salome, 2010). However, no process has been so relevant for the formation of social work in Chile as the establishment of the Chilean civil-military dictatorship in 1973, which constituted a turning point for the construction of discipline, training, and professional practice (Aguayo et al., 2018; Castañeda & Salome, 2010; Jimenez, 1982).

During Pinochet's dictatorship and according to the register of the Association of Social Workers of Chile (Colegio de Trabajadores Sociales de Chile, 2019), social work students and professionals were persecuted, arrested, made to disappear, and executed by the repressive organs of the State. At the institutional level, the dictatorship closed at least five of the 11 university programmes during 1973, the year of the coup d'état, and those that remained open had to cancel admissions for the first year or reduce their number of places (Iturrieta, 2018).

The impact of the dictatorship on social work did not only involve political persecution and the closure of schools. As a result of structural reforms and constitutional changes, in 1980, through the decree with the force of Law No. 1 and then with the Constitutional Organic Law on Education of 1990 (Law No. 19,682), it was established that the title of social worker lost its university status and could be granted by different institutions of higher education and not only by universities.

This change meant the definitive closure of various university schools, in addition to the proliferation of new training centres, which directly affected the quality of social work programmes (Iturrieta, 2018; Vivero, 2017). In effect, the appearance of new actors responsible for social work education contributed to its massification, which generated a strong social segregation in terms of the different levels of training, and lower selection levels (Riquelme & Garcés, 2016).

Even though after the recovery of democracy in 1990, little by little actions were taken to recognise the profession, the neoliberal reforms implemented in the military regime and administered by the democratic governments since 1990, generated a scenario for the teaching of social work that has been maintained for more than 30 years, with a high cost for the discipline from a union perspective and from the perspective of its development and strengthening (Aspeé, 2016).

In effect, regardless of the restitution of the exclusivity of the university degree, currently, most of the social work professionals graduate from professional institutes and technical training centres that have greatly proliferated throughout the country. These institutions deliver social work degrees after completing eight or four semesters of studies, without the need for an academic degree, limiting the training since they do not guarantee the development of a critical analysis of scenarios.

In order to present the case of social work practice training in Chile, this chapter will look particularly at university training in social work, which involves not only a professional degree but a university degree. This decision, beyond legal issues, is due to the fact that the tradition of social work training in Chile is university training (Iturrieta, 2018).

Soon to celebrate its centennial, social work education in Chile, according to the Ministry of Education (Mineduc, 2020), focuses on preparing professionals through academic programmes that last between nine and ten semesters. At the end of this period, the professionals receive a degree in social work and a social worker title, which qualifies them to practise the profession in direct and indirect intervention, in public and private settings, without any other requirements or specialisation.

In the same way, the enrolment of social work in university centres, at all levels, rose to 14,222 during 2019, and the number of graduates in 2018 was 2,251. The employability of social workers in the second year was 80%. Meanwhile, the average income during the first year of work reaches USD 890, which is relatively low in comparison with other four-year study programmes and, in practical terms, is equivalent to double the legal minimum wage set at USD 433 (Mineduc, 2020).

Currently, 49 higher education institutions offer training in social work and social service through 197 vocational training programmes that are almost entirely taught in face-to-face, daytime, and evening classes. It is important to note that, of the total number of institutions, 39 are universities and that, as of 2016, there is at least one university education centre that teaches social work in each region of the country (Mineduc, 2020).

Social Work Education in the Field

Traditionally, internships have been the core of social work training in Chile (Castañeda & Salome, 2010). In general, social work programmes have more than one practical course, including pre-practices – which are practices limited in time and methodology – and internships, which are carried out at the end of the training with the aim of integrating the knowledge, skills, and values acquired learned in the programme, in a professional setting.

Based on the observation of the curricula of university programmes accredited at the time by the National Accreditation Commission (CNA, 2020), it is possible to maintain that almost all of them, with the exception of one university, include practical courses, internships, and practice workshops, among others. Likewise, it is confirmed that every time that internships are considered in the study programmes, they are integrated as courses that are developed during one semester.

The same review of curriculum maps allows to establish that in general, the schools that offer practical courses have more than one practical course, usually three to six practical courses or internships. However, the differences in the programmes concern the orientation of the internships. Although almost all programmes conclude their training with an internship, the pre-internship courses, workshops, and internships, commonly developed between year three and year four of the career, have different orientations. Thus, some programmes divide their practical courses according to the project cycle (diagnosis, intervention, and evaluation internships); according to the methodology (case, group, and community); according to the beneficiaries (families, communities, and groups); and according to the level of intervention (micro and macro level).

In general, internship training in Chile involves the insertion of the student in an institution for one or more semesters, in which they are accompanied by a field supervisor. The internship also involves the student's participation in a workshop with other interns, which is facilitated by a university professor. Finally, practical courses also involve spaces for practice tutoring, which is a moment of individual work between the student and their professor (Escuela de Trabajo Social UC, 2017). While it is possible to identify other ways to organise social work internships, this model is the most common among schools of social work in Chile (Godoy, 2016).

Tutoring is a highly demanding academic and training experience for social work interns, which is based on the accompaniment and methodological advice by a professor. This accompaniment allows: to promote and positively reinforce strengths, to make visible and overcome the observed weaknesses, to improve the overall formation, to facilitate the cultural transmission, and to contribute to the development of Chilean education and research (Anabalón et al., 2018). The two-way relationship between student and professor is also highlighted by Castañeda and Salome (2010), who indicate that the tutoring relationship allows to accompany and observe the process of professional growth of students from a comprehensive human perspective, where ethical and value formation has a leading role.

In addition, workshops have been defined as moments of learning and collective support around peer discussion and collaborative-active learning (Escuela de Trabajo Social UC, 2017). In this space the student receives feedback from their professors and peers with the aim to promote collaboration, find joint answers to student problems, and improve the commitment to learning.

Based on a bibliographic review carried out at the ETSUC (UC School of Social Work) to develop teaching innovation in practical courses, it was possible to confirm that the North American and British literature does not include the concept of practical workshops, but rather refers to the concept of seminar, a space for collective discussion, where students receive feedback from older peers (Voshel & Hurand, 2016). In this way, the practical seminars are learning spaces that together allow students to develop professional competencies and skills. In this way, it is possible to argue that the workshop, the most common learning methodology in Latin America, shares with the seminar the idea of strengthening competencies, but differs from it in the ideas of collective learning, support, and containment of workshops.

As it has been pointed out, social work internship training implies the insertion of the student in a relevant organisation for social work. In this space, the student is accompanied by an institutional or field supervisor. In general, but not always, the role is occupied by a social worker. The link between the supervisor and the schools of social work is often based on trust (Godoy, 2016). because is a role that is exercised voluntarily and without remuneration most of the time.

However, due to the increasing complexity of the scenarios in which it intervenes, the role of the field supervisor is becoming increasingly important (Zuchowski, 2016). That is why we will focus our attention on this figure, which, despite its relevance, has received little attention from the literature in Chile and Latin America.

The Field Supervision in Internship Training

Practical experience in social work is one of the central components of social work training (Massaro & Stebbins, 2015) and a critical transition point into practice (Zuchowski, 2014). In this context, guidance, accompaniment, and modelling of competencies for adequate professional performance are fundamental for the students.

Much of the accompaniment in the professional practice and the modelling of competencies is provided to social work students in the agency where they develop their work in the field. These agencies are public and private organisations that provide various social services and are committed to integrating social work students into their daily work, designating a social worker or other social science professional as the person in charge. This professional has a fundamental role within the process of practice and assumes the task of accompanying, guiding, and modelling student competencies, serving as a technical counterpart to the academic supervisor. The field supervisor also receives other names such as practicum supervisor, fieldwork supervisor, training supervisor, external social work supervisor, etc.

Supervisors serve multiple functions. Miller, Donohue-Dioh, Larkin, Niu, and Womack (2018, p. 18) note that 'supervisors perform the integral function of socializing students in the practice of social work'. The literature distinguishes – albeit with different terminologies – three main functions, also called a triad of functions for effective supervision: i) the administrative or normative function that leads students to assume professional and ethical standards of operation in accordance with the organisation, ii) the educational or training function that allows the supervisee to become a professional by acquiring specific knowledge and professional skills, and iii) the restorative or support function that helps the supervisee to face difficult and stressful situations (Dan, 2017; Ketner et al., 2017).

The complexity involved in the balanced development of these functions indicates that supervision goes beyond the mere transfer of information and involves the reflective accompaniment and personalised modelling of professional skills that allow for the achievement of desirable standards of professional performance. The idea of a personalised process implies a relational component attached to the support function of supervision, which involves reflection on the practice and emotional support students (Ketner et al., 2017; Sugawara & Nikaido, 2014; Tebes et al., 2011; Tsui et al., 2017; Walker et al., 2008). In this sense, supervision gives way to a process of bilateral communication between the supervisor and the supervisee, involving emotions, dialogue, analysis, reflection, and a certain attitude (Runcan et al., 2012); and ultimately implies a shared exploration of the intervention in a context of trust, which highlights the strengths and vulnerabilities of the supervisee (Shea, 2019), but also makes visible the challenges and vulnerabilities of the professional practice in different contexts.

In the Chilean case, in general, few publications are found in relation to practical courses. This limitation is accentuated when it comes to research and publications about field supervision in social work. Notwithstanding the above, in this chapter it is possible to present the first results obtained from the teaching innovation project 'Virtual Community of supervision of professional practice: Articulating the evaluation and feedback of learning in Social Work'[1] of the School of Social Work of Pontificia Universidad Católica de Chile.

This project is focused on developing a training space for field practice supervisors. The first part of the project considered a supervisor profile's description among the various actors who are part of the practical course, particularly students and supervisors. In this framework, it is possible to point out that supervisors give high relevance to the functions of student performance feedback, the professional care space, and the guarantee of both the achievement of the students' learning objectives and the fulfilment of the institution's own intervention objectives. It should be noted that this perception about the main functions in the task of supervision is also shared by the students.

With respect to the knowledge required to perform the role of student supervisor, supervisors themselves recognise that knowledge of effective interventions, student assessment and feedback, and of the specific subject matter that they supervise is required. In addition, the design, implementation, and evaluation of social interventions seems to be quite relevant as well. Meanwhile, students identify student performance evaluation and feedback, subject matter expertise, and social intervention techniques as the most relevant knowledge supervisors should have. As per skills, supervisors emphasise the importance of competences such as self-efficacy, which is also significant for students, in addition to the ability to provide effective feedback on the practice. Finally, in terms of supervision values and attitudes, supervisors emphasise autonomy and assertiveness in professional practice, and students point out to the trainer attitude that supervisors should have, in addition to interest in the student, reflective capacity, and professional autonomy as significant guiding values of the supervisory practice (See Table 20.1).

In general, regarding the knowledge, skills, and attitudes needed to be a supervisor, there is agreement between students and professionals. However, it is striking that students make more demands on the attitudinal sphere while supervisors focus more on knowledge. This may be due to the expectations of the role. While supervisors recognise themselves as people who need to know in order to teach, students expect supervisors to be committed to their role. However, these results are not conclusive, and more evidence is needed in this area.

Table 20.1 Field Supervisor Knowledge and Skill Required

	Supervisors' Perception	*Students' Perception*
Supervisor knowledge	Effective interventions. Student evaluation and feedback Expertise in the specific subject matter that they supervise. Networking, design, implementation, and evaluation of social interventions.	Student evaluation and feedback. Expertise in the field that they supervise. Social intervention techniques.
Supervisor skills	Ability to motivate self-efficacy.	Ability to motivate self-efficacy. Ability to effectively provide feedback about the practice.

Source: Preliminary findings of the project 'Virtual Community of supervision of professional practice: Articulating the evaluation and feedback of learning in Social Work'. Pontificia Universidad Católica de Chile.

Along with the analysis related to the spaces of agreement and disagreement between supervisors and students, it is crucial to analyse the supervisor role's exercise. In this sense, the literature on the subject and the information we have from Chile allows us to establish that the role of supervisor is highly demanding, even more so when it is exercised in conditions limited by a particular model of social service organisations.

For this reason, in order to continue analysing the practice and the role of supervisors in Chile, it is necessary to understand the scenario where supervision is exercised, that is, organisations that pursue social welfare in the midst of a subsidiary state model that assigns social services from a neoliberal perspective.

Neoliberalism and New Public Management: the Scenario for Practical Social Work Education

In Latin America, during the last 25 years of the 20th century, in a context in which countries significantly increased their foreign debt, the adoption of neoliberal economic policy measures started in the 1980s as a way out imposed by the International Monetary Fund and the World Bank (Margheritis & Pereira, 2007; Panizza, 2009). Among the neoliberal economic policy reforms and state functioning imposed are the reduction of public spending, the privatisation of public enterprises and services, and the deregulation of internal labour markets, among others (Garretón, 2012; Harvey, 2005; Huerto, 2005).

Chile stood out among the countries that applied structural adjustments with greater extremeness (Ruiz, 2020), through a process facilitated by the absence of a democratic context and the pre-eminence of a minimum or sufficient rule of law to contain the arbitrariness, abuse of power, and systematic violations of human rights from the state administration (Falabella, 2015; Garretón, 2012; Harvey, 2005).

While from the economic policy point of view the Chilean process from the 1980s onwards was characterised by the neoliberal paradigm. From the administrative point of view, it was the New Public Management paradigm that was preferred (Morales, 2014). Thus, the implementation of the reforms of modernisation of the State, following the example of Margaret Thatcher in England or Ronald Reagan in the USA, had a social impact as a result of the integration of three market mechanisms into public policies (Cunill-Grau, 2012), which were i) public-private partnerships understood as agreements for the provision of services; ii) voucher systems that act as an access mechanism to social services – such as the provision of subsidies to guarantee access to education; and iii) outsourcing, which in the Chilean case can be observed in most child, adolescent, elderly, and disabled care services.

However, despite the fact that there are exceptions in Latin America, in the case of Chile, it is clear that with the support of the State, the presence of the private sector in public activities has strongly expanded. In fact, the phenomenon of outsourcing has a long history, but for the last three decades, it has been covering areas that in the past were provided by the State (Cunil-Graul, 2016)

Some examples of these reforms in Chile are related to public education, primary health, and child and adolescent care. Each of these areas of social care were stripped of the attention of the Central Government and the functions were transferred to the sub-national or local level or to private supporters under the logic of vouchers. In other words, the State left its proactive and guaranteeing role and transferred these functions to others, subsidising the demand that was effectively met. This mechanism generated the sustained weakening of public structures, public employment and, in short, the institutional capacity of the State in these areas of public policy.

Despite attempts by post-dictatorial governments to strengthen the social protection network, the neoliberal ethos has remained the basis of the Chilean development model (Muñoz & Pantazis, 2019). Although in the case of Chile there is no evidence regarding the effect of the new public management reforms on the professional practice of social work, international evidence agrees on the effects of such reforms. In concrete terms, neoliberal reforms have meant that social workers have seen their working conditions become precarious (Berg et al., 2008; Cademartori, 2018). Indeed, regarding subcontracting processes, workers, often without contracts, provide services for limited periods, limiting their working conditions. Similarly, the development of the profession can be limited by introducing competition in the provision of services, where cooperation between institutions and professionals is not a privileged criterion (Cunill-Grau, 2012), thus affecting collective learning.

Also, in the professional practice, objectives and quality are often compromised in order to act quickly and show effectiveness (Höjer & Forkby, 2011). Evidence also shows that there has been a tendency to over-bureaucratise the role and overestimate the role of budget in social work practice (Berg et al., 2008; Höjer & Forkby, 2011)

With regard to the above scenario, it is possible to argue that social work professionals who supervise interns do so in the face of the conditions described above. Thus, supervisors have the task of training in a context of job insecurity and precarious working conditions, with a large amount of administrative work and without much interaction with other actors in the community. This context, which, although it directly affects supervisors, is a challenge for all actors involved in the teaching of social work and must therefore be addressed collectively.

The Role of Field Supervision and the Challenges for Practical Social Work Training

Teaching and learning social work in the midst of social policies based on new public management is a double challenge. This is because those who assume the role of supervisor, which in the Chilean case are social work professionals whose main job is to work in agencies, are not only stressed by their work, but also by the expectations that the students and the teaching staff of the training teams have on their role.

In this way and considering the bibliographic review and previous research in the field, it is possible to identify certain actions that would help better address the supervision of practice in the Chilean case and other contexts where policies are developed under a neoliberal model. It is essential to mention that this article does not delve into structural reforms and union demands that should be promoted in relation to social work conditions – and which are also crucial to advancing the practical training of social work. Instead, this article focuses on practices that collaborate with the current scenario of professionals and that strengthen their role in order to allow for collective processes.

First, one of the fundamental challenges of supervision is the adjustment of expectations about the process. Supervisors recognise that it is beneficial for them to know both the expected learning, expectations, and responsibilities of students, as well as the responsibilities that the internship assigns to them and to the agencies (Massaro & Stebbins, 2015). This will necessarily require accessible and fluent communication mechanisms between the universities and supervisors, since adjustments must not only be made at the beginning of the practice, but permanently, since throughout the practice students face new and more complex challenges that require actions from supervisors.

For this reason, supervisors and professors must work to establish known limits with respect to the real possibilities of accompaniment, emphasising above all critical analysis. Therefore, recognising that the professionals will be action-oriented, it is necessary to clearly establish which spaces will be supported as a group with emphasis on reflective supervision.

Secondly, according to the value of reflective supervision and from a more relational perspective of supervision, the evidence indicates that an important challenge is the attunement with the emotional needs of students (Deal et al., 2011). Thus, it is necessary for field supervisors to build a space of care for them as well. This means that supervision can be an opportunity for professionals to analyse and manage care spaces for their own practice.

Developing the relational function represents a difficulty in an increasingly normative environment, where professional exercises tend towards the bureaucratic. The difficulty is greater when seeking to develop a reflective supervision that allows bilateral learning between supervisor and supervisee (Karpetis & Athanasiou, 2017; Tebes et al., 2011). For this reason, the schools of social work should promote the idea that supervision is a learning process for the supervisor as well, encouraging practices oriented to facilitate this process.

In this sense, and recognising the particular scenario in which internships are developed, it is necessary to take into consideration what was pointed out by Fazzi & Rosignoli (2016) who determined that supervision as a self-learning tool can be an important way for social workers to develop their professionalism in terms of critical reflection. The authors state that professionals who considered students as a source of learning and admitted their active participation in the intervention had spaces to reflect on the solutions adopted in their work as social workers and identified ways to improve the quality of their daily work. On the contrary, a more bureaucratic and normative supervision leads professionals to focus on tasks by limiting the reflective capacity in the professional practice and building a professional identity that moves away from the critical sense of discipline and operational autonomy, and instead focuses on the execution of tasks over which they have no control. In other words, when there is no reflective supervision, the professional identity is situated in a role of executing public policies or predefined social programmes within the framework of a neoliberal model.

In this sense, the key is in the professional experience and the attitude towards learning, since when supervisors conceive the professional identity as a search and constant learning from practice, they favour dual learning and therefore assume a reflective attitude (Fazzi & Rosignoli, 2016). This is extremely challenging in scenarios where social intervention is carried out within the framework of temporary subsidies for the implementation of social programmes in limited times, with a high turnover of personnel, low specialisation, and therefore with professionals that do not have the resources to respond to the multiple demands posed by the intersectionality of the users, which cannot be addressed through scattered interventions.

Therefore, it is the schools of social work that should present opportunities for the supervisor to develop these skills through the organisation of supervisor meetings, regular meetings with practical courses professors, access to the schools' resources, participation in professional care spaces, training processes, supervision of supervisors, and certainly a practical course programme that allows the implementation of these actions, while limiting administrative tasks and promoting reflective spaces.

Finally, one of the most critical challenges is to not lose sight of the fact that adequate supervision of practice processes and evaluation of student performance are interdependent elements that impact the quality of care, and which must be at the service of the subjects (Carraccio et al., 2016). This implies eliminating supervisory practices that exacerbate student learning and neglect the subject that gives it meaning. We believe that this is a great opportunity to connect supervisors with the purpose of intervention, giving emphasis to the responsibility of students in this task.

Conclusions

Supervision is a key task for the professional practice of social work in Chile and in the world. However, with regard to the precarisation of social services and the working conditions of social workers that can be observed in the Chilean reality, this becomes a highly stressful task. It is for this reason that the schools of social work must direct part of their efforts to strengthen the role of supervision and create training, supervision and support opportunities for supervisors. In the same way, the academic world must make progress in the production of international knowledge regarding this role, in order to facilitate its exercise in different contexts.

Supervising students generally operates as a demand for social worker interns that generates stress processes in the supervisors themselves. Therefore, we propose that schools develop training, administrative and care resources for the professionals themselves to perform the tasks of this role and other professional roles in an effective and motivating way.

More and more exhaustive information is required regarding field supervision in social work. The generation of knowledge about the role of field supervisors, their skills and the challenges they face in different organisational and political scenarios will allow to develop training processes that promote student learning, while maintaining the focus on the subject and consequently, the quality of care.

Finally, the disciplinary challenge is to maintain supportive supervision strategies that allow for reflective supervision, even in neoliberal contexts. Reflective supervision will contribute to the professional challenge of advancing towards scenarios of greater justice and universal guarantees; taking on the political dimension of the discipline, which until now had been overshadowed by the development model and which today, within the framework of the constituent process, has a fundamental role.

Note

1 The project is financed by the fund for Teaching Innovation 2020 of the Academic Vice-Rector's Office of Universidad Católica de Chile.

References

Aguayo, C., Cornejo, R., & López, T. (2018). *Luces y sombras del trabajo social chileno*. Espacio Editorial.
Anabalón, Y., Concha, M., & Mora, M. (2018). Tutorías académicas y Prácticas Profesionales: Invitación al desempeño profesional inicial en la formación trabajadores sociales. *Revista UCMaule, 54*, 51–64. https://doi.org/10.29035/ucmaule.54.51
Aspeé, J. (2016). Análisis longitudinal de la exclusividad universitaria del Trabajo Social en Chile. *Rumbos TS, 13*, 10–32.
Berg, E. E. b., Barry, J. J. J., & Chandler, J. J. P. (2008). New Public Management and Social Work in Sweden and England: Challenges and Opportunities for Staff in Predominantly Female Organizations. *International Journal of Sociology and Social Policy, 28*(3–4), 114–128. https://doi.org/10.1108/01443330810862188
Cademartori, F. (2018). Precarización laboral en el Estado y degradación de la fuerza de trabajo: análisis en trabajadoras vinculadas a la implementación de políticas sociales. *Trabajo y sociedad: Indagaciones sobre el empleo, la cultura y las prácticas políticas en sociedades segmentadas, 31*(31), 203–222. Universidad Nacional de Santiago del Estero. ISSN-e 1514–6871.
Carraccio, C., Englander, R., Holmboe, E. S., & Kogan, J. R. (2016). Driving Care Quality: Aligning Trainee Assessment and Supervision Through Practical Application of Entrustable Professional Activities, Competencies, and Milestones. *Academic Medicine, 91*(2), 199–203. https://doi.org/10.1097/ACM.0000000000000985
Caspi, J., & Reid, W. (2002). *Educational Supervision in Social Work - a task-centred model for field instruction and staff development*. Columbia Univesrity Press.

Castañeda, P., & Salome, A. M. (2010). Perspectiva histórica de la formación en trabajo social en chile. *Revista Electrónica de Trabajo Social, 8*, 68–92.

CNA. (2020). *Acreditacion Pregrado*. https://www.cnachile.cl/Paginas/Acreditacion-Pregrado.aspx

Colegio de Trabajadores Sociales de Chile. (2019). *Acto conmemorativo Día de los Derechos Humanos −10 de diciembre*. http://www.trabajadoressociales.cl/provinstgo/actgremial27.php

Cunill-Grau, N. (2012). ¿Qué ha pasado con lo público en los últimos 30 añios? Balance y perspectivas. *Reforma y Democracia, 52*, 5–44.

Cunil-Graul, N. (2016, October). La provision privada de servicios de proteccion social. Confrontando el debate anglosajon con los imperativos de America Latina. *Reforma y Democracia, 66*, 35–66.

Dan, V. (2017). An Exhaustive View on Supervision in Social Work: History, Evolution, Current Trends. *Revista de Asistenţă Socială, 2*, 147–159.

Deal, K. H., Bennett, S., Mohr, J., & Hwang, J. (2011). Effects of Field Instructor Training on Student Competencies and the Supervisory Alliance. *Research on Social Work Practice, 21*(6), 712–726. https://doi.org/10.1177/1049731511410577

Escuela de Trabajo Social UC. (2017). *Modelo de prácticas profesionales para la escuela de trabajo social uc*. Escuela de Trabajo Social UC.

Falabella, A. (2015). L'histoire du marché scolaire au Chili et l'émergence de la Nouvelle gestion publique: Le tissu politique de la dictature néo-libérale et des gouvernements de centre-gauche (1979–2009). *Educacao e Sociedade, 36*(132), 699–722. https://doi.org/10.1590/ES0101-73302015152420

Fazzi, L., & Rosignoli, A. (2016). Reversing the Perspective: When the Supervisors Learn from Their Trainees. *British Journal of Social Work, 46*(1), 204–221. https://doi.org/10.1093/bjsw/bcu112

Garretón, M. A. (2012). *Neoliberalismo protegido y progresismo limitado. Los gobiernos de la concertacion en Chile 1990–2010*. Santiago de Chile: Editorial Arcis,

Godoy, W. (2016). *Estrategias Didácticas En La Supervisión De Las Prácticas Profesionales En La Formación De Los Trabajadores Sociales* (p. 470). Chile: Un Estudio En Tres Universidades De Santiago, Región Metropolitana.

González, M. (2014). Inside Home. La visita domiciliaria de trabajadores sociales como estrategia de vinculación entre orden institucional y familia. Chile, 1925–1940. *Ammentu, 4*.

Harvey, D. (2005). *A Brief History of Neoliberalism*. Oxford University Press.

Höjer, S., & Forkby, T. (2011). Care for sale: The influence of New Public Management in child protection in Sweden. *British Journal of Social Work, 41*(1), 93–110. https://doi.org/10.1093/bjsw/bcq053

Huerto, M. (2005). El neoliberalismo y la conformación del Estado subsidiario. *Política y Cultura, 24*, 121–150.

Illanes, M. A. (2001). Ella en Lota-Coronel: poder y domesticación. El primer servicio social industrial de América Latina. *Mapocho, 49*(primer semestre), 141–148.

Iturrieta, S. (2018). Masificación, segmentación y fragmentación de la educación superior chilena: Bienestar subjetivo de profesionales. *Revista De Ciencias Sociales, 24*(3), 83–96.

Jimenez, M. (1982). Nueve años de historia de la Escuela de Trabajo Social: 1973–1982. *Revista de Trabajo Social, 38*, 59–66.

Karpetis, G., & Athanasiou, E. (2017). Training Fieldwork Supervisors of Social Work Students at a South European University: Evaluation of the Effectiveness of a Relational Psychodynamic Model. *Journal of Social Work Practice, 31*(1), 37–49. https://doi.org/10.1080/02650533.2015.1116436

Ketner, M., Cooper-Bolinskey, D., & VanCleave, D. (2017). The Meaning and Value of Supervision in Social Work Field Education. *Field Educator, 7*(2), 1-18.

Manrique, M. (1982). *De apostoles a agentes de cambio*. Centro Latinoamericano de Trabajo Social.

Margheritis, A., & Pereira, A. W. (2007). The Neoliberal Turn in Latin America: The Cycle of Ideas and the Search for an Alternative. *Latin American Perspectives, 34*(3), 25–48. https://doi.org/10.1177/0094582X07300587

Massaro, B., & Stebbins, M. (2015). Creating an Integrative Model of Education and Support for Field Instructors. *Field Educator, 5*(2), 1-6.

Miller, J., Donohue-Dioh, J., Larkin, S., Niu, C., & Womack, R. (2018). Exploring the Self-Care Practice of Practicum Supervisors: Implications for Field Education. *Field Educator, 8*(2), 1-20.

Mineduc. (2020). *Mi Futuro | Mineduc*. https://www.mifuturo.cl/

Miranda, P., Guerra, L., Calderón, M., & Cornejo, R. (2018). Organisational Social Work in Chile. Contributions of the Social Work Journal of the Pontificia Universidad Católica de Chile. *Revista de Asistenţă Socială, 4*, 25–39.

Morales, M. (2014). Nueva gestión pública en Chile: Orígenes y efectos. *Revista de Ciencia Politica, 34*(2), 417–438. https://doi.org/10.4067/S0718-090X2014000200004

Muñoz, G., & Pantazis, C. (2019). Social Exclusion, Neoliberalism and Resistance: The Role of Social Workers in Implementing Social Policies in Chile. *Critical Social Policy, 39*(1), 127–146. https://doi.org/10.1177/0261018318766509

O'Donoghue, K. B. (2010). *Towards the construction of social work supervision in Aotearoa New Zealans : A study of the perspectives of social work*. Massey University. https://mro.massey.ac.nz/handle/10179/1535

Panizza, F. (2009). *Contemporary Latin America: Development and Democracy Beyond the Washington Consensus*. ZedBooks. https://doi.org/10.1111/j.1470-9856.2010.00455.x

Petrila, A., Fireman, O., Fitzpatrick, L. S., Hodas, R. W., & Taussig, H. N. (2015). Student Satisfaction With an Innovative Internship. *Journal of Social Work Education, 51*(1), 121–135. https://doi.org/10.1080/10437797.2015.977175

Quiroz, M. (1998). *Antología del Trabajo Social Chileno*. Universidad de Concepción.

Riquelme, V. C., & Garcés, C. R. (2016). Los problemas del stock en campos profesionales difusos: Oferta educativa en Trabajo Social. *Estudios Pedagogicos, 42*(1), 37–52. https://doi.org/10.4067/S0718-07052016000100003

Ruiz, C. (2020). Estructura y conflicto social en la crisis del neoliberalismo avanzado chileno // Structure and social conflict in the crisis of Chilean advanced neoliberalism. *Espacio Abierto, 29*(1), 86–101.

Runcan, P. L., Goian, C., & Tîru, L. (2012). The Socio-communicational Style and the Need for Supervision of Professionals from the Social Services. *Revista de Cercetare Si Interventie Sociala, 37*, 180–195.

Shea, S. E. (2019). Reflective Supervision for Social Work Field Instructors: Lessons Learned from Infant Mental Health. *Clinical Social Work Journal, 47*(1), 61–71. http://search.ebscohost.com/login.aspx?direct=true&db=sih&AN=134786407&lang=es&site=ehost-live

Sugawara, E., & Nikaido, H. (2014). Properties of AdeABC and AdeIJK efflux systems of Acinetobacter baumannii compared with those of the AcrAB-TolC system of Escherichia coli. *Antimicrobial Agents and Chemotherapy, 58*(12), 7250–7257. https://doi.org/10.1128/AAC.03728-14

Tebes, J. K., Matlin, S. L., Migdole, S. J., Farkas, M. S., Money, R. W., Shulman, L., & Hoge, M. A. (2011). Providing Competency Training to Clinical Supervisors through an Interactional Supervision Approach. *Research on Social Work Practice, 21*(2), 190–199. https://doi.org/10.1177/1049731510385827

Tsui, M., O'Donoghue, K., Boddy, J., & Pak, C. (2017). From Supervision to Organisational Learning: A Typology to Integrate Supervision, Mentorship, Consultation and Coaching. *The British Journal of Social Work, 47*(8), 2406–2420. https://doi.org/10.1093/bjsw/bcx006

Universidad Catolica de Chile. (1933). *Memoria de la Universidad Católica de Chile 1930–1931–1932*. Universidad Catolica de Chile.

Vidal, P. (2011). Caracterización de las acciones del Trabajo Social. Cambios, Continuidades y Tensiones del Chile actual. *Revista Venezolana de Trabajo Social, VI*, 42–55.

Vivero, L. A. (2017). Influencia del neoliberalismo en el Trabajo Social chileno: discursos de profesionales y usuarios. *Revista Colombiana de Ciencias Sociales, 8*(1), 126. https://doi.org/10.21501/22161201.1940

Voshel, E. H., & Hurand, S. (2016). Utilizing Student/Peer-Facilitators to Create a Dynamic Field Seminar Learning Environment. *Field Educator, 6*(1), 1-8. http://ezproxy.puc.cl/docview/1790906183?accountid=16788

Walker, J., Crawford, K., & Parker, J. (2008). *Practice education in social work : A handbook for practice teachers, assessors and educators*. Learning Metters.

Zuchowski, I. (2014). Planting the Seeds for Someone Else's Discussion: Experiences of Task Supervisors Supporting Social Work Placements. *The Journal of Practice Teaching & Learning, 13*(1), 5–23. https://doi.org/10.1921/jpts.v13i1.807

Zuchowski, I. (2016). Getting to Know the Context: The Complexities of Providing Off-Site Supervision in Social Work Practice Learning. *British Journal of Social Work, 46*(2), 409–426. https://doi.org/10.1093/bjsw/bcu133

21
Let Me Count the Ways
Multiple Discourses in Understandings of Readiness for Practice in Social Work

Karene-Anne Nathaniel

This chapter presents findings that emerged from a process to unearth prevailing understandings of 'readiness' for social work practice in Trinidad. A focus group with students, educators, senior practitioners, field instructors, and allied professionals was used to generate data on the ways that participants made sense of the concept of readiness for practice in social work. Social constructionism provided the framework for interpreting the data, such that the multiple perspectives and discourses in these discussions were highlighted. Social constructionism posits that multiple versions of reality i.e. 'truths' exist with none having greater validity than any other. This chapter will explore these multiple truths and seek to reconcile whether they should all have equal influence in field assessments. Issues of power, identity, and perspective shape discourses and are also explored. The multiplicity presented shows the complexity of social work field education and evaluation.

The study that informs this chapter was conducted in Trinidad and explored understandings of the concept 'readiness for practice' in social work from multiple perspectives. As the primary researcher, I have particular interest in this topic because of my existing role as a social work educator at the St Augustine campus of the University of the West Indies in Trinidad (SAUWI). My philosophical base, that is, the value position that drives my commitment to scholarship in teaching and learning in social work is located in an on-going quest to explicate how 'good' (academically proficient) students may become 'good' (ethical, efficient, effective) social workers. Exploring 'readiness' is simply one leg of that quest, but I consider this to be a critical step in moving education and training closer to the realities of direct practice.

Trinidad is the larger island of the twin-island Republic of Trinidad and Tobago located at the southern-most end of the chain of islands known as the Caribbean. Social work in Trinidad has traditionally been practised through state agencies such as hospitals, clinics, and health centres, mental health institutions including addiction services, social welfare services, children's homes, court systems, prisons, and public schools. Over time, specialised areas of practice have also been introduced including child protection, youth services, poverty reduction, community development, HIV-AIDS and sexual health, social displacement, disability affairs, elder care, family services, the Family Court, the Children Court, mediation, employee assistance, and services to victims of crime. Social work practitioners are involved in meeting basic needs, crisis and disaster management, child protection, domestic violence, individual therapy, group work, community organisation, and policy development. Social workers in Trinidad and Tobago mainly provide ancillary services in the health, education, and justice systems. In Trinidad and Tobago, social work positions are largely filled by persons who have a tertiary-level qualification in social work namely a certificate or bachelor's degree in social work, but there have been instances where job specifications for some social work jobs have been non-specific and stipulated simply a social science degree. There are currently no licensing requirements for social workers, but medical and psychiatric social workers, employed within the public health system, must be registered with the Board for Professions Allied to Medicine.

Literature

Social work scholars have posited that social work practice is fuzzy, complicated (Parton 2000), and creates uncertainty about professional roles and value in society resulting in anxiety and defensiveness (Brand, Reith, & Statham 2005). The initial review of the literature seemed to indicate that 'readiness for practice' as a social work concept has remained unexplained. No study has been found that directly describes or operationalises readiness; neither has any of those reviewed suggested how it may be measured. This resonated with me because of the frequent interchangeable use of the term readiness with others like 'fitness to practice' and 'safe to practice' (Walton 2005). Considerable attention is given to what is required in preparing practitioners for the field, for example the values and skills needed to critically assess theories and methods on their applicability to practice and to use them effectively (Howard, McMillen, & Pollio 2003), the resolution of unresolved feelings associated with personal trauma (Lafrance & Gray 2004), working with diversity and across ethnic lines (Maxwell et al. 2003), building the ability to be conscious of oneself, one's learning and practice and the interaction of all these (Lu et al. 2011), and building learners' commitment to advocacy and the pursuit of social justice (Barlow & Coleman 2003).

Of note is the wide range of assertions and positions in the literature on what is required for professional development in social work. This is potentially problematic because universities, such as those in Trinidad, are expected to design training programmes that meet the needs of service users, supervisors/employers, and students, and to reliably assess successful completion of training (Walton 2005). The term readiness is repeated in the literature without explanation; for example, Moss et al. (2007) observe that the skills' laboratory forum has been used to (in part) assess students' readiness to practice but does not explain what this means or exactly how it will be determined.

The concept of 'readiness for practice' seems to have been interpreted by different scholars according to their particular research interest. This is significant in that it indicates variance in viewpoints on readiness, even in empirical studies, and that there is no single agreed definition. Interestingly, no study has been found that specifies 'readiness is …' or '… may be defined as …' or '… is understood as …' As such it could be an example of a *taken-for-granted* concept that consumes the critical attention of constructionist thinkers (Burr 2015; Neuman & Blundo 2000; van Bommel, Kwakman, & Boshuizen 2012). 'Readiness for practice' is implicit in the studies identified, and consistent with the focus of this paper and the study findings, multiple understandings are put forward in the social work scholarship.

Moreover, the literature relevant to this topic seems to fall into two main categories: how to actively prepare students/practitioners to practise social work and determining who is most appropriate for the profession. The literature shows that significant attention has been paid to what should go into making an effective social worker, namely personal traits and intrinsic abilities and attitudes, and knowledge and skills content that should be taught including capacities for working with selected special populations. Considerable work has also been done on monitoring the training 'product' that is theorising about the characteristics of those who should and who should not be accepted into the social work profession, including discourses about whether it is more appropriate to assess 'goodness-of-fit' for social work at selection or during the training process. However, few studies have been found that seem to consider process dynamics, that is, what happens in between these two ends of the education continuum.

This study sought to deconstruct understanding of readiness for practice in social work, and to ascertain the extent to which shared understandings exist across the landscape of the profession. Additionally, of particular concern is the repeated use of the concept 'ready' or 'not ready' in denoting practitioners' competence in practice (Pithouse & Scourfield 2002; Triseliotis & Marsh 1996). I contend that where there is wide disparity in meaning assigned to the concept 'readiness for practice' in social work, there may be no basis for using the term to classify practitioners' aptitude for professional practice.

Focus of the Study

This study has placed 'readiness for practice' on the table for open discussion with multiple shareholder groups and has attempted to deconstruct the concept into its constituent parts as understood from these different perspectives. The objective of the study was to explore understandings of the concept 'readiness for practice' in social work in Trinidad. The study endeavoured to generate findings that answer the research question 'what is meant by "readiness for practice" in relation to social work in Trinidad?' The findings will show whether the concept may be credibly used to qualify students' and practitioners' perceived capacity for practice. Additionally, the results also indicate where attention needs to be paid within the training process to improve 'goodness-of-fit' between learners'/practitioners' abilities and direct practice.

This study is timely because of the dramatic increase, within a fairly short timeframe, in the number of institutions in Trinidad offering undergraduate programmes in social work and the importance of streamlining those offerings within an empirical and pragmatic understanding of what students and agencies need. In addition, the Trinidad and Tobago Association of Social Workers (TTASW) has been working assiduously to formally regulate professional social workers; understanding the variable ways that readiness may be understood, demonstrated, and assessed will be important in formulating and implementing such standards. However, while the study was situated in Trinidad, it does not purport to prescribe 'readiness for practice' for Trinidad. Phenomena and experience are products of social processes and not predetermined by context or another external factor (Parton & O'Byrne 2000). The important role of context in social work education and practice is acknowledged in a global sense, but the study does not reduce readiness to a specific formula for Trinidad. Readiness was treated generically with no stated reference in interviews to regional or national dynamics.

Methodology

The selected method for gathering data for the study was the focus group to draw on the inter-subjective knowledge emerging from the synergy between participants (Padgett 2008). It was a mixed group comprised of representatives of many of the key shareholders in social work education and practice. This group generated a wide range of ideas and perspectives and in so doing commonalities, compatibilities, and contradictions surfaced. This was a purposeful convenient sample of attendees at a social work conference who randomly volunteered to participate in this open forum. Twenty-three persons participated in the discussion; they represented allied professionals, social work educators, students at different levels, social workers with different levels of experience, and social work supervisors from different settings. This group represented key shareholders in social work education and practice, but did not represent all actors; service users, social work employers, and the professional association were unrepresented. The study followed strict guidelines for ethics in qualitative research, including review board approval, consent procedures, protection of participants, and security of data. Content analysis using colour coding in a line-by-line process allowed the researcher to identify themes and interpret the data. The study did not reach for saturation of ideas but for diversity, therefore all responses form part of the findings and every contribution was treated as significant.

Findings

As the primary researcher, I made a purposive decision to approach data analysis so as not impose or search for distinct characteristics in the data, as in traditional, positivist approaches (Burr 2015; Taylor & White 2001), which could have produced a concrete literal definition of readiness. Instead, I sought a more fluid understanding, embracing diversity, depth, and complexity of meanings so that I could make the data most useful. These findings are a product of a process to understand how meanings of readiness have been constructed by these participants.

Characteristics of the 'Ready' Social Worker

The significance of age, life experiences, and personal characteristics, namely maturity and identity, in understanding, defining, and assessing readiness for social work practice was highlighted. There was some disagreement among the participants, with supervisors and allied professionals holding firm in their view that these aspects were critical, while educators, students, and practitioners maintained that the appropriate application of knowledge and skills was of higher priority. The group seemed to consider readiness within the discourse of 'what does one need in order to be a social worker'. The diversity within the group facilitated several perspectives on what was needed which were debated during the course of the discussion. The following excerpts are used to demonstrate this.

The first speaker (female in her early twenties) in responding to a preceding exchange about *maturity* as pivotal to readiness, understood *maturity* as *age*, and used her own growth process to say that her youth had not hindered her development as a social worker. For her, other aspects were important, such as professional knowledge, and she treated that as distinct from her personal development.

> I am fairly young and I hear people talking about maturity and knowing yourself, I am at that stage where I am still trying to find myself. So I wouldn't say that that is one of my requirements. I think I have the confidence to do social work but while I am finding myself, I think I have the knowledge base to help someone find themselves.

This perspective was challenged with a rhetorical question about how people without certain life experiences could help others work through such experiences. A non-social work trained allied professional seemed to be suggesting that social workers need to have considerable and similar life experiences to their clients in order to be ready for social work practice.

> How can she deal with it [adolescent problem] when she herself is still trying to find herself? How well can you guide somebody on parenting when you have not experienced parenting yourself?

However, trained social workers in the group were able to challenge this assertion from their own experiences, emphasising the importance of training, skills, and knowledge that equipped them for practice.

> Lack of experience has not impaired my ability to practise my skills. (Recent graduate)
> The skill that I have to have that really talks to readiness is the ability to engage what I have in relation to the person or situation before me. I am forming my understanding of something in the engagement itself. I have some information, about how children develop, how relationships work, and I engage that with a family around *their* issues, *their* interpretation of *their* situation and where *they* want to go. (Educator)

These responses suggest that maturity and life experience may not be approximated to, or substituted for, professional knowledge and skills. This discussion demonstrated the importance of having a mixed group to create a dialectic and generate inter-subjective knowledge. As the multiple voices confronted each other they were able to hear different perspectives and to use first-hand experiences to show how prevailing ideas about how social workers are supposed to be were flawed. These exchanges also show the diversity of experiences and viewpoints. In the challenging and counter-challenging that took place, no position emerged as either dominant or subordinate and it cannot be claimed that readiness connotes one thing and not something else. The diverse and contradictory ideas about the relevance of age, maturity, and life experience as traits of the 'ready' social worker are noteworthy.

What Do I Need to Become 'Ready for Practice' in Social Work?

The students and recent graduates in the focus group shared ideas and experiences that pointed to what students might need in order to develop 'readiness'. Younger students seemed to have a future orientation, focused on developmental needs and factors they believed could foster their 'readiness for practice'. Some student participants had as yet not been placed in agencies and this might have accounted for their attention to their anticipated learning and development. They seemed to view readiness within the discourse of (future) desired contributions to social work. These participants talked about what they wanted to learn, what they thought was important for them to become 'ready for practice'. There was an emphasis on skills, that is, learning how to do social work, over knowledge building, and, as demonstrated in the first response below, some recognition of the importance of self-development:

'One thing I want to learn how to do is how to apply what I learn in social work to myself first before other clients'. (Student 1)

'I want to learn how to assess situations properly, critical thinking, and being more open-minded'. (Student 2)

Mention was also made of the anticipated role of social work educators in their development, both in terms of instruction and evaluation.

> Feedback from lecturers really helps with developing our sense of readiness. If we are not doing the right thing and they tell us how to improve, then we know how to become ready or how ready or not ready we are.

Interestingly they also acknowledged their own responsibilities as learners in building their own sense of readiness, reflecting a conscientious approach to training and perhaps indicating that the process of becoming ready is organic and fluid.

'So, my responsibility is to gather as much information as is required to become ready to practice'. (Student1)

'I agree we have to be open, to take in what lecturers give us, to do research, to find experiences, to liaise with professional social workers, to get a feel of what they think. It's up to us'. (Student 2)

The data seemed to reflect anticipated readiness and what beginning social workers were looking forward to. Their responses reflect quasi-idealism, suggesting that if they were exposed to certain teaching and learning experiences, they could become 'ready' for social work practice. For beginning students their understandings of 'readiness for social work' seemed to be about capacity for making the difference that the profession tends to market.

Ways That 'Readiness' Was Compromised

There was noticeable distinction between younger students' responses and those of advanced students about to graduate; the latter reflected a seeming sense of disappointment or unfulfilled expectations from their field practice experiences. Their responses seemed more critical and past-oriented, emphasising external factors that blocked, limited, or eroded readiness. Their insights seemed to emerge from their observations and experiences in the field. As demonstrated in the following response, for these participants, it seems that the reality of practice had not matched with what they had expected.

'What we brought in, thinking this was social work, when you go out there it is not how you think it should be'.

Their understandings of readiness seemed to evolve as they interfaced with the real world of social work practice and seems to have created dissonance and a re-examining of what they believed social work to be. The next extract shows that, for these participants, this dissonance came about not only as their early expectations were unmet, but also as they looked for signs of what they were learning in practice. When they found that the reality did not match what they had learned, their disappointment was apparent.

> There's no nexus between what you were taught in theory – the caring, use of self, to be better, and change people's lives, change individuals and communities and even to change yourself, you don't get that outside when you are placed in the placements.

The students also seemed to look forward to a professional community of which they were to become a part and were disappointed to find that that did not exist in the way they had expected, as demonstrated in the following quote:

'There is no sense of social work community; there are groups, and cliques, Social Work Association, medical social work, but I don't feel like there is a clear community'.

It is feasible that, as students faced such disappointments, they could become cynical and disillusioned by the prospects of a view of practice that did not match their initial expectations. Their conversation about readiness seemed to be saying 'How can we be expected to get ready for practice when things are not as they should be?' Their newfound awareness of the practice of social work in the *real* world may actually reflect uncertainty about their readiness for such practice.

The conversation about readiness also seemed to float students' anxieties about being evaluated and this is strongly reflected in the extent of critical discussion about assessment. The participants raised critical questions about methods of assessment in social work, suggesting that students may be disadvantaged by the criteria being used to evaluate practice competence when there were inconsistencies between what they were taught and what they faced. In their opinion, numerous aspects of the task and educational environments needed to be revisited to enhance the potential of would-be practitioners.

The following response illustrates what the advanced students saw as a significant flaw in social work education. From this participant's perspective, the method of assessment through written examinations failed to capture her learning and professional growth.

> The theoretical in the classroom is judged at the end in a written exam specific to certain topics, not necessarily the totality of what you've learned or the experiences that you have gained in practicum to work together with it that you could bring to it … In the end you are judged on an exam that is not representative of all the work you have learned or what you have inculcated into yourself or what you have practiced and grown with.

A discourse of programme evaluation was apparent, informed by their own experiences and observations, in which they pointed to shortcomings in social work education. Would-be graduates in this study seemed to understand readiness as confidence and proficiency in practice, but also regard it as a product of a strong training programme that considered and incorporated a number of elements conducive to their all-round development.

Expected Behaviours and Attitudes

Experienced practice teachers reflected their expectations of the attitude and behaviours of a social work student. They identified what they considered to be favourable characteristics with particular emphasis on personal development and self-awareness. The group appeared to have also viewed readiness in the context of assessing students' potential for social work. For the most part, practice teachers focused on non-academic factors as characteristics of readiness. In the following excerpt, participants seem to value positive self-image and self-esteem.

> The hallmark of readiness is you have to be comfortable in your skin, who you are, because if not carefully managed in terms of yourself, if you look in the mirror and you are not pleased with who you see, it will manifest itself.

Later in the conversation, the possible disastrous consequences of concealing personal challenges in student-supervisor interactions were raised to reinforce this point, e.g.

'If I am masking all the time for you, and I am hurting, and I am in the helping profession, I will self-destruct'.

Practice teachers in this group affirmed the importance of self-awareness, but also seemed to be saying that they expected students to be open about their process of self-discovery and willing to self-disclose, so that their level of self-development could be evaluated in determining readiness. This message is interesting when compared with that of the senior students who seemed disillusioned by what they had seen in practice, a little sceptical about instructors' dependability, and therefore might be reluctant to share openly with practicum supervisors about their self-development and challenges. This could be a vicious circle.

In addition to personal factors, practice teachers also valued other non-academic abilities that reflected students' capacity for independent practice. Some emphasis was placed on 'initiative-taking' for example,

> 'Someone who is ready to take initiative ... you take initiative, we discuss, you get direction, good, you ready to practice'. (Practice teacher 1)
>
> A student who can use their initiative, that's a student who is ready, psychologically, they ready, they prepared, they take on that challenge. But if a person is hesitant, doubtful, they don't want to run that risk, they not ready. (Practice teacher 2)

A fine line seemed to exist between what the practice teachers considered to be desirable and what they expected from students. At one level, practice teachers were talking about certain preferred traits; then they seemed to want to see those demonstrated in very specific ways for assessment purposes. The voice of the practice teacher can be a powerful one in practicum interactions, but as the voice of the practice teacher saying, 'this is what we are looking for in social work students' converged with student voices in this study who said 'we did not get what we needed from our training experiences', issues of perspective and power also emerged, which could also have influenced the outcome of practicum interactions. The question of 'readiness for practice' or becoming 'ready' seemed to be superseded by the dynamics of training interactions.

The Dilemma of Selection and Training

Educators stressed the challenges of both nurturing readiness and ensuring that the most suitable persons entered the profession. They seemed to approach this discussion from a macro-perspective, regarding readiness within the discourse of achieving a good fit between the product of the educational process and the mission and mandate of social work.

The following response shows educators' concerns about candidates' suitability for the profession, a factor that is extensively discussed in social work scholarship.

> At the end of one semester there are those who we know we should not be grooming them to work with people who may or may not have issues, because we have picked up that there's a personality quirk that perhaps all the introspection and self-evaluation that we are going to do is maybe not going to make that much of a difference.

There is a suggestion in this excerpt that certain behaviours or traits are signs of 'unsuitability' and should debar someone from helping professions. While these remain unspecified, the likelihood exists that subliminal messages about suitability may impact judgments about readiness for practice. This was echoed later in the discussion, where participants seemed to take a goal-oriented stance in considering the kind of graduate a programme wants. Educators seemed to be saying that training programmes should consider the desired outcome of social work training in defining criteria for selection.

> Instead of at the end of the three years, 'readiness for practice' is really at the start of the three years 'is this really who we want to come in' bearing in mind what we want to put out at the end of the three years.

These voices seemed to allude to how to create 'ready' practitioners, in particular, people who can do what is required. One participant expressed some anxiety that trained social workers might not be able to fulfil social expectations in responding to crisis situations, and used third party feedback lamenting deficits in training to question whether social work education is responding to social needs. She asserted 'it's readiness for what?'

This last statement gets to the heart of meaning-making about readiness: are graduates of social work training programmes fit for purpose? As I listened to these different voices, I was able to expand that question to 'whose purpose?', and 'who defines the purpose'? As the social work educator participants wrestled with this concept, it was apparent that they too had been asking themselves questions about the role of social work education and educators.

As these five discourses are juxtaposed, the complexity of meaning-making about readiness is apparent. Each shareholder presents a multi-faceted perspective that cannot be subordinated to those of the others, that is, one cannot say that the viewpoint of educators, for example, is more or less important than that of students.

Discussion

'Readiness for Practice' Is a Plural Construct in Social Work

The most glaring finding in this study is the complexity in understandings of readiness. When I look at the trends in the focus group discussions, what stands out is how this singular topic stimulated plural conversations about key aspects of social work education and training and revealed numerous discourses. The literature also points to this complexity from the most basic level in use of the term readiness. Walton (2005), in advocating for preparation modules for, and assessment of, social work students prior to their first exposure to direct practice, groups readiness with preparation for practice, students' fitness to practice, and being safe to practice, which are arguably different constructs. Similarly, O'Connor, Cecil, and Boudioni (2009) talk about readiness as competence and note a further distinction between competence for practice (how people perform during training) and competence in practice (how they act in the *real world* once they become qualified). In addition, O'Connor, Cecil, and Boudioni (2009) look at another dimension: whether competence/readiness is present- or future-oriented; do these terms refer to how people practise today or to their ability to function as practice changes over time?

Therefore, in the simple use of language regarding this concept, the term readiness seems ambiguous yet, curiously, understood. This appears to be the quintessential definition of *taken-for-granted knowledge* (Burr 2015) in social work: within the profession, readiness remains unexplained while at the same time is used frequently and accepted as an appropriate term for describing various permutations of complex processes and experiences, for example, synergising academic knowledge and translating it into the capacity to relate to service users and use professional judgement (Giddings & Vodde 2003). Horwath and Thurlow (2004) explain 'professional judgment as the interpretive use of knowledge, practical wisdom, a sense of purpose, appropriateness and feasibility' (p. 9) requiring critical assessment of information, application of diverse knowledge and experience, reflectivity, and the ability to speak confidently about one's decisions. The literature is consistent with the study findings about the complex array of abilities required.

The data also showed that multiple perspectives on readiness coexist, and that constructs of readiness are informed by individual expectations, preferences and experiences. In essence, it may be risky to *take for granted* that everyone knows what everyone else means when one speaks of readiness for practice in social work. From my review of the literature, readiness is not described; neither is fitness nor safe to practice. This may be a testament to the fact that these phenomena are *taken-for-granted knowledge* within the profession. So, if understandings of readiness are taken as given, yet the phenomenon is highly complex, variable, and subjective, the question is: how are parties to social work education and practice able to decide who is ready or not?

Assessing Social Work Practice

Multiplicity and complexity are recurring traits in the different discourses on readiness; in motivation, in professional identity and socialisation, in power dynamics, in nurturance, in application, and all these come together to make for highly complex assessment practices and interactions. I also stated that the different facets in meaning-making about readiness seem to converge on the issue of practice assessment, and throughout the data the experience of being assessed seems at odds with the preparation they have received and sense of readiness.

Giddings and Vodde (2003) suggest that where supervision is perfunctory, practice teachers rely on student self-assessment reports to monitor progress; even then they are used mainly for formative evaluations and are incorporated into the summative assessment at the discretion of the practice teacher. Crisp, Green Lister, and Dutton (2006) question whether practice teachers are sufficiently knowledgeable to assess students; the power dynamics in assessment interactions can lead to undermine self-evaluation and lead to tacit acceptance of practice teachers' conclusions. However, there is also a contradiction in Crisp, Green Lister, and Dutton's argument; the authors posit that self-assessment can restore power, but they also observe that student self-assessments must be validated by practice teachers in order to factor into formal assessments and final grades. It appears that the core abilities that are valued in social work, such as reflectivity and self-evaluation and -regulation, could be eroded by experiences in training and practice. This seems to be reflected in the underlying frustration and cynicism in the message of students about to graduate: *how can I even speak of readiness for practice when my learning experiences have weakened my belief in my abilities?*

Participants also suggested that various aspects of social work, which could constitute readiness, are intangible and therefore cannot be measured, and were undecided about whether measurable criteria for readiness and social work practice as a whole are necessary. Taylor (2000) highlights that *non-academic* factor, for example life experience, maturity, commitment, and motivation, are pivotal in professional socialisation, mirroring critical aspects identified in this study, and are treated as important in social work education. If it is accepted that such non-academic, intangible qualities are essential for social work, and I aver that these are virtually impossible to measure because of the diversity of student motivation and experience, the profession may be better able to move towards developing methods for evaluating practice that are better suited to social work, for example consistent and widespread use of portfolios (Cournoyer 2013) and active service user involvement (Skilton 2011).

Critical Unanswered Questions Raised

In the course of this discussion, I have attempted to emphasise the span of complexity, in understandings of readiness revealed in the study, and the critical questions that have been raised further underscore these findings. It is clear from the data that readiness for practice in social work cannot be understood in isolation from numerous factors; namely, the personal and professional experiences of parties in social work education and practice, the dynamics of teaching and learning, power, professional, and personal identity, especially as they play out in practicum interactions, and, of particular significance, individual sense-making by all parties concerned about what professional practice entails and requires. To some degree, these seem to be understood as predictors of readiness development.

The questions raised by participants are simultaneously critical, Socratic and rhetorical; they indicate that this readiness conversation stimulated depth of thinking about social work education, practice and practitioners. Additionally, participants underscore the point that there are no clear-cut answers to many of the associated issues (endorsed by the literature) and that it is necessary to continuously pay attention to how these issues evolve over time and impact practice of the profession.

An underlying question in this critical conversation was which comes first? (as in the 'chicken and egg' dilemma). In terms of the importance of certain cognitive abilities, what Lu et al. (2011) refer to as meta-cognition skills, in applying personal, inter-personal, and theoretical learning to practice, do students need to be functioning at a nominal cognitive level upon entry, or are learning and practice designed to foster these skills? Must one resolve personal issues prior to embarking on social work training, or can training provide opportunities for reflection and growth, and the support to work on them along the way?

These critical questions, as well as the discussions of threats to readiness development and the challenges to assessing readiness invalidate the idea of readiness for practice as a concrete, measurable step towards conferring professional status. This message is consistent with social work scholarship; many of the associated concepts in social work have a wide range of interpretations, namely fit to practise, safe to practise, and readiness to practise (O'Connor, Cecil, & Boudioni 2009; Walton 2005), preparation for practice (Allen et al. 2010; O'Connor, Cecil, & Boudioni 2009), the call to social work (Daniel 2011; LeCroy 2012), suitability for social work (Barlow & Coleman 2003; Tam & Coleman, 2009; Unwin, Van Soest, & Kretzschmar 2006), and professional identity and professional socialisation (Ben Shlomo, Levy, & Itzhaky 2012; Miller 2013). This study reveals that all of these are tied up with understandings of readiness for practice, therefore a major consideration is the extent of ambiguity that prevails within the social work profession (and why is this so), as against directing attention on explicating one concept or another.

Conclusion

Interest in this topic was stimulated on the one hand by public outcry demanding *where are the social workers*? often in response to personal or community trauma brought on by disaster, abuse, and violence, particularly where children and youth are involved. In addition, I have been privy to expressed concerns from senior social workers, allied professionals, and others that social workers and social work students are not *ready* to practise when they come into the field. As a social work educator I have been cognisant of the changing profile of social work students in the last 15 years with increasing numbers of students who would be classified as millenials and Gen Zs (18–24) enrolling in the SAUWI programme. I have considered whether their young ages and lack of life experiences required specific support to get them ready to meet the demands of practice. Exploring understandings of readiness was thought to be a useful starting point to bridge any existing gaps between social work curricula and training and the needs of professional practice.

I previously regarded readiness as an indicator of fit between practitioner capabilities and what was required in practice, but I had also noted that the term was being used differentially by different actors, many times as an assessment of practitioner aptitude, and other times as a seeming indictment of the individual's personal characteristics and suitability for social work. Multiple expectations and messages about social work practice could create confusion and anxiety in the student. I started to question the breadth of interpretations of readiness, the different ways in which the concept was used and the spoken and unspoken expectations of the ready student. I began to wonder how these different interpretations were manifest in the assessment process and the extent to which these assessments could disadvantage students and newly qualified social workers. The study revealed that there are significant aspects of practice learning and evaluation that could disempower students, thus these insights could potentially raise concerns about equality and anti-oppression (universal values in social work with respect to service users) as they relate to social work students.

I have frequently made mention of the complexities in understandings of readiness revealed in this study. This is perhaps the most riveting finding of this research from which I have drawn certain conclusions. Numerous factors contribute to this complexity:

(i) the number of actors in social work education and practice, whose perspectives I purposively solicited for this research.
(ii) the active role of subjectivity, which I also valued highly.
(iii) the centrality of the individual both in sense-making about social work in general and in translating learning into practice; and
(iv) the numerous discourses in social worker development – professional identity, professional socialisation, reflectivity, professional gatekeeping, and the many dynamics of practicum and practice assessment, that have been revealed.

Several critical questions were raised by participants in the course of this study for which no clear answers were derived; the process of questioning and re-questioning positions and practices was instructive in revealing the several intersecting discourses in social work education and practice. However, there were points in the research where my own constructionist orientation was challenged by the allure of clear standards and measurable criteria for determining readiness and associated phenomena, such as suitability, fitness, and competence to practise, which could be universally and equitably applied. By the end of the study, I surmised that, in light of the complex and multi-dimensional nature of social work and the innumerable permutations of personal, inter-personal, interactional, environmental, and contextual elements involved, the quest for measurable indicators of readiness draws some attention away from process factors in education and training experiences through which the student develops capacity and confidence to practise.

While I appreciate the textural richness and welcome the dialectical quality apparent in the discussion, I also see this complexity as contributing to vagueness in meaning-making and in operationalising readiness. This ambiguity is a constant theme in the literature, extending from questions such as what social work is and what social workers do (Asquith, Clark, & Waterhouse 2005) right across the many discourses in social work. To objectify complexity does not imply that this is a problem; on the contrary, I argue that social work educators should claim it and underscore it. In this way, they are more likely to be aware of the full implications of the use of terms such as 'readiness', 'ready', and 'not ready' in denoting and evaluating practitioner capabilities. The question is, does the use of the term 'readiness' capture its fluid, organic, and plural identity, which the study revealed, or does it instead connote a static, fixed concept?

I posit that how readiness is used in the literature and in interactions takes for granted that there is collective and universal understanding of what it means and what it looks like. The assumption of taken-for-granted knowledge about concepts such as 'readiness for practice' is found to be a critical limitation of the move towards universal regulation in a profession that is grounded in the realities of local contexts.

Additionally, this study directs the profession away from terms such as 'readiness', 'ready', or 'not ready' which are static labels for practice capabilities and ripe with ambiguity. Instead, I have highlighted the constituent aspects of social work learning and practice, namely the many factors in the practicum experience; the process of professional socialisation and professional identity development; and implementing appropriate methods for social work practice assessments. These require concerted efforts to enhance the social work education outcome for students.

References

Allen, L., Donalds, S., Hinds, K. & McLean Cooke, W. (2010). Preparing to Practise: An Experiential Laboratory Approach for Beginning Social Work Students. *Caribbean Journal of Social Work, 8–9*, 78–95.
Asquith, S., Clark, C., & Waterhouse, L. (2005). *The Role of the Social Worker in the 21st Century. A Literature Review*. Edinburgh: Information and Analytical Services Division, Scottish Executive Education Department. Retrieved from http://www.scotland.gov.uk/Publications/2005/12/1994633/46334.
Barlow, C. & Coleman, H. (2003). Suitability for practice guidelines for students: a survey of Canadian social work programmes. *Social Work Education, 22*(2), 151–64.
Ben Shlomo, S., Levy D., & Itzhaky, H. (2012). Development of professional identity among social work students: contributing Factors. *The Clinical Supervisor, 21*(2), 240–255.
Brand, D., Reith, T., & Statham, D. (2005). *The Need for Social Work Intervention: A Discussion Paper for the Scottish 21st Century Social Work Review*. Web only: Information and Analytical Services Division, Scottish Executive Education Department. Retrieved from http://www.scotland.gov.uk/Resource/Doc/47121/0020810.pdf.
Burr, V. (2015). *Social Constructionism*. London: Routledge.
Cournoyer, B. R. (2013). *The Social Work Skills Workbook* (7th ed.). Belmont, CA: Brooks/Cole, Cengage Learning.
Crisp, B. R., Green Lister, P. & Dutton, K. (2006). Not Just Social Work Academics: The Involvement of Others in the Assessment of Social Work Students. *Social Work Education: The International Journal, 25*(7), 723–34.
Daniel, C. (2011). The path to social work: Contextual determinants of career choice among racial/ethnic minority students. *Social work education, 30*(8), 895–910.
Giddings, M. M., & Vodde, R. (2003). A Conceptual Framework for Foundation Practicum and Seminar: The Progressive Adaptation and Integrative Model. *Journal of Teaching in Social Work, 23*(1–2), 123–45.
Horwath, J., & Thurlow, C. (2004). Preparing Students for Evidence-based Child and Family Field Social Work: An Experiential Learning Approach. *Social Work Education, 23*(1), 7–24.
Howard, M. O., McMillen, C. J., & Pollio, D. E. (2003). Teaching Evidence-Based Practice: Toward a New Paradigm for Social Work Education. *Research on Social Work Practice, 13*(2), 234–59.
Lafrance, J. & Gray, E. (2004). Gate-keeping for Professional Social Work Practice. *Social Work Education, 23*(3), 325–40.
LeCroy, C. W. (2011). *The call to social work: Life stories*. Sage.
Lu, Y. E., Ain, E., Chamorro, C., Chang, C. Y., Feng, J. Y., Fong, R., ... & Yu, M. (2011). A new methodology for assessing social work practice: The adaptation of the objective structured clinical evaluation (SW-OSCE). *Social Work Education, 30*(02), 170–185.
Maxwell, J., Williams, L., Ring, K., & Cambridge, I. (2003). Caribbean Social Work Education. *Caribbean Journal of Social Work, 2*, 11–35.
Miller, S. E. (2013). Professional Socialization: A Bridge between the Explicit and Implicit Curricula. *Journal of Social Work Education, 49*(3), 368–86.
Moss, B. R., Dunkerly, M., Price, B., Sullivan, W., Reynolds, M., & Yates, B. (2007). Skills laboratories and the new social work degree: one small step towards best practice? Service users' and carers' perspectives. *Social Work Education, 26*(7), 708–722.
Neuman, K. & Blundo, R. (2000). Curricula Philosophy and Social Work Education: A Constructivist Perspective. *Journal of Teaching in Social Work, 2*(1/2), 19–38.
O'Connor, L., Cecil, B. & Boudioni, M. (2009). Preparing for Practice: An Evaluation of an Undergraduate Social Work 'Preparation for Practice' Module. *Social Work Education, 28*(4), 436–54.
Parton, N. & O'Byrne, P. (2000). What Do We Mean by Constructive Social Work? *Critical Social Work, 1*(1). Retrieved from http://www1.uwindsor.ca/criticalsocialwork/what-do-we-mean-by-constructive-social-work
Padgett, D. K. (2008). *Qualitative Methods in Social Work Research* (2nd ed.). Thousand Oaks, CA: Sage Publications Inc.
Parton, N. (2000). Some thoughts on the relationship between theory and practice in and for social work. *British Journal of Social Work, 30*(4), 449–463.

Pithouse, A., & Scourfield, J. 2002. Ready for Practice? The DipSW in Wales: Views from the Workplace on Social Work Training. *Journal of Social Work*, 2(1), 7–27.

Skilton, C. J. (2011). Involving Experts by Experience in Assessing Students' Readiness to Practise: The Value of Experiential Learning in Student Reflection and Preparation for Practice. *Social Work Education: The International Journal*, 30(3), 299–311.

Tam, D. M. Y. & Coleman, H. (2009). Construction and Validation of a Professional Suitability Scale for Social Work Practice. *Journal of Social Work Education*, 45(1), 47–63.

Taylor, I. (2000). Social work education.

Taylor, C. & White, S. (2001). Knowledge, Truth and Reflexivity: The Problem of Judgement in Social Work. *Journal of Social Work*, (1), 37–59.

Triseliotis, J. P. & Marsh, P. (1996). *Readiness to Practise: The Training of Social Workers in Scotland and Their First Year in Work*. Edinburgh: Scottish Office Central Research Unit.

Unwin, C. A., Van Soest D., & Kretzschmar, J. A. (2006). Key Principles for Developing Gatekeeping Standards for Working with Students with Problems. *Journal of Teaching in Social Work*, 26(1), 163–80.

van Bommel, M., Kwakman, K. & Boshuizen, H. P. A. (2012). Experiences of Social Work Students with Learning Theoretical Knowledge in Constructivist Higher Vocational Education: A Qualitative Exploration. *Journal of Vocational Education and Training*, 64(4), 529–42.

Walton, C. (2005). How Well Does the Preparation For Practice Delivered at the University Prepare the Student for Their First Practice Learning Opportunity in the Social Work Degree? *The Journal of Practice Teaching & Learning*, 6(3), 62–81.

22
Mental Shortcuts
Representativeness Heuristics in Evaluations and Social Work Practice Assessment

Karene-Anne Nathaniel

In her book *Practice Imperfect: Reflections on a Career in Social Work*, Rae Tucker Rambally (2002), a Trinidad national living and practising in the UK and Canada for more than 20 years, described her initiation to social work as driven by her own desire to help, her religious socialisation, and her early exposure to acts of giving in her family and community. She also admits that she was eager to engage directly with clients so she could help them and, because she had so much in common with them, she relied on her own experiences, and used herself as a reference to help them find solutions. While she acknowledged that her lack of formal training at times led to her feeling inadequate in practice, she seemed to express a 'readiness *to* practice' social work that was informed by her career aspirations, motivation, and own desire to serve. So even though Rambally lacked preparation, she was confident about her abilities; but would a practice assessor conclude that she was 'ready for practice'? What criteria would they use to determine whether she was 'ready' or not? And would all assessors agree on those criteria? These are the kinds of critical questions about the consistency of practice assessment in social work that evoked interest in this topic.

This chapter presents a conceptual discussion informed by findings from a focus group discussion with field educators on the island of Trinidad in the Caribbean, about their understandings of readiness for practice in social work and how, from their perspective, it should be assessed. This chapter builds on the findings of earlier work that highlighted variability in perspectives on acceptable practitioner behaviour, suitability, and fitness for practice, and expectations of different shareholders in education and practice. That study placed numerous shareholders in conversation with each other, and it was evident that each sub-group had a different perspective on what was important in nurturing and evaluating social work students and practitioners. Field educators play a crucial role in social work education as teachers, mentors, and assessors for social work students, and it can be said that they effectively shape the education product and the future of the profession. Therefore, this focus group was organised to provide a dedicated platform for them to discuss their perspectives.

DOI: 10.4324/9781003270119-26

Key Research Debates

Practice assessment in social work, together with suitability and fitness assessments, have been widely explored in the literature; there seems to be variability in formulations of what to look for and how to evaluate students and practitioners. Contemporary scholarship seems to be located within a discourse of *how does one become a professional social worker who is fit for purpose* as outlined in regulatory and accreditation standards. Simultaneously, there seems to be a resurgence of criteria-oriented studies (for example Lu, Ain, Chamorro, Chang, Feng, Fong, Garcia, Leibson Hawkins, & Yu 2011) that are purposed on creating scales or inventories for assessing practice, indicating possible revisiting of the positivist orientation that values objective measurements. For purposes of research, I focused on the concept of 'readiness for practice' which is regularly used as a blanket term to describe students' or practitioners' capabilities.

While 'readiness' has not been defined in the literature, implicit in different studies are variable ways of thinking about it. Some scholars frame it as a characteristic of professional competence (Le Maistre, Boudreau, & Paré 2006). Others take a pedagogical view and look at selected teaching/learning outcome based on selected instructional methods used (Smith & Van Doren 2004; Steffes 2004). Researchers have also considered self-assessment on the part of the student/practitioner in terms of self-efficacy, confidence, and feelings of competence to deal with the demands of practice that may not be externally observed or evaluated (Le Maistre, Boudreau, & Paré 2006; Mathias-Williams & Thomas 2002; Preston-Shoot 2003). Pithouse and Scourfield (2002) considered the extent to which practice assessors are satisfied that students have achieved the professional skills and aptitudes valued by the institution. It is this latter point, that of assessors being 'satisfied' which struck a chord with me, as in my mind 'satisfaction' speaks to a level of subjectivity that may not be quanti- or quali- fiable. Additionally, it is unclear how assessor 'satisfaction with performance' aligns with reflective practice and self-assessment on the part of the practitioner as highlighted by Le Maistre et al. (2006) and others. Constructionist thinking about discourses and identity and the role they play in interactions (Burr 2015) proved useful in analysing this dichotomy.

Conceptual Framework

An appreciation of discourses – how they manifest, how they intersect, and how they shape behaviour – is central to constructionist thinking, and proved highly valuable for framing the findings. Discourse is an important concept in constructionist theory, explained as representations of the world, of events, or of phenomena each consisting of multiple understandings of them (Burr 2015). Discourses are macro-constructs, created within any of a number of contexts, and can provide a platform for opinions and beliefs to give them particular meaning (White 2004). Each social phenomenon has multiple discourses that can vary by innumerable factors, and so the presentation and meaning of the phenomenon can also vary. Using the phenomenon 'readiness for practice' as the example, a social work student may posit that being ready means knowing what to do to help a client. The underlying discourse could be that knowledge and skills are fundamentals of readiness, or that readiness is understood as efficiency as a helper. From a different perspective, a field educator may say that readiness is about the practitioner's confidence in practice, which could be situated within a discursive context of self-identity or professional attitude as reflecting readiness.

Another important consideration is the relationship between discourse and power; each discourse confers power on some individual, group or community. Staying with the same illustration as above, the 'readiness as self-identity' or '… confidence in abilities' discourse situates power in each student/practitioner. Discourses such as 'readiness as ethical practice', '… taking instruction', '… attitude to authority' and '… accountability', position field educators in powerful roles in gatekeeping the profession; the gatekeeping responsibility also blurs the lines between mentor and assessor (Le Maistre, Boudreau, & Paré 2006).

Labelling a practitioner as 'ready' or 'not ready' may depend on the discursive orientation of the onlooker, that is, what is he/she looking for? From the angle of where the power lies, those in influential positions like field educators or line supervisors can make themselves heard more frequently. Those who are in positions of power (bearing in mind that as Foucault (1983) explains, power is not one-dimensional or one-directional), can adopt discursive positions informed by knowledge from any of a number of sources (e.g. own ideas or experiences, taken-for-granted knowledge, convention), and which are treated as truth because position-holders have influence. Understandings of readiness may be intertwined with such processes; versions of readiness that have been accepted and used to drive learning, instructional and evaluative practices may be applied uncritically, and overlook other truths that are equally significant.

The evaluation of social work abilities is made when performance is aligned with selected standards, e.g. in competency-based assessments. For me this raises questions about who determines these standards, are they universally applicable, and how are decisions made on whether performance matches standards. Heuristics of decision-making (or 'mental shortcuts') are used for making judgements in situations of ambiguity or uncertainty and are understood as flawed processes because they generate human error and biases (Tversky & Kahneman 1973, 1974 as cited in Belhekar 2017). Belhekar (2017) also cites Kahneman and Tversky (1972) that representativeness heuristics actively use stereotypes in decision-making and evaluations are based on the extent to which the subject exhibits similar characteristics. If practice capabilities are constructed out of social interaction, it may be more likely that evaluation of practitioner 'readiness' can be influenced by pre-existing biases and expectations, and subjective experiences, that is, by how people think, act, and interact. Although constructionists assert that multiple versions of reality exist with no one being more valid than the other, field educators and supervisors have legitimate authority to evaluate practice, so their 'truth' about practitioner or student performance is influential. Therefore, the risk that subjectivity and representativeness heuristics play a role in professional judgment is a concern for social work practice assessment.

Methodology

This was a basic small-scale qualitative study using a focus group consisting of ten experienced social workers with over three years' social work field education experience from a range of social work settings. As an exploratory study, the researcher did not reach for representativeness, transferability of findings, or saturation as desirable outcome. While the small scale of this study is a limitation as it is not possible to transpose the findings to all field educators in Trinidad, Crouch and McKenzie (2006) suggest that representativeness and sample size may be of little consequence where studies are more concerned with specific aspects of an issue or situation (as perceptions or viewpoints), than with establishing relationships between them and with some larger phenomenon or social problem. This study was limited to how these field educators, as agents of social work education and professional gatekeepers, made sense of 'readiness for practice' and its evaluation in social work.

Letters of invitation to participate were distributed to attendees at a biannual field educators' workshop at the University of the West Indies Trinidad Campus. Fifty unique individuals representing a cross section of social work and allied agencies attended these workshops and invitations were extended to all of them. The letter provided basic details about the study, and specified that interested persons with a minimum of three years of providing field instruction for social work students on placement could contact the primary researcher. The study was exempted from ethics committee approval as it did not involve vulnerable populations and posed negligible risk.

All final participants were female, representing four public agencies, two faith-based organisations, and two non-governmental organisations. Six of the ten participants were holders of bachelor degrees in social work, one had an MSW, and the other three had degrees in other social science disciplines. They all held their present positions for at least five years.

The focus group was held at an off-campus facility of the University of the West Indies. The discussion was free-form, loosely guided by two facilitators posing three core guiding questions: 1. *what is your understanding of 'readiness for practice' in social work in Trinidad;* 2. *what does a 'ready' social worker look like?* 3. *How do you know if a student/practitioner is ready or not?* The discussion was audio recorded and there was a rapporteur on hand. Data was transcribed and analysed using content analysis and colour coding in a line-by-line process to extract themes from the discussion. Open coding produced preliminary core ideas from the conversation around each question, e.g. statements about age and life experience were prominent for question 1, fearlessness for question 2, and self-awareness for question 3. Axial coding created clear themes around participants' use of subjective knowledge in their contributions, and memos made by the facilitators and during the coding process showed consistent threads in the insights provided. The findings presented represent the researcher's interpretation of not only what was shared, but the implications for students' assessment. Therefore, the discussion is more conceptual, as it looks beyond the actual text to determine common threads in the sense-making process, and possible consequences for student assessment.

Findings

As the focus group discussion unfolded, respondents put forward their own ideas, and certain threads were evident, namely, the significance of participants' past and current experiences in social work settings both as students and workers, and their individual sense of professional identity. The findings could be framed as answering the tacit question 'what have my experiences taught me about how to get myself/others ready for practice and what should I look for?' Additionally, respondents' sense of identity as professional social workers seemed to feature prominently, driving a discourse about what they thought they needed, or what they believe had contributed to strengthening their professional self-images. Reflectivity was apparent as they were able to integrate their experiences, sense of self, and understandings and expectations of social work, to construct ideas about how to promote and assess readiness. Field experience, that is, practicum, emerged primary and impactful in shaping participants' professional identity, as well as their understanding of what it means to be a 'ready' social worker.

The themes that follow represent notable threads in the conversation. Participants talked about their own preferences for instruction, what they expected from a 'ready' social worker, priorities in assessment, and examples of how they used of subjective knowledge in their sense-making.

Participants seemed to rely substantially on their own experiences as learners, mentors, and assessors in their approach to practice evaluation. Furthermore, a wide range of preferences and perspectives emerged. The diversity in experience shared created wide variation in understandings of readiness and expectations of students/practitioners. Participants' personal and professional identity, the centrality of lived experiences, whether as a student or practitioner, and the reflective process were seemingly intertwined in meaning making about readiness. Implicit in the discussion was the message: 'Who I am as a person and how I see myself as a social worker are functions of my experiences, whether positive or negative, and as I reflect on and make sense of those experiences, I come to a clearer understanding of how my own sense of readiness was achieved'. It was as though they each had a personal discourse that asked 'what worked/didn't work for me?' and they drew from those individual experiences and preferences, even expectations, about what education and training for the development of competence in practice, should entail. Additionally, participants identified methods and support systems that were, or could have been, beneficial to their development. They also examined the teaching methods they employed that achieved favourable results.

Preferences

The thread of 'preferences' shows a variation in priorities, targets for development, teaching strategies, which are seemingly informed by each participant's individual choices. As the participants exchanged ideas, the influence of their own preferences on their practice as field educators was apparent.

Teaching and Learning

Participants showed preference for interactive teaching methods, especially role playing. It is noteworthy that in this discussion the methods of social work education was emphasised over content, and preference for interactivity and experiential learning emerged. Participants spoke freely about how, in their own development, these activities, and the supportive feedback they received, helped them develop confidence as young practitioners, e.g.:

> 'role-plays which gave us an idea of what kind of cases we would meet'.
> 'simulated Case Conferences'.
> 'I [educator] do the role-playing and I would interact with the students, when they do anything I would give praises and I would support them and tell them they doing well'.

One field educator outlined in some detail her own approach to students to help foster their sense of confidence and self-awareness.

> I [educator] allow them [students] to share how they feel, if they feel good about what they did. I would encourage them to share how they feel about what went or didn't go well, why you think it did not go the way you wanted. Just letting them vent, not letting them feel like I know everything when I don't. Just letting them feel comfortable.

The educator seems to be stating a preference for open communication with students. She vividly describes mutuality in the student-supervisor interaction, permission to make mistakes, and the opportunity to practice reflectivity in a supportive environment is valued highly in a practicum agency.

Student Attitude to Learning

Participants reflected on their experiences as educators and observed students' apparent reluctance to be honest about their issues and needs, and a seeming distrust of the education process. There seemed to be a 'role of the learner' discourse, in which field educators were saying 'they (students) have to question and challenge and we have to be open to that'; and also 'they have to trust us, be honest and open about what their needs are and seek our help'. They also saw that being able to seek the necessary help to address personal difficulties whether or not they chose to disclose was an important responsibility students needed to embrace. Implicit in the data is the importance of the interpersonal and relational aspects of the learning environment in which students can openly and 'safely' explore their development with their field educator.

The ideas expressed here as preferences in determining practitioner readiness are not measurable or universal, but highly variable and fluid, and informed by individual sense-making, skills, and temperament. Similarly, students have different capacities, needs, and personalities, and there are numerous dynamics in the setting and interaction that affect behaviour, not the least of which are power and identity. A question may arise as to parity in practice assessments if students' performance is gauged against their responses to preferred teaching, learning, and capabilities identified by these field educators.

Assessing Readiness

Participants provided insight into what they viewed as the indicators of readiness. For this group, observable characteristics of readiness were readily identifiable and the data seemed to reflect accepted competencies, namely technical know-how in being able to carry out tasks, attitude to the work and clients, and self-confidence. There was a level of conviction in their statements, reflecting their assurance that they could identify a ready student:

'How I know that a student is ready? When they connect, when they are into it ... if the person can make a nice marriage between theory and practice'.

(Field Educator 1)

'Someone who is ready to take initiative ... you take initiative, we discuss, you get direction, good, you ready to practice'.

(Field Educator 2)

'And how you know their readiness is ... they eager ... if they can't wait, (student attitude is ...) 'They called me and I responded'.

(Field Educator 3)

I know you are ready when you have internalized the culture. So much so that you know what to say, when to say, you know who's in control, you know the customs and habits, what to deviate from. I know you are ready when you understand the culture and when you know boundaries.

(Field Educator 4)

It is noteworthy again that respondents spoke about their looking for what might be considered intangibles as indicators of competence. Additionally, different people seemed to value different traits and behaviours, and this was manifested again here in the discussion of assessment. I can see a challenge emerging when it comes to formal assessment in light of these multiple viewpoints and the conviction with which they are held by individual field educators as 'truth'. In my original musings about the topic of 'readiness for practice', I considered whether we were being totally fair to the student/practitioner in labelling them 'ready' or 'not ready' when the differentiation seemed to lie along a continuum from blurry to arbitrary, and clearly subjective.

The following two responses from an exchange in the field educators' group about how the students' temperaments allow for evaluation of their readiness, show how fixed ideas about personal characteristics can be flawed, and I think this reveals an inherent danger in the assessment of practice based primarily on personal traits and at the discretion of individual assessors.

> 'When a student is receptive to the learning ... When they challenge you as a practice teacher ... receptive and enthusiastic about the learning ... they have drive' (field educator 5).
>
> 'as well as you can be calm too, because my last student was, very ... seemed timid and when she was finished, the outcome was positive. That was just her personality' (field educator 6).

It seems that these preferences are closely tied to power and position in field placement interactions. Additionally, the data contains a number of intangible characteristics that can be open to interpretation, adding to an already complex interaction between the powerful practice teacher and the subordinate student whose practice needs to satisfy his/her supervisor in order to achieve a successful outcome.

It is instructive that field educators, reputedly the most powerful figures in the training environment in terms of assessing practice, specified variable, and subjective indicators of readiness. This can suggest that selected field educators might look for specific things, and begs the question whether in those situations there is room for uniqueness and innovativeness, in other words, can a student afford to be different? How does a student in this discursive and social context negotiate his/her brand of professional identity to the satisfaction of a supervisor who may be looking for specific yet esoteric qualities that are variable by person and situation?

How Do They Determine Whether a Practitioner Is Ready or Not? The Use of Subjective Knowledge in Assessment

Participants were asked to identify ways that readiness might be demonstrated or measured. Once again it was apparent that understandings of what it means to be 'ready for practice' and what that might look like, were drawn from respondents' individual experiences. The data was rich with anecdotes and personal insights which respondents used to justify their positions. To illustrate, in the following response, a field educator is making her point about the importance of being willing to learn and to seek direction, as a challenge to the stated view about the importance of age, maturity and life experience in developing 'readiness for social work'. The crux of her point seems to lie in her personal experience.

> When I first started in social work I was all of twenty-three and ... one of the things I learned was that I had to be 'ready' to learn. And I think that has to be the hallmark of any social worker when I would have a client, a couple who had been married for thirty plus years and had instances of domestic violence, and were concerned about how well I could answer that case, I had to acknowledge that I couldn't and I had to go to my supervisor for guidance on what to do.

Another respondent shared her opinion on students' motivation, which seemed to come from a different discourse and point of view.

> I think a lot of students at the undergraduate level are ready to hang a shingle when they graduate – to be a private practitioner more so than someone who will go out into the community or to provide services to distressed clients.

Of significance here is that how conclusions about readiness vary by individual perspectives. The apparent trends in the discussion seemed more significant than specific points raised by each person, in that, each response revealed a different perspective and conclusions that emanated from individual experiences. What seemed to be valid for these respondents were their work and life experiences, and the data reflects their confidence that the insights derived from their experiences provide a sound basis for their perspectives on 'readiness for social work'. My particular concern is whether, in light of these revelations, practice assessments are totally fair to the student and by extension to the profession.

To further reinforce this point, here is a response from a field educator:

'I love a student to challenge me … [describes a situation] student made me see my own bias and look another way. A student who is confident enough to challenge me is ready to practise'.

Another question arises however – to what extent do the power relations in social work practice settings allow for the kind of mutuality described here? There may be numerous variables that come into play to accommodate this kind of exchange, not the least of which is the nature of the agency, the level of the student, maturity, personality and temperament, the educator's sense of professional identity, and the resources available.

Expectations

One of my early observations that stimulated interest in this topic was that multiple expectations of social work and social workers abound, which may or may not be used to evaluate social work practice. Furthermore, power and position in practice settings can create a hierarchy of expectations, with certain ones given precedence or having greater influence on behaviour, and further complicating student-assessor interactions. In analysing the data, numerous expectations emerged – of students, of agencies, of field educators, of faculty, of society, and of the profession. The expectations expressed reflected multiple ideas about the anticipated role of the social worker, the capacities practitioners should have, and expected professional behaviour.

A senior field educator made the following statement:

> When they [new social workers] come in, they may have all these fancy ideas, but after one year they should know where they're going. When they're going forward they should have a better idea of the society where they are living.

Built into this statement is a tacit assumption about newly qualified social workers level of competence. Her use of the term *fancy ideas* in reference to practitioners' thinking about practice, connotes cynicism about a naïve outlook that new social workers come with. This presumption is followed up with her own expectation that within a year they should be grounded in reality. These findings suggest that understandings of readiness and evaluation of practitioners' abilities are driven by disparate, maybe unreasonable, expectations. In terms of understanding and assessing readiness, therefore, the prevalence of multiple, divergent expectations informed by subjective knowledge may be an important consideration.

Moreover, if there are multiple subjective perspectives on readiness, then how can it be reliably assessed? Whose 'truth' dominates in the real world of practicum and practice? Subjective realities may differ, as may what is preferred in training, traits, and capabilities: each person may be articulating different things and understanding differently what is involved. How can subjectivity be harnessed and incorporated into understandings of readiness and practice assessment so that all voices and positions can be heard and validated?

In summary, the findings showed the significance of subjective knowledge in understandings of readiness by considering data addressing perceived indicators of readiness, factors for promoting it, and practice assessment. Subjective knowledge seems to inform many of the decisions made in mentorship and assessment, and it has also been shown that there are prevailing expectations, also informed by individual experiences, about what is needed and how it should be measured. Within these ideas are power dynamics that influence identity and position and how people interact in practice settings. When we add subjectivity to these interactions, the process can vary widely and becomes increasingly complex. For the individual student or practitioner subject to these processes in practicum and professional practice interactions, this could be confusing and disadvantageous, and undermine professional identity formation.

Discussion

In this focus group discussion, participants discussed their understandings of readiness for social work practice by stressing non-academic factors. These included personal characteristics, namely age, maturity and life experience, self-awareness, and openness to confronting and addressing personal issues, with less attention to formal learning and academic abilities. While scholarship has tended to search for objective standards, or a scale or measure to aid in the evaluation process (see Barlow & Coleman 2003; Lafrance & Gray 2004; Lu et al., 2011; Tam & Coleman 2009; Unwin, Van Soest, & Kretzschmar 2006), the findings of this study seem more consistent with the literature on the criteria for determining suitability for social work. In writing about professional gatekeeping, Royse (2000) states that 'we (assessors) may differ on how wide or narrow the gate that opens to professional practice should be' (p. 24) and this statement seems to covertly acknowledge that subjectivity plays a significant role in practice assessment in social work.

The data showed that among these field educators, understandings of readiness are informed by individual expectations, preferences, and experiences. In the absence of a definition or common understanding of what it means to be 'ready for practice', and given the frequent use of the term, it seems that persons may take for granted that everyone knows what everyone else means when they speak of persons being 'ready' (or not) in social work. From my review of the literature, readiness is not described; neither is suitability, fitness, nor safe to practice. This may be a testament to the fact that collective understandings of these phenomena are also taken for granted. So, if understandings of readiness, as well as other terms used in student/practitioner evaluation are taken as given, yet the phenomena are variable and subjective, it is worth questioning the trustworthiness of assessment and evaluation protocols used by parties to social work education and practice.

I suggest that heuristics in assessment play an important part in determining readiness for practice in social work. Sunstein (2010) describes heuristics as a *rule of thumb* or mental shortcut people use when they need to answer a question, solve a problem, or make a decision for which there are no hard facts or clear guidelines, by focussing on one or two selected aspects. In this conversation, those aspects seem to be informed by their subjective experiences and sense-making about social work practice and professional identity. It appears to me that by applying heuristics to assessment, field educators and assessors make professional judgements about students' capacity for professional practice, in the face of the complex, multi-dimensional nature of social work, by honing in on such characteristics as maturity, self-awareness, and selected skills, derived from their own experiences, preferences, and expectations. Bordalo, Coffman, Gennaioli and Shleifer (2016) advance that in this approach to judgment, some information is overlooked for expediency, and it may not allow contextual factors to shape assessments. The findings suggest that for these participants, concerted attention is paid to non-academic factors, like personal traits and self-awareness, and formal learning may be deprioritised in practice assessment.

Furthermore, conclusions about who is ready or not ready for social work seem to be a product of the application of *representativeness heuristics* to assessment. Ritchie and Josephson (2018), 2Belhekar (2017) and Sunstein (2010) cite Tversky and Kahneman (1974) in discussing representativeness heuristics, , and describe a decision-making process in which individuals create an image or construct in their minds, which for them, represents a phenomenon (in this case a ready social worker). They then make decisions based on the extent to which what is before them resembles or is representative of that mental construct. When I consider the variation in perspectives revealed in the data, I have questioned, as one participant also asked, *how does one know one is right* (in one's assessment); in other words, how can parties be confident in their conclusions about student readiness or un-readiness, when there is so much to take on board – diversity, ambiguity, and many unknowns. I infer that they may be applying individual representativeness heuristics in their decision-making, that is, *rules of thumb* or mental shortcuts, using their own experiences, preferences, and expectations, to construct mental models of social worker 'readiness'.

Additionally, the extent to which another's behaviour, traits, and temperament are representative of those mental models, seems to inform professional judgment of who may be 'ready' or 'not ready' for social work. Sunstein (2010) and Ritchie and Josephson (2018) talk about the inherent risks in the heuristic process as it contributes to error and bias. If the mental representations are treated as universal principles, accepted unquestioningly, and used to make decisions that cannot be justified, they can lead to inaccuracies in assessment practice. Bordalo et al. (2016) warn that with this form of judgment, only representative characteristics come to mind, and contribute to bias and stereotyping that can disadvantage students. The authors go on to describe the pitfalls of stereotypes, namely that they can dismiss diversity, and divert attention from new information. Relative to the findings from this focus group conversation, I infer that where field educators' subjective experiences are the basis for representativeness heuristics in practice assessment, each assessor could have selected biases and a stereotype of a ready, suitable, fit, or competent social worker. Of even greater concern is Bordalo et al.'s (2016) observation that when people do not subject their judgments to scrutiny and new information, stereotypes may not change, leading assessors to 'over-react to information consistent with stereotypes, and under-react or even ignore information inconsistent with stereotypes' (p. 3). Therefore, shareholders in social work education and practice need to remain alert to how heuristic processes can compromise the trustworthiness of practice assessment and disadvantage students and practitioners.

Field educators in this focus group openly described their expectations and what they valued in social work students, which varied across the group. The possibility that representativeness heuristics and stereotyping could be at play in practicum interactions and assessment can be raised here again; field educators' expectations could be informing mental models of the 'ideal' social work student against which students could be compared. Finch and Taylor (2013) refer to the field educator's 'fantasy' (p. 251) about student capabilities which can lead to unrealistic expectations. Crisp et al. (2006) posit that even when the field educators' views are accurate, students may not trust the field educator to be objective in their observations, and rightfully so, as shown in this study. Critical feedback from the supervisor, even if they are on point, can be attributed to misinformation or misinterpretation of the students' behaviour. The dynamics of practicum interaction and relationship can be strained by mistrust and baseless evaluation, and further threaten practice outcome and professional identity. Participants also shared other challenges faced in supervising students, such as students' seeming disinterest in the work of the agency, or their academic and other commitments that take attention away from their taking full advantage of learning opportunities in direct practice. These, they believe, undermine readiness. Such observations and experiences can heighten field educators' stress and weaken their confidence in exercising supervisory authority in the practice setting adding to the complexity of social work practicum interactions.

Crisp, Green Lister, and Dutton (2006) question whether practice teachers are sufficiently knowledgeable to assess students, and posit that student self-assessment can stimulate empowerment. However, there is also a contradiction in Crisp et al.'s position. The authors also observe that student self-assessments often require validation by field educators in order to be considered in formal assessments and final grades. In my view, a field educator who has fixed ideas that are informed by his/her own experiences about what self-assessment should entail and include, might affirm points of agreement with his/her own ideas and invalidate divergent ones. This is an example of how representative heuristics in assessment can introduce bias and be disadvantageous to students. Also, by so doing so, core abilities that are valued in social work, such as practitioner reflectivity, self-evaluation, and self-regulation, could be undermined by the student's supervision and evaluation experiences.

Underpinning participants' statements was a tacit awareness of their authority as field educators in practice settings, and the limitations to exercising it. Burr (2015) asserts that social interactions within social contexts, coupled with individual motivation and perspective, lead people to construct meaning and act in ways that they think are most likely to achieve their desired outcome. For field educators, their identity as social workers and their level of commitment to both their profession and to their role as supervisor can influence their position in interactions with students. Their identity and position may be split between being nurturers of readiness and assessors of readiness and create intra-personal conflict in their exercise of power (Finch & Poletti 2014; Finch & Taylor 2013; Le Maistre, Boudreau, & Paré 2006; Regehr et al. 2002). The personal investment that they make to the profession and the students/practitioners they supervise can become intertwined with their own experiences and expectations and make the numerous aspects of this process highly subjective. All of this points to a reality that practice assessment in social work is a highly challenging process, therefore heuristics in decision-making, while inherently variable and problematic, may be a way to simplify it since heuristics are frequently used in situations of ambiguity to arrive at a conclusion (Ritchie & Josephson 2018; Belhekar 2017; Sunstein 2010).

Meaning making about readiness for practice in social work is generated in large measure within the context of practicum. A circular process is apparent in which the student's experiences, positive and negative, shape understandings of readiness for both him/herself and the field educator. Although not the focus of this study, it is worth pointing out that as the student completes training and assumes a field educator's role, prior practicum experiences can inform mentorship and assessment practices with the next generation of students, and the cycle continues. The subjectivity described is manifest in this cycle, along with opportunities and associated risks in practice assessment. The data did not reveal attention to formal guidelines for supervision or assessment in social work; emphasis was placed on individual experiences and impressions. The implications for incorporating the latter in practice assessments while abiding by agreed guidelines or standards need to be considered.

Conclusion

Heuristic bias in professional judgment of student/practitioner readiness and use of representativeness heuristics in decision-making have been put forward here as explanations for how the multiple and broadly diverse perspectives, preferences, and expectations held by field educators in this study have been used in generating understandings of readiness. Notably, the data seems to suggest that individual experiences informed individual representativeness heuristics, making it possible that every field educator can have different preferences and expectations, thereby potentially increasing complexity in conceptions of readiness and applications thereof in mentorship and assessment. As subjects of practice evaluation, students are beneficiaries of the conclusions drawn from these heuristic processes. Assessors' interpretations of their readiness (or fitness, suitability, or competence) for social work can positively and negatively affect their professional identity, confidence, self-efficacy, and long-term development.

Participants regarded maturity, self-awareness, and emotional competence as essential social worker attributes and, while the literature does not disagree, O'Connor, Cecil and Boudioni (2009) advocate for deliberate attention in social work curricula to fostering emotional maturity in students. Madden (2000) makes a crucial point:

> Faculty must avoid misinterpreting behaviour and emotions related to normal developmental issues and mistakenly viewing such characteristics as indicators of a student's unsuitability or unreadiness for professional practice.
>
> *(p. 144)*

It is clear, therefore, that assessors need to tread carefully in respect of the significance of non-academic factors such as age, maturity, and life experience when determining suitability and readiness for social work practice. Moreover, they may not be able to rely solely on their individual perspectives or opinions about how non-academic traits and abilities factor into social worker readiness, as to do so would increase the heuristic bias in practice assessment.

The findings of this focus group discussion suggest that understandings of readiness have been informed by the subjective knowledge of individual participants; in other words, it appears that readiness meant something a bit different for every field educator in this study. It can also mean something different in its application to individual students; in addition, readiness self-assessments will vary from one student to another. In exploring my findings in relation to the literature, I suggest that heuristics and representativeness heuristics play significant roles in meaning making about readiness, particularly in practice evaluation and perceived professional identity.

Therefore, social work professionals should be minded to pay attention to the content and process of practice assessments and to resist taking for granted that there is universal understanding of what one should look for. Such attention may avoid the tendency to determine practice capabilities through subjective mental shortcuts and variable stereotypes. It is apposite here to state that heuristic processes are natural and automatic for decision-making and also functional (Ritchie & Josephson 2018; Belhekar 2017; Sunstein 2010), as is taken-for-granted knowledge within a discipline or profession such as social work (Burr 2015). I am suggesting that it may be tenuous at best to qualify social workers' capabilities by highlighting selected elements based on individual preferences, expectations, or experiences. A critical dimension for such attention is the student's practicum experience. The findings show that practicum experiences can virtually *make or break* the preparation process and professional identity development and shape future field education practice and practice assessment.

The study points to the prevalence of heuristics or mental shortcuts in assessing readiness for practice in social work. Additionally, representativeness heuristics in decision-making offer an explanation for how field educators may use subjective experiences to create mental models, possibly stereotypes, that help them decide who is ready or not. Heuristic decision-making in social work practice assessment is likely to vary from person to person and, given the multiple non-academic aspects identified, can challenge consistency and trustworthiness of evaluations, and undermine professional identity. It is my hope that the findings of this study and the conceptual discussion presented prove instructive for social work scholars and field educators in alerting them to the power of subjective experience and its impact on their assessment practice; this can also stimulate reflectivity for field educators and initiate review of assessment guidelines and protocols in social work education.

References

Barlow, C. & Coleman, H. (2003). Suitability for Practice Guidelines for Students: A Survey of Canadian Social Work Programmes. *Social Work Education, 22*(2), 151–64.

Belhekar, V. M. (2017). Cognitive and Non-cognitive Determinants of Heuristics of Judgment and Decision-making: General Ability and Personality Traits. *Journal of the Indian Academy of Applied Psychology, 43*(1), 75.

Bordalo, P., Coffman, K., Gennaioli, N., & Shleifer, A. (2016). Stereotypes. *The Quarterly Journal of Economics, 131*(4), 1753–94.

Burr, V. (2015). *Social constructionism*. London: Routledge.

Crisp, B. R., Green Lister, P. & Dutton, K. (2006). Not Just Social Work Academics: The Involvement of Others in the Assessment of Social Work Students. *Social Work Education: The International Journal, 25*(7), 723–34.

Crouch, M., & McKenzie, H. (2006). The logic of small samples in interview-based qualitative research. *Social science information, 45*(4), 483–499.

Finch, J., & Poletti, A. (2014). 'It's Been Hell.' Italian and British Practice Educators' Narratives of Working with Struggling or Failing Social Work Students in Practice Learning Settings. *European Journal of Social Work, 17*(1), 135–50.

Finch, J. & Taylor, I. (2013). Failure to Fail? Practice Educators' Emotional Experiences of Assessing Failing Social Work Students. *Social Work Education: The International Journal, 32*(2), 244–58.

Foucault, M. (1983). The Subject and Power. In H. L. Dreyfus & P. Rabinow (Eds.), *Michel Foucault: Beyond Structuralism and Hermeneutics* (2nd ed., pp. 208–26). Chicago.

Lafrance, J. & Gray, E. (2004). Gate-keeping for Professional Social Work Practice. *Social Work Education, 23*(3), 325–40.

Le Maistre, C., Boudreau, S. & Paré, A. (2006). Mentor or Evaluator? Assisting and Assessing Newcomers to the Professions. *Journal of Workplace Learning, 18*(6), 344–54.

Lu, Y. E., Ain, E., Chamorro, C., Chang, C. Y., Feng, J. Y., Fong, R., Garcia, B., Leibson Hawkins, R., & Yu, M. (2011). A New Methodology for Assessing Social Work Practice: The Adaptation of the Objective Structured Clinical Evaluation (SW-OSCE). *Social Work Education, 30*(2), 170–85.

Madden, R. G. (2000). Creating a Bridging Environment: The Screening-In Process in BSW Programs. In P. Gibbs & E. H. Blakeley (Eds.), *Gatekeeping in BSW Programs* (pp. 135–48). Columbia University Press.

Mathias-Williams, R. & Thomas, N. (2002). Great Expectations? The Career Aspirations of Social Work Students. *Social Work Education, 21*(4), 421–35.

O'Connor, L., Cecil, B. & Boudioni, M. (2009). Preparing for Practice: An Evaluation of an Undergraduate Social Work 'Preparation for Practice' Module. *Social Work Education, 28*(4), 436–54.

Pithouse, A. & Scourfield, J. (2002). Ready for Practice? The DipSW in Wales: Views from the Workplace on Social Work Training. *Journal of Social Work, 2*(1), 7–27.

Preston-Shoot, M. (2003). Changing Learning and Learning Change: Making a Difference in Education, Policy and Practice. *Journal of Social Work Practice, 17*(1), 9–23.

Rambally, R. T. (2002). *Practice Imperfect: Reflections on a Career in Social Work*. Ste-Anne-de-Bellevue, Quebec: Shoreline Press.

Regehr, C., Regehr, G., Leeson, J. & Fusco, L. (2002). Setting Priorities for Learning in the Field Practicum: A Comparative Study of Students and Field Instructors. *Journal of Social Work Education, 38*(1), 55–64.

Richie, M., & Josephson, S. A. (2018). Quantifying Heuristic Bias: Anchoring, Availability, and Representativeness. *Teaching and Learning in Medicine, 30*(1), 67–75.

Smith, L. W., & Van Doren, D. C. (2004). The Reality-Based Learning Method: A Simple Method for Keeping Teaching Activities Relevant and Effective. *Journal of Marketing Education, 26*(1), 66–74.

Steffes, J.S. (2004). Creating Powerful Learning Environments: Beyond the Classroom. *Change: The Magazine of Higher Learning, 36*(3), 46–50.

Sunstein, C.R. (2010). Moral Heuristics and Risk. In S. Roeser (Ed.), *Emotions and Risky Technologies* (pp. 3–16). Accessed from http://link.springer.com/chapter/10.1007/978-90-481-8647-1_1#page-1.

Tam, D. M. Y. & Coleman, H. (2009). Construction and Validation of a Professional Suitability Scale for Social Work Practice. *Journal of Social Work Education, 45*(1), 47–63.

Unwin, C.A., Van Soest. D., & Kretzschmar, J.A. (2006). Key Principles for Developing Gatekeeping Standards for Working with Students with Problems. *Journal of Teaching in Social Work, 26*(1), 163–80.

White, R. (2004). Discourse Analysis and Social Constructionism. *Nurse Researcher, 12*(2), 7–16.

Part IV
Developing Competent Social Work Graduates: African Perspectives on Field Work Education

23
Contextualising Social Work Fieldwork Practicum
Innovations, Challenges, and Perspectives from Nigeria

Uzoma O. Okoye and Samuel O. Ebimgbo

Social work is regarded as a multifaceted profession that is usually practised in both public and private agencies with the focus to solve individuals, groups, and societal problems while also enhancing their social functioning and well-being. According to Dubois and Miley (1996:6) 'social work provides opportunities to work in many different settings with people whose problems, issues, and needs are diverse'. Notwithstanding the multifaceted nature of social work, it utilises scientific and systematic procedures to provide services to reduce problems in all human relationships (Uche, et. al, 2014; Pawar, et. al, 2004). In most cases, social workers offer services for a broad range of circumstances, such as crises (e.g. sudden illness or death); alcohol and drug abuse; lack of housing, money, food, or medical care; transitions such as retirement; and interpersonal problems such as marital conflict, domestic violence, older adults' maltreatment, and child abuse (Mishra, 2014; Gambrill, 1997). Usually, the practice of social work is carried out through the scientific method of helping, based on knowledge, understanding, and use of special techniques acquired through rigorous fieldwork practicum training (Bongo, 2015; Mishra, 2014).

Fieldwork practice entails engaging students in learning and developing their attitudes, values, knowledge, and skill needed in generalist social work practice. It can also involve providing opportunities for students to perform professional tasks in the field instruction and offer many situations in which students may have to apply concepts and principles learned in both class and field. In the field of learning, it is expected that theories and practice should be complementary and interdependent (Bogo, 2006; Ayala, et. al, 2018). Historically, most theories emanated from practice, precisely from closely observed experiences of people with their environments over time (Ebue & Agwu, 2017). The practice to a great extent validates theories, and equally improves on them (Bogo, 2015). Social work discipline is no exception to this development, hence the introduction of fieldwork practice as a prerequisite for the fulfilment of the award of diplomas or higher degrees in the discipline (Ajibo, Mbah, & Anazonwu, 2017). It is generally believed that fieldwork provides students with opportunities for first-hand engagement with several cases of clients. All of these have contributed to the reason why social work learning and studies all over the globe lay special emphasis on fieldwork experiences. However, these field experiences need not be the same as schools of social work which have the liberty of choosing how to go about their practicum. According to the Council of Social Work Education (2008) social work programmes can organise the required field instruction in different ways as long as degree programmes are educationally directed, coordinated, monitored, and meet the requirements of the Council on Social Work Education.

Social Work Fieldwork Practicum in Nigeria

The profession of social work is still young and uncommon in Nigeria. Historically, the profession came to be in Nigeria as a result of colonisation though Obikeze (2001) avers that the extended family system and social clubs were a primary replacement of welfare system services in the community before colonisation. Currently, social work in Nigeria has come a long way from just being a religious and voluntary offshoot to a professional discipline. As a new profession, social work still engages the methods or techniques which have been tested in the course of practice in other parts of the world (Uranta & Ogbanga, 2017). Also, the practice of social work in Nigeria aligns with the objectives and purposes of the social work profession worldwide as stated by Pincus and Minahan (1977). These objectives which have been carried over to fieldwork have helped to facilitate the dexterity of professionals to develop skills and capacities to regularly, effectively, and objectively deal with life situations obtainable in Nigerian society (Ekpe & Mamah, 1997).

In achieving or realising the purposes and objectives of social work, the practitioners are expected to operate within three levels of practice which include *micro, mezzo, and macro levels*. Under the micro level, the social worker is expected to deal with clients at individual and family levels. Common problems associated with this level of practice include housing; health care; transition; juvenile delinquency; mental health issues; alcohol and drug problems, among others (Eneh, et. al, 2017). In the mezzo level of practice, the practitioner deals with the group. This level is usually referred to as group work. The practitioner handles problems of clients in a group setting. Examples of groups in Nigeria include youth groups, groups of families with sick children, unemployment groups, neighbourhood groups, task forces, and support groups. Finally, under the macro level of intervention, a social worker deals with the community and this is most often tagged 'community development' in Nigeria. In this situation, the whole community is seen as the client of the social worker who works with them and not for them. Community workers mobilise, empower communities through their institutions, organisations, groups, leaders, advocates, and volunteers to achieve the desired objectives in the community (Ezeh et. al, 2017).

Although social work is a relatively new profession in Nigeria, its relevance is gradually becoming visible as the country tries to catch up with what other social workers are doing globally. Thus, various higher institutions in Nigeria are rapidly integrating social work as a course of study either as a fully-fledged department or sub-department. Some of these institutions include University of Nigeria, Nsukka, University of Ibadan, University of Jos, University of Benin, University of Ilorin, University of Lagos, Ebonyi State University, University of Calabar, among others. These institutions train students to become social workers at various levels such as ordinary level diplomas, bachelor's, and post-graduate. These students go through different classrooms and field instructors before they graduate. In the process of social work education in these institutions, students are sent out to various primary or secondary agencies to enable them to put into practice what they were taught in the classrooms.

The most common types of field placement associated with departments of social work in Nigerian higher institutions are block field placement and concurrent field placement.

Universities have the choice to choose the placement type they think will work best for them depending on where the university is located and the logistics they can handle. Under the block placement, students are allowed to undergo their classroom exercises for some time to acquire the necessary social work skills and competences and then placed in social service agencies with an approved learning plan for a length of time. This can be a whole academic semester, or during the long vacations, and it is supposed to last for at least 12 weeks. The students devote themselves full-time (five days per week: 8 am to 4 pm) to experiential learning in the agency. This type of field placement enables students to handle real-life cases, and their classroom instructors usually come around the agencies for on-the-spot supervision of the students. In Nigeria, some institutions like the University of Benin, University of Lagos, and University of Jos adopt this type of field placement. On the other hand, the concurrent field placement is when the students' time is divided between classroom learning and fieldwork experiences. This implies that both activities (classroom and field) are experienced simultaneously. Under the concurrent placement, typically, students are expected to be in the agency for two to three days per week and to take classes for two or three days. The exact proportion of time devoted to each set of learning experiences varies, depending on the type of academic term, the number of academic credits, and the students' level of study. This form of field placement permits the students to share ideas regarding the impending cases with fellow students as well as receiving directions or instructions from the supervisors. This type of field placement is what is being adopted at the University of Nigeria, Nsukka which is the focus of this chapter.

Social Work Field Practice at the University of Nigeria, Nsukka

The University of Nigeria, Nsukka is a federal university located in Enugu State which is one of the states in the South-Eastern part of Nigeria. The university was founded in 1955 and formally opened on 7 October 1960. University of Nigeria, Nsukka was the first fully-fledged indigenous and first autonomous university in Nigeria. Currently, the University of Nigeria, Nsukka has 102 academic departments including Social Work across 15 Faculties. Historically, the Social Work programme was established in 1976 in the Department of Sociology and Anthropology in the Faculty of the Social Sciences, University of Nigeria, Nsukka based on the request of the federal government to train and produce middle-level manpower who can man Social Welfare Departments in the Ministries. The University of Nigeria, Nsukka has therefore pioneered the training of university-level social workers in the country, to satisfy the need for this specialised manpower. It offered only a two-year diploma programme at first. In 1985, a three-year degree programme to absorb some of the graduates from the diploma programme started. In the 1986/87 academic session, a four-year undergraduate programme through JAMB and post-graduate programmes viz. the Post-graduate Diploma, M.Sc., and Ph.D. in Social Work commenced. In November 2001, the social work programme attained a sub-departmental status and in 2006, it was granted a full departmental status (Department of Social Work, 2015a). Currently, the department has an undergraduate student strength of 470 and 140 post-graduate students. In this chapter, however, the focus is on undergraduate students.

The Pattern of Fieldwork Practicum at the University of Nigeria, Nsukka

The type of field placement practised at the University of Nigeria, Nsukka is the concurrent field placement. The field practicum course time is divided between classroom learning and fieldwork experiences. The rationale is to allow the students to share their experiences regarding the issues they are having in their various agencies with their fellow students and classroom instructors in order to gain insights on how to proceed. In most cases during the field practicum class seminars, students may raise vital suggestions and opinions that may give fellow students ideas on how to handle the cases they have in their agencies more efficiently. Students are required to complete a total of 12 hours of field practicum every week in a semester. The fieldwork practicum begins at 7 am and ends at 1 pm every Tuesday and Thursday for an entire semester which is approximately 12 weeks. This aggregates to 144 hours a semester and 288 hours for a session (Department of Social Work, 2015b).

The students are assigned to various agencies within Nsukka town. Assigning students to agencies of practice is based on the objectives of the educational programme and the learning needs of students as assessed by the fieldwork placement team. Students are expected to write a weekly comprehensive report of their activities in the various agencies where the practicum is taking place. The report enables the lecturer to know what the student is doing in the agency and also give directions on areas where the student is not doing the right thing. These reports are usually kept confidential and must be written according to the format developed by Urbanowski and Dwyer (1988). This format is shown below:

Purpose of the Visit

Here the student is expected to state in clear language, their mission, intention, or/and aim of visiting the agency. This summarily involves all that they set out to achieve/accomplish in the agency for that particular fieldwork exercise.

Observation

The student is expected to give an account of all that is happening around them in the agency that has a direct or indirect bearing with the object/subject of intervention – be it the community, school, individual, hospital, etc. The bottom line here is that the student's scope of inference must be problem-specific.

Content

All that transpired between the student and their client in the course of the intervention constitutes the content. Put differently, it is a narrative account of what the student did in the field: how, when, and why.

Impression

This is a subjective expression of the student's goal assessment. Here the student is at liberty to state their feelings, cognitive judgment, and general expectations with regard to their client and the overall intervention process.

Worker's Role

Here the student is expected to describe all they did in the field, the skills, and methods/techniques they adopted in the intervention process. They are also expected to explain how and why such methods, skills, and techniques were adopted.

Next Plan of Action

The student social worker is expected here to state what will become their next line of action, or better still, what they intend to do in the next.

The above field practicum reporting format by Urbanowski and Dwyer (1988) was adopted by the department as a way of enabling students to be quite comprehensive in presenting their reports. This will give the classroom instructor ample opportunity to correct all the things the students are not doing right. The two semesters of fieldwork practice provide students with opportunities to apply generalist knowledge and skills in a broad spectrum of social agency settings in Nsukka. Students are exposed to a wide range of social work roles and responsibilities in their work within agencies and communities.

It is important to note that field practicum is carried out by students from their second year of study. The first-year students are exposed to what the department terms 'fieldwork orientation' during their first year. This involves visits to various social agencies within Enugu State and beyond. The rationale behind the orientation as stated in the field practicum manual (Department of Social Work, 2015) is to enable the students to achieve the following:

i. To understand the mission, structure, operation, and programmes of social service delivery system.
ii. To identify the strengths and needs of the community and population being served by the agency.
iii. To identify the central importance of developing and sustaining professional relationship with client systems of all sizes.
iv. To describe the multiple roles and responsibilities of the generalist social worker.

Each student is expected to visit at least four agencies and at the end of the semester, the students will be examined on the issues raised above as it relates to the agencies visited. Other areas that are usually covered during the examinations include:

i. Social work values and ethics and the significance of self-awareness.
ii. Significance of non-judgmental acceptance of clients of diverse backgrounds.
iii. Importance of supervision, accountability, and professional development.

At the end of the session, each student is expected to also turn in a 20-page report to the staff in charge of the field orientation on their observations and experiences during the field orientation visits. This constitutes a part of the student's final grade in the field practicum course.

Fieldwork Practicum Materials

The fieldwork practicum at the University of Nigeria, Nsukka provides additional structured learning opportunities that facilitate the integration of agency-based experiences with academic course work for the students. As a result of this, at the point of registration, students are given materials that guide them throughout the session.

The materials include the following:

The Fieldwork Manual

The manual provides the students with all the necessary information they need for effective practice. Such information includes the modalities for the first-year orientation programmes;

departmental policies concerning the field practice such as schedule and attendance, regulations, dress code, grades, and reports; roles of fieldwork class lecturer, agency supervisors, and the student. Other information contained in the manual are the field practicum reporting format; sample evaluation guidelines for agency supervisors; and the format for writing the field experience report.

The Logbooks

The second material given to the student is the logbook. This is meant for the documentation of the activities of the students with the client(s) in the course of intervention using the method outlined by Urbanowski and Dwyer (1988). The logbook which is a sort of a diary is usually submitted to the supervisor for assessment, observations, comments, and grading. The logbooks are submitted every Friday or fortnightly, depending on the classroom instructor's directives as to when it will be convenient to grade the logbooks. However, it must be graded to give the student a sense of direction on how he/she is faring in the course.

Agencies for Field Practicum at the University of Nigeria, Nsukka

Formal agencies for social work practice are not easy to come by in semi-urban and rural towns in Nigeria. Rather they are mainly located in the urban areas of Nigeria. This being the case, the department has over the years developed a system where students engage in the field practicum with 'agencies' that though not very popular in social work textbooks, have served the purpose of providing adequate training grounds for the students. These 'innovative' agencies include:

i. Market
ii. The university students' halls of residence
iii. Auto mechanic village

Apart from these three innovative agencies, other agencies include hospitals, schools, social welfare agencies, prisons, and communities. All these are in Nsukka town. In these agencies, students offer direct and indirect services to service users. Direct services entail the students working directly with individuals. They may also deal with families or small groups, larger groups, and also do community work. On the other hand, in indirect service, students perform services on behalf of people rather than directly with them. These might entail work in administration, designing, and evaluating programmes and developing procedures to improve the delivery of services and performing management duties. Below are some of the activities students perform in these agencies with excerpts from their field practicum logbooks.

Field Practicum at the Nsukka Main Market

The market is one of the innovative agencies for social work practicum at the University of Nigeria, Nsukka. Nsukka town has a big market situated in the centre of the town. The market is called Ogige Main Market. Apart from neighbourhood shops, the market is the only place where residents of Nsukka town and environs come to buy and sell. The market is administered by the Nsukka Local Government Authority. They also collect daily tolls from the traders. The market is divided into sections and each section is administered by a group of persons elected by members of the section. These sections are delineated by what they trade on. There is also a body elected by representatives of different sections that see to the day to day running of the market and report directly to the Nsukka Local Government Authority. This body is called the Ogige Market Amalgamated Traders Association of Nsukka (OMATAN). It is this body (OMATAN) that the students work with in the market. The students work with these market leaders by helping them to prioritise their needs especially with regard to what they need from the local government. Sometimes in conjunction with the market leaders, they organise awareness programmes in collaboration with different NGOs for market men and women on different issues such as hygiene, girl child education, sexual abuse, child labour, and so on. They also help to settle issues of human relationships that arise on a day-to-day basis in the market. For instance, in their daily transactions, many traders engage in one form of conflict or the other either with one another or with the customers. Thus, students on practicum settle disputes among the traders and also ensure that available social services (electricity, water, security, etc.) are evenly distributed among various sections of the market.

Summary of an intervention in the market:

> The student social workers were approached by one of the traders who complained about an increase in the electricity bill and non-placement of security agents close to his warehouse despite paying for the service. The social workers were able to meet with the executive members of the market to discuss how the trader's problem will be solved. In the first place, the executive members of the market were not happy about the report and were so eager to know the complainant which the social worker declined to reveal his identity. After much dialogue, the executive consented to reduce the electricity bill and also accepted to deploy security agents to other places that needed their operations. The next visit to the market, the light of the trader has been restored though the security agents have not been deployed. However, the trader was happy with restoring his light and still hope the security issues will be resolved soon as he continues to work with student social workers.

Field Practicum at the University/Campus Halls of Residence

The University of Nigeria, Nsukka halls of residence are among the innovative agencies for social work field practicum. The halls of residence were found to be an important agency because of many problems emanating from students' relationships with one another and school management. Part of the duties of students involves meeting with halls of residence students' administrator and supervisors to prioritise all the problems in the halls of residence, liaising between the halls of residence and different service units in the university, and also engaging in micro practice with individual students on various problems ranging from quarrels between roommates, attempted suicide, and academic problems. Usually, the students play advocacy roles as well as brokering and mediating roles. The services of social workers are not limited to the undergraduate halls of residence but also extend to post-graduate halls of residence. Students' social workers engage the school management, hall of residence leaders, and other stakeholders such as Dean of Student Affairs to ensure that these problems are ameliorated.

Summary of an intervention in a hall of residence:

> The student social workers who were sent to some of the undergraduate halls of residence observed that the cleaners attached to the halls of residence have not been paid for more than six months. They also discovered that students in the halls of residence especially the occupants of 3rd and 4th floors litter the environment and usually pour out dirty water from their floors down to the floors of the 1st. Also, the students litter the environment

with dirt because of a lack of waste bins. The cleaners also complained to social workers that students do not defecate at the toilets but prefer to defecate on the floor of the toilets which always constitute problem for the cleaners because of lack of water. The social workers reported to the school authority about the non-payment of the cleaners and the Bursar expressed shock because according to him, the contractor has been paid a long time ago. He immediately called the contractor and threatened to terminate his contract and he promised to pay the cleaners before the end of that day which he did. The social workers equally requested that water tanks be provided to the halls of residence to enable the students to fetch water to flush their toilets easily. They engaged all the students by teaching them the importance of maintaining a hygienic environment by not pouring dirty water from 3rd and 4th floors down to the 1st and ground floors. They also provided a system where offenders will be noted and made to pay a fine.

Field Practicum in the Nsukka Auto Mechanic Village

The Nsukka auto mechanic village is a location set aside by the Nsukka Local Government Authority for artisans who engage in different forms of car repairs and also sell different car spare parts. This location is being managed by the local government though the auto mechanics have their internal administration that consists of elected officers. It is these elected officers that the students work with in the auto mechanic village. The students work with these elected officers to prioritise their needs especially with regard to what the need from the local government. Sometimes they organise awareness programmes in collaboration with different groups on such issues like attitude to work, HIV/AIDS, empowerment etc. Issues of human relationships that arise on a day-to-day basis in the village especially concerning car owners and their auto mechanics, the boss and apprentice relationship, issues of theft, and so on are some of the problems the students attend to.

Summary of an intervention in the auto mechanic village:

> A student social worker who was posted the village reported the case of a car owner who is quarrelling with his auto mechanic because his car which he dropped with the auto mechanic for over one month is yet to be fixed. According to the student, the car owner came to the workshop and threatened to stop the auto mechanic from working since his car was not fixed. This resulted in a fracas that brought in the market security and social workers. In handling the case, the students heard from both parties. It was observed that the auto mechanic did not work on the car because he was bereaved and spent the money the car owner gave him for his car repairs on funeral expenses. The student then, with the help of the village security, pleaded with the car owner to give the auto mechanic some more funds to commence the repairs while the auto mechanic was made to sign an undertaking that he will be refunding the money weekly until the amount given to him is completely refunded. The auto mechanic also agreed to start repairs immediately and was made to apologize to the car owner for the inconvenience caused.

Field Practicum in Schools

The school is an institution where pupils/students are trained to acquire skills in reading and writing. The social work students can be assigned to any school either public or private primary or secondary institutions. School social workers aim to assist students arrest psycho-social/economic problems that affect them, their families, teachers, and all other action and target systems that could influence their academic and general growth (Okah, Onalu, & Okoye, 2017). These psycho-social problems are crucial risk factors for poor academic performance, poor self-esteem, poor adjustment, outside home environment, stealing, truancy, conflict with constituted authority or disobedience, and other behavioural problems (Ibobor & Ogbu, 2007; Uzuegbu, 2004).

Students are also sent to the Special School Nsukka for practicum. The special school is meant to provide education for students with disabilities. The school provides education and vocational services to the blind, deaf and dumb, autistic children, and children with Down syndrome. The students are usually referred to as 'special students'. Student social workers posted to the school help to create awareness to the public regarding the services the school renders and the clientele they serve. This they do through social media and other avenues like church announcements. They equally link the school to systems that provide them with resources for the effectual services. For instance, the students' social workers wrote to the Local Government Authority on the need to put a fence around the school and employ a gateman to ensure the safety of the children. The local government granted the request of the student social workers.

Summary of an intervention in a school:

> A group of students who are in senior secondary three approached one of the social work students posted in their school to seek assistance on the best way to excel in academics. According to them, they are finding it difficult to read, focus on academic activities, especially as they are in their final examination classes. In responding to the students' case, the social worker came up with some useful suggestions to the students such as making a personal timetable, forming a reading group or discussion group, and also ensuring that they are always in the class during lessons. In the next visit, the student social worker grouped the students and helped them develop a reading time table. After some weeks, some of the students recoded some improvement in their academic pursuits.

Field Practicum in the Hospital

The interest of the social workers in the hospital is to pay attention to the psycho-social issues of clients, while doctors and medical teams solve problems that involve treatment (Ajibo, Mbah, & Anazonwu, 2017). They are complementary to doctors and specialise in psychosomatic issues. Social workers help the hospital to get information on the history of the patient, providing counselling services to the patients, especially where the patients have social and psychological problems that are interfering with the treatment and recovery of the patients. The social worker also helps in planning programmes and formulating policies for the hospitals as well as providing after-care services to the client to ensure they do not relapse after treatment (Uzuegbu, 2004). The social worker also assists in raising funds for the treatment of the patients especially those classed as disadvantaged.

Summary of an intervention in a hospital:

> From the report of the students who are posted to one of the hospitals in Nsukka, when they got to the hospital, they met with people with many ailments but their attention was drawn to a young lady who had orthopaedic issues. The lady had not been receiving medical attention as a result of her inability to pay her bill which was to the tune of ₦750,000 ($2,143). The family is so poor and the students were told that the father had already sold part of his land to ensure that the daughter receives adequate medical care. Unfortunately, the funds the family raised were not enough. The students were able to link the client to

the resource systems that included relatives, churches, community members that assisted in paying off the hospital bills.

Field Practicum Practice in Nsukka Prison

Nsukka prison is the only correctional institution in Nsukka. Usually, the institution is meant for the rehabilitation and reformation of individuals who are considered offenders by the law. Students who are assigned to the Nigerian Prison, Nsukka, work with the prison welfare officers to ensure that inmates get justice and are at the same time rehabilitated. The students, together with the welfare officers, help inmates to link up with their family members, modify inmates' behaviours, create social acceptance for the offenders, and help ex-convicts to be re-integrated into society after their discharge.

Summary of an intervention in Nsukka prison:

> Some students were assigned to Nigerian Prison, Nsukka for their fieldwork practicum. The welfare officer linked them with an inmate who was involved in a theft at the general hospital Nsukka. He was arrested by the vigilante group, who handed him over to the police. The police charged him to court and he was granted bail. However, he could not meet his bail conditions and was being kept in the awaiting trial unit of the prison pending when his fulfilment of his bail conditions. In the process, he lost his father though unknown to him. The social workers traced his home and met with the family members to discuss his release. The social workers also met with some of the leaders in the community including the traditional rulers and the head of the vigilante group that arrested him. They were willing to facilitate his release but on a condition that the client be of good behaviour. The student social workers spent time counselling the client to ensure that he refrained from the unacceptable behaviours which the community members frowned upon. In the process of rehabilitating the young man, the news about his father's death was broken to him. This equally served as a measure to change him, knowing fully well that his father died from hypertension as a result of his behaviour. The social workers equally counselled him on the death of the father to prevent him from going into depression. After working with the client for one month, he was released. The student reported that they still maintain contact with the client to ensure that he is well re-integrated into society and also to be sure that he did not start the bad behaviour again.

Field Practicum in the Social Welfare Agency

In Nigeria, every local government council area has a social welfare agency. This agency is usually in charge of issues relating to children and families. Such cases that relate to child abuse and neglect, child adoption and fostering, marital problems, and teenage pregnancies are part of the issues that staff the social welfare agency are expected to resolve. Student social workers sent to this agency are expected with the guidance of staff to provide various services such as reconciliation of couples, premarital guidance and counselling, provision of financial assistance to distressed families through linkage to the necessary agencies, and supportive services to children to ensure optimal growth and development (Uzuegbu, 2004).

Summary of an intervention in the social welfare agency, Nsukka:

> A young widow in her 30s brought a case of maltreatment by her stepchildren after the death of her husband from a car accident. After the husband's funeral, the widow demanded

the release of the proceeds from the funeral along with the money the husband had in the bank as she was the next of kin. The stepson told her that there was no money remaining from the funeral. He also told her that the husband left nothing in the bank. From inquiries, the social workers discovered that the widow was just a housewife when the husband was alive and so had no source of income. However, the stepchildren put her in charge of harvesting and selling the cash crops in the family – she refused to take charge but rather she wanted the proceeds from the late husband's burial and money he left in the bank. The social workers noted that she was lazy but they were able to enhance her coping capacity by telling her that the cash crops would provide her with more assets than the funeral proceeds she was seeking. Since the stepchildren did not strip her of the husband's farms, the social workers advised her to harvest and process those cash crops and sell those products (such as palm oil, kernel, fruits) from their lands and also to cultivate the land to ensure that the proceeds are sold after harvest.

Challenges of Fieldwork Practicum in Nigeria

Social work remains a growing profession in Nigeria. However, despite the relevance of the profession to society, it seems that its importance is not recognised. This is the consequence of many factors. Such factors include the following:

Non-Professionalisation of Social Work

Unlike in many developed countries, social work services in Nigeria lie solely with the government. In other words, the government is the sole employer of social workers in Nigeria. This being the case, social workers cannot practise independently because the profession is not recognised by law unlike other professions that have laws backing them. As a result of the non-professionalisation of social work in Nigeria, there are regular conflicts between social workers and other professionals who claim they do what social workers do. This is owed largely to ignorance, and the lack of professionalisation sanctioned by law (Okoye and Ijiebor, 2013). Most jobs in the ministries, agencies, and parastatals meant for trained and qualified social workers are usually occupied by non-social workers. For instance, Okoye (2012) revealed that new government agencies and NGOs are currently assuming the roles of social welfare agencies with non-social workers as staff of these agencies. Certainly, cases may not always be handled in an unprofessional manner. The students on field practicum in some of these agencies usually report some unethical practices that occur within. Also, in one welfare agency Okoye (2012) reported that couples were being granted divorces by the Chief Welfare Officer who incidentally is a lawyer when such cases should have been referred to the courts. This is not surprising, because many of those who work in these agencies have academic backgrounds in sociology, psychology, counselling, and the law, but lack social work skills (Okoye, 2012).

Inadequate Supervision from the Agency

The majority of the agencies where our students go for field practicum are being manned by non-social workers who incidentally act as the field supervisors. This makes supervision at the agency not effective for the students who are undergoing training in these agencies. Miller et al. (2017) have emphasised the importance of field supervision in the training of social workers. It's been observed that the social work students are not being supervised and their report not being adequately checked through by the supervisors. However, the department from time to time tries to organise workshops for the field supervisors to bring them up to date with basic requirements. The Council on Social Work Education (2008) also noted that in many places assumptions are made by the expected supervisors on the performance of the students without really checking the students are ensuring a proper service delivery.

Inadequate Time Allocation

This is another challenge faced by the student social workers in the field of practice. The time factor affects fieldwork practicum in three ways. First, tertiary institutions in Nigeria are always plagued by a series of industrial action. As a result, the university academic calendar is in constant adjustment and readjustment. This to a great extent reduces the number of hours students can engage in practicum in various agencies during an academic session. Secondly, allotting 6 hours (7 am to 1 pm) a day and 12 hours a week to fieldwork seems inadequate. Some of these agencies do not commence their daily activities until past 10 am. Also, some of the agencies that commence their activities on time do not permit the interventions of student social workers to interfere with the agency activities. Thus, by the time the social work students are able to have an interaction with the client, their buses are ready to take them back to school by 1 pm.

Finally in the University of Nigeria, Nsukka, second-year students are expected to take some general courses, and some of them are done on fieldwork days. This often interferes with fieldwork practicum as students find it difficult to miss the lectures. Thus, student social workers who are involved in the general courses usually leave their field agencies to attend these lectures.

Lack of Knowledge about the Profession

Although the Department of Sociology and Anthropology, University of Nigeria, Nsukka, started teaching social work as a course in 1976, the profession is still not popular among individuals even within Nsukka. Though many social problems abound, seeking help outside the family and other community structures to solve a problem is still alien to many people in the country (Chukwu, Chukwu, & Nwadike, 2017). This factor is probably part of the reason why people still query the usefulness of the profession and what it entails to be a professional. Generally, Nigerians find it difficult to accept the services of social workers especially in sensitive situations. Also, some workers in various agencies usually have misconceptions regarding the scope of service of social workers. These misconceptions usually interfere with the expected roles and functions of students' social workers during field practicum (Amadasun, 2019). For instance, they are confused about the difference between charity work, volunteer, and social work services. Other misconceptions arising as to what social workers students should be doing in different agencies are highlighted by Okoye (2012) below:

i. On one occasion, students in a hospital setting were expected to contact friends and relatives of patients who were defaulting in payment of hospital dues. They were merely used as debt collectors.
ii. On another occasion, students posted to a home for motherless babies were made to wash nappies and mop dirty floors. When they protested, the management told them that it was the only job they could allow the students to do.
iii. In social welfare agencies, students were expected to collect child support from defaulting fathers and sometimes to participate in cases that involved dissolving marriages.

iv. There was one school where social work students were put in charge of 'catching' latecomers and flogging them. Some teachers also insisted that the students teach their classes and mark students' exams and tests.

Lack of Case Continuity

Most often, it is difficult for student social workers to complete their interventions with clients during a semester of field practicum since they must leave at the end of the semester for holidays. Case discontinuity, therefore, is largely influenced by semester holidays and sometimes by industrial action in the universities. At the end of the semester, these students who leave for holidays are more likely not to continue with the initial cases when they resume. This may probably be because the clients are no longer in the agencies or new cases may be assigned to them by the agency supervisor. The second factor that plays a crucial role in case discontinuity is the reassignment of students to different agencies at the end of the academic session. At the end of each academic session, the students are expected to be posted to another agency for their field experience. The agency may be similar to the one attended in the previous academic session but the location must be different. Thus, this can create case discontinuity.

Conclusion

The chapter has highlighted the social work fieldwork practicum in Nigeria with particular reference to the Department of Social Work, University of Nigeria, Nsukka. Field practicum is an integral part of social work training that should not be compromised even in places where placement in formal social agencies is not feasible. Therefore, innovative ways of doing field practicum are important to ensure that students benefit optimally. As a profession, social work aims at solving problems affecting different categories of persons in society. They equally ensure that the social functioning and well-being of individuals are enhanced. The social work interventions on individuals are performed by no other person than someone who has undergone the necessary social work training to acquire the knowledge, skills, and values needed for practice. This is what we have set out to give the students through field practicum in such places as the market, student halls of residence, and auto mechanic village – all in Nsukka. Although these placements come with their different challenges, the department is doing all within its means to surmount them. The chapter also noted that as a growing profession, social work is plagued with many challenges such as, lack of formal agencies, the time factor, and inadequate supervision among others. However, it is believed that some of these challenges will be overcome if social work is made a profession in Nigeria.

References

Ajibo, H., Mbah, F., & Anazonwu, N. (2017). Field practice in social work. In U. Okoye, N. Chukwu and P. Agwu (Eds.), *Social work in Nigeria: Books of readings* (pp. 112–121). Nsukka: University of Nigeria, Nsukka Press.

Amadasun, S. (2019). Mainstreaming a developmental approach to social work education and practice in Africa? Perspectives of Nigerian BSW students. *Social Work and Education*, 6(2), 196–207.

Ayala, J., Drolet, J., Fulton, A., Hewson, J., Letkemann, L., Baynton, M., ... & Schweizer, E. (2018). Field education in crisis: Experiences of field education coordinators in Canada. *Social Work Education*, 37(3), 281–293.

Bogo, M. (2006). Field instruction in social work. *The Clinical Supervisor*, 24(1–2), 163–193.

Bogo, M. (2015). Field education for clinical social work practice: Best practices and contemporary challenges. *Clinical Social Work Journal*, *43*(3), 317–324. https://doi.org/10.1007/s10615-015-0526-5

Chukwu, N., Chukwu, N., & Nwadike, N. (2017). Methods of social work practice. In U. Okoye, N. Chukwu, & P. Agwu (Eds.), *Social work in Nigeria: Books of readings* (pp. 47–63). Nsukka: University of Nigeria, Nsukka Press.

Council of Social Work Education, (CSWE). (2008). *In the purpose of a practicum*. Retrieved 8 April 2014 from http//www.pearsonhighered.com /showcase/swees/assets/moi GART9445 SE 05 CO1.PDF.

Department of Social Work, University of Nigeria, Nsukka. (2015a). *Revised undergraduate curriculum for the award of Bachelor of Science (BSc) degree in social work*. Nsukka: University Printing Press.

Department of Social Work, University of Nigeria, Nsukka. (2015b). *Fieldwork manual.*. Nsukka: University Printing Press.

Dubois, B., & Miley, K. K. (1996). *Social work an empowering profession*. Boston: Allyn and Bacon.

Ebue, M., & Agwu, P. C. (2017). Synergizing perspectives in social work: Blending critical theory and solution-focused model. *International Journal of Contemporary Research and Review*, *8*(9), 20263–20270.

Ekpe, C. P., & Mamah, S. C. (1997). *Social work in Nigeria: Colonial heritage*. Enugu: Unik Orient Print Ltd.

Eneh, J., Nnama-Okechukwu, C., Uzuegbu, C. & Okoye, U. (2017). Social work with families. In U. Okoye, N. Chukwu, & P. Agwu (Eds.), *Social work in Nigeria: Book of readings* (pp. 185–197). Nsukka: University of Nigeria Press Ltd.

Ezeh, C., Ugwoke, P., Ugwu, C., & Eya, O. (2017). Social work with communities. In Okoye, U., Chukwu, N. & Agwu, P. (Eds.). *Social work in Nigeria: Book of readings* (pp 172–181). Nsukka: University of Nigeria Press Ltd.

Gambrill, E. (1997). *Social work practice: A critical thinker's guide*. New York: Oxford University Press.

Ibobor, O. S., & Ogbu, A. I. (2007). The role of school social workers in national development. *International Journal of Development Studies*, *2*(2), 1–7.

Miller, J., Deck, S., Conley, C., & Bode, M. (2017). Field practicum supervisor perspectives about social work licensing: An exploratory study. *Field Educator*, *7*(1). 1–18.

Mishra, P. J. (2014). Social work field practicum: Opportunities with challenges. *International Journal of Multidisciplinary Approach & Studies*, *1*(5), 288–295.

Obikeze, D. S. (2001). Social work services in Nigeria in the emerging years. Lead paper presented at the Workshop on Social Services in Nigeria, University of Nigeria, Nsukka.

Okah, P., Onalu, C., & Okoye, U. (2017). Social work in school. In U. Okoye, N. Chukwu, & P. Agwu (Eds.), *Social work in Nigeria: Books of readings* (pp. 122–132). Nsukka: University of Nigeria, Nsukka Press.

Okoye, U. O. (2012). Trends and challenges of social work practice in Nigeria. In V. E. Cree (Ed.), *Becoming a social worker: Global narratives*. London: Routledge, Taylor and Francis Group.

Okoye, U. O., & Ijiebor, E. E. (March, 2013). The Nigerian Social Worker and the challenge of practicing in a multi-cultural society. Paper presented at the 2nd National Conference of the Nigerian Association of Social Work Educators (NASWE). On the theme Social Work Practice in a Diverse Society: Meeting the Challenges of Contemporary Nigeria from Wednesday 13th–Saturday 16th March, 2013 at The Banquet Hall, University of Benin, Benin-city.

Pawar, M., Hanna, G., & Sheridan, R. (2004). International social work practicum in India, *Australian Social Work*, *57*(3), 223–236.

Pincus, A., & Minahan, A. (1977). *Social work practice: Model and method*. Itasca, IL: FE Peacock.

Uranta, D. T., & Ogbanga, M. (2017). Issues in social work methods in contemporary projects in Africa. *International Journal of Management Research*, *3*(7), 60–68.

Urbanowski, M., & Dwyer, M. (1988). *Learning through field instruction: A guide for teachers and students*. Milwaukee, WI: Family Service America.

Uzuegbu, C. N. (2004). *Social work practice: An introduction*. Nsukka: Mike Social Publishers.

24
Social Work Field Education in Africa
The Case of Botswana

Lengwe-Katembula J. Mwansa

Field education in Africa, as part of social work education, goes back to the colonial times of the 1870s–1900 when social work was introduced to the continent. The 'Scramble for Africa' or 'Partition of Africa' at the Berlin conference in 1885, at which the rules of colonisation were agreed upon by the European countries, further entrenched their taking control of Africa. Effectively, colonialism in Africa meant the removal of power of the traditional rulers who controlled and directed the affairs of the territories, including the appropriation of their wealth. The colonists also introduced their own lifestyle and development paradigms, including social work and community development. Notably, they adopted an approach to governance called 'indirect rule', especially in Africa and Asia (Lugard, 1922). Indirect rule was a form of governance 'through pre-existing indigenous power structures'. For example, the 'British ruled Buganda through the traditional ruler, the Kabaka of Buganda' (Lugard, 1922). Indirect rule dealt successfully with issues such as shortages of staff, lack of funding, road networks, the hostility of tribes towards the colonialists, and racial arrogance. It was implemented through powerful rulers, kings, and monarchies, who were well-established and functional elements of native rule. Essentially, traditional governance was not disturbed or interrupted, but simply continued. It must also be noted that the chiefs and kings had a great deal of power and influence over their people who also had great respect for them. This is why the British, for example, in Nigeria and other territories used traditional power structures effectively to enforce authoritarian rule of the colonial establishment especially in the maintenance of law and order, collection of taxes, recruitment of labour for public works, road construction, trial and error (Lugard, 1922), and punishment of offenders.

Social work was introduced by the colonialists purportedly as an approach to development of the native lands through the use of local structures and institutions to empower the citizens through the perspective of strength. As a multi-dimensional social process, empowerment allows people to gain control and direct their own affairs of life. It is a process that liberates the people from fear and fosters the spirit of courage to decide on the solution over their lives, communities, and society by acting on issues to resolve them and bring about change (Cox et al. 2016). This fits in well with the strength perspective, which advocates for the people to bring about change through a combination of the right tendencies. According to Glicken (2007, p

52), the strength approach is a wellness model that attempts to identify and use clients' positive behaviours to overcome barriers or obstacles in order to bring about change and resolution of problems. The emphasis, according to this approach, is to dwell on the strengths rather than the weaknesses of the client. Further, in this approach, people are at liberty to act on issues or obstacles they define as important. They prioritise issues and act on them accordingly in order of importance and urgency.

For a continent that was in dire need of development, social work was an approach to development that was deemed to bring about a quality of life for the masses. Yet, colonialists adopted this model of development not because they wanted to bring development to the continent, but to fulfil their own interests, which were diametrically opposed to the welfare of the people. Their mission was first to plunder the wealth of the continent. But they needed a peaceful atmosphere to enable them to do so. The organising people and communities, and peace and order were necessary to achieve their goal. Managing various populations, which in several instances proved hostile to colonial rule, was a priority for the colonialists. Social work as an approach was therefore attractive to achieving this end. Methods such as community and locality development, and community practice, with its related methods of social planning and social action, are well suited to organising communities and groups of people in their structures.

Social work in Africa was introduced around the 19th and 20th centuries. As countries on the continent began to attain political independence, the need for social development became more urgent. The newly independent states were in a hurry to meet the expectations of the people. They found the social work approach attractive and promising, hence the adoption of the social work approach to social development. This led to the founding of training institutions for community development and later social work. Countries such as Egypt (1936 and 1946), Algeria (1942), Ghana (1950 and 1956), Nigeria (1951), Uganda (1954), Upper Volta (1956), Tanzania (1958), Zambia (1960), and Zaire (1962) (Yimam, ASWEA, 1974) established their training institutions with a view to training frontline workers and mid-level staff in community development to offer literacy, extension services, village development, and general development services to the people. In general, the training took the form of courses that led to a certificate, a diploma in community development, and finally a bachelor of social work or bachelor of arts degree.

Notably, all the established training institutions of community development at certificate, diploma, and later bachelor of social worker level had a strong component of field education (Yimam, 1974). This was based on the realisation that the social work profession, and indeed community development as a method, required trainees to have a practice component to expose them to the exigencies of the trade, based on the apprentice model of learning. From the information collected from 31 curricula of 26 institutions of learning in 19 countries of Africa (Yimam, 1974, p. ii-iii), all the institutions had either block field placement or concurrent fieldwork practice. For example, the Higher Institute of Social work in Cairo had fieldwork to allow learners gain insight into knowledge application and acquire skills of practice (Yimam, 1974, p 20). The School of Social Work Haile Selassie University offered a bachelor of social work and 'provided practical application of theory to practice 15 hours per week in social agencies through observation, specific assignments, direct service and orientation to community and country profile' (Yimam, 1974, p 25). The Oppenheimer Department of Social Services at the University of Zambia provided a full-time 16-week block field placement and concurrent fieldwork on a part-time basis during which learners consolidated their theoretical into practical knowledge through undertakings such as problem-solving, group processes, programme development, and professional learning and development (Yimam, 1974, p 105).

From the time of establishing the training institutions, it was clear in the minds of the founding fathers that field experience was a sine qua non for the training of frontline workers. It was felt that fieldwork education had to receive an appreciable amount of time for trainees to receive the necessary practice time to learn the art of service delivery. It was a general principle that one third of training time should be devoted to field education. Although this principle was established and offered a general guideline, there were variations from one institution to another. Nevertheless, it must be appreciated that from the beginning of social work in Africa field education has been regarded as a critical element of social work education and training.

It must also be mentioned that the programme of fieldwork education focused on helping the learner to apply the classroom knowledge based on theory to developing skills, techniques, and competencies through the existential conditions of training by working with clients. This of course was done under the guidance of the experienced agency staff. It was expected that under such circumstances, the learner would acquire greater maturity, and gain professional attributes and proficiency and cultural competencies. At the time it was felt that the service delivery was oriented towards the remedial rather than the developmental. It was therefore felt that efforts should be directed towards developmental services by aligning the national plan in the quest of meeting the needs of the people. According to Diallo, (1974, p 60):

> We were convinced that a successful social development allied with economic development depended to a great extent on the professional qualification and competence of those responsible for implementing the various programmes.

Although there were tremendous efforts and a great deal of enthusiasm to train the local staff in community development and social work, the materials were drawn from Europe and America and made no reference to the philosophy of life or the problem-solving processes of the indigenous people. Like any other group of people, Africans in their own environs had nurtured their universally accepted norms, values, beliefs, practices, and traditions. They had a well-defined indigenous knowledge base or systems which were employed whenever necessary. The training materials or the philosophy of education and training were all imported together with assumptions that were foreign and of course could not be attained. But perhaps more important was a phenomenon that Glicken (2007) refers to as a dual or parallel development of social work and social problems. Social work in Britain and North America came about because of the problems of life that emerged especially after the fall of the feudal system, the enclosure system, and the Industrial Revolution (Zastrow, 1993). Social work in that situation was a response to the existential experience of the time to help meet the human needs. The introduction of social work in Africa was motivated by ensuring the success of the colonial project imposed on the Africans.

Brief Information Background

The African continent consists of 55 sovereign states with varying levels of development, but they share a common history of colonialism and indeed of development of social work, as alluded to above. Ever since the attainment of the political independence, many states on the continent have not seen much improvement in the fortunes of the people. Africa continues to be ravaged by social ills including mass poverty, illiteracy, squalor, incessant internal strife and conflicts, unemployment, corruption, disease, especially HIV and AIDS, and now the rapidly evolving novel coronavirus/Covid-19 pandemic. Poverty in Africa has become endemic and manifests itself in facets such as hunger, chronic malnutrition, and poor health status, especially among children, who usually experience stunted and other growth disorders or fall prey to malnutrition. The poor in Africa live on US$1.25 per day. Its causes are multi-dimensional and poverty reduction and elimination strategies have largely eluded success. Many people in Africa cannot meet their basic human needs. However, the Brookings Institute examines the issue of why the numbers of impoverished people in Africa are increasing when African economies are growing:

> [the year] 2015 marks the 20th year since sub-Saharan Africa started on a path of faster economic growth. During that period, growth has averaged 5.2 percent per year. Meanwhile, the number of people on the continent reportedly living under $1.25 a day has continued to creep upwards from 358 million in 1996 to 415 million in 2011 – the most recent year for which official estimates exist (Brookings, https://www.brookings.edu/blog/africa-in-focus/2015/05/04/why-is-th).

Various reasons are given for this phenomenon, including the depth of African poverty; rapid population growth (2.6% per annum); inequality, which is said to be already at unusually high levels; the degree of mismatch between where growth is occurring and where the poor are; data quality (Chandy, 2015); and lack or inequality of opportunity (Stiglitz, 2016). Be that as it may, power and rampant corruption with their attendant greed lead to the concentration of wealth in the hands of the few, while the majority continue to wallow in absolute poverty. Those with power of sorts use it to control and suppress dissent so that they continue to plunder the wealth without hindrance. It is the privileged few who are not affected by the exigencies of hard economic times. Isabel do Santos, who was born in April 1973, emerged to be the wealthiest woman in Africa. According to Forbes, the only reason for her fortune (US$2.2 bn) was simply being the daughter of the former president José Eduardo dos Santos of Angola. In fact, even those elites around the former president at the time made fortunes, but could not compare with Isabel. Corruption on the continent has wound back the clock of development to when Africa was referred to as the Dark Continent.

Coronavirus began in Wuhan city in China in December 2019. Although coronavirus is currently an emerging global pandemic, it is an explosive, extremely dangerous health crisis, and therefore cannot be ignored as part of the context, given the potential it has already elicited in the leading developed countries of the world. Africa does not have the capacity to combat this deadly pandemic of coronavirus. Already the leading economy of the world, USA, does not seem able to deal with the malicious economic effects of the outbreak. The economies of China and Europe are all in tailspin. The socio-economic impact of the coronavirus on the African economies will be devastating. Most African countries have neither the capacity to fight the wide ranging impact of socio-economic effects of the coronavirus, nor the ability to mitigate its impact. This will negatively affect the already meagre social services on the continent. The impact of the coronavirus on human services will be felt for a long time to come on the continent, as elsewhere.

As stated above, many African countries share a common history in terms of the introduction of social work in Africa. So, it is easy for the writer to illustrate the development of social work by discussing a country, Botswana. As one of the poorest states in the world, Botswana was regarded as an outpost in the scheme of colonisation, except for the expansion of British political influence. It was a British protectorate from 1885 to 1966, when it attained independence from British rule. The population of Botswana at the time was 614,613 (Selected Statistical Indicators 1966–2016) enabling stakeholders to formulate policies, and plan and make decisions. Botswana has often been dubbed 'the miracle of Africa'. The discovery of diamonds in 1972 literally made Botswana a case of 'from rags to riches'. Prudent leadership in managing the newly found wealth, democratic governance based on the rule of law, transparency, and accountability made Botswana a shining example of a modern self-governing state in Africa. For several decades, it experienced one of the fastest growing economies in the world. Since then, Botswana has invested heavily in the development of infrastructure and human capital. Education has continued to enjoy the largest share of the national budget (Republic of Botswana, 2020).

Despite its splendid development record, and in contrast with many other African nations, Botswana continues to experience lopsided development, especially in terms of income inequalities and social injustice. According to the World Bank report (2019):

> Botswana has the fifth highest level of income inequality on the continent. Southern Africa itself has the highest income inequality in the world. For the rest of the sub-Saharan region, the Gini index of income inequality measurement ranges from 30 per cent in Ethiopia to 66 per cent in Seychelles. The laudable and impressive growth witnessed recently in Africa has unfortunately not been matched with a significant reduction in unemployment and poverty.

According to *Monitor*, Bobonong legislator Taulo Lucas (16 March, 2020, p 2) proposed a social justice commission to investigate and address the acute levels of inequality in the country. However, the motion was defeated in Parliament. But it is worth noting that poverty according to Lucas has become worse in the country with the national poverty rate standing at 16.3%.

> But the figures hide the regional poverty levels demonstrating the abject poverty. That Batswana live in [...] for example Kwenenge West with an average prevalence rate of 50.6%, Ngwaketse West with 40.3%, Kgaladi South with 39.5%, Gantsi with 36.3 % and Ngamiland West at 33.4.

Even though poverty has decreased considerably from previous levels, it remains one of the major impediments to human development. Botswana's human development index value stands at 0.728 and the country was ranked 94 in 2019 (UNDP, Human Development Report, 2019). This underscores the inequitable distribution of wealth, which leaves the majority with little resources to meet their basic human needs and are indeed they are vulnerable. Poverty is worse in rural areas, where in some cases it is estimated to be as high as 46 per cent. The worst group trapped in poverty are the children 'under 15 years', who represent nearly half of Botswana's poor and larger households.

This is the scenario under which social work has been practised in Botswana (World Bank, 2015).

The Context of Field Education

The introduction of social work in Botswana was heralded by the provision of social services in 1946 and was prompted by several reasons, including the need to integrate ex-servicemen from World War II, who had been absent from their villages, and the urbanisation and modernisation of the country, which changed the way of life and demanded new institutions to manage relationships and solving of the problems of life (Hedenquist, 1992). Initially, the slant of the services tended to be residual in outlook, but later changed to being developmental in nature, especially with the introduction of community development and later social work. The new services were located in the Department of Education and administered by one officer. Later the services were transferred to the Ministry of Local Government under the Department of Social and Community Development to foster a sense of self-help and self-reliance. The introduction of community development stimulated the need for voluntarism and training of more staff to spearhead community development. By 1971 there were 60 community development assistants (CDAs) and 13 assistant community development officers (ACDOs). The CDAs did not possess any training or experience, but had the enthusiasm and zeal to work under the ACOs. However, by 1973, the number of ACDOs had risen to 36. These were trained in Tanzania and Zambia on a ten-month certificate programme (Ferguson-Brown, 1996).

The ACDOs were the most highly trained in the Department of Social and Community Development. This is a significant development in social work and field education in Botswana. However, the Food for Work Scheme, which was introduced by the United Nations to fight the drought, relied on the ACDOs to lead the programme. Meanwhile, a one-year certificate course 'was set up at the Botswana Agriculture College to train the community development assistants. This institution continued to train the ACDOs until the programme was transferred to the University of Botswana in 1985' (Ferguson-Brown, 1996, p 75).

The University of Botswana was established in 1982 and then the Department of Social Work was founded in 1985 at the university (University of Botswana Calendar 1990-1991, pp. 34–37). The department began to offer a certificate in social work and a diploma in social work. This development led to the transfer of the training of community development assistants from Botswana Agricultural College to the Department of Social Work at the University of Botswana. And a year later, the degree in social work was introduced. The certificate in social work was eventually dropped in 1999. However, most of the staff in the department, as was common at the time in African countries, were non-citizen staff and Western-trained, as were the teaching materials. The development of social work in general and field education in particular were influenced largely by Western knowledge, values, skills, norms, competencies, and philosophy. Indigenous knowledge, value systems, and norms did not form part of the social work knowledge and practice.

The lack of indigenous staff created a hurdle in the development of social work because the non-citizen staff members were not familiar with the cultural nuances that require to be introduced in the teaching and practice of social work; for example, the problem-solving process, social institutions such as the 'BoKgosi' and 'Kgotla', and the co-related element of consultation (Nteseane & Solo, 2007). These are supreme institutions that need to be fully understood, appreciated, and adopted in the teaching and practice of social work. Such institutions are of immense interest and play a leading role in the life of the nation and therefore critical to the indigenisation of social work. Learners in field education have to be made to understand and appreciate such elements of culture and the part they play in the process of indigenisation of the social work profession.

It is also interesting to note that through various efforts the country preferred a philosophy of development that favoured a developmental (social development) approach to a residual one. It also strove to make people participate in development and make the process of decision-making bottom up instead of top to bottom in line with the philosophy of self-reliance and self-help. This augured well for the prevailing philosophy of social work education and training as envisaged by the founders of social work education in Africa (Tesfaye, document 6, ASWEA, 1973, Shawky, document 6, ASWEA, 1973, Anders, J.R. document 6, ASWEA, 1973; Diallo, Document 6, ASWEA, 1973). Many observers at the time found more merit in developmental social work or social development than the micro practice that found popularity in the West. Tribute must be paid to the founding members of staff of the Department of Social Work at the University of Botswana, who found merit in developmental social work. So fieldwork education was based on the community as a context of practice or a central organiser for social work education and practice. This was appropriate, given the nature of community life that prevailed in the country at that time (Ferguson-Brown, 1996).

In Africa, community provides the context of practice where 'social work is involved at the interface between the social services and the community' (Hutton, 1996, p 5). Communities have their particular social and cultural context in which social work is practised. Notably, communities are not static entities, but are dynamic, with rapid social change taking place. Within this context therefore, social development was chosen as an approach to be used by social work as conceived by the national development (Tesfaye, 1973), given its relevance in a developing situation. The concern here is not so much placed on residual or restoration of social functioning but on community response to meet the developmental needs of the group. This approach makes sense, given the meagre resources that are available in most countries of Africa. Priority in terms of allocation of resources should therefore be given to developmental and prevention needs rather than personalised curative services. However, the complex nature of modern life has made it necessary to establish new institutions that can facilitate the meeting of human needs. These new organisations include social services. Social work practitioners are concerned with a variety of social problems, including poverty, social injustice, social exclusion, violence, and unemployment, HIV and AIDS, family breakdown, mental health, and the evolving global health crisis of coronavirus. This is the context in which social work field education in Africa should be understood (Hutton & Mwansa, 1996).

Apprenticeship Model in Social Work Field Education

Many professions have adopted the apprenticeship model in teaching trainees or interns at various levels of learning. The model is said to be the backbone of many professions in terms of their learners becoming proficient in their work. Professions such as social work, medicine, nursing, teaching, and driving employ this model to teach their learners the existential knowledge of trade. This is an instructional programme in which the trainee has a 'hands-on' existential learning experience (Pratt & Johnson, 1998). This is intended for the learner to acquire familiarity, competence, and skill in a given trade. In this model, the learner undertakes the tasks under supervision. For example, in social work field education, the learner is given a hands-on existential learning in counselling by first observing and then is given the opportunity to undertake the task of counselling under supervision. The learner is expected to internalise several aspects of counselling, including listening, observation, empathy, encouragement, and flexibility (Hope & Timmel, 1999). But perhaps more importantly the apprenticeship involves the learner doing or carrying out an activity physically under the supervision of an experienced instructor. In other words, the learning process is a tangible exercise in which the learner has to perform the task, but based on the theoretical knowledge from the classroom. The learner engages in the activity but 'the processes of the activity are visible' (Pratt & Johnson, 1998). The idea is to undertake the task, derive the knowledge, but later examine the process with the supervisor to review how the process was executed. The supervisor explains concerns and smooths 'the rough corners', as it were, for the learner to take the necessary lessons. It is critical that the learner should experience this process of hands-on to appreciate how to perform the activity. This is in recognition that social work education consists of two major elements: classroom (theory) learning and fieldwork practice (University of Botswana Department of Social Work Fieldwork Manual (not dated); Royse & Rompf, 2007).

Although the apprenticeship model has been acclaimed as the backbone of many professional training systems, it does show some merits and demerits, which should be known by both the instructor and learner (https://opentextbc.ca/teachinginadigitalage/chapter/3-5-apprenticeship-learning-by-doing-1/). Here are some of the strengths:

- Teaching and learning are deeply embedded within complex and highly variable contexts, allowing rapid adaptation to real-world conditions.
- It makes efficient use of the time of experts, who can integrate teaching within their regular work routine.
- It provides learners with clear models or goals to aspire to.
- It acculturates learners to the values and norms of the trade or profession.

Here are some of the weaknesses:

- Much of a master's knowledge is tacit, partly because their expertise is built slowly through a very wide range of activities.
- Experts often have difficulty in expressing consciously or verbally the schema and deep knowledge that they have built up and taken almost for granted, leaving the learner often to have to guess or approximate what is required of them to become experts themselves.
- Experts often rely solely on modelling with the hope that learners will pick up the knowledge and skills from just watching the expert in action, and don't follow through on the other stages that make an apprenticeship model more likely to succeed.
- There is clearly a limited number of learners that one expert can manage, given that the experts themselves are fully engaged in applying their expertise in often demanding work conditions which may leave little time for paying attention to the needs of novice learners in the trade or profession' (https://opentextbc.ca/teachinginadigitalage/chapter/3-5-apprenticeship-learning-by-doing-).

The idea is not to exhaust the discussion of the model, but merely to bring out some of its salient features. Like any model or theory, there are strengths and weaknesses, but the choice remains with the user whether to apply such a system. But this is the model used in field instruction. However, it is important to remember, as Danbury (1994) indicates, that there has to be a distinction between what takes place in a classroom and what takes place in the field. A classroom provides knowledge in the form of theories, but training is the practical part of learning that takes place in the social agency in which practice knowledge is generated. The accumulation of such knowledge comes to form occupational experience, which is based on practice. This knowledge is replaced in terms of practice in any professional field.

This is hands-on field instruction (Danbury, 1994). In the years the writer has spent in training students in field education, often social agency staff where students are placed, complain about the students not being ready for the agency work (Danbury, 1994), usually because the learners are deemed to lack certain practice knowledge and therefore cannot stand on their own. But that is precisely the reason that they are taken to the field to learn through practice. Often this type of complaint is based on the conception that learners on field placement are not aware of the protocols, legislations, policies, and programmes or simply lack the knowledge and competencies expected by the practitioners of the social agencies. This, according to Danbury (1994), may suggest that lecturers do not adequately prepare learners for practice. This may not be the case at all. However, the Department of Social Work at the University of Botswana in partnership with various agencies trains learners in the Diploma in Social Work and Bachelor's degree in Social Work for 12 weeks and 9 (18 in total) weeks, respectively. The social agencies in the country provide the learning environment for the hands-on practice of social work under supervision.

Social Work Field Education

The content that follow comes largely from the fieldwork manual of the Department of Social Work, University of Botswana. The author has been teaching at the University for the past 29 years. While the document is the property of the department, the author, not in small measure, has contributed to its development. Therefore it is felt that liberal use would not be frowned upon. Field education at the University of Botswana takes place during the winter session after the academic year ends in early May. Field education usually overlaps with the first part of the academic year. Field education in the Department of Social Work is based on the mission statement:

> To provide a practice-centred approach to educating students in order to empower communities and individuals by focusing on their strengths, affirming their social and cultural diversity, promoting social justice, conducting applied research, and adopting critical perspectives to social issues.
>
> *(University of Botswana, Department of Social Work, fieldwork manual, p 4)*

The goal of the field education is:

> To offer practical, field-based experience that prepares social work students to be professionally responsible, gender sensitive and committed to culturally appropriate practice with a range of social systems, emphasizing interdependence, social justice, and empowerment approaches.
>
> *(University of Botswana, Department of Social Work, fieldwork manual, p 4)*

The diploma at the University of Botswana is a two-year programme of study, with the main objective of preparing learners for frontline social work practice at the grassroots level and who sometimes may get into middle management positions. However, the programme of study includes lessons on the individual, communities, groups, organisations, and social science courses. The learners undertake a 12-week fieldwork block placement at the end of the first year in May to mid-August. On the other hand, the Bachelor of Social Work at the University of Botswana provides professional education and practical training for preventing and ameliorating a wide range of undesirable social conditions by imparting knowledge in fields such as social and community development, youth and family welfare, and individual and communal life situations. The programme is a four-year study with two nine-week periods of fieldwork in the second and third levels. The programme covers a wide range of courses including professional social work interventions, human development and behaviour, communication theories and their applications. The curriculum is supported by the foundation courses of social sciences.

The department submits requests for field education placement to various agencies after consulting with learners of their preferences. Learners are expected to develop a learning contract, which is submitted to the field supervisor. Besides placing the student in appropriate social agencies, the department sets the areas for practice for the student to acquire skills, competencies, and knowledge of how to practise social work in line with the learning contract, which outlines student learning goals. Learners are placed in public, private, parastatal, non-governmental, community-based, and related social agencies. Initially, as indicated above, there was a serious challenge in finding suitable placements with acceptable quality supervision to meet the needs of the students.

The first learners in the programme to undertake field education went through trying times because the department could not find suitable supervisors in the agency. Remember what was said earlier about the training of the community development officers that many, if not all supervisors in the agencies had only a ten-month ACDO certificate qualification in community development. The lack of adequate supervisory abilities was the effect that was referred to earlier. In some cases, while the agency was suitable, they could not find a supervisor. This situation persisted for some time until the university trained adequate numbers of personnel with diplomas and bachelor's degrees to assume supervision in the social agencies. However, to mitigate this situation, the Department vigorously mounted field education supervisory workshops where some training was offered to all field supervisors. But it was not unusual for the academic supervisor to have administrative, educational, and supportive supervision (Kadushin & Harkness, 1992). The focus of training workshops was examination of the responsibilities of the department of social work; responsibilities of the host agency; responsibilities of the field supervisor; and student responsibilities. Each of these aspects had to be understood properly so as not to create wrong expectations. As many observers indicated, field education is an opportunity to initiate learners to the art of practice of social work through inculcation and assimilation of values, ethics, principles, competencies, and skills. The idea is to view field education as consciously planned activities that take place in an environment purposely set to make learners move from their level to another higher level in learning the actual practice. It denotes growth and development owing to the daily exercises, which turn theory into practice (Demba, 2012; Kaseke, 1986). In the process, the learner begins to appreciate the type of social work, namely micro (direct practice), mezzo, and macro (indirect practice). Essentially, field education provides the learner with an opportunity to develop and grow by way of applying classroom teaching to practical performance of social work under supervision.

The social agency is a partner in the training of social work professionals in the country. So, there are mutual expectations and roles that each must play in the process of field education of social work learners.

Social work field education is an integral part of social work training that is based on practice. This aspect of social work training takes place outside the classroom in a social work agency. The structure of the course is like any other subject with all the regulations and rules. The Field Work Coordinator reports to the Departmental Board for all matters related to the course including general academic regulations, regulations for awards and fellowships, examination regulations, and academic appeals procedures (University of Botswana Undergraduate Academic Calendar, 2019/2020). However, the day-to-day administrative matters are reported to the Head of Department for action. The bachelor of social work students spend 720 hours practical field experience while the Diploma students spend 480 hours practical field experience

Challenges and Prospects of Field Education

As stated earlier, the novel coronavirus or Covid-19 started in December 2019 in Wuhan city in China and was soon pronounced a global pandemic. It spread like wildfire throughout the world with varying degrees of impact. The world has continued to struggle to contain the virus but without much success. With the invention of Vaccination for COVID 19, the world started opening up again. However, one thing is certain that after all is said and done, life will never be the same. Covid-19 has brought about untold human misery and suffering through the tragic

Table 24.1 Timetable for fieldwork

January–March	Department prepares for fieldwork by contacting agencies and holding training fieldwork supervisory workshops
May:	Students begin fieldwork
June–July	Academic supervisors hold pre-arranged meeting(s) with students and field supervisors. The contract and the evaluation criteria are discussed and agreed upon
July	Field supervisors carry out mid-term placement evaluation with the students using the mid-term placement evaluation form. This evaluation form is to be completed before the academic supervisor's visit
August	Field supervisors complete the final student evaluation form. Students must ensure that the fieldwork co-ordinator receives this form together with the mid-placement evaluation form.
September	Students submit their daily log book, community project, and case study on individual intervention (which constitute the academic portfolio) to the field co-coordinator. These are assessed together with the field supervisor's input (20%) which both constitute the final grade for field work education.
December	Final fieldwork grades are submitted and feedback is provided to students on their work experience (fieldwork manual)

Source: University of Botswana, Department of Social work Fieldwork Manual (1994).

loss of human life of 371,000 globally so far (https://www.google.com/search?client=firefox-b-d&q=global+death+toll+cor) throughout the world, the destruction of economies with the accompanying loss of employment and livelihoods, and complete disorientation of human life with similar emotional frustration to that caused by HIV and AIDS. Although Africa has not yet reached the same scale of loss of human life and suffering, it is a matter of time before the bubble bursts.

One dreads to think about the impact of Covid-19 in Africa, especially in view of the current challenges of ill-health with meagre health resources, which cannot stand the huge negative impact of the pandemic. It has laid bare the vulnerabilities and contradictions in human relations especially in terms of human rights and issues of accessibility to resources in various societies in many spheres of life. The practice of social work has to deal with the issues of social justice in the post Covid-19 service delivery in the manner the elderly are treated and regarded. Many countries of Africa cannot withstand the impact of the pandemic. Health problems in Africa are exacerbated by the adverse consequences of climate change translating into massive poverty with the majority of the population living on US$1 per day, an energy crisis, squalor, hunger, unemployment especially among the youth being almost a crisis, and related problems of globalisation.

Social work field practice has to move from the usual peacetime practice sphere to a disaster sphere of practice to match the times that lie ahead for human life. Practitioners have to develop competencies, skills, and knowledge to work with individuals, families, groups of people, and communities to meet the challenges of disaster management that may become the way of life. Training in social work should pay attention to being sensitive and empathetic to various issues of life that continue to degrade the status of various groupings of humanity such as the marginalised, the poor, the elderly, the LBGT community, and children in need.

The present episodes of protests and violence across the USA after the vicious death of George Floyd, a black man, on 25 May 2020 is a constant reminder of the need for social work to remain resolute to the core values and principles of the profession especially the shared values of equity, inclusion, and social justice for all (Code of Ethics of the National Association of Social workers https://socialwork.utexas.edu/dl/files/academic-programs/other/nasw-code-of). Floyd's brutal killing by a white police officer is extremely unfortunate and is an example of 21st century institutionalised racism. The racially motivated killings of black people in the US continue to happen decades after the emancipation proclamation of 1863 (Glaude Jr, 2000; Goddu, 1997; Zafar, 1997). The training of social workers especially in Africa must make us aware of the negative forces still dominant in our spheres of life and emphasise equality for all people so that no section of society is left behind or discriminated against. Racism like any form of violence is a deadly 'virus' that must be wiped out. Crenshaw (1989) and Amanda Gorman (2017) talk of intersectionality as a framework of analysis of interlocking systems of power that negatively impact those who are most marginalised in society and suffer multiple forms of discrimination in relation to gender, classism, and race. The training of social workers must always aim for strategies and solutions that are inclusive and empowering to make the world a better place for all. Learners in social work must share the collective conscience that abhors any form of inequality and discrimination but work for social justice and dignity for all people.

The University of Botswana, like many public institutions of learning in Africa, has been entirely dependent on financial subventions from government since its establishment. We have also seen a gradual loss of funding over the years especially in the late 1990s which became more pronounced after the 2007–2008 global depression. The university budget was reduced and inadvertently departments were adversely affected including social work. From then on, the department lost the field work practice line budget to a faculty-wide allocation. This meant that the department had to compete for the meagre faculty allocation for fieldwork with other departments. This, as it can be appreciated, has created several challenges including difficulties in planning since the budget is not known until shortly before the start of field education. Planning for student visitation therefore cannot be ascertained, board and lodging cannot be pre-arranged, and supervision time has been curtailed which makes it difficult to undertake the usual supervisory visit. So fulfilling the hourly international expectation of practice becomes difficult to attain. In the process academic supervisors are exposed to fatigue due to long hours of driving without adequate rest in order to meet all learners within the shortest time possible lest some students may not be supervised. In addition, while the numbers of learners continue to increase the staff complement has been decreasing due to downsizing. The Department has tried to readjust in order to ensure that learning takes place under such circumstances but somehow quality tends to suffer. The Department has to find means and ways to ensure that adequate field work allocation is restored to provide the necessary conditions of teaching and learning. Fortunately, all the agency personnel from public, private, parastatal, non-governmental organisations, and community-based organisations who participate in teaching students during fieldwork do it voluntarily without any financial expectations. In fact participation in placement activity for any agency has been taken as a professional requirement. However, there is a need for constant workshops for the field supervisors to ensure that there is consistency in the understanding of the goals and expectations of field work training. The underfunding of fieldwork has also made it difficult to continue training agency fieldwork supervisors

Botswana, as a country, consists of rural and urban areas with the majority of people residing in rural areas and where the needs are greatest. Training of future social work practitioners must reflect this dichotomy in Botswana. However, while the Department has been determined to instruct students for the rural areas as well, there are challenges in finding suitable placement agencies with the necessary facilities including office space with resources such as chairs and computers, accommodation for students, and qualified field supervisors since those with a bachelor's degree tend to prefer urban areas. But some parts of the rural areas are remote or are settlements which are far-flung in the hinterland and very difficult to access because there is usually no public transport. These are communities that are on the margins of development with barely any development. Language is another issue of contention. While Setswana is widely spoken in the country these communities are usually inhabited by some minority groups of people that do not speak the language. For example, the first people (the Bushmen, part of the Khoisan group, San, Basarwa, or Khwe) of Botswana who speak their 'click' language called Khoisan are found in such communities or settlements. Most students do not know the language (https://www.google.com/search?client=firefox-b-d&q=what+language+do+the+basarwa+speak) and hence there are problems in communication which makes it difficult to work with such communities. The other problem is that the people in such communities tend to be nomadic and therefore not fixed in one place: it becomes a challenge to provide services.

Conclusion

Field work education has been duly recognised as a critical component of social work education and training since the inception of social work education in the early 1960s. Learners are therefore prepared to have practical experience before finally going out to practise through the method and theory of apprenticeship. There is a recognition, however, that social work was imported from western countries and has therefore many aspects that do not fit in the mode of practice in relation to the existing cultural context. It remains the responsibility of the educators and practitioners to make social work relevant to the practice setting. In some measure, field education should constantly endeavour to make learners aware of the necessity to adapt the practice of social work to the demands of the African context. There is also the need to think seriously how the practice of social work will apply itself to disaster reduction and management especially in view of the Covid-19 pandemic. It is vital that the practice of social work in Africa adapt the attitude of disaster preparedness in relation to social justice where human dignity can be observed. What role social work will take in the post Covid-19 era should be a focus of reflection by both practitioners and educators.

The dwindling resources in Africa for education will never get better. It remains a challenge for educators, learners, and practitioners to become innovative in finding resources for fieldwork pedagogy in particular. The current pandemic will simply worsen the bad situation on the continent. The economies in most African countries are weak and cannot withstand the onslaught of the pandemic. Education which is a pillar in development will be adversely affected. But this situation cannot be allowed because education offers some answers to the grim state of Africa.

References

Anders, J. R. (1973). *Social Work Training as a Means of Achieving National Goals in Africa In ASWEA Information Centre Addis Ababa*, June 1974 Document 7.

Code of Ethics of the National Association of Social Workers. https://socialwork.utexas.edu/dl/files/academic-programs/other/nasw-code-of

Cox, L.E., Tice, C. J., & Long, D. D. (2016). *Introduction to Social Work. An Advocacy-Based Profession*. Los Angeles: SAGE.

Chandy, L. (2015). 'Africa in Focus: Why is the number of poor people in Africa increasing when Africa's economies are growing?'. The Brookings Institution.

Crenshaw, K (1989). Demarginalizing the Intersection of Race and Sex: A Black Feminist Critique of Antidiscrimination Doctrine, Feminist Theory and Antiracist Politics. *University of Chicago Legal Forum, 1989*(1), Article 8.

Danbury, H. (1994). *Teaching Practical Social Work* (3rd Rev. ed.). Aldershot: Ashgate.

Dhemba, J. (2012). Fieldwork in Social Work Education and Training: Issues and Challenges in the Case of Eastern and Southern Africa. *Social Work and Society International Online Journal, 10*(1), 1–16.

Diallo, H. (1973) Constitution Of The Association of Social Work Education in Africa. Retrieved March 12, 2022, from https://archives.au.int/bitstream/handle/123456789/9497/CM%20698%28XXVI%29_E.pdf?sequence=1&isAllowed=y

Diallo, H. (1974). *Experience in the Setting up of a New School of Social Work in Curricula of Schools of Social Work and Community Development Training Centres in Africa*. Addis Ababa: ASWEA Information Centre. June 1974, Document 7.

Ferguson-Brown, H. (1996). The Origins of the Welfare and Community Development Programmes in Botswana. *Pula: Botswana Journal of African Studies, 10*(2), 66–82.

Glaude, E. S. Jr. (2000). *Exodus, Religion, Race and Nation in Early Nineteenth Century Black America*. Chicago, IL: University of Chicago Press.

Glicken, M. D. (2007). *Social Work in the 21st Century. An Introduction to Social Welfare, Social Issues, and the Profession*. Thousands Oak, CA: Sage.

Goddu, T. A. (1997). *Gothic America: Narrative, History and Nation* (6th ed.). New York: Columbia University Press.

Gorman, A. (2017). *How Amanda Gorman Became the Nation's First Youth Poet*. Retrieved June 12, 2020, fromhttps://www.google.com/search?client=firefox-b-d&q=Amanda+Gorman+and

Hedenquist, J. (1992). *Introduction to Social and Community Development Work in Botswana*. Botswana: Ministry of Local Government and Lands.

Hope, A, & Timmel, S (1999). *Training for Transformation: A Handbook of Community Workers*. Gweru: Mambo Press.

Hutton, M. (1996). *Community, Social Development and Social Change in Social Work Practice in Africa* (M. Hutton, & L.-K. Mwansa (Eds.). Gaborone: PrintConsult.

Hutton, M., & Mwansa, L.-K. (Eds.) (1996). *Social Work Practice in Africa, Social Development in a Community Context*. Gaborone: Printconsult.

Kadushin, A., & Harkness, D. (1992). *Supervision in Social Work*. Columbia University Press.

Kaseke, E. (1986). The Role of Fieldwork in Social Work Training. *Social Work Development and Rural Fieldwork in Journal of Social Development in Africa, 5*(3), 52–62.

Lucas, T. (16 March 2020). Social Justice Commission in the Monitor vol. 21. no. 10. Block 7, Plot 66450 Private Bag B0 340, Gaborone.

Lugard, L. F. J. (1922). *The dual mandate in British tropical Africa*. W. Blackwood and Sons.

Ntseane, D., & Solo, K. (2007). *Social Security and Social Protection in Botswana*. Gaborone: Bay Publishing.

Pratt, D., & Johnson, J. (1998). The Apprenticeship Perspective: Modelling Ways of Being. In D. Pratt, (Ed.), *Five Perspectives on Teaching in Adult and Higher Education*. Malabar, FL: Krieger.

Republic of Botswana, Ministry of Finance and Economic Development. (2020). *2020 Budget Speech by Dr. Thapelo Matsheka, Minister of Finance and Economic Development*. Gaborone: Government Printer.

Royse, D., & Rompf, E. (2007). *Field Instruction: A Guide for Social Work Students*. Boston: Pearson Education.

Shawky, A. (1973). *Political, Social and Economic Trends in Africa: Impact on Social Welfare in Africa In ASWEA Information Centre Addis Ababa*, June 1974 Document 7.

Stiglitz, J. E. (2016). *The Great Divide*. London: Penguin Random House.

Tesfaye, A. (1973). *Social Work Education in Africa: Trends and Prospects in Relation to National Development in Africa In ASWEA by Information Centre Addis Ababa*, June 1974, Document 7.

United Nations Development Programme. (2019). *Human Development Reports*. New York: United Nations Development Programme.

University of Botswana Calendar. (1990–1991). Gaborone. University of Botswana 1990-1991. Compiled by the Calendar Committee (Secretary: MD.D. Kuhlmann, Co-editors: Dr F.T.K. Sefe and Dr C.D. Yandila)

University of Botswana, Department of Social Work. (1994). *Fieldwork Manual*. Gaborone: University of Botswana.

World Bank Report. (2015). *Botswana Poverty Assessment*. Washington, DC: World Bank.

World Bank Report. (2019). *Poverty and Inequality: Botswana's Persistent Challenge*. Washington: World Bank.

Yimam, A. (1974). *Curricula of Schools of Social Work and Community Development Training Centres in Africa in ASWEA Information Centre Addis Ababa*, June 1974 Document 7.

Zafar, R. (1997). *We Wear the Mask: African Americans Write American Literature 1760–1870*. New York: Columbia University Press.

Zastrow, C. (1993). *Introduction to Social Work and Social Welfare* (5th ed.). California, USA: Brooks Cole.

25
Social Work Field Instruction in an Open and Distance Learning (ODL) Context

Boitumelo Joyce Mohapi

The International Federation of Social Work (IFSW) defines social work as

> A practice-based profession and an academic discipline that promotes social change and development, social cohesion, and the empowerment and liberation of people. Principles of social justice, human rights, collective responsibility and respect for diversities are central to social work. Underpinned by theories of social work, social sciences, humanities and indigenous knowledge, social work engages people and structures to address life challenges and enhance wellbeing.
>
> *(IFSW, 2014)*

The above indicates that social work is practice-based, meaning that social workers' training has a theoretical and practical work component, which is also referred to as field instruction, field placement, field education fieldwork, practicum, Work Integrated Learning (WiL), or internship (My Social Work Lab, 2011).

According to Kaseke (1991), social work was introduced globally to respond to the increased vulnerability of people caused by the Industrial Revolution and ensuing urbanisation. Colonial administrators introduced Africa's profession to counter urban areas' social issues (Kaseke, 1991). Before ushering in professional social work, welfare services were offered through either faith-based or traditional structures. The colonial administrators' reason for introducing welfare services was that social ills like destitution, prostitution, and drug abuse, if not dealt with, would cause disorder and instability in urban areas (Kaseke, 1991).

In Africa, social work education and training were launched in the 1920s and 1940s in Egypt and South Africa, respectively. The Jan Hofmeyer College was established in South Africa in 1924, and the Higher Institute for Social Work was established in Cairo in 1946. In West Africa, in Ghana, the School of Social Welfare in Accra was established in 1946, and the University of Ghana started teaching social work in 1956. In Southern Africa, the School of Social Work in Zimbabwe was established in 1964. The Oppenheimer College of Social Science in Zambia was made part of the University of Zambia in 1965.

In the North African region, the School of Social Work at the University of Khartoum in Sudan was established in 1969. In East Africa, a school of Social Work commenced in 1966 in

Ethiopia. In another Southern African country, in Botswana, the Department of Social Work was formed at the University of Botswana in 1985 (Mupedziswa & Sinkamba, 2014).

The growth of social work as an academic discipline in the African continent is also confirmed by Midgley (1981), who affirms that by 1973, the International Association of Schools of Social Work (IASSW) had registered 25 schools of social work from Africa. The number of social work training institutions has continued to grow, with institutions in Uganda, Kenya, Tanzania, Lesotho, and Swaziland.

Chitereka (2009) also asserts that social work is a young profession on the African continent. Mupedziswa (2005) maintains that social work was influenced and modelled according to the colonising powers' activities in Africa, and is focused on the remedial or curative approach. These colonising powers include Britain, France, and Portugal.

In Africa, social work now exists as a profession in many countries, like Zimbabwe, South Africa, Zambia, Ethiopia, Swaziland, Nigeria, Uganda, Ghana, Kenya, Tanzania, Rwanda, and Egypt training their social workers. This instruction is done in universities; most of them offer face-to-face training in social work. In South Africa, Open and Distance Learning (ODL) social work education is offered by the University of South Africa.

ODL social work training also recently emerged in Ethiopia (2008) at St. Mary's University (SMU) and supported by Indira Gandhi National Open University (IGNOU).

Vicary et al. (2018) point out that the phrase 'distance learning' itself is not a single concept, but is widely used as if it were. Collins (2008:423) defines distance learning as 'a perceived subset of open learning provided usually to individual learners and study materials delivered to their home either through hard copy materials, television or other media'.

Since distance education has become a platform for the delivery of education worldwide (Gabriel et al. 2015), the ODL system in India has emerged as a critical mode for providing education to large sections of society. With the spread in the information and communication technology sector, the classroom or campus boundaries are becoming blurred.

The ODL mode allows for easy access, affordability, broad reach across the country, and convenience for the population's marginalised and disadvantaged sections (Dash, 2018). The Indian system of ODL education is one of the largest globally, coming second after China. Although China has an extensive ODL system in social work, Leung (2007:392) asserts that

> The social work community in China … comprises academics and the top officials of the Ministry of Civil Affairs. Social work teachers often have neither formal pre-service social work training nor relevant practical experience. At best, they would have received limited on-the-job training in social work practice … It is thus difficult to rely on them to build social work knowledge and to demonstrate their value and contribution to society. The Ministry of Civil Affairs, for its part, has the desire to professionalise its own social welfare services, notably in the care of people with mental and physical disabilities, orphans and older people. But it may show little interest in supporting a generic social work practice.

Although China has a long history of offering social work in an ODL mode, the above indicates that there is still much work to reach all the vulnerable groups who may need social work services.

India also has an extensive distance education system, second only to China (University Grants Commission, 2017). Such pedagogy in India is offered by different training institutions, like the National Open University, Central Universities, State Open University, and State private universities.

Dash (2018) affirms that in India, distance education is also offered in various distance educational institutions (DEIS), and other entities like stand-alone institutions, professional associations, government institutions, and private institutions. The author further states that 'a new chapter in the field of distance education was opened in India with the establishment of Dr Bhim Rao Ambedkar Open University in Hyderabad in 1982 followed by the establishment of IGNOU at the national level by an act of parliament of India in 1985' (Dash, 2018:814). There are 17 open universities in India. From a single institution in 1962, the number of ODL establishments has reached 256. ODL constitutes over 22% of the total enrolment in higher education in India. (University Grants Commission, 2017).

The Indira Gandhi National Open University (IGNOU) started offering the Bachelor of Social Work (BSW) Programme through ODL mode in the year 2004 and the Master of Social Work (MSW) Programme in 2008, which is also being offered in Nepal and Ethiopia both in Hindi and English. Thus, the Indira Gandhi National Open University (IGNOU) system allows people from every walk of life to benefit from the ODL system. Some of the beneficiaries include retired persons, housewives, and people in employment.

The BSW and MSW programme in IGNOU was developed in response to requests from social service agencies across the country and the desire to reach the unreached by providing an accessible and affordable graduate and post-graduate education in social work (Dash, 2018). With its national network of student support services,

> IGNOU can provide the much-needed quality education that benefits thousands of individuals, social welfare, and development agencies across the country. To date, only about 25 universities in India offer social work education through ODL.

In Ethiopia, social work was offered through an ODL mode in 2008. This ODL mode of teaching social work was started at Saint Mary's University (SMU), with Indira Gandhi National Open University (IGNOU)'s support from India. This shift in the mode of teaching aimed to make social work education more accessible to students.

In South Africa, the University of South Africa (Unisa) is the only university offering the Bachelor of Social Work qualification in an ODL mode. This delivery model has implications for the field instruction component of the training, including field placements, supervision, and assessments.

Social Work Field Instruction

Because social work is a practice-based profession, field instruction forms part of its training. According to My Social Work Lab (2011), the history of social work field instruction in the United States of America dates back to the Charity Organisation Societies' era in the nineteenth century when social work students learned through apprenticeships. The apprenticeship training focused on learning by doing. By the end of the nineteenth-century social work, training began shifting from the apprenticeship training when schools of social work were being established in the United States of America. A social work practitioner named Mary Richmond argued that social workers' practical training needs to be supplemented by theory, paving the way for educationally based fieldwork practice. The schools of social work now had the opportunity to select the organisations where students were placed, which, in turn, made them control the quality of the practical work to which students were exposed. The trend in early social work education was that students would spend approximately half of their training in fieldwork settings, and the other half in the classroom.

Regarding fieldwork instruction in Africa, Gray et al. (2017) state that the focus should be on developmental social work. The authors avow that many educational establishments in southern and east Africa have made efforts to provide fieldwork placements that focus on developmental social work. The challenge that remains is that the majority of these fieldwork placements are in urban areas. In contrast, the majority of poor people in Africa live in rural areas. To ensure that students who undertake field instruction are conversant with developmental social work, training institutions need to make an effort to provide opportunities for placements in rural communities which will enable the students to work alongside development workers engaged in agricultural, water, sanitation, and infrastructural development programmes; primary healthcare provision, including child nutrition, maternal and child health, disability, AIDS and HIV interventions; micro-enterprise development; and adult education to enhance adult literacy.

Whilst field instruction placements in the rural areas of Africa are an ideal way of enhancing the students' knowledge of developmental social work, Hall (1990:18) notes that 'some students are reluctant to take on placements in rural areas, where conditions can be very demanding'. The reluctance of the students to work in such contexts is counterproductive in promoting developmental social work.

The International Federation of Social Workers (IFSW) has set standards that all social work training institutions must adhere to when conducting field instructions. These will be discussed in the next section.

Standards for Social Work Field Education

The International Federation of Social Work (IFSW, 2004) developed standards for social work field education. The IFSW (2004) stipulates that the following standards should be used to guide fieldwork education:

- There should be clear plans for the organisation, implementation, and assessment of both theory and field instruction.
- Service users should be involved in the planning and delivery of the programme.
- Indigenous or locally relevant social work education and practice should be recognised and developed. This knowledge should be based on different groups' traditions and cultures, but it should not violate human rights.
- The curriculum should continuously be reviewed and developed.
- Schools of social work should ensure that the curriculum assists social work students in developing critical thinking skills and becoming lifelong learners.
- The duration should be sufficient. Students' field education should also have the necessary complexity of tasks and learning opportunities to prepare students sufficiently for professional practice.
- The school of social work should have links with the agency where students are placed and coordinate the field placement.
- There should be an orientation for fieldwork supervisors.
- Fieldwork lecturers and supervisors should have the necessary qualifications and appropriate experience, as determined by the specific country's requirements and the social work profession's status in a specific country.
- Fieldwork lecturers should be included in curriculum development, and they should participate fully in this process.
- An educational institution training social workers should form partnerships with agencies where students are placed for fieldwork and service users. The agency and service users

should also be involved in decision-making about fieldwork education and assessing the student's fieldwork performance.
- The educational institution should provide fieldwork supervisors with a fieldwork manual. This manual should indicate the fieldwork standards, procedures, assessment criteria, and expectations.
- The educational institution should ensure that adequate and appropriate resources are provided for the qualification fieldwork component.

The IFSW standards described above clearly indicate that fieldwork instruction requires proper planning before it is undertaken. There should also be sufficient resources to ensure that fieldwork instruction is undertaken correctly, which has implications for human, financial, and other resources.

The South African Context

The early social welfare policies in South Africa were mainly prompted by colonialism and apartheid, which led to the development of welfare policies which were racially biased, and which enforced many social changes over traditional societies.

The process of industrialisation, which was heralded by the discovery of minerals in South Africa in the 1800s, also influenced the social and political structures of South Africa to change from being mainly farming communities to that of industrial communities. The effect of this was an increase in poverty, housing, and health problems.

Patel (2005) states the industrialisation processes and urbanisation brought about large-scale poverty, health, and housing problems. As a result, vulnerable groups like children, the poor, and persons with disabilities received social relief assistance. Their needs were met mostly through institutional care offered by faith-based organisations like the Dutch Reformed Church. That is why the first type of social legislation adopted addressed the needs of these vulnerable groups.

The first two child welfare organisations in the Cape and Johannesburg were established in 1908 and 1909. After establishing the Union of South Africa in 1910, welfare planning for white people in South Africa was initiated through the coordination of church and voluntary welfare organisations (Patel, 2005) which was the beginning of partnerships between government and voluntary organisations in the welfare sector.

The history of social welfare in South Africa can be traced back to 1929 when the Carnegie Commission was formed to investigate the 'poor white problem' (Patel, 2005). The Carnegie Commission recommended that a state welfare department should be established to overcome the fragmented approach to welfare services being rendered by different departments.

The first state department of welfare in South Africa was established in 1937. The purpose of this department was to restore malfunctioning individuals and families and to coordinate social services. This milestone is viewed as the beginning of the professionalisation of social work.

In this regard, McKendrick (1990) states 'it is in this period 1937–1950 that the effect of South African historical experience on the development of a social welfare philosophy and system can be seen most clearly'. This was the beginning of the government's involvement in welfare services, which had previously been rendered only by volunteer faith-based groups and community organisations. The focus of these welfare services was the alleviation of poverty.

Universities and religious colleges then followed by training social workers in the 1940s. (Patel, 2005).

The legislation, which provided the framework for delivery of welfare services in South Africa, was the Social and Associated Workers' Act, number 110 of 1978. It put in place mechanisms for control over the profession of social work and associated professions (Mckendrick, 1990), which granted social work full professional status.

The National Welfare Act (1978) made provision for the registration of welfare organisations and the establishment of a South African Welfare Council, which served in an advisory capacity to the minister of welfare on welfare matters, and regional establishment welfare boards for different race groups.

The welfare landscape had since changed when democracy was introduced in South Africa in 1994. New policies were introduced, as was a new constitution in 1996.

In South Africa, there are currently 16 universities offering social work training. Only one university amongst them, namely the University of South Africa (Unisa), offers social work training in a distance learning mode.

South Africa has a Council of Higher Education (CHE). The CHE is an independent statutory body established in Section 4 of the Higher Education Act (Act 101 of 1997). The mission of the CHE as the independent statutory quality council for South African higher education is to:

- Lead and manage quality assurance.
- Research and monitor trends and development.
- Initiate critical discourse on contemporary higher education issues and advise the minister on strategy and policy.

The Council for Higher Education (CHE) states that distance education, as a collection of methods, is concerned with finding ways to communicate and mediate the curriculum without necessarily requiring lecturers and students to be in the same place simultaneously (CHE, 2014:4). The CHE further states that distance education assumes a spatial separation of students and lecturers the majority of the time, which means that there are no students on campus for most or all of the time. In distance education, the emphasis is on teaching, learning, and assessment for students located in different places, who do not need to be physically present at the place where the lecturer is.

Universities have different options to choose from when offering distance education. The single-mode distance education is where all teaching, learning, and assessment is through distance or a dual mode where a contact university offers some of its courses in a distance mode. Another approach to distance education is a mixed approach, where courses are offered through contact teaching and distance education (CHE, 2014:4).

Social work is also a regulated profession in South Africa. All social work professionals and students (from the second year of study) must be registered with the South African Council for Social Service Professions (SACSSP).

The South African Council for Social Service Professions (SACSSP) is a statutory body established in Section 2 of the Social Service Professions Act 110 of 1978. Based on this Act's provisions, the SACSSP's comprehensive role is to determine, guide, and direct the authority body within the structure of social service professions in South Africa. The Council fulfils this role by setting the standards for education and training of practitioners and by taking policy resolutions as guidelines for the practising of the social service professions under its auspices (www.sacssp.co.za).

The SACSSP in conjunction with its professional boards guides and regulates the profession of social work in aspects of registration; education and training; professional conduct and ethical behaviour; ensuring continuing professional development; and fostering compliance with professional standards. It promotes and protects the integrity of the social service professions and the public's interest at large (www.sacssp.co.za).

To safeguard the public and the professions' integrity, no one may practise the social work profession without being registered with the South African Council for Social Service Professions as stipulated in the Social Service Professions Act 110 of 1978. Thus, registration is mandatory for social workers and student social workers who are studying social work.

To ensure that the training offered to student social workers meets quality assurance standards, the SACSSP (2020:21) has set norms and standards for fieldwork instruction, which have to be adhered to by all universities which offer social work training in South Africa. These norms and standards are set out in the table below.

The norms and standards of the SACSSP regarding social work field education clearly outline all the requirements for field education in South Africa. All educational institutions, agencies where students are placed, and the field education supervisors have to adhere to these norms and standards and display professional and ethical behaviour.

The existence of the Council of Higher Education and the SACSSP in South Africa is proof that South Africa has laws, policies, and systems to ensure quality in higher education, specifically in social workers' training.

The next section will focus specifically on the University of South Africa and its field education process.

The University of South Africa Fieldwork Education

The University of South Africa (Unisa) is the largest open distance learning institution in Africa and the most prolonged standing dedicated to distance education universities worldwide. The university enrols nearly one-third of all South African university students (www.unisa.ac.za). The university is founded based on the Higher Education Act 101 of 1997 and the University Statute.

Founded in 1873 as the University of the Cape of Good Hope, Unisa became the first public university to teach exclusively through distance education in 1946. Throughout the years, Unisa was perhaps the only university in South Africa to have provided all people with access to education, irrespective of race, colour, or creed.

Unisa has eight colleges, namely:

- Accounting sciences
- Agriculture and environment sciences
- Economics and management sciences
- Education
- College of Graduate Studies
- Human Sciences
- Law
- Science, Engineering, and Technology.

The Department of Social Work is an academic department based in the College of Human Sciences.

Since social work practice in South Africa is regulated by the SACSSP, there are specific criteria that fieldwork-training programmes have to adhere to in order to ensure quality assurance. The two leading role players in fieldwork education are the placement agency (management and supervisors/contact persons) and the university (national practical coordinator, social work lecturers).

Table 25.1 SACSSP Norms and Standards for Bachelor of Social Work Field Instruction

Norm	Standards
Practice experience is integral to the programme.	(a) A departmental policy on-field instruction is available that addresses, among others, hours per year, skills development activities, number of sessions of casework/group work/community work practice per level, reporting requirements, supervision, and a scaffolding approach. (b) The BSW field practice component is overseen by the Head of Department or Programme Leader and forms an integral part of its management activities. (c) Theory and practise are integrated at all levels. The theoretical modules are aligned with field instruction modules at each level. (d) Integrated field instruction is offered to students from the first year to the fourth year.
Practice experience appropriately supports the delivery of the programme and the achievement of the learning outcomes.	(a) Over the four years, students complete and provide evidence of at least 700 hours of actual social work in the field (excluding report writing). (b) Field education placements are structured so that students can cover all areas of the set outcomes and have access to a wide range of learning experiences in various practice environments that reflect the practice setting of social work practice. (c) Students have multiple opportunities (i.e., at more than only one year of study) to practice at each casework, group work, and community work levels. (d) The placements are well structured per year/level, to facilitate increased practice complexity, proficiency, and time in the field. (e) Logbooks are used in the entire field education experience of a student. (f) All second-level social work students are registered with the SACSSP before the commencement of their field education placement. (g) Students are oriented to each new placement. (h) Each student is assigned a suitable supervisor for the placement duration, such that all work is done under supervision. (i) Students gain experience at different placements each year. (j) Students who are more than one year over time have an individualised educational development plan.
The field education placement setting provides a safe and supportive environment.	(a) The agencies where students are placed have a safety policy in place and conduct periodic risk or safety assessments to ensure adherence to their policy. (b) Students undergo orientation to the placement's safety policy. (c) Cases allocated by the agency to a student are appropriate to his/her level of skill and competence, and the learning requirements of that level of study. (d) Field education placements have a policy regarding students' safety on aggression and sexual harassment from service users and placement staff. (e) Higher Education Institutions (HEIs) monitor the incidence of violence (muggings, assaults, rape etc.) as students move between the HEI and practice placements. (f) HEIs make efforts to reduce these incidents' likelihood and improve responsiveness to these incidents.

(*Continued*)

Table 25.1 Continued

Norm	Standards
The HEI must maintain a comprehensive and useful system for approving and monitoring all field education placements.	(a) Field education placement selection criteria and the accreditation process of placements are documented. (b) The programme has ongoing documented partnership arrangements (e.g., Memoranda of Understanding) with agencies, setting out the agency's roles and responsibilities, supervisors, HEI, and students. (c) Individual student placement contracts are in place for each student-placement pairing that sets out expectations, limitations, rules, rights, and grievance procedures. (d) A process for monitoring placements is documented and applied. (e) Student field education placements are terminated by the HEI at the end of the student placement. (f) Case files are appropriately and ethically stored, and cases are referred at the termination of field education placements. (g) Field education placements are terminated or re-contracted by the end of each academic year.
The field education placement providers have equality and diversity policies concerning students and how these will be implemented and monitored.	(a) The field education placement provider has proof of implementing the Employment Equity Policy for its staff profile. (b) Students are informed about the agency's policies on diversity, how to access them, and utilise them if they feel that they are discriminated.
Adequate numbers of appropriately qualified and experienced staff members are available to offer students appropriate supervision.	(a) Only SACSSP registered social workers, with at least two years' (three less than stipulated in the national Supervision Framework) practice experience, supervise students, except for supervisors of fourth-year students who require at least three years' practice experience. (b) Supervisors are oriented to the practical training requirements of the social work programme. (c) Supervisors receive regular in-service training from the HEI or agency relevant to supervision and/or the competencies required for the year group they supervise. (d) Supervisors involved in the formative and summative assessment are provided with appropriate training and guidance, which is CPD-accredited. (e) Supervisors are provided with professional development opportunities to enhance supervision quality (e.g., access to the university library, provision of course-related readings, CPD activities).
There are appropriately qualified and mandated staff at the HEI to manage field education experience of social work students at all levels.	(a) Sufficient academic staff are tasked to work on the field education programme. (b) Staff are mandated to coordinate and/or run the field education programme.

(Continued)

Table 25.1 Continued

Norm	Standards
Unethical conduct is managed.	(a) Students are not permitted to do fieldwork education until they are registered as student social workers with SACSSP. (b) Supervision and practice workshops address ethical conduct in practice. (c) Supervisors receive training on the ethics of providing supervision and supervisors' accountability for student conduct. (d) Mechanisms are in place to deal with unethical conduct by student social workers, academic staff, supervisors, or field education agency staff. (e) Service users are protected from unethical or unprofessional conduct by student social workers. (f) Severe cases of ethical misconduct are reported to the SACSSP.
The field has the opportunity to contribute to the quality of the BSW programme.	(a) Supervisors and field education agencies are invited (at least annually) to give feedback on various aspects of the BSW programme, including field education, supervision, preparation of students for practice, theory, course content, ethics, HEI-placement relations, and community projects.

Souce: Adapted from SACSSP Norms and Standards for the BSW (2020)

Before embarking on any practical work, students have to register with the SACSSP as student social workers, and they have to obtain police clearance to confirm that they do not have a criminal record.

During the first year of study, social work students at the University of South Africa are required to complete 40 hours of observation at an approved organisation under the supervision of a supervisor registered with the South African Council for Social Service Professions (SACSSP).

In the second year, the students have to undertake a maximum of 15 days of work-integrated learning at an approved organisation, also under the supervision of a social worker. In addition, second-year students have to attend practice sessions, offered in the form of workshops, which last six days.

The third-year students attend 18 days of practice sessions. They also have to complete 30 days of work-integrated learning at an approved organisation. The students have to conduct four casework sessions and four group work sessions. They are also expected to assess one community work project.

Final year social work students (fourth year) have to do work-integrated learning at an approved organisation from February to August in an academic year.

In the second week of February, the students have to spend one full week at the organisation they are assigned to (block placement). During this block placement, the students have to familiarise themselves with the organisation and negotiate with the organisation's contact person about the practical work they will do and the days they will spend at the organisation.

Thereafter they have to spend one or two days per week at the organisation, depending on the practical work (casework, group work, or community work).

The placement at organisations (Work Integrated Learning) provides an opportunity for social work students to acquire practical skills, knowledge, and professional values and develop a sense of professional identity. The practical work makes an essential contribution in preparing student social workers for the professional world of social work.

They then undergo oral assessments during September and October. The students also have to submit a portfolio of evidence (PoE) to display their work-integrated learning. When leaving the organisation, students are expected to do proper termination with all the people they have worked with.

The role players involved in the fieldwork instruction are the university, the placement organisation, the contact person at the organisation, the supervisor, and the student.

The University

The SACSSP has standards to which a university offering social work training must adhere. In terms of these standards, the university has to ensure that practice experience is part of its training. Therefore, the university has to have staff members who can manage students' field instruction at all levels. The fieldwork experience has to ensure that the learning outcomes set for the students are achieved and that the students are allowed to put into practice the theory they have learnt.

A university doing social work training has to put systems in place to manage any student's unethical conduct and have a system of approving and monitoring fieldwork instruction.

Unisa has a national coordinator for field instruction, who works with lecturers to manage work-integrated learning.

The roles of field instruction coordinator and the lecturers are negotiating with potential placement organisations to offer students an opportunity to do practical work and allocate students to organisations. They also allocate supervisors who will supervise the students' practical work. The students, supervisors, contact persons, and organisations are offered orientation regarding the Unisa expectations for student practical work.

The lecturers and field instruction coordinator also maintain regular contact with organisations to assess the placement's continued viability. The Unisa staff members also do the quality control of the students' work.

When there is misconduct or unethical issues, an ethics committee handles these matters and decides on the appropriate sanction in terms of the university's policies.

The Unisa lecturers also conduct practical work workshops in the different areas/provinces where students practise their skills.

The Placement Organisation

The SACSSP requires that those placement organisations have appropriately qualified staff members and appropriate policies to manage placements. The organisation should also contribute to the Bachelor of Social Work (BSW) programme.

The University of South Africa places students for fieldwork education in all the nine provinces of South Africa. The organisations offering students a place to do their practical work in casework, group work, and community work include non-government organisations, provincial government departments (for example, the departments of social development and correctional services), local government departments or municipalities, and faith-based organisations.

Students' practical work has to ensure that they practise the theory and skills they learned.

In this context, the organisation's role is to confirm placements at the organisation and inform the university if they have a specific request regarding placements. The organisation also has to allocate a qualified social worker as a contact person for the student. There has to be ongoing communication between the organisation and the university so that if difficulties arise, they can be resolved timeously.

The Practical Work Supervisor

The Unisa Department of Social Work appoints the practical work supervisor to assist social work students in organisations to implement their practical work. The supervisor has to be registered with the SACSSP as a social worker.

All appointed supervisors are mandated to attend an orientation workshop arranged by the Department of Social Work at Unisa. The workshop's focus is on the process of supervision, the theoretical content of the relevant modules, and the relevant administrative issues. This workshop is compulsory since all persons involved with the students' training must have a common understanding of the theory that the students are taught. The integration of this theory and practice is concerned.

The practical work supervisors meet with their allocated group of students on a weekly or basis. The main task of the supervisor is to help students to integrate social work theory and practice. They also have to offer professional guidance to the students regarding their practical work.

The Student

The student has to be registered as a student social worker with the SACSSP to undertake field instruction.

The student who is doing practical work is expected to attend workshops as stipulated in their study material. These workshops are compulsory and allow students to link theory with practical work. Simulations and role-plays are done during the workshops to offer students an opportunity to practice their skills.

A practical work guide is provided to students. This guide gives detailed information about the requirement for practical wok, the practical work curriculum, and the dates of the different activities that students have to complete.

As stated earlier, students are expected to do one full week of 'block placement' in February. Thereafter they have to spend one or two days per week at the organisation, depending on the practical work that they are doing. During the block placement, they have to identify potential clients (for casework) or the group's nature (for group work) that they need to run. The students also have to do community work.

The placement organisation has to give the student a field instruction *contract*. The contract has to specify the time that the student is expected to spend at the organisation. The contract also has to specify the student and the organisation's expectations and professional conduct.

The student is expected to keep a *logbook* completed weekly and signed by the contact person at the organisation.

The university also requires regular *feedback* about the student from the organisation. The organisation is provided with forms to complete for feedback.

Conclusion

Globally, India has an extensive system of ODL training, which includes the training of social workers through open and distance learning.

Social work in Africa was launched in the 1920s in South Africa and the 1940s in Egypt, but is now offered in many universities in Africa. South Africa and Ethiopia now offer social work training in an ODL mode.

The training of social workers has a field instruction component, and the standards for this are set by the International Federation of Social Work (IFSW).

In South Africa, the University of South Africa (Unisa) is in a unique situation as it is the only institution teaching social work in a distance learning mode.

The social work curriculum has a field instruction component, which necessitates contact between lecturers, students, and supervisors. The onslaught of the COVID-19 epidemic has reduced the amount of contact between people. Innovative ways had to be found to use video conferencing and other electronic media for workshops and meetings with students. The students also had to find alternative ways of reducing contact, like creating electronic groups and using other social media platforms. More innovative means of conducting field instructions should be explored to become a genuinely ODL institution. Further research needs to be conducted to explore whether students have access to the necessary technology and infrastructure.

References

Chitereka, C. (2009) Social work practice in a developing continent: The case of Africa. *Advances in Social Work, 10*(2), 144–156.

Collins, S. (2008). Open and distance learning in qualifying social work education in Britain and the USA: celebrating diversity and difference? *Social Work Education, 27*(4), 422–439.

Council on Higher Education. (2014). *Distance Higher Education Programmes In a Digital Era: Good Practice Guide*. Pretoria: Council on Higher Education.

Dash, B. M. (2018). Social work education through open and distance learning in India: Opportunities and challenges. *Social Work Education, 37*(6), 813–820.

Gabriel, N., Boahenamnd, K., & Boadi, M. O. (2015). Assessing the effectiveness of distance education within the context of traditional classroom. www.scrip.org/journal/ce

Gray, M., Agllias, K., Mupedziwa, R., & Mugumbate, J. (2017). The role of social work field education programmes in the transmission of developmental social work knowledge in Southern and East Africa. *Social Work Education, 36*(6), 623–635.

Hall, N. (1990). *Social work training in Africa: A fieldwork manual*. Harare: School of Social Work.

International Federation for Social Work (2004). Global standards for social work education and training. www.ifsw.org

International Federation of Social Work. (2014). *Global Definition of the Social Work Profession*. Document adopted at the IFSW General Meeting and the IASSW General Assembly in July 2014 www.ifsw.org

Kaseke, E.; (1991). Social work practice in Zimbabwe. *Journal of Social Development in Africa*. 6 (1), 33–45.

Leung, J. C. B. (2007). An international definition of social work for China. *International Journal of Social Welfare, 16*, 391–397.

McKendrick, B. W. (1990). *Introduction to social work in South Africa*. Pretoria: Haum Tertiary.

Midgley, J. (1981). *Professional imperialism: social work in the Third World*. London: Heinemann.

Mupedziswa, R. (2005). Challenges and prospects of social work services in Africa. In J. C. Akeibunor & E. E. Anugwom (Eds.), *The social sciences and socio-economic transformation in Africa* (pp. 271–317). Nsukka: Great AP Express Publishing.

Mupedziswa, R., & Sinkamba, P. (2014). Social work education and training in Southern and East Africa: yesterday, today and tomorrow. In C. Noble, H. Strauss, & B. Littlechild (Eds.), *Global social work: Crossing borders, blurring boundaries* (pp. 141–153). University of Sydney: Sydney University Press.

My Social Work Lab. (2011). *Field Instruction and the social work curriculum*. Pearson: Mysocialworklab. www.mysocialworklab.com.

Patel, L. (2005). *Social Welfare and Social Development*. Cape Town: Oxford University Press.

South African Council for Social Service Professions. (2020). *Norms and Standards for Bachelor of Social Work (BSW)*. Pretoria: South African Council for Social Service Professions.

South African Council for Social Service Professions. Accessed on May 27, 2021, from www.sacssp.co.za.

University Grants Commission. (2017). *Distance education bureau.* Accessed on January 7, 2021, from http://www.ugc.ac.in/deb/

University of South Africa. (2020). *Experiential learning programme /Placement organisation guideline.* Pretoria: University of South Africa.

University of South Africa. Accessed on May 28, 2021, from www.unisa.ac.za

Vicary, S., Copperman, J., & Higgs, A. (2018). Social work education through distance learning: The challenges and opportunities. *Social Work Education, 37*(6), 685–690.

26
Fieldwork Practice in Countries with Recently Introduced Social Work Training

Lessons from Lesotho

Sophia Thabane, Pumela Nomfundo Mahao, and Tšepang Florence Manyeli

Described as the signature pedagogy of social work training by the (USA) Council of Social Work Education, fieldwork practice is an integral component of social work training (Wayne, Bogo, & Raskin, 2010 in Simpson & Raniga, 2014). It presents an opportunity for experiential application of professional reflexivity, ethical conduct and reasoning as well as engagement with human vulnerability for the first time for some students. This two-dimensional training component, consisting of observation and application, places students in contact with social work clients' lived experiences, opening the opportunity to simultaneously test and hone classroom-acquired knowledge (Bogo, 2006; Dhemba, 2012; Hantman & Ben-Oz, 2014; Mwansa, 2011; Schmidt & Rautenbach, 2015; Simpson & Raniga, 2014; Tanga, 2013). In Lesotho, where the majority of social work students enter university directly from high school, it represents the developmental path from student to professional (Darkwa, 2007; Dhemba, 2012; Hantman & Ben-Oz, 2014; Mwansa, 2011). Thus, student experience of fieldwork practice can be as heuristic, didactic, and eye-opening as it can be humbling and traumatic, calling for deliberate planning and implementation along with ongoing oversight and reflection by all stakeholders: training institutions, placement agencies, and students alike (Bogo, 2006; Gray et al., 2018; Mwansa, 2011). The realities of training which include resource and practical considerations, however, often encumber implementation of the most relevant and efficacious approach to fieldwork practice, more so in countries such as Lesotho where professional social work training and practice are at an emerging stage (Darkwa, 2007; Dhemba, 2012; Gray et al., 2018; Mwansa, 2011).

Against the above background, this chapter shares the National University of Lesotho's (NUL) experiences of delivering the fieldwork practice component of social work training for almost 20 years (from 2001 to 2020) and documents lessons and possibilities for optimising use of human and other resources without compromising standards. The chapter opens with definitions of fieldwork practice, continues to describe the socioeconomic context of Lesotho, followed by selected theoretical perspectives on fieldwork practice and supervision. Fourth, it presents an overview of fieldwork practice at NUL and delineates how this was implemented upon inception of the programme as well as how it is implemented in a redesigned curriculum. Finally, lessons learnt in delivering fieldwork practice are followed by recommendations to universities on fieldwork format and coordination whether universities are planning on or whether they recently introduced social work training.

Fieldwork Practice in Social Work Training

A widely used definition of fieldwork practice is one by Hamilton and Else (1983 in Dhemba, 2012) who view it as, 'a consciously planned set of experiences occurring in a practice setting designed to move students from their initial level of understanding, skills and attitudes to levels associated with autonomous social work practice'. Hepworth, Rooney, and Larsen (2002) along with Bogo (2006) extend the definition by explaining that fieldwork engages students in supervised social work practice and provides real-life opportunities to apply theory to practice within practice settings. Lastly, authorities are in agreement that fieldwork practice should take place under direct supervision by trained and experienced social workers (Chui, 2010; Dhemba, 2012; Gray et al., 2018; Haanwinckel et al., 2018; Mwansa, 2011; Raskin, Wayne, & Bogo, 2008; Schmidt & Rautenbach, 2015; Simpson & Raniga, 2014; Tanga, 2013).

The Socioeconomic Context of Lesotho

'Basotho' refers to the native population of Lesotho. Lesotho is beleaguered by a myriad of socioeconomic concerns including pervasive incidence of poverty, inequality, unemployment, and high dependency ratio, all of which are compounded by a disquieting rate of HIV infection. According to the United Nations Development Programme (UNDP) (2018), Lesotho ranked 159/189 in compound Human Development Indicators. Country specific poverty statistics showed that 49.7% of the estimated population of 2,268,932 (World Population Review) was living below the National Poverty Datum Line in 2017, a 7% improvement from the previously recorded level of 56.6% in 2002. Disaggregated figures of the same year showed absolute poverty levels of 28.5% and 60.7% in urban and rural areas respectively with a country Gini-coefficient of 44.6 as well as dependency ratios of 2.0 and 2.8 for non-poor and poor respectively (World Bank, 2019:25, 32 & 63). Dependency ratios were exacerbated by prevailing unemployment rates of 24% of working age Basotho, attributable to massive retrenchment of Basotho from South African mines coupled with limited labour absorptive capacity of Lesotho's public and agricultural sectors (Tanga et al., 2017:153).

Lastly, Lesotho had the second highest HIV prevalence rate globally with more than a quarter or 25.6% of Basotho reportedly infected with HIV in the last National Demographic Health Survey, with age-disaggregated prevalence of almost half or 49.5% among females in the age group 35–39 years old and 46.9% among males in the 40–44 years old age group (Ministry of Health [Lesotho] and ICF Macro, 2016). On a positive note, national HIV treatment and management programmes have significantly reduced HIV-related mortality resulting in 68.9% of the population on HIV treatment with satisfactory viral load suppression (Ministry of Health [Lesotho], Centre for Disease Control and Prevention, and ICAP Columbia University of Public Health, 2017).

A combination of poverty, inequality, unemployment, and high dependency ratio is the impetus for various secondary social problems such as poor social services, childhood, and older persons' vulnerability, amongst others.

Theoretical Perspectives on Fieldwork Practice, Supervision, and Assessment

Fieldwork practice and supervision are best discussed from the starting point of two corresponding perspectives: Elton Mayo's Humanistic Theory of Management (Eriksson-Zetterquist et al., 2011) with Kadushin and Harkness (2002) typology of professional social work supervision. Elton Mayo's theory illuminated an otherwise under-recognised aspect of management studies, the human dimension. Implied in the results of Mayo's series of studies conducted in Hawthorne between 1927 and 1932 was that organisations ought to regard employees from an individualised psychosocial perspective before taking them as a homogenous group of workers. Kadushin and Harkness (2002) on the other hand promulgated a three-tier supervision typology of administrative, educative, and supportive supervision where the tiers are complementary and inextricable. Like Elton Mayo (Eriksson-Zetterquist et al., 2011), Kadushin and Harkness (2002) gave prominence to the human element at the workplace emphasising that professional supervision should not ignore workers' pre-acquired experiences and unmet needs which potentially impede or improve performance.

In Kadushin and Harkness' (2002) view, administrative supervision entails coordination of organisational functions to achieve the overarching organisational vision along with allocation of responsibilities and resources to facilitate implementation. Educative supervision is where superiors facilitate comprehension and compliance with organisational protocols for mission accomplishment and arrange for continued professional development as necessary. Supportive supervision is where supervisees' psychosocial needs, which may encumber performance, are taken into account and addressed to optimise performance. As expounded under recommendations below, present authors are in agreement that Elton Mayo's (Eriksson-Zetterquist et al., 2011) along with Kadushin and Harkness' (2002) management/supervision models are fundamental to university fieldwork practice implementation and oversight.

Finally, Simpson and Raniga (2014:180–182) promulgated the following five-stage fieldwork format: planning and preparation, beginning, middle, assessment, ending, and review, which as delineated below, present authors found consideration-worthy for universities planning on introducing social work training.

On supervision of fieldwork practice, Haanwinckel et al. (2018:947) described student fieldwork practice supervision as a medium through which training was translated into professional competence. They further quoted the following principles by Guerra and Braga (2009 in Haanwinckel et al., 2018) on which fieldwork practice supervision was grounded: insolubility of work and training; inextricability of theory and practice; integration of supervision; ethical underpinning; and technical social work knowledge. Additionally, Haanwinckel et al. (2018), who compared the role of social work fieldwork practice supervision in Brazil and England, advised that fieldwork practice supervision should ideally be congruent with students' varied training levels and be planned collaboratively by agency and university representatives.

Hantman and Ben-Oz (2014) on the other hand drew a distinction between social work classroom and field education explaining that classroom education built theoretical knowledge and was largely incumbent on students' cognitive abilities while field education was concerned with development of professional identity acquired through student–agency supervisor relational experiences. The authors further pointed out that the key to development of professional identity by students was role-modelling, which presupposes close interaction or mirroring of agency supervisors by students (Hantman & Ben-Oz, 2014). Hantman and Ben-Oz (2014:493) continued to quote Ronnestad and Skovholt's (2003 in Hantman & Ben-Oz, 2014) six-stage learner development facilitated by supervision during fieldwork practice: lay helper; beginning student; advanced student; novice student; experienced professional; and senior professional. The six-stage process is note-worthy for planning fieldwork implementation, supervision, and assessment.

Consistent with Hantman and Ben-Oz's (2014) thesis, Chui (2010) highlighted possible tensions between assessment of classroom and assessment of field education as the former focuses on recollection while the latter focuses on demonstrable competence, arguing that agency supervisors should work with university lecturers to achieve balanced assessment outcomes. Chui (2010) further propounded the following criteria for balanced assessment of fieldwork: relevance of competence to agency of fieldwork practice; clear, realistic, and measurable criteria adding that assessment scales should be multi-point with wide coverage of key competencies. Hence, fieldwork practice supervision and assessment should be a student and agency-specific process which, by all means, seeks to be objective and broad in coverage. Thus the indispensable component of social work training calls for supervisors to equally command academic accolades as well as personal attributes to appropriately guide students (Chui, 2010; Dhemba, 2012; Gray et al., 2018; Haanwinckel et al., 2018; Hantman & Ben-Oz, 2014; Simpson & Raniga, 2014; Tanga, 2013).

Finally, Chui (2010), Gray and Coates (2010), along with Raskin et al. (2008) questioned universality of prevailing international fieldwork practice standards, cautioning educators against blindly confining themselves to 'international' standards which may not necessarily be sensitive to circumstances in all world regions. Thus, they persuaded academics across the globe to generate empirical evidence of region-specific fieldwork practice standards to inform 'international' standards. Such standards should be developed collaboratively by educators, professionals, academic, and professional standards regulators and overseen by the latter (Chui, 2010; Gray & Coates, 2010; Raskin et al., 2008). African educators were further called upon to generate Africa-specific knowledge informing fieldwork practice as well as to create opportunities for cross-cultural fieldwork exposure (Gray & Allegritti, 2002; Gray & Coates, 2010; Mwansa, 2011; Schmidt & Rautenbach, 2015).

NUL Social Work Graduates since the Introduction of BSW

The Bachelor of Social Work (BSW) Programme was introduced in 2001 at the National University of Lesotho (NUL) culminating in its first graduate cohort of 18 candidates in 2005. The table below shows a fluctuating but increasing number of BSW graduates per year from academic year 2005/06 to 2018/19.

Table 26.1 Bachelor of Social Work Graduates from 2004/05 to 2018/19 academic years

Academic Year	Number of Graduates
2004/05	18
2005/06	24
2006/07	35
2007/08	Not readily obtainable
2008/09	Not readily obtainable
2009/10	Not readily obtainable
2010/11	93
2011/12	71
2012/13	85
2013/14	106
2014/15	67
2015/16	65
2016/17	59
2017/18	87
2018/19	90

Source: NUL Faculty of Social Science Annual Academic Records

Fieldwork Practice at NUL

In keeping with the curriculum, social work students are placed at a range of social welfare agencies responding to the above-described socioeconomic concerns (Dhemba, 2012; Tanga, 2013; UNDP, 2018; World Bank, 2019). Such agencies include government welfare service departments, hospitals and community health centres, local authorities together with international and local non-governmental organisations (NGOs) (Dhemba, 2012). NUL introduced an inception social work training programme in the 2001/2002 academic year and redesigned it in 2016/2017 to align it with international and academic standards, particularly with respect to fieldwork practice. Format/s of the fieldwork practice component in the inception and the redesigned programmes are discussed in turn below.

Format, Supervision, and Assessment of Fieldwork Practice in the Inception of the NUL Social Work Programme 2001–2017

Upon inception of the social work training programme in the 2001/2002 academic year, fieldwork practice was conducted twice a week in-semester alongside teaching, in the first three years of delivery of the programme until the 2004/2005 academic year when the university adopted three out-of-semester block-placements carried out between May and July, which is the end of the second semester. This change was necessitated by increased student enrolment numbers which could not all be accommodated by welfare agencies in Maseru, where the university is situated. In this inception programme, the out-of-semester block-placement fieldwork practice took place around the same time for first, second, and third year students with varying placement periods: four weeks for first and second year students followed by six weeks for third year students (Dhemba, 2012; Tanga, 2013). Thus, the major pitfall of introduction of block-placement in the inception programme was that it inadvertently but unavoidably reduced total placement hours for the entire programme as it could only be conducted during school holidays.

Assessment of fieldwork practice in the inception programme was based on students' oral and written reports, consistent with comparable countries in the Southern African region (Dhemba, 2012; Mwansa, 2011; Schmidt & Rautenbach, 2015; Simpson & Raniga, 2014; Tanga, 2013). Among other pertinent information, both reports contained mandatory reflection pieces on social work values, knowledge, as well as application of the skills base. Apart from oral and written reports, students were assessed through ongoing supervision by both agency supervisors and university lecturers (Dhemba, 2012; Tanga, 2013).

Challenges Encountered in Facilitating Fieldwork Practice in the Inception Programme

As alluded to, total practice hours in the inception programme did not add to the IFSW minimum stipulation, low numbers of qualified social workers compelled the university to place students under supervision by non-social workers while student enrolment numbers outweighed university human and other resources over time. Lastly, exacerbating an imperfect situation, fieldwork course coordination was compromised and the university/department did not have documented fieldwork practice guidelines while the agency and university assessment methods were somewhat incompatible. The challenges are discussed in detail subsequently.

Insufficient Practice Hours

The most fundamental limitation of the above-described fieldwork practice format was that total practice hours for all four training years did not add up to the IFSW stipulation of minimum 1000 practice hours as indicated under the fieldwork format above. Consequently, feedback from agency supervisors mentioned inadequacy of placement duration on the basis that it did not give students sufficient time to assimilate the range of content necessary to fully understand respective agencies, conduct thorough psychosocial assessments, plan and implement interventions effectively (Raskin et al., 2008). The agency supervisors further indicated that students could not familiarise themselves with all organisational aspects including agency functions, protocols, and procedures for delivering agency mandates. The time allocated was also reported as inadequate for well-considered normative and summative student performance evaluation (Chui, 2010; Haanwinckel et al., 2018; Hantman & Ben-Oz, 2014; Raskin et al., 2008).

Low Numbers of Qualified Social Workers Nationally

Secondly, while some agencies offered social work services, they did not employ qualified social workers, thus some students were supervised by non-social workers (Dhemba, 2012). This factor is widely acknowledged as weighing heavily on fieldwork practice in countries where the situation intersects with recent introduction of social work training such as Lesotho (Gray et al., 2018; Mwansa, 2011; Simpson & Raniga, 2014; Schmidt & Rautenbach, 2015). Student supervision by non-social workers deviated from the ideal, while the extent to which non-social workers could model and inculcate professional identity raised questions (Chui, 2010; Dhemba, 2012; Hantman & Ben-Oz, 2014; Gray et al., 2018; Schmidt & Rautenbach, 2015; Simpson & Raniga, 2014).

Increased Student Enrolment Numbers Relative to Human and Financial Resources

As indicated on Table 26.1, student enrolment numbers increased steadily over time while human and other resources were not accordingly adjusted, impacting training on several levels. Firstly, increased student numbers necessitated more placement agencies with social work professionals, which was difficult considering the low numbers of qualified social workers nationally at that time (Dhemba, 2012; Tanga, 2013). In addition, human and financial resource limitations featured strongly as impediments to effective and timely student supervision (Dhemba, 2012; Tanga, 2013). Delayed disbursement or non-allocation of funds for lecturers' meals, transportation, and accommodation during fieldwork practice supervision often hindered lecturers' timely supervision visits to all practice agencies. With increased enrolment numbers, more days and more funds had to be dedicated to lecturer supervision. In some cases 'supervisory visits' to local agencies were conducted after students' completion of fieldwork practice while students placed outside Lesotho received no university supervision on account of financial constraints. Delayed supervision and/or absence of ongoing oversight may have contributed to students' unsatisfactory/unprofessional behaviour, perhaps on account of demotivation. There is yet no empirical evidence explaining the observed students' unprofessional conduct during fieldwork practice in Lesotho.

Thus, increased student enrolment numbers coupled with inadequate resources impacted negatively on effectiveness of supervision along with overall programme quality (Chui, 2010;

Gray & Allegritti, 2002; Gray & Coates, 2010; Raskin et al., 2008). This led to increased workload for social work lecturers since the staff complement remained the same despite increased student enrolment. To counteract resource limitations, NUL revised tuition fees after inception of the programme, frustrating students' financial plans. Adjusting fee structures after programme inception tend to be lengthy bureaucratic processes, which should be circumvented by predicting programme costs before inception.

Weak Fieldwork Course Coordination

In relation to student enrolment numbers and effective student supervision and support, NUL also experienced a challenge of fieldwork practice coordination. The task was undertaken by one of the lecturers, who also managed a teaching load. This position, as observed by Dhemba (2012), effectively increased concerned lecturers' overall workload and potentially compromised coordination efforts. It is worth mentioning an incident of misunderstanding between the university and some agencies. Fieldwork practice components of different university training programmes are organised differently. As a result, agencies at which social work is a secondary function such as health and educational institutions were sometimes confused by the disparate weekly practice hours and expectations of students from different study programmes such as counselling, pharmacology, and social work. The Department of Social Work therefore received complaints to the effect that some students were not abiding by stipulated practice hours. Such misunderstanding could be avoided by clear fieldwork practice guidelines and through communication by a designated university coordinating body.

Absence of Written Fieldwork Practice Guidelines and Difficulty in Reconciling Agency and University Assessment Reports

A further challenge encountered in the inception programme was absence of written fieldwork practice guidelines for use by agency supervisors and students (Chui, 2010; Haanwinckel et al., 2018). Hence agency supervisors were not clear of standards and expectations per year of training and even for the entire compliment of fieldwork practice (Haanwinckel et al., 2018; Raskin et al., 2008). As a result, agency supervisors guided and graded students largely based on their discretion, without consistency or uniformity, a problematic situation as opined by several authorities (Chui, 2010; Mwansa, 2011; Tanga, 2013).

Additionally, agency supervisors' pre-designed assessment forms were exclusively narrative, without opportunity for awarding quantitative grades. The foregoing assessment method posed a challenge of reconciliation with university assessment as the former was exclusively qualitative while the later was quantitative. Resultantly, lecturers were tasked with quantifying agency supervisors' reports. The final fieldwork practice mark, awarded by the university, comprised of compounded agency supervisors' assessment outcomes as quantified by university lecturers together with oral and written fieldwork report marks in a 20:20:60 ratio.

Format, Supervision, and Assessment of Fieldwork Practice in a Redesigned NUL Social Work Training Programme

To address the above-listed challenges pertaining to inception fieldwork practice format and standards, a new social work training programme was introduced in the 2017/2018 academic year. Some issues, however, such as containment of student enrolment numbers are still under consideration. A discussion of NUL's revised fieldwork practice hours, student supervision by qualified social workers, fieldwork coordination by a designated staff member along with practice and assessment follows.

Revision of Field Practice Hours and Student Supervision by Qualified Social Workers

Firstly, the inception programme format was reconsidered to address insufficient practice hours along with challenges of supervision by non-social workers. The redesigned programme requires students to undertake a total of six months or 1000 practice hours under supervision by qualified social workers only (Darkwa, 2007; Gray et al., 2018; Haanwinckel et al., 2018; Hantman & Ben-Oz, 2014; Mwansa, 2011; Simpson & Raniga, 2014). To achieve this, second year students are placed for eight weeks or two months (320 practice hours) at the end of the second semester followed by a placement period of 17 weeks or four months (680 practice hours). Secondly, while NUL still uses the block-placement format, it limits groups of students on fieldwork to one group at a time. Reduced student numbers at a time implies a wider range of agencies to select from, hence as much as possible only those agencies with qualified social workers are considered.

In areas with few agencies and/or few qualified social workers, NUL makes arrangement for a lecturer to provide ongoing supervision or source supervision from qualified social workers in the same area (Haanwinckel et al., 2018; Hantman & Ben-Oz, 2014). It should be mentioned that the supervision arrangement with qualified social workers nationwide to supervise students in their respective areas but not their employment agencies is a non-remunerative collegial arrangement. NUL Social Work Department is in the process of requesting remuneration for qualifying social workers supervising students outside such social workers' employment agencies.

Fieldwork Course Coordination

To strengthen coordination, NUL appointed a Fieldwork Practice Coordinator to perform all coordination functions including preparing students for fieldwork, generating a list of selected placement agencies and facilitating liaison with agencies, managing number of students per agency in line with agency capacity as well as planning and organising the fieldwork component (Chui, 2010; Haanwinckel et al., 2018; Hantman & Ben-Oz, 2014). All communication with placement agencies is channelled through the coordinator for a streamlined, consistent approach. While the coordinator still manages a teaching load, the teaching load has been reduced to account for the coordination role.

Fieldwork Practice Guidelines and Assessment

In addition to strengthened course coordination, the redesigned programme came up with Fieldwork Practice Guidelines together with a quantitative-scores assessment report format for both agency and University supervisors. The guidelines, which were intended for lecturers, agency supervisors as well as students, conform to empirically tested ones (Mwansa, 2011; Tanga, 2013) while the assessment guidelines meet Chui's (2010) multi-point, broad-based, agency-specific assessment criteria.

In line with Tanga's (2013) call for standardised nationwide fieldwork practice format, the afore-mentioned fieldwork guidelines give agency supervisors a suggested sequence of how to organise fieldwork on weekly and monthly bases without being prescriptive. The assessment report format on the other hand is an eight-point mixed quantitative/qualitative tool covering personal traits, professional competencies, knowledge about agency (functions and protocols), foundation skills in social work, ethical awareness, and administrative competencies (Chui, 2010). These tools are included as annexes to the chapter as follows: Annexure I: NUL Fieldwork Practice Guidelines and Annexure II: NUL Fieldwork Practice Assessment Format.

For the purpose of assessment, at the end of each fieldwork placement block, students present both oral and written reports. The final fieldwork mark comprises an aggregate of marks awarded by agency supervisors and university lecturers as thus:

i)	Agency supervisor	15 marks
ii)	Lecturer (field supervision)	15 marks
iii)	Lecturer (student's oral presentation)	20 marks
iv)	Lecturer (student's written report)	50 marks
v)	Total	100 marks

Lessons Learnt

In a small, economically challenged country such as Lesotho, with few social services agencies, it is not advisable to send all groups of social work students on fieldwork at the same time as they compete for spaces with other students from other programmes at NUL as well as students from other institutions, lowering efficacy thereof. Secondly, fieldwork practice should be considered part of a continuum of training where classroom learning prepares students for and builds up to competent practice. NUL makes efforts to maintain such a continuum and as a result of improvements made in the redesigned programme and delivery thereof, coupled with introduction of new relevant courses, the feedback received from agency supervisors regarding student performance has been encouraging. This is testimony that thorough student preparation through various taught courses is equally instrumental in grooming students for both fieldwork and professional practice.

Secondly it cannot be overstated that fieldwork practice requires deliberate human and other resource planning. To improve quality and efficacy therefore, it should be accorded the necessary and sufficient financial, administrative, and human resources (Darkwa, 2007; Dhemba, 2012; Gray et al., 2018; Mwansa, 2011; Tanga, 2013). There has to be manageable student enrolment numbers to ensure that they are all placed in relevant agencies and under appropriate professional supervision (Haanwinckel et al., 2018; Hantman & Ben-Oz, 2014; Schmidt & Rautenbach, 2015; Simpson & Raniga, 2014).

Recommendations

The perennial marginalisation of fieldwork practice in social work training lamented by pioneers of African social work scholarship (e.g. Kaseke 1990 in Dhemba, 2012; Mupedziswa, 1997 in Dhemba, 2012) and again noted by present authors is the premise from which recommendations to schools with recently introduced and planned programmes are postulated.

In addition to the above-discussed changes to NUL fieldwork practice format therefore, the following recommendations are put forth for all universities planning and those in the early stages of social work training. These are followed by a recommendation to all social work academia. The present authors, some of whom have been delivering the social work training programme at NUL for nearly 20 years, accumulated valuable lessons over the years. This was largely on account of prevailing socioeconomic trends in Lesotho which saw globally unchallenged incidences of social vulnerability trends such as unemployment and HIV-related morbidity and mortality coupled with shrinking budget allocations for social services including education (Ministry of Health [Lesotho] and ICF Macro, 2016; World Bank, 2019). The following insights were hence garnered from lessons learnt and achievements made within a relatively short time, against considerable socioeconomic challenges. The recommendations to universities cover two main areas: fieldwork practice administration as well as a four-stage fieldwork practice format.

Recommendations to Universities with Recently Introduced and Those Planning to Introduce Social Work Training Programmes

Fieldwork Practice Administration

Planning

Firstly, universities ought to be cautioned: the fieldwork practice component of social work training is a costly undertaking on human and other resources (Darkwa, 2007; Mwansa, 2011; Schmidt & Rautenbach, 2015; Simpson & Raniga, 2014; Tanga, 2013). In countries such as Lesotho, the cost of fieldwork practice is potentially exacerbated by inadequate infrastructure in terms of roads, electricity, and uneven distribution of service agencies between cities and rural areas (where many social work students are resident and where welfare services are most needed). Often, communications infrastructure is often similarly inadequate in such contexts. Thorough planning with projections in terms of finances and student enrolment numbers is hence strongly called for during the programme planning stage (Gray et al., 2018).

Financial plans should include a detailed human resources element. To afford fieldwork practice the centrality it warrants in terms of implementation and oversight thereof, the authors are in agreement of necessity of two administrative sections for fieldwork practice coordination: a University Fieldwork Practice Department as well as a Department Fieldwork Practice Coordinator. The purpose and functions of the foregoing sections are outlined subsequently.

University Fieldwork Practice Department

Firstly, there should be a University Fieldwork Practice Department to manage agency selection and provide ongoing supportive supervision to students across respective universities. The understanding is that agency selection and supportive supervision are fortes of administration and student counselling respectively. Allocating both responsibilities to lecturers has the effect of neglecting altogether or diminishing attention given to the tasks because the lecturers' chief mandate is lecturing and research. The benefit of such university departments is that they would promote special attention to fieldwork planning and ongoing oversight as motivated by Haanwinckel et al. (2018). They would serve as points of contact between universities and agencies. Lastly, such departments would communicate the distinction to agencies pertaining to the different expectations of students from varying study programmes to avoid misunderstanding.

Workers in the fore-mentioned department would be trained in administration as well as student counselling and may only coordinate agency selection and provide supportive supervision as promulgated by Kadushin and Harkness (2002). The understanding here is that educational and administrative supervision would be provided by lecturers from relevant programmes and agency supervisors respectively (Kadushin & Harkness, 2002). Apart from social work, university programmes with field practice components which would be served by the department include education, law, nursing, and pharmacology. The propounded University Fieldwork Programmes Department would hence serve all university programmes which have fieldwork practice components. The benefit of this recommended department would be to mainstream and ensure prioritisation of fieldwork practice programmes by universities.

Social Work Department Fieldwork Practice Coordinator

In addition to the University Fieldwork Practice Department, universities should appoint a Social Work Department Fieldwork Practice Coordinator. For the coordinator, each training level of students registered for fieldwork practice would represent the equivalent of a taught course in terms of teaching load. This means that if two training levels go for attachment, the coordinator would be considered to have a teaching load of two courses. The rationale for Departmental Coordinators would be to circumvent scenarios where fieldwork becomes additional loads for lecturers, restricting focused attention to it (Dhemba, 2012; Haanwinckel et al., 2018; Schmidt & Rautenbach, 2015; Simpson & Raniga, 2014; Tanga, 2013). Such a coordinator should hold similar educational qualifications as lecturers.

The coordinators' functions would be to guide students' fieldwork practice plans and to provide summative assessment consistent with Kadushin and Harkness' (1991) educational supervision. Normative assessment in the form of ongoing supervision on the other hand would be provided by both agency supervisors along with the entire compliment of social work lecturers as is already the case in Lesotho and in many African universities as reported (Dhemba, 2012; Mwansa, 2011; Tanga, 2013).

Supervision Outsourcing

A major issue which encumbers fieldwork practice in countries with newly introduced social work training is the scarcity of academically qualified agency supervisors trained as social workers (Dhemba, 2012; Gray et al., 2018; Simpson & Raniga, 2014). This is a factor in Lesotho as mentioned above. For countries in the same situation as Lesotho, therefore, it is recommended that universities should engage trained social workers from outside placement agencies to provide administrative supervision on a weekly basis. Two conditions are necessary for this to be executed efficiently: placement agencies should be amenable to the option and such supervisors should be qualified social workers conversant with respective agency functions. Retired social workers along with qualified social workers not working in social work agencies may be co-opted for this purpose.

Here, again, the role of University Fieldwork Placement Departments as liaisons between universities and agencies becomes significant. It would be the role of such departments within universities to negotiate terms of office for outsourced supervisors while outsourced supervisors would be expected to uphold social work principles and to work hand in hand with agency supervisors.

Fieldwork Practice Format Options

In keeping with IFSW minimum of 1000 practice hours required for conferment of BSW, and still under administration, two fieldwork practice formats are described here for consideration: a two-part block fieldwork practice format whereby students are attached with agencies for two separate periods or an academic year-long placement during the final year of study.

TWO-PART BLOCK FIELDWORK PRACTICE FORMAT

The first placement period can be during school holidays followed by a longer in-semester placement. School holidays fieldwork practice may be necessitated by the reality that social work students in the early years of training may be required to register for common courses with other programmes.

ONE-PART ACADEMIC YEAR-LONG FIELDWORK PRACTICE FORMAT

The second placement format is an academic year-long placement undertaken during the final year of study. As explained, concurrent fieldwork was found to be problematic on several levels by NUL and is not encouraged.

Recommended Four-Stage Fieldwork Format

Finally, present authors found Simpson and Raniga's (2014) five-stage student supervision typology expounded above worthy of consideration by universities. The present authors slightly modified the typology into the following four-stages discussed in turn below and summarised on a table thereafter: planning, inception, implementation, and conclusion. The proposed four stages further underscore necessity for a designated departmental fieldwork coordinator.

Stage One: Planning

Planning is the key to success of any exercise. For the success of this stage, students should have an idea of the spectrum of social services agencies before selection and commencement of fieldwork practice. This point is made consistent with Hoffman's (1990 in Simpson & Raniga, 2014) caution that placement agency selection ought to be systematic rather than expedient. Various BSW curricular have an 'Introduction to Social Work Practice Module' at the foundation stages of training, often in the first semester. For systematic selection, therefore, it would be worthwhile to incorporate specific information on welfare agencies and their functions. In this manner students will gain insight on respective agencies and later make informed selection based on the learning interests.

Where there are Master's of Social Work students, many of whom may be employed in welfare agencies while also studying, they could be requested to give presentations to first year BSW students explaining the functions of their employment agencies. Another effective strategy for facilitating beginning students' awareness of social services agencies is to include first year students when senior students make oral fieldwork presentation reports. Finally, it is advisable that students should draft fieldwork plans with assistance from lecturers before commencement of fieldwork.

Stage Two: Inception

Inception is where students begin fieldwork practice at agencies with university-approved fieldwork practice plans in hand. The planning stage of fieldwork practice should entail student induction into agency functions and protocols for implementing such functions. Subsequent to induction, agency students and agency supervisors should discuss (and modify as relevant) university-approved and fieldwork practice plans drafted by students.

Stage Three: Implementation

Inception should be followed by implementation, the main fieldwork practice part. Reference is made to Table 26.2's fieldwork process guidelines for an example of a time-framed schedule of tasks which may guide agency supervisors and students on how to go about the implementation stage of fieldwork guided by written plans agreed upon by departmental fieldwork practice coordinators and agency supervisors. Apart from student implementation of plans, the key feature of fieldwork practice implementation is ongoing student supervision by all responsible parties. Agency supervisors should provide administrative supervision while University Fieldwork Practice Departments provide supportive supervision and social work lecturers provide educational supervision. Universities' attention is brought to the rising trend of student burnout, largely on account of inability to balance social and academic responsibilities, calling for ongoing supportive supervision. Administrative and educational supervision should take place on a weekly and monthly basis respectively.

Stage Four: Conclusion

The conclusion stage of fieldwork practice should commence at practice agencies with informing clients of students' impending departure as is the requirement in all instances of direct intervention (DuBoi and Miley, 2005). It is also the stage of summative evaluation wherein students present oral and written reports with oversight from recommended offices of Department Fieldwork Practice Coordinators.

To conclude the recommendations section, it is stressed that universities should strive for a minimum of monthly one-on-one and weekly structured supervision. Weekly supervision may be individual or group supervision depending on university preference. With the increasing pattern of internationalisation, universities should make provision for supervision of international students placed outside counties of operation. As a cost management strategy, communication technology is an important option to make use of for weekly and monthly supervision of students. In 2021 and beyond it cannot be excusable for students to not receive university supervision because of distance.

Recommendations to All Social Work Academics

While the present authors, all of whom are social work academics, are in agreement that 'information-scarcity' and 'under-documentation' are somewhat overused adjectives in academic reports, the authors are equally in agreement on the dearth of research evidence on fieldwork pedagogy and research globally. Apart from such a paucity, much of the empirical evidence found while researching for this chapter was out of date. Hence, the authors make a clarion call to all social work academics to prioritise fieldwork practice through empirical research and academic conferences to share experiences, ideas, and possibilities for improvement of this pivotal social work training component. As pointed out, factors associated with student burnout and misconduct during fieldwork should also be understudied and documented to preempt them. Strategies for African-specific fieldwork practice should be empirically investigated (Gray & Allegritti, 2002; Gray & Coates, 2010). Finally, academics are urged to interrogate contextual relevance of set 'international' standards to make input to the standards (Raskin et al., 2008).

Table 26.2 Summary of above-recommended fieldwork format

Recommended fieldwork practice stage	Description of stage	Responsible Party
Planning	Students are introduced to functions of a spectrum of welfare agencies in their country or region.	Lecturer responsible for 'Introduction to Social Work Practice' or its equivalent.
	Beginning students attend fieldwork practice oral report presentation session by senior students.	Departmental Fieldwork Practice Coordinator and students.
	Students select placement agencies.	University Fieldwork Practice Department.
	Universities communicate with agencies to request placement of students.	University Fieldwork Practice Department.
	Students draft fieldwork plans with guidance from Department Fieldwork Practice Coordinator.	Departmental Fieldwork Practice Coordinator and students.
Inception	Induction to agency describing agency functions and implementation protocols.	Agency supervisor.
	Presentation of pre-drafted fieldwork practice plans to agency supervisor for adjustment/improvement/change as necessary.	Agency supervisor and students.
Implementation	Ongoing supportive supervision.	University Fieldwork Practice Department.
	Implementation of fieldwork practice plans as agreed upon between by agency supervisor and student.	Students.
	Ongoing report writing.	Students.
	Ongoing administrative supervision.	Agency supervisor.
	Ongoing educational supervision.	University supervisors.
Conclusion	Drafting of final fieldwork practice report.	Students.
	Oral presentation of report by students.	Department Fieldwork Practice Coordinator.
	Summative evaluation of students' oral and written reports.	Department Fieldwork Practice Coordinator.

Source: Author

Conclusions

Fieldwork practice ingrains professional reflexivity and ethical reflection while aiding assimilation of theoretical and empirical content through contextual application. It is, however, often encumbered by resource limitations (Darkwa, 2007; Dhemba, 2012; Gray et al., 2018; Mwansa, 2011; Schmidt & Rautenbach, 2015; Tanga, 2013). Since resource limitations can be expected to be a permanent feature of higher education delivery, efforts should be made to prioritise fieldwork practice through careful planning and viable cost containment strategies to optimise its efficacy as well as student developmental gains.

References

Bogo, M. (2006). Field instruction in social work: A review of the research literature. *The Clinical Supervisor, 24*(1), 163–193.

Chui, E. W. T. (2010). Desirability and feasibility in evaluating fieldwork performance: Tensions between supervisors and students. *Social Work Education, 29*(2), 171–187.

Darkwa, O. K. 2007. Continuing social work education in an electronic age: The opportunities and challenges facing social work educators in Ghana. *Professional Development, 2*(1), 38–43.

Dhemba, J. 2012. Fieldwork and social work education and training: Issues and challenges in the case of Eastern and Southern Africa. *Social Work and Society, 10*(1), 1–12.

DuBois, B., & Miley, K. K. (2005). *Social Work: An Empowering Profession*. Boston: Pearson.

Eriksson-Zetterquist, U., Mullern, T., & Styhre, A. 2011. *Organizational Theory: A Practice-based Approach.* Oxford: Oxford University Press.

Gray, M., & Coates, J. (2010). Indigenization and knowledge development: Extending the debate. *International Social Work, 53*(5), 1–15.

Gray, M., & Allegritti, I. (2002). Cross-cultural practice and the indigenization of African social work. *Social Work/Maatskaplike Werk, 38*(4), 234–336.

Gray, M., Agllias, K., Mupedziswa, R., & Mugumbate, J. 2018. The expansion of developmental social work in Southern and East Africa: Opportunities and challenges for social work field programmes. *International Social Work, 61*(6), 974–987.

Haanwinckel, I. B. Z., Fawcett, B., & Garcia, I. A. B. 2018. Contrasts and reflections: Social work field supervision in Brazil and England. *International Social Work, 61*(6), 943–953.

Hantman, S., & Ben-Oz, M. (2014). There are no shortcuts: Trusting the social work training process. *Journal of Social Work, 14*(5), 491–505.

Hepworth, D. H., Rooney, R., & Larsen, J. A. (2002). *Direct Social Work Practice: Theory and Skills*. New York: Brooks/Cole.

Kadushin, A., & Harkness, D. (2002). *Supervision in Social Work*. New York: Columbia University Press.

Ministry of Health [Lesotho] and ICF Macro. (2016). *Demographic and Health Survey Lesotho 2014*. Maseru.

Ministry of Health [Lesotho], Centre for Disease Control and Prevention (USA) and ICAP Columbia University of Public Health (UK). (2017). *Lesotho Population Based HIV Impact Assessment 2016–2017*. Maseru.

Mwansa, L. (2011). Social work education in Africa: Whence and whither? *Social Work Education, 30*(1), 4–16.

Raskin, M. S., Wayne, J., & Bogo, M. (2008). Revisiting field education standards. *Journal of Social Work Education, 44*(2), 173–188.

Schmidt, K., & Rautenbach, J. V. (2015). Field instruction: Is the heart of social work education still beating in the Eastern Cape? *Social Work/Maatskaplike Werk, 52*(4), 589–610.

Simpson, B., & Raniga, T. (2014). Student supervision. In E. Engelbrecht (Ed.), *Management and supervision of social workers: Issues and challenges within a developmental social development paradigm*. Hampshire: Cengage Learning.

Tanga, P. T. (2013). The challenges of social work field training in Lesotho. *Social Work Education: The International Journal, 32*(2), 157–178.

Tanga, P. T., Bello, H. M., Makatjane, T. J., & Tsikoane, T. 2017. Economic globalization, HIV and AIDS and gender dimensions in the Lesotho textile and garment industry. In N. Dumais (Ed.), *HIV/AIDS Contemporary Challenges*. London: Intech Open.

United Nations Development Program [UNDP]. (2018). *Human development indices and indicators: Lesotho 2018 statistical indicators update*. UNDP.

World Bank and [Lesotho] Bureau of Statistics. (2019). *Lesotho Poverty assessment: Progress and challenges in reducing poverty*. The World Bank.

World Population Review. (n.d.). Population live. Available at: http//www.worldpopulationreview.com. (last accessed September 2018).

Annexure I: NUL Fieldwork Practice Guidelines

Timeframe	Activity/Task	Responsible Person/s
End of first week of placement	Prepare a mutually agreeable learning plan with specific tasks assigned to the student; these should be in line with the agency functions and objectives of fieldwork outlined below.	Student and Agency Supervisor
On weekly basis throughout the placement	Hold periodic, pre-scheduled structured supervision sessions to assess the students' performance and progress. Weekly structured supervision sessions are recommended but the frequency may be determined by individual supervisors based on the nature of tasks assigned to students.	Agency supervisors
Monthly	Write monthly process reports for the purpose of ongoing assessment.	Student
Final month of placement	Write a final field placement report which should first be approved and shared with the agency supervisor before submission to the University.	Student
At the end of placement	Give an oral presentation at the University covering key performance areas and assignments conducted throughout the fieldwork.	Student

Source: Authors

Annexure II: NUL Fieldwork Practice Assessment Format

	Parameters	Areas	Rating out of 3	Comments/Areas of Improvement
1.	Personal traits	Honesty, confidence when interacting with clients, reliability, punctuality, diligence, sincerity/passion/ eagerness to serve vulnerable populations, pro-activeness, sensitivity to the plight of others, and adherence to dress code.		
2.	Professional competencies	Ability to establish and maintain relationships with clients agency staff, coworkers and supervisor, empathy, warm positive regard for clients and their circumstances.		
3.	Knowledge of agency	Knowledge about agency, functioning, policies and strategic plans, programmes, systems and activities, services, clients, networking with other organisations.		

(Continued)

Annexure II: Continued

	Parameters	Areas	Rating out of 3	Comments/Areas of Improvement
4.	Foundation skills	Listening, questioning/interviewing, record keeping, and report writing. Ability to conduct thorough psychosocial assessments using appropriate theoretical frameworks. Competence in intervention planning, implementation, and evaluation.		
5.	Ethics, principles, and values	Competence in upholding ethics, principles, and values.		
6.	Theoretical knowledge and techniques	Ability to integrate theoretical knowledge with practice, appropriate use of practice methods and models of social work practice as relevant.		
7.	Administration	Development of professional attitude to assigned tasks, ability to plan and manage work with minimal supervision, ability to make decisions and apply own initiatives, ability to demonstrate resourcefulness, and respond appropriately to demands of a given situation. Eagerness to learn, ability to take instructions, sense of responsibility and professional commitment, working cooperatively in a team, ability to write reports and meet deadlines, recording daily activities and case studies, ability to do office administration work, participation in agency meetings, taking minutes, and representing agency in stakeholders' meetings.		
8.	Please mention any particular outstanding competencies, attributes or achievements by student during attachment		(Rating out of 2)	
TOTAL	-			-

Source: Authors

27
Social Work Field Education
A Comparative Study of South Africa and Eswatini

Boitumelo Joyce Mohapi, Felicity Besong Tabi, and Zee Catherine Masuku

The chapter presents a critical review of the role of social work field education programmes as a medium to transfer practical knowledge in social work practice in Eswatini and South Africa. It further discusses a brief overview of the location and the socioeconomic outlook of the Kingdom of Eswatini and the Republic of South Africa, the rationale of the study, the relevance of social work field education, challenges encountered in social work field education, and a brief comparative aspect of the role of fieldwork education between South Africa and Eswatini.

Situated between South Africa and Mozambique, the Kingdom of Eswatini, with about 1.1 million citizens, is considered a low-middle-income country in which 69% of the population live below the national poverty line. In addition to its high levels of poverty, unemployment, and inequality, its Gini coefficient at 0.51% seems to be relatively high according to world standards (Central Statistics Office, 2017; Ministry of Economic Planning and Development 2006; Dhemba & Nhapi, 2020). Compounded with these clusters of social challenges, the call for intervention has been eminent. Hence, the need to implement social services and developmental projects to improve these prevailing conditions of life amongst the Swazi people. Therefore, with the hope of managing these social challenges, (Government of Eswatini, 2016) aims to initiate programmes that will improve social services and developmental projects through community intervention schemes, self-help capacitation programmes in collaboration with non-governmental organisations (NGOs) (Dhemba & Nhapi, 2020).

Focusing on the drive to address the need for social services, poverty eradication, and social development in the country, Dhemba and Nhapi (2020) articulated that, in 2014/15, two institutions of higher learning, namely the University of Eswatini (UNESWA), and the Eswatini Medical Christian University (EMCU) introduced the Bachelor of Social Work degree. They also incorporated fieldwork education in their programmes to prepare prospective social work graduates for the challenge on the ground. However, this is still at its infant stage and not entirely known and appreciated. Therefore, it is not yet evident whether the social work graduates from these institutions dispense the knowledge they acquired (Dhemba & Nhapi, 2020) because of the lack of understanding of what social work entails and its importance.

Since its emergence during the latter part of the 19th century (Midgley, 1981), social work evolved into professional practice in several countries across the globe (IASSW, 2002). Being a practice-based profession and an academic discipline that enhances social transformation, development, cohesion, and the empowerment of people (International Federation of Social Work, 2014), the need for proper education and training in all aspects of the profession is paramount because the social work profession engages with people in communities, social organisations, and families. Thus, social workers work in various public and private organisational settings such as schools, correctional facilities, family programmes, infant, child, youth, adult, and older adult programmes. These programmes serve homeless people, medical settings, housing, residential care, advocacy, community organisation, and many more settings, attempting to remediate change and, at times, prevent social problems in communities. They plan and institute change by using many professional skills and techniques to help people and families function more capably.

As part of a student's training to become a professional social worker, social work students must internalise social work values and ethics, develop skills, a sense of professional self, and learn the fundamentals of social work practice with all client systems. Thus, the kind of knowledge needed for social work includes both theoretical and practical. Importantly, guided by the ethics, values, scholarly inquiry, and practice principles of the social work profession, the objective of the two institutions mentioned earlier is to educate and prepare students to become effective, ethical, and competent generalist social workers by providing quality learning opportunities in the promotion of social, economic, and environmental justice for diverse populations in the Kingdom of Eswatini and abroad.

For the above reasons, fieldwork is an essential component in the training of social workers (Wayne et al., 2010). The fieldwork experience is intended to enhance student learning within all areas of service delivery. Fieldwork thus entails supervised learning experiences in a wide range of social work practice settings which allow theory learnt during formal lectures to be integrated with real-life challenges. The goal is to achieve competency in the exit level outcomes under the learning outcomes set out in the fieldwork curriculum. However, the fact that acquiring this goal demands progressive professional training and education, there is a need for structural changes and acceptable professional guidelines to ensure the acquisition of professional social workers (Healy & Meagher, 2004; Weiss et al., 2004), that are locally, regionally, and internationally capacitated to serve.

One of such changes is that the social work field education system in Eswatini that has been chiefly Western-oriented (Kreitzer, 2012; Mabundza, 2017) and hence may consider embracing a paradigm shift in its quest to realise and maximise effective social work education and transfer of knowledge. It is imperative to emphasise that the Kingdom of Eswatini is very much culture-oriented, implying that social support and relief efforts that depict social work operation must align with the norms and values of its people (Mabundza, 2017). With this in mind, the role of social work field education programmes in the transfer of social work knowledge can only be achieved through the implementation of models that will effectively translate the foreign colonial theoretical understanding of social work to suit the local context of practical needs (Dominelli & Bernard, 2003; Healy, 2001; Mabundza, 2017). However, the social work profession in the country is still at its infant stage. Unlike in South Africa and many other countries across the globe where the recognition, establishment, and training of social workers were adopted many years ago, the social work profession gained such recognition and its establishment in Eswatini recently, in 2014.

Nevertheless, the origin of social welfare services in Eswatini dates back to 1952. The Department of Social Welfare (DSW) was established in 1977 and was mandated to provide integrated services to improve the Swazi nation's quality of life, particularly the poorest and most vulnerable. In 2009, the Social Development Policy was adopted. The scope of the DSW mandate expanded further following the adoption of the Social Development Policy (SDP) (Deputy Prime Minister's Office, Kingdom of Eswatini, 2012, p. 7).

Despite the previous development, the training of social work professionals has been quite a challenge. And in 2014/15, two institutions of higher learning in the kingdom introduced the Bachelor of Social Work degree. However, this programme borrowed heavily from Western theories and practice, and three years later, it was challenged by the notion that ideas and methods conveyed directly from the West might present future challenges as it seemingly disregards the cultural, political, and social differences that exist in developed and developing countries such as Eswatini (Mabundza, 2017). The critique is that African – implicitly Eswatini – social work should be rooted in its values and indigenous structures and approaches by incorporating Western and African theories and practices. A further emphasis was that Swazi scholars and educators should improve learning materials and develop case studies using local examples that speak to the Swazi context. Additionally, these institutions were advised to carry out evidence-based research to inform policymakers on matters of importance regarding the profession of social work (Mabundza, 2017).

South Africa is located at the southern tip of Africa. The country is bordered by Namibia, Botswana, Zimbabwe, Mozambique, Eswatini, and Lesotho. The country's mid-year population is estimated to have increased to 59.62 million in 2020, according to the report released by Statistics South Africa (Statistics South Africa, 2020). Two oceans surround the country.

The distance between South Africa and Eswatini is 1192 kilometres or approximately 12 hours' travel on land. Both countries are in the Southern African Region, close to each other.

Although South Africa is ranked as a middle-income economy globally, there is a lot of inequality and poverty. Zegeye and Maxted (2002) explain that inequality in South Africa is not only found between rich and poor people, but it is also evident in the unequal benefits and opportunities for different people in society.

In this regard, Schenck and Louw (2010) state that South Africa is both a first world and third world nation because the income inequality is growing at an alarming rate.

Social work has a critical role in alleviating poverty and contributing to Sustainable Development Goal 1, which aims to end poverty in the world.

In South Africa, the Jan Hofmeyer College was one of the first institutions established in 1924 to offer formal training to social workers.

Rationale for the Study

It is important to indicate here that the purpose of this chapter is a comparative study between South Africa and Eswatini, focusing on the role of social work field education programmes in the transfer of knowledge in social work practice. As noted earlier, one may assume that Eswatini at its infant stage may benefit through lessons learnt from South Africa, whose field education programme is at its advanced stage. Nevertheless, it is noteworthy that social work field education and training as a medium through which social challenges and developmental initiatives can be enhanced through social work practice is a dire need in Eswatini.

Thus, promoting an effective fieldwork education may bring about positive change to the communities through social work practice. Importantly, Weiss and Welbourne (2008) highlight that Chile, Germany, Spain, India, the United States, the United Kingdom, and South Africa provide comprehensive explanations of the profession of social work. This study was carried out by social work educators and academics well-known in the area and have previously published in social work and were requested to contribute their thoughts and expertise on the area. Their data was utilised to compare and contrast the differences and similarities that they have as various countries. Given this evidence, South Africa is ideally placed by location and experience to model a developmental approach in enhancing the social work field education in Eswatini due to its proximity.

The Role of Social Work Field Education

Social work field education is paramount for the prospective social work professional (Noble, 2011) because in fieldwork student social workers are trained to practice and manage diverse types of needs in an evolving challenging world. The concept of field education is to enable social work students to acquire practical knowledge and simultaneously understand the dynamics of how social workers apply professionalism in practice (Shulman, 2005; Bogo et al., 2020), which can be done with the assistance of field work supervisors. During the practicum, field educators or supervisors are expected to help students integrate theory into practice, thereby enhancing their professional knowledge (Bogo et al., 2020). The translation of theoretical knowledge in social work into practical knowledge (Gray et al., 2010) for positive transformation of challenging life experiences remains the fundamental objective of social work practice. For Tackett et al. (2001), field education programmes in social work bring students in training with the realities on the ground where they experience practical knowledge and interact with others in the community at large.

The International Federation of Social Work (IFSW, 2004) has set global standards for field education in social work. They include the following:

- Field education should be sufficient in the duration and complexity of tasks and learning opportunities to ensure that students are prepared for professional practice.
- There should be planned coordination and links between the school and the agency/field placement setting.
- There should be an orientation for fieldwork supervisors or instructors.
- Field supervisors or instructors who are qualified and experienced should be appointed, as determined by the development status of the social work profession in any given country. There should also be an orientation for fieldwork supervisors or instructors.
- The field instructors should participate in curriculum development.
- A partnership should be formed between the educational institution and the agency (where applicable) and service users in decision-making regarding field education and evaluating student's fieldwork performance.
- A field instruction manual that details its fieldwork standards, procedures, assessment standards/criteria, and expectations should be made available to field instructors and supervisors.
- There should be adequate and appropriate resources to meet the needs of the fieldwork component of the programme.
    (IFSW, 2014)
    The above standards indicate that all institutions which train social workers should invest enough resources in the field education of the student social workers.

Recent studies indicate the importance and expansion of social work practice in recognising and promoting social work field education and training to address social challenges right down to the grassroots of modern society (Gray et al., 2017). This paradigm shift towards adequate fieldwork knowledge and practice in social work calls for stakeholders in Africa, and specifically Eswatini, to raise the bar in fieldwork education and practice to meet the current socio-economic challenges in the country and continent at large (Nhapi & Dhemba, 2020). For too long the reliance on social work operation that focuses on theory and service to social needs within the urban vicinities has not been fruitful (Hall, 1990; Mupedziswa & Kubanga, 2016) in the African continent where the brunt of extreme poverty, lack of basic education and primary health care is lagging primarily in rural areas. Moreover, the realities of droughts, HIV/AIDS, and other social challenges have seriously destroyed the social well-being of most Swazi people, thereby exposing the vulnerable groups – comprising both the old and young – to severe social disadvantages. In this regard, one is compelled to submit that the local society must recognise and promote social work field education and practice to eradicate the social ills and disadvantages plaguing the populace.

Studies have confirmed that when students acquire knowledge through practice in the community under the supervision and mentorship of qualified field instructors, they can integrate theory and practice. This exposure allows them to demonstrate social work competencies and professionalism (Bogo, 2010; Finch et al., 2019). Input from social work graduates echoes the view that field education is the most important element in their study that prepares them for future practice (Bogo et al., 2020). Thus, field education remains central and complements social work education in respect to the preparation of professional practice (Wayne et al., 2010, p. 161). Field education in social work is considered to be the 'signature pedagogy of social work education' (Council on Social Work Education [CSWE], 2008, 2015a).

Social work education and training in Eswatini are currently provided by the University of Eswatini (UNESWA) and the Eswatini Medical Christian University (EMCU) that both started offering the speciality in 2014. With EMCU, the social work education programme is a four-year Bachelor of Social Work degree. Because the social work education training is composed of theory and practice, EMCU, from the outset, ensured that fieldwork education was part of the complete programme. However, despite this initiative, the fieldwork education and training programme has not been as successful as envisaged due to several limiting factors comprising the lack of appropriate placement agencies, lack of qualified onsite supervisors, lack of qualified social workers in the few institutions that carry out social work activities, and the shortage of placement agencies (Nhapi & Dhemba, 2020). Nevertheless, the realities with fieldwork challenges should not be undermined, as Parrish (2020) decried the fact by stating a need for more relevant scholarship on the prevailing circumstances.

In South Africa, social work education and training are offered by 16 public universities and one private college. They are:

Nelson Mandela University
North West University (Mafikeng, Potchefstroom, and Vaal)
Stellenbosch University
University of Cape Town
University of Fort Hare (East London and Alice)
University of Free State
University of Johannesburg
University of KwaZulu-Natal
University of Limpopo
University of Pretoria
University of South Africa
University of Venda
University of Western Cape
University of Witwatersrand
University of Zululand

Walter Sisulu University
South African College of Applied Psychology.
(asaswei.org.za)

All these institutions offer a four-year bachelor's degree, master's, and doctoral qualifications.

Critical Analysis of the Role of Social Work Field Education Programme between South Africa and Eswatini

As highlighted above, the role and importance of social work field education for the transfer of knowledge are critical for effective service delivery in the said speciality. Therefore, it remains imperative to understand how this aspect of the social work profession is recognised and implemented in South Africa and Eswatini for knowledge base improvement and expansion. In this regard, this section of this chapter will discuss the differences and challenges that exist between South Africa and Eswatini in their social work field education programmes for the transfer of theoretical knowledge into practice as an objective in line with the needs of the profession (Social Work Task Team, 2017). UNESWA and EMCU, as institutions of higher education, have continued to promote the implementation of effective social work field education programmes for prospective social work graduates in Eswatini since the commencement of the programme in 2014. However, the following limiting factors to effective fieldwork education and training in the country have been identified as mentioned above.

Social Work Field Education in South Africa

The South African Council for Social Service Professions (SACSSP) has set norms and standards for field education in social work. All universities teaching social work have to adhere to these standards. They are summarised below (SACSSP, 2020, p. 21).

Practice Experience Is Integral to the Programme

This means that each university has to have a policy in place regarding field instruction. This policy has to stipulate the hours of field education, and it should form part of the management activities of the department. Furthermore, field instruction should be offered at all levels of study, and it should be aligned to the theoretical modules taught (SACSSP, 2020, p. 21).

Practice Experience Appropriately Supports the Delivery of the Programme and the Achievement of the Learning Outcomes

Over the four years of social work training, students have to complete 700 hours of practical work. This should include micro, macro, and meso work and should be done in various environments that reflect the country's context. The fieldwork should follow a 'building block' approach, where learning increases in complexity for each year of study. All social work students should be registered with the SACSSP from the second year of research, and they have to keep logbooks as evidence of their practical work. All students doing practical work have to be assigned a qualified supervisor.

The Practise Placement Setting Provides a Safe and Supportive Environment

All field education organisations should have a policy on safety, aggression, and sexual harassment, and students have to be orientated to this policy. The universities need to monitor the cases of violence which occur as the students move between the university and the field placement organisation. The instances that are allocated to students should also be appropriate to their level of study.

The Higher Education Institution Must Maintain a Comprehensive and Effective System for Approving and Monitoring All Placements

There should be memoranda of understanding (MOUs) between the university and the field placement organisation. Contracts for students should also be in place. Files should be ethically stored, and there should be a proper termination process at the end of the students' placement.

The Placement Providers Have Quality and Diversity Policies Concerning Students, Together with How These Will Be implemented and Monitored

The placement organisation should have an employment equity policy, and students should have access to these policies and diversity policies.

Adequate Numbers of Appropriately Qualified and Experienced Staff are Available to Offer Students Appropriate Supervision

Supervisors working with students should be registered with the SACSSP and have more than two years of experience. Supervisors working with fourth level students should have more than three years of experience. The university placing students at organisations should train the supervisors on what is required.

There are appropriately enough mandated staff at the HEI to manage the field experience of social work students at all levels

Each university should have staff who are allocated to control the field instruction programme.

Unethical Conduct Is Managed

Students are not allowed to do practical work unless they are registered with the SACSSP. The issue of ethical conduct should be emphasised by the university and the field placement organisation. There should be processes to deal with unethical behaviour, and misconduct cases should be reported to the SACSSP.

The Field Has the Opportunity to Contribute to the Quality of the BSW Programme

Supervisors should be invited to give feedback on the Bachelor of Social Work programme.

Social Work Field Education in Eswatini

Working towards similar objectives in furthering and enhancing the social work profession in Eswatini, the institutions of higher learning mentioned above in line with government requirements formulated independently but somehow similar social work field education programmes that strive to comply with international standards. Hence, the following key areas of importance are discussed.

Compulsory Fieldwork Experience

Even in the absence of a regulating body, higher education institutes have policies in place that guide their fieldwork programmes. Field education programmes have been designed to complement theory and practice. It is envisaged that all students undertaken social work education must satisfactorily complete the required period set for field education before graduating (UNESWA, Department of Sociology & Social work, 2017, pp. 8–9; EMCU, Department of Social work, n.d.).

Contact Time and Learning Hours

Students in the area of social work begin their fieldwork practice in their second year and continue it until they graduate in their fourth year. Students are placed in various organisations around the country throughout the months of July and August after they finish their exams at the conclusion of the academic year. The field work practicum lasts for six weeks. Throughout the six-week term, students are required to collaborate with the supervisor. Students must work with the supervisor for at least eight hours every day, Monday through Friday. Students are required to follow the organisation's principles, rules, and regulations while on the job. All concerns relating to field work must be discussed with the field instructor. Generally, students are required to complete 240 hours of field work each academic year, which averages to 40 hours weekly.

Field Education Structure

In Eswatini, field education is designed and managed by the department head in collaboration with other professional staff members of the department. However, to ensure success and expected objectives, the said field education programmes are expected to be coordinated by designated qualified staff from the department of social work under the guidance of the head of department or field instructor.

Criteria for Choosing an Organisation for Field Placement

Considering the challenges already mentioned above and the availability of the appropriate agencies or organisation to place students for practicum in the country, these institutions have put down policy for scrutiny to ensure suitability for students' field training. However, achieving the objective of this endeavour has not been quite fulfilling considering the absence of the appropriate agencies that are willing to absorb students for fieldwork.

The Practice Placement Setting Provides a Safe and Supportive Environment

In this regard, these institutions have implemented strategies to ensure that students are safe in the various organisations they undertake fieldwork. To accomplish this outcome, frequent site visits and constant communication are expected to be practised between the fieldwork coordinator and the students in the field.

Quality Assurance

To ensure that students acquire the right quality and standard of field education, these institutions have made it mandatory that field education instructors or supervisors are qualified and experienced social workers with at least a bachelor's degree in social work. However, this requirement for field supervisors is also challenging due to the shortage of qualified professionals in the country. Because of this challenge of social work professionals in the country to assist in fieldwork education, these institutions are often under pressure to ensure that their students are placed in the appropriate agencies to acquire the expected quality field training envisaged.

To maintain standards and expected outcomes as envisaged towards their social work education training, the institutions have made it possible that the field coordinators regularly engage with the field supervisors to ascertain what is happening in the field. During such times, feedback from the field is gathered, and interventions are provided where necessary. Later in class, when students are back from the field, depending on the need.

Memorandum of Understanding

Under the policy guidelines for their field education programmes, these institutions have put Memorandums of Understanding or a draft memorandum with the various agencies offering placements for their students. This agreement guarantees a legal corporation between these institutions and the multiple organisations providing placement for their students, ensuring continued placement opportunities for students.

Student Orientation and Ethical Issues

To ensure success in the fieldwork programmes, the institutions have policies that indicate that social work students should be briefed and educated on the frequent challenges on the field and the conditions of operations. The briefing usually includes what is expected of the students in the field and what is expected of their prospective supervisors. Additionally, key ethical aspects are brought to their understanding and the need to comply. In this regard, Bogo et al. (2020) assert that it is of utmost importance to remember that before students are sent out for fieldwork, they must be prepared to face the realities in the field, including the information about field procedures and conditions of operations.

Field Work Curriculum and Implementation

It is essential to mention that although UNESWA and EMCU both integrate fieldwork education in their training programmes for social workers (Dhemba & Nhapi, 2020), the curriculum for fieldwork, however, is slightly different with little or no significant disparity in terms of professionalism. However, where the challenge lies again is the lack of adequate professional help during fieldwork education. It is worth reiterating that field supervisors' role is crucial for fieldwork training to be meaningful. For success, the field instructors must provide students with an emotionally supportive relationship while completing their field practice as students. The field supervisor is also in charge of disseminating ideas and perspectives and taking into account the experiences of students (Bennett et al., 2013; Wang & Chui, 2016; Gair et al., 2015; Haanwinckel et al., 2018). An honest, transparent relationship between the field supervisor and student is vital since it allows the field supervisor to be approachable, trustworthy, and listen to the challenges of the student while providing them with a non-judgemental environment free of stress, helplessness, and intimidation (Brodie & Williams, 2013; Coohey et al., 2017; Bailey-McHale et al., 2019; Ross et al., 2019). However, in situations where field supervisors are not social workers, the aforementioned goals may not be achieved.

It is, however, safe to indicate that the above highlight is still not attainable in Eswatini due to the shortage of the available skills in social work field education and training, mainly because the profession is still at its infant stage and not quite known by the majority of the Swazis and corporate entities. Moreover, the absence of the right and experienced fieldwork education and training supervisors in the country compromises field experience in certain areas. And seemingly because the Department of Social Welfare that is responsible for all social service activities in the country has not yet integrated (Dhemba & Nhapi, 2020) and contextualised professional social work operations in the country, standardisation of field education remains challenging. This makes it surmountable to contextualise or indigenise the social work education and practice in the country. More so, with the absence of a professional regulating body for social work in the country, practical knowledge transfer remains challenging.

Unlike in South Africa and other developing countries, the social work knowledge base is mixed, comprising the Western and indigenous knowledge (Weiss-Gal & Welbourne, 2008), which poses specific difficulties to acquire the expected outcome as a result of differences in economic viability and cultural practice compared to Western societies. On the contrary, social work education in Eswatini is currently characterised by imported knowledge because there is yet no local framework or indigenous knowledge-based capacity to integrate imported knowledge in social work theory to suit local customs and values. This observation seemingly falls in line with the experiences elsewhere; for example, developing countries have managed to incorporate these dual systems of social work practice. However, a number of authors have indicated a need for the indigenisation of social work practice for better results (Gray et al., 2017). The contextualisation of knowledge usually provides a positive response and cooperation from the indigenous groups.

Challenges Encountered in Fieldwork Education in Social Work

In fieldwork practice, schools of social work encounter a variety of issues ranging from student placement to performance evaluation. As a rule of thumb, it is pointless to have theory without practice because fieldwork in social work education and training is critically relevant for the transfer and increase in practical knowledge for the professional (Dhemba, 2012; Gray & Collett van Rooyen, 2002; Gray et al., 1996; Green, 1999; Hall, 1990; Hochfeld et al., 2009; Mamphiswana & Noyoo, 2000; van Rooyen & Gray, 2000) in social development. Hence acquiring social work theory without practice virtually leads to poor service delivery, defeating the ultimate expectation of the helping profession. As a measure to address the reasons for the mediocre performance of social work in Africa, several authors (Gray et al., 2014; Mupedziswa & Kubanga, 2016; Osei-Hwedie, 1993, 1995, 1996a, b) have concluded that there is a need to indigenise social work for a better outcome in the continent. And this implies the transformation of theoretical knowledge in social work into meaningful indigenous social work practice that suits local cultural groups of the African people. In this regard, it is observed that it is time to contextualise colonial-imported social work knowledge into that which local social work professionals may use to acquire meaningful sociocultural empowerment and development amongst the poor, vulnerable, and marginalised rural communities.

However, based on the situation on the ground, one may argue that this current innovative dispensation in social work education for effective fieldwork application is yet to be realised in Eswatini because of the shortage of expert knowledge of social work practice in the field.

In Eswatini, the theoretical knowledge that social work graduates acquire at the university are seemingly not being utilised as expected due to inadequate recognition of the profession exacerbated by the absence of a regulating body and unemployment. Without the opportunity for graduates to contextualise theoretical knowledge into practice, graduates may not acquire the necessary fieldwork experience that could necessitate the transfer of knowledge to others through field training (Dhemba & Nhapi, 2020). In the Kingdom of Eswatini, culture has a powerful influence in all spheres of life. Therefore, an effective social work practice must blend with cultural norms and values. Conversely, in South Africa, the integration of theory and fieldwork practice has been practised for quite a long time with lots of transitional and educational experiences. Although one may highlight the fact that South Africa and many other African countries may be going through what one may call a transitional period in the combination of theory and practice contextually, one may assert that Eswatini can learn from South Africa and integrate this experience into their quest to enhance social work education in its entirety in the kingdom.

Opportunities to Practice

The challenge of finding a suitable agency or organisation for fieldwork practice is a significant problem for social work students in both countries. Still, maybe to a broader extent, in Eswatini, being a small country with limited organisations that provide social services, it is usually challenging for tertiary institutions to place students out for fieldwork training timeously and for the appropriate required length of time for fieldwork practice. This challenge is critical because it affects students' chances of gathering adequate fieldwork education and experience. Providing enough time for field education and practice in social work is very important for transferring knowledge and expertise (Tackett et al., 2001; Gault et al., 2000). Based on experience, one may argue that insufficient time allocation for field education compromises the social work student's overall practical knowledge. Experience points out that without practical wisdom, students may complete their studies with a lack of confidence in their ability to face practical situations onsite (Wayne et al., 2010, p. 161; Bogo et al., 2020). This situation in Eswatini may not be the same as in South Africa, considering that the latter has a much bigger economy and corporate space and institutions in which social work students can be accepted to undertake field education and training. With their much-informed awareness and knowledge of the social work profession and the availability of a regulating council, field education and training provisions are more advanced than in Eswatini.

Location of Placement Agencies

Another challenging issue is finding the right agency that will provide the appropriate quality and level of field training required for a set of students at a particular time of their study. Experiences on the ground in Eswatini indicate that the very agencies capable of offering positions for placement to social work students are most often found within the country's urban areas. Unfortunately, this practice does not usually provide opportunities for students to acquire broad-based valuable practical knowledge available in fieldwork education within rural areas. Observations in this regard, by other commentators, agree that there is much to learn in social work field education outside urban areas that genuinely complement social work practice, with individuals, groups, and rural communities for a better society (Hall, 1990; Mupedziswa & Kubanga, 2016). However, because Eswatini has a tiny economy that has seriously been affected by poverty and massive unemployment, sponsorship for internship programmes and travelling to the rural areas for fieldwork is very limited.

Students who are fortunate to have placement positions in these agencies remain in the offices for most of their time during their fieldwork practice. Financial viability to support students' allocation for practicum is a global crisis, based on studies confirming that often practicum opportunities for students are limited due to financial support to agencies taking in students (Bogo et al., 2020). This observation is common in Western countries (CSWE, 2015b; Gushwa & Harriman, 2019; Ayala et al., 2018; Tam et al., 2018; Baginsky et al., 2019; Cleak & Zuchowski, 2019; Hay et al., 2019), just as it is the case in developing and poorer countries too because the effects are more significant in the poorer countries. Considering the number of social needs evident around the rural areas, social work students could benefit more in their field education experience if they had the opportunity to practise more often in the rural communities.

The issue of a rural bias regarding placement organisations is found both in South Africa and Eswatini, although the situation appears to be more extreme in Eswatini.

Education and Qualification of Field Supervisors

As earlier indicated above by Dhemba and Nhapi (2020), the shortage of qualified supervisors for fieldwork practice is a significant impediment in the drive for excellence and training in social work field education in Eswatini. The reason for the disparity is that social work is still a relatively new profession in the country. As such, the desire to source skilled social work experts into the country is not encouraging since knowledge of the profession and its role in society is still lacking.

On another note, the majority of the social work graduates in the country that ought to be on the field are unemployed. Unfortunately, positions and activities that are to be occupied by social workers are taken by non-social workers hence limiting these trained social workers to explore fieldwork activities and eventually increasing their knowledge in fieldwork and developmental social work practice (Dhemba & Nhapi, 2020). Furthermore, the few who have found jobs do not typically perform social work since the organisations for which they work do not often comprehend what social work practice requires.

Additionally, this unfortunate circle of events seriously affects fieldwork education and training as the inadequacy of theoretical knowledge becomes obvious without the use of it. Moreover, for social work and fieldwork education to be meaningful, it must be indigenised to suit the local context of social challenges (Manyama, 2018), and this necessitates a greater understanding and knowledge of what the social work profession entails.

As earlier mentioned, anyone can claim to be a social worker and even work as one because they had acquired some training in counselling or social sciences from institutions that claim to be training social workers because of the absence of a professional regulatory body in the country. Additionally, one must painfully mention that the sad reality on the ground is that even some of those that assume the responsibility in most of the agencies that provide placement for social work students in fieldwork practice are not qualified social workers. In this regard, one can only imagine the challenges and frustration that prospective social workers experience during their fieldwork practice. Like in South Africa, where the social work profession is well known and appreciated, such that the academic curriculum and guideline for fieldwork is regulated to suit local needs, the situation in Eswatini is different, as mentioned above. Dhemba and Nhapi (2020), articulate that the Department of Social Development that oversees social services activities is not quite flexible yet regarding the integration and accommodation of effective social work practice.

As mentioned earlier, in South Africa supervisors who supervise the student in the field practice organisations must have a Bachelor of Social Work qualification (as a minimum). They are also required to have at least two years of experience supervising first to third level students and a minimum of three years' experience supervising fourth level students. It is also a statutory requirement that they should be registered with the SACSSP.

Conclusion

South Africa and Eswatini are neighbouring countries in the Southern African Region. They have a vast difference in population numbers, with Eswatini having just more than one million and South Africa's population exceeding 59 million. Eswatini is entirely landlocked, whereas two oceans surround South Africa.

The Kingdom of Eswatini is providing social work training in two universities in the country, intending to alleviate poverty, unemployment, enhancing primary healthcare services and social development. However, the benefits of professional social work services are not yet in motion. In South Africa, social work training is offered in 16 public universities and one private college. The International Federation of Social Work has set Global Standards for Field Education, and the South African Council for Social Service Professions, a statutory body, has developed norms and standards for field practice. These norms and standards guide the field practice undertaken by students from first to fourth level.

The practice of social work in South Africa is regulated by the Social Service Professions Act (110 of 1978).

It can be said that despite the availability of acceptable social work education and training in Eswatini, there is still a considerable gap for close in terms of field education and the transfer of knowledge and practice in the social work profession. Due to the shortage of qualified professionals and the appropriate field placement agencies in the country, fieldwork advancement is seriously negatively affected. In South Africa, the profession is well known and respected with a professional body that oversees the social work practice for the transfer of knowledge and development. Therefore, the social work field education and training in Eswatini needs attention for positive transformation.

References

Ayala, J., Droplet, J., Fulton, A., Hewson, J., Letkemann, L., Baynton, M., Elliott, G., Judge-Stasiak, A., Blaug, C., Gérard Tétreault, A., & Schweizer, E. (2018). Field education in crisis: Experiences of field education coordinators in Canada. *Social Work Education*, *37*(3), 281–293. https:/ /doi.org/10.1080/02615479.2017.1397109

Baginsky, M., Manthorpe, J., & Hickman, B. (2019). Social work teaching partnerships: A discussion paper. *Social Work Education*, *38*(8), 968–982. https://doi.org/10.1080/02615479.2019.1616685

Bailey-McHale, J., Bailey-McHale, R., Caffrey, B., MacLean, S., & Ridgway, V. (2019). Using visual methodology: Social work students' perceptions of practice and the impact on practice educators. *Practice*, *31*(1), 57–74. https://doi.org/10.1080/09503153.2018.1476477

Bennett, S., Mohr, J., Deal, K. H., & Hwang, J. (2013). Supervisor attachment, supervisory working alliance, and affect in social work field instruction. *Research on Social Work Practice*, *23*(2), 199–209. https://doi.org/10.1177/1049731512468492

Bogo, M. (2010). *Achieving competence in social work through field education*. University of Toronto Press.

Bogo, M., Sewell, K. M., Mohamud, F. & Kourgiantakis, T. (2020). Social work field instruction: A scoping review. *Social Work Education*, *10*(1080), 1–33. https://doi.org/10.1080/02615479.2020.1842868

Brodie, I., & Williams, V. (2013). Lifting the lid: Perspectives on and activity within student supervision. *Social Work Education*, *32*(4), 506–522.

Central Statistical Office. (2017). *Swaziland national housing and population census preliminary report*. Mbabane: Central Statistical Office.

Cleak, H., & Zuchowski, I. (2019). Empirical support and considerations for social work supervision of students in alternative placement models. *Clinical Social Work Journal*, 47(1), 32–42.

Coohey, C., Dickinson, R., & French, L. (2017). Student self-report of core field instructor behaviors that facilitate their learning. *Field Educator*, 7(1), 1–15.

Council for Social Work Education [CSWE]. (2008). *Educational policy and accreditation standards*. Washington, DC: National Association of Social Workers.

Council for Social Work Education [CSWE]. (2015a). Educational policy and accreditation standards (EPAS). Author. Available: http://www.cswe.org/getattachment/Accreditation/Accreditation-Process/2015-EPAS/2015EPAS_Web_FINAL.pdf.aspx. (Accessed, 19/05/2021).

Deputy Prime Minister's Office, Kingdom of Eswatini. (2012). *Proposed organizational structure*. Mbabane: Department of Social Welfare.

Dhemba, J. (2012). Fieldwork in social work education and training: Issues and challenges in the case of Eastern and Southern Africa. *Social Work & Society: International Online Journal*, 10(1), 1–16.

Dhemba, J. & Nhapi, T. (2020). Social work and poverty reduction in Southern Africa: The case of Eswatini, Lesotho and Zimbabwe. *Social Work & Society*, 18(2).

Dominelli, L. & Bernard, W. T. (2003). *Broadening horizons: International exchanges in social work*. Aldershot: Ashgate.

Eswatini Medical Christian University, Faculty of Applied Social Sciences, Department of Social Work. (n.d.). *Field education guidelines*. Mbabane.

Finch, J., Williams, O. F., Mondros, J. B., & Franks, C. L. (2019). *Learning to teach, teaching to learn* (3rd ed.). Alexandria, VA: Council on Social Work Education.

Gair, S., Miles, D., Savage, D., & Zuchowski, I. (2015). Racism unmasked: The experiences of Aboriginal and Torres Strait Islander students in social work field placements. *Australian Social Work*, 68(1), 32–48.

Gray, M. & Coates, J (2010). 'Indigenization' and Knowledge Development: Extending the Debate. International Social Work, 53(5), 613–627

Gault, J., Redington, J., & Schlager, T. (2000). Undergraduate business internships and career success: Are they related? *Journal of Marketing Education*, 22, 45–53.

Gray, M., & Collett van Rooyen, A. J. (2002). The strengths perspective in social work: Lessons from practice. *Social Work/Maatskaplike Werk*, 38, 225–233.

Gray, M., O'Brien, F., & Mazibuko, F. (1996). Social work education for social development. *Journal of Social Development in Africa*, 11, 33–42.

Gray, M., Kreitzer, L., & Mupedziswa, R. (2014). The enduring relevance of indigenisation in African social work: A critical reflection on ASWEA's legacy. *Ethics and Social Welfare*, 8, 101–116.

Gray, M., Agllias, K., Mupedziswa, R., & Mugumbate, J. (2017). The role of social work field education programmes in the transmission of developmental social work knowledge in Southern and Eastern Africa. *Social Work Education*, 36(6), 623–635.

Green, S. (1999). The matrix of social work practice: Implications for the transformation of social work education. *Social Work/Maatskaplike Werk*, 35, 29–38.

Gushwa, M., & Harriman, K. (2019). Paddling against the tide: Contemporary challenges in field education. *Clinical Social Work Journal*, 47(3), 17–22.

Haanwinckel, B. Z., Fawcett, B., & Garcia, J. A. B. (2018). Contrasts and reflections: Social work fieldwork supervision in Brazil and England. *International Social Work*, 61(6), 943–953.

Hall, N. (1990). *Social work training in Africa: A fieldwork manual*. Harare: School of Social Work.

Hay, K., Maidment, J., Ballantyne, N., Beddoe, L., & Walker, S. (2019). Feeling lucky: The serendipitous nature of field education. *Clinical Social Work Journal*, 47(1), 23–31.

Healy. K., & Meagher, G. (2004). The reprofessionalisation of social work: Collaborative approaches for achieving professional recognition. *British Journal of Social Work*, 34, 243–260.

Hochfeld, T., Selipsky, L., Mupedziswa, R., & Chitereka, C. (2009). *Developmental social work education in southern and east Africa*. Johannesburg: University of Johannesburg, Centre for Social Development in Africa.

IASSW. (2002). *Directory*. Southampton, UK: IASSW.

Ife, J. (2001). *Human rights and social work: Towards rights-based practice*. Cambridge: Cambridge University Press.

International Federation of Social Work. (2004). Global standards for the education and training of social workers. www.ifsw.org

International Federation of Social Workers. (2014). Global definition of social work. Available: http://ifsw.org/policies/definition-of-social-work/ (Accessed 02 April 2021).

Kreitzer, L. (2012). *Social Work in Africa: Exploring culturally relevant education and practice in Ghana*. Calgary: University of Calgary Press.

Mabundza, L. (2017). Indigenisation of social work curriculum in Swaziland. In *Rethinking social work in Africa: Decoloniality and indigenous knowledge in education and practice*. Johannesburg: OR Tambo Conference Centre.

Mamphiswana, D., & Noyoo, N. (2000). Social work education in a changing socio-political and economic dispensation: Perspectives from South Africa. *International Social Work, 43*, 21–32.

Manyama, W. (2018). Where is developmental social work as social work practice method in Tanzania? The case of the Dar es Salaam region. *International Journal of Social Work, 5*(2), 43–57.

Midgley, J. (1981). *Professional imperialism: Social work in the third world*. London, Heinemann.

Mupedziswa, R., & Kubanga, K. (2016). Developing social work education in Africa: Challenges and prospects. In I. Taylor, M. Bogo, M. Lefevre, & B. Teater, (Eds.), *Routledge international handbook of social work education*, (pp. 119–130). London: Routledge.

Nhapi, T. G., & Dhemba, J. (2020). Embedding the developmental approach in social work education and practice to overcome poverty: The case of Southern Africa. *Greenwich Social Work Review, 1*(1), 11–20. https://doi.org/10.1177/0020872820944998

Noble, C. (2011). Field Education: Supervision, Curricula and Teaching Methods. In C. Noble, & M. Henrickson, (Eds.), *Social Work Field Education and Supervision across Asia Pacific* (pp. 3–22). Sydney University Press.

Osei-Hwedie, K. (1993). The challenge of social work in Africa: Starting the indigenisation process. *Journal of Social Development in Africa, 8*, 19–30.

Osei-Hwedie, K. (1995). *A search for legitimate social development education and practice models for Africa*. Lewiston, NY: Edwin Mullen.

Osei-Hwedie, K. (1996). The indigenisation of social work education and practice in South Africa: The dilemma of theory and method. *Social Work/Maatskaplike Werk, 32*, 215–225.

Parrish, D. E. (2020). From the editor—message from the new editor-in-chief: Hope and possibility on the horizon. *Journal of Social Work Education, 56*(1), 1–4.

Ross, B., Ta, B., & Grieve, A. (2019). Placement educators' experiences and perspectives of supervising international social work students in Australia. *Australian Social Work, 72*(2), 188–205.

Schenck, C. J., & Louw, H. (2010). Poverty. In L. Nicholas, J. Rautenbach and M. Maistry (Eds.), *Introduction to Social Work*. Cape Town: Juta.

Shulman, L. S. (2005). Signature pedagogies in the disciplines. *Daedalus, 143*(3), 52–59.

Social Work Task Team. (2017). *Field education manual and policies*. Kwaluseni, Eswatini: Department of Sociology and Social Work.

South African Council for Social Service Professions. (2020). *Norms and standards for bachelor of social work (BSW)*. Pretoria: South African Council for Social Service Professions.

Statistics South Africa. (2020). 2020 Mid-year population estimates. www.statsa.gov.za.

Tackett, J., Wolf, F., & Law, D. (2001). Accounting interns and their employers: Conflicting perceptions. *Ohio CPA Journal, 60*, 54–56.

Tam, D. M. Y., Brown, A., Paz, E., Birnbaum, R., & Kwok, S. M. (2018). Challenges faced by Canadian social work field instructors in baccalaureate field supervision. *Journal of Teaching in Social Work, 38*(4), 398–416.

University of Swaziland, (2017). Field Education Manual and Policies. Department of Sociology and Social Work.

Van Rooyen, C. A. J., & Gray, M. (2000). Social work education in South Africa: Changing contexts, changing content. *Social Work Africa, 1*, 19–26.

Wang, Y., & Chui, E. (2016). An exploratory path model of social work students' satisfaction with field education experience in China. *Social Work Research, 40*(3), 135–145.

Wayne, J., Bogo, M., & Raskin, M. (2010). Field education as the signature pedagogy of social work education. *Journal of Social Work Education, 46*(3), 327–339.

Weiss, I., Spiro, S., Sherer, M. & Korin-Langer, N. (2004). Social work in Israel: Professional characteristics in an international comparative perspective. *International Journal of Social Welfare, 13*, 287–296.

Weiss-Gal, I., & Welbourne, P. (2008) The professionalization of social work: A cross-national exploration. *International Journal of Social Welfare, 17*, 281–290. https://doi.org/10.1111/j.1468-2397.2008.00574.x

Zegeye, A. & Maxted, J. (2002). *Our dream deferred: The poor in South Africa*. Pretoria: South African History Online and Unisa Press.

28
Professionalisation of Social Work in Eswatini
A Comparative Study Between South Africa and Eswatini

Boitumelo Joyce Mohapi, Felicity Besong Tabi, and Zee Catherine Masuku

The professionalisation of any career or profession is an important element of recognition and appreciation for purposes of establishing and respecting ethical guidelines, professional development, and status (Weiss-Gal & Welbourne, 2008). Since its inception towards the later part of the 19th century (Midgley, 1981) social work has progressively developed into a profession that has been in practice in well over 144 nations (IASSW, 2002). As a result, the social work profession is gaining popularity globally (Healy & Meagher, 2004; Weiss et al., 2004), irrespective of the continuous arguments for and against its professional status (Illich, 1977; Reisch & Andrews, 2001; Simpkin, 1979; Walker & Beaumont, 1981).

In fact, Chitereka (2009) notes that social work exists as a profession in most African countries, including South Africa, Zimbabwe, Zambia, Ethiopia, Nigeria, Uganda, Ghana, and Kenya, Tanzania, Rwanda, and Egypt. These countries train their own social workers. Notably, in different countries, social work retains distinct features, and this variety is intriguing. With this observation however, one may highlight the fact that the professionalisation of social work in some countries is still a challenge. Despite these challenges, the social work profession remains an important practice-based profession that delivers social services to the majority of people.

According to the International Federation of Social Work (IFSW), social work is

> A practice-based profession and an academic discipline that promotes social change and development, social cohesion, and the empowerment and liberation of people. Principles of social justice, human rights, collective responsibility and respect for diversities are central to social work. Underpinned by theories of social work, social sciences, humanities and indigenous knowledge, social work engages people and structures to address life challenges and enhance wellbeing.
>
> *(IFSW, 2014)*

The above definition indicates that social work integrates academic knowledge with practice to enhance people's lives. The profession of social work can make a considerable contribution to the achievement of the Sustainable Development Goals (SDGs) in Africa. According to the United Nations Development Programme (UNDP, 2015), the SDGs are 'a set of seventeen goals which imagine a future just fifteen years off that would be rid of poverty and hunger, and safe from the worst effects of climate change. It's an ambitious plan'. Social work's role in supporting vulnerabilities is also emphasised by Kang'ethe (2014), who states that 'Social work is a humanistic profession, and it is also a discipline that it has the potential to address the different kinds of vulnerabilities that are faced by communities'.

Although most of the SDGs can be addressed by the involvement of social workers, the profession is especially critical in addressing the following goals:

- Goal number 1: End extreme poverty in all forms
- Goal number 2: End hunger, achieve food security and improved nutrition, and promote sustainable agriculture
- Goal number 3: Ensure healthy lives and promote well-being for all ages
- Goal number 4: Ensure inclusive and equitable quality education and promote lifelong learning opportunities for all
- Goal number 5: Achieve gender equality and empower all women and girls
- Goal number 8: Promote sustained, inclusive and sustainable economic growth, full and productive employment and decent work for all

This discussion seems to confirm the uniqueness of the social work profession embodied in 'the duality of the profession's person and environment mandate' whereby social workers are professionally mandated to assist in making the community conducive for people and at the same time assist in making people function properly within the community (Segal, Gerdes, & Steiner, 2019, p. 3).

Since social work undoubtedly provides a professional approach to addressing social issues, it is imperative for the profession to be professionalised by each country providing its services in order to allow professionally qualified personnel apply its knowledge base to assist communities in addressing social problems. Operationally, professionalisation according to Mohan (1996, p. 3) refers to the creation of a distinct body of knowledge; the existence of a distinct set of specialised abilities; a recognised training programme within or endorsed by tertiary education with controlled entry; an ethical standard; and a corporate entity or union with the ability to determine competence. The author adds that, selflessness, a devotion to service, status, responsibility, and integrity are among the less visible qualities of professionalisation.

The aim of this chapter, therefore, is to present a comparative analysis of the professionalisation of social work in Eswatini and South Africa, with the hope of advancing a roadmap for social work professionalisation in Eswatini, based on lessons learned from South Africa where social work is professionally regulated as will be discussed below. Secondly, commentators like Weiss and Welbourne (2008), reiterate that South Africa is one of the countries that provides extensive understanding of the profession of social work. Given this information, South Africa is in a stronger position to lead the way in terms of professionalising social work in Eswatini. The analysis will be performed with the aid of certain recognised values or features that can be used to make comparisons based on standards observed in other countries including South Africa that had long recognised and promoted professionalisation. These values include: public recognition; monopoly over types of work; competing roles of the profession; professional autonomy; knowledge base; professional education; social work professional-regulating organisations; and ethical standards.

Study Context

The current state of social work is better understood in the country's demographic composition and social structure that may impact on the results of the study. Eswatini is a landlocked country that is almost surrounded by South Africa and Mozambique on the east. The current population is 1,170,790, 30% of which is urban (Eswatini Demographics, 2020). Most of the country is rural, with peri-urban areas in the main cities.

South Africa is located at the southern tip of Africa, surrounded by two oceans. The country is bordered by Namibia, Botswana, Zimbabwe, Mozambique, Eswatini, and Lesotho. The country's mid-year population is estimated to have increased to 59.62 million in 2020, according to the report released by Statistics South Africa. (Statistics South Africa, 2020). Although South Africa is ranked as a middle-income economy globally, there is a lot of inequality and poverty.

The distance between South Africa and Eswatini is 1192 kilometres or approximately 12 hours travel on land. Both countries are in the Southern African Development Community (SADC) region and are close to each other.

History of Social Work Development

When Swaziland/Eswatini became independent during the post-colonial era in 1968, she took membership with the United Nations and a signatory of the Social Welfare Convention (Kanduza & Mkhonza, 2003). Social welfare origin in Eswatini dates back to 1952, during the colonial era by the British, before independence. Nationally, the Department of Social welfare is 'ultimately responsible for the provision of social development services and programmes' (DSW policy, 2009). The Department of Social Welfare was established in 1977 under the Care Service Order of 1977 in the Ministry of Home Affairs (MOHA) to reduce poverty and other social problems.

Regardless of the introduction of social work to support the Department of Social Welfare's national goal of improving the socioeconomic conditions of the Swazi people, they continue to face insurmountable obstacles. Eswatini is in desperate need of holistic professional social work intervention programmes, given the country's socioeconomic issues, including HIV and AIDS, poverty, and joblessness (Dhembe & Naphi, 2020), as well as the current Covid-19 pandemic.

Because economically and ecologically vulnerable communities are continually faced with acute resource scarcity (Shajahan & Sharma, 2018), technical and social support efforts must be implemented using the best professional practices if desired outcomes are to be achieved. Despite the government's initiative to provide social work education and training in the country in order to address the country's numerous social concerns, a good outcome of this endeavour may only be realised when future social workers are given the opportunity to work professionally (Weiss-Gal & Welbourne, 2008). Service delivery in the social work field can be difficult without a professional founding.

The early social welfare policies in South Africa were mainly influenced by colonialism and apartheid. This led to the development of welfare policies that favoured one racial group over others and enforced many social changes over traditional societies. The discovery of minerals in South Africa and industrialisation in the 1800s influenced the social and political environment in the country. The country moved from comprising of mainly farming communities to being largely industrialised communities. This resulted in rising levels of poverty in the country, with accompanying housing and health problems.

According to Mckendrick (1990), the history of social welfare in South Africa can be traced back to 1929. This was when the Carnegie Commission probed the 'poor white problem' (Patel,

2005). One of the recommendations of this commission was that state welfare departments should be launched to mitigate the disjointed approach to the rendering of welfare service, which different state departments rendered.

The first government department of welfare in South Africa was established in 1937. Its main aim was to restore broken families and individuals and to coordinate social services. This step was viewed as a milestone in the professionalisation of social work in South Africa.

Concerning the above, McKendrick (1990) states, 'it is in this period 1937–1950 that the effect of South African historical experience on the development of a social welfare philosophy and system can be seen most clearly'. This marked the beginning of the state's involvement in welfare services, which had up to that period been performed only by volunteer church groups and community organisations. The focus of these services was to reduce poverty. Later on, universities and religious colleges followed by training social workers (Patel, 2005).

Legislative Framework for Social Welfare Delivery

In South Africa, the legislation that provided the framework for delivering welfare services was the Social and Associated Workers' Act, 110 of 1978. This law enabled the development of a mechanism for controlling the profession of social and associate professions and granted social work full professional status.

The registration of welfare organisations was facilitated by the National Welfare Act (1978). It also enabled the institution of a South African Welfare Council that served in an advisory capacity to the minister of welfare-on-welfare issues and the establishment of regional welfare boards for the various race groups in South Africa.

In Eswatini, the legislative framework for delivering social welfare services includes the Department of Social Welfare created in 1952 in Eswatini (Her Majesties Stationery Service, 1962, 1968). The Department of Social Welfare was established in 1977 under the Child Care Service Order (CCSO) of 1977. This order regulates the following child care functions:

- To make provision for orphaned, destitute, homeless and abandoned children
- To protect children from abuse or ill-treatment
- To remove children from the custody or care of unfit persons or from conditions that are physically or morally harmful to them or likely to be so harmful
- To perform other humanitarian services for children's welfare as authorised by the Ministry.

The Shift to Professionalism

The welfare landscape had since changed in 1994 when democracy was introduced in South Africa. The White Paper for Social Welfare (1997) was introduced and is based on the following principles:

- Securing basic welfare rights
- Equity
- Non-discrimination
- Democracy
- Improved quality of life
- Human Rights
- People-centred policies
- Investment in human capital

- Sustainability
- Inter-sectoral collaboration
- Decentralisation of service delivery
- Quality services
- Transparency and accountability
- Accessibility
- Appropriateness
- Ubuntu

As mentioned above, in Eswatini, the Department of Social Development DSW, was established after the country gained independence. The circumstances under which social welfare has developed has forced Eswatini 'to adopt a system of social welfare provision based on modern thinking, drawing its principles from the tradition of the Poor Laws of Britain' (Kanduza & Mkhonza, 2003, p. 11). The services provided by DSW services have mainly focused on grants for vulnerable groups. In the 2000s, particularly with the challenges caused by HIV and AIDS, there were policy and legislative changes within the DSW.

The adoption of the National Development Social Policy (2009) highlighted the emphasis for the DSW to shift from social welfare to social development to ensure clients are sufficiently empowered and eventually self-sustainable (DSW Strategic Plan 2011–2015). The refocus from a welfare to developmental approach therefore requires the department to engage in social work, community development, and social assistance. Presently, the DSW services include 'comprehensive social welfare services focusing on all vulnerable groups (families, older persons, disabilities, children, ex-servicemen, substance abuse people, persons affected with HIV/AIDS)' (DSW, 2009), in addition, to providing social security systems to the most vulnerable, orphaned and vulnerable children school bursary and old age grants.

It is worth noting that, although the policy was adopted in 2009, 12 years later, it seems as though service delivery in Eswatini is still remedial and not developmental. "Social development leads to an improvement to people's quality of life" (Chitereka, 2009, p. 154). Unfortunately, because of this drawback, the Eswatini citizens still appear to be in the early stages of recognising the significance or worth of social work in the country. Chitereka further asserts that 'once people see real changes in their lives because of social work intervention, they will ultimately respect the profession and value social work services'. (p. 154)

Distinction between Social Work and Paraprofessionals

The title 'social worker' in the South African context is a protected title. No person without the requisite qualification and registration with the South African Council for Social Service Professions (SACSSP) may use the title or practice as such. Section 15 (1) of the Social Service Professions Act 110 of 1978, as amended states, that: "no person shall in any manner whatsoever, practice the profession in which a professional board has been established, unless he or she has been registered under this Act as a Social Worker." Any person in violation of this section shall be subjected to prosecution. The title social work is bestowed to all graduates from accredited Schools of Social Work. In South Africa, the prerequisite is a four year Bachelor's Degree Qualification (on an NQF Level 7 or 8). The SACSSP requires both these educational levels to register on the SACSSP database (Social Service Professions Act 110 of 1978).

In South Africa, there is also a distinct difference in the operational expectations of social workers and social auxiliary workers. For example, social auxiliary workers provide a supervision-based supportive service because they are only allowed to work under the supervision of a social worker. Social workers, on the other hand, because of the nature and extent of their qualification and specialist offerings, can provide a range of services.

The term 'social auxiliary work' in terms of the regulations relating to the registration of social auxiliary workers as described in the Social Service Profession Act of 1978, as amended 'is an act or activity being practiced by a Social Auxiliary Worker under the guidance and control of a Social Worker and as a supporting service to a Social Worker in order to achieve the aims of social work'.

Section 15 (1) of the Social Service Professions Act also states that "no person shall in any manner whatsoever practice in a profession in which a professional board has been established unless he or she has been registered under this Act as a Social Worker". In other words, the Social Auxiliary Worker is an assistant to the Social Worker and cannot function without supervision by the registered Social Worker.

> "The Social Auxiliary Worker must have a Further Education and Training (FET) Certificate in Social Auxiliary Work at National Qualification Framework Level (NQF Level) 4 or 5, or education and training in Social Work that is equivalent to NQF Level 4 or 5 registered with the South African Qualifications Authority; or a Certificate in Social Auxiliary Work which the council awarded to a person who successfully completed the study course in Social Auxiliary Work offered by the SACSSP and in respect of which the holder of the qualification was enrolled for such qualification before 30 June 2006 or received written approval by the council for enrolment at a later date as determined by the Council (Section 18 (2) of Social Service Profession Act, Act 110 of 1978 as amended: rules regulating to the qualifications for registration as a Social Auxiliary Worker)"
>
> *(www.dsd.gov.za)*

In Eswatini, the title 'social worker' is not a protected title owing to the absence of a regulatory body of practice. As a result, many non-social workers use the title and practice as such. This situation seems to substantiate the fact that, until social work is professionalised in Eswatini, its future is questionable because, as Mohan (2018, p. 21) puts it, 'all work is "social"'.

However, there is consensus that there is a need for social auxiliary workers at grassroots level where there is no DSW coverage. But, in practice those positions are occupied by non-professionals who have 'O' level (high school certificate) and below. Often they have received short term certified training. At one point, a recommendation was made for Eswatini to borrow from social auxiliary curriculum training from neighbouring countries such as South Africa (UNICEF, 2010).

In Eswatini, several paraprofessionals have obtained a 'working with children, families, and communities at risk' certificate, and others have the Psychosocial Support Certificate. This certificate is currently being rolled out in two of the country's pre-primary, primary, and secondary school training colleges.

However, the government of Eswatini prioritised social work in 2013 and provided funding to train social workers through a government scholarship managed by the Ministry of Labour and Social Security. The Government offers a Social Work scholarship locally and in South Africa (Ministry of Labour and Social Security, 2013).

Professional Registration and Regulation of Social Work Practice

A study by Weiss and Welbourne (2008) determined that to obtain a recognised social work qualification requires a recognised professional course that is at least three years or longer. They further found that entrance requirements on the type of degree vary depending on the country.

Presently, in South Africa bachelors, master's, and doctoral degree qualifications can be obtained. However, in Eswatini, only the bachelor's degree is offered. With these degrees being offered presently, now the diploma in social work is less in demand.

In establishing a theoretical framework to distinguish professional and non-professional occupations and as well identifying factors that affect their growth, the trait and power approaches are briefly discussed (Hall, 1994; Macdonald, 1995) in order to throw light on values observed in analysing professionalisation in Eswatini and South Africa.

Two Approaches to Professionalisation

In this discussion two approaches (the trait and power approaches), will be looked at briefly to synthesis the concept of professionalisation in social work.

With the trait or tribute approach, the word 'profession' refers to a collection of distinguishing characteristics that differentiate 'professions' from 'occupations' (Hall, 1994; Hugman, 1996; Popple, 1985), implying that this method operationalises the concept by defining essential characteristics or core traits. Citing Green, Abbott (1999), and Hall (1994) we highlight five important attributes: a systematic body of knowledge; professional authority recognised by its clientele; community sanction; a regulatory code of ethics; and a professional culture sustained by formal professional associations, must be considered in order to validate professionalisation. Whereas there is no unanimous agreement on the most important traits (Millerson, 1973; Popple, 1985), it is generally understood that the trait or attribute approach has always been the framework for adjudicating the professional status of social work (Weiss-Gal & Welbourne, 2008). According to Greenwood (1957), social work is considered to be a profession on the bases of the above-mentioned attributes.

With the power approach, Freidson (1907) believes professions to be occupations having a prominent sense of authority in the social structure within their practice's jurisdiction, allowing them to exert control about what constitutes their practice. In the same vein, Johnson (1972), defined professions as careers in which the employer maintains control over a variety of parts of the operations, including: the most important aspects of their job; the selection, training, and licencing of members; and autonomy in determining the kind of services and who is allowed to receive them. Besides, the power approach has enjoyed prominence in the field of social work in recent decades (Abbott, 1999; Hopps & Collins, 1995), exploring the level of monopoly that social work has enjoyed in service delivery (Giarchi & Lankshear, 1998; Johnson & Yanca, 2001; Popple, 1995).

Contextual Analysis of Professionalisation of Social Work between South Africa and Eswatini

An analytical discussion of the professionalisation of social work in Eswatini and South Africa will be explored based on the two approaches to professionalisation stated above, while focusing on the following values: public recognition, monopoly over types of works; competing roles of the profession; professional autonomy; knowledge base; professional education; social work professional-regulating organisations and ethical standards.

Public Recognition

One indicator of public recognition that an occupation is a profession is the existence of laws and licencing procedures establishing entrance criteria, barring those who do not meet those criteria from working in or assuming the title of the profession (Hardcastle, 1990; Greenwood, 1957; Specht, 1988). A crucial missing element in the professionalisation of social work in Eswatini is the absence of a council to regulate the profession. This has negatively impacted service delivery and ultimately results in the low professional status of the profession among the public.

Unlike in some other countries that have regulating authorities, anyone professing to be a social worker in Eswatini is allowed to practise so long as they are able to find work. This situation is quite critical because it has been observed that there have been occasions where non-social workers have been employed in positions that were to be occupied by social workers (Dhemba & Nhapi, 2020). Moreover, because social work is relatively new, the majority of the population and corporations do not seemingly recognise it or, more importantly, do not grasp what it comprises. In South Africa however, it is mandatory that all social workers must be registered with the South African Council for Social Services Professions. Without licencing, no social worker is permitted to practice (Weiss-Gal & Welbourne, 2008).

In South Africa, registration with the South African Council for Social Service Professions (SACSSP) is a prerequisite for professional practice and a legal requirement as prescribed by the Social Service Professions Act 110 of 1978. Currently, there are 37138 registered social workers and 12397 registered auxiliary social workers (SACSSP, 2021).

In contrast, Eswatini lacks a quality assurance component to regulate social work practice. The exact numbers of qualified social workers in the country are unknown. It is estimated that there are approximately 200 skilled social workers nationally. The government employs about the majority of social workers in the country, while the rest are employed by other government ministries, NGOs, or remain unemployed. A council specific to social work in Eswatini would ensure quality assurance based on professional and academic qualifications. After all, 'professional associations enhance the professional identity, visibility, growth, and development of the professions they represent' (Global Alliance, 2015).

Monopoly over Types of Work

According to Greenwood (1957), an occupation may be considered to be a profession when it commands exclusive rights to execute specific tasks and function within its jurisdiction of operations. The monopoly of certain specified tasks in social work as a requirement for professionalisation is non-existent in Eswatini. Because it is a relatively young profession in the country, obtaining such exclusive rights to carry out specific categories of operation is quite challenging. This appears to be one of those regulations that may need considerable effort and procedures to be approved in the country. With reference to South Africa, one may not be too sure about the level of monopoly social work enjoys. However, based on a cross-cultural study on professionalisation done by Weiss-Gal and Welbourne (2008), it was found that South Africa and none of the other countries featured in the study had – or exercised the right to monopolise – specific work categories in respect of their professional status. However, in Eswatini, one may ascertain that the situation is exacerbated by the lack of a professional body regulating social work practice, unlike South Africa.

Competing Roles of the Profession

Several authors (Gray & Mazibuko, 2002; Healy & Meagher, 2004; McDonald et al., 2003), assert that professionalisation in this regard may be considered in terms of how an occupation is able to neutralise or suppress competition from other specialists that might be able to provide similar services closely related to social work. According to Weiss-Gal and Welbourne (2008), this threat to social work practice is very real, especially when it comes to knowledge and skills that may be easily integrated into social work disciplines. This scenario is prevalent in Eswatini. In fact, there is very serious confusion when it comes to the work social workers are supposed to be doing (Dhemba & Nhapi, 2020). This threat to the profession of social work in Eswatini requires an immediate response if the new profession is to be fully acknowledged and given the professional standing it deserves. However, this problem appears to be universal, as both Lymbery (2001) and McDonald et al. (2003) agree that this threat to the social work profession is a global phenomenon that has been observed in many Western countries. Because it is considered a global issue, there is reason to suppose that South Africa may be experiencing some amount of it, even if minimal, due to the country's professional regulatory body for social work.

Professional Autonomy

This aspect of professional autonomy in the professionalisation of social work requires the professional social worker enjoy and exercise the right to make work-related decisions based on his or her own professional knowledge and expertise without the interference of or dependence on those who know nothing about the profession (Weiss-Gal & Welbourne, 2008). Experience in the field indicates that often social workers' professional autonomy is consumed by repressive leaders of organisations or institutions for which they work as a result of their working conditions. In this respect they are forced to comply or act against their professional values in order to comply with organisational objectives, procedures, and regulations (Compton & Galaway, 1999; Hugman, 1996; Howe, 1980; Jones, 2001; Reisch & Wenocur, 1986). This condition of work in the field of social work is not uncommon in Eswatini, and is prevalent in some institutions because of the lack of adequate awareness and proper understanding of what social work profession entails.

More so, some of the organisations that employ social workers do not really provide social work-related services. According to on-the-ground experience, most social workers take advantage of these job opportunities, owing to the country's unemployment rate and a lack of proper social work job classifications. Furthermore, because social work is still a relatively new profession in the country, most agencies involved in social welfare activities, including social work practice, are managed by non-social workers. Resultantly, those social workers who work under them may eventually feel a lack of autonomy in their professional activities. On the other hand, studies have confirmed that most social service agencies in South Africa and some other nations are led by qualified social workers, which may allow for professional autonomy in those organisations (Weiss-Gal & Welbourne, 2008).

Knowledge Base

With respect to knowledge base capabilities regarding professionalisation, Weiss-Gal and Welbourne (2008) assert that knowledge base refers to the understanding and level of professional knowledge of social workers in the field pertaining to defined work specialties. This comprises different categories of social work services such as social problems in connection with poverty, child abuse and neglect; knowledge on vulnerable groups of people; expertise in intervention strategies to individuals and communities; information concerning the interaction between different groups of people and so forth. In this regard, the ability to integrate theory and practice effectively is expected of the professional social worker.

In Eswatini, it is safe to state that the level of social work training provided by institutions of higher learning is standard and competitive enough for graduates to perform effectively as social workers. However, social workers in most countries including Eswatini may not be adequately equipped in advanced techniques to deal with challenges such as HIV and AIDS (Kang'ethe, 2014) and drug abuse that is ravaging the young population in the country, necessitating the development and empowerment of the social work sector in the country to address the issues (Swaziland State of the Youth Report 2015).

Importantly, there is a need to integrate theory and practice in social work in order to maximise professionalism (Gray et al., 2014; Mupedziswa & Kubanga, 2016; Osei-Hwedie, 1993, 1995, 1996a, b), which is still quite a challenge in Eswatini. Weiss-Gal and Welburne (2008) identified a blend of Western and indigenous knowledge imported into most of the surveyed countries, and that contextualisation was required in order to improve results. South Africa is said to be ahead of the curve in this area due to its expertise and professional organisation of social service structures, which Eswatini might learn from.

Professional Education

Hugman (1995) maintains that acquiring a reasonable tertiary professional education in social work is an essential requirement for professional practice. Since its inception in Africa social work has gone through progressive training and transformed into a professional knowledge-based occupation in the continent (Midgley, 1981; Chitereka, 2009). As a prerequisite for professionalisation, both undergraduate and postgraduate qualifications are required for anyone to be considered a professional social worker in Eswatini and South Africa. But the difference between the two countries is that in Eswatini, its implementation is lagging behind since the profession is not regulated by a professional council while in South Africa it is regulated by the SACSSP.

In Eswatini, social workers with undergraduate qualification are trained locally in UNESWA and EMCU, while those with postgraduate qualification are trained abroad. Dhemba and Nhapi (2020) add that tertiary social work education in Eswatini commenced in 2014, with the establishment of four-year Bachelor of Social Work (BSW) programmes at the two local universities, the University of Eswatini (UNESWA) and Eswatini Medical Christian University (EMCU). Currently, there is no social work association in the country that the students can take membership of. Several attempts were made to establish a social work association, as late as 2016, but none have been successful to date.

The situation is different in South Africa, where several universities provide social work education up to postgraduate levels, as well as advanced platforms for professional practice, as observed by Weiss-Gal & Welbourne (2008). Established in 1924 in South Africa, the Jan Hofmeyer College was one of the first institutions to train social workers. Currently there are 16 public universities and one private college offering a social work qualification in South Africa. They are all affiliated to the Association of South African Social Work Education Institutions (ASASWEI). These universities are:

Nelson Mandela University
North West University (Mafikeng, Potchefstroom and Vaal)
Stellenbosch University
University of Cape Town
University of Fort Hare (East London and Alice)
University of Free State
University of Johannesburg
University of KwaZulu-Natal
University of Limpopo

University of Pretoria
University of South Africa
University of Venda
University of Western Cape
University of Witwatersrand
University of Zululand
Walter Sisulu University
South African College of Applied Psychology
(asaswei.org.za)

The aims of ASASWEI are:

- To facilitate collaboration and exchange of information on social work education, training research and practice with relevant networks (governmental and non-governmental) on national, regional, and international levels.
- To develop strategies that enhance the recognition of social work as a profession.
- To promote recognition of the contribution of social work to social and economic development and the transformation of South African society.
- To support the development of appropriate and locally specific research, theory and practice. Contribute to developing and implementing social welfare and education policies in the South African context.

(ASASWEI, 2021)

Registration and Regulation of Social Work Education

In Eswatini, the Eswatini Higher Education Council (ESHEC) under the Ministry of Education regulates all tertiary institutions. In the absence of a social work accreditation body or council in Swaziland, all social work training is governed by the Ministry of Education and the Training Qualification Framework (European Union, 2016). ESHEC has approved the social work programmes at UNESWA and EMCU.

In South Africa, the Council for Higher Education (CHE) is an independent statutory body established in Section 4 of the Higher Education Act (Act 101 of 1997). As an independent statutory quality council, the CHE focuses on quality assurance, research, and monitoring, initiating critical discussions on contemporary higher education issues, and advising higher education ministers in current matters.

The CHE conducts institutional audits for all universities as a quality assurance measure. The audit looks at institutional policies, systems, procedures, strategies, and resources utilised to support teaching and learning, research, and community engagement. The audit also examines the academic support services in place at higher education institutions (CHE, 2021).

Social Work-Regulating Organisations

Weiss-Gal and Welbourne (2008) argue that most nations have established national and local professional bodies to regulate the social work profession in their respective countries as an important condition for professionalisation in social work. In South Africa, for example, as stated above, there is a professional association that regulates the membership of social workers in both government and private practice (Gray & Mazibuko, 2002; Mazibuko & Gray, 2004), to ensure that social work is conducted in a professional manner. However, as previously stated, this is not the case in Eswatini. And because Eswatini lacks this critical instrument to govern and ensure competent professional practice of social work, the profession's worth and importance in the country appears to be substantially affected. As a result, professional social work practice in Eswatini is in desperate need.

Professional regulatory organisations, particularly at the national level, play an important role in encouraging professional growth through knowledge sharing using various methods, as well as establishing and enforcing ethical rules while ensuring the advancement of quality social education (Weiss-Gal & Welbourne, 2008). Furthermore, these authors argue that these professional bodies protect both the members' and the consumers' interests in social work services.

Ethical Standards

This professional feature as a criterion for social work professionalisation has been recognised a very significant requirement to be considered in most countries (Weiss-Gal & Welbourne, 2008) where social work is practiced. The authors also stated that an ethical code in social work practice was established in South Africa in the 1980s (Weiss-Gal & Welbourne, 2008), but none exists in Eswatini at the moment due to the novelty of the profession and a seemingly lack of other professional tools to enhance it. In contrast to Eswatini, this demonstrates how far the profession has progressed in South Africa.

Conclusion and Recommendations for the Way Forward

Looking back, this chapter has reflected on the current situation of social work professionalisation in Eswatini and South Africa, identified gaps, and then critically explored the nexus between these gaps and service delivery. It should be stated that this chapter does not argue that social work anywhere is a non-success. Instead, this study sought to offer a thorough yet fair overview of the profession's strengths and weaknesses as it is currently practised in both nations and to come up with ideas for how to strengthen it. While social work in South Africa has grown into a sustainable profession over time, in Eswatini, social work is a relatively new profession. In both countries however, social work professionals render their services in government departments of social welfare, hospitals, schools, probation services, police, and correctional facilities just to name a few.

Social work has relentlessly expanded its positive impact in society, working to enhance the dignity and self-sufficiency of the marginalised people it serves. Reflecting on the definitions of social work and the SDGs discussed earlier, one may state that, social work is hence placed in a broader perspective of the 'social ordering' of society and the strategies that are designed to bring and/or maintain social order. Social ordering systems include the welfare system and policy of the nation, health, education, and security systems. Social ordering is of great importance to society because of the unpredictability of human behaviour. Behaviours such as robbery, abuse, neglect, assault, terrorism, and trafficking destabilise the social order to a greater or lesser extent and require intervention by government and other organisations.

Social work is one of the strategies used for such interventions. Social work is therefore far more than just doing good works based on religious convictions, philanthropy, or humanism. Given this evidence, it is absolutely imperative for each country where social work is practised to grant social work the professional status and autonomy it deserves by professionalising the profession. Meanwhile, social workers in Eswatini could form a strong association that aims to increase public awareness about social work and use that as leverage to lobby for professionalisation in the government and other sectors.

Based on the discussion above, a case has been made for Eswatini's introduction of a social work regulatory body to standardise practice and ethical conduct as a matter of urgency. In this instance, a social work council would define practice standards and academic qualifications to regulate social work. This would ensure that qualified social workers are employed and the quality-of-service delivery can be of a professional standard. Based on observation from this discussion, one may suggest that there is quite a number of lessons that Eswatini can emulate from South Africa, since South Africa has lots of experience on social work activities' processes and professional expertise on the occupation. With the introduction of a professional body, there will be opportunities for social workers to grow in the profession for service delivery and professional protection. This will enable government to enjoy good returns on investment on social work education in the country and also provide opportunities for employment of social worker as well as the attraction of highly qualified social workers.

Additionally, maybe the government needs to have a clear absorption plan for new social work graduates over a five-year period of time. In addition, there is need to closely monitor professionalisation closely as well as the repayment of study loans. It is timely for Eswatini to have an Auxiliary Social Work programme that will be at foundational level and is specific to Social Work. Ideally, it should be linked to the Bachelor of Social Work degree, so that it is the entry point to the profession. More importantly, Eswatini, like other African countries, is part of the global social work community. Over the past few years, social work has expanded to virtually every corner of the world (Darkwa, 2007). It is thus imperative for Eswatini to professionalise social work in order to meet regional and international standards.

References

Abbott, A.A. (1999). Measuring social work values: A cross-cultural challenge for global practice. *International Social Work, 42*, 455–470.
Austin, D. (1983). The Flexner myth and the history of social work. *Social Service Review, 57*, 357–377.
Bamford, T. (1990). *The future of social work*. Basingstoke: Macmillan.
Brij, M. (2018). *The future of social work: Seven pillars of practice*. Thousand Oaks: SAGE, Publications.
Chitereka, C. (2009). Social work practice in a developing continent: The case of Africa. *Advances in Social Work, 10*(2),144–56.
Chitereka, C. (2009). Social work education, training and employment in Africa: The case of Zimbabwe *Journal Ufahamu: A Journal of African Studies, 35*(1), 149–154.
Compton, B.R, & Galaway, B. (1999). *Social work processes* (6th ed.). Pacific Grove: Brooks/Cole Publishing.
Council for Higher Education. (n.d.). Legislative and policy mandate. www.che.ac.za.
Council of Higher Education. (2021). *HISTORY OF THE CHE*. Retrieved from www.che.ac.za
Darkwa, O. K. (2007). Continuing social work education in an electronic age: The opportunities and challenges facing social work educators in Ghana. *Professional Development, 2*(1), 38–43.
Department of Social Development. (1997). *White paper on social welfare*. Pretoria: Department of Social Development.
Deputy Prime Minister's Office. (2009). Social welfare department. Policies. Available: http://www.gov.sz/index.php/ministries-departments/the-deputy-prime-minister-s-office/social-welfare-department. (Accessed, 10/07/2021).
Dhemba, J., & Nhapi, T. (2020). Social work and poverty reduction in Southern Africa: The case of Eswatini, Lesotho and Zimbabwe. *Social Work & Society, 18*(2), 1–13.
Dominelli, L., & Bernard, W. T. (2003). *Broadening horizons: International exchanges in social work*. Aldershot: Ashgate.
Eswatini Demographics. (2020). Population of Eswatini. Available: https://www.worldometers.info/world-population/swaziland-population/. (Accessed, 09/07/2021).
European Union (2016). *Training needs assessment of the department of social welfare Mbabane*.

Flexner, A. (1915). Is social work a profession? In: National Conference of Charities and Corrections, Proceedings of the National Conference of Charities and Corrections at the 42nd Annual Session, May, held in Baltimore, MD.

Freidson, E. (1970b). *Professional dominance: The social structure of medical care.* New York: Atherton Press.

Gault, J., Redington, J., & Schlager, T. (2000). Undergraduate business internships and career success: Are they related? *Journal of Marketing Education, 22,* 45–53.

Giarchi G, & Lankshear, G. (1998). The eclipse of social work in Europe. *Social Work in Europe, 5,* 25–36.

Global Social Service Workforce Alliance. (2015). *The state of the social service workforce report.* Washington, DC: Global Social Service Workforce Alliance.

Government of Swaziland. (2009). *National Social Development Policy Mbabane.* Government of Swaziland.

Government of Swaziland. (2012). *Children's Protection and Welfare Act Mbabane.* Government of Swaziland.

Government of Swaziland. (2012) *DSW Strategic Plan 2011–2015.*

Gray, M., & Mazibuko, F. (2002). Social work in South Africa at the dawn of the new millennium. *International Journal of Social Welfare, 11,* 191–200.

Greenwood, E. (1957). Attributes of a profession. *Social Work, 2,* 5–45.

Hall, R. (1994). *Sociology of work.* California: Pine Forge Press.

Hardcastle, D. (1990). Legal regulation of social work. In *Encyclopaedia of Social Work* (18th ed.) (1990 supplement). Silver Spring: NASW.

Healy, K, & Meagher, G (2004). The reprofessionalisation of social work: Collaborative approaches for achieving professional recognition. *British Journal of Social Work, 34,* 243–260.

Her Majesty's Stationary Office. (1962). Swaziland - Report for the Year 1961". London: Crown Printers. 1962., "Swaziland Report for the Year. 1968". London: Crown Printers. 1968. . "Swaziland Report for the Year. 1962". London: Crown Printer.

Hopps, J, & Collins, P. (1995). Social work profession overview. In: Edwards R. (Ed.), *Encyclopaedia of social work* (19th ed.). Washington, DC: NASW.

Howe, E. (1980). Public professions and the private model of professionalism. *Social Work, 25,* 179–191.

Hugman, R. (1996). Professionalization in social work: The challenge of diversity. *International Social Work, 39*(2), 131–147.

Iarskaia-Smirnova, E., & Romanov, P. (2002). 'A Salary is not important here': The professionalization of social work in contemporary Russia. *Social Policy and Administration, 36,* 123–141.

Illich, I. (1977). *Disabling professions. London, New Hampshire, Salem. International social work: Professional action in an interdependent world.* New York: Oxford University Press.

International Association for Schools of Social Work. (2002). *Directory.* Southampton, UK: IASSW.

Ife, J. (2001). *Human rights and social work: Towards rights' based practice.* Cambridge: Cambridge University Press.

International Federation of Social Work. (2004). *Ethics in social work, statement of principles* Available: http://www.ifsw.org/en/p38000324.html. (Accessed 13/032008).

International Federation of Social Work. (2014). *Global Definition of the Social Work Profession.* Available: https://www.ifsw.org/global-definition-of-social-work/ (Accessed, 20/06/2021).

Johnson, T. (1972). *Professions and power.* London: Macmillan.

Johnson, L., & Yanca, S. (2001). *Social work practice: A generalist approach* (7th ed.). Boston: Allyn and Bacon.

Jones, C. (2001). Voices from the front line: State social workers and New Labour. *British Journal of Social Work, 31,* 547–562.

Kanduza, A. M, & Mkhonza, S. T. (2003). *Issues in the economy and politics of Swaziland since 1968 webster print.* Matsapha.

Kang'ethe, S. M. (2014). Exploring Social Work Gaps in Africa with Examples From South Africa and Botswana. *Journal of Social Sciences, 41*(3), 423–431.

Lymbery, M. (2001). Social work at the crossroads. *British Journal of Social Work, 1,* 369–384.

Lyons, K. (1999). *International social work: Themes and perspective.* Aldershot: Ashgate.

Lyons, K. (2006). Globalisation and social work: International and local implications. *British Journal of Social Work, 36,* 365–380.

Macdonald, K. (1995). *The sociology of the professions.* London: Sage.

Mazibuko, F., & Gray, M. (2004). Social Work professional associations in South Africa. *International Social Work, 47,* 129–142.

McDonald, C., Harris, J., & Wintersteen, R. (2003). Contingent on context? Social work in Australia, Britain and the USA. *British Journal of Social Work, 33,* 191–208.

McKendrick, B. W. (1990). *Introduction to social work in South Africa.* Pretoria: Haum Tertiary.

Midgley, J. (1981). *Professional imperialism: Social work in the third world*. London: Heinemann.

Midgley, J. (2001). Issues in international social work: Resolving critical debates in the profession. *Journal of Social Work, 1*, 21–35.

Millerson, G. (1973). *The qualifying associations: A study in professionalization*. New York: Humanistic Press.

Ministry of Sports, Culture, and Youth Affairs. (2015). *Swaziland State of the youth report 2015*. Swaziland: UNFPA.

Mupedziswa, R., & Kubanga, K. (2016). Developing social work education in Africa: Challenges and prospects. In I. Taylor, M. Bogo, M. Lefevre , & B. Teater (Eds.), *Routledge international handbook of social work education* (pp. 119–130). London: Routledge.

Osei-Hwedie, K. (1993). The challenge of social work in Africa: Starting the indigenisation process. *Journal of Social Development in Africa, 8*, 19–30.

Osei-Hwedie, K. (1995). *A search for legitimate social development education and practice models for Africa*. Lewiston, NY: Edwin Mullen.

Osei-Hwedie, K. (1996b). The indigenisation of social work education and practice in South Africa: The dilemma of theory and method. *Social Work/Maatskaplike Werk, 32*, 215–225.

Patel, L. (2005). *Social welfare and social development in South Africa*. Cape Town: Oxford University Press.

PEPFAR. (2012) *Social welfare systems strengthening assessment report Mbabane*. PEPFAR.

Popple, K. (1995). *Analysing community work: Its theory and practice*. Buckingham: Open University Press.

Popple, P. (1985). The social work profession: A reconceptualization. *Social Service Review, 59*, 560–577.

Reisch, M., & Wenocur, S. (1986). The future of community organization in social work: Social activism and the politics of professional building. *Social Service Review, 60*, 70–93.

Republic of South Arica. (1978). *National welfare Act 110 of 1978*. Pretoria: Office of the Prime Minister.

Republic of South Africa. (2007). *Hon T Mbeki: State of the Nation Address*. www.gov.za

Segal E A, Gerdes K E, & Steiner S. (2019) *An introduction to the profession of social work : Becoming a change agent*. Boston: Cengage Learning.

Shajahan, P., & Sharma, P. (2018). Environmental justice: A call for action for social workers. *International Social Work, 61*(4), 476–80.

Simpkin, M. (1979). *Trapped within welfare: Surviving social work*. London: Macmillan.

Skidmore, R., Thackeray, M., & Farley, O. (1997). *Introduction to social work* (7th ed.). Boston: Allyn and Bacon.

South African Council for Social Service Professions. www.sacssp.co.za

Specht, H. (1988). *New directions for social work practice*. New York: Prentice Hall.

Statistics South Africa. (2020). *2020 Mid-year population estimates*. Retrieved from www.statssa.gov.za

Swaziland Government (2013). Ministry of labour and social security: General information for the award of scholarship in Swaziland. Available: http://www.gov.sz/index.php/services-sp-1938984530/76-labour-a-social-security/labour-a-social-security/409-scholarship-department. (Accessed, 10/07/2021).

Tackett, J., Wolf, F., & Law, D. (2001). Accounting interns and their employers: Conflicting perceptions. *Ohio CPA Journal, 60*, 54–56.

The International Association Of Schools Of Social Work. (2021). *Association of South African Social Work Education Institutions (ASASWEI)*. Retrieved from www.asaswei.org

Unicef (2010) Preliminary Capacity Gap Assessment Of The Social Welfare Sector In Swaziland: Inception Report. Mbabane. Unicef

Walker, H., & Beaumont, B. (1981). *Probation work: Critical theory and socialist practice*. Oxford: Basil Blackwell.

Weiss, I., Spiro, S., Sherer, M., & Korin-Langer, N. (2004). Social work in Israel: Professional characteristics in an international comparative perspective. *International Journal of Social Welfare, 13*, 287–296.

Weiss-Gal, I., & Welbourne, P. (2008). The professionalization of social work: A cross-national exploration. *International Journal of Social Welfare, 17*, 281–290.

Welbourne, P., Harrison, G., & Ford, D. (2007). Social work in the UK and the global labor market: Recruitment, practice and ethical considerations. *International Social Work, 50*, 27–40.

United Nations Development Programme. (2015). Sustainable development goals. Available: https://www.undp.org/sustainable-development-goals. (Accessed, 09/07/2021).

Index

Note: Page numbers in *italics* indicate figures and page numbers in **bold** indicate tables in the text

Abbott, A. A. 409
academic colonisation 117
Adaikalam, F. 140
ADBU *see* Assam Don Bosco University
'Adivasi' (tribal) 22
Ahn, B. 143
Alptekin, K. 185
Anti-oppressive practice 212
Antiracist Social Work 212
Aristotle 17, 21
Assam Don Bosco University (ADBU) 26–27; Community Counselling Centre 30; community engagement projects of 29–34, **31–33**; Department of Social Work 29; fieldwork education at 27–29; Life Skill Education and Awareness Programme 30; *Swastyayan* 30
Association of Social Workers of Chile 288
Atal, Y. 57
Aung, U. T. 281
Ayllu 225
Aymara people 223–225, 227, 229, 232–234, 236

Bachelor of Social Work (BSW) 39, 41
Baikady, R. 199
Bailey, K. R. 141
Baines, D. 175, 177
Baker, L. 98
Baldoni, J. 144
Barbados *see* Cave Hill Campus Barbados
BASW *see* British Association of Social Workers
Beck, C. T. 58
Behring, Elaine 211
Belhekar, V. M. 315, 322
Ben-Oz, M. 374
Bernasconi, S. S. 175
Bethany Society 57
Bhanti, R. 95
block placement, at Cave Hill Campus Barbados 255–256; advantages and disadvantages of 261–262; organisation of 256–258

bodhi, S. 26, 35
Bodhi, S. R. 140–142
Bogo, M. 253, 257, 259, 372, 396
Bolgün, C. 186
Bordalo, P. 321–322
Boroujerdi, M. 56
Botcha, R. 95
Botswana, social work field education in 343–355; apprenticeship model 349–352; assistant community development officers 348; background 345–347; challenges and prospects of 352–355; community development assistants 348; context of 347–349; overview 343–345; University of Botswana 348, 351, 354
Boudioni, M. 307, 324
Bourdieu, P. 212
Brechin, A. 20
Bright, C. 261
British Association of Social Workers (BASW) 242
Brydon, K. 281
Bryman, A. 270
Buchanan, C. 258
Burney, Ansar 120
Burr, V. 323
Butcher, H. 104
Butterfield, Alice K. 27
Byram, M. 232

Cain, A. 232
Çalis, N. 182
Canadian Association for Spirituality and Social Work 145
Caribbean Internship Programme (CIP) 261
Castañeda, P. 290
Cave Hill Campus Barbados 252–263; block placement 255–256; block placement, advantages and disadvantages of 261–262; BSc Social Work 254; Cave Hill programme, Cave Hill programme faced by 254; field integrative seminar 258–259; international and regional field placements 260–261; organisation of block

419

Index

placement 256–258; preparation of students for internship 259–260; quality assurance review of social work programme, recommendation of 257–258; *Social Work Field Education Manual* 255; social work programme 254; student's learning goals 255–256; support to field supervisors 259–260; undergraduate social work programme, internship within 253
CCC *see* Community Counselling Centre
Cecil, B. 307, 324
Cerna, C. 225
Ceylon School of Social Work 78
Chang, M. 56
Charity Organization Society 182
Chhapra, Mushtaq 120
Chhipa, Muhammad Ramzan 120
Child Care Service Order (CCSO) 406
Chile: clinical social work in 209–221; Constitutional Organic Law on Education of 1990 288–289; development model 294; indigenous peoples in 224–236; professional practice model 240–244; School of Social Work at ETSUC 239–244; schools of social work 220; social work education in 288–291; social work in 239; social work practicum in 287–296; *see also* clinical social work, in Chile; social work practicum in Chile
China, social work field education in: challenges for 200–204; development of 198–199; lack of available practice placement agencies 201–202; lost focus on practice teaching 200–201; overview 197–198; practice standards, lack of 202; social work education council, lack of 202–203; structure and content of 200; trained educators and supervisors, lack of 203; trained supervisors at placement agency, lack of 203–204
Chitereka, C. 358, 403
Christensen, J. M. 279
Chui, E. W. T. 374, 378
Cieszkowski, August 18
clinical social work, in Chile 209–210, 219; Division of Disease Prevention and Control 214; emergency of 213–219; increasing complex needs 213–215; social policy implementation 215; state organisation, type of 215–219
Coates, J. 142, 236, 269, 274, 281
Coffman, K. 321–322
Cohen, A. P. 104, 113
Coholic, D. 142
Collins, S. 358
Committee On Socio Economic and Health Development Assam (COSEHDA) 57
community, definition of 104
community-based open setting field work 65; stakeholders of 65

Community Counselling Centre (CCC) 30
community engagement projects, of ADBU 29–34, **31–33**; competence in practice 35; context-specific social work practice 35; contribution to national development 36; dialoguing in 35; fieldwork evaluation in 36–37; partnerships 36; peoples' participation in 34; sustainability of 36
community mapping 105–106
community social work methods in Sri Lanka 102–113; community mapping 105–106; community social work students, future scope for 111–113; empowerment-oriented social work 109–111; overview 102–103; Participatory Rural Appraisal 106; risk analysis 108–109, *109*; slums and shanties/low-income settlements/urban underserved communities 103–104; SWOT analysis 106–108, **107**
competency: demonstration of 43, 50–51; identification of 43, 46–49; linkage to theoretical knowledge 43, 46–49; social work 166
competency-based field practicum of KMC 39–40; developmental context 41–42; evaluation context 42; historical context 40–41
competency-based field work pedagogy of KMC 42–43, *51*; acquisition of ability to practise skills and knowledge 43; competency-based learning placement 43; developing learning experiences 43; measurement of performance 43
competency-based learning 39–40, 42
competency-based pedagogy 42
competency-based practice and behaviour 43, 49–50
concurrent fieldwork in open setting community 65, 66; concurrent fieldwork community, opportunities for 68; entry point activities 67–68; field selection 67; fieldwork supervision 73; first day at community open setting 70; frequency of field visit 67; group conference 73–74; individual conference 73; meeting key people 67; orientation of trainees before fieldwork 68–70; own fieldwork setting 74; rapport building 67–74; real-time feedback 73; regular visits to community 70–73
context-specific social work practice model 2, 35
continuous professional development (CPD) 139–140
Corbett, J. 105
Cornelius, L. J. 143
Corrigan, P. 211
Cortes, H. 225
Cossom, J. 93
Costello, S. 281
Council on Social Work Education (CSWE) 1, 39, 94, 157–159, 330; field practice as 'signature pedagogy' 182, 252
Cournoyer, B. R. 244

Index

COVID-19 pandemic, in India 13; prescription for prevention of 16; response in Mumbai 15–16
Crenshaw, K. 354
Crisp, B. R. 269, 282, 308, 322, 323
Critical Social Work 212
Crouch, M. 315
CSWE *see* Council on Social Work Education

Daivayaparsya (spiritual or faith therapy) 97
Danbury, H. 350
dansel 111
Dash, B. M. 95, 139, 142, 359
decolonisation, definition of 96
Delgado, M. 105
Desai, A. S. 63
Desai, M. M. 139
Devi, Tharani 72
Dhemba, J. 377, 388, 399, 412
Diaguita 224
Diallo, H. 345
Direction of Institutional Analysis and Planning of the Pontificia Universidad Católica de Chile (DAIP) 218
distance educational institutions (DEIS) 359
Doel, M. 95, 252
Donohue-Dioh, J. 291
DuBois, B. 329
Dutton, K. 308, 323
Dwyer, M. 332–334

eclecticism 176
eluwün (burial) 225
eluwün (burial of the dead) 233
empowerment: definition of 109–110; principles in 110
empowerment-oriented social work 109–111
Estalayo, M. M. 212
estancia 225
Eswatini, professionalisation of social work in 403–415; approaches to professionalisation 409; contextual analysis of professionalisation of social work 409; Department of Social Development 407; legislative framework for social welfare delivery 406; National Development Social Policy 407; professional registration and regulation of social work practice 408–409; recommendations 414–415; shift to professionalism 406–407; social work and paraprofessionals, distinction between 407–408; social work development, history of 405–406
Eswatini, social work field education in 394–400; challenges encountered 397–398; compulsory fieldwork experience 395; contact time and learning hours 395; Department of Social Welfare 389–390; education and qualification of field supervisors 399–400; Eswatini Medical Christian University 388; field education structure 395; field work curriculum and implementation 396–397; memorandum of understanding 396; opportunities to practice 398; organisation for field placement, criteria for selecting 395–399; overview 388–389; placement agencies, location of 398–399; quality assurance 396; role of social work field education programme, analysis of 393; social welfare services, origin of 389–390; student orientation and ethical issues 396; University of Eswatini 388
Eswatini Medical Christian University (EMCU) 388, 396, 412
ethnic-cultural diversity 223
ETSUC *see* Pontifical Catholic University of Chile
extra-judicial killings (EJKs) 177

Faleolo, M. 281–283
Feminist Social Work 212
Ferreira, S. B. 144
Field Action Projects (FAPs) 139
field practicum in Srilanka: block 84; Master of Social Work, opportunities and challenges for 85–89; orientation to, benefits of 82; recommendations for improvement at NISD 90; social work students and supervisors, challenges experienced by 81; subjects offered at NISD **89**
field supervisor 290, 291; knowledge and skill required **292**
field work: guidelines **56**; practice abilities in 1; recognition as pedagogy 1
fieldwork education 1, 2, 14, 26; in ADBU, Assam (India) 27–29; in Africa 7–8; challenge in India 54; in global south 3–4; in Latin American 7; in social work 3
fieldwork in India, challenges in 54–63; indigenisation 55–56; mushrooming of social work institutes 54; overview 54–55; social work and field work practices in North-East India 57–62
Field Work Practicum Learning Plan 40
Finch, J. 322
Fleury, Sonia 212
Floyd, George 353
Flynn, C. 267, 268
Flyvbjerg, B. 58
Fook, J. 62, 211, 212
Fouché, C. 280
Francis, A. P. 146
Freidson, E. 409
Freire, Paulo 18

Gadamer, H. 21
Gangadhar, B. S. 141
García, R. 215

Index

GASW *see* Georgian Association of Social Workers
Geng, G. 258
Gennaioli, N. 321–322
Georgia, establishment of social work in 153–168; Advanced Year of Field Education 163; Council on Social Work Education 157–159; CSWE-accredited programme 158; development of scientific social work, opportunities for 156; Georgian Association of Social Workers 154; Government of Georgia 153; implicit curriculum 158–159; international standards of field education 156–159; Law on Social Work 155; macro-level reforms in 153–154; Master of Social Work Programme Director 164, 167; MSW programme, assessment criteria for field education of 159–166, **160–161**; NGO sector 156; overview 153–154; policy documents affecting social work education 154–155; selection of agencies, criteria for 164–165; selection of field instructors, criteria for 165; Social Work Competencies 158; social work education 155–156; social work educators 156; Social Work Practice Seminar 162–163; social work workforce 155–156
Georgian Association of Social Workers (GASW) 154
Giddings, M. M. 308
Glicken, M. D. 343, 345
Global Standards for Social Work Education and Training (GSSWET) 157, 158, 253
Google Scholar 138
Gorman, Amanda 354
Graham, J. 142
Gray, M. 142, 236, 268, 269, 281, 282, 374
Great Depression 265
Green Lister, P. 308, 323
Greenwood, E. 409, 410
Greif, G. L. 143
group conference (GC) 73–74
Growing Seed 57
GSSWET *see* Global Standards for Social Work Education and Training
Gulalia, P. 141, 142
Guna theory 97
Gundermman, H. 225

Haanwinckel, B. Z. 373, 380
Hall, N. 77, 360
Hall, R. 410
Hantman, S. 373, 374
Haq, Abrar ul 120
Harkness, D. 37, 381
Hayward-Jones, J. 266
Hazare, Anna 98
Healy, K. 15
Hepworth, D. H. 372

Hetherington, T. 142, 236
Higher Education Support Programme 156
Higher National Diploma in Social Work (HDipSW) 80
Hilali-Ahmer Cemiyeti 183
Horwath, J. 307
Hossain M. A. 268
Huang, Y. 57, 63
Hugman, R. 412
huilliche 224
Hull Jr, G. H. 252

IASSW *see* International Association of Schools of Social Work
IFSW *see* International Federation of Social Workers
IJSW *see* Indian Journal of Social Work
India: Bharatiya Curriculum 93; 'Bharatiyakaran' of social work education 93; Council on Social Work Education 1, 39, 94; COVID-19 pandemic in 13; field work in, challenges faced in 54–63; indigenous model of social work education 92–93; praxis fieldwork model in Kerala 18–22; social work curriculum in 92–93; social work in 14–16; social work models/practices, need for revamping 97–98; social work practice in 138–146; social work values 98; Tata Institute of Social Sciences 92; *see also* fieldwork in India, challenges in; social work field education in India; social work practice in India
Indian Journal of Social Work (IJSW) 139, 142
indigenisation 268
indigenous peoples in Chile 223–236; Aymara 223–225, 227, 229, 232–234, 236; cultural competencies 234–236; cultural identity 232–234; Diaguita 224; historical and socio-demographic aspects 224–226; indigenous cultural practices 228, **230**; indigenous cultural practices, study of 227–232; intercultural competence 232; Mapuche 223, 224, 227, 229, 232, 233, 236; overview 223; personal wellbeing index 229; population in poverty and social exclusion *226*; social work and 226; subjective wellbeing 229, 230, **230**, **231**
Indira Gandhi National Open University (IGNOU) 359
individual conference (IC) 73
Indo-Global Social Service Society (IGSSS) 57
Industrial Revolution 265, 345, 357
International Association of Schools of Social Work (IASSW) 77, 157, 189, 282, 358
International Association of Universities 30, 282
International Federation of Social Workers (IFSW) 55, 77, 157, 182, 189; International Social Work Code of Ethics 275; social work, definition of 172, 357, 403; social work as human

rights profession 172; standards for fieldwork education 360–361
Islary, Jacob 29
Ituarte, A. I. 216

Jabeen, T. 118
Janci Rani, P. R. 72
Japa 97–98
Jebaseelan, A. 94
Jebaseelan, U. S. 141
Jeyarani, J. S. 141
Jeyarani, S. J. 94
Johnson, E. J. 141
Jones, J. 145
Jones, J. F. 92
Josephson, S. A. 322

Kadambari Memorial College of Science and Management (KMC) 39–40; Field Work Learning Plan (2016) 41; learning plan 49
Kadushin, A. E. 37, 97, 381
Kamasua, K. 267, 268
Kang'ethe, S. M. 404
Kaseke, E. 95, 357
katawün (ear piercings) 225
Katz, P. 94
Khan, Abdul Bari 120
Khan, Akhter Hameed 120
Khan, Imran 120
kiñe eluwün 233
Kirst-Ashman, K. K. 252
KMC *see* Kadambari Memorial College of Science and Management
KMC social work, competency-based 40; developmental context 41–42; evaluation context 42; historical context of 40–41
Kreitzer, L. 282
Kripa Foundation 57
Kulkin, H. 143
küme mongen 236
küpan (kinship) 233

lafkenche 224
Lager, P. B. 260
Lakshmi, Vijaya 141
Larkin, S. 291
Larsen, J. A. 372
Latin America, social work in 239; Alliance for Progress 210; reconceptualisation 209–212; social work and state 212
Lawani, B. T. 54, 55
Lawihin, D. 267–269, 280, 281
LEAP *see* Life Skill Education and Awareness Programme
Lee, J. A. 110
Le Maistre, C. 314
Leonard, P. 211

Leung, J. C. B. 358
LGBRIMH *see* Lokopriya Gopinath Bordoloi Regional Institute Mental Health
Life Skill Education and Awareness Programme (LEAP) 30
Lokopriya Gopinath Bordoloi Regional Institute Mental Health (LGBRIMH) 57
Louw, H. 390
Lovai, B. 267
low-income settlements 103–104
Lu, Y. E. 309
Lucas, Taulo 347
Lydon, M. 105
Lymbery, M. 411

macro practice of social work 65–66
Madden, R. G. 324
mafutün (matrimony) 225
Mahaweli Development programmes 78
Makhubele, J. C. 97
Malena, C. 119
managerialism 14
Manschardt, Clifford 55
Mapuche people 223, 224, 227, 229, 232, 233, 236
mapudungun 225
mapulugün 233
Mapundungung 233
marginalised community 15
Markovic, Mahilo 18
Marxist Social Work 212
Master's of Social Work (MSW) 27; in Chile 216; fieldwork structure **28**; at Ilia State University 153, 167; in Indira Gandhi National Open University 359
Maternity Benefit Act 61
Matthew, G. 54
Mavely, Stephen 29
Maxted, J. 390
Maxwell, J. 257
Mayo, Elton 373
McDonald, C. 411
McKendrick, B. W. 361, 405, 406
McKenzie, H. 315
Midgley, J. 55, 92, 96, 358
Miley, K. K. 329
Miller, J. 291, 339
Minahan, A. 330
Minimol 141
Monash University Human Research Ethics Committee (MUHREC) 271
Moss, B. R. 300
mudukku (slums) 103–104
Mullaly, B. 20
Mullaly, R. 20
Mungai, N. 281, 282
Muñoz, W. 225
Munoz-Guzman, Carolina 7

Index

Munson, C. E. 240, 243, 246
Mupedziswa, R. 97, 358
Myerhoff, B. 59
My Social Work Lab 359

nagche 224
Nagpaul, H. 97
Narayan, L. 142
Narzary, Victor 27, 29, 30
National Association of Social Workers: professional supervision, definition of 260
National Institute of Social Development (NISD) 76–77, 79, 82; BSW Handbook of 77; field practicum and 86; field practicum at, recommendations for improvement of 90; field work practicum subjects offered at **89**; Field Work Unit at 77; School of Social Work, field work unit of 90–91
National University of Lesotho (NUL) 371; Bachelor of Social Work (BSW) Programme 374; field practice hours and student supervision, revision of 378; fieldwork course coordination 378; fieldwork practice assessment format **386–387**; fieldwork practice at 375; fieldwork practice guidelines **386**; Fieldwork Practice Guidelines and Annexure II 379; Social Work Department 378; social work programme 2001–2017 375; Social Work Training Programme, redesigned 278; student enrolment numbers, increase in 376–377; weak fieldwork course coordination 377
National Youth Project 57
Nations Sustainable Development Goals 279
Nayak, L. M. 141
NEFSA 57
Neville, A. 118
New Frontiers in Social Work Education 139
Nhapi, T. 388, 399, 412
Nigeria, social work fieldwork practicum in 330–341; block field placement 330–331; case continuity, lack of 341; challenges of 339–341; community development 330; in hospital 337–338; inadequate supervision from agency 339–340; inadequate time allocation 340; knowledge about profession, lack of 340–341; non-professionalisation of social work 339; Nsukka auto mechanic village 336; in Nsukka prison 338; in schools 336–337; in social welfare agency 338–339; social work 330; University of Nigeria, Nsukka 331–335
Nikku, R. B. 280, 282
NISD *see* National Institute of Social Development
Niu, C. 291
North East Network (NEN) 57
North East Research and Social Work Networking (NERSWN) 57
NUL *see* National University of Lesotho

Obikeze, D. S. 330
Ogige Market Amalgamated Traders Association of Nsukka (OMATAN) 335
Okoye, U. O. 339, 340
OMATAN *see* Ogige Market Amalgamated Traders Association of Nsukka
Open and Distance Learning (ODL) 357–369; in China 358; Dr Bhim Rao Ambedkar Open University in Hyderabad 359; in India 358, 359; Indira Gandhi National Open University 359; social work education 358; social work field instruction 359–360; social work training 358; in South Africa 359–368; standards for social work field education 360–368
Open Society Foundation Academic Fellowship Programme 156
orientation field placement 79–80; challenges and opportunities 81–82

Pachamama 225
Padmore, J. 141
Pakistan, social work in 116–136; academic colonisation 117; administrative issues 128–135, *129*; charity and social development 117–118; common perceived perception of social workers 124; field work concerns 130–133, *131*; Gilgit-Baltistan 122; ineffective professional growth and recognition of social work practice 127; job market of social workers 128–130; KPK province 122; low recognition 126; Ministry of Social Welfare 118; new fields new avenue, need of 134–135; nexus between public and private sector 119–121; NGO sector 119–120; professional challenges 126; quest for ideology and identity 126; 'The Social Welfare Project' 118; social work and social welfare in, introduction to 116–117; social work association 127, *127*; social work education, birth of 119; social work literature, availability of 133–134; social work practice and voluntary social work 119–121; social work profession, challenges for 124–126, *125*; social work programme in, study of 121–135; social work training 120–121; United Nations, role of 116, 119; Village Aid programme 130; welfare policies 120
Panda, B. 141
Papua New Guinea (PNG) 265–285; contemporary social work education in 265; cultural and linguistic diversity of 266; curriculum, connecting 284; global and local social issues, connecting 274–275, 278–279; global expectations and local policies, connecting 279–280; global expectations and standards, connecting 275; global-local connectedness in field education, achieving 277–278; global social work education

standards in, study of 270–283; governance and policy systems for localisation 277; graduates with culturally relevant skills, developing 273–274; knowledge building, research for 276; linking global and local approaches to practice 281–282; literature on indigenisation and localisation of social work 268–269; local application of global standards 282–283; local-global knowledge for integration in field education 274–277; Melanesian knowledge and wisdom 272–273; organisation, connecting 284–285; practice settings, connecting with 276–277; social care and support models 276; Social Workers Association, role of 285; social work practice and education in 267–268; strategic recommendations 284; university and community, link between 280–281; urbanisation in 266

Papua New Guinea Social Workers Association (PNGSWA) 267, 283
Paracka, S. 141
Participatory Rural Appraisal (PRA) 106
Patel, L. 361
Pathak, B. 98
Pawar, M. 139
Pawson, R. 144
Payne, M. 60
pedagogy: competency-based 42; field work recognition as 1; signature, fieldwork as 16–18
Pedagogy of the Oppressed (Freire) 18
pelpath (shanties) 104
personality 58
pewenche 224
Pfau, Ruth 120
Philippines, social work in 170–181; College of Social Work and Community Development 173, 174; field instruction programme 170–171; overview 170–171; social justice and human rights *see* social justice and human rights, in Philippines; social work profession 170; University of the Philippines 173; *see also* social justice and human rights in Philippines
Pincus, A. 330
PMJDY *see* Pradhan Mantri Jan Dhan Yojana
PNGSWA *see* Papua New Guinea Social Workers Association
poesis 18
Polit, D. F. 58
political consciousness 177–178
Ponnuswami, I. 146
Pontifical Catholic University of Chile (ETSUC) 239–244; professional practice model 240–244; School of Social Work at 239–244
Powell, F. 26, 29, 34, 37
PRA *see* Participatory Rural Appraisal
Practice Imperfect: Reflections on a Career in Social Work (Rambally) 313

Pradhan Mantri Jan Dhan Yojana (PMJDY) 72
Pranayama 98
praxis: being collaborative 21–22; collaboration 21–22; critical action in 20–22; definition of 18; dividends of 23; fieldwork model in Kerala 18–22; reflexivity 19–20, 22; theory of 17–18
professional practice, standardisation of 182
professional practice model, of ETSUC 240–244; problem statement 242; professional skills and technical knowledge 242–244
professional supervision, definition of 260
professor 240; axis of management 249–250; axis of supervision 249; axis of training 249; effective supervision, aspects for 243; Munson's activities and skills identified by **248**; professional abilities of, research on 244–250; professional practice 242; social work curriculum, contributions to 248–250; soft and professional skills of 245–248, **247, 248**; successful supervision, basic elements of **248**
programmes, projects, and activities (PPAs) 174
Prolegomena zur Historiosophie (Cieszkowski) 18
Promotion and Advancement of Justice, Harmony and Rights of Adivasis (PAJHRA) 57
Puig, C. 246
Pulla, V. 280, 282
Purbanchal University (PU) 40; Bachelor of Social Work at 39; social work programme 41
pvñeñelche 229

Radical Social Work in Britain 212
Ramakrishna Mission 57
Rambally, Rae Tucker 254
Ranaweera, A. 78
Raniga, T. 373, 382
Rashtriya Gramin Vikas Nidhi (RGVN) 57
Raskin, M. S 374
'ready for practice,' in social work 313–324; assessing readiness 318–319; conceptual framework 314–315; heuristics in assessment 321–322; key research debates 314; multiple expectations of social work and social workers 320–321; overview 313; as plural construct in social work 307; preferences 317; readiness of practitioner 319–320; requirements for 303–305; small-scale qualitative study 315–319; student attitude to learning 317–318; subjective knowledge in assessment 319–320; teaching and learning 317
Reagan, Ronald 293
Reamer, F. G. 144
reflexive praxis 19–20, 22, 23
reflexivity 58
Rehmatullah, S. 133
ResearchGate 138
Reyes-Quilodran, Claudia 7
Reynolds, R. R. 54

Index

Richie, M. 322
Richmond, Mary 359
Ring, K. A. 255, 261, 262
risk analysis 108–109, *109*
Rizvi, Adeeb 120
Rock, L. F. 255, 258, 261, 262
Rooney, R. 372
Rossiter, A. 20
Roy, Shehzad 60, 95, 120
Royse, D. 321
Ruby, J. 59
rural camp, in Sri Lanka 80; challenges for 85; opportunities for 85
Rush, E. 281, 282

SACSSP *see* South African Council for Social Service Professions
Sáez, L. N. 212
Sahin, F. 186
Salome, A. M. 290
Samad, A. 268
Saqib, Amjad 120
Satvavajaya (psychotherapy) 97
Sawdon, D. 95
Schenck, C. J. 390
Schiff, M. 94
School of Social Work at the Pontificia Universidad Católica de Chile (SSWPUC) 217, 220
Sehman, H. 194
Seneh 57
SHALOM 57
Shardlow, S. 95, 252
Sharma, Riju 27, 29
Sharma, S. 140
Shawky, A. 96
Shenar-Golan, V. 113
Shishu Sarothi 57
Shleifer, A. 321–322
shramadana (donating labour) 111
signature pedagogy, in social work education 182; field education 158; fieldwork as 16–18; of social work training 371; theory of praxis 17–18
Simpson, B. 373, 382
Sindh Institute of Urology (SIUT) 120
Singh, Rajendra 98
Singh, R. R. 140
Sinha, D. 96
Sinha, J. B. P. 96
Sinkamba, R. P. 97
Sirumbayi, Ponnu 71
SIUT *see* Sindh Institute of Urology
skill development: of students and practitioners 4–5
skills and knowledge: acquisition of ability to practise 43, 49–50; integration of 43
Smith, J. 145

social justice and human rights in Philippines: awakening of fieldwork students on socio-political realities 174–175; commitment 178–179; creating sites for dissent 179–180; extra-judicial killings 177; field instruction for future social workers 175; as ideological moorings of social work 172; overview 170–171; political consciousness, raising 177–178; social work education, locus of field instruction in 172–174; spaces for resistance 179–180; theory, role of 176
social work 13, 23; COVID-19 response in Mumbai 15–16; critical 15; decolonising field work training in 96–97; definition of 111, 172, 357, 403; emancipatory approach 14, 15; field work practices 3, 94–96; field work training of 39; in Georgia 153–166; *see also* Georgia, establishment of social work in; in India 14–16; macro practice of 65–66; maintenance approach 14; as practice-based profession 119; practitioners 3; profession 2; relationship between theory and practice 4; Therapeutic helping approach 14
social work curriculum 92–93; Bharatiya Curriculum 93; Bharatiyakaran of 93; western 93
social work education 1; challenge in global south 2; in classrooms 26; in developing world 2; fieldwork as signature pedagogy in 16–18; in India *see* India; in Pakistan 116–136; in Sri Lanka 76–91; tacit knowledge building in 4
social work field education 3; in Africa 343–355; basic components of 192; in developing Asia 6–7; local models of 4; role of 391–393; South Africa *vs.* Eswatini 388–400; standards for 360–368; in Turkey 182–195
social work field education in India: challenges for 200–204; development of 198; lack of available practice placement agencies 201–202; lost focus on practice teaching 200–201; overview 197–198; practice standards, lack of 202; social work education council, lack of 202–203; structure and content of 199–200; trained educators and supervisors, lack of 203; trained supervisors at placement agency, lack of 203–204
social work practice in India 138–146; challenges to 142; fieldwork practicum, strengthening 141–142; future prospects 142; indigenous literature in social work 139–140; journey of social work 139–142; overview 138; supervision and spirituality 144–145; supervision in fieldwork, importance of 140–141; supervisory processes and mentoring 142–143; Virtual Field Placements 144; virtual placements and e-learning, incorporation of 143–144; zone of proximal development 145–146

social work practice in Trinidad, readiness for: assessment of 308; critical unanswered questions 308–309; expected behaviours and attitudes 305–306; literature, review of 300–301; overview 299–300; 'ready for practice' as plural construct in social work 307; 'ready for practice' in social work, requirements for 303–305; 'ready' social worker, characteristics of 302–303; selection and training, dilemma of 306–307; study of 301–309

social work practicum in Chile 287–296; field supervision, role of 294–295; field supervision in internship training 291–293; neoliberalism and new public management 293–294; overview 287–288; practical social work education 293–294; practical social work training, challenges for 294–295; social work education 288–291; social work education in field 289–291; supervision 296

social work training 371–384; all social work academics, recommendations to 383; difficulty in reconciling agency and university assessment reports 377; facilitating fieldwork practice in inception programme, challenges in 375; field practice hours and student supervision, revision of 378–379; fieldwork practice administration 380–382; fieldwork practice format options 381–382; fieldwork practice guidelines and assessment 378–379; fieldwork practice in 372; four-stage fieldwork format, recommended 382–383; insufficient practice hours 376; lessons learnt in 379; low numbers of qualified social workers 376; Open and Distance Learning 358; overview 371–372; in Pakistan 120–121; recommendations for 379–384, **384**; redesigned NUL programme 278; signature pedagogy of 371; social work department fieldwork practice coordinator 381; socioeconomic context of Lesotho 372; *see also* National University of Lesotho; student enrolment numbers, increase in 376–377; supervision outsourcing 381; theoretical perspectives on 373–374; University Fieldwork Practice Department 380–381; weak fieldwork course coordination 377; written fieldwork practice guidelines, absence of 377

South Africa: Council of Higher Education 362, 363; legislative framework for social welfare delivery 406; National Welfare Act (1978) 362; Open and Distance Learning in 359; Social Service Professions Act 110 of 1978 363, 400, 406, 408, 410; social welfare policies in 405; South African Council for Social Service Professions 362–363, **364–366**, 366–368, 407; South African Welfare Council 362; University of South Africa fieldwork education 363–367; University of the Cape of Good Hope 363

South Africa, social work field education in 393–394; achievement of learning outcomes 393–394; Jan Hofmeyer College 390, 412; practice experience 393–394; role of social work field education programme, analysis of 393

South African Council for Social Service Professions (SACSSP) 362–363, 393, 394, 410; norms and standards for bachelor of social work field instruction **364–366**; placement organisations, requirement of 367–368; practical work supervisor with 368; standards for university offering social work training 367; student registered with 368

Southern African Development Community (SADC) 405

spirituality 144–145

Sri Lanka, social work education in 76–91; Ceylon School of Social Work 78; concurrent placement 80; existing field education programmes 79–82; Higher National Diploma in Social Work programme 80; human settlements and service delivery 80; *Mahaweli* Development programmes 78; MSW field practicum, opportunities and challenges for 85–89; National Institute of Social Development 76–77; *see also* National Institute of Social Development; orientation field placement 79–82; orientation to field practicum, benefits of 82; poor student–supervisor relationship 83–84; rural camp, challenges for 85; rural camp, opportunities for 85; rural camp in human settlements 85; Social Work Diploma programme 78; social work field practice, history of 78; social work students and supervisors in field practicum, challenges experienced by 81; supervision, challenges of 82–83; *see also* community social work methods in Sri Lanka; field practicum in Srilanka

Sri Lanka Institute of Social Work 78

Sri Lanka Qualifications Framework 80

Sri Lanka School of Social Work 76–77

structural inequalities 15

Structural Social Work in Canada 212

student–supervisor relationship 83–84

Subedar, I. S. 95

subjective wellbeing (SWB) 229

suma qamaña 236

Sunstein, C. R. 321, 322

Sustainable Development Goals (SDGs) 404

Swargiary, Bibharani 27

Swastyayan 30

SWOT analysis 106–108, **107**

tacit knowledge building 4

Tackett, J. 391

Tanga, P. T. 379

Index

Tata Institute of Social Sciences (TISS) 92, 139, 145
Taylor, I. 308, 322
Tempus/Tacis Programme of Europe 156
Thatcher, Margaret 293
theoria 18
Thurlow, C. 307
Tirupura, B. 142
Tomanbay, I. 184
Topping, A. 145
Trevelyan, C. 211
Trevithick, P. 23
Trinidad *see* social work practice in Trinidad, readiness for
Trinidad and Tobago Association of Social Workers (TTASW) 301
TTASW *see* Trinidad and Tobago Association of Social Workers
Turkey, social work field education in 182–195; applied research courses 188; Association of Schools of Social Work 186; College of Social Work at Hacettepe University 184; Department of Social Work and Social Services 184; field practice courses on social work 189; fundamental problems of social work education 192–193; graduate programmes 191–192; Hacettepe University Department of Social 194; Higher Education Institutions Examination 184; overview 182–183; Social Services Academy 184–186; social work as profession and discipline in, historical background of 183–184; social work field practice 189, 190; social work field practice locations 193; structure and content of social work education 184–194; Student Selection and Placement Center 184; supervision 193–194; Türkiye Sosyal Hizmet Uzmanlar Derneği 185, 186; university degree for social worker 184; Yükseköğretim Program Atlas 184
tuwün (place of birth) 233

underserved community 103–104
UNESCO 231
UNICEF 49
United Nations Development Programme (UNDP) 404
United Nations Human Development Index 266
University of Eswatini (UNESWA) 388, 396, 412
University of Nigeria, Nsukka: agencies for field practicum at 334–339; fieldwork practicum materials 333–334; pattern of fieldwork practicum at 331–333
University of the West Indies 253
Urbanowski, M. 332–334

'Vandavasi' (nontribal) 22
Veneracion, M. C. J. 55
Vergara, J. I. 225
VFP *see* Virtual Field Placements
Vicary, S. 358
Virtual Field Placements (VFP) 144
Vodde, R. 308
Voorhees, R. 48
Vygotsky, L. S. 145

Wairire, G. G. 281, 282
Walton, C. 307
Wattis, J. 145
Weil, M. 97
Weiss-Gal, I. 390, 404, 408, 410–412
Welbourne, P. 390, 404, 408, 410–412
wenteche 224
we xipantu (new year) 225
WhatsApp 256
Williams, J. 143
Willie, C. V. 104
Womack, R. 291
Wong, Y.-L. R. 96

Xiong, Z. 269, 282

Yip, K. 55, 269
Yoga 97
Yolcuoglu, I. 194
Yuktivyapasrya (rational therapy) 97
Yunong, H. 269, 282

Zegeye, A. 390
Zhang X. 57, 63
zone of proximal development (ZPD) 145–146
Zoom 256
ZPD *see* zone of proximal development